Family Patterns

Gender Relations

Third Edition

Family Patterns

Gender Relations

Edited by Bonnie Fox

OXFORD
UNIVERSITY PRESS

8 Sampson Mews, Suite 204, Don Mills, Ontario M3C 0H5
www.oupcanada.com

Oxford University Press is a department of the University of Oxford.
It furthers the University's objective of excellence in research, scholarship, and education by publishing worldwide in

Oxford New York
Auckland Cape Town Dar es Salaam Hong Kong Karachi
Kuala Lumpur Madrid Melbourne Mexico City Nairobi
New Delhi Shanghai Taipei Toronto

With offices in
Argentina Austria Brazil Chile Czech Republic France Greece
Guatemala Hungary Italy Japan Poland Portugal Singapore
South Korea Switzerland Thailand Turkey Ukraine Vietnam

Oxford is a trade mark of Oxford University Press
in the UK and in certain other countries

Published in Canada by Oxford University Press

First Published 2009

Library and Archives Canada Cataloguing in Publication

Family patterns, gender relations / edited by Bonnie J. Fox. — 3rd ed.

Includes index.
ISBN 978-0-19-542489-8

1. Family. 2. Sex role. I. Fox, Bonnie, 1948–

HQ734.F2417 2008 306.85 C2008-903577-1

Cover image: PhotoAlto/Veer

Oxford University Press is committed to our environment.
This book is printed on acid-free paper ∞.
Printed and bound in the United States of America.

6 7 - 14 13 12

Contents

Preface ix

Acknowledgements xi

PART ONE **Putting 'Family' in Perspective 1**

Chapter 1 Conceptualizing 'Family' 3
Meg Luxton and Bonnie Fox

Chapter 2 The Unnatural Family 21
Felicity Edholm

Chapter 3 Is There a Family? New Anthropological Views 29
Jane Collier, Michelle Z. Rosaldo, and Sylvia Yanagisako

PART TWO **Diverse Family Patterns 41**

Section 1 Foraging Societies: Communal 'Households' 42

Chapter 4 Women in an Egalitarian Society: The Montagnais-Naskapi of Canada 43
Eleanor B. Leacock

Section 2 Agricultural Societies: The 'Family Economy' 55

Chapter 5 The Family Economy in Modern England and France 56
Louise A. Tilly and Joan W. Scott

Chapter 6 Patriarchal Relations of Production in Nineteenth-century Ontario 85
Marjorie Griffin Cohen

Section 3 Industrial Capitalism: The Rise of Breadwinner–Homemaker Families 97

Chapter 7 Dynamics of Kin in an Industrial Community 99
Tamara K. Hareven

Chapter 8 Domesticity 111
Nancy F. Cott

Chapter 9 Putting Mothers on the Pedestal 118
Maxine L. Margolis

Section 4 From 1950s Breadwinner–Homemaker Families to Twenty-first Century Diversity 136

Chapter 10 Sexuality and the Post-war Domestic 'Revival' 137
Mary Louise Adams

Chapter 11 Wives and Husbands 156
Meg Luxton

Chapter 12 As Times Change: A Review of Trends in Family Life 180
Bonnie Fox with Jessica Yiu

PART THREE Elements of Family 209

Section 1 Sexuality: Negotiating Adult Intimacy 210

Chapter 13 Heterosexuality: Contested Ground 212
Mariana Valverde

Chapter 14 Navigating Sexual Terrain: Legacies of the Sacred and the Secular in the Lives of French-Canadian Women 219
Tish Langlois

Chapter 15 One Is Not Born a Bride: How Weddings Regulate Heterosexuality 236
Chrys Ingraham

Section 2 Marriage and Domesticity: Becoming Family 241

Chapter 16 'Here Comes the Bride': The Making of a 'Modern Traditional' Wedding in Western Culture 242
Dawn H. Currie

Chapter 17 Veering Toward Domesticity 259
Kathleen Gerson

Chapter 18 Education, Work, and Family Decision-making: Finding the 'Right Time' to Have a Baby 277
Gillian Ranson

Section 3 **Parenthood and Childcare: Taking on Gendered Responsibilities** 290

Chapter 19 When the Baby Comes Home: The Dynamics of Gender in the Making of Family 292
Bonnie Fox

Chapter 20 Motherwork, Stress, and Depression: The Costs of Privatized Social Reproduction 310
Harriet Rosenberg

Chapter 21 'Like a Family': Reproductive Work in a Co-operative Setting 325
Diana Worts

Chapter 22 Opting into Motherhood: Lesbians Blurring the Boundaries and Transforming the Meaning of Parenthood and Kinship 343
Gillian A. Dunne

Section 4 **The Gender-divided Work Involved in Maintaining Families** 365

Chapter 23 Household Labour and the Routine Production of Gender 367
Scott Coltrane

Chapter 24 Lesbians at Home: Why Can't a Man Be More Like a Woman? 385
Gillian A. Dunne

Chapter 25 Moneywork: Caregiving and the Management of Family Finances 417
Sandra Colavecchia

Chapter 26 The Politics of Family and Immigration in the Subordination of Domestic Workers in Canada 428
Sedef Arat-Koc

Chapter 27 Family Coping Strategies: Balancing Paid Employment and Domestic Labour 453
Meg Luxton

PART FOUR **Families Negotiating Change, Changing Families 475**

Chapter 28 From Hong Kong to Canada: Immigration and the Changing Family Lives of Middle-class Women from Hong Kong 477
Guida Man

Chapter 29 Gender, Generation, and the 'Immigrant Family': Negotiating Migration Processes 496
Gillian Creese, Isabel Dyck, and Arlene Tigar McLaren

Chapter 30 Transforming Rural Livelihoods: Gender, Work, and Restructuring in Three Ontario Communities 509
Belinda Leach

PART FIVE **Other Family Matters 523**

Chapter 31 Confronting Violence in Women's Lives 525
Rosemary Gartner, Myrna Dawson, and Maria Crawford

Chapter 32 Children's Adjustment to Divorce 543
Frank F. Furstenberg and Andrew J. Cherlin

Chapter 33 Lessons from Europe: Policy Options to Enhance the Economic Security of Canadian Families 552
the Shelley A. Phipps

Index 575

Preface

The third edition of *Family Patterns, Gender Relations* focuses on understanding the patterns and dynamics in the relationships through which people care for children, themselves, and each other. In exploring the social relations through which family is created and maintained, we also focus on how these relationships are shaped by their larger social context and especially by the way society is organized. Because the relations that sustain families are typically gendered, the book is as much about gender as it is about family.

The book begins by challenging assumptions that families are somehow determined by 'human nature'. Chapter 1 introduces the book, with a definition of family that accommodates the significant cross-cultural and historical variations in family patterns and a sketch of an (historical-materialist) approach for understanding these differences. In Chapters 2 and 3, social anthropologists dispel any notion that nuclear families and conventional gender roles are natural, and thus universal, in human societies.

Part Two highlights historical variations in family patterns, and includes a chapter describing family patterns in foraging societies. My objective in including so many social-historical pieces is not to sketch the history that created current patterns but, rather, to promote an understanding of how family patterns are related to their political-economic context. Understanding how marital relationships, motherhood, household composition, extended kin relations, and other elements of family are influenced by the economy and by how people earn their subsistence, as well as by powerful gender ideologies and other important aspects of social context, is central to any sociological analysis of family.

Concluding the discussion of variations in family organization across different types of economy are two chapters on the 1950s and a chapter describing long-term trends in variables shaping families—from average age at marriage and the percentage of people married and living common law to divorce rates. Idealized images of family shape people's expectations, if not their daily experiences, of family. Those images often derive from mythical notions of the 1950s. Chapter 10, from Mary Louise Adams's *The Trouble with Normal*, describes the 1950s promotion of an image of 'the family' as a symbol of stability and security (i.e., the 'bedrock of society') and the sources of that idea. Chapter 11, from Meg Luxton's *More Than a Labour of Love*, examines the nature of relationships between wives and husbands in families where the man is the breadwinner and the woman is a full-time homemaker. Together these chapters begin the critical discussion of family that characterizes the rest of this book.

Part Three, the 'Elements of Family', explores how social organization impacts women's and men's lives as they make and maintain families (and the intimate relations at their core) and includes discussions of marriage, motherhood, caregiving, money management, and housework. The social forces and processes moving people to create heterosexual nuclear families are explored, as are the relations and dynamics common to those families. But single mothers, lesbian couples, and heterosexual couples trying to share the work of parenting are also discussed. And Chapter 26 discusses the changed composition of many middle- and upper-class families: it explores the implications of their increasing reliance on a paid domestic worker. Finally, Chapter 27 addresses the issue of the incompatibility of employment and family responsibilities, and the options families have for coping with it, in the context of cutbacks in social services.

The chapters in Part Four take up the challenges presented by immigration and economic restructuring, with articles that examine both the challenges that are posed and how family members handle them. Issues of gender, race, and class, as well as social support, figure prominently in these descriptions and analyses. Finally, the first two chapters in Part Five address problems not uncommon in Canadian families: men's violence against women, and the negative impact of divorce on children. Solutions to the problems many families are facing are taken up again in the last chapter, which compares the approach to social policy that has been taken by Canadian governments to policy approaches common in Europe.

Creating this edition of the anthology proved to be especially challenging because there are chapters in the second edition that I still find useful in my own course and because many topic areas seemed to be in sore need of up-to-date Canadian material—especially racial, ethnic, and class diversity in family patterns; immigration and families; sexuality; native families; divorce; and comparative social policy. In the end, I replaced 15 chapters from the second edition with more contemporary essays, five of which were written specifically for this book. In addition, three chapters have been revised and updated (Chapters 1, 12, and 26). Altogether, 21 of the chapters were either written by Canadians or are about Canada or Canadians. As in earlier editions, I used non-Canadian material only when I thought it was too good to leave out.

Many people contributed to the third edition. Meg Luxton sat with me for three days last December in order to jointly rewrite the first chapter of this book. I thank her for that dedication as well as for years of conversation that have kept my passion for studying family alive. I thank Sedef Arat-Koc for revising her wonderful chapter. Thanks go to Gillian Creese, Arlene McLaren, Isabel Dyck, Tish Langlois, Sandra Colavecchia, and Diana Worts for writing chapters for this book; to Rod Beaujot, Zenaida Ravanera, and Monica Boyd for answering my questions about demography; and to John Fox for taking the time to design the figures in my demography chapter. And I send a heartfelt thanks to Ann Marie Sorenson who gave me a course reduction this year—without which this book could not have been completed. As well, thanks go to Patrizia Albanese, Sara Dorow, Judy Taylor, Adam Green, Anna Korteweg, and anonymous reviewers for their helpful suggestions. Finally, I thank other colleagues and students at the University of Toronto (especially those who took my 'Families' course in 2006–07) whose enthusiasm for the book and for my course convinced me to do another edition.

The people at Oxford have also been marvellous and I thank them wholeheartedly. Several editors watched me miss deadlines without criticizing. In the end, Jennifer Charlton skilfully handled the job of editor. My thanks go to her, to Amanda Maurice for skilful copyediting, and to Phyllis Wilson for managing the production of the book.

I dedicate the book to Jesse as he begins his adventures in university and the world beyond. Every day, he reminds me that being a mother is the best thing I've ever done.

Acknowledgements

Mary Louise Adams. 'Sexuality and the Post-war Domestic "Revival"', in *The Trouble with Normal: Postwar Youth and the Making of Heterosexuality* (Toronto: University of Toronto Press, Inc.), 18–38. Copyright © 1997. Reprinted with permission of the publisher.

Sedef Arat-Koc. 'The Politics of Family and Immigration in the Subordination of Domestic Workers in Canada', revised version of 'In the Privacy of Our Own Home', *Studies in Political Economy* 28 (Spring 1989). Reprinted by permission of *Studies in Political Economy*.

Marjorie Griffin Cohen. 'Patriarchal Relations of Production', in *Women's Work, Markets, and Economic Development in Nineteenth-century Ontario* (Toronto: University of Toronto Press, Inc.), 42–58. Copyright © 1988. Reprinted with permission of the publisher.

Jane Collier, Michelle Z. Rosaldo, and Sylvia Yanagisako. 'Is There a Family? New Anthropological Views', in *Rethinking the Family: Some Feminist Questions*, eds Barrie Thorne with Marilyn Yalom (Boston: Northeastern University Press). Copyright © 1992 Institute for Research on Women and Gender, Stanford University. Reprinted with permission by University Press of New England, Hanover, NH.

Scott Coltrane. 'Household Labour and the Routine Production of Gender', *Social Problems* 36, 5: 473–90. Copyright © 1989 The Regents of the University of California. Reprinted with permission of University of California Press.

Nancy Cott. 'Domesticity', in *The Bonds of Womanhood* (New Haven, CT: Yale University Press). Copyright © 1977. Reprinted with permission of the publisher.

Dawn H. Currie. '"Here Comes the Bride": The Making of a "Modern Traditional" Wedding in Western Culture', *Journal of Comparative Family Studies* 24, 3 (Autumn 1993): 403–19. Reprinted with permission.

Gillian A. Dunne. 'Lesbians at Home: Why Can't a Man Be More Like a Woman?', in *Lesbian Lifestyles* (London: MacMillan, 1996), 178–225. Reproduced with permission of Palgrave Macmillan.

Gillian A. Dunne. 'Opting into Motherhood: Lesbians Blurring the Boundaries and Transforming the Meaning of Parenthood and Kinship', *Gender & Society* 14, 1 (Feb.): 11–35. Copyright © 2000 Sociologists for Women in Society. Reprinted by permission of SAGE Publications, Inc.

Felicity Edholm. 'The Unnatural Family', in *The Changing Experience of Women*, eds Elizabeth Whitelegg et al. (Oxford: Blackwell Publishing, 1982). Reprinted with permission of the publisher.

Frank F. Furstenburg and Andrew J. Cherlin. 'Children's Adjustment to Divorce', in *Divided Families: What Happens to Children When Parents Part* (Cambridge, MA: Harvard University Press, 1991). Reprinted with permission of the publisher.

Rosemary Gartner, Myrna Dawson, and Maria Crawford. Excerpts from 'Woman Killing: Intimate Femicide in Ontario, 1974–1994', in *Resources for Feminist Research* 26, 3, 4 (1998). Reprinted by permission.

Kathleen Gerson. 'Veering Toward Domesticity', in *Hard Choices: How Women Decide About Work, Career, and Motherhood* (Berkeley: University of California Press). Copyright © 1986 The Regents of the University of California. Reprinted with permission of the publisher.

Tamara K. Hareven. 'Dynamics of Kin in an Industrial Community', in *Families, History, and Social Change* (Boulder, CO: Westview Press), 52–69. Copyright © 2000. Reprinted by permission of Westview Press, a member of Perseus Books Group.

Chrys Ingraham. 'One Is Not Born a Bride: How Weddings Regulate Heterosexuality', in *Introducing the New Sexuality Studies*, eds Steven Seidman, Nancy Fischer, and Chet Meeks (London: Routledge), 197–201. Copyright © 2006. Reproduced by permission of Taylor & Francis Books, UK.

Tish Langlois. 'Navigating Sexual Terrain: Legacies of the Sacred and the Secular in the Lives of French-Canadian Women', unpublished PhD diss., University of Toronto, 2008. Reprinted with permission of the author.

Belinda Leach. 'Transforming Rural Livelihoods: Gender, Work, and Restructuring in Three Ontario Communities', in *Restructuring Caring Labour*, ed. Sheila Neysmith (Toronto: Oxford University Press Canada), 210–25. Copyright © 2000. Reprinted by permission of the publisher.

Eleanor B. Leacock, ed. 'Women in an Egalitarian Society: The Montagnais-Naskapi of Canada', in *Myths of Male Dominance* (New York: Monthly Review Press, 1981), 33–8, 44–50, 51–4, 57–62. Reprinted by permission of the publisher.

Meg Luxton. 'Wives and Husbands', in *More Than a Labour of Love: Three Generations of Women's Work in the Home* (Toronto: Canadian Scholars' Press, Inc./Women's Press, 1980). Reprinted by permission of Canadian Scholars' Press, Inc.

Guida Man. 'From Hong Kong to Canada: Immigration and the Changing Family Lives of Middle-class Women from Hong Kong', in *Voices: Essays on Canadian Families*, 1st edn, ed. M.M. Lynn (Toronto: Nelson Education Ltd). Copyright © 1996. Reproduced by permission <www.cengage.com/permissions>.

Maxine L. Margolis. 'Putting Mothers on the Pedestal', in *Mothers and Such: View of American Women and Why They Change* (Berkeley: University of California Press, 1984). Reprinted with permission. Maxine L. Margolis is Professor Emerita of Anthropology at the University of Florida.

Shelley A. Phipps. 'Lessons from Europe: Policy Options to Enhance the Economic Security of Canadian Families', in *Family Security in Insecure Times*, Vol. II (Ottawa: Canadian Council on Social Development, 1996). Reprinted with permission.

Gillian Ranson. 'Education, Work, and Family Decision-making: Finding the "Right Time" to Have a Baby', *Canadian Review of Sociology and Anthropology* 35, 4 (1998): 517–33. Reprinted with permission of Blackwell Publishing.

Harriet Rosenberg. 'Motherwork, Stress, and Depression: The Costs of Privatized Social Reproduction', in *Feminism and Political Economy*, 1st edn, eds Heather Jon Maroney and Meg Luxton (Toronto: Nelson Education Ltd). Copyright © 1987. Reproduced by permission <www.cengage.com/permissions>.

Louise A. Tilly and Joan W. Scott. 'The Family Economy in Modern England and France', in *Women, Work and Family* (New York: Holt, Rinehart and Winston, 1978). Reprinted by permission.

Mariana Valverde. 'Heterosexuality: Contested Ground', in *Sex, Power and Pleasure* (Toronto: Canadian Scholars' Press, Inc./Women's Press, 1985). Reprinted by permission of Canadian Scholars' Press, Inc.

Diane Worts. '"Like a Family": Reproductive Work in a Co-operative Setting', unpublished PhD diss., University of Toronto, 2003. Reprinted with permission of the author.

PART ONE

Putting 'Family' in Perspective

Chapter 1

To orient us in our examination of families, this chapter discusses how family is thought about in everyday life, in legal and political terms, in popular culture, and in sociological studies. Over the last several decades, there have been some dramatic and important changes that have challenged earlier understandings of families and have forced us to rethink common-sense assumptions. Women's mass movement into the paid labour force unsettled a long-standing division of work that shaped the organization of families. The women's movement, the gay, lesbian, and trans movements, and other equality-seeking groups also created new gender and family relationships as they struggled to gain equal rights. As well, significant economic changes have made life more precarious for most people. Since the 1980s, governments have rejected many established welfare-state policies that provided a modest safety net for most people, and instead implemented an array of neo-liberal policies. Neo-liberalism starts from a commitment to unrestricted capitalist investment, the free market, and private profit making. One of its main assumptions is that 'private choice is better than public regulation as a mechanism for allocating resources and ordering social affairs' (Phillipps 2000: 1). Accordingly, the deregulation of employment has resulted in more and more jobs without security, and thus the requirement that people work harder and longer. As a result, family life has become more pressured and uncertain.

This chapter looks at the ways family has been thought about and offers an approach to the study of family that we find useful. It asks how we might conceptualize family as we try to understand cross-cultural variations and historical changes, as well as the changes that we are living through today.

Conceptualizing 'Family'

Meg Luxton and Bonnie Fox

When people use the term *family* they usually assume that what they mean by it is clear. Yet depending on the context the term has a variety of meanings. An adult man who talks about working to support his family probably means his wife and young children. An adult woman who plans to quit her job to have a family is referring to children. A recent immigrant to Canada who says he misses his family may mean his wife and children who have not yet immigrated, or he may live with his nuclear family but still miss his parents, in-laws, and siblings who were part of his daily life before he came to Canada. A university student going home to spend the holidays with her family likely means her parents and siblings. Someone who explains that their family was killed in the Holocaust probably means an extended kin group. Still someone else who describes a group of friends as 'my real family' is identifying people who provide significant emotional and personal support. At the same time, when a play or film is advertised as 'family entertainment', the implication is that few people will find it offensive. And when politicians claim to support 'family values', they usually mean something quite different from gays and lesbians who claim 'we are family too'.

These diverse usages show how slippery the term is. In this paper, we review common-sense and formal definitions of family as well as some of the practical implications of these definitions. We also review the social forces that create families, showing how they produce certain kinds of understandings and limit others. After reviewing dominant sociological perspectives on family and feminist critiques of them, we propose a way of approaching the study of family that both accommodates the diverse family patterns that are common today and promotes understanding.

The Familiar and the Commonsensical

We suggest that the complexities, contradictions, and confusions surrounding the way *family* is used occur in part because families are so familiar and our everyday definitions of family so taken for granted. At the same time, several decades of change have disrupted prevailing assumptions about families and thus caused some confusion.

Almost everyone is a member of a family and lives for significant periods of time in a family, so they assume that they know very well what *family* means. The nuclear family has been such a widely accepted form for so long in Canada that getting married, having children in the context of marriage, and living as a nuclear family seem natural. In fact, the heterosexual nuclear family based on marriage so dominates popular culture—in spite of sizeable numbers of common-law couples and lone parents as well as increasing numbers of same-sex couples—that even people who grew up in families configured differently sometimes assume there is only one 'real' kind of family. Moreover, family relationships are often so emotionally profound and so deeply tied to unconscious feelings that the assumptions of those who grew up in nuclear families are hard to question. For many people, the pattern of marriage and nuclear families is so taken for granted that it seems to be a product of nature. Nevertheless, notions that the nuclear family is a natural unit must be interrogated if for no other reason than that they have important practical consequences for most of us.

The ease with which people accept marriage norms and nuclear-family forms also comes from the way ideas about marriage and 'the family' are central to common-sense ideologies. The belief that biology is a 'given', that it determines various social phenomena—such as institutions like 'the family' as well as personality and behaviour—is strong in this culture. Thus, the biology of reproduction seems to 'naturally' produce the heterosexual nuclear-family pattern, including conventional gender divisions of work and responsibility. Increasingly, however, the relative importance of biological relations and social ties is debated. Disagreements are especially heightened when financial responsibility and custody arrangements are at stake. Fathers who have never taken care of their children can make custody claims on the strength of their biological relationship. Single mothers are pressured to name the biological father when registering the birth of their child and in some cases have been denied access to social assistance if they fail to name the father. And there are debates about whether sperm donors have the right to privacy or whether their biological offspring have the right to know the identity of the donor. These ambiguities about biology reinforce cultural confusions about family, but they have yet to significantly challenge deeply held beliefs about the determining nature of biology.

Definitions of family are also hard to clarify because there is often a confusion of common-sense ideas, moral judgments, and actual practices. For many people, the fact that the majority of women and men marry and live as couples, especially if they have or want to have children, for example, reinforces the idea that families should be based on heterosexual, monogamous couples. Such beliefs may easily lead to moral assessments that those who do not live in such relationships are inferior, or immoral, or to be pitied (Adams 1997). Moreover, it is often assumed that other family patterns cause problems, especially for children (Arnup 2005).

The dominance of beliefs that assume the heterosexual nuclear family is the ideal, or norm, makes life difficult for anyone who lives differently. Single people or those who live in extended kin groups may be considered peculiar; childless couples are sometimes pitied or considered selfish, while single mothers are subject to considerable hostility, especially when they need social support; gay, lesbian, bi, and trans people are subject to harassment and their relationships are often not respected or validated. Deep desires to be socially acceptable or to conform to parental wishes motivate many people to get married and form nuclear families. Others may find such social pressures painful, offensive, and oppressive, but may respond by fighting for social acceptance and legitimacy. Such struggles have led to changes in how families are understood. There is no longer a legal distinction made between 'legitimate' and 'illegitimate' children; and gay and lesbian marriages are now recognized. These struggles, the public debates they evoke, and the changing practices they make possible produce new complexities and uncertainties about family forms and definitions.

As understandings about family have become more contentious, the political stakes have risen. On the one hand, neo-liberal theory is indifferent to how people organize their personal lives and families. On the other hand, its advocates have mobilized 'family-values' discourses to promote their central idea that 'families' and not the state are responsible for people's welfare. Because neo-liberalism holds individuals responsible for their own well-being, it tolerates a wide range of personal strategies as long as they ensure that the individuals concerned are not likely to make demands on state services. From that perspective, gay and lesbian marriages (which, like heterosexual marriages, hold partners responsible for each other's well-being) may be more acceptable than young women becoming single mothers (who will probably need state support while their children are young).

Yet, as states motivated by neo-liberalism cut spending on social services, spokespeople argued that families should take responsibility for their own care and survival. In 1994, for example, the newly elected Conservative Ontario Premier, Mike Harris, justified his government's plans to cut welfare and social services by insisting that people should rely less on government services and more on families, friends, neighbours, and communities (Luxton 2006: 264). However, the idea that families should and can be self-reliant is problematic in a period when few families can rely on one income, employed parents have to juggle the competing demands of paid employment and family responsibilities, and many people face longer workweeks, unemployment, and poverty (Bezanson 2006). Right-wing, 'pro-family' groups have played on people's anxieties and anger about these social changes and focused those feelings on changing family patterns. They blame many social problems on those who do not conform to heterosexual nuclear-family forms, especially mothers who take on paid employment. Such groups have very effectively invoked 'the family' to symbolize a mythical (and lost) past and lobbied for a return to 'traditional family values'—a reassertion of the importance of heterosexual nuclear families in which women are home full-time (Coontz 1992; Gairdner 1992).

Formal Definitions

Inequities arise from some contemporary definitions of family. For example, *family* is a legal term involving particular definitions that entail specific rights and obligations for certain people. Biological and adoptive parents are required to provide material support and emotional nurturing for their children and are normally entitled to custody of, or access to, those children. Other people who may have deep emotional relations with children are not recognized in the law. Thus, a woman who may have lived with her divorced lover's children on a daily basis and cared for them for years has no legal claim to them while the father's parents do—even though they may have seen the children only once a year as they grew up. An estranged father may have greater access to a child's school record and confidential discussions with the teachers about the child's performance at school than the person who has cared for the child every day after school for years. State-regulated institutions such as schools or hospitals use marriage and family relations to determine which people will be informed and consulted about the status of a person in the institution. Critically ill patients may find that family members with whom they have had little contact are admitted to their rooms and entitled to make significant medical decisions, whereas friends who have provided daily support and who best know their wishes are excluded. Similarly, even when someone designates an heir in a will, the 'immediate family' has some legal grounds to challenge that will and claim a right to the inheritance. Finally, until 1999 in Ontario, a wife of only weeks was entitled to a widow's pension while a same-sex lover of 20 years was not. Only recently are same-sex partners gaining the rights and privileges that heterosexual spouses have always enjoyed. In the 1990s, same-sex partners of employees of the federal government became eligible for benefits such as health care and Canada Pension (Larson, Goltz, and Munro 2000). In 1997, British Columbia became the first jurisdiction in North America to extend the definition of spouse to include same-sex partners living together for at least two years (Larson et al. 2000). And only since June 2005 have same-sex partners been able to marry in Canada. As gay and lesbian couples have fought for the right to be treated the same as other couples, they have changed our definition of family.

Similarly, definitions of family embedded in immigration law have shaped immigration to Canada, but new Canadians also challenge our definitions of family. Under current legislation, a Canadian citizen or permanent resident may sponsor her or his spouse, common-law or conjugal partner, or dependent children to come to Canada as permanent residents. They can also sponsor their parents, grandparents, and certain other specified close kin. But other categories of people are excluded, even if they have the same or more important relationships. Refugees who have raised children not legally theirs are refused the right to bring those children with them. People coming from societies that recognize multiple spouses may have to select only one spouse to conform to Canadian law. At the same time, waves of immigrants have brought different ways of thinking about families to Canada: they have raised new questions about how marriage partners are best chosen, they have argued that extended kin groups are important networks of emotional and material support that warrant loyalty and legal recognition, and their assumptions about families have expanded prevailing ideas.

These examples show that the way we conceptualize family matters. Embodying deeply held cultural assumptions, the concept informs legislation, policies, and practices that govern our lives. It also shapes decisions we make as individuals about how to live our lives. And it limits or expands our imaginations as we think about the future.

Standard definitions of family centre on a number of characteristics to identify a kind of social unit—rather than focus on social relationships involved in specific activities and bearing special emotional significance. The former tendency makes apparent sense to governments, which need to count and classify their populations to assess the need for social services, and even to social scientists when their chief concern is classification. However, a comparison of the definitions used by Statistics Canada in the

1980s and in 2006 shows how even definitions based on a social unit have changed in response to changes in social practices and social relations. In the 1980s, Statistics Canada's definition of a census family was: 'A husband and wife (with or without children who are unmarried), or a lone parent with one or more children who have never married (regardless of age), living in the same dwelling unit.' This was differentiated from an economic family, which was a group of two or more people who were related to each other by blood, marriage, or adoption and who lived in the same dwelling. In both definitions, if a woman and man lived together they were treated as if married, regardless of their legal status (Statistics Canada 1984: viii–ix, Table 4).

These definitions have been revised. A census family is now considered to be a married couple and the children, if any, of either or both spouses; a couple living common law and the children, if any, of either or both partners; or, a lone parent of any marital status with at least one child living in the same dwelling. All members of a particular census family live in the same dwelling. A couple may be of opposite or same sex. Children may be children by birth, marriage, or adoption (regardless of their age or marital status) as long as they live in the dwelling and do not have their spouse or child living in the dwelling. Grandchildren living with their grandparent(s), but with no parents present, also constitute a census family (Statistics Canada 2006a). An economic family refers to a group of two or more persons who live in the same dwelling and are related to each other by blood, marriage, common law, or adoption. A couple may be of opposite or same sex. Foster children are included. By definition, all persons who are members of a census family are also members of an economic family. Examples of the broader concept of economic family include the following: two co-resident census families who are related to one another are considered one economic family; co-resident siblings who are not members of a census family are considered as one economic family; and nieces or nephews living with aunts or uncles are considered one economic family (Statistics Canada 2006b).

While the new definitions recognize lesbian and gay partnerships and marriages, in restricting *family* to spouses or partners and people related by blood or adoption, and by insisting on co-residence, these definitions exclude some people. As Margrit Eichler (1988) has argued, when definitions based on form, rather than actual social relations or activities and functions, are used to establish eligibility for policies supposed to support families, they can threaten the welfare of individuals and undermine the economic bases of some families. When definitions of family are not based on activities and functions—much less the social relations responsible for them—biology and legal status are easily accepted as determinants of family. As a result people choosing to live collectively, friends sharing financial resources and providing each other necessary daily support, and people in other types of relationships who share material resources, provide daily support services, and have deep emotional connections are all excluded. When used to set policy on access to loved ones, such definitions can separate needy people from those who give them care and support (e.g., visiting rights in hospitals).[1]

It is generally problematic to specify relationships determined by blood, marriage, or residence and exclude some social relationships of exactly the same nature.[2] Anthropologists have shown persuasively that family and kinship are social creations and not products of biology (see Sahlins 1976; Goody 1976; Collier, Rosaldo, and Yanagisako 1982; see Chapter 3). Even in the simplest human societies, biological ties do not establish the domestic groups that provide mutual support and nurturance of children (Lee 1979). Throughout human history, the composition and organization of domestic groups have varied tremendously. In other words the group that lives together, co-operates to produce its subsistence, and cares for children has not always consisted of people tied by blood or marriage. Logically, then, social functions and not biological and/or residential relations might be the way to identify family.

Different Approaches to Conceptualizing Family

Statistics Canada's definition of family has changed as gays, lesbians, feminists, and immigrants have insisted it must. So, too, theoretical approaches to the study of family have changed. In the 1950s and 1960s, American sociologist Talcott Parsons advanced arguments about 'the family' that reflected the familistic ideology that seemed to have captivated so many Americans and Canadians. He assumed that relations of marriage and blood are the only ones that truly involve (and can involve) a strong commitment to people's welfare, and especially to the nurturance of children.

Advancing a structural-functionalist argument, Parsons argued that societies have to perpetuate themselves biologically and socially in order to continue. He insisted that 'the family' is the unit best suited to have and care for children and to ensure the well being of adults, and therefore that 'the family' was essential and universal. For Parsons, 'the family' involved a heterosexual nuclear unit in which there is a division of labour based on gender, with the man assuming the 'instrumental' role and the woman the 'expressive' role—the breadwinner–homemaker family, in other words (Parsons and Bales 1955; see Zelditch 1960). Of course, his argument about the essential nature of this family was tautological: once the heterosexual nuclear family is defined as the best unit for child rearing its necessity is given. The provocative question of whether it *is* best for children to grow up in nuclear families is one this argument sidesteps. In emphasizing the functional nature of the division of household labour by gender, Parsons's work rationalized the gender inequality characteristic of the 1950s in the US and Canada. Moreover, in writing about the division of labour based on gender in terms of 'roles', Parsons adopted language that implied a universal, and separate but equal, gender order in families: he obscured the power imbalance inherent in gender divisions in heterosexual nuclear families, as well as the work involved in homemaking and childcare (Thorne 1982). Further, by asserting that the family form predominant among white, middle-class Americans was functional and natural, Parsons paved the way for those who insisted that other family forms—especially those common in the African-American community (Stack 1974)—were deviant or inadequate.

Influential though it was, Parsons's work was soundly criticized and largely dismissed some time ago by many sociologists (see Morgan 1975). The theme of a functional fit of family to society could not predict the changes that are now so evident in families. Nevertheless, partly because Parsons's arguments were so close to common-sense views of family, they retained their influence on family sociology. And they continue to appear in popular debate. So-called family-values proponents use them as they argue that 'the family' (i.e., the heterosexual, breadwinner–homemaker family) is the 'bedrock of society'. Politicians and religious leaders who resisted gay and lesbian marriage, and some sociologists with a conservative political agenda, have a perspective on family very similar to Parsons's (Popenoe 1993; see Chapter 12).

Parsons's assumption that what was functional (or good) for society was good for the individual could not withstand feminist critique of the way nuclear families were organized. Indeed, sociology had to reconceptualize family after feminist theorists (writing in the 1960s and 1970s especially) made a public issue of the private oppression of full-time housewives (see Friedan 1963; Luxton 1980). Insisting that women's experience of marriage was very different from men's—that private housework was isolating, unrewarding, and connected with economic dependency; and that there was a power differential central to marriage (which too often was expressed through men's violence against their wives)—feminist social scientists irrevocably transformed sociology's depiction of family life (Barrett and McIntosh 1982; Cheal 1991; Fox 1997; Mandell and Duffy 1988; Thorne and Yalom 1982; see Bernard 1972; Hartmann 1981; Mitchell 1966; Oakley 1974; Rowbotham 1973; Smith 1973). Because of feminist arguments, the understanding that men, women, and children have different experiences of family life, that inequality and power differentials are typically built into family organization, that family is sustained by work, and that the economy influences what goes on in families are important assumptions many sociologists now bring to the study of family.

Since the 1980s, significant social change has prompted new sociological approaches to studying family. A majority of women are now in the paid labour force—and thus have some degree of choice about committing to a long-term relationship, or remaining in one. At the same time, neo-liberal governments have deregulated the labour market, so jobs have become less secure and more demanding of our time and energy than they used to be (Jacobs and Gerson 2004; Presser 2003; Shalla and Clement 2007). These changes have meant that families are subject to more stress. As divorce has become more accepted and readily available, people are more likely to leave problematic relationships. Thus, more people are likely to live alone for significant periods of their lives. And people's life courses are more diverse than they used to be (Beaujot 2000; Jones, Marsden, and Tepperman 1990). In turn, individualizing forces in society have been mirrored by a shift in the theoretical approaches of some sociologists toward a focus on the individual (Cheal 1991: 132).

For example, Elisabeth Beck-Gernsheim (2002) in *Reinventing the Family* argues that family life, which used to be governed by tradition, is giving way to 'life as a planning project'. That is, people are not only 'refusing lifelong plans, permanent ties, [and] immutable identities' but are increasingly involved in perpetual choice making and decision taking about how they will fashion and re-fashion their lives. The image she creates is of individuals moving in and out of families throughout their lives.

Turning attention to the individual rightly acknowledges individualizing forces in society; it also highlights individual agency. Doing both is important. But there are problems inherent in focusing exclusively on individuals and their choices. One key problem is that most people still live in families and have lasting family relationships. And despite increasing diversity in family patterns and in individuals' personal histories, there are still regularities in family life. Most people believe that their emotional needs are best met by finding a partner. For many women especially, life is incomplete if they don't have children, and most assume that they should be married or in a stable partnership in order to parent effectively (McMahon 1995). Yet when heterosexual couples become parents, gender divisions in their relationship—especially divisions involving work and responsibility—are usually strengthened (Fox 2001; Walzer 1998). Gender divisions are also tragically revealed by ongoing patterns of men's violence against their women partners (Gartner, Dawson, and Crawford 1998; see Chapter 31). Thus, any consideration of family life needs to be attentive to these and other patterns that are common to families.

Another problem with a focus on individual choice is that it encourages analysis that ignores the many ways in which people's circumstances, and thus the organization of society, shape and constrain their lives. For example, Canadian women who wish to have children find it very difficult to be parents on their own—given the need to both provide care and earn a livelihood in a society that gives parents relatively little support with childcare. Moreover, analyses that focus on individual choice, and emphasize our ability to make choices, have the inadvertent effect of implying individual responsibility for any consequences that our choices might produce. For example, women who choose to have a baby often find themselves at home full-time feeling exhausted, stressed, and isolated for reasons that involve the social context of motherhood in this society (Rosenberg 1987; see Chapter 20). Blaming women for these feelings would be sociologically naïve as well as insensitive and unfair.

Avoiding these problems, but also responding to individualizing trends, some sociologists have concluded that because people's experiences of family life and the kinds of families they live in are so varied, there is no such thing as 'the family'. Instead they argue that the family does not exist. Rather, they argue that family is essentially a symbol system or ideology (Barrett and McIntosh 1982; Gittins 1985). In short, for some writers, family is a set of ideas; and in this society we are all subject to a hegemonic (or dominant) ideology about families. Specifically, familism, which sees the nuclear family as universal and necessary, constitutes an ideology that characterizes Western capitalist societies (Barrett and McIntosh 1982).

A recent study by physical scientists at the Center for Systems Integration and Sustainability at Michigan State University in the US illustrates how pervasive and problematic familistic ideology can be (Lu and Liu 2007). The authors show that smaller households use more resources and generate more garbage than larger households. From these findings they jump to an unwarranted and startling conclusion. They do so because they frame their analysis with an unexamined assumption about the essential nature of nuclear families. Based on data from 12 countries, they argue that because divorce resulted in 7.4 million more households, divorce is a key contributor to increased resource consumption and thus climate change! Rather than argue for more support for collective living arrangements, which would be even less wasteful than nuclear-family households, they argue:

> As global human values continue to shift toward greater autonomy and choice, the environmental impacts of increasing divorce will continue unless effective policies to minimize household dissolution are implemented. . . . The environmental impact of divorce and other lifestyles such as separation should be considered when making personal choices and government policies. (Lu and Liu 2007: 20633)

This conclusion offers a stunning example of the ways in which familial ideology and political bias can distort scientific analysis.

Familial ideology has a strong hold in this culture. But equating family with familistic discourse is problematic. Although it is true that symbol systems make social life meaningful and therefore profoundly shape our lives, it is also the case that there is a material reality to personal life that must be understood. There are social processes and social relations involved in family—which often assume patterned regularity—that cannot be reduced to sets of ideas, however intricately they are bound up with ideas.

Forces Creating Families

Ideology is certainly one of the key social forces that move people to make families. Rayna Rapp (1982) has argued that family is the ideological, normative concept that recruits people to household relations of production, reproduction, and consumption. In addition to ideological forces creating families, there are other cultural factors and also emotional and material factors that promote family formation.

The ideological and cultural forces that idealize couples and families are increasingly subtle and hard to pin down. In a market culture that presents us with so many options, it seems that people are confronted with endless choices about how to live. Nevertheless, the strong belief that only people related by blood or marriage can be truly committed to each other is a critical force pulling people together to form families. As well, marriage remains one of the markers of adult status and parenthood confirms it further (Fox forthcoming; McMahon 1995). Many young adults experience pressure from those around them to marry and have children.

As well, popular culture—from the music and advertising industries to Hollywood production companies—frequently relies on glorifications of romantic love to sell their products. And the wedding industry is once again making huge profits (Ingraham 2006; Currie 1993; see Chapter 16). In popular TV series like *Sex and the City* and *Desperate Housewives*, women dedicate themselves to finding or keeping a man, however mixed their feelings are about men, however troubled the lives of the heterosexual couples around them, and however satisfying, supportive, and even loving their friendships are with each other. In movies made for a teenage and young adult male audience (like *Knocked Up* and *Superbad*) comedic plots centre on the powerful lure of sex that propels boys toward girls in spite of the apparent social chasm that seems to separate them, their painful awkwardness with each other, and the close relationships boys have with each other.

Heterosexuality is another social force pulling women and men together and into creating families. Heterosexuality is no more biologically determined than are heterosexual families (Blumenstein and Schwartz 1989; Seidman 2003; Weeks 1981; Valverde 1985; see Chapter 13). An array of social forces create heterosexuality as the normative sexual pattern, and these forces also promote family. The subtle and unsubtle repression of 'inappropriate' sexual and gender expression in children and young people—especially boys—and the eroticization of relationships between girls and boys, women and men, produce men and women who are likely to be drawn to each other. In turn, the complicated dynamics of romantic love are so compelling that people get married far more readily than seems rational given the responsibilities it entails.

Less apparent than ideologies of romantic love, gender remains a major social force pulling women and men together to form families. Because social arrangements continue to create gender differences—whether these involve individual characteristics or different opportunities and experiences—they promote the mutual dependence of women and men. Some researchers have argued that a variety of social processes—including social pressures—produce girls who learn how to care for others, and to do the 'emotion work' central to intimacy, and boys who do not (Cancian 1985; Kimmel 1999; Reitsma-Street 1998). Certainly, persistent differences in the material positions of women and men are sufficient to cause interdependence between them. Women and men still fare differently in the labour force as is evidenced by the gender gap in earnings connected to the ongoing gender segregation of jobs (Brooks, Jarman, and Blackburn 2003). Of course, many women now earn enough to support themselves and to have a choice about whether or not to commit to a long-term relationship with a man. But fewer women earn enough to support themselves and children—as the high poverty rates of lone mothers make clear. The dependence of women with children on men is reinforced by the meagreness of the support extended to women with babies and young children by the state and the community (Wall 2001). In short, motherhood continues to reinforce women's dependence on men. That men are dependent on women to create and sustain family relationships is also apparent in the difficulties men often have maintaining relationships with their children after divorce (Arendell 1995). Thus, the gender differences that are fostered by the way society is currently organized promote the formation of heterosexual families.

Other cultural and social organizational factors do the same. Although being single is increasingly acceptable, and indeed glorified in popular culture, many social institutions and practices still make daily life easier for couples. It is often more difficult for people to function socially as singles. In some communities ('great for raising a family') single people feel excluded from informal social life that is based on couples. Even in large cosmopolitan cities, people may feel awkward or uncomfortable eating in a restaurant or going to the movies by themselves. More concretely, people travelling on their own sometimes have to pay a singles surcharge. And the construction of houses and even apartments or condominiums invariably feature one and not two 'master bedrooms' (often with attached bathrooms): housing stock assumes that people live as couples or as single adults and barely accommodates adult friends wishing to live together. These social facts and experiences that penalize single people make having a partner and being in a family more attractive. In many ways, the social world is organized around the nuclear-family unit. Fairly devoid of community, this society creates the need for people to form families—and not just for the sake of caring for children. Of course, the desire to have children provides a compelling incentive to establish a partnership, given both the assumption that children are best cared for when they have two parents living together and the difficulties that lone mothers have caring for their children and earning subsistence.

In short, families are products of ideologies (especially those of normative heterosexuality, romantic love, motherhood, and familism itself), culture, and social and economic organization (especially the gender inequality characteristic of the labour market). These forces recruit people to share their resources, have and raise children, and care for each other. Family, in turn, gives children a claim on social resources and ensures social reproduction.

Interestingly, those forces that have recruited most people to form heterosexual nuclear families have weakened in recent decades. Women are choosing to have children on their own, same-sex couples are creating families and raising children, and women as well as men are dedicating themselves to their careers and avoiding long-term relationships. Heterosexuality is no longer the only socially accepted form of sexual expression or foundation of committed relationships (Arnup 2005; Carrington 1999; Weston 1991). The ideologies of romantic love and even motherhood—as women's primary career, often entailing full-time work and relegating all else to the background—now compete against some other ideas, albeit only vaguely developed ones. And the majority of women do not need men economically the way they did decades ago (Coontz 2005).

Yet in this society family remains an important social institution. The emotional connection that so ties people of different generations and households together 'til death do us part'—more so than marriage it seems—must be central to our conceptualization of family. The power of familism, and kinship ideology in general, in this society attests to the tremendous intensity of the psychic connections among close family. As others have argued, the privatization of family life in this society, and the exclusivity of the mother–child relationship, is no doubt behind this intensity (Mitterauer and Sieder 1982; Coontz 1988).[3]

Toward Definition and Conceptualization

In order to study family in the context of rapid social change, we find it most useful to think of family as the relationships that bring people together on an ongoing and daily basis to share resources for the sake of caring for children and each other. Certainly, the care of children is at the heart of what we mean by family. More broadly, we think it most productive to think of family as the relationships that mobilize resources, especially for the sake of generational and daily reproduction. And while we have emphasized the social forces that influence people, we must emphasize that people *actively create* their families. Focusing on the relationships that gather and redistribute resources, and thus provide for people's daily sustenance, highlights the material aspects of the social relations that constitute families as productive and reproductive units.

Arguably, what family most fundamentally involves is the maintenance of life on a daily and generational basis. In conceptualizing and studying family, then, it is more useful to consider the social relationships and processes by which people's ongoing needs are met than to focus on blood and legal status. Specifically, *family* refers to the social relationships that people create to care for children and other dependants daily and also to ensure that the needs of the adults responsible for these dependents are met. Feminist social scientists refer to this work as 'social reproduction' (Gill and Bakker 2003; Bezanson and Luxton 2006). Barbara Laslett and Johanna Brenner (1989: 382–3) have explained what social reproduction means as follows:

> Among other things, social reproduction includes how food, clothing, and shelter are made available for immediate consumption, the ways in which the care and socialization of children are provided, the care of the infirm and elderly, and the social organization of sexuality. Social reproduction can thus be seen to include various kinds of work—mental, manual, and emotional—aimed at providing the historically and socially, as well as biologically, defined care necessary to maintain existing life and to reproduce the next generation.

In every social system there is a relationship between the way people produce their subsistence and wealth—food, shelter, clothing, and other goods, including the tools to produce those goods—and the way the human population is produced across generations, and daily. This relationship is never simple or direct. However, the type of work people do to sustain life—whether that involves foraging, pastoralism, agriculture, industrial or post-industrial capitalism—creates conditions for certain patterns of child-bearing and rearing. In a similar way, certain practices of child-bearing and rearing both require and make possible other types of work (Seccombe 1992; 1993).

For example, women in foraging societies tend to bear children at later ages, at greater intervals, and thus have comparatively fewer numbers of live births per woman than women in peasant societies (Howell 1979). And because there is little wealth to inherit in foraging societies, there is neither social concern over the legitimacy of children nor control over women's sexuality (Leacock 1981). Instead, all children are welcomed as members of the society and the group as a whole tends to accept responsibility for children (Turnbull 1962; Lee 1979). In such societies, because children are cared for collectively and also because work is under the control of the worker, women are not required to concentrate on childcare instead of participating in the other work necessary to sustain community life (Lee 1979; Leacock 1981; see Chapter 4).

In contrast, peasant farmers who individually hold land and must produce their subsistence by working that land tend to have more children in smaller intervals. As a result, women become more tied to child rearing and do work that is compatible with childcare (Draper 1975; Harris 1981; Tilly and Scott 1978; see Chapter 5). In societies where kin groups own great wealth, inheritance becomes a major social concern and certain children are clearly designated as the legitimate heirs of specific individuals. In many agricultural societies where kin membership in the father's lineage both entitles the individual to rights in the land and its produce and legitimates the individual's claim to inheritance rights, children's legitimacy is ensured by powerful social controls over women's sexuality (Lerner 1986).

Today, as an evolving legacy of life in advanced capitalist economies, the number of children per woman is very low (see Chapter 12). This is understandable given that parents do not have the means to ensure their children's material success (e.g., land they can pass on to sons who will farm it as their parents did). Indeed, parents now believe they must devote enormous amounts of energy preparing their children emotionally and intellectually to succeed in systems that are beyond their control (i.e., the schools and then the labour market) (Hays 1996; Wall 2004). Amidst long-term decline in birth rates, the state in most capitalist societies has assumed a variety of pro-natalist policies (e.g., anti-abortion laws, family allowances) to induce (white) women to have children. Meanwhile, until recently, women have devoted much of their lives to raising their children. Household responsibilities were too great to combine this with waged work, and employers deliberately refused to employ married women (Strong-Boag 1988). Now, since there is both need and opportunity for married women to hold jobs, most women must juggle employment with domestic responsibilities defined as theirs (Hochschild 1989; Luxton and Corman 2001; see Chapter 27).

Aside from the relationship between the organization of production and the organization of reproduction, the nature of wealth and the requirements of production have also been related systematically to the form, composition, and structure of households. Thus, in societies where people had to forage daily to meet subsistence needs, a near-communal organization in which scarce resources were shared, and economic decisions were made collectively, was the wisest survival strategy (Leacock 1981; see Chapter 4). In contrast, in the feudal and early modern periods, as in earlier Roman and Germanic societies—when agricultural and artisanal production were the bases of the economy—the household was the organizing centre for economic production. Indeed, the word *economy* comes from the Greek word for household. In medieval times, recruitment to the household and household membership were dictated primarily by changing household labour requirements. All workers and servants had the same position in families as biological children: they were under the authority of the male property owner and household head (Mitterauer and Sieder 1982).

The subsequent separations of place of residence and site of production for household use, on the one hand, and site of production of goods and services for the market, on the other—which occurred as capitalism developed—generated a major transformation in households and families. Among other things, the separation destroyed the ease with which parents had previously been able to coordinate childcare and their other work. From the nineteenth century, middle-class European, Canadian, and American households increasingly became centres exclusively for raising children and doing domestic labour (Davidoff and Hall 1987; Mintz and Kellogg 1988; Ryan 1981; see Chapter 9).

Today, the household, or residential unit, is often the unit of social reproduction. That is, it is a unit of production, reproduction, and consumption in which people work and pool resources so as to ensure that their own and their dependants' subsistence and emotional needs are met. But this is not always the case. For instance, women commonly have coped with poverty and financial insecurity—and raised their children despite these struggles—by creating support networks of kin and non-kin that extend across households and involve the pooling of all kinds of resources (from money to clothing to time). Decades ago, Carol Stack (1974) documented such a pattern of coping in poor African-American communities, whose men faced nearly impossible obstacles to achieving the role of breadwinner. Similar patterns exist in other cultures (Tanner 1974; Rogers 1980) and, in a modified form, have also existed in traditional, white working-class communities in Western industrial societies (Young and Willmott 1957; Gans 1962). And today, families across all social classes often rely daily on the help and support of kin, friends, and/or paid domestic workers (nannies, babysitters, and women who clean) (Hansen 2005). Carol Stack's (1974: 32) definition of family is therefore worth considering: 'Ultimately I defined "family" as the smallest, organized, durable network of kin and non-kin who interact daily, providing domestic needs of children and assuring their survival.' Because the relationships responsible for social reproduction in our society vary in content, at least by social class, sexual orientation, and race, such a broad definition is useful.

A Look at Social Reproduction

A peculiarity of the development of industrial and post-industrial capitalism is that paid labour that produces subsistence goods and unpaid domestic labour came to be physically separated and socially differentiated. In the process, traditional divisions of labour between women and men took on new significance: women's work was increasingly privatized (i.e., done in a private situation and defined as 'the family's' responsibility). It developed a new character as paid work left the home and women themselves were increasingly defined in terms of domestic qualities (Davidoff and Hall 1987; Coontz 1988). In turn, because housework is privatized it was virtually ignored as *work* until feminism revised our thinking. Nevertheless, household work is essential not only to family members' maintenance but also to the capitalist economy.

Household work involves housework—that is, all the chores necessary to maintain people physically (from meal preparation to clothing care), childcare (from changing diapers to listening to an upset teenager), adult care (from nursing the sick to providing emotional support), and 'making ends meet' (balancing incoming money against the needs of household members). Although it is apparent that this work is necessary to household members' well-being, it is less obvious that it is also central to the operation of the marketplace. In this economy, employers are not responsible for the daily recuperation of their labour force—unlike in feudal economies where landlords had some obligations to their peasants and master craftsmen housed and fed their apprentices. Thus, the domestic labour that rejuvenates the worker's ability to work is not only important to his or her success in the labour market but is also important to the employer.

Since World War II in Canada and the United States, when households are unable to make ends meet, the state typically has provided a safety net of minimal assistance, at least for the short term. Yet, unlike in Europe, there has been persistent reluctance by the state to assume the responsibilities of social reproduction; consistently, law and policy have enforced families' assumption of those responsibilities (Eichler 1988; Morton 1988; Cameron 2006; Bezanson 2006). Accordingly, state provision of good quality daycare is unlikely—though perhaps partly because of the specific nature of the work of caring for children (Blumenfeld and Mann 1980). At the same time, in a society where the public sphere seems increasingly inhospitable and even dangerous, there is some ambivalence on the part of parents about shifting children's daytime care from the home to community facilities. Given the alternatives presented by a society increasingly dominated by the marketplace, the comforts of a private haven, nourishing home-cooked meals, etc., remain attractive. All that is entailed by privatized social reproduction seems essential to the quality of life in a society that is essentially anti-social.

Of course, women do the vast majority of the tasks that create the house as a comfortable home and the family as a supportive environment (Luxton 1980; see Chapters 11 and 27). Indeed, women do the bulk of this work even when they also have full-time employment (Bianchi, Robinson, and Milkie 2006; Marshall 2006). This gendered division of household responsibility constitutes a serious concern for us all: those women balancing the demands of family and employment (and they represent the majority of Canadian women) have less sleep, less leisure, and less time for friends than men; and they experience considerable stress trying to coordinate two fundamentally incompatible kinds of jobs (Hochschild 1989; 1997).

We must confront the question of how much longer women can continue their balancing act in the context of very little substantial change in the organization of paid work and occupational careers, community services, and gender ideology. We must also ask how families can endure when the demands of paid employment—working longer and harder with less security—means people have less time and fewer resources for family life (de Wolff 2006). In turn, these questions raise another: Is it possible, in a capitalist society, to de-privatize family life so that the responsibilities are shared by the society as a whole rather than held by individuals (i.e., women)?

Before we can tackle such large questions, we need a firm understanding of both contemporary and historical family patterns. The lessons to be gained from examining history should contribute to an understanding of the social forces shaping family organization today. Unless these are understood and assessed as structural obstacles to change or forces promoting change, we cannot successfully move on to tackle current problems and explore avenues of change for solving them. Our hope is that with the conceptualization of family that we have proposed (and that emerges from feminist theory), fruitful questions about family will arise, including ones about the nature of current changes in family life and obstacles to a family organization that ensures people's well-being and empowerment. Perhaps we can even begin to find answers to our questions.

Notes

1. The emphasis in Eichler's criticism is that family membership and treatment as a family member handicaps individuals. Individuals' marital or family status—and not their personal characteristics—establish their eligibility for state benefits: family relationships may disqualify people for benefits (e.g., a handicapped person loses disability if attached to a spouse with a reasonable income). Eichler's solution is to treat people as individuals in terms of claims on social resources. We agree, but are concerned about the implicit juxtaposition in her argument between individual and collective/community. The social forces that individualize and isolate us are so strong that advocating another such force is unsettling. The problem, as Eichler points out, is that the state is seeking to shift responsibility for people's welfare onto families and simultaneously undermining them. Promotion of universal social services, as well as guaranteed individual access to them and to a decent income, would alleviate the problem.
2. The term *blood* continues in both popular and scholarly usage to connote genetic ties.

3. In turn, we suspect that the emphasis placed upon biology in this society (which generates belief in sociobiological explanations of social phenomena without any evidence, for example) is emblematic of these same emotional bonds among parents and children and the ideology that expresses them.

References

Adams, M.L. 1997. *The Trouble with Normal: Post-war Youth and the Making of Heterosexuality* (Toronto: University of Toronto Press).

Arendell, T. 1995. *Fathers and Divorce* (Thousand Oaks: Sage).

Arnup, K. 2005. 'Lesbian and Gay Parents', in *Canadian Families: Diversity, Conflict, and Change*, eds N. Mandell and A. Duffy (Toronto: Harcourt Brace).

Barrett, M., and M. McIntosh. 1982. *The Anti-social Family* (London: Verso).

Beaujot, R. 2000. *Earning & Caring* (Peterborough: Broadview Press).

Beck-Gernsheim, E. 2002. *Reinventing the Family* (Cambridge: Polity Press).

Bernard, J. 1972. *The Future of Marriage* (New Haven: Yale University Press).

Bezanson, K. 2006. *Gender, the State, and Social Reproduction* (Toronto: University of Toronto Press).

———, and M. Luxton, eds. 2006. *Social Reproduction: Feminist Political Economy Challenges Neo-liberalism* (Montreal and Kingston: McGill-Queen's University Press).

Bianchi, S., J. Robinson, and M. Milkie. 2006. *Changing Rhythms of American Family Life* (New York: Russell Sage Foundation).

Blumenfeld, E., and S. Mann. 1980. 'Domestic Labour and the Reproduction of Labour Power: Towards an Analysis of Women, the Family and Class', in *Hidden in the Household: Women's Domestic Labour under Capitalism*, ed. B. Fox (Toronto: The Women's Press).

Blumenstein, P., and P. Schwartz. 1989. 'Intimate Relationships and the Creation of Sexuality', in *Gender in Intimate Relationships: A Microstructural Approach*, eds B.J. Risman and P. Schwartz (Belmont, CA: Wadsworth Publishing Co.).

Brooks, B., J. Jarman, and R. Blackburn. 2003. 'Occupational Gender Segregation in Canada, 1981–1996', *Canadian Review of Sociology and Anthropology* 40, 2: 197–213.

Cameron, B. 2006. 'Social Reproduction and Canadian Federalism', in *Social Reproduction*, eds K. Bezanson and M. Luxton (Montreal and Kingston: McGill-Queen's University Press).

Cancian, F. 1985. 'Gender Politics: Love and Power in the Private and Public Spheres', in *Gender and the Life Course*, ed. A. Rossi (New York: American Sociological Association).

Carrington, C. 1999. *No Place Like Home: Relationships and Family Life among Gays and Lesbians* (Chicago: University of Chicago Press).

Cheal, D. 1991. *Family and the State of Theory* (Toronto: University of Toronto Press).

Collier, J., M. Rosaldo, and S. Yanagisako. 1982. 'Is There a Family? New Anthropological Views', in *Rethinking the Family: Some Feminist Questions*, eds B. Thorne and M. Yalom (New York: Longman).

Coontz, S. 1988. *The Social Origins of Private Life* (London: Verso).

———. 1992. *The Way We Never Were: American Families and the Nostalgia Trap* (New York: Basic Books).

______. 2005. *Marriage, a History: From Obedience to Intimacy, or How Love Conquered Marriage* (New York: Viking).

Currie, D. 1993. '"Here Comes the Bride": The Making of a Modern Traditional Wedding in Western Culture', *Journal of Comparative Family Studies* 24, 3 (Autumn): 403–19.

Davidoff, L., and C. Hall. 1987. *Family Fortunes: Men and Women of the English Middle Class 1780–1850* (London: Hutchinson).

de Wolff, A. 2006. 'Bargaining for Collective Responsibility for Social Reproduction', in *Social Reproduction* (Montreal and Kingston: McGill-Queen's University Press).

Draper, P. 1975. '!Kung Women: Contrasts in Sexual Egalitarianism in the Foraging and Sedentary Contexts', in *Toward an Anthropology of Women*, ed. R. Reiter (New York: Monthly Review Press).

Eichler, M. [1983] 1988. *Families in Canada Today* (Toronto: Gage).

Fox, B. 1997. 'Another View of Sociology of the Family in Canada: A Comment on Nett', *Canadian Review of Sociology and Anthropology* 34, 1: 93–9.

———. 2001. 'The Formative Years: How Parenthood Creates Gender', *Canadian Review of Sociology and Anthropology* 38, 4: 373–90.

———. Forthcoming. *When Couples Become Parents* (Toronto: University of Toronto Press).

Friedan, B. 1963. *The Feminine Mystique* (New York: Dell).

Gairdner, W. 1992. *The War Against the Family: A Parent Speaks Out* (Toronto: Stoddart).

Gans, H. 1962. *The Urban Villagers* (New York: Free Press).

Gartner, R., M. Dawson, and M. Crawford. 1998. 'Woman Killing: Intimate Femicide in Ontario, 1974–1994', *Resources for Feminist Research* 26, 3, 4.

Gill, S., and I. Bakker, eds. 2003. *Power, Production, and Social Reproduction: Human In/security in the Global Political Economy* (London: Palgrave Macmillan).

Gittins, D. 1985. *The Family in Question: Changing Households and Familiar Ideologies* (London: Macmillan).

Goody, J. 1976. *Production and Reproduction: A Comparative Study of the Domestic Domain* (Cambridge: Cambridge University Press).

Hansen, K. 2005. *Not-so-nuclear Families* (New Brunswick, NJ: Rutgers University Press).

Harris, O. 1981. 'Households as Natural Units', in *Of Marriage and the Market*, eds K. Young, C. Wolkowitz, and R. McCullough (London: CSE Books).

Hartmann, H. 1981. 'Capitalism, Patriarchy, and Job Segregation by Sex', *Signs* 1, 3: 137–70.

Hays, S. 1996. *The Cultural Contradictions of Motherhood* (New Haven: Yale University Press).

Hochschild, A. 1989. *The Second Shift: Working Parents and the Revolution at Home* (New York: Avon).

———. 1997. *Time Bind: When Work Becomes Home & Home Becomes Work* (New York: Metropolitan Books).

Howell, N. 1979. *Demography of the Dobe Area !Kung* (New York: Academic Press).

Ingraham, C. 2006. *White Weddings: Romancing Heterosexuality in Popular Culture*, 2nd edn (New York: Routledge).

Jacobs, J., and K. Gerson. 2004. *The Time Divide: Work, Family, and Gender Inequality* (Cambridge, MA: Harvard University Press).

Jones, C., L. Marsden, and L. Tepperman. 1990. *Lives of Their Own: The Individualization of Women's Lives* (Toronto: Oxford University Press).

Kimmel, M. 1999. 'Masculinity as Homophobia: Fear, Shame, and Silence in the Construction of Gender Identity', in *Men and Power*, ed. J. Kuypers (New York: Prometheus Books).

Larson, L., J.W. Goltz, and B.E. Munro. 2000. *Families in Canada: Social Contexts, Continuities and Changes* (Toronto: Prentice Hall Allyn & Bacon).

Laslett, B., and J. Brenner. 1989. 'Gender and Social Reproduction: Historical Perspectives', *Annual Review of Sociology* 15.

Leacock, E. 1981. *Myths of Male Dominance: Collected Articles on Women Cross-culturally* (New York: Monthly Review Press).

Lee, R. 1979. *The !Kung San Men, Women, and Work in a Foraging Society* (New York: Cambridge University Press).

Lerner, G. 1986. *The Creation of Patriarchy* (Oxford: Oxford University Press).

Lu, E., and J. Liu. 2007. 'Environmental Impacts of Divorce', PNAC 104, 51: 20629–34.

Luxton, M. 1980. *More Than a Labour of Love: Three Generations of Women's Work in the Home* (Toronto: The Women's Press).

———. 2006. 'Friends, Neighbours, and Community: A Case Study of the Role of Informal Caregiving in Social Reproduction', in *Social Reproduction*

Feminist Political Economy Challenges Neo-liberalism, eds K. Bezanson and M. Luxton (Montreal and Kingston: McGill-Queen's University Press).

———, and J. Corman. 2001. *Getting By in Hard Times: Gendered Labour at Home and on the Job* (Toronto: University of Toronto Press).

McMahon, M. 1995. *Engendering Motherhood: Identity and Self-transformation in Women's Lives* (New York: The Guilford Press).

Mandell, N., and A. Duffy. 1988. *Reconstructing the Canadian Family: Feminist Perspectives* (Toronto: Butterworths).

Marshall, K. 2006. 'Converging Gender Roles', *Perspectives* (July), Cat. No. 75-001-XIE (Ottawa: Statistics Canada).

Mintz, S., and S. Kellogg. 1988. *Domestic Revolutions: A Social History of American Family Life* (New York: The Free Press).

Mitchell, J. 1966. 'Women: The Longest Revolution', *New Left Review* 40: 11–37.

Mitterauer, M., and R. Sieder. 1982. *The European Family* (Oxford: Basil Blackwell).

Morgan, D. 1975. *The Family and Social Theory* (London: Routledge & Kegan Paul).

Morton, M. 1988. 'Dividing the Wealth, Sharing the Poverty: The (Re)formation of "Family" in Law in Ontario', *Canadian Review of Sociology and Anthropology* 25, 2.

Oakley, A. 1974. *Woman's Work: The Housewife, Past and Present* (New York: Pantheon Books).

Parsons, T., and R.F. Bales. 1955. *Family, Socialization and Interaction Process* (New York: Free Press).

Phillipps, L. 2000. 'Tax Law and Social Reproduction: The Gender of Fiscal Policy in an Age of Privatization', unpublished paper from SSHRC-funded project 'Feminism, Law, and the Challenge of Privatization', Toronto, Osgoode Hall Law School, York University.

Popenoe, D. 1993. 'American Family Decline, 1960–1990: A Review and Appraisal', *Journal of Marriage and the Family* 55, 3: 527–42.

Presser, H. 2003. *Working in a 24/7 Economy: Challenges for American Families* (New York: Russell Sage Foundation).

Rapp, R. 1982. 'Family and Class in Contemporary America: Notes Toward Understanding of Ideology', in *Rethinking the Family: Some Feminist Questions*, eds B. Thorne and M. Yalom (New York: Longman).

Reitsma-Street, M. 1998. 'Still Girls Learn to Care: Girls Policed to Care', in *Women's Caring: Feminist Perspectives on Social Welfare* (Toronto: Oxford University Press).

Rogers, B. 1980. *The Domestication of Women: Discrimination in Developing Societies* (London: Tavistock).

Rosenberg, H. 1987. 'Motherhood, Stress, and Depression: The Costs of Privatized Social Reproduction', in *Feminism and Political Economy: Women's Work, Women's Struggles*, eds H.J. Maroney and M. Luxton (Toronto: Methuen).

Rowbotham, S. 1973. *Woman's Consciousness, Man's World* (Harmondsworth, UK: Penguin Books).

Ryan, M. 1981. *Cradle of the Middle Class: The Family in Oneida County, New York, 1790–1865* (Cambridge: Cambridge University Press).

Sahlins, M. 1976. *The Use and Abuse of Biology* (Ann Arbor, MI: University of Michigan Press).

Seccombe, W. 1992. *A Millennium of Family Change: Feudalism to Capitalism in Northwestern Europe* (London: Verso).

———. 1993. *Weathering the Storm: Working-class Families from the Industrial Revolution to the Fertility Decline* (London: Verso).

Seidman, S. 2003. 'The Introduction and the Rise of a Heterosexual Identity', in *The Social Construction of Sexuality* (New York: W.W. Norton & Co.).

Shalla, V., and W. Clement, eds. 2007. *Work in Tumultuous Times: Critical Perspectives* (Montreal and Ithaca: McGill-Queen's University Press).

Smith, D.E. 1973. 'Corporate Capitalism', in *Women in Canada*, ed. M. Stephenson (Toronto: New Press).

Stack, C. 1974. *All Our Kin: Strategies for Survival in a Black Community* (New York: Harper & Row).

Statistics Canada. 1984. *1981 Census of Canada. Economic Families in Private Households, Income and Selected Characteristics*, Cat. No. 93–937 (Ottawa: Supply and Services).

———. 2006a. <http://www.statcan.ca/english/concepts/definitions/cen-family.htm>.

———. 2006b. <http://www.statcan.ca/english/concepts/definitions/eco-family.htm>.

Strong-Boag, V. 1988. *The New Day Recalled: Lives of Girls and Women in English Canada, 1919–1939* (Markham: Penguin).

Tanner, N. 1974. 'Matrifocality in Indonesia and Africa and among Black Americans', in *Woman, Culture and Society*, eds M.Z. Rosaldo and L. Lamphere (Stanford: Stanford University Press).

Thorne, B. 1982. 'Feminist Rethinking of the Family: An Overview', in *Rethinking the Family: Some Feminist Questions*, eds B. Thorne and M. Yalom (New York: Longman).

———, and M. Yalom, eds. 1982. *Rethinking the Family: Some Feminist Questions* (New York: Longman).

Tilly, L., and J. Scott. 1978. *Women, Work and Family* (New York: Holt, Rinehart and Winston).

Turnbull, C. 1962. *The Forest People* (Garden City, NY: Doubleday).

Valverde, M. 1985. *Sex, Power and Pleasure* (Toronto: Women's Press).

Wall, G. 2001. 'Moral Constructions of Motherhood', *Gender & Society* 15, 4: 592.

———. 2004. 'Is Your Child's Brain Potential Maximized? Mothering in an Age of New Brain Research', *Atlantis* 28, 2: 41–50.

Walzer, S. 1998. *Thinking about the Baby: Gender and Transitions into Parenthood* (Philadelphia: Temple University Press).

Weeks, J. 1981. *Sex, Politics, and Society: The Regulation of Sexuality Since 1800* (New York: Longman).

Weston, K. 1991. *Families We Choose: Lesbians, Gays, Kinship* (New York: Columbia University Press).

Young, M., and P. Willmott. 1957. *Family and Kinship in East London* (Baltimore: Penguin).

Zelditch, M. 1960. 'Role Differentiation in the Nuclear Family', in *A Modern Introduction to the Family*, eds N. Bell and E. Vogel (New York: The Free Press).

Chapter 2

Perhaps the most important assumption about 'the family' in popular culture is that the nuclear pattern is somehow natural, and therefore universal. The nuclear family seems to follow from the biology of reproduction. This essay challenges all assumptions about universal family patterns. It examines aspects of family life that seem to us to be nearly inevitable—like the relationship between mother and child—and instead shows tremendous diversity across human societies. Felicity Edholm's discussion raises the challenge that we should always question the seemingly unquestionable.

The Unnatural Family

Felicity Edholm

. . . It was, and still is, widely argued that some form of the family, and, in some cases, of the nuclear family, was universal and was found in all societies. Only recently has this accepted wisdom been challenged and it has still not been dislodged. One major reason for its resilience in anthropology, apart from the crucial political, economic, and ideological significance of the family in the nineteenth- and twentieth-century Western world, is that groups very similar to those which we identify as the family do exist in the majority of societies known to anthropologists. Furthermore, anthropologists have tended to assume that an adequate explanatory definition of any given social or cultural trait can be extended to similar traits in other cultures. But as one anthropologist has commented: 'because the family seems to be the predominant unit we must not be bemused into thinking that it is the "natural" or "basic" one' (Fox 1967: 38). . . .

It is usually assumed that the family, a co-residential unit containing parents and their own children, is the natural primary unit within which domestic and sexual relations and socialization will take place; that relationships between members of a family are unique and specific, and are recognizably different from relationships with individuals outside the family; that there is, at least for the early years of life, an inevitably deep and necessary dependence between a mother and her children, and that there is some sense of obligation and interdependence between those who are members of the family, particularly between parents and children; that incest taboos operate within the family unit; and that property, status, and positions pass within the family. It is also usually assumed that there is considerable interdependence, both social and sexual, between men and women and that this is revealed within the family/the household.

The most critical areas of kinship to examine in order to have some understanding of the family are those which offer the greatest challenge to preconceptions and which have significant effect on the construction of kinship relations insofar as they affect the assumptions we have outlined above. Five areas will be explored: conception, incest, parent/child relations and adoption, marriage, households and residence.

Conception

The question of who our kin, our relations, are is answered in numerous ways, even for the primary parent–child relation. Notions of blood ties, of biological connection, which to us seem relatively unequivocal, are highly variable. Some societies of which we have anthropological record recognize only the role of the father or of the mother in conception and procreation. The other sex is given some significance but is not seen, for example, as providing blood . . . as having any biological connection. Only one parent is a 'relation', the other parent is not. In the Trobriand Islands, for example, it is believed that intercourse is not the cause of conception; semen is not seen as essential for conception (Malinowski 1922). Conception results from the entry of a spirit child into the womb; the male role is to 'open the passage' to the womb, through intercourse, and it is the repeated intercourse of the same partner which 'moulds' the child. A child's blood comes from its mother's side and from her siblings, her mother and mother's brother, not from the father. A child will not be related by blood to its father, but will look like its father since he has through intercourse created its form. Fathers continue after birth to have a very close and intimate relationship with their children and it is this contact which also is seen as creating the likeness, as moulding the child in his/her father's image.

Other societies recognize the crucial importance of semen in the formation of a child, but believe that it is essential for conception that either the semen of more than one man is involved—or that fertility is only possible given a mixture of different semen; thus a newly married woman in Marind-Anim society (in New Guinea) is gang-raped at marriage and on subsequent ritual occasions (Van Baal 1966). Semen is understood as being necessary for growth throughout childhood and adolescence and elaborate male homosexual activities ensure that adolescent boys are in receipt of semen.

The Lakker of Burma on the other hand consider that the mother is only a container in which the child grows; she has no blood connection with her children, and children of the same mother and different fathers are not considered to be related to each other (Keesing 1976). These cases are extreme but have important implications in that they indicate not only that relations which seem to us to be self-evidently biological are not universally seen as such. 'Natural', 'biological' relations are not inevitably those which organize human relations at a very fundamental level since what is understood as 'biological' is socially defined and therefore is expressed in different ways.

Incest

Incest is another area of human relations which is widely discussed in terms of some kind of innate, instinctive abhorrence for sexual relations with 'close kin' and is often attributed to a subconscious realization of the genetic danger of inbreeding. (It is not uniformly accepted that inbreeding is inevitably disadvantageous.)

Incest taboos, defined as prohibitions on sexual relations between individuals socially classified as kin, as relations, are nearly universal. But the prohibition does not inevitably apply to the individuals whom we would identify as primary kin. The most dramatic exceptions to incest are found in certain royal dynasties (Egypt, Hawaii) where inbreeding (brother–sister) was enforced in order to keep the purity of the royal line, as well as in Ptolemaic and Roman Egypt where apparently father–daughter and brother–sister sexual relations were relatively common. In most other known societies, sexual relations between those socially recognized as 'biologically' related are taboo. The Trobrianders, for example, do not consider the children of one father and different mothers to be related and sexual relations between those children are thus entirely legitimate, whereas sexual relations with women who have the same mother, or whose mothers are siblings, is taboo. The Lakker of Burma do not consider that the children of the same mother have any kinship links. 'Incest' does not apply to these non-kin and sexual relations are permitted. In other societies in which, for example, the category of mother or sister is extended to include all males or females of the same generation who are descended through one parent from a common grandfather, or great-grandfather, it is frequently this whole group which is sexually unavailable. It is the social definitions of significant kinship relations that are important in defining incest rather than any concept of natural, biological imperatives militating against sexual intercourse within a 'natural family unit'.

Parent/Child Relations: Adoption

It is nearly universally accepted in all anthropological texts on the family, however prepared they are to accept the fact that the nuclear family is not ubiquitous, that the 'mother–child tie is inevitable and given', that the 'irreducible and elementary social grouping is surely the mother and her children'. This is seen as determined by the imperatives of infantile dependence and the need for breast milk and is also related to other psychological needs on the part both of the mother and of the child. It is in this context instructive to consider the implications of the widespread practice of adoption. In many societies, children do not live with their 'real' parents, but often stay with their mothers until some time after they have been weaned, when, as they say in N. Ghana, they have 'gained sense' (at about six). However, throughout Melanesia and Polynesia, children are adopted just after weaning or, in some instances, well before—a phenomenon which is considered as absolutely acceptable. In some instances babies are adopted and breast-fed by their adopted mother. Margaret Mead (1935: 193) describes such a situation among the Mundugumor in New Guinea: 'even women who have never borne children are able in a few weeks, by placing the child constantly at the breast and by drinking plenty of coconut milk, to produce enough, or nearly enough, milk to rear the child, which is suckled by other women in the first few weeks after adoption'.

In Tahiti, young women often have one or two children before they are considered, or consider themselves to be, ready for an approved and stable relationship. It is considered perfectly acceptable for the children of this young woman to be given to her parents or other close kin for adoption while she is freed to continue what is seen as the 'business of adolescence'. The girl can decide what her relationship to the children will be, but there is no sense in which she is forced into 'motherhood' because of having had a baby; 'motherhood' in such a situation can be seen as a status reached by women at a particular stage of development, as involving a psychological and social readiness, not something inevitably attached to the physical bearing of children.

In nearly all the societies in which adoption of this kind is common (and where anthropologists have discussed it at length) it is clear that the adopted child will still maintain contact with its 'natural' parents and will know what their relationship to each other is. A Tahitian man (himself adopted) was asked about children's relations to their parents: 'if you are not adopted you are grateful to your biological mother because she gave birth to you. On the other hand, when you are taken in your infancy by somebody it isn't worthwhile to think any more about your mother. The woman who took you in is just the same as your biological mother. Your gratitude is because you were an infant and you were taken' (in Levy 1970: 81). One of the interesting aspects of this definition of the relationship between parents and children is the sense in which it is seen as so critically dependent on gratitude—from child to parent—since it is recognized that adults choose to bring up the child and do not have a necessary sense of responsibility or instinctive love for it. The implications of such attitudes for all social relations are clearly considerable.

Again, in most of these societies it is agreed that the adopted child is more the foster father's than the true father's. Margaret Mead (1935), writing on the Manus of New Guinea, described the very considerable personality similarities she saw between fathers and their adopted children. The relationship between fathers and children is extremely close; fathers feed and spend a lot of time with their children. The 'likeness', of which the Trobriand Islanders speak, between father and children, is also, in many other Melanesian and Polynesian societies, seen as due to the close personal contact between them. The father–child relationship is seen as a crucial and, above all, as a social relationship, one which is created by social contact, not one which exists because of a 'blood relationship'. In Tahiti, it is considered an ultimate shame for adopted children to leave the house of their adopted parents since the relationship between those who have lived together and have grown 'familiar' ('matau') with each other (the essential ingredient for all good relations) is seen as inevitably far closer than that between biological, 'natural' parents.

It is instructive in this context to consider the United Nations' study on the *Adoption of Children in Western Nations* in which it is argued that in the West, society attributes 'a sacred character . . . to family bonds' (Levy 1970). The extent to which this attribution is ideological is even more evident once we have understood the extraordinary narrowness of our definitions of familiar, 'natural' relations.

Marriage

It has been claimed that some form of marriage is found in all human societies. The definitions of marriage, however, again give some indication of the kind of complexity that is involved in the attempt to provide universals. One famous definition by Goodenough (1970: 12–13) defines marriage in these terms:

> Marriage is a transaction and resulting contract in which a person (male or female, corporate or individual, in person or by proxy) establishes a continuing claim to the right of sexual access to a woman—this right having priority over rights of sexual access others currently have, or may subsequently acquire, in relation to her (except in a similar transaction) until the contract resulting from the transaction is terminated, and in which the woman involved is eligible to bear children.

Other definitions stress, above all, the significance of marriage in determining parentage—in allocating children to different groups. The definitions have to be understood in relation to the kinds of social arrangements which are entirely inconsistent with our notions of marriage.

The Nayar of northern India provide one of the most problematic cases of 'marriage' (Schneider and Gough 1972). The basic social group among the Nayar is the Taravad, a unit composed of men and women descended through the female line from a common ancestress. Thus it is brothers and sisters, mothers and children who cohabit. A child becomes a member of the mother's Taravad, not the father's. A Nayar girl was involved, before she reached puberty, in a formal ritual with a man from an equivalent caste to her own, and then was able to take as many lovers as she wished; the 'husband'—the man who had been involved in the ritual—only had a very minimal ritual attachment to his 'wife', although he too could be one of her lovers. (Not all lovers came from the same caste.) Husbands and fathers, in such a context, are entirely peripheral to the domestic life of their wives and children—and never cohabit.

Among the Nuer of the Nile Basin, one of the most common forms of marriage is what has been called 'ghost' marriage (the anthropologist Evans-Pritchard who worked among the Nuer estimates that nearly 50 per cent of all marriages correspond to this form). Ghost marriage refers to the situation in which a man dies unmarried or with no children of his own. If this happens, a close kinsman (related to him through his father's line) will marry a wife 'to his name' and children born of this union will be seen as the dead man's children. A man who has been involved in marrying this way and bearing children for another man will, when he dies and if he has not contracted a second marriage in his own name—only possible if his wife dies—have to become in his turn a proxy father and a subsequent ghost marriage will be contracted. If a married man dies his widow then should ideally be married by a brother or close male kin of the dead man and, again, children born of this union will be considered to be those of the dead man, not of the living husband.

The Nuer also have another contractual form of 'marriage' in which an old and important, usually barren, woman may marry a younger woman. Nuer marriages are contracted through the 'husband' giving the bride price (cattle) to the wife's group. The children born to this younger woman will then, for particular purposes such as inheritance, be considered as the children of the old woman; their 'father'. Marriages of this kind indicate the importance among the Nuer both of becoming a parent, or rather a male parent, in order to become an ancestor—for only 'fathers' with offspring are remembered and have status as ancestors—and also of the inheritance of property. Nuer marriages also demonstrate that the marriage indicates a contract between a group of related 'men', who are seen in some sense as equivalents, and a woman married to one of them.

These two widely differing examples illustrate one of the other critical elements in the relations defined by marriage: the difference between the 'legally' recognized father or mother and the person who was involved in conception, or birth. In both the cases cited above, the person we would see as the father, he who had impregnated the woman, is not given any social recognition at all; it is the person, not necessarily male, who is given the social position of father who is recognized through the ritual of 'marriage'. The two males are distinguished in the anthropological literature thus: the biological father is the *genitor*, the biological mother the *genetrix*, the 'socially' recognized father the *pater*, the socially recognized mother the *mater*. In cases of polyandry, where a woman is 'married' to more than one man, as is the case among the Toda, one of the men will perform a ritual which makes him the *pater*, and the child and subsequent children will belong to this group. In some of the societies (very few) in which polyandry exists, it is a group of brothers who share a wife. In some cases a group of sisters will be 'married' to a group of brothers and in such situations the children belong to the family group. Individual paternity is thus socially less important than membership of a family unit.

Paternity is of crucial importance in societies in which status, positions, and property are transmitted through the male line. The notion of the group, related through the male line, can in some societies have such force that sexual relations between a woman and any male from the same group as that into which she was born (and such a group can include a considerable number of individuals, all the descendants of a common great-grandfather, for example) are regarded as incestuous. We can see with the example of the Nayar (although the Nayar do constitute an exceptional case) that paternity has far less social significance if all important social attributes are gained through inheritance down the female line. (It is important to recognize that such a system of inheritance does not imply that men are marginalized . . . but that it is brothers rather than husbands who are the significant social males.)

Even in situations in which the attribution of paternity is so important we cannot simply assume that the concepts of legitimacy and illegitimacy are clear-cut. In many societies of this kind there are all kinds of arrangements for the allocation of children—which are not wholly dependent on the concepts of the determining factor of parenthood.

Household and Residence

Our conception of what constitutes the family is dependent not only on what we have called kinship ties but equally in terms of residence, domestic units, or households. Given the range of kinship relations that we have briefly explored, it is inevitable that a wide range of different residential patterns exist. Moreover, households will not only be composed of individuals whose relations to each other are based on different criteria but the size and composition over time of such households will vary, as will their relation to production, to other units, and to social positions.

There are three basic forms of residence as isolated by anthropologists: vivilocal, where a married couple and their children live with the kin of the husband; matrilocal, where the couple live with the kin of the wife; and neolocal, where the couple live independently of either group of kin. This scheme is however further complicated by the fact that in many societies in which descent is traced through the female line (matrilineal societies), the children might initially live with the mother and father with the father's kin, and then later move to live with their mother's kin; in other words, with their mother's brothers, those from whom they will inherit property, status, or position. Often in such societies (such as the Trobriand Islanders) daughters never live with their mother's kin—they stay with their fathers until they marry and then move to their husband's kin. The complication of residence patterns is considerable—one of the factors which these different patterns demonstrate is that households as units of parents and their children are not a necessary or permanent social arrangement. The extent to which individuals are identified with any one household, both as children and as adults, varies considerably. In most matrilineal societies men will circulate and often a man will split his available time and space between kin and conjugal roles. In some societies of this kind, men will live alternately in two places, or will frequently visit two different units, or move at different stages from one to another. In the case of the polyandrous Toda, a woman married to different men will circulate between their different households (Rivers 1906). Children similarly will shift residence in many societies—in many instances, because of the 'institution' of fostering whereby, from the age of about five, children are sent to be brought up by non-parental kin. Claims to have a foster child are formally expressed as the rights held by a man in his sister's children—and by a woman in her brother's daughter—but it is much more extensive than this, and there are many instances of children living with their grandparents (Goody 1969: 192). Households then can often be extremely fluid units, with shifting membership.

In most of the known societies of the world, monogamy is the exception rather than the rule. Some anthropologists claim that over 90 per cent of the world's cultures involve plural polygamous marriages. We have already referred to polyandry, one woman with several husbands, but by far the most common form of polygamy is polygyny—one man with several wives.

In some polygynous societies, almost invariably those in which descent is traced through the male line, households consist of a series of relatively self-contained living quarters in which a man and his wives, each with her own children, live, one wife in a relatively autonomous domestic unit. In others, domestic arrangements are dominated by a group of brothers with their wives and their offspring.

The domestic existence of each smaller unit within such a group is determined by the existence of the larger group and is ultimately dependent on the authority of those males who are in control of the unit as a whole.

In such situations it is again difficult to arrive at a useful definition of such a unit if we are concerned to consider households purely as kinship entities. Is such a mother and children unit an entity or is it a sub-household within a much larger household?

The Tiv of Nigeria provide an example of this latter form of 'household'. Tiv kinship groups live in compounds, a circular arrangement of huts and granaries, in the centre of which is an open space—'the centre of Tiv family life'. The compound head is the senior, eldest man. He settles disputes, supervises the productive activities of the group, and controls magic. His several wives live in separate units in the compound which is also inhabited by his junior children, unmarried daughters, and married sons and their families. In addition, there may be a younger brother and his family, and/or outsiders.

As is argued by the anthropologists involved, while in a sense each wife who has a separate hut and her children constitute a separate domestic unit, the larger compound group—a patrilineal extended family augmented by outsiders—is the central domestic unit of everyday Tiv life and of collective economic enterprise (Bohannon and Bohannon 1968).

It is only when we consider the household in terms of this latter—its productive capacities—that we can make sense of this kind of domestic unit usually found in agricultural communities. Households and domestic units are not only an arrangement of people related to each other through parent–child ties, but in societies such as the Tiv, they form units of production and have to be analyzed and understood as such.

Kinship ties have thus been seen by some anthropologists as constituting the relation of production. The Tiv compound, for example, is essentially a means of reuniting and controlling necessary labour, both productive and reproductive. Clearly, households in many societies have to be analyzed as units of production and consumption, and as providers of labour. The form of the household must therefore be analyzed in terms of the economic structure of the society as a whole and cannot simply be seen as a unit containing the 'family', essentially defining sets of affective relations. Precisely because the Western ideal of the nuclear family is so ideologically and spatially separated from wage labour, the recognition of the profound economic significance of household formation in other societies has posed considerable problems for anthropologists. It has been even more difficult for Western sociologists to re-examine the economic role of the family within their own society in the light of the understanding gained through anthropological analysis.

Polygynous households of the kind described above are common in Africa, south of the Sahara, and however different their form, they are usually crucial productive units. In New Guinea, very different domestic arrangements exist and these cannot be analyzed in terms of the same economic determinants. In Marind-Anim and many other New Guinea societies, domestic organization constructs very considerable separation between men and women. Special men's houses provide the focal point for all male life (often including sleeping and eating) and there are often stringent taboos on women having access to such houses and, in general, on contact between males and females.

Conclusion

The family, particularly the nuclear family, can be seen, through comparative analysis, as just one very specific means of organizing the relations between parents and children, males and females. It is not, as has so often been claimed, some kind of 'natural' instinctive and 'sacred' unit. Even the bond between mothers and their own children, which is seen in almost mystic terms as the fundamental biologically determined relationship, can be seen as far less important than we are generally led to believe. Universal definitions of human relations must be constantly questioned and the whole notion of the 'natural' must, in terms of human relations, be challenged, and the 'unnatural'—in these terms the social construction of relationships—must be fully recognized.

References

Bohannon, P., and L. Bohannon. 1968. *Tiv Economy* (Northwestern University Press).

Carroll, V. 1970. *Adoption in Eastern Oceania* (The University of Hawaii Press).

Evans-Pritchard, E.E. 1951. *Kinship and Marriage among the Nuer* (Oxford: Clarendon Press).

Fox, R. 1967. *Kinship and Marriage* (Harmondsworth, UK: Pelican).

Goodenough, W.H. 1970. *Description and Comparison in Cultural Anthropology* (Chicago: Aldine Publishing).

Goody, J.R. 1969. *Comparative Studies in Kinship* (London: Routledge & Kegan Paul).

Keesing, R.M. 1976. *Cultural Anthropology, a Contemporary Perspective* (New York: Holt, Rinehart and Winston).

Levy, R.I. 1970. 'Tahitian Adoption as a Psychological Message', in *Adoption in Eastern Oceania*, ed. V. Carroll (The University of Hawaii Press).

Malinowski, B. 1922. *Argonauts of the Western Society* (London: Routledge & Kegan Paul).

Mead, M. 1935. *Sex and Temperament in Three Primitive Societies* (New York: William Morrow & Co.).

Rivers, W.H.R. 1906. *The Todas* (New York: Macmillan).

Schneider, D., and E.K. Gough. 1972. *Matrilineal Kinship* (Berkeley: University of California Press).

Van Baal, J. 1966. *Dema: Description and Analysis of Marind-Anim Culture (South New Guinea)* (The Hague: Martinus Nijhoff).

Chapter 3

This essay takes up where the last left off—with the insight that family is not determined by biology, and in fact is socially constructed. Specifically, anthropologists Jane Collier, Michelle Z. Rosaldo, and Sylvia Yanagisako argue that 'family' is an idea situated in the development of complex societies with distinct public and private spheres. Their discussion addresses the question why family is seen as so important in industrial-capitalist societies.

The work of Bronislaw Malinowski has most influenced anthropologists' thinking about family. So, a consideration of his ideas is central in this article. While Malinowski's work may be unfamiliar to sociology students, his ideas have had a strong impact on sociological approaches to the study of family life: Talcott Parsons was his student. And Parsons's structural-functionalist perspective on nuclear families—which held them to be the best arrangement for raising children and for meeting the emotional needs of adults—has had a lasting influence on how we think about family, both in popular culture and in sociology.

Is There a Family? New Anthropological Views

Jane Collier, Michelle Z. Rosaldo, and Sylvia Yanagisako

This essay poses a rhetorical question in order to argue that most of our talk about families is clouded by unexplored notions of what families 'really' are like. It is probably the case, universally, that people expect to have special connections with their genealogically closest relations. But a knowledge of genealogy does not in itself promote understanding of what these special ties are about. The real importance of The Family in contemporary social life and belief has blinded us to its dynamics. Confusing ideal with reality, we fail to appreciate the deep significance of what are, cross-culturally, various ideologies of intimate relationship and, at the same time, we fail to reckon with the complex human bonds and experiences all too comfortably sheltered by a faith in the 'natural' source of a 'nurture' we think is found in the home.

This essay is divided into three parts. The first examines what social scientists mean by The Family. It focuses on the work of Bronislaw Malinowski, the anthropologist who first convinced social scientists that The Family was a universal human institution. The second part also has social scientists as its focus, but it examines works by the nineteenth-century thinkers Malinowski refuted, for if—as we shall argue—Malinowski was wrong in viewing The Family as a universal human institution, it becomes important to explore the work of theorists who did not make Malinowski's mistakes. The final section then draws on the correct insights of nineteenth-century theorists to sketch some implications of viewing The Family not as a concrete institution designed to fulfill universal human needs but as an ideological construct associated with the modern state.

Malinowski's Concept of the Family

In 1913, Bronislaw Malinowski published a book called *The Family among the Australian Aborigines* in which he laid to rest earlier debates about whether all human societies had families. During the nineteenth century, proponents of social evolution argued that primitives were sexually promiscuous and therefore incapable of having families because children would not recognize their fathers (Morgan 1877). Malinowski refuted this notion by showing that Australian Aborigines, who were widely believed to practise 'primitive promiscuity', not only had rules regulating who might have intercourse with whom during sexual orgies but also differentiated between legal marriages and casual unions. Malinowski thus 'proved' that Australian Aborigines had marriage, and so proved that Aboriginal children had fathers, because each child's mother had but a single recognized husband.

Malinowski's book did not simply add data to one side of an ongoing debate. It ended the debate altogether, for by distinguishing *coitus* from conjugal relationships Malinowski separated questions of sexual behaviour from questions of the family's universal existence. Evidence of sexual promiscuity was henceforth irrelevant for deciding whether families existed. Moreover, Malinowski argued that the conjugal relationship, and therefore The Family, had to be universal because it fulfilled a universal human need. As he wrote in a posthumously published book:

> The human infant needs parental protection for a much longer period than does the young of even the highest anthropoid apes. Hence, no culture could endure in which the act of reproduction, that is, mating, pregnancy, and childbirth, was not linked up with the fact of legally founded parenthood, that is, a relationship in which the father and mother have to look after the children for a long period, and, in turn, derive certain benefits from the care and trouble taken. (Malinowski 1944: 99)

In proving the existence of families among Australian Aborigines, Malinowski described three features of families that he believed flowed from The Family's universal function of nurturing children. First, he argued that families have to have clear boundaries, for if families were to perform the vital function of nurturing young children, insiders had to be distinguishable from outsiders so that everyone could know which adults were responsible for the care of which children. Malinowski thus argued that families formed bounded social units, and to prove that Australian families formed such units, he demonstrated that Aboriginal parents and children recognized one another. Each Aboriginal woman had a single husband, even if some husbands occasionally allowed wives to sleep with other men during tribal ceremonies. Malinowski thus proved that each Aboriginal child had a recognized mother and father, even if both parties occasionally engaged in sexual relations with outsiders.

Second, Malinowski argued that families had to have a place where family members could be together and where the daily tasks associated with child rearing could be performed. He demonstrated, for example, that Aboriginal parents and their immature children shared a single fire—a home and hearth where children were fed and nurtured—even though, among nomadic Aborigines, the fire might be kindled in a different location each night.

Finally, Malinowski argued that family members felt affection for one another—that parents who invested long years in caring for children were rewarded by their own and their children's affections for one another. Malinowski felt that long and intimate association among family members fostered close emotional ties, particularly between parents and children, but also between spouses. Aboriginal parents and their children, for example, could be expected to feel the same emotions for one another as did English parents and children, and as proof of this point Malinowski recounted touching stories of the efforts made by Aboriginal parents to recover children lost during conflicts with other Aborigines or with white settlers and efforts made by stolen Aboriginal children to find their lost parents.

Malinowski's book on Australian Aborigines thus gave social scientists a concept of The Family that consisted of a universal function, the nurturance of young children, mapped onto (1) a bounded set of people who recognized one another and who were distinguishable from other like groups; (2) a definite physical space, a hearth and home; and (3) a particular set of emotions, family love. This concept of The Family as an institution for nurturing young children has been enduring, probably because nurturing children is thought to be the primary function of families in modern industrial societies. The flaw in Malinowski's argument is the flaw common to all functionalist arguments: because a social institution is observed to perform a necessary function does not mean either that the function would not be performed if the institution did not exist or that the function is responsible for the existence of the institution.

Later anthropologists have challenged Malinowski's ideas that family always includes fathers, but, ironically, they have kept all the other aspects of his definition. For example, later anthropologists have argued that the basic social unit is not the nuclear family including father but the unit composed of a mother and her children: 'Whether or not a mate becomes attached to the mother on some more or less permanent basis is a variable matter' (Fox 1967: 39). In removing father from the family, however, later anthropologists have nevertheless retained Malinowski's concept of The Family as a functional unit and so have retained all the features Malinowski took such pains to demonstrate. In the writings of modern anthropologists, the mother–child unit is described as performing the universally necessary function of nurturing young children. A mother and her children form a bounded group distinguishable from other units of mothers and their children. A mother and her children share a place, a home and hearth. And finally, a mother and her children share deep emotional bonds based on their prolonged and intimate contact.

Modern anthropologists may have removed father from The Family, but they did not modify the basic social science concept of The Family in which the function of child rearing is mapped onto a bounded set of people who share a place and who 'love' one another. Yet it is exactly this concept of The Family that we, as feminist anthropologists, have found so difficult to apply. Although the biological facts of reproduction, when combined with a sufficiently elastic definition of marriage, make it possible for us, as social scientists, to find both mother–child units and Malinowski's conjugal-pairs-plus-children units in every human society, it is not at all clear that such Families necessarily exhibit the associated features Malinowski 'proved' and modern anthropologists echo.

An outside observer, for example, may be able to delimit family boundaries in any and all societies by identifying the children of one woman and that woman's associated mate, but natives may not be interested in making such distinctions. In other words, natives may not be concerned to distinguish family members from outsiders, as Malinowski imagined natives should be when he argued that units of parents and children have to have clear boundaries in order for child-rearing responsibilities to be assigned efficiently. Many languages, for example, have no word to identify the unit of parents and children that English speakers call a 'family'. Among the Zinacantecos of southern Mexico the basic social unit is identified as a 'house', which may include from one to 20 people (Vogt 1969). Zinacantecos have no difficulty talking about an individual's parents, children, or spouse; but Zinacantecos do not have a single word that identifies the unit of parents and children in such a way as to cut it off from other like units. In Zinacantecos society, the boundary between 'houses' is linguistically marked, while the boundary between 'family' units is not.

Just as some languages lack words for identifying units of parents and children, so some 'families' lack places. Immature children in every society have to be fed and cared for, but parents and children do not necessarily eat and sleep together as a family in one place. Among the Mundurucu of tropical South America, for example, the men of a village traditionally lived in a men's house together with all the village boys over the age of 13; women lived with other women and young children in two or three houses grouped around the men's house (Murphy and Murphy 1974). In Mundurucu society men and women ate and slept apart. Men ate in the men's house, sharing food the women had cooked and delivered to them; women ate with other women and children in their own houses. Married couples also slept apart, meeting only for sexual intercourse.

Finally, people around the world do not necessarily expect family members to 'love' one another. People may expect husbands, wives, parents, and children to have strong feelings about one another, but they do not necessarily expect prolonged and intimate contact to breed the loving sentiments Malinowski imagined as universally rewarding parents for the care they invested in children. The mother–daughter relationship, for example, is not always pictured as warm and loving. In modern Zambia, girls are not expected to discuss personal problems with, or seek advice from, their mothers. Rather, Zambian girls are expected to seek out some older female relative to serve as confidante (Shuster 1979). Similarly, among the Cheyenne Indians who lived on the American Great Plains during the last century, a mother was expected to have strained relations with her daughters (Hoebel 1978). Mothers are described as continually admonishing their daughters, leading the latter to seek affection from their fathers' sisters.

Of course, anthropologists have recognized that people everywhere do not share our deep faith in the loving, self-sacrificing mother, but in matters of family and motherhood, anthropologists, like all social scientists, have relied more on faith than evidence in constructing theoretical accounts. Because we *believe* mothers to be loving, anthropologists have proposed, for example, that a general explanation of the fact that men marry mother's brothers' daughters more frequently than they marry father's sisters' daughters is that men naturally seek affection (i.e., wives) where they have found affection in the past (i.e., from mothers and their kin) (Homans and Schneider 1955).

Looking Backward

The Malinowskian view of The Family as a universal institution—which maps the 'function' of 'nurturance' onto a collectivity of specific persons (presumably 'nuclear' relations) associated with specific spaces ('the home') and specific affective bonds ('love')—corresponds, as we have seen, to that assumed by most contemporary writers on the subject. But a consideration of available ethnographic evidence suggests that the received view is a good deal more problematic than a naïve observer might think. If Families in Malinowski's sense are *not* universal then we must begin to ask about the biases that, in the past, have led us to misconstrue the ethnographic record. The issues here are too complex for thorough explication in this essay, but if we are to better understand the nature of 'the family' in the present, it seems worthwhile to explore the question, first, of why so many social thinkers continue to believe in Capital-Letter Families as universal institutions and, second, whether anthropological tradition offers any alternatives to a 'necessary and natural' view of what our families are. Only then will we be in a position to suggest 'new anthropological perspectives' on the family today.

Our positive critique begins by moving backward. In the next few pages, we suggest that tentative answers to both questions posed above lie in the nineteenth-century intellectual trends that thinkers like Malinowski were at pains to reject. During the second half of the nineteenth century, a number of social and intellectual developments—among them, the evolutionary researches of Charles Darwin, the rise of 'urban problems' in fast-growing cities, and the accumulation of data on non-Western peoples by missionaries and agents of the colonial states—contributed to what most of us would now recognize as the beginnings of modern social science. Alternately excited and perplexed by changes in a rapidly industrializing world, thinkers as diverse as socialist Frederick Engels (1955) and bourgeois apologist Herbert Spencer (1973)—to say nothing of a host of mythographers, historians of religion, and even feminists—attempted to identify the distinctive problems and potentials of their contemporary society by constructing *evolutionary* accounts of 'how it all began'. At base, a sense of 'progress' gave direction to their thought whether, like Spencer, they believed 'man' had advanced from the love of violence to a more civilized love of peace or, like Engels, that humanity had moved from primitive promiscuity and incest toward monogamy and 'individual sex love'. Proud of their position in the modern world, some of these writers claimed that rules of force had been transcended by new rules of law (Mill 1869), while others thought that feminine 'mysticism' in the past had been supplanted by a higher male 'morality' (Bachofen 1861).

At the same time, and whatever else they thought of capitalist social life (some of them criticized, but none wholly abhorred it), these writers also shared a sense of moral emptiness and a fear of instability and loss. Experience argued forcefully to them that moral order in their time did not rest on the unshakable hierarchy—from God to King to Father in the home—enjoyed by Europeans in the past (Fee 1974). Thus, whereas Malinowski's functionalism led him to stress the underlying continuities in all human social forms, his nineteenth-century predecessors were concerned to understand the facts and forces that set their experiential world apart. They were interested in comparative and, more narrowly, evolutionary accounts because their lives were torn between celebration and fear of change. For them, the family was important not because it had at all times been the same but because it was all at once the moral precondition for, the triumph of, and the victim of, developing capitalist society. Without the family and female spheres, thinkers like Ruskin feared we would fall victim to a market that destroys real human bonds (Ruskin 1907). Then again, while men like Engels could decry the impact of the market on familial life and love, he joined with more conservative counterparts to insist that our contemporary familial forms benefited from the individualist morality of modern life and reached to moral and romantic heights unknown before.

Given this purpose and the limited data with which they had to work, it is hardly surprising that the vast majority of what these nineteenth-century writers said is easily dismissed today. They argued that in simpler days such things as incest were the norm; they thought that women ruled in 'matriarchal' and peace-loving states; or, alternatively, that brute force determined the primitive right and wrong. None of these visions of a more natural, more feminine, more sexy, or more violent primitive world squares with contemporary evidence about what, in technological and organizational terms, might be reckoned relatively 'primitive' or 'simple' social forms. We would suggest, however, that whatever their mistakes, these nineteenth-century thinkers *can* help us rethink the family today, at least in part because we are (unfortunately) their heirs, in the area of prejudice, and partly because their concern to characterize difference and change gave rise to insights much more promising than their functionalist critics may have thought.

To begin, although nineteenth-century evolutionary theorists did not believe The Family to be universal, the roots of modern assumptions can be seen in their belief that women are, and have at all times been, defined by nurturant, connective, and reproductive roles that *do not* change through time. Most nineteenth-century thinkers imaged social development as a process of differentiation from a relatively confused (and thus incestuous) and indiscriminate female-oriented state to one in which men fight, destroy their 'natural' social bonds, and then forge public and political ties to create a human 'order'. For some, it seemed reasonable to assume that women dominated, as matriarchs, in the undifferentiated early state, but even these theorists believed that women everywhere were 'mothers' first, defined by 'nurturant' concerns and thus excluded from the business competition, co-operation, social ordering, and social change propelled and dominated by their male counterparts. And so, while nineteenth-century writers differed in their evaluations of such things as 'women's status', they all believed that female reproductive roles made women different from and complementary to men and guaranteed both the relative passivity of women in human history and the relative continuity of 'feminine' domains and functions in human societies. Social change consisted in the acts of men, who left their mothers behind in shrinking homes. And women's nurturant sphere was recognized as a complementary and necessary corrective to the more competitive pursuits of men not because these thinkers recognized women as political actors who influence the world but because they feared the unchecked and morally questionable growth of a male-dominated, capitalist market.

For nineteenth-century evolutionists, women were associated, in short, with an unchanging biological role and a romanticized community of the past, while men were imaged as the agents of all social process. And though contemporary thinkers have been ready to dismiss manifold aspects of their now-dated school of thought, on this point we remain, perhaps unwittingly, their heirs. Victorian assumptions about gender and the relationship between competitive male markets and peace-loving female homes were not abandoned in later functionalist schools of thought at least in part because pervasive sexist biases make it easy to forget that women, like men, are important actors in *all* social worlds. Even more, the functionalists, themselves concerned to understand all human social forms in terms of biological 'needs', turned out to strengthen earlier beliefs associating action, change, and interest with the deeds of men because they thought of kinship in terms of biologically given ties, of 'families' as units geared to reproductive needs, and, finally, of women as mere 'reproducers' whose contribution to society was essentially defined by the requirements of their homes.

If most modern social scientists have inherited Victorian biases that tend ultimately to support a view uniting women and The Family to an apparently unchanging set of biologically given needs, we have at the same time failed to reckon with the one small area in which Victorian evolutionists were right. They understood, as we do not today, that families—like religions, economies, governments, or courts of law—are *not* unchanging but the product of various social forms, that the relationships of spouses and parents to their young are apt to be different things in different social orders. More particularly, although nineteenth-century writers had primitive society all wrong, they were correct in insisting that *family* in the modern sense—a unit bounded, biologically as well as legally defined, associated with property, self-sufficiency, with affect and a space 'inside' the home—is something that emerges not in Stone Age caves but in complex state-governed social forms. Tribal peoples may speak readily of lineages, households, and clans, but—as we have seen—they rarely have a word denoting Family as a particular and limited group of kin; they rarely worry about differences between legitimate and illegitimate heirs or find themselves concerned (as we so often are today) that what children and/or parents do reflects on their family's public image and self-esteem. Political influence in tribal groups in fact consists in adding children to one's home and, far from distinguishing Smith from Jones, encouraging one's neighbours to join one's household as if kin. By contrast, modern bounded Families try to keep their neighbours out. Clearly their character, ideology, and functions are not given for all times. Instead, to borrow the Victorian phrase, The Family is a 'moral' unit, a way of organizing and thinking about human relationships in a world in which the domestic is perceived to be in opposition to a politics shaped outside the home, and individuals find themselves dependent on a set of relatively non-contingent ties in order to survive the dictates of an impersonal market and external political order.

In short, what the Victorians recognized and we have tended to forget is, first, that human social life has varied in its 'moral'—we might say its 'cultural' or 'ideological'—forms, and so it takes more than making babies to make Families. And having seen The Family as something more than a response to omnipresent, biologically given needs, they realized too that Families do not everywhere exist; rather, The Family (thought to be universal by most social scientists today) is a moral and ideological unit that appears not universally but in particular social orders. The Family as we know it is not a 'natural' group created by the claims of 'blood' but a sphere of human relationships shaped by a state that recognized Families as units that hold property, provide for care and welfare, and attend particularly to the young—a sphere conceptualized as a realm of love and intimacy *in opposition* to the more 'impersonal' norms that dominate modern economies and politics. One can, in non-state social forms, find groups of genealogically related people who interact daily and share material resources, but the contents of their daily ties, the ways they think about their bonds and their conception of the relationship between immediate 'familial' links and other kinds of sociality, are apt to be different from the ideas and feelings we think rightfully belong to families we know. Stated otherwise, because our notions of The Family are rooted in a contrast between 'public' and 'private' spheres, we will not find that Families like ours exist in a society where public and political life is radically different from our own.

Victorian thinkers rightly understood the link between the bounded modern Family and the modern state although they thought the two related by a necessary teleology of moral progress. Our point resembles theirs not in the *explanations* we would seek but in our feeling that if we, today, are interested in change, we must begin to probe and understand change in the families of the past. Here the Victorians, not the functionalists, are our rightful guides because the former recognized that *all* human social ties have 'cultural' or 'moral' shapes and, more specifically, that the particular 'morality' of contemporary familial forms is rooted in a set of processes that link our intimate experiences and bonds to public politics.

Toward a Rethinking

Our perspective on families therefore compels us to listen carefully to what the natives in other societies say about their relationships with genealogically close kin. The same is true of the natives in our own society. Our understanding of families in contemporary American society can be only as rich as our understanding of what The Family represents symbolically to Americans. A complete cultural analysis of The Family as an American ideological construct, of course, is beyond the scope of this essay. But we can indicate some of the directions such an analysis would take and how it would deepen our knowledge of American families.

One of the central notions in the modern American construct of The Family is that of nurturance. When anti-feminists attack the Equal Rights Amendment, for example, much of their rhetoric plays on the anticipated loss of nurturant, intimate bonds we associate with The Family. Likewise, when pro-life forces decry abortion, they cast it as the ultimate denial of nurturance. In a sense, these arguments are variations of a functionalist view that weds families to specific functions. The logic of the argument is that because people need nurturance, and people get nurtured in The Family, then people need The Family. Yet if we adopt the perspective that The Family is an ideological unit rather than merely a functional unit, we are encouraged to subject this syllogism to closer scrutiny. We can ask, first, what do people mean by nurturance? Obviously they mean more than mere nourishment—that is, the provision of food, clothing, and shelter required for biological survival. What is evoked by the word nurturance is a certain kind of relationship: a relationship that entails affection and love, that is based on co-operation as opposed to competition, that is enduring rather than temporary, that is non-contingent rather than contingent upon performance, and that is governed by feeling and morality instead of law and contract.

The reason we have stated these attributes of The Family in terms of oppositions is because in a symbolic system the meanings of concepts are often best illuminated by explicating their opposites. Hence, to understand our American construct of The Family, we first have to map the larger system of constructs of which it is only a part. When we undertake such an analysis of The Family in our society, we discover that what gives shape to much of our conception of The Family is its symbolic opposition to work and business, in other words, to the market relations of capitalism. For it is in the market, where we sell our labour and negotiate contract relations of business, that we associate with competitive, temporary, contingent relations that must be buttressed by law and legal sanctions.

The symbolic opposition between The Family and market relations renders our strong attachment to The Family understandable, but it also discloses the particularity of our construct of The Family. We can hardly be speaking of a universal notion of The Family shared by people everywhere and for all time because people everywhere and for all time have not participated in market relations out of which they have constructed a contrastive notion of the family.

The realization that our idea of The Family is part of a set of symbolic oppositions through which we interpret our experience in a particular society compels us to ask to what extent this set of oppositions reflects real relations between people and to what extent it also shapes them. We do not adhere to a model of culture in which ideology is isolated from people's experiences. On the other hand, neither do we construe the connection between people's constructs and people's experiences to be a simple one of epiphenomenal reflection. Rather, we are interested in understanding how people come to summarize their experience in folk constructs that gloss over the diversity, complexity, and contradictions in their relationships. If, for example, we consider the second premise of the aforementioned syllogism—the idea that people get 'nurtured' in families—we can ask how people reconcile this premise with the fact that relationships in families are not always simple or altruistic. We need not resort to the evidence offered by social historians (e.g., Philippe Ariès [1962] and Lawrence Stone [1977]) of the harsh treatment and neglect of children and spouses in the history of the Western family, for we need only read our local newspaper to learn of similar abuses among contemporary families. And we can point to other studies, such as Young and Willmott's *Family and Kinship in East London* (1957), that reveal how people often find more intimacy and emotional support in relationships with individuals and groups outside The Family than they do in their relationships with family members.

The point is not that our ancestors or our contemporaries have been uniformly mean and non-nurturant to family members but that we have all been both nice and mean, both generous and ungenerous, to them. In like manner, our actions toward family members are not always motivated by selfless altruism but are also motivated by instrumental self-interest. What is significant is that, despite the fact that our complex relationships are the result of complex motivations, we ideologize relations with The Family as nurturant while casting relationships outside The Family—particularly in the sphere of work and business—as just the opposite.

We must be wary of oversimplifying matters by explaining away those disparities between our notion of the nurturant Family and our real actions toward family members as the predictable failing of imperfect beings. For there is more here than the mere disjunction of the ideal and the real. The American construct of The Family, after all, is complex enough to comprise some key contradictions. The Family is seen as representing not only the antithesis of the market relations of capitalism; it is also sacralized in our minds as the last stronghold against The State, as the symbolic refuge from the intrusions of a public domain that constantly threatens our sense of privacy and self-determination. Consequently, we can hardly be surprised to find that the punishments imposed on people who commit physical violence are lighter when their victims are their own family members (Lundsgaarde 1977). Indeed, the American sense of the privacy of the things that go on inside families is so strong that a smaller percentage of homicides involving family members are prosecuted than those involving strangers (Lundsgaarde 1977). We are faced with the irony that in our society the place where nurturance and non-contingent affection are supposed to be located is simultaneously the place where violence is most tolerated.

There are other dilemmas about The Family that an examination of its ideological nature can help us better understand. For example, the hypothesis that in England and the United States marriages among lower-income ('working-class') groups are characterized by a greater degree of 'conjugal role segregation' than are marriages among middle-income groups has generated considerable confusion. Since Bott observed that working-class couples in her study of London families exhibited more 'segregated' conjugal roles than 'middle-class' couples, who tended toward more 'joint' conjugal roles, researchers have come forth with a range of diverse and confusing findings (Bott 1957). On the one hand, some researchers have found that working-class couples indeed report more segregated conjugal role relationships—in other words, clearly differentiated male and female tasks as well as interests and activities—than do middle-class couples (Gans 1962; Rosser and Harris 1965). Other researchers, however, have raised critical methodological questions about how one goes about defining a joint activity and hence measuring the degree of 'jointness' in a conjugal relationship (Zelditch 1964; Turner 1967; Platt 1969). Platt's findings that couples who reported 'jointness' in one activity were not particularly likely to report 'jointness' in another activity is significant because it demonstrates that 'jointness' is not a general characteristic of a relationship that manifests itself uniformly over a range of domains. Couples carry out some activities and tasks together or do them separately but equally; they also have other activities in which they do not both participate. The measurement of the 'jointness' of conjugal relationships becomes even more problematic when we recognize that what one individual or couple may label a 'joint activity', another individual or couple may consider a 'separate activity'. In Bott's study, for example, some couples felt that all activities carried out by husband and wife in each other's presence were

> similar in kind regardless of whether the activities were complementary (e.g., sexual intercourse, though no one talked about this directly in the home interview), independent (e.g., husband repairing something while the wife read or knitted), or shared (e.g., washing up together, entertaining friends, going to the pictures together). It was not even necessary that husband and wife should actually be together. As long as they were both at home it was felt that their activities partook of some special, shared family quality. (Bott 1957)

In other words, the distinction Bott drew among 'joint', 'differentiated', and 'autonomic' (independent) relationships summarized the way people thought and felt about their activities rather than what they were observed to actually do. Again, it is not simply that there is a disjunction between what people say they do and what they in fact do. The more cogent point is that the meaning people attach to action, whether they view it as coordinated and therefore shared in some other way, is an integral component of that action and cannot be divorced from it in our analysis. When we compare the conjugal relationships of middle-income and low-income people, or any of the family relationships among different class, age, ethnic, and regional sectors of American society, we must recognize that our comparisons rest on differences and similarities in ideological and moral meanings as well as differences and similarities in action.

Finally, the awareness that The Family is not a concrete 'thing' that fulfills concrete 'needs' but an ideological construct with moral implications can lead to a more refined analysis of historical change in the American or Western family than has devolved upon us from our functionalist ancestors. The functionalist view of industrialization, urbanization, and family change depicts The Family as responding to alterations in economic and social conditions in rather mechanistic ways. As production gets removed from the family's domain, there is less need for strict rules and clear authority structures in the family to accomplish productive work. At the same time, individuals who now must work for wages in impersonal settings need a haven where they can obtain emotional support and gratification. Hence, The Family becomes more concerned with 'expressive' functions and what emerges is the modern 'companionate family'. In short, in the functionalist narrative, The Family and its constituent members 'adapt' to fulfill functional requirements created for it by the industrialization of production. Once we begin to view The Family as an ideological unit and pay due respect to it as a moral statement, however, we can begin to unravel the more complex, dialectical process through which family relationships and The Family as a construct were mutually transformed. We can examine, for one, the ways in which people and state institutions acted, rather than merely reacted, to assign certain functions to groupings of kin by making them legally responsible for these functions. We can investigate the manner in which the increasing limitations placed on agents of the community and the state with regard to negotiating the relationships between family members enhanced the independence of The Family. We can begin to understand the consequences of social reforms and wage policies for the age and sex inequalities in families. And we can elucidate the interplay between these social changes and the cultural transformations that assigned new meanings and modified old ones to make The Family what we think it to be today.

Ultimately, this sort of rethinking will lead to a questioning of the somewhat contradictory modern views that families are things we need (the more 'impersonal' the public world, the more we need them) and, at the same time, that loving families are disappearing. In a variety of ways, individuals today *do* look to families for a 'love' that money cannot buy and find; our contemporary world makes 'love' more fragile than most of us hope and 'nurturance' more self-interested than we believe (Rapp 1978). But what we fail to recognize is that familial nurturance and the social forces that turn our ideal families into mere fleeting dreams are *equally* creations of the world we know *today*. Rather than think of the ideal family as a world we lost (or, like the Victorians, as a world just recently achieved), it is important for us to recognize that while families symbolize deep and salient modern themes, contemporary families are unlikely to fulfill our equally modern nurturant needs.

We probably have no cause to fear (or hope) that The Family will dissolve. What we can begin to ask is what we *want* our families to do. Then, distinguishing our hopes from what we have, we can begin to analyze the social forces that enhance or undermine the realization of the kinds of human bonds we need.

References

Ariès, P. 1962. *Centuries of Childhood*, trans. R. Baldick (New York: Vintage).

Bachofen, J.J. 1861. *Das Mutterrecht* (Stuttgart).

Bott, E. 1957. *Family and Social Network: Roles, Norms, and External Relationships in Ordinary Urban Families* (London: Tavistock).

Engels, F. 1955. *The Origin of the Family, Private Property and the State*, in *Karl Marx and Frederick Engels: Selected Works*, Vol. II (Moscow: Foreign Language Publishing House).

Fee, E. 1974. 'The Sexual Politics of Victorian Social Anthropology', in *Clio's Consciousness: Raised*, eds M. Hartman and L. Banner (New York: Harper & Row).

Fox, R. 1967. *Kinship and Marriage* (London: Penguin).

Gans, H.J. 1962. *The Urban Villagers* (New York: Free Press).

Hoebel, E.A. 1978. *The Cheyennes: Indians of the Great Plains* (New York: Holt, Rinehart and Winston).

Homans, G.C., and D.M. Schneider. 1955. *Marriage, Authority, and Final Causes* (Glencoe, IL: Free Press).

Lundsgaarde, H.P. 1977. *Murder in Space City: A Cultural Analysis of Houston Homicide Patterns* (New York: Oxford University Press).

Malinowski, B. 1913. *The Family among the Australian Aborigines* (London: University of London Press).

———. 1944. *A Scientific Theory of Culture* (Chapel Hill: University of North Carolina Press).

Mill, J.S. 1869. *The Subjection of Women* (London: Longmans, Green, Reader and Dyer).

Morgan, L.H. 1877. *Ancient Society* (New York: Holt).

Murphy, Y., and R. Murphy. 1974. *Women of the Forest* (New York: Columbia University Press).

Platt, J. 1969. 'Some Problems in Measuring the Jointness of Conjugal-role Relationships', *Sociology* 3: 287–97.

Rapp, R. 1978. 'Family and Class in Contemporary America: Notes Toward an Understanding of Ideology', *Science and Society* 42: 278–300.

Rosser, C., and C. Harris. 1965. *The Family and Social Change* (London: Routledge & Kegan Paul).

Ruskin, J. 1907. 'Of Queen's Gardens', in *Sesame and Lilies* (London: J.M. Dent).

Shuster, I. 1979. *New Women of Lusaka* (Palo Alto, CA: Mayfield).

Spencer, H. 1973. *The Principles of Sociology*, Vol. I, *Domestic Institutions* (New York: Appleton).

Stone, L. 1977. *The Family, Sex, and Marriage in England 1500–1800* (London: Weidenfeld & Nicolson).

Turner, C. 1967. 'Conjugal Roles and Social Networks: A Re-examination of a Hypothesis', *Human Relations* 20: 121–30.

Vogt, E.Z. 1969. *Zinacantan: A Mayu Community in the Highlands of Chiapas* (Cambridge, MA: Harvard University Press).

Young, M., and P. Willmott. 1957. *Family and Kinship in East London* (London: Routledge & Kegan Paul).

Zelditch Jr, M. 1964. 'Family, Marriage and Kinship', in *A Handbook of Modern Sociology*, ed. R.E.L. Faris (Chicago: Rand McNally), 680–707.

PART TWO

Diverse Family Patterns

Section 1 Foraging Societies: Communal 'Households'

To understand family patterns, it is important to get a sense of the dynamic relationship between the way production is organized, on the one hand, and the way the social relations involved in sexuality, reproduction, child rearing, and daily consumption are organized, on the other. The chapters in Part Two of this book aim to tell us something of the nature of that relationship. When we compare gender and family patterns in societies based on foraging, agriculture, and industrial capitalism we see some significant contrasts. From these, we can begin to see how different ways of acquiring a livelihood involve different gender relations and different family patterns. For example, the co-operation, sharing, and dependence on a group larger than the nuclear unit, which are central to survival in foraging societies, have clear implications for the gender relations and living arrangements typical in them. This conclusion is clear in Eleanor Leacock's description of a foraging community native to Quebec and Newfoundland and Labrador.

Chapter 4

These selections from the writings of the late anthropologist Eleanor B. Leacock provide rich descriptions of gender and family relations among the Montagnais-Naskapi, an Aboriginal people who survived by hunting and gathering. Leacock's research involved close examination of the 'Jesuit Relations' (diaries kept by the Jesuits working in the seventeenth century in what is now Quebec, and Newfoundland and Labrador); it also included her own fieldwork in Labrador during the 1950s and 1960s. The parts of her essays presented here provide us not only with descriptions of 'family' and gender relations in a foraging society but also a sketch of her argument about how the ways foragers acquired their livelihood (i.e., their 'economy') shaped both their family organization and the gender relations typical in their society. Accordingly, she also provides vivid descriptions of how family and gender changed as these people abandoned hunting for trapping and trading with Europeans (and as the Jesuits, working on behalf of France as well as their Church, devoted themselves to undermining Native traditions).

Leacock describes a society in which people lived in small groups and acquired their subsistence by co-operating with each other daily. She indicates a division of labour based on gender, but which did not entail systemic gender inequality. The autonomy that women had in this society, Leacock argues, was related to the dependence all people had on the group: because people depended on each other daily—because co-operation and generosity were central to daily subsistence—people accorded each other considerable freedom. This autonomy, and the absence of private property, formed the basis of the gender egalitarianism common in foraging societies.

For much of the year, the Montagnais-Naskapi lived in small hunting groups, which functioned as 'families' do in our society. It is important to note that the composition of these units—about which Leacock writes elsewhere—consisted of several nuclear-family units, which were not necessarily related by blood. This kind of larger unit, containing several nuclear families, is common in foraging societies, as well as in horticultural societies. Thus, evolutionary psychologists, who claim that blood ties (and the desire to protect biological offspring) formed the basis of lasting ties and family units over the course of human evolution, are ignoring evidence on the nature of the kinds of societies in which humans evolved. For the Montagnais-Naskapi, hunting groups were the units of production, consumption, child rearing, and residence as long as the Montagnais-Naskapi were hunters. As Leacock points out, these units constituted 'the economy'. Because women played a central role in them, they played a central role in the economy.

Women in an Egalitarian Society: The Montagnais-Naskapi of Canada

Eleanor B. Leacock

In the past, the Montagnais-Naskapi of the eastern Labrador Peninsula lived by hunting moose, caribou, beaver, bear, hare, porcupine, and other small game; by fishing, and by catching water fowl. The Indians hunted with bows and arrows, spears, and a variety of traps.

Meat that was not eaten was smoke-dried for storage. In the summer they gathered nuts, berries, and roots.

The Montagnais-Naskapi lived in tents constructed of 20 to 30 poles, converging at the top and covered with large rolls of birch-bark and animal hides. A tent might be shared by about 18 people. They wore breechcloths, leggings and moccasins, and robes with detachable sleeves, made from leather by the women. In the winter, travel was by foot on snowshoes and long narrow sledges, which were dragged along forest trails by a cord strung across the chest. Canoes made of birch-bark were used in the summer.

Until very recently, the Montagnais-Naskapi still lived for the most part in tents, wore moccasins, and often the women retained their traditional hairstyle with the hair wound on two little wooden knobs over the ears. They manufactured their own canoes, snowshoes, fish spears, sleds, and toboggans using the 'crooked knife'—a sharpened steel file, curved upwards at the end and hafted in a piece of wood. They seldom settled in one place for more than a few weeks; entire families moved hundreds of miles or more in the course of a year.

The Indians spoke their own language, told their own stories, and taught their children to read and write in the phonetic script they developed long ago when European books and letters gave them the idea. Thus, many anthropologists considered the Indians' use of some modern technology, and their adoption of some Western social and religious practices, to be the sum total of the changes that have taken place in their lifestyle.

However, a close study of the observations made centuries ago by traders and missionaries shows what profound changes have taken place in the way the Montagnais-Naskapi live. Le Jeune, a Jesuit missionary, lived with a Montagnais band in the winter of 1633–4 and his accounts give a picture of their life in the days when they depended on hunting not only for food but for everything from clothes to snowshoe webbing. Three or four families, usually related, lived together in a single, large tent; men, women, and children travelled together, each working and contributing to the group to the extent he or she was able.

Le Jeune relates that three tent groups joined forces and decided to winter together on the south shore of the St Lawrence River some miles below Quebec. Leaving their canoes at the coast, they went inland and travelled about, shifting their camp 23 times in the period from 12 November to 22 April. The winter was a hard one, since the lack of snow made it impossible to trace moose successfully. One of the three tent groups left the other two so that they might spread out over a wider area.

Eventually a heavy snowfall alleviated the situation, and large game was killed in sufficient numbers so that some of the meat could be dried and stored. In the spring, the tent group Le Jeune was with split up temporarily, some members keeping to the highlands to hunt moose, the others following the stream beds where beaver were to be found. Gradually the entire party collected again at the coast where the canoes had been cached.

Within the group, the social ethic called for generosity, co-operation, and patience, and Le Jeune commented on the good humour, the lack of jealousy, and the willingness to help that characterized daily life. Those who did not contribute their share were not respected, and it was a real insult to call a person stingy.

The Montagnais had no leaders; the 'chiefs' Le Jeune referred to were apparently men of influence and rhetorical ability. Everyone was impressed with the skill of the speaker who put forth the Montagnais view of French-Indian relations when he greeted Champlain in 1632. Such men were spokesmen, who acted as intermediaries with the French or with other Indian groups, but they held no formal power, a situation the Jesuits tried to change by introducing formal elections. . . .

Important matters were resolved through considered discussion. Le Jeune was impressed by the patience with which people listened as others spoke, rather than all talking at once. At that time leadership in specific situations fell to the individual who was most knowledgeable. For instance, during Le Jeune's stay when food was scarce and the Indians had to move in search of it, he wrote: 'When our people saw that there was no longer any game within three or four leagues of us, a Savage, who was best acquainted with the way to the place where we were going, cried out in a loud voice, one fine day outside the cabin: "Listen men, I am going to mark the way for breaking camp tomorrow at daybreak."'

The principle of autonomy extended to relations between men and women. Though some observers saw women as drudges, Le Jeune saw women as holding 'great power' and having 'in nearly every instance . . . the choice of plans, of undertakings, of journeys, of winterings'. Indeed, independence of women was considered a problem to the Jesuits, who lectured the men about 'allowing' their wives sexual and other freedom and sought to introduce European principles of obedience.

Compare this lifestyle with that of an Indian man living to the northeast of Quebec a few decades ago, who depended upon the produce of his trapline for most of his livelihood. He worked within a definite territory which was probably passed down to him by his father, father-in-law, or another older relative. During the trapping season he left his family at a permanent camp, or perhaps even at the fur trading post, and he travelled back and forth along his line of some 300 to 400 steel traps, preferably in the company of a partner or grown son, but at times alone. Only in the summer did he join his fellow band members at the trading post, and only in this season would all the trappers live together with their families for a reasonably long period of time.

The change in this Indian's life had come about because he was no longer primarily a hunter. He was first and foremost a trapper, dependent upon the goods his furs procured for him at the local trading post. True, his ancestors always hunted and traded furs. Avenues of exchange and communication in Aboriginal America had apparently been kept open from time immemorial. However, this trade was primarily for luxury items and for social purposes. It was not of great economic importance; the economy of the Indians was still based almost entirely on hunting for immediate use.

Then Europe, breaking the bonds of the small, self-contained feudal communities of the Middle Ages, slowly began to develop into a commercial and urban civilization. Explorers covered the earth; trade with American Indians, and the fur trade in particular, was of no small importance. Even before the end of the sixteenth century, British and French companies were competing among themselves for a monopoly of the St Lawrence trade.

To the Indians, the trade opened up a source of new and more effective tools and weapons, of cloth which did not have to be tanned and worked, and of foods which could be more readily transported and stored. However, it demanded an unending flow of furs, and trapping fur-bearing animals began to displace the hunting of large game in the Indian economy. Within a few generations the Indians near the earliest trade centres around Quebec had become dependent upon trade goods as the mainstay of their existence. When the fur-bearing animals in their immediate area became scarce, they became the middlemen between the Europeans and the Indians who lived farther to the north and west.

On the face of it, there seems little reason why it should make much difference when men turned to trapping rather than hunting as a major pursuit. But through the fur trade it came to supersede and replace all other basic economic activities. And tending a trapline was a more individual type of activity than hunting. When men became trappers, the sexual definition of functions and spheres of interest became sharper, for the wife and children began to be set apart as the family who were provided for, as compared to the men who were the providers. At the same time, there was a breaking up of the 'family bands' (the two or three tent groups that usually stayed together) into smaller units approaching the 'nuclear' family.

A connected change that took place in Montagnais-Naskapi life was an increasingly clear-cut differentiation between the spheres of men's work and women's work. In the past, both sexes were almost continuously engaged in satisfying the immediate needs of the extended family group. There was a rough and ready division of labour, based on expediency, with the men doing most of the large game hunting and the women preparing the food, making the clothes and tents, and tending the small children. When necessary, the women helped with the hunting, and if a woman was busy elsewhere, a man would readily look after the children. *The Mistassini Diaries*, written a century ago by Hudson's Bay Company members, mention Indian women in western Labrador who were the heads of families and even handled their own traps.

The lack of a marked division of labour prevailed until recently in the camp of the Northwest River Indians. A man and his wife would come together from the woods, each carrying a log. A father and daughter might saw wood together. A man might hold a fussing child while the mother calmly did something else, feeling no compulsion to take over. A whole family would go off in a canoe to pull in the fishnets. Two young women would pick up some guns and go off to hunt rabbits. It is only when one comes to the technical processes that one noticed a division of skills that seems to be rigid: the men were the woodworkers, making the canoes and snowshoes, and the women handled the skins, scraping, tanning, working, and sewing them.

Another change that can be observed among the Montagnais-Naskapi is a shift toward smaller family units. Only on rare occasions did two or three Indian families of eastern Labrador still share a tent. One result of the breaking up of large 'extended' families into smaller units, based on a married couple and their children, was that the circle of people upon whom the children depend began to shrink. Le Jeune reveals the feelings of a seventeenth-century Indian father, who chided the French, saying, 'Thou hast no sense. You French people love only your own children; but we love all the children of our tribe.' In 1950, however, there was a growing emphasis among the Indians on having one's 'own' son who will help one on the trapline.

On the other hand, it must be said that the general loving attitude toward all children still prevailed. Time and again one noticed an adult's casual and spontaneous concern for the needs of whatever child happened to be around. Nor could one pick out an orphan or 'adopted' child by the way he or she was treated. Such children were in no way set apart from the life of the group but were gratefully taken in and cherished by another family.

These are only a few of the developments that have been taking place in Montagnais-Naskapi life. Any number of others could be studied—changing forms of property and attitudes toward possessions, courtship practices, recreation and amusement, methods of child rearing, and so on. However, the same fundamental point would be made by examination of any important area of living: that the Montagnais-Naskapi Indians are not a people who simply accepted some European traits and rejected others but a people who actively adjusted their whole way of life to meet the demands of a new occupational calling.

By 1950, most Montagnais-Naskapi had moved into relatively large centres of permanent settlement. Three important towns were Schefferville, near a large interior iron mine; Seven Islands, a railhead on the St Lawrence River; and Happy Valley, near the Goose Bay Air Base on the eastern coast. While most Indians who lived in these towns were wage labourers at the enterprises near their homes, work was often seasonal, and some still derived a major part of their income from winter trapping. Many young Indians were moving to cities for work and schooling and some were joining local and national Indian groups that concern themselves with the problems and futures of Native Canadians. As part of this future many young Indians found that they wanted to retain some of the Indian tradition of a close group life, in tune with the waters and forests, the animals and bird life, the natural surroundings of their ancestors.

❖

What was the status of the Montagnais-Naskapi women in the early seventeenth century when the French were establishing a foothold in the upper St Lawrence valley? As is often the case, a look through accounts written at the time yields contrasting judgments. One may read that 'women have great power . . . A man may promise you something and if he does not keep his promise, he thinks he is sufficiently excused when he tells you that his wife did not wish him to do it' (Thwaites 1906, 5: 179). Or one may read that women were virtual slaves:

> The women . . . besides the onerous role of bearing and rearing the children, also transport the game from the place where it has fallen; they are the hewers of wood and drawers of water; they make and repair the household utensils; they prepare the food; they skin the game and prepare the hides like fullers; they sew garments; they catch fish and gather shellfish for food; often they even hunt; they make the canoes, that is, skiffs of marvelous rapidity, out of bark; they set up the tents wherever and whenever they stop for the night—in short, the men concern themselves with nothing but the more laborious hunting and the waging of war . . . Their wives are regarded and treated as slaves.

Fortunately, the ethnohistorical record for the Montagnais-Naskapi is full enough so that contradictions between two statements such as these can be resolved. The view that the hard work of Native American women made them slaves was commonly expressed by European observers who did not know personally the people about whom they were writing. The statement about female authority, however, was written by a man who knew the Montagnais-Naskapi well and recognized that women controlled their own work and made decisions accordingly. Paul Le Jeune, superior of the Jesuit mission at Quebec, had spent a winter in a Montagnais lodge in order to learn the language and understand the culture of the people he was supposed to convert and 'civilize'. He commented on the ease of relations between husbands and wives in Montagnais society, and explained that it followed from 'the order which they maintain in their occupations', whereby 'the women know what they are to do, and the men also; and one never meddles with the work of the other' (5: 133). 'Men leave the arrangement of the household to the women, without interfering with them; they cut and decide and give away as they please without making the husband angry. I have never seen my host ask a giddy young woman that he had with him what became of the provisions, although they were disappearing very fast' (6: 233).

Le Jeune sought to change this state of affairs, and he reported to his superiors in Paris on this progress in 'civilizing' the Montagnais-Naskapi through what became a fourfold program. First, he saw permanent settlement and the institution of formally recognized chiefly authority as basic. Second, Le Jeune stressed the necessity of introducing the principle of punishment into Montagnais social relations. Third, central to Le Jeune's program was education of Montagnais-Naskapi children. . . . Montagnais-Naskapi culture posed a stumbling block for the Jesuits in that the Montagnais did not practise corporal punishment of children. Le Jeune complained, 'The Savages prevent their instruction; they will not tolerate the chastisement of their children, whatever they may do, they permit only a simple reprimand' (5: 197). Le Jeune's solution was to propose removing the children from their communities for schooling: 'The reason why I would not like to take the children of one locality in that locality itself, but rather in some other place, is because these Barbarians cannot bear to have their children punished, even scolded, not being able to refuse anything to a crying child. They carry this to such an extent that upon the slightest pretext they would take them away from us, before they were educated' (6: 153–5).

Fourth, essential to Le Jeune's entire program was the introduction of European family structure with male authority, female fidelity, and the elimination of the right to divorce. Lecturing a man on the subject, Le Jeune said the man 'was the master and that in France women do not rule their husbands' (5: 179). The independence of Montagnais women posed continual problems for the Jesuits. Le Jeune decided that

> it is absolutely necessary to teach the girls as well as the boys, and that we shall do nothing or very little, unless some good household has the care of this sex; for the boys that we shall have reared in the knowledge of God, when they marry Savage girls or women accustomed to wandering in the woods will, as their husbands, be compelled to follow them and thus fall back into barbarism or to leave them, another evil full of danger. (5: 145)

Le Jeune's account of his problems, successes, and failures in introducing hierarchical principles into the ordering of interpersonal relations among the Montagnais-Naskapi affords a clear record of the personal autonomy that was central to the structure and ethics of their society—an autonomy that applied as fully to women as to men.

Montagnais-Naskapi Economy and Decision-making

The Montagnais-Naskapi lived by hunting and trapping wild game—caribou, moose, beaver, bear, hare, porcupine, and water fowl, by fishing, and by gathering wild berries and other vegetable foods. Like foraging peoples everywhere, they followed a regular pattern of seasonal movement according to the provenience of the foods on which they depended. The Montagnais with whom Le Jeune worked summered on the shores of the St Lawrence River, where groups of several hundred people gathered to fish, socialize, and make and repair canoes, snowshoes, and other equipment. In the fall, groups of some 35 to 75 people separated out to ascend one or another of the rivers that emptied into the St Lawrence. During the winter hunting season, these bands might split up into smaller groups in order to spread out over a wide area in search of game. However, they kept in touch with each other so that if some were short of food, they could turn to others for help.

The smallest working unit was the group that lived together in a large cone-shaped lodge—some 10 to 20 people, or, in Western terms, several nuclear families. In early times, as later, residential choices were probably flexible, and people moved about in accord both with personal likes and dislikes and with the need for keeping a reasonable balance in the working group between women and men and young and old. Upon marriage, however, a man ideally moved into his wife's lodge (Thwaites 1906, 31: 169). Accordingly, mentions of a Montagnais man's family might include the man's wife's sister, or a son-in-law, or a father-in-law (6: 125; 9: 33; 14: 143–5). Yet three brothers and their wives shared the lodge in which Le Jeune lived. Le Jeune is silent about the relationships among the wives who, judging from hunting-group compositions in recent times, could easily have been sisters or parallel cousins.[1] In any case, Le Jeune's diary shows that the arrangement was not permanent.

Ethnographic evidence as well as the *Jesuit Relations* indicates that decisions about movements were made by the adult members of whatever group was involved. There is no question about women's importance in making such decisions. In fact, one recorder stated that 'the choice of plans, of undertakings, of journeys, of winterings, lies in nearly every instance in the hands of the housewife' (68: 93). Individuals might be chosen as spokespersons to mediate with the French, but such 'chiefs' held no formal authority within the group. Le Jeune noted that 'the Savages cannot endure in the least those who seem desirous of assuming superiority over the others; they place all virtue in a certain gentleness or apathy' (16: 165).

> They imagine that they ought by right of birth, to enjoy the liberty of wild ass colts, rendering no homage to anyone whomsoever, except when they like. They have reproached me a hundred times because we fear our Captains, while they laugh at and make sport of theirs. All the authority of their Chief is in his tongue's end; for he is powerful insofar as he is eloquent; and, even if he kills himself talking and haranguing, he will not be obeyed unless he pleases the Savages. (6: 243)

Le Jeune was honest enough to state what he saw as the positive side of Montagnais egalitarianism:

> As they have neither political organization, nor office, nor dignities, nor any authority, for they only obey their Chief through goodwill toward him, therefore they never kill each other to acquire these honours. Also, as they are contented with mere living, not one of them gives himself to the Devil to acquire wealth. (6: 231)

In his final judgment, however, Le Jeune remained bound by his culture and his missionizing commitment: 'I would not dare assert that I have seen one act of real moral virtue in a Savage. They have nothing but their own pleasure and satisfaction in view' (6: 239–41).

The Jesuit Program for Changing Montagnais Marriage

As indicated above, Le Jeune's original assumption—that he could win the Montagnais to Christianity through converting the men—changed when he learned how far Montagnais family structure was from that of the French. He realized that he would have to give special attention to women as well as men if he was to eliminate the Montagnais' unquestioned acceptance of divorce at the desire of either partner, of polygyny, and of sexual freedom after marriage.

'The young people do not think that they can persevere in the state of matrimony with a bad wife or a bad husband', Le Jeune wrote. 'They wish to be free and to be able to divorce the consort if they do not love each other' (16: 41). And several years later, 'The inconstancy of marriages and the facility with which they divorce each other are a great obstacle to the Faith of Jesus Christ. We do not dare baptize the young people because experience teaches us that the custom of abandoning a disagreeable wife or husband has a strong hold on them' (22: 229).

Polygamy was another right that women as well as men took for granted: 'Since I have been preaching among them that a man should not have more than one wife, I have not been well received by the women; for, since they are more numerous than the men, if a man can only marry one of them, the others will have to suffer. Therefore, this doctrine is not according to their liking' (12: 165). And as for the full acceptance of sexual freedom for both women and men, no citation can be more telling of the gulf between French and Montagnais society than Le Jeune's rendition of a Montagnais rebuff:

> I told him that it was not honourable for a woman to love anyone else except her husband, and that this evil being among them, he himself was not sure that his son, who was there present, was his son. He replied, 'Thou hast no sense. You French people love only your own children; but we love all the children of our tribe.' I began to laugh, seeing that he philosophized in horse and mule fashion. (6: 255)

Converts to Christianity wrestled with the dilemmas posed by the French faith. A recently married young man wished to be faithful to his wife but felt himself 'inclined toward infidelity'. Deeply disturbed by his criminal wish, he entreated to be imprisoned or publicly flogged. When his request was refused, 'He slips into a room near the Chapel and, with a rope that he finds, he beats himself so hard all over the body that the noise reaches the ears of the Father, who runs in and forbids so severe a penance' (22: 67).

❖

In 1640, eight years after Le Jeune's arrival in New France and the setting up of a Jesuit mission, the governor called together a group of influential Montagnais men, and 'having recommended to the Christians constance in their marriages—he gave them to understand that it would be well if they should elect some chiefs to govern them' (18: 99). Accordingly, the Montagnais sought advice from the Jesuits, who supervised the election of three captains. The men then 'resolved to call together the women to urge them to be instructed and to receive holy Baptism'. The women were used to holding councils of their own to deal with matters of concern to them and reported surprise at being lectured to by the men:

> Yesterday the men summoned us to a council, but the first time that women have ever entered one; but they treated us so rudely that we were greatly astonished. 'It is you women', they said to us, 'who keep the Demons among us; you do not urge to be baptized . . . when you pass before the cross you never salute it, you wish to be independent. Now know that you will obey your husbands and you young people know that you will obey your parents, and our captains, and if any fail to do so, we will give them nothing to eat.' (18: 107)

Women's responses ranged from zealous compliance to rebelliousness. An incident illustrating compliance with a husband's wishes, and suggesting the internalization of guilt, occurred when a Christian woman joined some 'games or public recreation' of which her husband did not approve:

> Having returned, her husband said to her, 'If I were not Christian, I would tell you that if you did not care for me you should seek another husband to whom you would render more obedience; but having promised God not to leave you until death, I cannot speak to you thus, although you have offended me.' This poor woman asked his forgiveness, without delay, and on the following morning came to see the Father

> who had baptized her, and said to him, 'My Father, I have offended God, I have not obeyed my husband; my heart is sad; I greatly desire to make my confession of this.' (18: 35)

Other women continued to have lovers, to solicit married men to take a second wife, and to defy or leave their husbands. One convert complained, 'My wife is always angry; I fear that the Demons she keeps in my cabin are perverting the good that I received in holy Baptism.'. . .

Another particularly revealing incident offers an important comment on Montagnais ethics, and indicates the growing distance between the missionized Montagnais, with their acceptance of corporal punishment, and the unconverted. A Jesuit called some 'chief men' together and, after commending them on putting a stop to 'the disorderly conduct that occasionally occurred among them', expressed astonishment at their permitting a young baptized woman to live apart from her husband. The captain responsible for her replied that 'he had tried all sorts of means to make her return to her duty and that his trouble had been in vain; that he would, nevertheless, make another effort.' The Jesuit father counselled him to consult his people and decide upon what was to be done for such disobedience: 'They all decided upon harsh measures. "Good advice", they said, "has not brought her to her sense; a prison will do so." Two captains were ordered to take her to Kebec and . . . have her put in a dungeon.' The woman fled, but they caught her and tried to take her by canoe to Quebec. At this

> some Pagan young men, observing this violence, of which the Savages have a horror, and which is more remote from their customs than heaven is from Earth, made use of threats, declaring that they would kill anyone who laid a hand on the woman. But the Captain and his people, who were Christians, boldly replied that there was nothing that they would not do or endure in order to secure obedience to God. Such resolution silenced the infidels.

To avoid being imprisoned, the woman 'humbly begged to be taken back to Saint Joseph, promising thenceforward she would be more obedient'. Le Jeune stated,

> Such acts of justice cause no surprise in France, because it is usual there to proceed in that manner. But, among these peoples . . . where everyone considers himself from birth, as free as the wild animals that roam in their great forest . . . it is a marvel, or rather a miracle, to see a peremptory command obeyed, or any act of severity or justice performed. . . .

Long-range Impact of the Jesuit Program

. . . Perhaps no incident in the *Relations* more poignantly reveals the cultural distance to be spanned by Montagnais converts than that in which a French drummer boy hit a Montagnais with his drumstick, drawing blood.

> The Montagnais onlookers took offence, saying, 'Behold, one of thy people has wounded one of ours, thou knowest our custom well; give us presents for this wound.' The French interpreter countered, 'Thou knowest our custom; when any of our number does wrong, we punish him. This child has wounded one of your people; he shall be whipped at once in [their] presence.' When the Montagnais saw the French were in earnest about whipping the boy, they began to pray for his pardon, alleging he was only a child, that he had no mind, that he did not know what he was doing; but as our people were nevertheless going to punish

> him, one of the Savages stripped himself entirely, threw his blanket over the child and cried out to him who was going to do the whipping: 'Strike me if thou wilt, but thou shalt not strike him.' And thus the little one escaped. (5: 219)

This incident took place in 1633. How was it possible that scarcely 10 years later, adults could be beating, withholding food from, and even, if the report is accurate, doing such things as throwing hot ashes on children and youths? Above, I have referred to the punitiveness toward the self and others that accompanied the often tormented attempt on the part of converts to reject a familiar set of values and replace it with another. This psychological response is familiar. To say this, however, merely presses the next question: Why did some Montagnais feel so strongly impelled to make this attempt? The answer is that the Jesuits and their teachings arrived in New France a full century after the economic basis for unquestioned co-operation, reciprocity, and respect for individual autonomy began to be undercut by the trading of furs for European goods. On the basis of new economic ties, some Montagnais-Naskapi were interested in attaching themselves to the mission station and the new European settlement, thereby availing themselves of the resources these offered. By the same token, some were prepared to accept the beliefs and ritual practices of the newcomers, and to adopt—or attempt to adopt—new standards of conduct.

Elsewhere, I have documented the process whereby the stockpiling of furs for future return, to be acquired when the trading ships arrived, contradicted the principles of total sharing based on subsistence hunting, fishing, and gathering (Leacock 1954). The process has subsequently been well described for the Canadian sub-Arctic generally, and it has been pointed out that parallel processes are involved when a horticultural people become involved in exchange relations with a market economy (Murphy and Steward 1955).

At the same time that the fur trade was undercutting the foundation for Montagnais-Naskapi values and interpersonal ethics, the terrible scourge of epidemic disease, the escalation (or introduction) of warfare, and the delusion of relief from anxiety offered by alcohol were also undermining Montagnais-Naskapi self-assurance. Alfred Goldsworthy Bailey (1969) has described the effects of these developments in a review of the conflict between European and eastern Algonkian cultures during the sixteenth and seventeenth centuries. Fear of disease, particularly smallpox which raged in the decade after the priests' arrival, was only equalled by fear of the Iroquois. The prolonged and intricate torture of Iroquois prisoners, into which women entered with even more zeal than men, was a grim expression of profound fearfulness and anger. Alcohol, which temporarily elated the spirits, led to fights around the European settlement; in 1664 there is a reference to a case of rape committed under its influence (48: 227).

This is not to say, however, that Montagnais-Naskapi society as a whole was thoroughly disrupted. The violence that occurred around the European settlement contrasts not only with the friendliness, gaiety, and lack of quarrelling that Le Jeune described during the winter he spent in the interior in 1633–4 but also with the general co-operativeness and goodwill—albeit laced with raucous banter and teasing—that characterized Montagnais-Naskapi life in later centuries in the rest of the Labrador Peninsula. Quebec was, after all, a gateway to the North American interior, and fur trading posts and mission stations pushed ever westward. The non-racist policy of building a French colony in part with re-socialized Indians was abandoned and replaced by a hardening colour line. In time, all Montagnais-Naskapi became Catholic, but without the closer supervision of the Jesuits, they retained established religious practices and added Catholic sacraments and prayer. During the summer of 1951, the 'shaking-tent rite', in which a religious practitioner converses with the gods, both gaining useful information and entertaining the audience in the process, was still being practised in eastern Labrador.

The pace of change in most of the Labrador Peninsula was slow, as Indians living far from centres of early settlement and trade gradually became drawn into a fur-trapping economy. In the summer of 1950, I was able to document the final stages of transition in southeastern Labrador, at a time when the next major change was about to transform life for French and English fishermen and fur trappers as well as Montagnais-Naskapi hunter trappers; a railroad was being built into a huge iron mine deep in the north central part of the peninsula. When I was there, conditions in the north woods were still such that the traditional Montagnais-Naskapi ethic of co-operativeness, tolerance, and non-punitiveness remained strong.

What about the relations between women and men? . . . Burgesse (1944) has written that

> labour is fairly equitably divided between the sexes under the economic system of the Montagnais. Each sex has its own particular duties but, within certain limits, the divisions between the types of work performed are not rigid. A man would not consider it beneath his dignity to assist his wife in what are ordinarily considered duties peculiar to the woman. Also, women are often enough to be seen performing tasks which are usually done by men. On being questioned in regard to this aspect of their economics, the Montagnais invariably reply that, since marriage is a union of co-equal partners for mutual benefit, it is the duty of the husband to assist his wife in the performance of her labours. Similarly, it is the duty of the wife to aid the husband. . . .
>
> The Montagnais woman is far from being a drudge. Instead she is a respected member of the tribe whose worth is well appreciated and whose advice and counsel is listened to and, more often than not, accepted and acted upon by her husband. (4–7) . . .

Women retained control over the products of their labour. These were not alienated, and women's production of clothing, shelter, and canoe covering gave them concomitant practical power and influence, despite formal statements of male dominance that might be elicited by outsiders. In northern Labrador in the late nineteenth century, dependence on trading furs for food, clothing, and equipment was only beginning. Band cohesion was still strong, based on the sharing of meat, fish, and other necessities, and on the reciprocal exchange of goods and services between women and men.

By the middle of this [twentieth] century, the economic balance had tipped in favour of the ultimate dependence upon the fur trade (and, in many cases, wage labour) throughout the entire Labrador Peninsula. The Montagnais-Naskapi lived in nuclear-family units largely supported by the husband and father's wages or take from the trapline. Nonetheless, the resources of the land were still directly used, were still available to anyone, were acquired co-operatively insofar as it was most practical, and were shared. Furthermore, partly through their own desire and partly in accord with the racist structure of Western society, the Montagnais-Naskapi maintained their status as a semi-autonomous people and were not separated into an elite minority versus a majority of marginal workers. Thus, a strong respect for individual autonomy and an extreme sensitivity to the feelings of others when decisions were to be made went with a continuing emphasis on generosity and co-operativeness, which applied to relations between as well as within the sexes.

In my own experience living in a Montagnais-Naskapi camp, I noted a quality of respectfulness between women and men that fits Burgesse's characterization. I also observed such behaviour as an ease of men with children, who would take over responsibility even for infants when it was called for, with a spontaneity and casual competence that in our culture would be described as 'maternal'. Nonetheless, men were 'superior' in ways commonly alluded to in anthropological literature. The few shamans who still practised their art (or admitting practising it to an outsider) were men; band chiefs were men; and patrilocality was both an ideal and statistically more common among newlyweds than matrilocality. In short, Montagnais-Naskapi practice at this time fitted what is considered in the anthropological literature to be usual for people who live (or have recently lived) by direct acquisition and use of wild products; strongly egalitarian, but with an edge in favour of male authority and influence.

Seventeenth-century accounts, however, referred to female shamans who might become powerful (Thwaites 1906, 6: 61; 14: 183). So-called outside chiefs, formally elected according to government protocol to mediate with white society, had no more influence within the group than their individual attributes would call for; and matrilocality had only recently given way to patrilocal, post-marital residence. As markedly different as Montagnais-Naskapi culture continued to be from Western culture, the ethnohistorical record makes clear that it had been constantly restructuring itself to fit new situations and that the status of women, although still relatively high, has clearly changed.

Note

1. Parallel cousins are the children of two sisters or two brothers (and their spouses). Children of a brother and a sister (and their spouses) are called 'cross-cousins'. As is common in many kin-based societies, the Montagnais-Naskapi terms for parallel cousins were the same as for siblings, while the terms for cross-cousins, who were desirable marriage partners, connoted something like 'sweetheart' (Strong 1929).

References

Bailey, A.G. 1969. *The Conflict of European and Eastern Algonkian Cultures, 1504–1700* (Toronto: University of Toronto Press).

Burgesse, J.A. 1944. 'The Woman and the Child among the Lac-St-Jean Montagnais', *Primitive Man* 17.

Leacock, E. 1954. 'The Montagnais "Hunting Territory" and the Fur Trade', *American Anthropologist* 78.

Murphy, R.F., and J.H. Steward. 1955. 'Tappers and Trappers: Parallel Processes in Acculturation', *Economic Development and Cultural Change* 4.

Strong, W.D. 1929. 'Cross-cousin Marriage and the Culture of the Northeastern Algonkians', *American Anthropologist* 31.

Thwaites, R.G., ed. 1906. *The Jesuit Relations and Allied Documents*, 71 vols (Cleveland: Burrows Brothers).

Section 2 Agricultural Societies: The 'Family Economy'

Years ago, researchers laid to rest the myth that pre-industrial families were typically extended (i.e., consisting of three generations living together under one roof). Yet the dynamics of pre-industrial households, which have been described by social historians studying peasant and artisan households from medieval times through the eighteenth century, cast a new perspective on the matter. Although the nuclear-family pattern may have been dominant at any point in time across much of Europe, its existence was premised on cross-generational ties (through which land—the prerequisite of marriage—was passed). So, while mortality limited the chances that children would live with their grandparents, extended kin ties were fundamental to family existence. Moreover, nuclear families' continued existence was often predicated on the willingness or need of other households to take in their children at various points in their childhood and youth, as well as on the labour of people who lived in the household but were not related by blood or marriage (e.g., farm workers, servants, etc.). In short, there was nothing self-contained or privatized about nuclear families in pre-industrial Europe. They bore little resemblance to nuclear families today—in their composition, degree of stability, the care of children, and the emotional tenor of households.

Chapter 5

What follows is a selection from Louise Tilly and Joan Scott's book *Women, Work and Family*, which examines women's work on farms and in urban shops in England and France between 1700 and 1950. The selection contains a fine description of the dynamics of pre-industrial households in the eighteenth century. At the time, land was being purchased in large amounts by commercial capitalists (for the production of wool) and many peasants thus lost the land that allowed them to produce their daily subsistence; in turn, they were forced into waged work. Tilly and Scott, however, describe the life of peasant farmers and urban craftspeople—and specifically, 'the family economy'. For these people, living in a pre-industrial economy, households were both units of production and units of consumption, and thus in continual need to balance the supply of labour against the requirements of consumption; they did so by altering household composition. But the enduring and essential core of these households was the married couple: women and men worked together to support their families.

We learn from Tilly and Scott's summary of their research that the work of producing subsistence so dominated daily life in pre-industrial households in England and France that much of the nature of family life, and likely even the quality of personal relationships, was dictated by economic considerations and pressures. The residents of households came and left as labour requirements changed, marriages were delayed as couples waited to acquire the property necessary to support a new household, and in general the interests of households took precedence over the interests of the individuals in them. High death rates also shaped the lives of children and adults—in dramatic ways.

Tilly and Scott's detailed description of the position of women—both single and married—gives us a pretty clear picture of one side of the division of labour based on gender. Because women did essential work, Tilly and Scott suggest (as some other historians have argued) that there was a 'rough equality' between husbands and wives. In contrast, other historians point to the gross inequality in the legal status of married women and men, including legal approval of husbands' use of violence against 'disobedient' wives, and cultural definitions of husbands as household authorities, to argue that gender relations were patriarchal—that is, that men with property exerted authority and control over the women and children in their households.

The Family Economy in Modern England and France

Louise A. Tilly and Joan W. Scott

Economy and Demography

In the cities and the countryside of eighteenth-century England and France economic life was organized on a small scale. The visual image one gets from reports of the period is of small farms dotting the countryside and of small shops lining the crowded narrow streets of cities. . . . The centre of life for rural people, whatever the size of their holding, was a farm. The centre of the farm was the household in which they lived and around which work was organized.

For those engaged in rural and urban manufacturing the household was both a shop and a home. . . . In the craft shop and on the land most productive activity was based in a household, and those labouring often included family members. This form of organization is often referred to as the household or domestic mode of production. It had important consequences for family organization. The labour needs of the household defined the work roles of men, women, and children. Their work, in turn, fed the family. The interdependence of work and residence, of household labour needs, subsistence requirements, and family relationships constituted the 'family economy'.

The specific form of the family economy differed for craftsmen and peasants. And in the city and the country there were important differences between the prosperous and the poor, between those families with property and those who were propertyless. Nonetheless, in all cases production and family life were inseparably intertwined. And the household was the centre around which resources, labour, and consumption were balanced.

Rural Economies

Most people lived in rural areas and worked in agriculture during the eighteenth century. Estimates based on scattered local studies show that in 1750 agriculture employed about 65 per cent of all English people and about 75 per cent of the French population (Cipolla 1976: 74). The forms of agricultural organization differed in France and England.

In France, the most typical rural household in the eighteenth century was the peasant household. In the course of the century the pressures of increased population and of high rents and taxes drove many families off the land or left them severely impoverished. . . . Some families barely subsisted on their land, others not only produced for themselves but marketed a crop of grapes, grains, olives, and the like. Some families manufactured cloth or clothing to supplement their earnings. Others hired themselves out as part-time labourers as well as tilled their own soil. Whatever the expedients they adopted to make ends meet, these rural people remained peasants, and the family's life ultimately was organized around the property, no matter how small the holding (Baehrel 1961; Goubert 1965b: 148; Hufton 1974; 1975).

The composition of the peasant household could vary considerably over the years. At any time those living and working together constituted a 'family' whether or not they were related by blood. 'The peasant concept of the family includes a number of people constantly eating at one table or having eaten from one pot . . . peasants in France included in the concept of the family the groups of persons locked up for the night behind one lock' (Thorner, Kerblay, and Smith 1966; Flandrin 1976: 103).

Although the terms *family* and *household* were often used interchangeably, and although servants took their meals with family members, the number of non-kin in the household of a propertied peasant depended on the composition of his own family. The propertied peasant had to balance labour and consumption. His resource—land—was fixed. The amount of work to be done and thus the number of labourers needed changed in the course of the family's life cycle. A young couple could adequately provide for its own needs, with the assistance perhaps of some day labourers at planting and harvest times. As children were born, they also had to be fed, and the availability of the mother to work away from the hearth decreased. The consumption needs of the family exceeded its labour power, and so at this point outside labour was recruited. Young men and women were added to the household as servants. They usually worked in exchange for room and board, rarely for cash wages. They were available for work because their own families either could not support them or did not need their labour. (One study suggested that 30 per cent of all rural workers in England at the end of the seventeenth century were servants, and that 60 per cent of all those fifteen to twenty-four years old in rural England were servants.) As the peasant's own children grew up, the need for outside help diminished. When several children lived in the household, there might be more labour available than the size of the landholding warranted. At this point, farmers might rent or buy additional land. More typically, in the land-poor regions of western Europe, children would leave home to seek employment. They usually worked in other households as servants (Macfarlane 1970: 209; Berkner 1972; Kussmaul-Cooper 1975b).

In England some people still supported themselves on small farms during the eighteenth century, but they were a decreasing group. The growth of agricultural capitalism, particularly in the form of sheep-herding to produce wool for sale, led to the enclosure of large areas of land and the gradual, and violently resisted, dispossession of small farmers. Despite their protests and resistance, English farmers lost the struggle to retain their land and their right to farm it (see Thompson 1975 and Hay et al. 1975 for details). By 1750 land ownership was concentrated 'in the hands of a limited class of very large landlords, at the expense both of the lesser gentry and the peasants . . .' (Hobsbawm 1968: 15).

The dispossessed became agricultural labourers working for wages on the large farms, or they turned to cottage industry. Those involved in cottage industry worked at home on account for a merchant entrepreneur. In England the typical form of cottage or domestic industry was wool and, later, cotton weaving. In both England and France, merchants brought raw materials to rural cottages and then picked up the woven cloth which they had finished in towns or large villages. By having cloth woven in the countryside, the merchants managed to escape the control of the guilds, organizations of urban craftsmen, which closely supervised production in the cities. Although cottage weavers, like agricultural labourers, worked for wages, they worked in their own households, controlling the pace and organization of production. The family was the unit of production and of consumption, the household was the locus of work and residence. The family economy thus existed in the cottages of domestic weavers (and hosiers and nail or chain-metal workers) as it did in the households of propertied peasants.

Agricultural labourers, on the other hand, left home to earn wages elsewhere. 'Thus an amazing number of people have been reduced from a comfortable state of partial independence to the precarious condition of hireling' (Davies 1965: 41). Family members often worked together. And the aim of everyone's work was to secure enough to support the family, both by bringing home some cash and by labouring in exchange for food. Among these families, family membership meant shared consumption, but not shared production. In this case the family economy became a 'family wage economy'. The unit's need for wages, rather than for labourers, defined the work of family members.

Work in Urban Society

Cities in both England and France had similar economic and occupational structures in the early modern period. They were essentially centres of consumer production and of commerce. The dominant form of activity differed from city to city. Yet city life differed markedly from life in the country. Gathered within city walls was a diverse population linked by an exchange of goods, services, and cash.

The varieties of urban life can be illustrated by examining several cities. For the early modern period, we will describe York, England, and Amiens, France. Both these cities were typically 'pre-industrial' in economy and social structure. York was a Cathedral town, engaged in commerce, while the principal business of Amiens was small-scale, largely artisanal textile manufacture. . . .

The specific jobs available to men and women differed according to the economic structure of each city. In York most manufacture involved luxury products: bell casting, glass painting, and pewter and clock making were among those listed. . . . Although the fortunes of the city (once the 'second capital' of English society) seemed to be declining by the end of the eighteenth century, it remained a centre of handicrafts and trade. . . .

In the provincial capital of Amiens most people were engaged in the woollen trades. Various tax lists enable us to determine the occupations of others in the city, although these lists give out a partial description, since only the wealthier people in the city were taxed. Most artisans and shopkeepers on the lists were in textiles, food, and the building trades. A list from 1722 indicates a number of servants, too (Deyon 1967: 546).

Despite differences in specific trades in each city, the forms of organization were similar. Economic units were small, often overlapping with households. The scale of production was also small, for the quality and quantity of activity in commerce and manufacture were controlled by guild or other forms of regulation and by the availability of only limited amounts of capital. Life was more specialized in urban than in rural society. Food and clothing production, for example, was carried on in separate settings from the households of most urban residents. Rather than make most of what it needed, the urban family bought what it needed in the market or in shops. Shoemakers, for example, made shoes for sale, but they purchased their other clothing and food. Because of this division of labour, urban families were involved in many more consumer activities than their rural counterparts, and cash was regularly used as a means of exchange.

Manufacture and trade, however, were geared primarily to the demand of the local population. Hence the production of food and clothing and the construction of housing were the largest urban manufacturing sectors. Together they employed, according to one estimate, from 55 to 65 per cent of a city's working population (Cipolla 1976: 75).

In Amiens, as in York, guilds regulated the training and activities of skilled craftsmen. The number of workers in a trade was limited and, except in a few cases such as millinery and shawl making, the masters and apprentices were male. Craftsmen often worked at home or in small shops assisted by family members, apprentices and journeymen, and servants. Indeed, the dynamic of the self-employed artisan's household was much like that of the peasant's, for labour supply and consumption needs had to be balanced. An artisan had to produce and sell enough goods so that he could feed his family. Competition from others in the trade was controlled by guilds, which limited the numbers of those who became masters. Yet labour demands were variable within a trade; some work was seasonal, there were periods of great activity, other periods of slump. An artisan's family members often served as extra hands, as unpaid assistants in time of high demand. In addition, if family members alone could not furnish the necessary labour, an artisan hired assistants, who lived in the household as long as their labour was needed. On the other hand, if he could not use the labour of his family members at his trade, a craftsman often sent them off to find work elsewhere. His children joined another household as apprentices or domestic servants.

Although craftsmen produced most goods in workshops in their homes and used their families as labour units, the economy of the city provided many opportunities for work away from home. Men and women earned wages as servants or as street merchants, or as assistants to artisans or construction workers. The wage workers included journeymen who had no chance to advance to mastership, masters who had lost their small capital in bad times and now worked for others, daughters and sons of craftsmen whose shops could not absorb their labour, migrants to the city, unskilled workers, and widows with no capital but with a family to support.

Servants formed a substantial portion of urban populations in the seventeenth and eighteenth centuries. Their precise numbers are often difficult to determine since they were not always listed separately in tax and demographic records. Nonetheless, from those records which clearly identified servants, it has been estimated that perhaps 16 per cent of those between the ages of fifteen and sixty-five in European cities in this period were servants. Hufton suggests that in eighteenth-century French cities, servants could represent as much as 13 per cent of the working population. In Aix in 1695, some 27 per cent of the working population were servants. The term *servant* designated a broad category of employment (Hufton 1974: 4). Any household dependent, whether performing domestic or manufacturing tasks, was a servant. There were servants in the households of the rich and in the households of craftsmen and petty artisans. They were young men or women who joined a family economy as an additional member. Indeed the language used to describe servants denoted their dependent and age status. 'Servant' was synonymous with 'lad' or 'maid'—a young, unmarried, and therefore dependent person.

Wage labourers, on the other hand, lived in households of their own, bound together, like the families of agricultural labourers, by the need to earn money which would pay for their subsistence. Their presence in cities is attested to by the rolls of charitable organizations, which gave them bread when they could not earn enough, and by the complaints of guilds against their activity. Petty artisans, unskilled and casual labourers, carters, and street hawkers were commonly listed. In Paris in 1767, when an Order-in-Council enjoined the registration of non-guild members selling food, clothing, or lodging to the public, the list included 'retailers and repairers of old clothes and hats, of rags and of old ironware, buckles and hardware . . . sellers of medicines for eyes, corns, and assorted afflictions. . . '. The inventory of lawsuits against non-guild members in York in 1775 included many of these same trades (Allison and Tillot 1961: 216; Kaplow 1972: 45). In the families of wage labourers, all members old enough to seek employment did so.

The work of each person brought little remuneration; the combined earnings of family members were often barely enough for the support of the group. In these families, individuals sold their labour power in order to support the family unit; they were 'in fact if not in principle . . . proletarian[s]' (Landes 1969: 44). Theirs was a 'family wage economy'.

Production and Consumption

In both England and France, in city and country, people worked in small settings, which often overlapped with households. Productivity was low, the differentiation of tasks was limited. And many workers were needed. The demand for labour extended to women as well as men, to everyone but the youngest children and the infirm. Jobs were differentiated by age and by sex, as well as by training and skill. But among the popular classes, some kind of work was expected of all able-bodied family members. The work of individuals was defined by their family positions. An observer of twentieth-century French peasants described their household economy in terms which also portray peasant and artisan families in the seventeenth and eighteenth centuries: 'The family and the enterprise coincide: the head of the family is at the same time the head of the enterprise. Indeed, he is the one because he is the other . . . he lives his professional and his family life as an indivisible entity. The members of his family are also his fellow workers' (Mendras 1970: 76). But whether or not they actually worked together, family members worked in the economic interest of the family. In peasant and artisan households, and in proletarian families, the household allocated the labour of family members. In all cases, decisions were made in the interest of the group, not the individual. This is reflected in wills and marriage contracts which spelled out the obligation of siblings or elderly parents who were housed and fed on the family property, now owned by the oldest son. They must work 'to the best of their ability' for 'the prosperity of the family' and 'for the interest of the designated heir' (Bernard 1975: 30). Among property-owning families the land or the shop defined the tasks of family members and whether or not their labour was needed. People who controlled their means of production adjusted household composition to production needs. For the propertyless, the need for wages—the subsistence of the family itself—sent men, women, and children out to work. These people adjusted household composition to consumption needs. The bonds holding the proletarian family together, bonds of expediency and necessity, were often less permanent than the property interest (or the inheritable skill) which united peasants and craftsmen. The composition of propertied and propertyless households also differed. Nevertheless, the line between the propertied and the propertyless was blurred on the question of commitment to work in the family interest.

One of the goals of work was to provide for the needs of family members. Both property-owning and proletarian households were consumption units, though all rural households were far more self-sufficient than urban households. Rural families usually produced their own food, clothing, and tools, while urban families bought them at the market. These differences affect the work roles of family members. Women in urban families, for example, spent more time marketing and less time in home manufacture. And there were fewer domestic chores for children to assist with in the city. In the urban family, work was oriented more to the production of specific goods for sale, or it involved the sale of one's labour. For the peasant family, there were a multiplicity of tasks involved in working the land and running the household. The manner of satisfying consumption needs thus varied and so affected the kinds of work family members did.

When the number of household members exceeded the resources available to feed them, and when those resources could not be obtained, the family often adjusted its size. Non-kin left to work elsewhere when children were old enough to work. Then children migrated. Inheritance systems led non-heirs to move away in search of jobs, limited positions as artisans forced children out of the family craft shop, while the need for wages led the children of the propertyless many miles from home. People migrated from farm to farm, farm to village, village to town, and country to city in this period. Although much migration was local and rural in this period, some migrants moved to cities, and most of these tended to be young and single when they migrated. . . . Village compatriots tended to live near one another. Young men and boys often migrated to be apprenticed to a craftsman who himself came from their village. Young women and girls followed their brothers to Amiens and became domestic servants (Deyon 1967: 7–10).

Migration increased in times of economic crisis, when food was scarce and when, even with everyone working, families could not feed all their members. The precariousness of life in rural and urban areas in the seventeenth and eighteenth centuries has been documented dramatically in studies such as those by Pierre Goubert and Olwen Hufton. These studies have shown that large numbers of ordinary people barely survived on the fruits of their labour. At the end of a lifetime of work, an artisan or peasant might have nothing more than a few tools or the small piece of land with which he began. Simply feeding one's family in these circumstances was a constant preoccupation. An increase in the price of bread, the basic staple in the diet of the popular classes, could easily make a family's earnings inadequate for its survival. . . .

Even if the price of bread remained stable, other factors might unbalance a family's budget.

Agricultural or trade depressions could severely strain a family's resources. At these times there were bread riots as people collectively sought food for their families. If matters did not improve, individual families might send children off to seek their fortunes away from home, as servants, apprentices, or vagrants. Sometimes the father of the family left home in search of work. He thereby relieved the household of the need to feed him, since he could contribute nothing to its support. He also left the family to an uncertain, but probably poverty-stricken, future.

If the adult members of the family could continue working, then young children were sent away to restore the balance between consumption and work. When families were desperate, parents might expose or abandon a last-born child. Older children, still too young to work productively, were sent off also, to whatever their fate might hold. Fictional characters such as Hansel and Gretel and Hop-O'-My-Thumb, children deliberately lost by parents who could not feed them, had real counterparts. Deyon's study of seventeenth-century Amiens indicates that during food shortages in 1693–4 and 1709–10 the number of abandoned children rose. These were not only infants but children as old as seven (Deyon 1967: 357). Another recent study of the records of charity in eighteenth-century Aix-en-Provence reveals that children were regularly enrolled at an orphanage because their families could not feed them. Only a third of these were actually orphans. Once a child entered the orphanage, he or she was likely to be joined by a sibling. In other cases, a child would return home and be replaced in the orphanage by a sibling. Families used the orphanage as a temporary measure, enrolling a child and then withdrawing him or her as economic circumstances allowed. Hence one girl entered the Aix orphanage in 1746, 'rejoined her family briefly in 1747, then returned . . . later left again, and . . . re-entered . . . in 1755' (Fairchilds 1976: 10).

The location and organization of work differed among the households of rural and urban people and among the propertied and the propertyless. So did the levels of consumption vary and the manners of satisfying family needs. Yet in all cases the family was both a labour unit and a consumption unit, adjusting its size and assigning work to its members to meet its needs in both spheres.

Demography: Marriage

The demographic patterns of early modern England and France reflected the need to balance people and resources. Death frequently influenced these patterns. Perhaps the most sensitive indicator of the relationship between resources and population was the age at which couples married. The precise age at marriage varied from city to country and from region to region depending on inheritance laws and on specific conditions. Yet among the popular classes the crucial differences were between the propertied and the propertyless.

Marriage was, among other things, an economic arrangement, the establishment of a family economy. It required that couples have some means of supporting themselves and, eventually, their children. For peasant children this meant the availability of land; for artisans, the mastery of a skill and the acquisition of tools and perhaps a workshop. Wives must have a dowry or a means of contributing to the household. Among families with property these resources most often were passed on from generation to generation.

In England, inheritance by the oldest son prevailed. In France this custom of primogeniture was not universal. In some areas of France, particularly in the west, an heir and his wife lived with his parents, in a stem family arrangement. In northern France, on the other hand, a young man had to postpone marriage until a house was vacant. This meant until the death of one or both parents. Land was passed to one child—usually, though not necessarily, the oldest son. He paid his siblings a cash settlement which represented their share of the family land. A brother could use his money to buy some land of his own or to set himself up in a trade. A sister used her money as a dowry. Often the heir had to mortgage the property to pay off his sisters and brothers. Sometimes, too, the money was not available. Then the heir's siblings might remain on the family farm as unmarried labourers in their brother's household, working in exchange for room and board. 'A peasant reckons this way; my farm can feed no more than one, at most two, sons; the others may have to remain unmarried or seek their fortune elsewhere' (Braun 1966: 46; see also Flandrin 1976: 180–1).

Among artisans, trade regulations prevented early marriage. Apprentices and journeymen were not allowed to marry until they had completed their training. In some cases, the duration of apprenticeship was as much a function of the artisans' desire to control workers' access to their trade as it was of the difficulty of the skills taught. Apprentices' and journeymen's associations reinforced the control by expelling from their ranks anyone who married. A young man was ready to marry only when he had an established niche in the system of production.

The need for a dowry meant that young women, too, often had to wait for the death of their parents to receive a settlement. In the weaving centre of Manchester, for example, in the period 1654–7, more than half of the girls marrying for the first time had recently lost their fathers. Other girls, those who worked to accumulate savings for a dowry, had to spend many years gathering a small sum (Armengaud 1975: 145).

The result of these requirements was a relatively late age at marriage in both England and France; women were generally twenty-four or twenty-five years old, men twenty-seven. The late age at marriage of women meant that couples had fewer children than they would have had if the woman had been nineteen or twenty at marriage. If she married at twenty-five, the woman was actively engaged in child-bearing for only a portion of her fertile years. (There was little sexual intercourse outside of marriage, and very low rates of illegitimacy. During the eighteenth century in France, the illegitimacy rate increased from 1.2 to 2.7 per cent of all births.) Thus relatively late marriage functioned as a kind of birth control, in the sense that it limited the size of the completed family (Goubert 1965a; Henry 1965).

Among the propertyless, there were no resources to inherit. When a young man and woman were able to earn wages, they could marry. Not only must an individual be able to work, however, but work which paid wages must be available. (Servants, for example, could not marry since a requirement of their jobs was that they live in the household they served, that they remain unmarried, and that they receive much of their payment in room and board, not cash.) One study has shown that in Shepshed, England, during the seventeenth century, the coming of domestic industry provided jobs and cash wages and led to a lowered age of marriage (Levine 1976; see also Braun 1966). In other areas, the growth of commercial agriculture, and the consequent demand for agricultural labourers, may have had the same effect.

Among the poorest, marriage sometimes did not take place at all. The absence of property and the lack of any expectation that it would be acquired, made legalization of sexual relationships unnecessary. From the seventeenth century comes this comment on the urban poor: 'They almost never know the sanctity of marriage and live together in shameful fashion' (Fairchilds 1976: 33). These people, however, were exceptions. In general, those without property did marry. They married younger than their peasant and artisan counterparts and, as a result, their wives bore more children over the course of the marriage. But most expected to be able to live on the fruits of their labour. A couple marrying in Amiens in 1780 acknowledged their poverty, but wrote a contract anyway, agreeing that if they did manage to make some money, the future bride would have 'by preciput 150 livres of the estate and the survivor would have the bed and bedclothes, . . . his or her clothes, arms, rings, and jewels' (Deyon 1967: 254).

Some people never married, of course. In general, permanent celibacy was more common in cities than in the country. There were examples of unmarried brothers or sisters remaining sometimes on farms with a married sibling. More commonly, however, these individuals migrated to a city in search of work. The occupational structure of particular cities often determined the marital fate of many of its migrants. In Lyons, for example, the women who came to work in the silk industry greatly outnumbered the men. As a result, during the eighteenth century, some 40 per cent of adult women were still single at age fifty in that city. (In towns where men outnumbered women, more women were married.) In Amiens, with its mixed occupational structure, 20 per cent of the women over forty in one wealthy parish were single at death. The rate was 13 per cent in two poorer parishes. Domestic servants in the wealthy parish account for the difference. Cities housed most people whose occupations by definition precluded marriage—members of religious orders, soldiers, servants, and prostitutes were typically urban residents (Deyon 1967: 42; Armengaud 1975: 30; see also Knodel and Maynes 1976).

Birth and Fertility

Once a couple married, at whatever age, they began to have children. About half of all first babies were born less than a year after their parents' marriage. Studies of French villages indicated that subsequent children were then born about twenty-five to thirty months apart. This interval was apparently the result of two factors, postpartum abstinence from intercourse, and nursing, which postpones the onset of ovulation. Among working-class families in cities, birth intervals were shorter because mothers sent their children to wet nurses rather than nursing them themselves and because infant mortality was high. In both cases, women became fertile sooner than they would have if they had nursed an infant. In Amiens, for example, in a parish of small shopkeepers, artisans, and workers, children were born about two years apart. In Lyons, where work in the silk industry demanded a great deal of a mother's time and where children were regularly sent to wet nurses, birth intervals were even shorter: births occurred there at the rate of one per year (Wrigley 1969: 124; Armengaud 1975: 52; Flandrin 1976: 197).

There is some evidence to indicate that couples sometimes practised deliberate birth control. One study, of the English village of Colyton in Devon in the seventeenth century, seems to show that couples were deliberately limiting the size of their families. Its author, E.A. Wrigley, suggests that a longer than usual interval between the next-to-last and the last birth is an indicator of attempted fertility control. This first attempt of couples to avoid conception failed, of course, but the longer birth interval is evidence of their effort. Such control as there was was probably achieved by means of *coitus interruptus*, or withdrawal, the most widely known and widely practised technique (Wrigley 1966: 123). Most other studies, however, using the same kinds of data and the same method of family reconstitution, do not point to deliberate family limitation before the late eighteenth century. Yet complete families were not large: four or five children at most, more often only two or three who lived to adulthood. Why?

First, standards of nutrition and health were very low. Analyses of the diet of the popular classes in this period show consistent evidence of malnutrition, a factor which inhibited conception and which promoted miscarriage. Poor nutrition of a mother increased the likelihood that her infant would be stillborn or weak. And it affected the supply of milk she had to nurse it. In addition, poor nutrition made many women infertile before forty or forty-five—the usual age of menopause (Meuvret 1965; Le Roy Ladurie 1969).

Second, mortality rates were very high. If infants did not die at birth because of unsanitary or crude childbirth procedures, they died within the first year of life. Young children, too, died in large numbers. Finally, many marriages were shortened by the death of one of the spouses. Childbirth resulted in a high incidence of maternal death. In one fishing village in France, one-third of all marriages were broken by death within fifteen years. Men's opportunities for remarriage were usually greater than those of women. As a result, women did not engage in intercourse during all of their fertile years and hence did not bear children. Given the odds that death would strike a young child or a spouse, there was little need to employ birth control (Armengaud 1975: 53). Death was the natural regulator of family size in early modern England and France.

Death and Mortality

Premature death was a frequent experience of family life in this period. Death rates nearly matched birth rates, producing a very slow growth of population. The crude birth rate was about 35 per thousand; the death rate 30 per thousand. Moreover, until around 1730, there were years with dramatically high death rates, reaching 150,300, and even 500 per thousand in some localities. These deaths were the result of widespread crop failures and consequent starvation, or of epidemics of diseases like the plague. The last plague epidemic struck in southern France in 1720–2 (Cipolla 1964: 77; Clarkson 1971: 28–9), but new diseases caused killing epidemics well into the twentieth century. Demographers usually place the end of extreme and widespread mortality due to disease and starvation in the early eighteenth century.

Yet even in relatively stable times, death rates were very high by modern standards—a rate of 30 per thousand is more than triple the present-day rate in western Europe. Studies of French villages show that about one-quarter of all infants born alive died during their first year of life, another quarter died before they reached the age of twenty. Urban death rates were even higher. In Amiens, for example, during the seventeenth century, 60 to 70 per cent of all burials were of persons under twenty-five. Although rates varied from parish to parish and among villages, the overall situation was similar in England and France. Goubert aptly summarized the mortality experience of pre-industrial families: 'It took two births to produce one adult' (Goubert 1965a: 468).

The life expectancy at birth for people in this period was thirty years. Of course, that figure included infant and child mortality. If a person lived to age twenty-five, the likelihood was much greater than at birth that she or he would live to fifty or sixty. Yet, although systematic evidence is hard to accumulate, it is clear that adult mortality was also quite high. The figures on orphans and widows are revealing in this connection. Laslett's analysis of the English village of Clayworth found that during the period 1676–88, '32 per cent of all resident children [under 14] had lost one or both of their parents'. A study of all children in households in nineteen English communities from 1599 to 1811 indicates that some 20 per cent were orphans. For France, Jean Fourastié has drawn a hypothetical portrait of family life for a man at the end of the seventeenth century. In that situation marriage would be broken by the death of a spouse after an average of twenty years. The average age of a child orphaned in this way would be fourteen years (Fourastié 1959: 427; Laslett 1974; Armengaud 1975: 74–7).

Many children were left orphans when their mothers died in childbirth. Ignorance of the need for sanitary conditions, the crude attempts of midwives to force a baby from the womb, and the general poor health of pregnant women made for high rates of maternal mortality. Age-specific mortality tables drawn for small seventeenth- and eighteenth-century villages show women dying in larger numbers than men between ages twenty-four and forty—the child-bearing years. In Amiens, in the parish of Saint-Rémy in 1674–6, fifty-three women and forty men aged fifteen to forty-five died. In another parish in 1665–8, deaths were recorded for ninety-one women and only fifty-two men in that age range (Deyon 1967: 39).

The death of a parent left not only orphans but widows or widowers. The existence of these people is attested to by notices of second marriage, particularly of men, and by charity rolls and tax lists, on which widows' names predominated. Fourastié's calculations show that 1,000 men married at age twenty-seven and surviving to age fifty, nearly half would have lost their wives. Many of these men would have remarried and would have also lost a second wife. (The calculations for women would be similar except that fewer widows remarried.) Overall, in eighteenth-century France 'at least 30 per cent of all marriages were second weddings for one of the partners'. Most parishes had many widows in them. In Châteaudun, at least half of the seamstresses and spinners listed on tax rolls in 1696 were widows. In eighteenth-century Bayeux, over 46 per cent of all textile workers in the linen and woollen trades were widows (Fourastié 1959: 425; see also Couturier 1969: 64; Lebrun 1971: 190; Hufton 1974: 116; Baulant 1976: 105). The poor widow, struggling to support her children, was a familiar figure in the towns and villages of the period.

Early modern populations could do little medically to control mortality. Nutrition was poor, little was known about hygiene, and medical science had not developed. In 1778, a French demographer noted that 'it is still a problem whether medicine kills or saves more men' (Armengaud 1975: 70; see also Dupaquier 1976). The result was that every person who survived to adulthood experienced the loss of close relatives: a father, mother, sisters, and brothers. Few children knew their grandparents, few grandparents lived to see the birth of a first grandchild. Orphanhood, widowhood, and the loss of children were common experiences. In calculations about family size, about fertility and household labour supply, the expectation of death played an important part.

These, then, were the economic and demographic characteristics of England and France during the seventeenth and eighteenth centuries. Agriculture was more important than manufacturing, and most people lived in rural areas. In France, small-scale property holding and artisanal manufacture were typical. In England, by 1750, there had been consolidation of agricultural holdings and a consequent increase in the size of farms, on the one hand, and in the proportion of people without property, on the other hand. Work in both countries was relatively undifferentiated and productivity was low. On the demographic side, fertility and mortality were both high, so population growth was very slow. A relatively high age of marriage and a degree of non-marriage served to reduce fertility. From the perspective of the household, most aspects of life were affected by the need to maintain scarce resources and consumers in a delicate balance. Family life and economic organization were inseparably entwined. Premature death was a familiar experience in each household. Within this context were shaped the position and activities of women.

Single Women in the Family Economy

Most single women belonged to households, either as daughters or servants. Most were young, but whatever their age, single women were regarded as dependants of the household in which they lived and worked. Under the domestic mode of production most work was organized around a household, the basic unit of which was a married couple. Girls either worked at home or for another family. If they were to escape this state of dependency, they had to marry, for single adult women were effectively children. The language of the day equated a girl with a maid, a maid with a servant. Age, marital status, and occupation were inseparably intertwined.

Single women were often effectively servants for their families, if not in the households of strangers. Those employed in other areas, textiles for example, usually lived with a family or with other women like themselves. Even in religious orders, single women joined a family of celibate sisters. Prostitutes usually lived in groups. Economically it was extremely difficult to be single and independent. In the best of jobs female wages were low, one-third to one-half of what men's were (Hauser 1927; Hufton 1975). The only way for a woman to achieve a measure of economic security, as well as adult status, was to marry. If she did not marry, her position was anomalous. If she became a nun, of course, she gained protection and recognition, although her role and autonomy were limited. An unmarried woman outside a convent was vulnerable to material hardship and sexual exploitation.

Although aggregate figures are not available for this period, local studies indicate that in rural areas marriage took place at a relatively late age and nearly all women did marry. In urban areas, rates of celibacy among women could be higher because of differences in sex ratios and as a result of the concentration of specialized occupations for single women (Hollingsworth 1969: 160–8). Most of these occupations, like domestic service or religious orders, involved a family-like dependency.

Single Women's Work

All women began their working lives as daughters, serving the family economy of which they were a part. The specific jobs they did were a consequence of their family's place in the productive process, of the nature of the enterprise in which it was engaged.

A daughter began assisting at home as soon as she was able to work. Indeed, at an early age, her role was no different from that of male children, and many accounts make no distinction when describing children's work. Girls and boys were given small tasks to do as early as four or five years of age. In rural areas they cared for farm animals and helped at harvesting and gleaning. In cottages where families engaged in rural industry, young children washed and sorted wool or learned to spin. . . . As they grew older, girls usually assisted their mothers, boys their fathers. In agricultural areas, daughters helped with dairying, cared for poultry, prepared food, and made cloth and clothing. During planting and harvesting they joined family members and hired hands in the fields. . . .

In cities also, daughters worked for their families. The craftsman's household was also his workshop and his family members were among his assistants, whether he wove silk or wool, sewed shoes or coats, made knives, or baked bread. . . . If the father worked elsewhere, daughters assisted their mothers as market women, laundresses, or seamstresses. When she worked at home a daughter served a kind of apprenticeship to her mother, learning the domestic, agricultural, or technical skills she would need as an adult.

Not all girls remained working at home until marriage, however. The labour needs of her family defined the type of work a daughter might do at home, but also whether or not she would remain there. Family labour was differentiated by age and sex. So, if a family had no need for a daughter's labour, she would be sent to a job somewhere else. Peasants with two or three working children and more than one daughter would send younger daughters away to earn their keep. Weavers, who needed several spinners to supply thread for their looms, jealously guarded their daughters at home, while bakers or shoemakers whose sons, male apprentices, and wives were an ample labour force, regularly sent their daughters away. Families thus adjusted their labour supply by sending off daughters not suited for certain work and taking on male apprentices in their stead.

The ability of a family to feed its children was another influence on where a daughter worked. For subsistence farmers with small holdings, the cost of maintaining a daughter might be greater than the value of her labour. It would be cheaper to hire and feed a few local labourers during the harvest season than to provide for one's own child all year long. Moreover, in time of economic crises, the numbers of 'surplus children', those who could not be supported, would grow, and daughters and sons would be sent off to seek jobs as servants or apprentices.

Death was yet another factor which sent daughters to work away from home. The death of a parent often left the widow or widower less means to support the children. In the French town of Châteaudun during the sixteenth to eighteenth centuries, for example, daughters of wine growers remained at home until marriage. They participated in all aspects of domestic and household work and were given ample dowries when they married. The death of a father, however, immediately changed the pattern. At that point, the mother took up a trade and sold the family holding or passed it to one of her sons. Daughters who were too young to marry or 'who could not marry immediately became chambermaids in town or farm servants in the country'. The luckiest of these found places at the homes of other wine growers (Couturier 1969: 181).

The remarriage of a widowed parent could also result in the dislocation of the children of the first marriage, either because the step-parent resented feeding and caring for children who were not his or her own or because conflicts and jealousies became unbearable. Folk tales such as Cinderella and Snow White capture an aspect of these relationships. . . .

Even if both parents were alive, however, the economic resources of the family might be insufficient for the establishment of more than one child with the means to live independently as a married adult. Daughters needed a dowry, and families customarily provided them with it. In rural areas, depending on laws of inheritance, a girl was given either a sum of money or movable property, usually household and farm furnishings. Again depending on local practices, she might receive a full settlement at her marriage or be promised a payment after the death of her parents. In cities, craftsmen gave their daughters household furnishings, cash, skills, or tools. In country and city, the size of the family contribution to a dowry or settlement was very small among the lower classes. Often, the family's contribution had to be supplemented. An artisan's daughter had an advantage over her rural counterpart in this situation, for the skills she had were highly valued. Unlike the heavy manual labour of a farm, trade skills guaranteed a lifetime of relatively high wage-earning possibilities or of assistance to one's husband at his trade. These were acceptable as substitutes for the dowry required of rural girls. But, in either case, if a dowry was needed for a woman's contribution to a marriage and the family (or some other source) could not provide it, a girl had to earn it herself (Clark [1919] 1968: 194; Hufton 1975: 9).

When for one or a combination of reasons daughters left home to work, they usually entered another household. In the country, domestic service was the typical occupation of a young girl. Of course, in areas of rural textile manufacture, particularly in England, in the early eighteenth century, spinners were in great demand. It took the work of four spinners to supply thread enough for one weaver. One Englishman complained about 'Maid-Servants who choose rather to spin, while they can gain 9s/week by their Labour than go to service at 12d a week to the Farmer's Houses as before' (Clark [1919] 1968: 115–16). Spinsters lived either at home or in the weaver's household. But even in areas where spinning and lacemaking jobs were available, girls sometimes went into service at age twelve or thirteen, after having done textile work as a child. Cities offered other opportunities and urban-born girls took advantage of them. Such girls might be apprenticed to a crafts- or tradeswoman. Others might work for wages in a local enterprise, usually related to textile or garment manufacture. . . . But in cities, as in the country, the main occupation for young girls was domestic service. In Ealing in 1599, for example, almost 'three-quarters of the female children [between ages fifteen and nineteen] seem to have been living away from their parents', most often as servants (Macfarlane 1970: 209; Perrot 1975: 425).

In a period when most productive activity was organized within or around a household, service was the major occupation for young, single women. Service involved a variety of chores, not only the ones the twentieth century associates with domestic work. A servant was a household dependant who worked in return for board and wages. The low cost of her labour, the availability of young, single women to work, the need in producing households for an extra hand, made the employment of a servant a fairly common practice. Service was the customary means by which households exchanged labour supply and balanced their own labour and consumption needs.

In upper-class families a girl 'in service' was a maid of one kind or another, a laundress, charwoman, serving maid, or nursemaid. In household productive units she was an extra hand, available to do whatever work was required. She might be a dairymaid or harvester on a farm; in textile towns she was 'a resident industrial employee'. In Lyons, for example, a *servante* did domestic chores and helped prepare the silk to be woven. As with a daughter, the nature of the family enterprise defined her work, except that a servant girl usually did the dirtiest and most onerous of the chores that needed to be done (Le Roy Ladurie 1969: 477; Hufton 1975: 3). In return for her work she was fed, housed, and clothed and paid a wage at the end of her term, which usually lasted a year. This meant that a servant had little or no money to spend on herself during the year and was entirely dependent on her employers. The year term also meant frequent moves for a girl from one household to another. Moves might be even more frequent for some girls. Employers might fire them at any point, refusing to pay anything for their services. The failure of a small business inevitably sent the servant girl packing, with no payment of her wages, no matter how long she had worked.

When daughters left home to work they did not always sever family ties. Their parents often helped them find jobs, and provided homes for them between terms of service. One study suggests that female farm servants in England returned to their families far more frequently than did males (Kussmaul-Cooper 1975a: 6). Moreover, kin networks were a common means used by those seeking jobs. In the country, peasants and agricultural labourers sought work for their daughters at neighbouring farms or in a nearby village or large town. . . .

A girl's ability to maintain contact with [her] family depended on how far she had journeyed from home. . . . In general, . . . the continuing demand for cheap female labour in towns and on farms made it possible for most girls to remain within a short distance of home, sustained by occasional visits, by parcels of food, and by the expectation of returning there to marry.

The death of a girl's parents, of course, modified this pattern. Orphans were on their own, lacking family connections to help them find work or to sponsor their migrations. Without resources, with no one to turn to for help, orphans had to settle for whatever work they could find, throwing themselves on the mercy of an employer, a charitable organization, or the state. They were more vulnerable, more open to exploitation, more likely to end up in trouble as criminals, prostitutes, and mothers of illegitimate children. A sixteenth-century English magistrate described the 'dells' of his day as delinquent girls on the road 'through the death of their parents and nobody to look after them . . .' (Pinchbeck and Hewitt 1969: 99). In a society where family membership was important for economic and social survival (as well as for social identity), the lack of a family had only negative effects.

The work of a young single woman was circumscribed by a limited range of occupational opportunities. The type and location of her work was defined by her family's needs. A daughter worked, as everyone did in lower-class families in this period, to help support the unit of which she was a part. In addition, her work prepared her for marriage, by giving her training and skills and sometimes also by enabling her to accumulate the capital she needed for a dowry.

Courtship and Marriage

A girl was ready for marriage when she had accumulated some capital or received it from her family, when she was ready to help establish a productive unit, a household. The amount was not necessarily very large. In France, some cash, a bed, sheets, and some pots were frequently all a girl brought to her new household. . . . Often a girl's small earnings supplemented the family contribution.

Unless she migrated far away, or unless she was an orphan, a girl's marriage usually involved her family in a variety of ways. First, her family's economic situation limited her choice of a husband to someone of roughly comparable means. The size of the dowry the family promised or provided was a reflection of its property holdings or trade prosperity. An artisan's craft position was itself an important consideration, for access to a tightly controlled craft might be gained for a son-in-law. Among property-owning peasants, parents often vetoed suitors whose family holdings did not measure up to their own. Marriage was a chance to extend or renew family capital. Less directly, parental and community expectations imbued children with the idea that they would repeat their parents' experience. They usually did not expect to rise in the world, only to remain at their parents' level. Hence they sought partners among their social and economic peers.

Second, the parental community of residence and work was most often the one within which a girl found a husband. In rural areas, young women met young men in the village, at local social gatherings, or in the household of an employer. In France, the *veillée* offered young people a means of meeting one another, under the watchful eye of parents and neighbours and in activities which were usually segregated by sex. The *veillée* was the rural custom of gathering in the largest, warmest barn on cold winter evenings. The animals and the groups of people created warmth, and the company an occasion for socializing. 'People sat on benches, chatting, laughing, complaining about taxes and tax collectors, gossiping about young men and women . . .' (Flandrin 1976: 106).

In the city, a girl might marry an apprentice or journeyman in her father's shop, or the son of another craftsman. Networks of labour and trade were important sources of marriage partners. In Amiens, such 'corporative endogamy' was the rule. Young men in the same trades married one another's sisters with great frequency; apprentices married their master's daughters or widows (Deyon 1967: 340). But apprentices or journeymen might also choose a servant girl in the household. The small capital she had saved from her service brought to the couple the possibility of buying a loom and setting up a shop of their own (Hufton 1975: 7–9). Since social, occupational, and family life were so closely intertwined, one's associate at work often became a marriage partner.

Among the propertyless, of course, marriage crossed occupational lines, but geographic endogamy was the norm. Artisans and peasants as well as the unskilled and propertyless tended to marry others from the same parish or a neighbouring one. . . .

Social and geographic endogamy had important implications for marriage and for premarital sexual behaviour. It meant that family and communal ties, as well as the relationship between the two individuals, bound a couple together and governed their behaviour. In many areas, engaged couples began sleeping or living together before marriage. Local custom varied, of course. In areas of France and England, studies have documented the practice. In addition, the fact that rates of prenuptial conception tended to be higher in cities than in rural areas suggests that such cohabitation was more common in cities. Premarital sexual activity was tolerated because marriage was expected to and usually did take place. Hence, although some brides were pregnant at the altar, bastards were relatively few. Using marriage and birth registers from seventy-seven parishes in rural England, from 1540 to 1835, P.E.H. Hair found that between one-third and one-sixth of all brides were pregnant at their weddings (Hair 1966; Hollingsworth 1969: 194). Indeed, pregnancy often seems to have precipitated a couple's marriage. In small village communities, or among groups of urban craftsmen, families could put a great deal of pressure on a young man who had begun to regret his choice of a mate and was hesitating about marriage. Such social pressure tended to ensure that marriage usually followed engagement, especially if pregnancy intervened.

The women who bore illegitimate children were often those with no ties to their families of origin. Several English studies have indicated that most illegitimate births came from the poorest and most vulnerable women in the community. One study suggests the existence of a subgroup of 'bastard bearers' (Laslett and Oosterveen 1973: 284). These were people whose sexual behaviour was not that different from their more prosperous counterparts. The difference was that 'the relatively more secure position [of the better-off] meant that their behaviour was more certain of ultimate legitimation' (Levine and Wrightson 1980). In other words, prosperous parents were in a better position to enforce the promise of marriage which had compromised their daughters. On the other hand, girls with no parents or those who were a long distance from home were most vulnerable. Servant girls in cities were often open to exploitation by their employers or by young men they met. Indeed, rates of illegitimacy and of child abandonment were highest among domestic servants. These women could not appeal to parental, religious, or community authority to help them make a seducer keep his promise.

Young women were protected not only by their parents but by community institutions as well. In many rural areas, the rituals of courtship and marriage involved vigilant groups of young people who regulated the morals and sexual activity of the village. Adolescent boys particularly policed the behaviour of courting couples, sometimes even influencing a man's choice of a mate. A wide discrepancy in the ages of the couple, for example, or promiscuity or adultery, could attract the ridicule of local youths. They would engage in elaborate rituals, following the couple, mocking them, singing profane songs under the woman's window. A bad-smelling bush planted before a girl's door indicated her low moral standing. A group of young men might fight or fine strangers courting local girls (Davis 1971; Gillis 1974: 20). Unwed mothers as well as married men who seduced single girls would be 'charivaried' or, in England, hear the sound of 'rough music' at their door. . . . In the village community these proceedings had the effect of legal sanctions. The charivari set and enforced standards of acceptable sexual conduct. Natalie Davis has pointed out that they also regulate the activities of the youths themselves, preventing too-early marriage and premarital promiscuity.

Organizations of craftsmen, too, watched over the activities of journeymen and apprentices. The rules of journeymen's organizations included the requirement that members not marry until they had completed their training and were in a position to help support a family. Guilds also had rules which prohibited young men from seducing girls and which enforced their regulations with fines and expulsion (Cadet 1870: 118, citing S. Daubie). Of course, those outside the guild structure were not subject to such rules. In general, the movement of people into, out of, and within cities made the regulation of sexual and social behaviour more difficult, especially among the unskilled. Hence rates of illegitimacy were higher in cities, and concubinage was a more common practice.

A woman's courtship and her marriage involved her family in a number of important ways. A young man usually asked a young woman's family for her hand. Then the families of the engaged couple assembled to draw up a contract which specified the economic terms of the marriage. The wedding was celebrated by family and community members. In the country, whole villages turned out to eat, drink, and dance in celebration of the consecration of a union; in cities all the craftsmen of a particular trade (many of whom were also related) attended the festivities. Among the propertyless and the unskilled the wedding might be less elaborate, but dancing was free and people could clap and sing if there was no money to hire music. These rituals and festivities marked the couple's entry into adulthood, the creation of a new family, the beginning of an independent existence. Among property holders marriage might ally two families and joint property holdings. In the lower ranks of society marriage was simply the establishment of a new family economy, the unit of reproduction and of work without which 'one cannot live' (Armengaud 1975: 144; Stone 1975: 48–9).

The characteristics of marriage among the popular classes clearly were different from those in the upper classes. Among wealthy families there was strict parental control over marriage. Parents sought to preserve their status and wealth by allying their children with a limited group of similarly wealthy families. Children's marriages extended networks of power and influence. The lineage must be protected, the patrimony enlarged and transmitted from one generation to the next. In these cases property was the basis for status and political power, hence family control over children's marriages was vital for the preservation of the elite position of aristocrats or local notables. There was, for example, a close association between the transmission of wealth and political power in Vraiville, a French village studied by Martine Segalen. There all the mayors for ten generations were descendants of, or married to, one of the thirteen most eminent families (Segalen 1972: 104). The families carefully chose spouses for their children from among a very small group of large property holders.

Among the popular classes parental consent and family contracts did not mean the same thing. Within the social and economic limits already described, individual choice of a spouse was permitted. Parental consent functioned as a verification of the couple's resources. Parents wanted to be sure a child would find his or her new family situation roughly equal to that of the family or origin. Moreover, the contract involved not the acquisition of resources for the patrimony but the surrendering of resources by families to the new family. Families, rather than the individuals to be married, drew up the contracts because they were the units of social identification and of membership for all individuals. The children were leaving one family to establish another and they were transferring their resources, their means of support, from one household to another. Relatively few persons, men or women, went through an intermediate stage of independence—economic or social—as they passed from their family of origin to their family of procreation. Individuality in the modern sense was socially and legally limited.

The age of marriage was constrained by the fact that family and social resources were limited. Like their husbands, wives were expected to bring a contribution to the marriage, in the form of capital, household furnishings, or marketable skills. Marriage itself signified the beginning of a new enterprise, of an economic partnership of husband and wife. It was 'the founding of a family' (Armengaud 1975: 144). And it was the emergence of this new family, the recreation of a social and economic unit, the beginning of a new enterprise that families and communities celebrated at a wedding.

During the time she was single a young woman usually worked in a household. Family labour and consumption needs determined whether or not she worked at home. But wherever she worked, she was dependent on the household in which she lived. Her work was both a means of contributing to her family's economy and a means of supporting herself. It also prepared her for marriage by helping accumulate the resources she would need to establish a family of her own.

Married Women in the Family Economy

The married couple was the 'simple community of work, the elementary unit' in the pre-industrial household (Gouesse 1972: 1146–7). The contribution of each spouse was vital for the creation and survival of the family. From its outset, marriage was an economic partnership. Each partner brought to the union either material resources, or the ability to help support each other. Peasant sons brought land, craftsmen brought their tools and skill. Daughters brought a dowry and sometimes a marketable skill as well. The dowry of a peasant or artisan daughter was usually a contribution to the establishment of the couple's household. These might include 'a bit of cash, furniture, linen, tools. Sometimes a loom, one or two skeins of wool, several pounds of wool and silk, a boat, a thousand eels for a fish merchant, sometimes a house or part of a house in the city, a meadow and some plots of land in the country' (Deyon 1967: 341).

Among the propertyless there was only the promise of work and wages. In Amiens in 1687, François Pariès, a mason, and Marie Hugues declared in their contract that they had no material possessions and that 'they are mutually satisfied with their well-being and with one another' (Deyon 1967: 254). The point was that the wife as well as the husband made an economic contribution (or a promise of one) which helped set up the new household. In addition, however, it represented a commitment to help support the new family. The resources brought to the marriage were only a beginning. The continuing labour of each partner was required to maintain the couple and, later, its children. In the course of a lifetime, the work of husband and wife was the major source of the family's support. Families were productive and reproductive units, centres of economic activity, and creators of new life. Married women contributed to all aspects of family life and thus fulfilled several roles within their households. They engaged in production for exchange and production for household consumption, both of which contributed to the family's economic well-being. And they performed the reproductive role of bearing and raising children.

Married Women's Work

A married woman's work depended on the family's economic position, on whether it was involved in agriculture or manufacturing, whether it owned property or was propertyless.

But whether labour or cash were needed, married women were expected to contribute it. The fact that a woman bore children influenced the kind of work she did, but it did not confine her to a single set of tasks, nor exclude her from participation in productive activity. The organization of production in this period demanded that women be contributing members of the family economy. It also permitted women to control the time and pace of their work, and to integrate their various domestic activities.

Within the pre-industrial household, whether on the farm or in the craft shop, among property holders and wage earners, there was a division of labour by age and by sex. The levels of skill expected of children advanced with age, with young children performing the simplest and crudest chores. Certain kinds of heavy work were reserved for men, but women also did many heavy tasks which today are considered too arduous for females. Hauling and carrying were often women's tasks. Rural and urban wives sometimes had occupations of their own, or they shared their husbands' occupations performing specified tasks within the productive process. Indeed, the jobs women did reflected the fact that they performed several functions for the family. The normative family division of labour tended to give men jobs away from the household or jobs which required long and uninterrupted commitments of time or extensive travel, while women's work was performed more often at home and permitted flexible time arrangements.

Rural women

On farms, men worked in the fields, while women ran the household, made the family's clothes, raised and cared for cows, pigs, and poultry, tended a garden, and marketed surplus milk, vegetables, chickens, and eggs. A French peasant saying went: 'No wife, no cow, hence no milk, no cheese, neither hens, nor chicks, nor eggs . . .' (Armengaud 1975: 75). The sale of these items often brought in the only cash a family received. Women's participation in local markets reflected their several family roles. They earned money as an outgrowth of activities concerned with family subsistence; and they might use the money to purchase food and supplies for their families. Their domestic and market activities overlapped, and both served important economic functions for the family. Moderately prosperous farm families owed their success to a variety of resources, not the least of which was the wife's activity. . . .

Wives of propertyless labourers also contributed to the family economy. They themselves became hired hands, 'working in the fields and doing all kinds of hard jobs'. Others became domestic textile workers. Still others alternated these activities. When Vauban, justifying his fiscal recommendations under Louis XIV, described the family of an agricultural labourer, he emphasized the importance of the wife's ability to earn money: 'by the work of her distaff, by sewing, knitting some stockings, or by a bit of lacemaking, according to the region' (Morineau 1972: 236; see also Flandrin 1976: 113). Without this and her cultivation of a garden and some animals, 'it would be difficult to subsist'. Home work most commonly involved spinning or sewing. Lacemaking, straw plaiting, glove making, knitting, and needlework were the major areas of domestic manufacture. Pinchbeck estimates that lacemaking alone employed as many as 100,000 women and children in seventeenth-century England. About a million women and children worked in the clothing trades as a whole in England in that period (Pinchbeck [1930] 1969: 203; Clark [1919] 1968: 97). And in France, as rural industry took hold in some areas, the numbers of women employed in spinning rose. Women earned low wages spinning, perhaps five sous a day in Picardy at the end of the seventeenth century (Guilbert 1966: 30–1). Male weavers earned double that amount. Yet the individual wage a married woman could earn was less important than was her contribution to a joint effort. Spinning and weaving together were the complementary bases of the family economy.

When no home work was available, a wife marketed her household activities, shopping for others at the market, hawking some wares: extra pieces of linen she had woven or lengths of thread she had spun and not used. Rural women also became wet nurses, nursing and raising the children of middle-class women and of urban artisans who could afford to pay them. In the countryside around Paris and around the silk-weaving centre of Lyons, for example, wet nursing was a common way for a rural woman to earn some additional money while caring for her own child. In areas around big cities in France particularly, this might be an organized enterprise. In Paris, for example, men or women (called *meneurs* or *messagères*) located rural nurses, recruited urban babies, then transported the infants in carts to the country, where they often remained until they were three or four years old, if they survived infancy. One late eighteenth-century estimate places at about 10,000 the number of Parisian infants sent out to nurse. Maurice Garden suggests that close to a third of all babies born in Lyons (some 2,000 of 5,000 to 6,000) were carted off to the countryside. Until the late eighteenth century these included the children of the upper classes as well as of artisan and shopkeeping families (Garden 1970: 324). Most often, however, the more prosperous families hired wet nurses who lived in the household. The wet nurse 'business' was most developed, it appears, in large pre-industrial urban centres where married women played an active role in artisan and commercial enterprise. There was little supervision of the nurses in this period. The job could be fairly lucrative and demand was high, so some women 'nursed' babies long after their own children had grown and their milk dried up.

Married women, then, would often alternate different kinds of work, putting together a series of jobs in order to increase their earnings or to earn enough to help their families survive. Indeed the absence of employment for the wives of wage earners was often given as the reason for a family's destitution.

Although women tended to work at or near home, they did not do so exclusively. On farms, the rhythm of the seasons with their periods of intensive labour brought women into the fields to sow and harvest, as well as to glean. . . . In areas where small property holders worked as agricultural labourers or as tradesmen, women tended the family plot and men worked away from home 'except for about a week in hay harvest, and for a few days at other times, when the gathering of manure or some work which the women cannot perform' required the men's assistance (Pinchbeck [1930] 1969: 20). In the vineyards of the Marne 'the wife [was] really the working partner of her husband: she share[d] all of his burdens', cultivating the grapes (Flandrin 1976: 113).

On the other hand, there was household work which included the entire family. In villages in France, for example, the kneading and preparation of bread (which was baked in a communal oven) 'mobilized the energies of everyone in the house every other week in the summer and once a month in winter' (Bernard 1975: 30). And the winter slaughter of a pig took all family members and sometimes some additional help. When the farm or the household needed labour, it incorporated all hands, regardless of sex, in periods of intense activity. At other times, though work roles were different, they were complementary. The family economy depended upon the labour of both husband and wife.

Urban women

Wives of skilled craftsmen who worked at home usually assisted their husbands, sharing the same room, if not the same bench or table. The wife sometimes prepared or finished materials on which the husband worked. Thus wives spun for their weaver husbands, polished metal for cutlers, sewed buttonholes for tailors, and waxed shoes for shoemakers. Sometimes a wife's work was identical to her husband's. . . . If the wife was not her husband's constant companion at the loom, however, or if spinning was her customary job, she still must be able to take his place when he had other tasks, when he was ill, or when he died. . . . The fact that all family members worked together and benefited jointly from the enterprise meant that some jobs were learned by both sexes and could be interchangeable. It meant, too, . . . that the family's joint economic activity was the first priority for everyone.

If the products made at home were sold there, then a craftsman's wife was usually also a shopkeeper. She handled transactions, kept accounts, and helped supervise the workers in the shop. Many of these women hired servants to free them from 'the routine of domestic drudgery'. When work pressed, as it did in the Lyonnais silk trade (where the typical female occupation was silk spinning or assistance with weaving), mothers sent their infants off to nurses rather than break the rhythm of work in the shop (Clark [1919] 1968: 156; see also Hufton 1975: 12).

Yet, if a wife was her husband's indispensable partner in many a trade, and even if her skill equalled his, she remained his assistant while he lived. Married women were granted full membership in certain guilds only after their husbands had died and then so long as they did not remarry. Occupational designations in all but the food and clothing trades usually were male. Women were referred to as the wives of the craftsmen, even when they were widows and practising in the trade on their own. Hence, Mrs Baskerville, a widow of a printer and letter founder, 'begs leave to inform the Public, . . . that she continues the business of letter founding, in all its parts, with the same care and accuracy that was formerly observed by Mr Baskerville' (Pinchbeck [1930] 1969: 284–5). The practice reflected a family division of labour which undoubtedly took into account a woman's domestic tasks: her other activities might claim her time, while the husband could be a full-time craftsman. In addition, in the most skilled trades, an investment in long years of training might be unwise for a woman in the light of the lost time, the illnesses, and the higher mortality of women usually associated with childbirth (Deyon 1967: 39). The exclusion of women also represented a means of controlling the size of a craft. Only when labour was scarce were women permitted to practise certain trades. . . . By and large, in the home-based skilled trades, married women were part of the family labour force.

Some women did have crafts or trades of their own in the cities of England and France in 1700. Most of these were associated with the production and distribution of food and clothing. The all-female *corporations* in seventeenth-century France include seamstresses, dressmakers, combers of hemp and flax, embroiderers, and hosiers. In addition, there were fan and wig makers, milliners, and cloak makers (Guilbert 1966: 21–2). Lists from English cities are similar.

In many of these trades women regularly took on apprentices. In millinery, for example, an apprenticeship lasted from five to seven years and required a substantial fee. The women ran their enterprises independently of their husbands, whose work often took them away from home. . . .

Women were represented, too, in the retail trades, assisting their husbands and running their own businesses as well. In England, brewing once was a female monopoly. It was so no longer by the eighteenth century, but women still practised the trade. Women were also bakers, grocers, innkeepers, and butchers. At least one woman butcher in eighteenth-century London 'lived by killing beasts in which . . . she was very expert' (Pinchbeck [1930] 1969: 295).

By far the most numerous group of married women working independently were the wives of unskilled labourers and journeymen. They were women in precarious economic situations, since their husbands never earned enough money to cover the household needs. These women had no skills, nor did they have capital for goods or a shop. No family productive enterprise claimed their time. So they became petty traders, and itinerant peddlers selling such things as bits of cloth or 'perishable articles of food from door to door' accompanied by their children (Clark [1919] 1968: 150, 290; Hufton 1974). The street was their shop; their homes were their workplaces; and their work required no investment in tools or equipment. On the list of non-guild members in Paris cited on page 62 there were 1,263 women and only 486 men. The women were lodging-house keepers and retailers or 'repairers of old clothes and hats, of rags and old ironware, buckles and hardware' (Kaplow 1972: 45). When they did not sell items they had scavenged or repaired, they sold their labour, carting goods, water, or sewage, doing laundry, and performing a host of other unskilled services which were always in demand in the city and usually outside the control of the guilds. Their work was an aspect of 'the economy of makeshift' which characterized their entire lives. As such, the time spent earning wages was sporadic and discontinuous. . . .

The time required of women differed greatly in different situations. During harvesting and planting, wives worked day and night in the fields. Wives of urban butchers and bakers spent many hours in the family shop. Lyons' silk spinners paid others to nurse their babies. Women doing casual labour had to spend long hours earning a few pence or sous. Yet the work of most married women permitted a certain flexibility, some control over the time and pace of work. Some studies estimated that in the course of a year, a woman probably spent fewer days at cash-earning activities than did her husband. While a man worked about 250 days a year, a woman worked about 125 to 180 days. The studies, based on contemporaries' analyses of family budgets of French weavers in 1700 and agricultural labourers in 1750, assumed that a married woman worked less 'because of the supplementary demands of her sex: housekeeping, childbirth, etc.' (Morineau 1972: 210, 221). In the fields, women could stop work to nurse a baby or feed a young child. In craft and retail shops, they could allocate some time for domestic responsibilities. In addition, they could include young children in certain aspects of their work, teaching them to wind thread or clean wool. Those who walked the street selling their wares were invariably accompanied by their children. Yet rather than 'working less', as contemporaries described it, it seems more accurate to say that demands on women's time were more complex. In this period, the type of work women did meant that even if home and workplace were not the same, a woman could balance her productive and domestic activities.

Widows

We have described so far a 'normal' situation, in which both husband and wife were alive. Yet mortality statistics indicate that quite frequently death changed this picture. The death of a husband disrupted the family division of labour and left the wife solely responsible for maintaining the family. Sometimes, of course, there were children to assist her, to run the farm, or earn some wages. But often they were too young or too inexperienced to contribute much.

In the best of circumstances, a widow gained the right to practise her husband's craft. She became legal representative of the family, and her mastery and autonomy were publicly recognized. . . .

Widowhood, however, was usually a difficult situation. Deprived of a husband's assistance, many women could not continue a family enterprise and instead sought new kinds of work. In the French town of Châteaudun, for example, wives of vineyard owners, who had managed the household side of the family enterprise while their husbands lived, took in sewing and spinning when they died. The wife could not do the heavy work of harvesting the grapes herself. And she could rarely afford to pay hired help. The few opportunities for her to earn money—usually as a seamstress—were poorly paid and were insufficient to keep up the activities of the vineyard (Baulant 1976: 106). In cities, women who did the most onerous jobs were often widows whose need led them to take any work they could find. Many of these women were unable to support themselves despite their work, for wages were so low. The jobs available to these women—as seamstresses, or unskilled workers—were notoriously poorly paid. Hence it was impossible for women and their families to live on earnings alone. So they often sent their children off to charitable institutions, or to fend for themselves. Widows and orphans made up the bulk of names on charity lists in the seventeenth and eighteenth centuries. . . .

Remarriage was clearly the happiest solution for a widow, since an economic partnership was the best means of survival. Widows and widowers did remarry if they could. One study of the Parisian region found that in the sixteenth, seventeenth, and eighteenth centuries men remarried within a few months or even weeks of their wives' deaths (Baulant 1976: 104). Among the lower classes, the rates of remarriage were much higher than among the upper classes, who were protected from penury by the money or property specifically designated for widowhood in marriage contracts. Prosperous widows were sometimes prevented from remarrying by children who did not want their inheritance threatened. If she could find a husband, a second marriage for a widow of the popular classes meant a restoration of the household division of labour. If she had a craft shop or some land, a widow might attract a younger man eager to become a master craftsman or a farmer. (As the husband of a master's widow a man was legally entitled to take over the mastership.) But if she had no claim to property or if she had to relinquish those claims because of the difficulty of maintaining the enterprise alone, she would marry a man whose economic situation was considerably worse than her first husband's. In these instances, farm wives, for example, would become agricultural field labourers or, perhaps, spinners (Couturier 1969: 139).

In most cases, however, widows failed to find new spouses and they had to manage on their own. Widowers more often chose younger, single women as their second wives. A widow's advanced age or the fact that she had children lessened her chances of finding a husband. (Sometimes the price of remarriage was the abandonment of her children, since a prospective husband might be unwilling or unable to contribute to their support. But even this alternative might be preferable to the precarious existence of a widow on her own who might have to abandon her children anyway.) The charity rolls and hospital records of the seventeenth and eighteenth centuries starkly illustrate the plight of a widow with young children or of an elderly widow, desperately struggling and usually failing to earn her own bread. 'Small wonder', comments Hufton (1974: 117), 'the widow and her brood were common beggars. What other resource had they?'

Although there were fewer of them (they either remarried or simply abandoned their children), widowers too were on the charity lists. Like the widows, these men had great difficulty supporting themselves and their dependent children. Such men and women were eloquent testimony to the fact that the line between survival and starvation, between poverty and destitution, was an extremely thin one. They clearly demonstrate as well that two partners were vital to family survival. The family division of labour reflected an economy based on the contributions of husband and wife. The loss of one partner usually meant the destruction of the family economy. Although the jobs they performed may have differed, the work of husband and wife were equally necessary to the household. It was this partnership of labour that struck one observer in eighteenth-century France:

> In the lowest ranks [of society], in the country and in the cities, men and women together cultivate the earth, raise animals, manufacture cloth and clothing. Together they use their strength and their talents to nourish and serve children, old people, the infirm, the lazy and the weak. . . . No distinction is made between them about who is the boss; both are . . . (Hufton 1974: 38)

It is not entirely clear that a partnership of labour meant there existed a 'rough equality' between husband and wife in all areas of family life (this is the position of Power 1975: 34). It is clear, however, that the survival of the family depended on the work of both partners. . . . Tasks performed were complementary. The differentiation of work roles was based in part on the fact that women also had to bear children and manage the household, activities which were necessary, too, to the family economy. The family economy reproduced itself as the basic economic unit of production. Children were important as well for the sustenance of aged and dependent parents.

Married Women's Domestic Activity

The wife's major domestic responsibility was the provision of food for the family. The work of all family members contributed directly or indirectly to subsistence, but wives had a particular responsibility for procuring and preparing food. In the peasant family, 'the duties of the mother of the family were overwhelming; they were summed up in one work: food' (Le Roy Ladurie 1969: 481). In the unskilled labourer's home, too, the wife raised chickens, a cow, a pig, or a goat. Her garden supplemented the miserable wages she earned sewing and those her husband made in the fields. Urban wives frequented markets, where they haggled and bargained over the prices of food and other goods. Some also kept small gardens and few animals at home. Whether she grew food or purchased it—whether, in other words, she was a producer or consumer—the wife's role in providing food served her family. A wife's ability to garden and tend animals, or to bargain and to judge the quality of items for sale, could mean the difference between eating decently and not eating at all. In more desperate circumstances, women earned the family's food by begging for it or by organizing their children to appeal for charity. They supervised the 'economy of makeshift', improvising ways of earning money or finding food, and going without food in order to feed their children. One curé in Tours compared such women to 'the pious pelican of the *Adoro Te*, who gave her blood to feed her young'. Hufton's careful study of the poor in eighteenth-century France has led her to conclude that 'the importance of the mother within the family economy was immense; her death or incapacity could cause a family to cross the narrow but extremely meaningful barrier between poverty and destitution' (Hufton 1971: 92).

Food was the most important item in the budgets of most families. Few families had any surplus funds to save or to spend on anything other than basic necessities. A French artisan's family, for example, whose members earned 43 sols a day, spent in 1701 approximately 36 sols on food: bread, herring, cheese, and cider. Poorer families ate less varied fare. Rural and urban wage earners in eighteenth-century France could spend more than half of their income on bread alone (Lefebvre 1962: 218; Morineau 1972: 210; Hufton 1974: 46–8).

The fact that she managed the provision of food gave the wife a certain power within the family. She decided how to spend money, how to allocate most of the family's few resources. She was the acknowledged manager of much of the monetary exchange of the family and her authority in this sphere was unquestioned. Legally, women were subordinate to their husbands. And some were clearly subject to physical mistreatment as well. Recent studies of criminality, violence, and divorce among the lower classes during the seventeenth and eighteenth centuries indicate that wife beating occurred and that women were at a disadvantage in seeking redress in court.

The law tolerated male adultery and punished it in females; and it also tolerated violence by men against their wives (Abbiateci et al. 1971; Castan 1974; Phillips 1976). The studies, of course, focus on examples of family breakdown and disharmony which reached the criminal courts. They do not, therefore, adequately describe the day-to-day dealings of husband and wife, nor do they detail *distribution* of power within the household. Yet it is precisely the distribution that is important. Men had the physical and legal power, but women managed the poor family's financial resources. Within the households of the popular classes there seem to have been not just one but several sources of power. Men did not monopolize all of them. Wives' power in the household stemmed from the fact that they managed household expenditures for food. Among families which spent most of their money on food this meant that the wife decided how to spend most of the family's money. . . .

Childbirth and Nurture

The role of food provider was an important aspect of a married woman's productive economic activity and it was also tied to her reproductive role. For it was she who bore and nurtured children, she who clothed and cared for them. Children were the inevitable consequence of marriage; child-bearing was an exclusively female activity. Married women expected to spend much of their married lives pregnant or caring for young children. High infant mortality rates and ensuing high fertility meant that at least two-thirds of a wife's married years involved reproductive activity. For women the risks and pain of childbirth, the need to spend some time nursing an infant, the supervision and feeding of children were all part of the definition of marriage.

The activities surrounding childbirth were almost exclusively performed by females. Midwives sometimes assisted at the birth of a child. These were usually local women who had 'inherited' the few skills they had from their own mothers or from another woman in the community. But a midwife's services cost money and often women simply helped another, with no previous training or experience. The lack of knowledge contributed to maternal and infant disability and death. . . .

Well into the nineteenth century babies were delivered by untrained women. As Hufton (1974: 14) has put it, 'The actual birth of the child was surrounded by a "complicity" of females.' Childbirth created a bond among women. They not only shared the experience but also assisted and nursed one another as best they could.

Yet after the birth of a baby, in the list of household priorities the care of children ranked quite low. Work and the provision of food for the family had first claim on a married woman's time. In the craft shop or on the farm, skilled or unskilled, most labour was time intensive. Men and women spent the day at work, and what little leisure they had was often work related. Hence in the rural *veillée* people would gather in barns on winter evenings to keep warm, to talk, but also to repair farm tools, to sew, to sort and clean fruit and vegetables. In cities when women were not formally employed or when their paid work was through, they put in long hours spinning, buying and preparing food, or doing laundry. Household tasks were tedious and no labour-saving technology lightened the chores of a working woman. She simply did not have time to spare to devote specifically to children. The demands of the family enterprise or the need to earn wages for the unskilled could not be postponed or put aside to care for children, who, in their earliest years, represented only a drain on family resources. Busy mothers in French cities sent their babies out to be nursed by wet nurses if they could afford it. . . . Death rates among children put out to nurse were almost twice as high as among infants nursed by their own mothers. Even infants who remained at home, however, did not receive a great deal of care. The need for special attention for young children simply was not recognized. As Pinchbeck and Hewitt (1969: 8) have put it, 'Infancy was but a biologically necessary prelude to the sociologically all-important business of the adult world.' . . .

The position of children in a family was the result of several factors: high infant and child mortality rates and a relative scarcity of both time and material resources. The likelihood was great that a child would die before it reached maturity. Parents' treatment of their children clearly took these odds into account. They often gave successive children the same name, anticipating the fact that only one would survive. Since the life of any child was so fragile, there was no reason to try to limit or prevent pregnancy. Moreover, as two historians have put it:

> The high rates of mortality prevailing amongst children inevitably militated against the individual child being the focus and principal object of parental interest and affection. . . . The precariousness of child life also detracted from the importance of childhood as an age-status. In a society where few lived to grow old, age was of less significance than survival. (Pinchbeck and Hewitt 1969: 7)

The needs of family economy and not children's individual needs or the needs of 'childhood' determined whether or not children remained at home from infancy onward. If they were not put out to a wet nurse, children might be sent into service or apprenticeship at age seven or eight. They were expected to work hard and were sometimes subjected to harsh treatment by their masters and mistresses. (Court records are full of accounts of young servants and apprentices fleeing from cruel employers.) On the other hand, if the family needed their labour, children worked at home.

Children were a family resource only if their labour could be used. In propertied families, of course, one child was also important as an heir. As soon as they were able, young children began to assist their parents in the work of the household. In time of scarcity, those not working might be abandoned or sent away, for they were of limited usefulness to the household as it attempted to balance labour and food.

As family labourers, children were accorded no special treatment. They simply worked as members of the family 'team'. Their interest and their needs were not differentiated from the family interest. The mother's services to the family were therefore services to them as well. Although she spent time as a child-bearer, a mother allocated little time to activities specifically connected with child rearing. Children were fed and trained to work in the course of the performance of her other responsibilities. Married women allocated their time among the three major activities. The organization of production in this period permitted them to integrate their activity, to merge wage work, production for household consumption, and reproduction.

Production was most often located in the household, and individuals for the most part controlled the time and pacing of their work. Production for the market was often an outgrowth of production for household consumption. Although household chores were time-consuming, they did not demand a broad range of skill or expertise. Childbirth interrupted a woman's routine and claimed some of her time, but after a few days, a woman was usually back to work, taking time out only to nurse the infant. Views of children and standards of childcare were such that children were either sent away at a young age or were incorporated into adult routines and adult work. Hence it was possible for a married woman to earn wages or to produce for the market, to manage her household, and to bear children. Each activity influenced the others, but no single activity defined her place nor claimed all of her time. In the course of her lifetime, indeed in the course of a year or a day, a married woman balanced several types of activity and performed them all. She was the cornerstone of the family economy.

References

Abbiateci, A., et al. 1971. *Crimes et criminalité en France, XVIIe–XVIIIe siècles* (Paris: Colin).

Allison, K.J., and P.M. Tillot. 1961. 'York in the Eighteenth Century', in *A History of Yorkshire*, ed. P.M. Tillot (London: The Institute of Historical Research).

Armengaud, A. 1975. *La famille et l'enfant en France et en Angleterre du XVIe au XVIIIe siècles: Aspects démographiques* (Paris: Société d'édition d'enseignement supérieur).

Baehrel, R. 1961. *Une Croissance: La Basse Provence rurale (fin du XVIe siècle–1789)* (Paris: SEVPEN), 109–20.

Baulant, M. 1976. 'The Scattered Family: Another Aspect of Seventeenth-century Demography', in *Family and Society*, eds R. Forster and O. Ranum (Baltimore: Johns Hopkins).

Berkner, L. 1972. 'The Stem Family and the Development Cycle of the Peasant Household: An Eighteenth Century Austrian Example', *American Historical Review* 77 (Apr.): 398–418.

Bernard, R.-J. 1975. 'Peasant Diet in Eighteenth-century Gevaudan', in *Diet from Pre-industrial to Modern Times*, eds Forster and Forster (New York: Harper & Row).

Braun, R. 1966. 'The Impact of Cottage Industry on an Agricultural Population', in *The Rise of Capitalism*, ed. D. Landes (New York: Macmillan).

Cadet, E. 1870. *Le Mariage en France* (Paris: Guillamin).

Castan, Y. 1974. *Honnêteté et relations sociales en Languedoc (1715–1780)* (Paris: Plon).

Cipolla, C. 1964. *The Economic History of World Population*, rev. edn (Baltimore: Penguin).

———. 1976. *Before the Industrial Revolution: European Society in the Eighteenth Century* (New York: Norton).

Clark, A. [1919] 1968. *The Working Life of Women in the Seventeenth Century* (London: G. Routledge & Sons; reissued by Frank Cass).

Clarkson, L.A. 1971. *The Pre-industrial Economy of England, 1500–1750* (London: Batsford).

Couturier, M. 1969. *Recherches sur les structures sociales de Châteaudun, 1525–1789* (Paris: SEVPEN).

Davies, D. 1965. 'The Case of Labourers in Husbandry, 1795', in *Society and Politics in England, 1780–1960*, ed. J.F.C. Harrison (New York: Harper & Row).

Davis, N. 1971. 'The Reasons of Misrule: Youth Groups and Charivaris in Sixteenth-century France', *Past and Present* 50: 42–75.

Deyon, P. 1967. *Amiens, Capitale provinciale: Etude sur la société urbaine au 17e siècle* (Paris, The Hague: Mouton).

Dupaquier, J. 1976. 'Les Caractères originaux de l'histoire démographique française au XVIIIe siècle', *Revue d'histoire moderne et contemporaine* 23 (Apr.–June).

Fairchilds, C. 1976. *Poverty and Charity in Aix-en-Province, 1650–1789* (Baltimore: Johns Hopkins University Press).

Flandrin, J.-L. 1976. *Familles: Parenté, maison, sexualité dans l'ancienne société* (Paris: Hachette).

Fourastié, J. 1959. 'De la vie traditionnelle à la vie "tertiare"', *Population* 14.

Garden, M. 1970. *Lyon et les lyonnais au XVIIIe siècle* (Paris: Les Belle-Lettres).

Gillis, J.R. 1974. *Youth and History* (New York: Academic Press).

Goubert, P. 1965a. 'Recent Theories and Research on French Population between 1500 and 1700', in *Population in History: Essays in Historical Demography*, eds D.V. Glass and D.E.C. Eversley (Chicago: Aldine).

———. 1965b. 'The French Peasantry of the Seventeenth Century: A Regional Example', in *Crisis in Europe, 1540–1660: Essays from Past and Present*, ed. T. Aston (London: Routledge & Kegan Paul) and *Beauvais et le Beauvaisis*.

Gouesse, J.-M. 1972. 'Parenté, famille et mariage en Normandie aux XVIIe et XVIIIe siècles', *Annales: Economies, Sociétés, Civilisations* 27.

Guilbert, M. 1966. *Les Fonctions des femmes dans l'industrie* (Paris, The Hague: Mouton).

Hair, P.E.H. 1966. 'Bridal Pregnancy in Rural England in Earlier Centuries', *Population Studies* 20 (Nov.): 233–43.

Hauser, H. 1927. *Ouvriers du temps passé* (Paris: Alcan).

Hay, D., et al. 1975. *Albion's Fatal Tree* (New York: Pantheon).

Henry, L. 1965. 'The Population of France in the Eighteenth Century', in *Population in History: Essays in Historical Demography*, eds D.V. Glass and D.E.C. Eversley (Chicago: Aldine).

Hobsbawm, E.J. 1968. *Industry and Empire: An Economic History of Britain since 1750* (London: Weidenfeld and Nicolson).

Hollingsworth, T.H. 1969. *Historical Demography* (London: The Sources of History Limited in Association with Hodder and Stoughton Ltd.).

Hufton, O. 1971. 'Women in Revolution, 1789–1796', *Past and Present* 53.

———. 1974. 'Women and Marriage in Pre-revolutionary France', unpublished paper.

———. 1974. *The Poor of Eighteenth Century France, 1750–1789* (Oxford: Clarendon Press).

———. 1975. 'Women and the Family Economy in Eighteenth Century France', *French Historical Studies* 9 (Spring): 1–22.

Kaplow, J. 1972. *The Names of Kings: The Parisian Laboring Poor in the Eighteenth Century* (New York: Basic Books).

Knodel, J., and M.J. Maynes. 1976. 'Urban and Rural Marriage Patterns in Imperial Germany', *Journal of Family History* 1 (Winter).

Kussmaul-Cooper, A. 1975a. 'The Mobility of English Farm Servants in the Seventeenth and Eighteenth Centuries', unpublished paper, University of Toronto (cited with permission).

———. 1975b. 'Servants and Laborers in English Agriculture', unpublished paper, University of Toronto (cited with permission).

Landes, D. 1969. *The Unbound Prometheus* (Cambridge: Cambridge University Press).

Laslett, P. 1974. 'Parental Deprivation in the Past: A Note on the History of Orphans in England', *Local Population Studies* 13 (Autumn): 11–18.

———, and K. Oosterveen. 1973. 'Long-term Trends in Bastardy in England: A Study of the Illegitimacy Figures in the Parish Registers and in the Reports of the Registrar General, 1461–1960', *Population Studies* 27.

Lebrun, F. 1971. *Les Hommes et la mort en Anjou aux 17e et 18e siècles* (Paris, The Hague: Mouton).

Lefebvre, G. 1962. *Etudes Orléannaises*, Vol. I (Paris: CNRS).

Le Roy Ladurie, E. 1969. 'L'Amenorrhée de famine (XVIIIe–XXe siècles)', *Annals: ESC* 24e Année (Nov.–Dec.): 1589–601.

Levine, D. 1976. 'The Demographic Implications of Rural Industrialization: A Family Reconstitution Study of Shepshed, Leicestershire, 1600–1851', *Social History* (May): 177–96.

———, and K. Wrightson. 1980. 'The Social Context of Illegitimacy in Early Modern England', in *Bastardy and Its Comparative History*, ed. P. Laslett (Cambridge: Cambridge University Press).

Macfarlane, A. 1970. *The Family Life of Ralph Josselin* (Cambridge: Cambridge University Press).

Mendras, H. 1970. *The Vanishing Peasant: Innovation and Change in French Agriculture*, trans. J. Lerner (Cambridge, MA: MIT Press).

Meuvret, J. 1965. 'Demographic Crisis in France from the Sixteenth to the Eighteenth Century', in *Population in History: Essays in Historical Demography*, eds D.V. Glass and D.E.C. Eversley (Chicago: Aldine).

Morineau, M. 1972. 'Budgets populaires en France au XVIIIe siècle', *Revue d'histoire économique et sociale* 50.

Perrot, J.-C. 1975. *Genèse d'une ville moderne: Caen au XVIIIe siècle* (Paris, The Hague: Mouton).

Phillips, R. 1976. 'Women and Family Breakdown in Eighteenth Century France: Rouen 1780–1800', *Social History* 2 (May): 197–218.

Pinchbeck, I. [1930] 1969. *Women Workers and the Industrial Revolution, 1750–1850* (London: G. Routledge; reissued by Kelley).

———, and Hewitt, M. 1969. *Children in English Society*, Vol. I (London: Routledge & Kegan Paul).

Power, E. 1975. *Medieval Women* (Cambridge: Cambridge University Press).

Segalen, M. 1972. *Nuptialité et alliance: Le Choix du conjoint dans une commune de l'Eure* (Paris: G.P. Maisonneuve Larose).

Stone, L. 1975. 'The Rise of the Nuclear Family in Early Modern England', in *The Family in History*, ed. C. Rosenberg (Philadelphia: University of Pennsylvania Press).

Thompson, E.P. 1975. *Whigs and Hunters* (London: Allen Lane).

Thorner, D., B. Kerblay, and R.E.F. Smith, eds. 1966. *A.V. Chayanov on the Theory of Peasant Economy* (Homewood, IL: Richard D. Irwin).

Wrigley, E.A. 1966. 'Family Limitation in Pre-industrial England', *Economic History Review*, 2nd series, 19 (Apr.): 89–109.

———. 1969. *Population and History* (London: Cambridge University Press).

Chapter 6

Descriptions of the staple-exporting economy on which Canada was built usually focus on trade relations and ignore the work relations through which families produced their daily food. As in England and France in the eighteenth century, couples living in Ontario in the nineteenth century built and sustained their families through hard daily work that featured men's and women's mutual dependence and complementary responsibilities. Nevertheless, property relations, in Ontario as in England, cast women in a very different position than that of their male partners. This selection from Marjorie Cohen's book *Women's Work, Markets and Economic Development in Nineteenth-century Ontario* makes the argument that the gender relations characterizing family farms in pre-industrial Ontario were patriarchal. Cohen's focus on the gender inequality inherent in production relations in Ontario complements Tilly and Scott's description of the gendered relations of work and family life in England and France.

Patriarchal Relations of Production in Nineteenth-century Ontario

Marjorie Griffin Cohen

Patriarchal productive relations can be defined as the organization of labour in which males, as husbands, fathers, and even sons and brothers, have power over the productive activities of their children, wives, and sometimes their sisters and mothers. This power was not confined simply to non-waged labour in the home but, since family labour was the most prevalent form of labour in the pre-industrial period, it will be the focus of my discussion of patriarchal productive relations.

Patriarchy

In the agricultural sector, the non-waged labour of family members was the most important source of labour power. The significance of family labour to agricultural production is well known, but the social relations of this type of production are rarely considered.[1] The concept of a family economy implies an indivisibility of income and a community of effort that does not easily lend itself to the type of class analysis possible when the object of study is waged labour. Yet the issue of ownership and control of labour is as significant in the family economy as it is in more identifiably capitalist relationships.

In most analyses of productive relations the issue of ownership is understood to be critical to establishing power and control. The very principles of organization of labour within a society are based on who does and who does not own the means of production: ownership implies not simply possession but all the social institutions developed to recognize property rights. How property relations are recognized by society is most directly evident in the laws which protect property relations. But the issue of ownership extends beyond the strictly legal aspects of control, for all of the social standards, customs, and the entire complex of human relations are influenced by this fundamental relationship. The significance of who owns property at any stage in the development process has been summed up by Oscar Lange: 'It is the ownership of the means of production which decides the ways in which they are used and which thereby determines the forms taken by co-operation and the division of labour. Moreover the ownership of the means of production determines the issue of who owns the products, and hence decides how they are distributed.'[2]

The usual analysis of class relations deals with those clearly identified through market activity. That is, class interests are evident when owners are employers and workers receive wages. When there is no waged labour present, such as in simple or independent commodity production, the ownership is usually treated as being vested in the group which performs the labour—the family. When ownership by the family is understood to be communal, the issue of systematic domination and exploitation in the production process cannot be admitted as a possibility. Whatever accumulation of capital occurs is not seen as an expropriation of anyone's surplus labour if it is assumed that the group shares in ownership.

However, the family in nineteenth-century Ontario was not an egalitarian unit and neither custom nor law considered that the family *per se* owned the means of production. Only under exceptional circumstances did women own the means of production. For the most part property was owned by the male head of the family. Wives and children were the proletariat of the family farm, the workers whose labour was rewarded according to the good fortune or goodwill of the owner. The significance of male control over female labour has been obscured because of the conjugal relationship, their mutual dependence, and their shared standard of living, yet female labour was not in a position of equality with male labour in the family economy where the ownership and control of property were in the hands of the male alone.

The important point to be made here is that the question of power through property relations in general is not unique to capitalist relations, but is crucial to understanding productive relations within the family economy as well.[3] Male control over labour was established through the power of ownership. In the family economy the issue of power was complicated by the personal relationships of the family and the fact that the male head of the family was clearly part of the labouring unit. But his position was distinct from the others; all surplus produced by the non-waged workers who did not share in ownership was, in effect, expropriated by the owner.[4] Whatever accumulation of capital occurred was legally his. Non-waged family workers had certain rights with respect to their membership in the family: children and wives could claim support from their fathers or husbands, but the general understanding was that this support was their right, less by virtue of their contribution than by virtue of their economic helplessness. They had no legal rights to what they produced through their labour even though the contribution of family members was critical to the success or failure of the economy of the family unit.

The implications of patriarchal productive relations were distinct for different forms of labour within the family unit. While male and female children and wives were all labourers subject to the authority of the male owner of the means of production, there were significant differences in the duration and extent of patriarchal dominance. Until the father died or gave his property away he exerted considerable control over his children's labour. But male and female children were treated differently, particularly with regard to their ultimate relationship to property. For women, both as children and as wives, patriarchal control took a different form than it did for men in that it did not cease with the passing of time, but was likely to continue throughout their lifetimes.

The Law

Male domination in property issues was stipulated in law in nineteenth-century Ontario. The rights of women to own property and even to claim ownership of the product of their own labour were severely restricted. Single women over 21 years of age and widows were, by law, given the same rights as males over property. But inheritance practices and social and legal restrictions with regard to occupation and appropriate behaviour meant that most property was controlled by males. For single women the period of time during which they were likely to be legally free from the control of either a husband or a father was non-existent or comparatively short. . . . For most women the property protection for single women was irrelevant.

The labour a single woman provided on the property of a male relative generally was understood to have been freely provided and did not provide the woman with either a claim on the property or a claim to a wage. Paul Craven's study of court cases in nineteenth-century Ontario indicates that the law upheld the assumption that any work a woman performed for a member of her family was part of her natural duty. In one striking case, where a woman unsuccessfully sued her brother for wages for the work she had performed for several years on his farm, the judge was explicit in this regard:

> Nothing was more natural than an unmarried young woman should live with and keep house for her brother, especially while he was also unmarried, and that without the idea of hiring or wages entering into the mind of either. It would be we fear a mischievous doctrine to lay down that in every case in which a niece, or cousin, or sister-in-law is proved to be living in a farmer's house, treated in every way as one of the family, and assisting in the work of doing all or most of the housework, she could, in the absence of any evidence whatsoever as to hiring or wages, be held entitled to the direction of a judge that the law in such a case implied a promise to pay.[5]

Until 1859 married women in English Canada had no right to property in their own name. This legal disability was based on English common law where, in the words of the English jurist Sir William Blackstone, 'the husband and wife are one and that one is the husband'.[6] Upon marriage women were considered the responsibility of their husbands and in this respect the law recognized it as the wife's legal right to be supported by the husband.[7] But the price of protection was the loss of independence of action, and of ownership and legal control over the products of a woman's labour. Even the primary products of her labour, her children, were legally under her husband's control. Until about the mid-nineteenth century, she could not claim them as her own under any circumstances and even when her husband died she would not automatically be recognized as the legal parent. Her husband could, if he wanted, appoint someone other than their mother as their legal guardian. In fact, anything a woman might produce, sell, or earn through her labour was legally the property of her husband and she could not use or dispose of it without his approval.

By mid-century, legislation was enacted to expand women's rights with regard to both their children and their property. In 1855 an act was passed giving women in Ontario the possibility of obtaining custody of their children under 12 years of age in cases where the judge 'saw fit'.[8] It followed similar custody legislation passed in England in 1839. In some cases, the courts rendered progressive interpretations of the law and women were not only awarded custody of their children but also provision for their maintenance. However, in the majority of cases, courts upheld the idea that the common law rights of fathers over their children were not abrogated by enactment of the new legislation. According to legal historian Constance Backhouse, improved custody rights for women had less to do with women's rights, *per se*, than with the growing recognition of the need to protect children and to award custody in their interests.[9]

In response to considerable pressure from women, the Ontario government in 1859 passed An Act to Secure to Married Women Certain Separate Property Rights.[10] This Act gave women rights to property they had owned before marriage which had not been covered by a marriage contract or settlement. However, a wife's earnings still belonged to her husband, and while the law legally entitled her to make a will, her heirs could only be her husband or her children.[11] Once again, while the intent of the law seemed fairly clear, the tendency of the courts was to continue to uphold a husband's control over his wife's property, including her ability to make contracts and to convey her land.[12] The Married Women's Act of 1872 extended women's property rights somewhat. With this Act, married women were permitted to own and administer separate property and to enter into contracts as though they were unmarried.[13] However, they were not given increased control over family property; rather, women's power existed only with regard to property that was distinctly in their name alone. With the Married Women's Property Act, a woman's earnings were considered her separate property. However, this provision was limited to earnings specifically arising out of the woman's employment in a trade or occupation where her husband had no proprietary interest. So while a married woman would be permitted to retain the earnings she might receive from production on her own land, from waged work, or from any special literary or artistic talent she might possess, she would not be legally entitled to the income from her labour on the family enterprise because the family property was still legally the husband's. The change in the law regarding women's property did not change the control a man could exercise over his wife's labour. His consent was still needed if she wanted to work for wages or engage in some sort of business on her own.[14] Nevertheless, throughout the second half of the nineteenth century the law was gradually improved so that its intent in providing greater property protection was clear. By the end of the century, women's separate property rights were considerably more secure than they had been at mid-century.

Inheritance

While family practices may have mitigated the practical effects of the law for some women in their daily lives, the significance of male legal superiority became especially clear when the husband or father died. An examination of the wills in one county—Stormont, Dundas, and Glengarry, Ontario—for two periods, from 1800 to 1811 and from 1850 to 1858, gives a clear indication of the tenuous claim women had on all forms of property.[15] The wills indicate not only the infrequency with which property was transferred to women but also the understanding of the will maker that the family property was entirely his. This particular county was chosen because records of wills are available from the early period of settlement and a comparison can therefore be made between inheritance practices when land was relatively plentiful and when it became more scarce. For the purposes of this study it would have been preferable to use data from a county more oriented toward wheat production, but since such counties were settled later, the changes in inheritance practices over a fairly long period of time (i.e., from mid-century when data are available to the end of the century) also reflected changes in legislation regarding women's property rights. While the changes in inheritance are significant in indicating the relative strength of patriarchal control as the economy became more industrialized and laws changed, at this point I want to focus on patriarchal control of all forms of property before legislative changes occurred.

Although Stormont, Dundas, and Glengarry County did not generate the wealth typical of wheat-exporting counties farther west, the economy in the early period relied heavily on timber exports and later was strongly influenced by the staple-exporting trade of other sections of the province.[16] To establish the validity of using information from this county as an indication of the general nature of female inheritance in the first half of the nineteenth century, I have also examined the wills of a wheat staple-exporting county, Wellington, for comparison. . . . Since the inheritance pattern in Wellington County indicates that men there were no more generous in their distribution of property to the women in their families, it is fairly reasonable to assume that the infrequency with which property was transferred to women in Stormont, Dundas, and Glengarry was not atypical.

Wives' Inheritance

In 1801 the Surrogate Court for the Eastern District of Ontario received a petition from Mary Links for permission to administer the estate of her husband, Matthew, who had died intestate. The inventory of his property indicates that not only were all the farm stock and implements considered to be his possessions but all of the household items as well. Since these items are usually the tools of women's labour, their express ownership by the husband is noteworthy. Included in the inventory were the following: '1 collender, half a dusen of knives and forkes, 1 dusen of spunes, 1 candle stick and snuffer, 2 chairs, 3 tin canasters, 1 cuking glass, 1 frying pan, 1 dresser, 3 tin tumblers'.[17] This inventory was not an isolated instance. In most cases men did not leave wills, so the court, usually after petition from a relative, would assign someone to be an administrator of the estate and would order an inventory of property to be taken. The inventories overwhelmingly indicate that household utensils, furniture, and linens were the property of the husband.

Widows were legally able to own property, but inheritance practices were such that males exerted considerable control over their wives after their deaths. Only in rare circumstances in the first half of the nineteenth century was a woman given total control over her husband's property when he died. In the wills of males in Stormont, Dundas, and Glengarry County, Ontario, for the two periods studied, women inherited their husband's property outright in only 6 to 8 per cent of the cases (Table 6.1). Women appear to have been given complete control of the property to dispose of without restriction only when there were no children of the husband living. But generally even if there were no children, directions were explicit about what should be done with the property after the wife's death.

Frequently, the wife was given the use of the property for her lifetime, with instructions for further inheritance clearly laid out. In the early nineteenth century this was a much more common practice than later. In Stormont, Dundas, and Glengarry about one-third of the wills from 1800 to 1811 stipulated that the wife should have the estate for her lifetime. By mid-century the proportion had dropped to one-sixth.

Even when wives were left the right to the estate for life, there were many restrictions laid out. Some men were quite specific about what the wife could do with the land, including instructions about whether or not she could cut

Table 6.1 Bequests to Wives in Wills by Males,* Stormont, Dundas, and Glengarry, Ontario, 1800–11 and 1850–58 (%)

	1800–11		1850–58	
Wife inherits outright	8		6	
Wife granted usufruct	30		16	
Children inherit major portion	46		55	
(a) son to support mother		14		19
(b) wife inherits portion		32		35
No mention of wife	16		23	
Wife disinherits upon remarriage	30		35	

*There was one woman who died with a will in the 1800–11 period and three with wills in the 1850–58 period.

Sample size: 1800–11 = 37; 1850–58 = 31.

Source: Public Archives of Ontario, Wills Collection, GS 1-1251; GS 1-1253.

timber. But the most restrictive practice was the tendency for husbands to tie their wife's use of the property to what they felt was the appropriate way for her to live the rest of her life. It was fairly common practice for men to deprive their wives of the right to inheritance if they should remarry. For example, one farmer left his wife the management of the income from the farm for as long as she remained his widow:

> In case my wife should remarry then in that case my executors herein after named and whom I also appropriate as Trustees for my children shall then take the sole management of the said farms and stock and rent or let the same or shares as they see fit and apply the said income to the benefit of my children whom they shall take the management of and see them educated and placed in such situation as said income will admit of and to give my widow a cow and four sheep with a bed and bedding and for her to have no more to say of my affairs. But if she remain my widow and so continues after the children are all educated and of age she shall still have during her natural life the one-half of the income of the said farm on which we at present reside.[18]

Roughly a third of the wills made by men in Stormont, Dundas, and Glengarry during the first half of the nineteenth century specifically limited wives' inheritance to the period they remained widows. This practice appears to have been widespread throughout Ontario, although in counties farther west the proportion of wills which explicitly forbid remarriage by mid-century was somewhat smaller.[19]

While the threat of disinheritance undoubtedly gave women few options for the future, they did have some choice over whether they would adhere to their husbands' wishes that they not remarry. But some husbands even went so far as to stipulate that their wives would lose all property rights if they cohabited.[20] Over the issue of the guardianship of children, the husband's will was paramount. Women had no legal right to the guardianship of their children, either while the husband lived or when he died, and when he died he was entitled to designate anyone he chose as guardian.[21] Usually the mother was named as guardian, but it was not at all uncommon for the oldest son or some other male relative to be put in control of the younger children, should the wife remarry. George Crites's instructions in his will of 1804 is typical of caveats found in many wills. 'If my widow should marry I hereby obligate my said son George to bring up and maintain the rest of my children that are not able to do for themselves and use the best endeavour to see them instructed in reading and writing.'[22] Considering that his wife, upon remarriage, was to be disallowed the produce of the land and stock, the furniture, and the third part of the land which her husband had left her for life, her ability to care for these children would have been severely limited. The point remains that even if she had wished to, or if a new husband were prepared to assume responsibility for their maintenance, she would not have been permitted legally to assume this responsibility.

The issue of dower rights is particularly interesting with regard to a widow's claim to her husband's property. In theory a woman was to receive one-third of her husband's real and personal property upon his death, unless he designated in his will that her portion be larger. In practice this was less strict than the law would indicate. Dower clearly did not mean that a woman would inherit one-third of the estate outright. As mentioned earlier, it was usual for a man to stipulate who would receive his property after his wife died, even if she was to have control of it during her lifetime. The exceptions to this practice are so rare that they are remarkable in themselves. For example, although Donald Fraser left his land to his grandson, his wife was given use of the household furniture, stock, and farming implements for her life. Her husband, in addition, permitted her to dispose of this property after her death 'as she may think proper amongst her children with the consent of the majority of the executors'.[23] Alexander McGruner did not leave his estate to his wife for her life but trusted her judgment to a degree which was extraordinary for his time and circumstances. McGruner willed that his land be divided among his male children and that 'the dividing of the same to my said children be according to the judgment and discretion of my wife as she may think and see most suitable when said children come of age'. He also permitted his wife to take what she would need when the lands were divided 'and arrangements should take place so that as my widow she may not be dependent in her advanced age'.[24]

It was rare for a husband to be concerned about his wife's dependency as she aged. Generally the husband ensured that his wife would be dependent upon her children through the conditions of his will. In a substantial number of the wills a son was specifically ordered to support his mother. One man, in a will which was not at all uncommon, left instructions for the care of his wife. The two sons were to share all of his property

> except the lower front room in the home which I have for the use of my wife Catherine as long as she is my widow and likewise she is to have a decent maintenance of the place suitable to her condition. But if she will marry she shall have what property she brought to my home and no more, neither will she have any title to hire, rent, or let the room to any other person or persons but for her own use only, then to be the property of my sons aforesaid.[25]

Generally the wills did not describe in detail how the wife would be maintained. Rather, sons were simply instructed to maintain their mother for life or as long as she remained a widow. In some cases it was specified that the support be 'in a kind, comfortable and respectable manner' or suitable to her sex and station in life.[26]

Clearly the conditions of dower could be satisfied without specifically settling how much a widow would receive. And whatever protection dower gave a woman, it did not extend beyond her widowhood. The vague stipulation that the wife should be provided for by the heirs of the estate increased from 14 per cent of the wills in the beginning of the century to almost one-fifth by mid-century. This practice could be a reflection of the general tendency for estates to be settled on one son as land became more scarce and farm sizes decreased.[27]

The effect of making women so dependent on their sons could create real hardship and loss of position. Frances Stewart described her widowhood as a period of extreme dependency where she was never 'allowed . . . to think or act but as . . . guided or directed'.[28] While widows may have appeared to have exchanged dependency on their husbands for dependency on their sons, the loss of position in the family could drastically change their real circumstances. Susanna Moodie claimed that in some families, especially those newly in the middle class, a widow was little more than a drudge:

> the mother, if left in poor circumstances, almost invariably holds a subordinate position in her wealthy son's or daughter's family. She superintends the servants, and nurses the younger children; and her time is occupied by a number of minute domestic labours, that allow her very little rest in her old age. I have seen the grandmother in a wealthy family ironing the fine linen or broiling over the cook-stove while her daughter held her place in the drawing room.[29]

In these circumstances the women rarely had any alternative but to submit to the conditions in their children's households.[30]

The most common inheritance practice and one reflected in about a third of the wills studied was for the wife to inherit for her lifetime a portion of the estate, with the bulk to go to the children. If the farmer was relatively wealthy her inheritance would include land, but if the farm was small the usual practice was for one son to inherit the land, with the mother receiving the produce from a specific portion of it. John Munro was a wealthy farmer who willed that his wife be supported from the income from the property and be given the use of the house until her son married. When the son married he was to repair another house on the property for his mother's use, but if she decided to live with any of her children she was to continue to receive the same allowance from the estate 'in order to compensate them for her support'. While John Munro envisaged this income from the estate as ultimately belonging to whoever cared for his wife, he urged his children to give their mother enough so that 'she may have what will be sufficient to keep her comfortable during her lifetime'. John Munro obviously felt somewhat guilty about his treatment of his wife and explained why she was not given control over his will: 'I should have appointed her executrix, but being sensible of her disposition I conceived it dangerous to the interest of the family.'[31]

Occasionally the will stipulated that the wife's share was to be in lieu of dower. In a few cases there appears to have been a conscious effort to see that the wife's one-third interest was actually what she received. But for the most part the wife's rightful and legal claim seems not to have been an issue. The fact that very few women made wills and none, during the periods examined, contested the wills of their husbands indicates the lack of control women had over property.[32] Women's main security in property rights was their husbands' sense of duty to provide for them after they died.

Daughters' Inheritance

Patriarchal control placed sons and daughters on significantly different footings as labourers in the family economy. The labour of sons was more likely to result in a substantial share of the father's assets than the labour of daughters. In an economy where labour was scarce and land relatively plentiful, the ability of the father to retain the labour of his children often was crucial to the success or failure of the family enterprise.[33] The father was frequently able to assure his labour supply through the promise of land transference to his sons. When there were sons and daughters in the family, the daughters seldom shared equally in the distribution of the family property when the father died (Table 6.2). This could be a reflection of the greater value placed on the labour of male children and the desire to retain these services as long as possible, or it could reflect the social and legal restrictions which would have meant that any part of the estate left to a daughter would ultimately have

Table 6.2 Bequests to Daughters in Wills by Males,* Stormont, Dundas, and Glengarry, Ontario, 1800–11 and 1850–58 (%)

	1800–11	1850–58
Daughters not mentioned	38	25
Daughters left all	3	3.5
Daughters inherit equally	8	14
Daughters given lesser portion of land	22	3.5
Daughters paid small sum; given chattels, personal property, furniture; or to be maintained by brother	30	54

*There was one woman who died with a will in the 1800–11 period and three with wills in the 1850–58 period.

Sample size: 1800–11 = 37; 1850–58 = 31.

Source: Public Archives of Ontario, Wills Collection, GS 1-1251; GS 1-1253.

been controlled by her husband. Most likely both these factors influenced a father's decision to exclude his daughters from a substantial share of his estate. The sexual division of labour whereby females tended to work most often at tasks associated with family subsistence and household maintenance would undoubtedly have made the daughter's labour appear less valuable to the farmer than the labour of sons, who would be more associated with labour directed toward the market.

The division of property among sons took a variety of forms. Sometimes it was given to the oldest son outright, but more frequently it was divided among the sons in a way so that each would have some property.[34] While the more or less equal division of land among sons was fairly common in the early part of the nineteenth century, the effect of this sort of property transfer over time, coupled with land scarcity in certain areas, meant that smaller and smaller parcels of land were being transferred. In order to pass on enough land to ensure an adequate 'man/land' ratio, repeated subdivisions of land had to be avoided.[35]

To this end a type of land transfer known as the 'English-Canadian' system of inheritance developed.[36] In this system the bulk of the estate would be passed on to a single son, usually the oldest, and he in turn was obliged to settle certain amounts on other children in the family. Sometimes though, the younger sons were given lesser amounts of land and the principal inheritor was obliged only to provide the daughters with some amount specified in the will. Generally the daughters did not fare well regardless of the system of inheritance. In 1803, Adam Johnston of Cornwall, Ontario, left his sons equal shares of his 400-acre estate. His daughters Nancy, Margaret, Janet, Jane, and Mary-Ann were to be given 'one shilling if demanded'.[37] While this appears to have been a particularly spiteful way to single out daughters in a will, this may not have been the intention. In a large proportion of the wills daughters were not mentioned at all.[38] But sometimes their omission is explained by the father as a consequence of their having already received what he thought appropriate.[39] The usual practice was for a father to settle some form of property or money on a daughter as her dowry when she married. Sons who inherited the bulk of the estate were frequently instructed to maintain their sisters until they were married, at which time they were to be given a cow or some sheep, sometimes with a little money as well.

The majority of wills either did not mention daughters or specified a legacy which was a small sum of money, some personal property, a portion of the family furniture when the mother died, or a cow, pig, or sheep.[40] In the early part of the century almost a third of the wills left some portion of the land to daughters. Generally this consisted of a small part of the total estate, with the major part going to the male heirs. But by mid-century, no doubt because of the scarcity of land in the district, the practice of leaving any land at all to daughters was drastically reduced. While over one-fifth of the wills in the early period left daughters a small parcel of land from the estate, by mid-century this was reduced to less than 5 per cent.

The striking feature of the wills is the extent to which it is assumed that daughters would be totally dependent on a male, either a brother or a husband, for support. The few exceptions to this practice are interesting for what they indicate about women's work. Duncan McDonald, for example, wanted to ensure that his wife and daughters would have some source of income for themselves. In his will, although he left everything to his son with the usual caveat that he provide the women with 'sufficient fuel, provisions and other necessaries usual with their sex and station', the son was further instructed to see that each daughter receive one cow and one fatted hog each year to dispose of as she wished. He also specified that 'the females [are] to have all poultry and the produce as their sole property'.[41]

A female had little recourse in law if she felt that her inheritance was an unfair reflection of her contribution to the family economy. Craven's study gives the example of one woman who had lived and cared for her father for years under the assumption that she would inherit from him when he died. Her suit for recompense for her labour was not found in her favour because, as the judge commented, 'this young woman could not be living anywhere else more properly than with her aged and infirm parent; and if she did acts of service, instead of living idly, it is no more than she ought to have done in return for her clothes and board, to say nothing of the claims of natural affection which usually lead children to render such services.'[42]

Ownership

The concentration of ownership of the means of production in the household by males meant that women's labour throughout their lives would be subject, either directly or indirectly, to male power and authority. No part of their productive activity could escape the potential power of male domination. In this respect the issue of ownership of property in the family economy is considerably more all-encompassing than the power over labour exercised by capitalist ownership. The capitalist employer exercised control over the labour purchased, but the subsistence production of the wage worker in the family economy was distinct, separate, and beyond the employer's control. In the family economy the means of production and the means of subsistence were inseparable: women had no productive sphere beyond the power of male authority. Although the effects of patriarchal productive relations were often obscured by the close personal relationships and the interdependence of family members in the family economy, and while the degree of oppressive male dominance undoubtedly varied from household to household, the general effect of male ownership was to exercise control over female labour. . . . In this section the intention has been to establish women's alienation from the system of ownership. As daughters, wives, mothers, and widows, they were dependent on the will of fathers, husbands, sons, and brothers.

In the transference of property the tenuous claim women had on the means of production was most obvious. Susanna Moodie's comment that 'death is looked upon by many Canadians more as a matter of business, and change of property into other hands, than as a real domestic calamity'[43] is something of a mystery to historians who feel that, considering what happened when property changed hands, there was a domestic calamity.[44] Many women certainly experienced real grief when a father or a husband died, but their relationship to property was likely to change little. Perhaps Susanna Moodie was thinking less of the sentiments of widows than of children when she spoke of their calm anticipation of a relative's death. For sons with a prospect of inheritance it could not have been calamitous. For daughters, whatever change in property occurred was likely to affect them to a small degree. If any property was settled on them, it would be more likely to occur when they married than when their father died.

A widow's position was considerably more precarious. While there was a possibility of increased control of property through the provisions of the husband's will, there was also the more likely possibility that her situation would deteriorate if the terms of the will made her dependent on her children. In another respect Susanna Moodie's analysis is apt for the wife as well as for the children. For the most part the intention of men's wills appears to have been that wives would maintain essentially the same position relative to property that they held while the husband was alive.

Notes

1. In the major study on labour in Canadian agriculture there is a brief reference to the labour of unpaid family workers, but for the most part the author chooses to see farm units which did not hire labour as being 'owner-operated', and refers only to the labour performed by the male owner. George Haythorne, *Labour in Canadian Agriculture* (Cambridge, MA: Harvard University Press, 1960).
2. Oscar Lange, *Political Economy,* Vol. I, trans. A.H. Walker (Oxford: Pergamon Press, 1963), 16–17.
3. James A. Henretta, 'Families and Farms: Mentalité in Pre-industrial America', *William and Mary Quarterly* 35 (Jan. 1978): 21.
4. Max Hedley, in his studies of family farms in twentieth-century western Canada, points to the inequalities in productive relations which are concealed by the term 'family farm'. He says: 'we need to recognize that while there is private ownership of the means of production by an individual who applies his own labour to the productive process, there is also a considerable amount of labour by non-owners of the means of production. The commodities produced by this labour do not belong to the actual producer but to the owners of the means of production; therefore, any surplus labour embodied in them is in effect expropriated.' Max Hedley, 'Relations of Production of the "Family Farm": Canadian Prairies', *Journal of Peasant Studies* 9 (1981): 74.
5. *Redmond v. Redmond* (1868), 1 *Upper Canada Queen's Bench Reports* 220, cited by Paul Craven, 'The Law of Master and Servant in Mid-nineteenth-century Ontario', in *Essays in the History of Canadian Law,* Vol. I, ed. David H. Flaherty (Toronto: Osgoode Society, 1981), 177.
6. Margaret E. MacLellan, 'History of Women's Rights in Canada', in *The Cultural Tradition and Political History of Women in Canada*, Royal Commission on the Status of Women in Canada, No. 8, p. 1.
7. Linda Silver Dranoff, *Women in Canadian Life: Law* (Toronto: Fitzhenry & Whiteside, 1977), 26.
8. Constance B. Backhouse, 'Shifting Patterns in Nineteenth-century Canadian Custody Law', in *Essays in the History of Canadian Law*, ed. David H. Flaherty, 212–48.
9. Ibid., 213.
10. Constance B. Backhouse, 'Married Women's Property Law in Nineteenth-century Canada', unpublished paper (Apr. 1987).
11. Sheila Kieran, *The Family Matters: Two Centuries of Family Law and Life in Ontario* (Toronto: Key Porter, 1986), 51.
12. For a full discussion of the specifics of the law and how it was subsequently interpreted by the courts, see Backhouse, 'Married Women's Property Law in Nineteenth-century Canada'.
13. Similar acts permitting married women to own and control property were passed by other provinces in the following years: British Columbia, 1873; Manitoba, 1875; Newfoundland, 1876; Nova Scotia, 1884; Northwest Territories, 1886; New Brunswick, 1896; Prince Edward Island, 1896; Saskatchewan, 1907; Alberta, 1922. MacLellan, 'Women's Rights', 4.
14. National Council of Women of Canada, *Women of Canada: Their Life and Work*, ed. Isabel Aberdeen (Ottawa: Queen's Printer, 1900), 39.
15. Bruce S. Elliott correctly points out the dangers in looking only at wills for inheritance patterns. They tend to be more representative of the wealthy than the poor, the old rather than the young, and the sick rather than the healthy. 'Sources of Bias in Nineteenth-century Ontario Wills', *Histoire sociale/Social History* 17, 35 (May 1985).
16. For information on the significance of this area as a supplier of waged labour in the timber camps on the Ottawa [River] see Arthur R.M. Lower, *Great Britain's Woodyard: British America and the Timber Trade, 1763–1867* (Montreal: McGill-Queen's University Press, 1973), 188; also, for the effect of increased immigration to more westerly points of [the] province on income generating activities in Dundas, see James Croil, *Dundas; or, A Sketch of Canadian History* (Montreal: B. Dawson & Son, 1861), 152.
17. Public Archives of Ontario [hereafter PAO], Wills Collection [hereafter WC], GS 1-1251, Mary Links, 1801.

18. PAO, WC, GS 1-1253, William Cassidy, 1853.
19. See . . . David Gagan, *Hopeful Travellers: Families, Land, and Social Change in Mid-Victorian Peel County, Canada West* (Toronto: University of Toronto Press, 1981), 55.
20. PAO, WC, GS 1-1253, Hugh Shaw, 1853.
21. The right of married women to guardianship of their children was introduced in provincial statutes from 1910 to 1923. MacLellan, 'Women's Rights', 5.
22. PAO, WC, GS 1-1251, George Crites, 1804.
23. PAO, WC, GS 1-1253, Donald Fraser, 1853.
24. PAO, WC, GS 1-1253, Alexander McGruner, 1857.
25. PAO, WC, GS 1-1251, John Saver, 1811.
26. PAO, WC, GS 1-1253, Adam Cockburn, 1854; PAO, WC, GS 1-1264, Robert Valance, 1890.
27. Gagan, *Hopeful Travellers*, Ch. 3.
28. E.S. Dunlop, ed. *Our Forest Home: Being Extracts from the Correspondence of the Late Frances Stewart* (Toronto, 1889), 80–1.
29. Susanna Moodie, *Life in the Clearings vs. the Bush* (New York: DeWitt & Davenport, 1855), 291–2.
30. Moodie seemed to see this as a matter of will more than of necessity, saying 'they submit with great apparent cheerfulness, and seem to think it necessary to work for the shelter of a child's roof, and the bread they eat'. Ibid., 292.
31. PAO, WC, GS 1-1251, John Munro, 1800.
32. Women were given the right to dispose of property by testament in Ontario in 1801. Susan Altschul and Christine Carron, 'Chronology of Legal Landmarks in the History of Canadian Women', *McGill Law Journal* 21 (Winter 1975): 476.
33. Gagan, *Hopeful Travellers*, 44; Folbre, 'Patriarchy', 6; see also Lawrence Stone, 'The Rise of the Nuclear Family in Early Modern England: The Patriarchal State', in *The Family in History*, ed. Charles E. Rosenberg (Philadelphia: University of Pennsylvania Press, 1975), 13–57, for a discussion of inheritance as a means of strengthening patriarchy.
34. Herbert J. Mays, in a study of the settlement of Gore near Toronto, has shown that acquiring land through inheritance, rather than direct sales, became increasingly significant for males by mid-century as land became more scarce and the population aged. '"A Place to Stand": Families, Land and Permanence in Toronto Gore Township, 1820–1890', *Historical Papers* (1980): 185–211.
35. Gagan, *Hopeful Travellers*, 50.
36. A.R.M. Lower, *Canadians in the Making: A Social History of Canada* (Toronto: Longmans, Green & Company, 1958), 336.
37. PAO, WC, GS 1-1251, Adam Johnston, 1803.
38. From 1800 to 1811 in Stormont, Dundas, and Glengarry County, 38 per cent of the wills filed did not leave a bequest to daughters. In some of these families there may have been no daughters, but still the percentage is high. By 1850–58 the proportion had dropped to 25 per cent.
39. PAO, WC, GS 1-1264, John McKercher, 1890.
40. In the early part of the century this accounted for more than two-thirds of all wills. By mid-century almost four-fifths of the wills either neglected daughters altogether or gave them only very small bequests.
41. PAO, WC, GS 1-1253, Duncan McDonald, 1850.
42. *Sprague and Wife v. Nickerson* (1844), 1 *Upper Canada Queen's Bench Reports* 284, cited by Craven, 'The Law of Master and Servant', 177.
43. Moodie, *Life in the Clearings*, 138.
44. Rosemary R. Ball, '"A Perfect Farmer's Wife": Women in 19th Century Rural Ontario', *Canada: An Historical Magazine* 3 (Dec. 1975): 16; Gagan, *Hopeful Travellers*, 50–1.

Section 3 Industrial Capitalism: The Rise of Breadwinner–Homemaker Families

There are long-standing debates among sociologists about the impact of industrial capitalism on working-class families. Influential early arguments held that the process whereby families lost their ability to support themselves—most commonly, when peasants and family farmers lost their land—produced a breakdown of traditional family patterns. The erosion of a 'family economy' meant the breakup of families as working groups. The need for wages meant migration in search of work and the separation of individuals from their kinship networks and village communities, and often the separation of husbands and wives. Meanwhile, early industrial capitalists relying on cheap labour often hired women and children to work in their factories. Thus, economic partnerships of husbands and wives, and supervision of children's work by parents, gave way to the abuses and exploitation characteristic of early factories. The daily stress and struggle associated with poverty put additional strains on spousal relationships at a time when husbands and wives were negotiating their new circumstances. Historical evidence indicates that husbands' violence against their wives and men's abandonment of women and children were not rare events in urban, working-class families.

Family and industrial work were not entirely at odds for the working class in the nineteenth century, however. Family was not just altered in the profound changes associated with industrialization; as well, much about family shaped the industrialization of work. Sonya Rose's research (reported in Limited Livelihoods*) shows that the gendered* *relations of authority and divisions of work characteristic of patriarchal household production served as the model that factory owners adopted as they organized their workplaces: men supervised women and children, skilled work (and the training for it) was reserved for men and boys, machinery was built for one sex or the other, and men earned higher wages than women. Some early industrialists even adopted a paternalistic strategy of management to undermine worker resistance to the exploitation inherent in their situation.*

Moreover, even though old patterns were unsettled, nuclear families persisted, and usually retained their hold on their members: for example, daughters often delayed their marriages because their parents needed the earnings they brought home. Because working-class men were unable to earn wages sufficient to support a family, the earnings of sons and daughters, and the shopping, cooking, budgeting, and other domestic skills of housewives, were critical to the livelihood of families. Moreover, kinship networks were important during the nineteenth century, as extended-family members played a vital role in people's migration to factory towns and their survival strategies once there. Not only was family and kinship central to working-class livelihood but the authority of male household heads was undermined in an economy where men were both 'wage slaves' and inadequate providers, and their children earned money essential to the household. Family members were dependent on each other for survival, and in a way that undermined patriarchy (i.e., men's household authority).

Skilled male workers, however, struggled to protect their earnings and their jobs, in a context of rapid economic restructuring (in which capitalists used low-paid women workers to undermine their position). They campaigned for a 'family wage' which would enable them to support their wives and children. As an organized group, they also regularly took action to exclude women from 'skilled' and high-paying jobs. Thus, new notions of gender and family developed as working-class men responded to their position in the labour market.

At the same time, a middle class composed of businessmen, professional men and their families was developing. For the most successful people in this class—especially the capitalists able to build factories—work was moving outside the household, and thus the nature of the household was changing. In response, a gender ideology known as 'separate spheres' developed, which provided an explanation of the dramatically changed social landscape. The developing separation between public and private sectors was seen as mirroring differences between men and women, which were increasingly understood to be natural. Meanwhile, the emerging middle class embraced domesticity as an identity and moral code. The 'cult of domesticity' provided 'family men'—who were also profit-seeking capitalists—a positive identity in its equation of family with virtue and especially caring.

The three chapters that follow describe both working-class and middle-class experiences in the nineteenth century. The selection from Tamara Hareven's work discusses her research findings on how working-class families survived and adapted to the difficulties of dependence on waged work in nineteenth-century factories. The selections from the work of Nancy Cott and Maxine Margolis are about the middle class. Nancy Cott describes the domestic and gender ideals that developed in the nineteenth century which have had lasting influence. The chapter by Maxine Margolis describes the many changes that led to new ideas about domesticity and gender, especially new definitions of motherhood.

Chapter 7

In the 1970s, sociologist Tamara Hareven did extensive research on French Canadians who migrated to Manchester, New Hampshire, between 1880 and 1930 to work in a large textile mill located there. She found that kin served as an 'informal recruitment and hiring agency' that helped people migrate, find housing and jobs, and learn the skills essential to success in the mill. In fact, relatives often worked side by side in the mill—assisting each other in their work—and lived near each other in the town. The selection below describes the ongoing kinship support that occurred among relatives, as well as the sacrifices individuals made for the sake of their parents, children, and siblings.

Dynamics of Kin in an Industrial Community

Tamara K. Hareven

Kin Assistance in Critical Life Situations

The interdependence of kin in the factory was part of a larger role that kin fulfilled as the very source of security and assistance in all aspects of life. Within the family, relatives provided major support over the entire life course, both on a routine basis and in times of stress. Kin assistance was essential both in coping with the insecurities dictated by the industrial system, such as unemployment and strikes, and in coping with personal and family crises, especially death.

The basic axis of kin assistance, both in families living in nuclear households and in extended ones, was that of siblings with each other and parents with their children. Most mutual assistance among kin was carried out between brothers and sisters and between adult children and aging parents, even after they had left their common household. Older brothers and sisters were expected to care for their younger siblings as a matter of course, even to act as surrogate parents in the event of the death of a parent. Given the wide age spread of children within the family, it was not unusual for the oldest child to be about the age at which he or she could have been a parent of the youngest child.

Grandmothers and aging aunts cared for grandchildren and for nieces and nephews, without necessarily living in the same household. They also cooked meals, cleaned house, and mended clothes when a mother was working. Older female relatives assisted young women in childbirth and took care of the other children in the family while the mother was recovering. Relatives cared for each other during illness (at a time when people rarely stayed in hospitals). Relatives reared orphans, along with their own children, and also took in invalids and retarded family members. Male relatives helped each other in the repair and maintenance of their apartments or homes; when they owned farmland outside the city, they co-operated in planting and harvesting. They shared tools and implements, traded services and transportation.

As siblings left home and established their own households, modes of assistance in the nuclear family were broadened to include extended kin. In addition to this basic interaction of the core siblings and parents, nuclear families were enmeshed in larger kinship networks that often spanned two or three generations and were expanded through marriage. The distance of the relationship affected, of course, the intensity of the interactions. Instead of close involvement with child rearing, health care, and the collective work and maintenance of the household, assistance was of a more casual nature. The level of obligation varied depending on how closely kin were related. In times of crisis or in the absence of other sources of support, however, more distant kin often took on major responsibilities as well.

Even though nuclear families resided in separate households, they extended their reach beyond the household by sharing and exchanging resources and labour with their kin. Autonomous nuclear households drew their strength and support from extended kin. Living in proximity to one's kin was essential for survival, particularly in periods when transportation was difficult or when a shortage in housing occurred. Despite the predominance of the nuclear household, relatives opened up their homes to each other during periods of transition or need. Some newlywed couples initially lived either with their parents, usually the wife's parents, or with an older brother and sister. Couples often shared housing temporarily with relatives after their arrival in Manchester or during periods of scarcity. Generally, however, they adhered to the custom of separate residence of the nuclear family from extended kin. They lived near each other, often in the same building, separate but available in time of need.

The social space of the Simoneau family in Manchester illustrates the conscious effort of kin to reside near each other and the flexibility kin exercised in extending to each other temporary help with housing. When the oldest son first arrived to settle in Manchester in 1908, he lived in a boarding house. When his widowed father and younger siblings joined him two years later, the family lived in a tenement close to the mills. Shortly thereafter, they moved to the West Side of Manchester to be near other relatives. His father married a woman from his hometown who lived nearby in Manchester. She brought her niece, who had been living with her, into the household. The niece later married the oldest Simoneau son.[1]

As each of the Simoneau sons and daughters married, they set up separate residences within several blocks of their father's house. When only two unmarried teenage children remained, the father moved to the nearby village of Goffstown. Because commuting to work in the mill was difficult for the young daughter still living at home, she moved in with her married sister in Manchester. The father lived in Goffstown until his death, at which point the youngest son moved to Boston. The other siblings continued to live in proximity to each other. Two brothers and their wives shared housing temporarily, first during the 1922 strike, when a brother lost his home because of unemployment, and again after the shutdown of the Amoskeag, when another brother sold his home and moved to Nashua to seek work. Upon his return, he and his family moved in with the oldest brother for a limited period while looking for their own place to live.

The experience of people who had no relatives to assist them demonstrates the bitter price paid for isolation from kin. Lottie Sargent's father, for example, had no relatives in the city. After his wife died in childbirth, he took Lottie as a baby to bars and clubs, where the 'ladies of the night' kept an eye on her. Eventually, he placed her in the orphanage until he remarried; then he took her into his newly established household. Another example of the consequences of isolation from kin is provided by Cora Pellerin, who had no relatives in Manchester to take care of her two daughters. When both she and her husband were working in the mill, she had a housekeeper. But during her husband's prolonged illness, she had to place the children in the Villa Augustina, a Catholic boarding school. To both Cora and her daughters, it was a heart-rending experience:

> I had never been to a school with the nuns. It was hard for me to put them in there. It is a big, big building, and it seemed that it was

> just like a jail. That's the way I felt inside. I used to go and see them every Wednesday night, and they'd come home every Saturday. They'd have supper with me and leave every Sunday afternoon at four o'clock. If they didn't come, it was because they'd been bad and were being punished. I used to cry on my way home. I wiped my eyes before seeing my husband because if he'd notice it, he'd take the girls out. (*Amoskeag*: 211)

Even though a systematic measure for the consistency of kin assistance is not available, it is clear from the interviews that assistance from distantly related kin was frequent. The people interviewed were conscious of kinship ties that often included extended kin to whom one might be related through in-laws or cousins. Thus, in addition to the actual communication with kin, the mental kinship map, which was often reinforced by an elaborate genealogy, encompassed distantly related kin as well.

The fluidity and informality in the functions and roles of kin in Manchester was characteristic of the overall kinship structure in American society. Normatively defined in American culture, rather than legislated, the obligations among extended kin have always been flexible and voluntary (Parsons 1943: 22–8). The boundaries for extended kin were loosely defined, centering on the nuclear family as a focus. Goode characterizes kin in contemporary American society as 'ascriptive friends'. Kin are involved in mutual reciprocity as friends, but 'they may not intrude merely because they are relatives' (Goode 1963: 76):

> There is no great extension of the kin network. . . . Thus the couple cannot count on a large number of kinfolk for help. Just as these kin cannot call upon the couple for services. . . . Neither couple nor kinfolk have many *rights* with respect to the other, and so the reciprocal *obligations* are few. . . . the couple has few moral controls over their extended kin, and these have few controls over the couple. (italics in original; Goode 1963: 8)

As opposed to more generationally defined kinship systems in traditional agrarian societies, where the place of each member was more clearly determined within the kinship system and where obligations among kin were more rigidly legislated and defined, the extended kinship system in Manchester (and in the United States generally) was loosely defined. Kin relations and obligations revolved around individuals or the nuclear family.

In Quebec, children's opportunities and obligations were ranked in relation to inheritance practices,[2] whereas French Canadians in Manchester adopted a more flexible and voluntary system. However, they followed several basic implicit rules governing kin assistance, which also specified that nuclear-family members (and later parents and their adult children) were first in priority for assistance. Customarily, couples also drew a line between in-laws and their family of orientation. The closest kin connections followed a mother–daughter dyad—adult women were usually engaged in closer exchanges with their own mothers than with their mothers-in-law and drew explicit boundaries with their husbands' families.

This sequence of priorities usually led to a multi-layered pattern of kin interaction over the life course. As younger children grew up, older siblings helped them find jobs. They aided younger sisters, especially in preparing for marriage and in setting up households. In addition, they cared for aging parents and often continued to assist their siblings later in life. Older children thus were sometimes caught in a squeeze between helping younger siblings and caring for aging parents simultaneously. Marie Anne Senechal, for example, had no sooner finished rearing her younger siblings than she encountered the responsibility of caring for her aging father and continuing to aid her siblings in their adult years.

Within each family or kin group, one member, usually a woman, emerged as the 'kin keeper'. Larger networks had several kin keepers, but within a nuclear family, the task usually fell upon one member. Most commonly, the oldest daughter or one of the older daughters was cast in the role of kin keeper when a crisis arose, such as the death of the mother. Ora Pelletier viewed herself as a kin keeper (even though she was not the oldest daughter):

> But if they need me, if they have any trouble or you know they're in trouble or they're worried about something or if they need a recipe or something they always call me like if I was the mother . . . No matter what happens you know they will call me and ask me. Ask me for advice, or, 'Do you remember how Mom used to do this or that?' (interview with Ora Pelletier)

Kin keepers usually retained their role throughout their lives. Although needs and responsibilities changed, their centrality to the kin group as helpers, arbiters, and pacifiers continued over life and became even more pivotal with age. Kin keepers were at times designated by parents in advance or were thrust into that position by circumstances and by their skills and personalities. Given the wide age spread of children within the family, designating the oldest or middle children as kin keepers was an important strategy for large families.

Some kin keepers remained single because the responsibility of care extended and escalated as they grew older. They commanded greater authority among their siblings, nieces, and nephews and were in the centre of family communication. Kin keepers kept track of different family members who immigrated or who married and left town; they scheduled family reunions and celebrations of birthdays and anniversaries. When adult siblings were in conflict with each other, kin keepers tried to resolve the feud by acting as intermediaries.

Kin keeping thus carried with it prestige and respect, in addition to the many tasks and services. For a woman, in particular, this position also bestowed a power and influence she rarely held within her nuclear family, where the father was the source of authority and the final arbiter. But kin keeping was also confining and bestowed many obligations on the person so designated.

Marie Anne Senechal explained how she became a kin keeper. The oldest daughter, she was left at age 20 with 11 children, including two infants, when her mother died. She opposed her father's plan to place the non-working children in an orphanage, and along with her work in the mill, she took charge of them. Committed to rearing her siblings, Marie Anne allowed her sister, two years her junior, to get married, knowing that this decision sealed her own fate—the entire care of the home would be on her shoulders forever. 'It's my fault that my sister got married. I should have told her not to. She was 18, and she was the one who was taking care of the house. She asked for my advice, and I said, "Well, an old maid doesn't have a very good name.". . . I pushed my sister to get married.' But the sister's departure was not free of guilt. 'When she left with him [her husband], all of us were at the window; all the little kids. She never forgot our faces in the window. As long as she lived, she always said, "Marie Anne, why did I get married and leave you all by yourself?"' (*Amoskeag*: 280–1).

Florida Anger, the oldest daughter, helped with the rearing of her younger siblings even though both parents were alive. She and her sisters and brothers worked together in the mill, and her parents assigned her the task of making sure her siblings actually went to work and stayed with their jobs. She also helped at home with child rearing and housework. After they married, her younger sisters turned to her for assistance, especially during the illness and death of a child of one of her sisters. Throughout their adult lives, her brothers and sisters sought her help. She mediated the quarrels over the use of their father's insurance money and his car after his death and subsequently tried to reconcile her feuding siblings when petty conflicts arose.

How were the multiple patterns of kin assistance that extended over the entire life course and flowed back and forth across a wide geographic region enforced? Why did kin assist each other over long time periods? What prepared them to pay the high personal cost of self-sacrifice that often led to the postponement or denial of marriage for women?

The most eloquent explanation advanced for kin assistance has been the theory of exchange relations, which Michael Anderson employs in his study of nineteenth-century textile workers in Lancashire (1971). His emphasis on instrumental relationships is particularly relevant to this study. Using economic exchange theory, Anderson argues that the basis for kin assistance was exchange in services and in supports during critical life situations. The motives that led kin to help each other, he argues, were 'calculative': parents aided their children with the expectation of receiving assistance in old age; and more distant kin helped each other in the hope of receiving returns when they were in need. These calculative relationships were reinforced by strong societal norms dictating mutual obligations among relatives. Anderson thus sees kin assistance as a series of exchanges revolving around self-interest and reinforced by social norms.[3] Although the time period is different, the Manchester workers share several characteristics with Lancashire's labourers. In both communities, kin provided the almost exclusive source of assistance for a low-resource population with a high proportion of migrants. However, the interviews of former Manchester workers, which provide crucial information on their own perceptions of instrumental relationships, make it clear that certain aspects of kin assistance cannot be entirely explained by economic exchange theory.

In the context of Manchester, instrumental relationships fell into two categories: short-term routine exchanges in services and assistance in critical life situations and long-term investments in exchanges along the life course. In addition to those forms of assistance previously discussed, kin provided money on a short-term basis and traded skills, goods, and services. For example, mill workers supplied their relatives with cheap cloth and received farm products in exchange. Plumbers and masons traded services with each other, and storekeepers exchanged merchandise for medical or legal assistance from relatives.

Long-term investments were more demanding and less certain in their future returns, and the most pervasive exchange along the life course was that between parents and children—old-age support in return for child rearing. Under conditions of frequent migration, exchanges across the life course also occurred among aunts and uncles and their nieces and nephews, with the former frequently acting as surrogate parents for their newly arrived young relatives in Manchester. Such exchanges were horizontal as well as vertical. Horizontally, aunts and uncles were fulfilling obligations to or reciprocating the favours of brothers or sisters by taking care of their children; vertically, they were entering into exchange relationships with their nieces and nephews, who might assist them later in life. Godparents also represented long-term exchanges. Because godparents assumed obligations of future assistance to their godchildren, the people selecting them preferred relatives or non-relatives with resources.

Although the benefits of short-term exchanges are easily understandable, it is difficult to accept calculative motives as the exclusive base of long-term kin assistance, especially when the rewards were not easily visible. For example, those women who substantially delayed or even sacrificed an opportunity for marriage to fulfill their obligation to care for younger siblings or aging parents did so for no apparent reward. Men and women supported members of their nuclear families even when a more distant relative might have been a better long-term contributor to an exchange bargain. These forms of kin behaviour exceed benefits that could be measured by economic exchange.

Young family members who subordinated their own careers to family needs did so out of a sense of responsibility, affection, and familial obligation rather than with the expectation of eventual gain. Within this context, kin assistance was not strictly calculative. Rather, it expressed an overall principle of reciprocity over the life course. Reciprocity, as Julian Pitt-Rivers (1973) defines it,

> is undifferentiated in that it requires that a member of the group shall sacrifice himself for another, that kinsmen shall respect preferential rules of conduct toward one another regardless of their individual interests. Such reciprocity as there is comes from the fact that other kinsmen do likewise. Parents are expected to sacrifice themselves for their children but they also expect that their children will do the same for theirs. The reciprocity alternates down the chain of generations, assuming that the grand parental generation will be repaid in the persons of the grandchildren. (101)

The sense of duty to family was a manifestation of family culture—a set of values that entailed not only a commitment to the well-being and self-reliance or survival of the family but one that took priority over individual needs and personal happiness. The preservation of family autonomy was valued as a more important goal than individual fulfillment. Family autonomy, essential for self-respect and good standing in the neighbourhood and the community, was one of the most deeply ingrained values: it dictated that assistance be sought among kin. Few of the people interviewed turned for help to the church, ethnic mutual-aid associations, public welfare, or charity. (It must be remembered that given the stigma attached to receiving charity, many may not have admitted they were aided in this manner.) The first significant acceptance of public welfare occurred in the 1930s when workers turned to the Federal Emergency Relief Administration and the Works Progress Administration after enduring weeks of unemployment and the subsequent shutdown of the mills.

In a regime of insecurity, where kin assistance was the only continuing source of support, family culture by necessity dictated that family considerations, needs, and ties guide or control most individual decisions. Collective family needs were not always congruent with individual preferences. Migrating to Manchester, locating jobs and housing, and conversely leaving the mills and returning to Canada were all embedded in family strategies rather than in individual preferences.

At times, such family decisions ignored individual feelings to a degree that would seem callous from the vantage point of our times; Mary Dancause, for example, was at age four sent back by her parents to live with relatives in Quebec when she had an eye disease. When she reached age 12, her parents uprooted her from a loving environment in Quebec to bring her back to Manchester to take care of younger siblings. She recalled her bitterness and loneliness: 'I was so lonesome, I cried so much, you won't believe it. My mother would be working in the kitchen and I would be talking to myself: "I want to go back, I want to go back"' (interview with Mary Dancause).

Her older brother, who had also been left behind but who was not summoned back, decided to strike out on his own for Manchester. When he knocked on his parents' door, his father did not recognize him. 'There was a knock at the back door. "We don't want anything", Father said, and he banged the door. So my brother went around to the front. He rang the bell, and my father said, "It's you again." Brother said, "Wait a minute, can I talk to you?" He told him, "I'm your son"' (*Amoskeag*: 51).

Both career choices and economic decisions were made within the family matrix. Families might be described as being composed of units that were switched around as the need arose. Each unit was relied upon and used when appropriate. Following such strategies, families timed the movement of members in response to both individual schedules and external conditions. Family strategies revolved around a variety of decisions: when to migrate, when to return, when those who were left behind should rejoin the family in Manchester, who should be sent to explore other working opportunities, who should be encouraged to marry, and who should be pressured to stay at home.

The subordination of individual needs to family decisions did not always take place without conflict. Many interviewees who had made personal sacrifices expressed long-repressed anger and pain during the interview. Anna Fregau Douville, for example, as the last child of working age who could support her parents, left school and started working at age 14 and postponed her own marriage. When Anna finally announced she was going to get married, her sisters pressured her to cancel her engagement, claiming that her fiancé was a drunkard. Actually, 'they were scheming to get me to support my folks until they died. . . . But my mother told me, "Anna, don't wait too long. What if I die or your father dies? Then you'd insist on staying with me, and you'll lose your boyfriend."' She got married and lived two houses away from her parents. Although Anna was determined to live her life independently of her family, she was never quite free of guilt. Having grown up in a large family where she experienced first-hand the pressures imposed by kin, Anna subsequently set strict boundaries with her husband's family immediately following her marriage: she refused to pay her mother-in-law's debts and made it clear to her husband and her in-laws that they could not rely on her to compensate for their extravagances:

> I put my foot down the first year that I got married. . . . When his parents used to come and visit me and ask to borrow money . . . I said, 'Listen, I don't go down to your house to bother you. I'm happy with my husband and get the hell out. Don't ever come here and try to borrow anything from him or from me.' . . . My husband agreed with me. He said, 'I'm glad that you can open up with them. I couldn't talk that way to my own family.' (*Amoskeag*: 291)

Interestingly, despite her resentment of extended family obligations and her own bitterness toward her siblings, Anna Douville kept the most complete family albums and follows the traditional Quebec custom of maintaining a family genealogy. Her personal resentment of the intrusions of kin into her own privacy was divorced from her ideological commitment to keeping a complete family record for posterity.

Anna's refusal to provide assistance to her husband's family represented a common pattern among women who had been deeply enmeshed in responsibilities with their own kin. Once they married, they refused involvement with their husbands' relatives to avoid taking on new obligations, having just emerged from their own families' burdens. Cora Pellerin, for example, postponed her marriage until the death of her fiancé's ailing mother rather than join his household and take on the responsibility of caring for her. When she married, Cora closed her home to her husband's older sister. She allowed her housekeeper to give her husband's sister an occasional meal, but she did not admit her as a regular member of the household even though her sister-in-law could have acted as a babysitter and a housekeeper. Eventually, her sister-in-law moved to a convent (interview with Cora Pellerin).

Marie Anne Senechal, who spent most of her life rearing her own siblings and finally married when she was in her sixties, drew a firm line with her husband's sister. Even though she allowed her own siblings to live in her house, she would not tolerate her sister-in-law. Marie Anne drove her out of the house, finally, after provoking a quarrel. Ora Pelletier, whose six older sisters worked in the mills, was ostracized by her siblings ever since she cashed in their father's insurance policy after his death and used the money for her own needs. She felt entitled to the money because she was the last remaining daughter at home and had taken care of her father until his death. Alice Olivier still resented being sent to work in the mill at age 14 while her two brothers were sent to the seminary at Trois-Rivières in Canada. At age 60, she returned to high school to fulfill her old dream of an education. The interview took place just at the point when she was about to graduate from high school. After all these years she finally confronted her mother, asking her why she had sent her to work instead of letting her stay in school (*Amoskeag*: 268–9).

And Marie Anne Senechal, who defended her lifelong sacrifices for her family without any aura of martyrdom, finally wiped away a tear at the end of the interview and said: 'I thought I'd never marry. I was 67 years old when I got married. . . . It was too much of a wait, when I think of it now, because I would have been happier if I'd got married. . . . I knew I wasn't living my own life, but I couldn't make up my mind'. . . (*Amoskeag*: 281–2).

Migration and the Continuity of the Kinship System

Although historians and sociologists have long recognized the importance of kin in communities of destination in facilitating migration and settlement, less attention has been paid to the role of relatives remaining in the communities of origin. Kin who remained in Quebec fulfilled a crucial function in providing backup assistance and security for the migrating family. Availability of continued support in the community of origin was therefore an essential consideration in the decision to migrate.

The networks of relatives, besides serving as important backups, also enabled workers to experiment with different employment opportunities, to send their sons to scout for better jobs, and to marry off their daughters. 'Long-distance' kin, like those nearby, were sources of security and assurance in times of crisis and often served as a refuge. Some people who worked until their later years of life retired to their villages of origin. Some unmarried pregnant women, for whom life in Manchester was unbearable because of shame and social pressure, went to live in convents in Quebec until their children were born and then either remained there or returned to work in Manchester. Some parents left young children with relatives in Quebec until they found jobs and housing in Manchester. Others sent sick children back to Quebec to recuperate with relatives.

This interaction between immigrants in Manchester and their kin in Quebec leads to a revision of existing models of the territoriality of kin. Most recent historical studies of kinship in the industrial environment have focused on geographic proximity as the chief measure of kin interaction. Elizabeth Bott's (1957) model of urban networks emphasizes residence in the same neighbourhood as the most salient feature of kin interaction.[4] Although the Manchester data offer important examples of the interconnectedness of kin with neighbourhood, which is central to Bott's model, they also reflect kin as mobile units transcending the specific boundaries of one neighbourhood or community.

Manchester's French-Canadian textile workers had many of the same characteristics listed by Bott as generally conducive to the formation of strong kinship networks: neighbourhood proximity; similarity in work (particularly where one industry dominates the local employment market), occupational status, and migration patterns; and lack of opportunity for social mobility. Despite their common characteristics, the Amoskeag's French-Canadian workers differed considerably from London's East Enders in their interaction with kin. The Manchester study reveals that strong ties over several generations can still be maintained under conditions of kin dispersion.

In Manchester, as in mid-nineteenth-century and twentieth-century East London or Preston, kinship networks were embedded in the city's neighbourhoods. But the social space of French-Canadian kin extended from Quebec to Manchester and spread over New England's industrial map. French-Canadian kinship behaviour in Manchester thus demonstrates the importance of intensive kin networks in one's immediate neighbourhood and workplace, as well as persistence of distant kinship ties laced through a larger geographic region.[5] Geographic distance did not disrupt basic modes of kin co-operation but led, rather, to a revision of priorities and forms of assistance. Under certain conditions, migration strengthened kinship ties and led to new kin functions, which evolved as changing conditions dictated. . . .

Continuities and Discontinuities in the Functions of Kin

To understand fully the role of kin in twentieth-century Manchester, one must place it in historical perspective. Ideally, the kinship patterns of French Canadians in Manchester should be compared to those of their communities of origin in rural Quebec. Unfortunately, only two studies of kinship in Quebec are available for comparison: an ethnographic study of the village of St Denis by Horace Miner (1939) and a more recent study of urban kinship ties in Montreal by Philippe Garigue (1967).[6]

Were the kinship patterns characteristic of St Denis transported to Manchester? In the absence of a full-fledged comparison of family structure, demographic behaviour, women's labour-force participation, and family economy for Manchester and the Quebec parishes of origin, it would be impossible to answer this question conclusively. This discussion is limited, therefore, to a comparison with the kinship patterns found in Quebec by Miner and Garigue, respectively. In rural St Denis, kin were at the base of the organizational structure. They controlled the channels of land transmission and all major aspects of assistance and discipline. Symbols of kin permeated religious life, and reverence for ancestors constituted an important component of socialization. Even marriage partners were chosen within the kinship network. Kin directed and dominated most important career decisions. In outlining the stages of the family cycle in rural Quebec, Miner stressed the farmer's perception of the interrelatedness of generations: 'Life is like a turning wheel. The old turn over the work to the young and die, and these in turn get old and then turn the work to their children. Yes, life is like a wheel turning' (Miner 1939: 85). Particularly important for comparative purposes is Miner's emphasis on the interchangeability of sons for inheritance rather than on primogeniture. The father decided which son would inherit the farm and launched the other sons into the outside world by providing them with assistance to migrate to the towns to find jobs or by helping with their education. After the father's death, the other brothers customarily left the household, because it was considered a disgrace to live in a brother's home. Also important, for comparative purposes, was the prevalence of mutual assistance and shared effort, especially among brothers who farmed in the same village or in nearby villages.

Migration to Manchester shifted the economic base of the family from landholding to industrial work. It therefore disrupted the basic territorial continuity and the interlocking of generations within the family cycle. The move to an industrial economy obviously exposed the French-Canadian immigrants to different occupational careers and economic organization. Accordingly, it necessitated a reorganization of family roles and a redefinition of kinship rules. The stem family structure found by Miner in St Denis was not present in Manchester. As indicated earlier, sons and daughters in Manchester tended to set up their own households after marriage even though they did not move far away from their parents. At most, some spent the first two years of marriage in their parents' household. Once removed from the land, fathers in Manchester lost the bargaining power and control they had held by virtue of their land ownership. Thus, the move to industrial cities may have weakened the patriarchal authority of traditional rural families.

However, despite this major change, migration to Manchester did not result in a breakdown of kinship ties. Traditional family structures were not disrupted through the migration of sons and daughters. Migration was an essential component of the family cycle in Quebec. Non-inheriting sons left home to work in cities, often in textile towns such as Trois-Rivières. Daughters usually entered domestic service or textile work. Migration to Manchester was, therefore, part of the larger historic pattern of rural–urban migration of Quebec sons and daughters at specific stages of the family cycle.

The factory system in some ways reinforced family ties. Industrial work allowed adult sons and daughters to remain in the parental household until marriage and to establish their own households nearby after marriage. In this respect, life in an industrial town (provided the entire nuclear family had migrated) offered greater opportunities for cohesion and contact among relatives throughout their lives. The dispersal of children by inheritance practices did not affect families in Manchester. As long as employment in the mills was available, children and parents continued to work in the same place, thus allowing continued interaction with parents as well as siblings.

Life in the industrial town added new functions to an already long repertory of kin interaction. The legacy of rural Quebec to industrial Manchester—the principle and practice of kin solidarity—was extremely significant in the adaptation of rural workers to industrial conditions. Once villagers left the land, their kin ceased to be the exclusive organizational base of social life and lost many of their sanctions. However, a corporate view of family life and an orientation to a collective family economy was maintained in Manchester, at least in the first generation. The principle of resource exchanges across the life course took new forms, such as the provision of housing, childcare, the teaching of skills, and brokerage within the factory.

A comparison of the organization and behaviour of kin in Manchester with that of kin in urban Quebec communities is also illuminating. Garigue (1956) found large kinship networks in Montreal, which were vitally linked with relatives in their rural community of origin, as well as in a number of other French-Canadian communities. These networks did not contain scattered nuclear families but instead exhibited concentrations in each location of kin clusters that, as part of a larger network, maintained contact with each other in several different communities. Individuals and nuclear families generally migrated to join a specific cluster. Migrants often moved to a certain urban community because other relatives lived there. The pattern outlined by Garigue places kinship ties in Manchester into a larger world of French-Canadian networks, a cell in a larger series of clusters—many located in Quebec.

This examination of the kinship patterns in Manchester and its comparison with Quebec raises crucial historical questions: What changes in kinship patterns resulted from migration and settlement in new communities? What behaviours were transferred with modifications and which remained intact? Answers hinge on an overall understanding of the transmission of pre-migration organizations and traditions to new settings. A systematic distinction between complete transfers of traditional patterns or their modification and new adaptation will considerably advance our understanding of the role of kin in adaptation to modern, industrial life.

The French-Canadian case in Manchester suggests that what has been considered a survival of pre-modern patterns may also represent modern responses to new industrial conditions. French-Canadian immigrants initially transported kinship ties and traditional practices of kin assistance to Manchester. They subsequently adapted their kin organization to the industrial system by developing new modes of interaction and new functions.

Although the basic kinship ties had been imported from rural Quebec, their functions, responsive to the demands of industrial production, were different from those customarily performed by kin in rural society. Functioning in an industrial environment required a familiarity with bureaucratic structures and organizations, adherence to modern work schedules, planning in relation to the rhythms of industrial employment, specialization in tasks, and technological skills. The roles assumed by kin—hiring young relatives and manipulating the pace of production—required a mastery of 'modern' processes, a high level of expertise, and sophistication. The role of kin in these areas, as well as in the more personal areas, such as housing, required a comprehension of the complexity and diversity inherent in an urban industrial system. The selective use of kinship ties by the workers of Manchester represented, therefore, both earlier practices and their modification.

The selectivity used by immigrants in adapting their traditional ties and resources to industrial conditions is most significant in this process. Modernization theory has frequently viewed integration with kin as an obstacle to geographic mobility and adaptation to modern ways (Moore 1965; Inkeles and Smith 1974). The Manchester case suggests, rather, that kin not only facilitated migration to industrial communities but also served as agents of adaptation and modernization by providing role models and by offering direct assistance. Under the insecurities of the factory system, the selective use of kinship was part of survival strategies and under certain circumstances also facilitated mobility.

Notes

1. These patterns of residence were reconstructed from city directories and addresses listed in the Amoskeag Company's employee files.
2. For definitions and descriptions of traditional kinship systems, see Fox (1967), Arensberg and Kimball (1968), Fortes (1969), and Lèvi-Strauss (1969). For a historical analysis of legal changes governing American family and kinship organization, see Farber (1973).
3. For a theoretical discussion of the instrumentality of kin in modern society, see also Bennett and Despres (1960).
4. Bott's model has been subsequently applied to a variety of neighbourhood and community studies in England and the United States, most notably Michael Young and Peter Willmott's study of East London (1957) and Herbert Gans's study of Boston's West End (1962).

5. Compare also with Litwak's assertion that geographic propinquity is not an essential condition for the maintenance of extended kinship ties (1960).
6. Recently, the extent to which St Denis is representative of most rural Quebec communities has been questioned. No comparable studies for other Quebec communities are available, however.

References

Anderson, M.S. 1971. *Family Structure in Nineteenth-century Lancashire* (Cambridge, UK: Cambridge University Press).

Arensberg, C.M., and S.T. Kimball. 1968. *Family and Community in Ireland*, 2nd edn (Cambridge, MA: Harvard University Press).

Bennett, J.W., and L.A. Despres. 1960. 'Kinship and Instrumental Activities', *American Anthropologist* 62: 254–67.

Bott, E. 1957. *Family and Social Network: Roles, Norms, and External Relationships in Ordinary Urban Families* (London: Tavistock).

Farber, B. 1973. *Family and Kinship in Modern Society* (Glenview, IL: Scott Foresman & Co).

Fortes, M. 1969. *Kinship and the Social Order* (Chicago: Aldine Publishing Co).

Fox, R. 1967. *Kinship and Marriage: An Anthropological Perspective* (London: Penguin).

Garigue, P. 1956. 'French-Canadian Kinship and Urban Life', *American Anthropologist* 58: 1090–1101.

———. 1967. *La vie familiale des Canadiens Français* (Montréal: Les Presses de l'Université de Montréal).

Goode, W. 1963. *World Revolution and Family Patterns* (New York: Free Press).

Inkeles, A., and D. Smith. 1974. *Becoming Modern: Individual Change in Six Developing Countries* (Cambridge, MA: Harvard University Press).

Lèvi-Strauss, C. 1969. *The Elementary Structures of Kinship* (Boston: Beacon Press).

Litwak, E. 1960. 'Geographical Mobility and Extended Family Cohesion', *American Sociological Review* 25: 385–94.

Miner, H.M. 1939. *St Denis: A French-Canadian Parish* (Chicago: University of Chicago Press).

Moore, W.E. 1965. *Industrialization and Labor: Social Aspects of Economic Development* (Ithaca, NY: Cornell University Press).

Parsons, T. 1943. 'The Kinship System of the Contemporary United States', *American Anthropologist* 45: 22–38.

Pitt-Rivers, J. 1973. 'The Kith and the Kin', in *The Character of Kinship*, ed. J. Goody (Cambridge, UK: Cambridge University Press).

Chapter 8

This chapter, selected from social historian Nancy Cott's *The Bonds of Womanhood*, describes the domestic ideals that developed in the nineteenth century. Cott also argues that the image of Home as a 'haven in a heartless world' (in the words of the late Christopher Lasch) represented a reaction to the popular perception that industrial workplaces featured exploitative relationships and general immorality—and that, more generally, capitalism was an immoral economic system. Far from subverting capitalism, however, this domestic ideology provided rationalization for it.

Cott also describes the gender ideals that were closely connected to domesticity. Just as men were beginning to be defined as 'breadwinners', women were increasingly defined in terms of domesticity. Historians Leonore Davidoff and Catherine Hall (in *Family Fortunes*) have argued that domesticity also represented a 'badge of social class'—a code of conduct and set of values that signified the moral superiority of a developing white middle class.

The only issue that Cott does not explore here is that of the source of these ideas. The evidence is that middle-class women themselves were forging an identity amidst the erosion of the family economy, and using this domestic ideology to claim status for themselves and increase their own power in the household.

Domesticity

Nancy F. Cott

In 1833, when Esther Grout returned to Hawley, Massachusetts, from her travels in search of employment, and wrote in her diary 'Home is sweet'—'there is no place like home'—those phrases were freshly minted clichés (Grout 1833). A host of New Englanders were using the printed word to confirm and advance her sentiments. Essays, sermons, novels, poems, and manuals offering advice and philosophy on family life, child rearing, and women's role began to flood the literary market in the 1820s and 1830s, with a tide that has not yet ceased. These early works fall into five categories. There were those primarily on the mother's (less frequently, the father's) responsibilities, such as the Reverend John S.C. Abbott's *The Mother at Home*, Lydia Maria Child's *The Mother's Book*, William Alcott's *The Young Mother*, and Theodore Dwight's *The Father's Book*. A closely related group, including Herman Humphrey's *Domestic Education*, Louisa Hoare's *Hints for the Improvement of Early Education*—a fictional version—Catherine Sedgwick's *Home*, offered principles for child rearing. Others such as Sally Kirby Fales's *Familiar Letters on Subjects Interesting to the Minds and Hearts of Females* and Lydia H. Sigourney's *Letters to Young Ladies* assess women's social role in a general way. A fourth sort more specifically considered the appropriate education for women: Abigail Mott's *Observations on the Importance of Female Education* and Almira Phelps's *The Female Student*, for instance, did so. A slightly different number, with titles such as *The Young Lady's Home* or *The Young Lady's Friend*, followed the etiquette tradition, prescribing manners for women and men.[1] At the same time, magazines addressing an audience of 'ladies' multiplied rapidly, carrying essays, stories, and advice of a similar domestic slant. Despite some minor differences and contradictions among the views expressed in this rash of words, altogether they revealed a single canon—of domesticity.

The central convention of domesticity was the contrast between the home and the world. Home was an 'oasis in the desert', a 'sanctuary' where 'sympathy, honour, virtue are assembled', where 'disinterested love is ready to sacrifice everything at the altar of affection'. In his 1827 address on female education, a New Hampshire pastor proclaimed that 'It is at home, where man . . . seeks a refuge from the vexations and embarrassments of business, an enchanting repose of affection: where some of his finest sympathies, tastes, and moral and religious feelings are formed and nourished—where is the treasury of pure disinterested love, such as is seldom found in the busy walks of a selfish and calculating world.' The ways of the world, in contrast, subjected the individual to 'a desolation of feeling', in the words of the *Ladies' Magazine*; there 'we behold every principle of justice and honour, and even the dictates of common honesty disregarded, and the delicacy of our moral sense is wounded; we see the general good, sacrificed to the advancement of personal interest, and we turn from such scenes, with a painful sensation . . .' (Burroughs 1827: 18–19; *Ladies' Magazine* 1830a).

The contradistinction of home to world had roots in religious motives and rhetoric. Christians for centuries had depreciated 'the world' of earthly delights and material possessions in comparison to Heaven, the eternal blessings of true faith. In the 1780s and 1790s, British Evangelicals doubled the pejorative connotation of 'the world' by preferring bourgeois respectability above the 'gay world' of aristocratic fashion. Living in an era of eroding public orthodoxy, they considered family transmission of piety more essential than ever to the maintenance of religion; consequently, they conflated the contrasts of Heaven versus 'the world' and bourgeois virtue versus the 'gay world' with the contrast between the domestic fireside and the world outside.[2] In that tradition, when Esther Grout wrote in her diary, 'oh how sweet is retirement. The pleasantest & I think some of the most profitable moments of my life have been spent in retirement', she was referring to her withdrawal from the world in solitary religious devotion and *also* to her repose *at home* (Grout 1830).

The rhetorical origins of the contrast between home and world demand less interpretation than the canon of domesticity built upon it. That contrast infused the new literature because, in simplest terms, it seemed to explain and justify material change in individuals' lives. Between the Revolution and the 1830s, New England's population became more dense and more mobile, its political system more representative and demanding of citizens, its social structure more differentiated, and its economic structure more complex than in earlier years when the business of 'the world' had mostly taken place in households. Economic growth and rationalization and the entry of the market mechanism into virtually all relations of production fostered specialized and standardized work and a commercial ethic. Because of regional division of production and marketing, agriculture production itself became more specialized and more speculative. The farmer's success was not in his own hands when he produced for distant markets. In handicrafts the functional differentiation of wholesale merchant, retail merchant, contractor or 'boss', and pieceworker replaced the unified eighteenth-century pattern in which an artisan made and sold his wares from his residence. Masters (now employers) and their journeymen or apprentices no longer assumed a patriarchal relationship; wages and prices defined their relationship to one another and to the merchants above them. Trends such as the decline of traditional determinants of deference, the assertion of an individualist ethos, increasing extremes of wealth and poverty, and replacement of unitary association networks by pluralistic ones, indicated deep change in social relations (Common 1909; Montgomery 1968; Fischer 1974). Differentiation and specialization characterized this transformation of society. These were portrayed and symbolized most powerfully in the separation of production and exchange from the domestic arena—the division between 'world' and 'home'.

The canon of domesticity encouraged people to assimilate such change by linking it to a specific set of sex roles. In the canon of domesticity, the home contrasted to the restless and competitive world because its 'presiding spirit' was woman, who was 'removed from the arena of pecuniary excitement and ambitious competition'. Woman inhabited the 'shady green lanes of domestic life', where she found 'pure enjoyment and hallowed sympathies' in her 'peaceful offices'. If man was the 'fiercest warrior, or the most unrelenting votary of stern ambition', 'toil-worn' by 'troubled scenes of life', woman would 'scatter roses among the thorns of his appointed track'. In the 'chaste, disinterested circle of the fireside' only—that is, in the hearts and minds of sisters, wives, and mothers—could men find 'reciprocated humanity . . . unmixed with hate or the cunning of deceit' (*Ladies' Magazine* 1830b; Cary 1830: 4.7; *The Discussion* 1837: 225–6; *Ladies' Companion* 1840). The spirit of business and public life thus appeared to diverge from that of the home chiefly because the two spheres were the separate domains of the two sexes.

In accentuating the split between 'work' and 'home' and proposing the latter as a place of salvation, the canon of domesticity tacitly acknowledged the capacity of modern work to desecrate the human spirit. Authors of domestic literature, especially the female authors, denigrated business and politics as arenas of selfishness, exertion, embarrassment, and degradation of soul. These rhetoricians suggested what Marx's analysis of alienated labour in the 1840s would assert, that 'the worker . . . feels at ease only outside work, and during work he is outside himself. He is at home when he is not working and when he is working he is not at home' (Marx [1844] 1967: 292–3). The canon of domesticity embodied a protest against that advance of exploitation and pecuniary values. Nancy Sproat, a pious wife and mother who published her own family lectures in 1819, warned that 'the air of the world is poisonous. You must carry an antidote with you, or the infection will prove fatal.' (A latter-day Calvinist, she clearly gave 'the world' dual meaning, opposing it to both 'home' and 'Heaven'. Her antidote, likewise, was a compound of domestic affection and religious faith.) No writer more consistently emphasized the anti-pecuniary bias of the domestic rhetoric than Sarah Josepha Hale, influential editor of the Boston *Ladies' Magazine* from 1828 to 1836 and subsequently of *Godey's Lady's Book* in Philadelphia. 'Our men are sufficiently money-making', Hale said. 'Let us keep our women and children from the contagion as long as possible. To do good and to communicate should be the motto of Christians and republicans.' She wished 'to remind the dwellers in this "bank-note world" that there are objects more elevated, more worthy of pursuit than wealth'. 'Time is money' was a maxim she rejected, and she urged mothers to teach their children the relative merits of money and of good works.[3]

Yet the canon of domesticity did not directly challenge the modern organization of work and pursuit of wealth. Rather, it accommodated and promised to temper them. The values of domesticity undercut opposition to exploitative pecuniary standards in the work world by upholding a 'separate sphere' of comfort and compensation, instilling a morality that would encourage self-control, and fostering the idea that preservation of home and family sentiment was an ultimate goal. Family affection, especially maternal affection, was portrayed as the 'spirit indefatigable, delighting in its task', which could pervade the 'regenerate' society. Furthermore, women, through their reign in the home, were to sustain the 'essential elements of moral government' to allow men to negotiate safely amid the cunning, treachery, and competition of the marketplace.[4] If a man had to enter the heart-less and debasing world, his wife at home supplied motive and reward for him, to defuse his resentment:

> O! what a hallowed place home is when lit by the smile of such a being; and enviably happy the man who is the lord of such paradise. . . . When he struggles on in the path of duty, the thought that it is for *her* in part he toils will sweeten his labours. . . . Should he meet dark clouds and storms abroad, yet sunshine and peace await him at home; and when his proud heart would resent the language of petty tyrants, 'dressed in a little brief authority', from whom he receives the scanty remuneration for his daily labours, the thought that she perhaps may suffer thereby, will calm the tumult of his passions, and bid him struggle on, and find his reward in her sweet tones, and soothing kindness, and that the bliss of home is thereby made more apparent. ('Essay on Marriage' 1834)

The literature of domesticity thus enlisted women in their domestic roles to absorb, palliate, and even to redeem the strain of social and economic transformation. In the home, women symbolized and were expected to sustain traditional values and practices of work and family organization. The very shrillness of the *cri de coeur* against modern work relations in the canon of domesticity meant that women's role in the home would be inflexibly defined.

Recoiling from the spirit of self-interest and self-aggrandizement they saw in the marketplace, rhetoricians of domesticity looked to the home for a sanctuary of 'disinterested' love; because women at home presumably escaped exposure to competitive economic practices, they became representatives of 'disinterestedness'. (In fact, women at home who engaged in 'given-out' industry, as increasing numbers did, brought the economic world into the home.) More profoundly and authentically, married women represented 'disinterestedness' because they were economically dependent. Because their property and earnings by law belonged to their husbands, married women could not operate as economic individuals.[5] Wives lacked the means and motive for self-seeking. The laws of marriage made the social model for striving for wealth irrelevant to them. Beyond equating wives' economic dependence with disinterestedness, the canon of domesticity went a further step and prescribed women's appropriate attitude to be selflessness. The conventional cliché 'that women were to live for others' was substantially correct, wrote the author of *Woman's Mission*, for only by giving up all self-interest did women achieve the purity of motive that enabled them to establish moral reference points in the home (*Woman's Mission* 1840: 48–52). Thus women's self-renunciation was called upon to remedy men's self-alienation.

Furthermore, the canon of domesticity required women to sustain the milieu of task-oriented work that had characterized earlier family organization. This requirement made service to others and the diffusion of happiness in the family women's tasks. Women's household service alone remained from the tradition of reciprocal service by family members. Since it highlighted that aspect of women's role, the canon of domesticity in its early formulation directed them not to idleness or superficial gentility but to a special sort of usefulness. Sarah Hale maintained, for instance, that women's principles of unselfishness and magnanimity should be manifest in their acts of service. A female author of *Letters on Female Character* similarly preferred to view woman as 'a rational being, whose intelligent and active exertions are to afford a perennial source of comfort to mankind', rather than as a romantic goddess to be worshipped (*Ladies' Magazine* 1830b: 445; Cary 1830: 174).

Assuming that women would be happy insofar as they served others and made them happy, these writers reinforced women's orientation toward interpersonal goals in the emotional realm rather than self-reliant accomplishment.[6] 'In everything I must consult the interest, the happiness, and the welfare of *My Husband*', Eunice Wait of Hallowell, Maine, wrote on the day she married a Universalist evangelist, '. . . may it be my constant study to make him contented and happy, and then will my own happiness be sure' (Cobb 1822). In a similar vein Mary Orne Tucker congratulated herself, after four years of marriage, on her husband's happiness at home: 'His *happy home* I say, and I say it too with *pride*, and *pleasure*; it is no small compliment to my own abilities, to my own powers to please, my temper is somewhat wayward, but I hope it has not been discovered in scenes of domestic life, to shine as a good wife, is an object of my highest ambition, there are many humble duties to fulfill and to fulfill them with honour and chearfulness [*sic*] is a consideration which ought not to be beneath the notice of every reflecting woman.'[7]

The amorphousness of such requirements as 'to please' or 'to serve' did not make women's role any less demanding. Ironically, the rhetoric that intended to distinguish 'home' and 'woman' from 'the world' and 'man' tended to make the two spheres analogous and comparable. It was the paradox of domesticity to make women's work roles imitate men's; despite the intent to stress how they differed, domestic occupations began to mean for women what worldly occupations meant for men. A businessman in a *Godey's Lady's Book* story admonished his young wife, who had repeatedly neglected to have his midday meal ready on time:

> Your error lies in a false idea which you have entertained, that your happiness was to come somewhere from out[side] of your domestic duties, instead of in the performance of them—that they were not part of a wife's obligations, but something that she could put aside if she were able to hire enough servants. I cannot, thus, delegate my business duties to anyone; without my governing mind and constant attention, everything would soon be in disorder, and an utter failure, instead of prosperity, be the result of my efforts. By my carefulness and constant devotion to business, I am enabled to provide you with every comfort; surely, then, you should be willing also to give careful attention to your department, that I may feel home to be a pleasant place. (Arthur [1841] 1972: 169)

Business provided one analogy, politics another. 'I think it is my humble desire to be as a wise Legislator to my little province', wrote Susan Huntington, a minister's wife who knew the domestic canon by heart before publications rehearsed it, 'to enact as few statutes as possible, & those easy and judicious—to see that all things are done at the proper time, & in the proper way, so far as is practicable, that our family may be a quiet, well organized, regular family' (Huntington 1819).

Defining it as her province, the canon of domesticity made woman's household occupation her vocation. The very attempt to immobilize woman's role in the home transformed her household duties into a discrete, specialized, and objective work role. Domesticity as a vocation meant, furthermore, that woman's work role imitated man's while lacking his means of escape. If man could recover from his work 'at home', woman's work was 'at home'. She provided for his relief. Since her sex role contained her work role, for her there was no escape. 'A law of her being' appointed her vocation, according to the canon. 'To render *home* happy, is woman's peculiar province; home is *her world*.' She was 'neither greater nor less than man, but different, as her natural vocation is different, and . . . each is superior to each other in their respective departments of thought and action.' Even if woman's vocation was 'natural', however, it required preparation and instruction. Not only the numerous books of advice to the wife and mother but also new institutions to educate girls for those roles heralded the rationalization of women's domestic occupations into a 'profession'.[8]

Notes

1. All of the titles mentioned were published in New England (primarily Boston) between 1830 and 1840 except Hoare's, published in London in 1819, republished in New York, 1820, and then in Salem in 1829; Mott's, published in New York in 1825; and Sedgwick's 1835 novel—though a New Englander she published with Harper & Bros in New York.
2. For examples of Evangelical writings see T. Gisborne, *An Enquiry into the Duties of the Female Sex* (London, reprinted Philadelphia, 1798), and H. More, *Stricture on the Modern System of Female Education,* Vol. I, 9th edn (London, 1801); see also M.G. Jones, *Hannah More* (Cambridge, 1952); Gordon Rattray Taylor, *The Angel-makers: A Study in the Psychological Origins of Historical Change, 1750–1850* (London: Heinemann, 1958), esp. 12–36; Christopher Hill, 'Clarissa Harlowe and Her Times', *Essays in Criticism* 5 (1955): 320; Keith Thomas, 'The Double Standard', *Journal of the History of Ideas* 20 (1959): 204–5; and I. Watt, 'The New Woman, Samuel Richardson's Pamela', in *The Family: Its Structure and Functions*, ed. R.L. Coser (New York: St Martin's, 1964), 286–8.
3. Mrs N. Sproat, *Family Lectures* (Boston, 1819); *Ladies' Magazine* 3 (Jan. 1830): 42–3; (July 1830): 325; 3 (Feb. 1830): 49–55. Hale maintained that women's empire in the home was 'purer, more excelled and spiritual than the worldly scope of regulating by laws the intercourse of business', *Ladies' Magazine* 5 (Feb. 1832): 87. Cf. Catherine Beecher's declaration in *Suggestions Respecting Improvements in Education* (Hartford, CT, 1829), 53: 'The dominion of woman [in contrast to man's] may be based on influence that the heart is proud to acknowledge.'
4. *Woman's Mission* (New York, 1840): 20–1; *The Discussion:* 225. Cf. Mary Ryan's conclusion in 'American Society and the Cult of Domesticity, 1830–1860' (PhD diss., University of California, Santa Barbara, 1971), esp. 70–1, that the literature of domesticity of the 1840s included a complete theory of the psychologically specialized and socially integrative functions of the family in industrial society. Ryan observes that women in the home instilled in their husbands and children national values and an ethic of social control; 'by sustaining their husbands through the discomforts of modern work situations, and gentry restraining them from antisocial behaviour, American women facilitated the smooth operation of the industrial system'. The nineteenth-century definition of 'social integration' was 'the moral power of woman' (70, 337).
5. Nor did wives, on the whole, fail to understand their dependence: 'First when I received the $5 bill I kissed it', a Cambridge woman wrote to her absent husband in thanks, 'because it seemed to me proof that my dear Husband did not lose me from his mind as soon as from his sight: then, I thought I would use it very prudently.' Elizabeth Graeter, Cambridge, MA, to Francis Graeter, 14 Aug. 1836, Hooker Collection.
6. In children's books in the 1840s, there is a discernible contrast between the achievement motivation encouraged in boys and the affiliation motivation encouraged in girls. J.S.C. Abbott's *The School Boy,* for instance, stressed that the boy must aim for correctness and truth, even at the expense of popularity. Girls' books by Lydia Maria Child and Lydia Sigourney also advocated purity and correct principle, but stressed that girls should

attain these by loving others, treating them nicely, following the Golden Rule, etc. In his *Rollo* series, Jacob Abbott portrayed Rollo (nine years old) as an independent little man who followed the truth and wished to succeed but made Rollo's sister Jane passive, cautious, nervous, and dependent on her brother. Bernard Wishy discussed these books in *The Child and the Republic* (Philadelphia, 1968), 57–8.

7. She continued, 'I am every day amply repaid for all my endeavors to please, every look from my master is certificate of my success, and the plaudit of my own conscience affords sweet peace.' Diary of Mary Orne Tucker, 1 May 1802.
8. Quotations from *Ladies' Magazine* 3 (May 1830): 218; Caleb Cushing, 'The Social Condition of Woman', from the *North American Review*, Apr. 1836, reprinted in *Essays from the North American Review*, ed. Allen Thorndike Rice (New York, 1879), 67. Catherine Beecher popularized the idea that wife-and-motherhood was woman's 'profession' in [the] mid-nineteenth century, but that usage began, I believe, with Hannah More's *Strictures on the Modern System of Female Education*, originally published in 1799 and widely read by women in the United States for decades after. More wrote, 'The profession of ladies, to which the bent of their instruction should be turned, is that of daughters, wives, mothers, and mistresses of families' (Vol. 1, 9th edn [London, 1801], 112).

References

Arthur, T.S. [1841] 1972. 'Sweethearts and Wives', *Godey's Lady's Book* 23 (Dec.), reprinted in *Root of Bitterness: Documents of the Social History of American Women*, ed. N.F. Cott (New York: Dutton, 1972).

Burroughs, C. 1827. *An Address on Female Education, Delivered in Portsmouth, N.H., Oct. 26, 1827* (Portsmouth).

Cary, V. 1830. *Letters of Female Character*, 2nd edn (Philadelphia).

Cobb, E.H.W. 1822. Diary, Vol. 1 (10 Sept.): 29, BPL.

Common, J.R. 1909. 'American Shoemakers, 1648–1895', *Quarterly Journal of Economics* 24: 39–84.

The Discussion of the Character, Education, Prerogatives, and Moral Influence on Women (Boston, 1837).

'Essay on Marriage'. 1834. *Universalist and Ladies Repository* 2 (Apr. 19): 371.

Fischer, D.H. 1974. 'America: A Social History', Vol. 1, 'The Main Lines of the Subject 1650–1975', unpublished MS, esp. Ch. 4: 42–3; Ch. 12: 20–2.

Grout, E. 1830. Diary (13 Sept.), Pocumtuck Valley Memorial Association Library Collections, HD.

———. 1833. Diary (4 Aug.), Pocumtuck Valley Memorial Association Library Collections, HD.

Huntington, S.M. 1819. Diary (14 June), SML.

Ladies' Companion. 1840. 'Influence of Woman—Past and Present', 13 (Sept.).

Ladies' Magazine. 1830a. 'Home' by L.E., 3 (May): 217–18.

———. 1830b. Quotations from 'Woman', probably by S.J. Hale, 3 (Oct.): 441, 444.

Marx, K. [1844] 1967. 'Alienated Labor', in *Writing of the Young Men on Philosophy and Society*, eds and trans. L.D. Easton and K.H. Guddat (Garden City, NY: Anchor Books, 1967).

Montgomery, D. 1968. 'The Working Classes of the Pre-industrial American City', *Labor History* 9: 3–22.

Women's Mission. 1840 (New York).

Chapter 9

The feature of family life that is perhaps most difficult to get perspective on is the mother–child relationship. Intensive mothering, in which children assume a priority in their mothers' lives, seems to us the only way to raise children. This selection traces the historical development of the ideas that define motherhood as we know it. American anthropologist Maxine Margolis (writing in the 1980s) situates the rise of new ideas about childhood and motherhood in the changes occurring in households, and thus family life, in the nineteenth century, as an economy based on household production gave way to an industrial-capitalist society. The broad changes she describes occurring in the United States were happening in Canada as well, and they made for significant changes in family patterns.

The erosion of the family economy (referred to as the 'domestic economy' here), which not only provided women with a critical productive role but also allowed both parents to train their children for adulthood, established the context for new definitions of women's role and parenting. What is not clear in Margolis's discussion, though, is who produced this ideology. Margolis emphasizes the imposition of these ideas on women. In contrast, social historian Mary Ryan, in *Cradle of the Middle Class*, has shown that middle-class women themselves had a hand in fashioning these ideas—in reaction to the erosion of their role in producing household subsistence and in anticipation of the need to prepare their children for a quickly changing economy (in which parents were losing the possibility of passing on either land or skills to the next generation).

Social historians know less about what social relations and daily life were like for middle-class North Americans than they do about cultural ideals. Canadian historian Francoise Noel (in *Family Life and Sociability in Upper and Lower Canada, 1780–1870*) has, however, searched through diaries and personal correspondence for evidence about the personal lives of propertied middle- and upper-class families in Upper and Lower Canada between 1780 and 1870. She describes marriages based on love and companionship, as well as property sufficient to support an independent household. The love and affection she finds between spouses, and the concern about children's development and grief over their death, indicate strong similarities with couples today. But the incredible sociability of these nuclear families stands in contrast with the ideals of privacy and independence that became so central to family life in the twentieth century. According to Noel, nineteenth-century couples met and even honeymooned in the company of family, especially parents; and they celebrated traditional holidays in large gatherings of family and friends. Members of extended families stayed with each other for long visits, and neighbours and friends were in and out of each other's homes frequently. Noel argues that mutual assistance—among neighbours especially—was very important to family life in Canada at that time.

Putting Mothers on the Pedestal

Maxine L. Margolis

> Motherhood as we know it today is a surprisingly new institution. In most of human history and in most parts of the world even today, adult, able-bodied women had been, and still are, too valuable in the productive capacity to be spared for the exclusive care of children.
>
> Jessie Bernard
> *The Future of Motherhood*, 1974

Debates about the conflict between motherhood and work have lessened in intensity over the last decade as millions of middle-class wives and mothers have taken jobs and as employment for these women has become the norm rather than the exception. But these developments have not met with unanimous approval. Just think of the demand by groups like the Moral Majority for a return to 'traditional family values', code words for the presence of a full-time housewife–mother in the home. Nevertheless, biting denunciations of working mothers—so common during much of this century—are much less frequent today. Most women are pleased to be living in an era in which they are free to take a job or even pursue a career and in which their economic contribution to their families is recognized. They probably feel less uneasy about working because it is no longer an article of faith that their employment is harmful to their children. But what is often overlooked is that this is not the first time in American history when work and motherhood were thought compatible and when women's productive activities were seen as essential to their families' well-being.

Ideas about the 'correct' maternal role have often changed over the last 250 years in the United States. Not until the nineteenth century, for example, did a child's development and well-being come to be viewed as the major, if not the sole, responsibility of his or her mother, who was then urged to devote herself full-time to her parental duties. In contrast, during the eighteenth century child rearing was neither a discrete nor an exclusively female task. There was little emphasis on motherhood *per se* and both parents were simply advised to 'raise up' their children together.

These and other changes in ideas about motherhood are not isolated cultural artifacts resulting from random ideological fashions. I will argue that these value changes were and are moulded by changes in the nature of the family and the American economy. I intend to review the process whereby motherhood as a full-time career for middle-class women first arose as women's role in the domestic economy diminished, 'work' was removed from the household, the family became more isolated from the larger community, the need for education and skilled children increased, and the birth rate declined. As a result of these developments, with minor variations, the exclusivity of the mother–child dyad and the incessant duties of motherhood emerged beginning in the 1830s as givens in American child-rearing manuals and other prescriptive writings aimed at the middle class.

One of the principal factors that have influenced the middle-class mother's role and the ideology surrounding it is the decline of domestic production. During the colonial period when women were responsible for the manufacture and use of a wide variety of household products essential to daily living, women could not devote themselves full-time to motherhood. But in the early nineteenth century, as manufacturing left the home for the factory, middle-class women found themselves 'freed up' to spend more time on childcare. And before long they were told that such full-time care was essential.

The daily presence or absence of men in the home also shaped the American definition of motherhood. During colonial times when men, women, and children all worked together in or near the household, there were no firm distinctions in parental responsibilities. It was the duty of both parents to rear their children, and fathers were thought to be especially important to a proper religious education. But when a man's work began to take him away from the home for most of the day—an arrangement that began with the onset of industrialization nearly 200 years ago—child-rearing responsibilities fell heavily on the mother. And, once again, middle-class mothers were told that this was in the nature of things.

Household size and its contacts with the outside world have also influenced the mother role. Prior to the nineteenth century, when most households were larger than the nuclear family, when they consisted of more people than just a married couple and their children, the presence of other adults who could take a hand in childcare diluted maternal responsibility. Because the household was the site of both life and work, because there was a constant coming and going of people, the mother–child tie was but one of many relationships. As the country industrialized in the nineteenth century, however, the home and the place of work became separate. Women then remained as the only adults in the household and the mother–child relationship was thrown into sharp relief. Mothers took on all the burdens of childcare, and their performance of these tasks became a major concern. Why? Because the middle-class mother was advised that she and she alone had the weighty mission of transforming her children into the model citizens of the day.

Fertility rates also influence the mother role, but not always in the way one might expect. It seems logical that the more children a woman has the more she will be defined by her maternal role, for the care and feeding of a large brood demand so much time. But this was not always the case. The emphasis on motherhood in the nineteenth century *increased* as fertility among the middle class *decreased*. One explanation of this anomaly lies in what has been called the 'procreative imperative' (Bernard 1974: 7; Harris 1981: 84). This refers to the promotion of cheap population growth by powerful elements in society which benefit from the rearing of 'high quality' children. As industrialization continued, the need for skilled labour correspondingly increased. Thus, the reification of maternity during the nineteenth century reflects a dual attempt to stem the falling birth rate in the middle class and increase the quality of children through long-term mother care. The emphasis on maternity was also a way of solving what became known as 'the woman question'. Once a woman's productive skills were no longer needed, what was to occupy her time? The answer was summarized in a single word: *motherhood*.

This preoccupation with motherhood and the corollary assumption that an exclusive mother–child relationship is both natural and inevitable is by no means universal. Ethnographic evidence clearly points out the variability of childcare arrangements and the ideologies that justify them. One study of 186 societies from around the world, for example, found that in less than half—46 per cent—mothers were the primary or exclusive caretakers of infants. In another 40 per cent of the societies in the sample, primary care of infants was the responsibility of others, usually siblings. An even more striking finding is that in less than 20 per cent of the societies are mothers the primary or exclusive caretakers *after* infancy. The authors of this study conclude: 'According to our ratings, in the majority of these societies mothers are not the principal caretakers or companions of young children' (Weisner and Gallimore 1977: 170; for information on cross-cultural differences in child-rearing values see Lamber, Hamers, and Frasure-Smith 1979).

How are we to explain this conclusion which contradicts the deeply held modern American belief in the central role of the mother in childcare? A number of factors are involved in the explanation, but one clue is that the living arrangement we take so much for granted—the married woman's residence in a nuclear-family household made up exclusively of parents and children—is extremely rare cross-culturally. Such households are found in only 6.1 per cent of the societies listed in the massive Human Relations Area Files, the largest systematic compilation of cross-cultural data in the world (Weisner and Gallimore 1977: 173). So in the majority of societies other kin present in the household relieve the mother of some of the burden of childcare.

Another factor that influences the degree of maternal responsibility is the nature and location of women's productive activities. In societies with economies based on hunting and gathering or agriculture, young children typically are taken care of by an older sibling or by their mother or other female relative while these women are gathering or gardening. But in industrial societies where the workplace and the household are separate, production and childcare are incompatible. It is in these same societies—ones in which women's activities typically are limited to the domestic sphere—that we find the duties of parenting weighing most heavily on the mother (Brown 1970: 1073–8; Klevana 1980).

A study of mothers in six cultures points up the relative rarity of Western industrial childcare patterns. In the American community represented in the study, 92 per cent of the mothers said that they usually or always took care of their babies and children by themselves. The other five societies displayed considerably less maternal responsibility for childcare. In the words of the authors: 'The mothers of the US sample have a significantly heavier burden (or joy) of baby care than the mothers in any other society.' They explain: 'Living in nuclear families isolated from their relatives and with all their older children in school most of the day the [American] mother spends more time in charge of both babies and older children than any other group' (Minturn and Lambert 1964: 95–7, 100–1, 112–13).[1]

These studies suggest that the preoccupation of American experts with the mother–child relationship almost certainly is a result of social and economic developments in the United States and Western industrialized societies in general, societies that are characterized more than most others by exclusive mother–childcare arrangements. What we have come to think of as inevitable and biologically necessary is in great measure a consequence of our society's particular social and economic system. We are certainly not unique in believing that our brand of mother–child relationship is natural and normal. People in every culture firmly believe that *their* child-rearing practices stem from nature itself (Berger and Luckmann 1966: 135).[2]

Raise up Your Children Together: The Colonial Period to 1785

A distinct maternal role would have been incompatible with the realities of life during colonial times. The mother–child relationship was enmeshed in the myriad daily tasks women performed for their families' survival. They kept house, tended gardens, raised poultry and cattle, churned milk into butter and cream, butchered livestock, tanned skins, pickled and preserved food, made candles, buttons, soap, beer, and cider, gathered and processed medicinal herbs, and spun and wove wool and cotton for family clothes. The wives of farmers, merchants, and artisans were kept busy with these duties and the wives of merchants and artisans often helped in their husbands' businesses as well. Child rearing therefore largely centred on teaching children the skills needed to keep the domestic economy going. Child rearing was not a *separate* task; it was something that simply took place within the daily round of activities. It is little wonder that in 1790 a New England mother could write that her two children 'had grown out of the way' and are 'very little troble [*sic*]' when the younger of the two was still nursing (quoted in Cott 1977: 58; quoted in Bloch 1978b: 242).

The agrarian economy of the seventeenth and eighteenth centuries presented no clear-cut separation between the home and the world of work; the boundary between the pre-industrial family and society was permeable. Male and female spheres were contiguous and often overlapped, and the demands of the domestic economy ensured that neither sex was excluded from productive labour. Fathers, moreover, took an active role in child rearing because they worked near the household. Craftsmen and tradesmen usually had their shops at home and farmers spent the long winter months there. The prescriptive literature of the day rarely or imprecisely distinguished between 'female' or domestic themes and the 'masculine' world of work. The few colonial domestic guides addressed both men and women under the assumption that they worked together in the household (Sklar [1841] 1977; Ariès 1965).

Scholars now agree that the colonial family was not an extended one as was once thought; the best estimates are that at least 80 per cent were nuclear (but not nuclear in the same way as the small isolated nuclear family of the industrial era). The colonial family was nuclear in the formal sense in that parents and children were at its core, but mothers and fathers usually were not the only adults living in the household. Some families took in maiden aunts, or perhaps an aged parent, others had apprentices or journeymen, while domestic servants were common in the households of the prosperous. Moreover, because the typical colonial couple had six to eight offspring, children ranging from infancy to adolescence were commonly found in the same household. Finally, the practice of 'putting out' children and taking others in ensured that at least some children were not brought up exclusively by their parents. What is central to the discussion here is that during the colonial period children's relationships were not nearly as mother-centred as they later came to be in the smaller industrial variant of the nuclear family. Given the composition of the colonial American household, children must have received support from and been disciplined by a number of adults—their parents, apprentices or servants, older siblings, and perhaps other relatives as well (Demos 1970; Greven 1973; Bloch 1978b; Degler 1980: 5).

Children themselves were hardly recognized as a separate human category in the American colonies of the seventeenth and eighteenth centuries. 'There was little sense that children might somehow be a special group with their own needs and interests and capacities', writes one historian. Virtually all of the child-rearing advice of the day emphasized that children were 'meer Loans from God, which He may call for when He pleases'. Parents were told to bring up their children as good Christians and discipline was emphasized, but no mention was made of developing the child's personality, intelligence, or individuality. Quite to the contrary, most sermons dwelt on the importance of breaking the child's 'will' (Wadsworth [1712] 1972; Mather [1741] 1978; Demos 1970: 57–8).

Some children were 'put out' to work as early as six or seven years of age, and those who remained with their parents were expected to help with household chores. Girls as young as six could spin flax and boys helped in farming tasks or fetched wood. Childhood was at best a span of years lasting considerably less than a decade. Even had a family wanted a prolonged, leisurely childhood for its offspring, this was a luxury few could afford (Calhoun [1917] 1960; Demos 1970: 141).

Since infant mortality rates were high, parents expected to lose some of their children. Infant mortality in the seventeenth century, for example, ranged from 10 to 30 per cent in different parts of the colonies; this high rate was acknowledged in the sermons of the day. . . .

Although not a great deal is known about seventeenth- and eighteenth-century advice on child rearing and parental roles—the few manuals of the period were of English origin—we can glean some indication of parental duties in the American colonies from the sermons of the day. In a 1712 sermon entitled 'The Well-ordered Family, or, Relative Duties', Benjamin Wadsworth, pastor of the Church of Christ in Boston, distinguished mothers' responsibilities from fathers' when he urged the former to 'suckle their children'. But then he went on to say: 'Having given these hints about Mothers, I may say of Parents (Comprehending both Father and Mother) they should provide for the outward supply and comfort of their Children. They should nourish and bring them up.' In the lengthy discussion of religious instruction and the teaching of good manners and discipline that followed, all of Wadsworth's injunctions were addressed to 'Parents'. . . .

Colonial clergymen were generally consistent in their sermons treating parental roles. Fathers were to supervise the secular and religious education of their children, teaching them to fear and respect God, but mothers also were advised of their responsibilities in this training. Both parents were admonished to set good examples for their children, and both were held responsible for their children's general well-being. Except for the greater authority bestowed on the father as head of the family, the prescribed roles for parents made no important distinctions on the basis of sex. Similarly, even in funeral sermons for women, there was little mention of motherhood as opposed to the more generalized concept of parenthood. In the few sermons specifically addressed to mothers, the duties laid out were the same as those addressed to both parents, and 'none of these were distinctly maternal obligations' (Frost 1973; Masson 1976; Bloch 1978a: 106; Ulrich 1979).[3]

To be sure, women were thought to have special ties to their children during infancy, and infants were described as 'hers' by both men and women. The realities of reproduction were certainly recognized, and here we find special advice to mothers. A number of clergy inveighed against the practice of wet nursing, which in fact was quite rare in the American colonies. In describing the duties of a righteous woman, Cotton Mather admonished: 'Her care for the Bodies of her Children shows itself in the nursing of them herself. . . . She is not a Dame that shall scorn to nourish in the world, the Children whom she has already nourished in her Womb.' Wet nursing was condemned because it was thought contrary to God's will and dangerous to the physical health of the child, not because it was believed to interfere with the development of a bond between mother and child. Some ministers actually warned women against 'excessive fondness' for their children (Mather [1741] 1978: 105; Bloch 1978a: 105; Norton 1980: 90, 94).

Once children reached the age of one or two, when their survival was more certain, all directives regarding child rearing were addressed to *both* parents. Fathers were expected to take a larger role once children reached an educable age. This was particularly true among the Puritans, who believed that the 'masculine' qualities of religious understanding and self-discipline were essential in child rearing. One of the few distinctions made in the sermons of the day was in vocational training; this was the responsibility of the parent of the same sex as the child, although sometimes responsibility was removed from the family entirely. Children, particularly boys, often were sent out at age nine or 10 to apprentice in other households, while children from other families were taken in to serve as apprentices (Ryan 1975: 60; Bloch 1978a: 107; 1978b: 242; Kessler-Harris 1981: 29).

A cult of motherhood did not exist because it would have been incongruous in this setting. Women were far too busy to devote long hours to purely maternal duties, and fathers, older siblings, and other adults were also on hand to see to children's needs and discipline. Moreover, because of high mortality rates, a woman was not likely to become obsessive about her children, some of whom would not survive to adulthood. It is not surprising that, as one scholar had remarked of the colonial period, '. . . motherhood was singularly unidealized, usually disregarded as a subject, and even at times actually denigrated'. Although women bore and cared for very young children, this role received less emphasis in the prescriptive literature than nearly any other aspect of women's lives. Motherhood, when it was discussed at all, was merged with the parental, domestic, and religious obligations of both sexes (Bloch 1978a: 101, 103–4).

The Transition: 1785–1820

The cult of motherhood is usually associated with the middle and late nineteenth century, but we can see its roots in the prescriptive literature of the very late eighteenth century and the first decades of the nineteenth century. During these years the earliest hints of a special and distinct maternal role began appearing in sermons, domestic guides, medical volumes, and child-rearing manuals; for the first time writers began stressing the critical importance of maternal care in early childhood.

It is significant that these years also witnessed the beginnings of the industrial revolution. Markets slowly expanded, agriculture efficiency increased, transportation costs decreased—all developments that led to greater specialization in the economic division of labour. What is centrally important to my argument is that home industry, which typified the colonial period, began to wane. Gradually home manufacture for family use was replaced by standardized factory production for the wider market. The first industry that moved from the home to the factory was textile manufacture, one of women's traditional household tasks. As early as 1807 there were a dozen large textile mills in New England, and by 1810 farm families could buy cloth in village shops and from itinerant peddlers (Smith 1796: 58; Brownlee 1974: 77; Ryan 1975: 91; Cott 1977: 24).

The replacement of homespun by manufactured goods was nonetheless a gradual process. In 1810, Secretary of Treasury Albert Gallatin estimated that 'about two-thirds of the clothing, including . . . house and table linen used by the inhabitants of the United States, who do not reside in cities, is the product of family manufactures'. In terms of monetary value this was about ten times the amount produced outside the home. Class membership and place of residence were primary factors in the reduction of home manufacture; more prosperous families, urban dwellers, and those living in the older settled areas of the east led the way in the substitution of store-bought goods for homemade ones (quoted in Degler 1980: 361).

While women's role in the domestic economy gradually diminished, important changes also were taking place in the family. By the late eighteenth century the domestic sphere had begun to contract; there were fewer servants than there had been earlier, the practice of taking in apprentices and journeymen had all but ceased, and with the expansion of economic opportunities fathers were spending less time at home. The physical separation of the home and the place of work already was under way for artisans, merchants, and professionals. But while fewer adults remained in the household, children were now living in it until they reached adolescence. With the demise of the 'putting out' system, middle-class children were no longer apprenticed to other families and by 1820 they generally lived at home until about the age of 15. The nuclear family itself became smaller as the birth rate declined, particularly in the more densely populated eastern regions of the country. A study of Gloucester, Massachusetts, found that women who married before 1740 had an average of 6.7 children, while those who married after that date averaged 4.6 children. Similarly, by the late eighteenth century in Andover, Massachusetts, women typically had five or six children when their grandmothers had averaged seven or eight (Greven 1970; Bloch 1978a: 114; 1978b: 251; Degler 1980).

Not only was the middle-class household smaller in size but with the onset of industrialization it was no longer a wholly self-contained unit whose members were bound by common tasks. For the first time the place, scope, and pace of men's and women's work began to differ sharply. As a distinct division of labour gradually arose between the home and the world of work, the household's contacts with the outside decreased. By the first decades of the nineteenth century the term *home* had come to be synonymous with *place of retirement or retreat* (Cott 1977).

Ideologies about the nature of children also began to change. By 1800 the Calvinist belief in infant damnation had begun to give way to the Lockean doctrine of the *tabula rasa*, which stressed the lack of innate evil (or good), and the importance of experience in moulding the child. In 1796 one physician wrote, 'that any children are born with vicious inclinations, I would not willingly believe'. Children, at least middle-class children, began to be seen as individuals. They were no longer viewed as 'miniature adults' whose natural inclinations toward evil had to be broken: childhood was becoming a distinct period in the life cycle. The dictum that children were to be treated as individuals with special needs and potentials requiring special nurturing placed a new and heavy responsibility on parents; failure in child rearing could no longer 'be blamed on native corruption', explains one historian (Smith 1796: 108; Frost 1973: 87; Slater 1977).

These altered views of children coincided with the decline of the birth rate in the late eighteenth and early nineteenth centuries. The decline in New England, for example, was greatest between 1810 and 1830, and, according to one scholar, during these years 'the new sensibility toward children first became highly visible' (Slater 1977: 73). But the lower birth rate, implying fewer children per family and perhaps more attention paid to each child, only partially explains the fundamental change in thinking about children. Both the gradual redefinition of women's role and the redefinition of childhood were linked to larger societal changes affecting middle-class life.

The prescriptive literature on childcare in these years was in many ways transitional between the stark dicta of the colonial clergy and the effusive writings of the later nineteenth-century advice givers. Prior to about 1830 such literature did not enjoy mass circulation but appeared in periodical articles, printed sermons, and occasional treatises. All of it came under the rubric 'domestic education' and was written by ministers, physicians, and parents for a white, middle- and upper-middle-class audience. Most pertinent here was the transitional image of the role of middle-class mother. Motherhood in fact was being revamped. Duties that had once belonged to both mothers and fathers or to fathers alone were now becoming the near exclusive province of mothers. One historian of the period notes that 'now fathers began to recede into the background in writings about the domestic education of children'. Treatises on the treatment of childhood diseases, diet, hygiene, and exercise for young children now addressed mothers alone. Some of the medical texts also offered advice on the psychological management of young children, stressing for the first time the importance of the mother's influence during the impressionable years (Slater 1977; Bloch 1978a: 112–13).

Arguments against wet nursing also took on a new cast. Whereas earlier commentators condemned the practice for its ill effects on a child's health, writers now added that wet nursing tainted the child's character. One of the earliest references to a special relationship between mother and child appears in this context. A 1798 tract printed in England (but read in America) urged women to nurse their children so as to avoid 'the destruction, or at least the diminution of the sympathy between mother and child'. Nursing was no longer simply a woman's religious duty but the key to her future happiness as well. 'Those children who are neglected by their mothers during their infant years', wrote Dr Hugh Smith in 1796, 'forget all duty and affection toward them, when such mothers are in the decline of life.' The same author exalted in the joys of breast-feeding: 'Tell me you who know the rapturous delight, how complete is the bliss of enfolding in your longing arms the dear, dear fruits of all your pains!' (Smith 1796: 54, 57; quoted in Frost 1973: 72).

Another early guide is Dr William Buchan's *Advice to Mothers*, published in Boston in 1809. The growing importance of the maternal role is obvious here. 'The more I reflect on the situation of a mother, the more I am struck by the extent of her powers', wrote Dr Buchan. Clearly not all mothers are equal: 'By a mother I do not mean the woman who merely brings a child into the world, but her who faithfully discharges the duties of a parent—whose chief concern is the well-being of her infant.' But mothers walked a narrow line between neglect and overindulgence. 'The obvious paths of nature are alike forsaken by the woman who gives up the care of her infant to a hireling . . . who neglects her duties as a mother; and by her who carries these duties to excess; who makes an idol of her child' (Buchan [1809] 1972: 3, 77). This is the first mention of a theme that was to be heard over and over again in the prescriptive writings of the nineteenth and much of the twentieth centuries. Mothers must be ever on guard to do their job properly—always lurking in the background of the advice books were the pitiful figures of mothers who had failed, mothers who had not taken their duties seriously, or mothers who had performed them with excessive zeal. . . .

Emphasis on the mother role was not limited to advice manuals. Between 1800 and 1820 a new theme appeared in many New England sermons: mothers are more important than fathers in shaping 'the tastes, sentiments, and habits of children'. One New Hampshire minister proclaimed in 1806: 'Weighty beyond expression is the charge devolved to the female parent. It is not within the province of human wisdom to calculate all the happy consequences resulting from the persevering assiduity of mothers.' While sermons of the day did not deny all paternal responsibility, they made clear that raising children was a specialized domestic activity that was largely the province of mothers. As one scholar of the period notes, this 'emphasis departed from (and undermined) the patriarchal family ideal in which the mother, while entrusted with the physical care of her children, let their religious, moral, and intellectual guidance to her husband' (quoted in Cott 1977: 86; quoted in Bloch 1978a: 112).

Although little is known about the actual child-rearing practices in the early nineteenth century, it is clear that the aim of the advice manuals and the sermons dealing with the topic was to increase the amount of time and attention mothers devoted to infants and small children. For the first time in American history the care of young children was viewed as a full-time task, as a distinct profession requiring special knowledge. What had once been done according to tradition now demanded proper study. Even arguments favouring women's education now came to be couched in terms of the woman's role as mother; women were to be educated because the formation of the future citizens of the republic lay in their hands (Sicherman 1975: 496). It is ironic, indeed, but by no means coincidental, that as their sphere narrowed and became more isolated, middle-class women were told that their sphere's importance to the future of the new nation was boundless.

Historian Ruth H. Bloch notes that economic factors exercised a 'push–pull' effect on child-rearing responsibilities. As the domestic production of middle-class mothers began to wane and their domestic work lost its commercial value, fathers began to spend more and more time working outside the home, as did other adults who had once resided in the household (Bloch 1978b: 250). Women, left alone at home with their children, who were now living there until adolescence, began to assume almost complete responsibility for childcare. The prescriptive literature, with its newly expanded definition of motherhood, was thus a response to these structural changes in society. In essence, as the female role in domestic production declined, the middle-class woman was told to focus on reproduction.

Motherhood, A Fearful Responsibility: 1820–70

The concept of the mother role which prevailed from the late eighteenth century to about 1820 was, in the words of one historian, 'a rare and subdued hint of the extravagant celebration of motherhood to come' (Abbott 1833: 162; Calhoun [1918] 1960: 52; Ryan 1975: 126). Beginning in the 1820s and gaining momentum in the 1830s and 1840s, a flood of manuals and periodical articles gave advice on the maternal role, exulted in the joys of motherhood, and told women that good mothering was not only the key to their own and their children's happiness but crucial to the nation's destiny as well.

This period between 1820 and 1860 was one of rapid industrialization; industrial production in fact doubled every decade. . . . The most salient change occurring during these years was the eventual demise of the self-sufficient household. The growth of industry, technological advances, improvements in transportation, and the increasing specialization of agriculture made more goods available, and the household became more and more reliant on the market to meet its needs. In simple terms, the period between 1820 and 1860 witnessed the substitution of store-bought goods for home-manufactured goods, and this development had a profound impact on women's work. Even as early as the 1820s women's domestic production had diminished in scope and variety to the extent that they were left with only a residue of their former household duties. In New England by 1830 home spinning and weaving were largely replaced by manufactured textiles, and by mid-century women's productive skills had become even more superfluous; butter, candles, soap, medicine, buttons, and cloth were widely available in stores. By 1860 women's contribution to household production continued to a significant extent only in remote frontier regions. The noted feminist and abolitionist Sarah Grimké remarked on the decline of home manufacture in 1838: 'When all manufactures were domestic, then the domestic function might well consume all the time of a very able-bodied woman. But nowadays . . . when so much of woman's work is done by the butcher and the baker, by the tailor and the cook, and the gas maker . . . you see how much of woman's time is left for other functions' (Cott 1977; Ehrenreich and English 1978; quoted in Degler 1980).

The removal of production from the home to the factory led to the breakdown of the once close relationship between the household and the business of society. For the first time 'life', that is, the home, was divided from 'work'. Not only had the two spheres become separate, they were now seen as incompatible; the home was a retreat from the competitive world of commerce and industry, a place of warmth and respite where moral values prevailed. The business of the world no longer took place at home.

These economic and social developments were of course not unique to the United States. A similar series of events occurred in England in the seventeenth century. There, in the words of one scholar of the period, 'the old familial economic partnership of husband and wife was being undermined. The wife was being driven from her productive role. The concept of the husband supporting his family was replacing mutuality in earning power . . . [the wife's] place might still be in the home, but her husband was no longer an integral part of it' (Thompson 1974: 75).

The American household continued to shrink throughout the nineteenth century. By 1850 the ancillary household members had moved out—an unmarried sister might be teaching school in town and greater numbers of domestic servants were leaving the middle-class household to take factory jobs. . . . Part of this decrease, however, resulted from a falling birth rate.

Ideas about the nature of children continued to evolve. The neutral *tabula rasa* of the first decades of the nineteenth century was supplanted by the idea of the 'sweet angels of the Romantic era'. After 1830 children were routinely depicted as beings of great purity and innocence. They were naturally close to God and their virtuous proclivities had only to be gently moulded to ensure eternal salvation. Closely allied with this idealized image of the young was the conviction that *mothers and mothers alone* had the power to transform malleable infants into moral, productive adults. For this reason many warned against the dangers of hiring nurses, for even the best nurse was never an adequate substitute for the mother herself. Only a mother's care and influence, not that of fathers, older siblings, relatives, or servants, could fulfill the special physical and spiritual needs of the growing child. Motherhood had not only become a career-like responsibility but the responsibility had grown longer and longer in duration. By the mid-nineteenth century middle-class children remained at home until well into adolescence, and throughout the century there was a tendency to prolong dependence. Children left home at a later and later age (Slater 1977; Wishy 1968: 40; Degler 1980: 69).

Some scholars claim that the nineteenth century's concern with the child as an individual and with proper child-rearing methods was the result of a decline in infant mortality. Parents, they argue, became more certain that their children would grow to adulthood and so were willing to invest more time and energy in them. Historian Carl Degler faults this thesis, citing data that suggests that infant mortality did not decline. In fact, infant mortality might even have been higher than the official statistics indicate with the likelihood of a high mortality rate among unreported births. One could argue on this basis that at least part of the growing concern for the child was because infant mortality rates did remain so high. Catherine Beecher and other manual writers contended that proper childcare would help to prevent the deaths of infants and young children (Beecher [1841] 1977; Degler 1980: 72–3).

Population growth from reproduction did in fact decline steadily as the birth rate fell throughout the nineteenth century. By 1850 the average white woman was bearing only half as many children as her grandmother had. Even more striking is the 50 per cent decline in the completed fertility rate for the century as a whole; it fell from 7.04 children per white woman in

1800 to 3.56 in 1900. The question, of course, is why did women bear fewer children? In the words of anthropologist Marvin Harris, in an industrializing, urbanizing society children 'tend to cost more and to be economically less valuable to their parents than children on farms' (Degler 1980: 181; Kessler-Harris 1981: 34; Harris 1981: 81).

Children in agrarian societies cost relatively little to raise and they help out by doing a variety of tasks even when they are young. But in cities the expense of rearing children increases as does their period of dependency; most or all of the items a child needs must be purchased, and schooling is required before the child can become economically independent. In essence, urban children contribute less and cost more. Therefore, as the nineteenth century progressed, the shift in the costs and benefits of having children particularly affected the middle class, whose children required longer and longer periods of socialization before they could make it on their own outside the home. The rearing of 'quality' children, children who enjoyed a long period of dependency while they were schooled to take their 'rightful' position in society, was an ever more costly process. Is it any wonder then that the average middle-class family had fewer and fewer children as the century progressed?

The immense outpouring of advice manuals and other prescriptive writings after 1830 cannot be adequately explained by continued high levels of infant mortality or even by the fact that women were having fewer children and simply had the time to make a greater investment in each one. Another factor in the advice-giving boom was the nation's slowly growing need for children who would be reared to become professionals or to take the business and management positions being created by the industrializing process. What better and cheaper way to accomplish this than by urging middle-class women to devote many years and large quantities of their (unpaid) time and energy to nurturing the future captains of business and industry?

Another key to understanding the paeans to motherhood is the falling fertility rate of the middle class. But the relationship is by no means a simple one. It seems logical that if women had been taking these paeans seriously they would have had more rather than fewer children, and it is of course naïve to assume that fertility decisions are made on the basis of advice books. I believe the line between the two is as follows: as fertility declined among the white middle class, there was growing alarm in certain quarters. Where were the future leaders in business and industry to come from? Who was going to manage the nation's burgeoning industries? At a time when the fertility of the non-white and the foreign-born was higher than that of native-born whites, the country's elite feared that the 'backbone' of the nation was being diluted by 'lesser types'. The glorification of maternity which was directed at potential mothers of the 'backbone', was an attempt, albeit an unsuccessful one, to encourage their reproductive activity.[4]

Scholars are not certain just how people in the nineteenth century controlled their fertility, but there is evidence that American women began practising abortion more frequently after 1840. One historian estimates one abortion for every 25 or 30 live births during the first decades of the century, a proportion that rose to about one in every five or six live births during the 1850s and 1860s. Most contemporary physicians agreed that the primary motive for abortion was control of family size, and they cited as evidence the fact that by far the largest group practising abortion was married women. It is significant that prior to the nineteenth century there were no laws prohibiting abortion during the first few months of pregnancy. The procedure was not illegal until 'quickening', that is, until the first movements of the fetus are felt at about four months. The first laws banning abortion were passed between 1821 and 1841; during those two decades 10 states and one territory specifically outlawed its practice. By the time of the Civil War nearly every state had laws prohibiting abortion at all stages of fetal development (Gordon 1977: 52, 57n; Mohr 1978: 50, 20).

I do not think that mere coincidence accounts for concern about the falling birth rate, laws banning abortion, and the publication of numerous childcare manuals and articles lauding the maternal role, all appearing at roughly the same time. The outpourings of the advice givers reflected the wider anxiety about middle-class women's declining fertility and sought to counteract it by dwelling on the joys of motherhood for their white, middle-class audience.

The contraction of women's productive activities in the now smaller and more isolated nuclear household provided the necessary setting for this expanding emphasis on the mother role. There was now a sizeable, literate audience of homebound women who could be advised of the importance of motherhood and given suggestions of time-consuming methods for its proper discharge. In short, as the domestic sphere contracted and middle-class women found their lives increasingly centred around their husbands and children, they were advised of the gravity of their redefined role. What higher calling was there than shaping the future leaders of the nation?

Maternal Ideals

A number of recurrent themes in nineteenth-century child-rearing manuals and periodical articles were only weakly developed or were entirely absent from the prescriptive writings of an earlier era. Foremost among these are that childcare is the exclusive province of women, that motherhood is their *primary* function, and that mothers, and mothers alone, are responsible for their children's character development and future success or failure. By the 1830s motherhood had been transformed into a mission so that 'the entire burden of the child's well-being in this life and the next' was in its mother's hands (*The Ladies' Museum* 1825; Sunley 1963: 152). These themes, moreover, were not limited to child-rearing manuals. Popular novels, poems, and biographies of famous men all stressed the important role of the mother in shaping her child's fate. Middle-class women were told that they had it in their power to produce joy or misery, depending on how they performed their parental duties. These sentiments were echoed in a burgeoning literature on 'female character' which claimed that women were innately nurturant, domestic, and selfless, all qualities that made them 'naturals' at child rearing.

One of the most striking features of the child-rearing advice of the mid-nineteenth century is the disappearance of references to fathers. While some earlier tracts were addressed exclusively to mothers, most were written for 'parents', and there was even an occasional 'advice to fathers' manual. This shift from *parental* to *maternal* responsibility is evident in Philip Greven's collection of sermons, treatises, and other sources of advice on child rearing dating from 1628 to 1861 (Greven 1973). The first eight excerpts, originally published between 1629 and 1814, are all addressed to 'parents'. It is not until John Abbott's 1833 essay 'On the Mother's Role in Education' that the maternal role is highlighted and mothers are given the primary responsibility for childcare.

Mothers were offered abundant advice on the feeding, dressing, washing, and general management of infants and young children. They were told how to deal with teething, toilet training, masturbation, and childhood diseases. But the mother's physical care of her children was a minor task compared to her job of socializing them. Women were advised that their every thought and gesture, no matter how seemingly inconsequential, carried a message to the child. Women were to be ever on their guard lest they impede their offspring's moral development.

Many writers stressed the sentimental benefits of an activity that received no material rewards. 'How entire and perfect is the dominion over the unformed character of your infant. Write what you will, upon the printless tablet, with your wand of love', wrote Mrs Sigourney in *Letters to Mothers* (1838).

Women's education is justified, some advice givers claimed, because of women's influence on the next generation. *Maternal* education, however, was what they really sought. In an 1845 tome, for example, Edward Mansfield cited three reasons for educating women: 'that they should as *mothers*, be the fit teachers of infant men. That they should be the fit teachers of American men. That they should be the fit teachers of Christian men' (Mansfield 1845: 105; emphasis in original).

Motherhood, as depicted in the prescriptive writings of the mid-nineteenth century, was a full-time occupation demanding time-consuming unpaid labour. 'It truly requires all the affection of even a fond mother to administer dutifully to the numerous wants of a young child', wrote William Dewees. Mrs Sigourney agreed. She saw a mother as 'a sentinel who should never sleep at her post', recommending that women get household help to perform manual tasks so that the mother 'may be able to become the constant directress of her children'. There is no question that mothering was work; infants should be fed on demand, and toilet training and 'moral education' should begin at a few months of age. Cleanliness was stressed and clothes were to be washed often and changed as soon as they got dirty. Furthermore, the good mother would keep careful records of her children's behaviour and development. The Reverend Abbott told mothers to 'study their duty', while Mrs Sigourney urged women to 'study night and day the science that promotes the welfare of our infant' (Abbott 1833: 169; Sigourney 1838: 28, 82, 87; Dewees 1847: 64–5).

Mothers, according to the advice givers, were perfectly suited to care for their children; no one else could do the job as well or, one might add, as cheaply. As far as the mother's duties permitted, she was to 'take the entire care of her own child', advised the popular domestic writer, Lydia Maria Child. During the first 'sacred' year, concurred Mrs Sigourney, 'trust not your treasure too much to the charge of hirelings. Have it under your superintendence night and day. The duty of your office admits of no substitute.' But what of other family members? Are they of no help? Yes: 'brothers and sisters, the father, all perform their part, but the mother does the most', opined the author of a *Parents Magazine* article, who went on to issue a stern warning. Children whose mothers did not 'take the entire care of them' faced real danger; a mother 'cannot be long relieved without hazard or exchanged without loss' (Child [1831] 1972: 4; Sigourney 1838: 16, 32, 87; *Parents Magazine* 1841: 156).

A corollary of the focus on mothers was the disappearance of fathers from the child-rearing manuals of the nineteenth century. Advice books assumed that children spent most of their time with their mothers, not their fathers, even though by law and custom final authority was patriarchal. Paternal responsibilities were rarely spelled out. For example, in answering the question 'Is there nothing for fathers to do?' Reverend Abbott responded that there are many paternal duties 'which will require time and care'. But the only duties he actually stipulated for fathers were 'to lead their families to God' and to teach their children to 'honour' their mother. Although some advice givers saw fathers as the primary disciplinarians in the family, others urged mothers to punish their children's misbehaviour before fathers returned home in the evening. Even daily prayers, once led by the father as head of the household, had now become the province of the mother (Abbott 1833: 155–6).

The occasional references to fathers in the prescriptive writings of the day either remarked on their sovereignty in the home or noted their real responsibilities outside of it. A father's duties, advised the *Ladies' Companion*, are 'the acquisitions of wealth, the advancement of his children in worldly honour—these are his self-imposed tasks'.

❖

By the mid-nineteenth century a gooey sentimentality had come to distinguish motherhood from fatherhood. A sample from a 'ladies' magazine' of the day reveals the tone: 'Is there a feeling that activates the human heart so powerful as that of maternal affection? Who but women can feel the tender sensation so strong? The father, indeed, may press his lovely infant to his manly heart, but does it thrill with those feelings which irresistibly overcome the mother?' (*Ladies' Literary Cabinet* 1822: 5).

These patterns of ideological change are also apparent in an analysis of sixteenth- to nineteenth-century child-rearing responsibilities in England. English manuals of the sixteenth and seventeenth centuries told parents to 'co-rear' their children: eighteenth-century manuals depicted mothers as the primary child rearers but expressed some anxiety about this; by the nineteenth century mothers were the primary rearers 'without anxiety' (Stewart, Winter, and Jones 1975: 701).

In America by mid-century good mothering was not only essential to the well-being and future of the child but the lack of such exclusive care was considered a threat to the very moral fibre of the nation. 'The destiny of a nation is shaped by its character', Reverend Beckwith proclaimed, 'and that character . . . will ever be found to be molded chiefly by maternal hands.' 'When our land is filled with pious and patriotic mothers, then will it be filled with virtuous and patriotic men', agreed Reverend Abbott. But it is clear that women's contribution to the young republic was to be indirect. In the words of Daniel Webster: 'It is by promulgation of sound morals in the community, and more especially by the training and instruction of the young that woman performs her part toward the preservation of a free government . . . '(Abbott 1833: 153; Beckwith 1850: 4; quoted in Kuhn 1947: 34).[5] As part of the effort to convince middle-class women of their crucial role in the nation's destiny—a role wholly dependent on the diligent performance of their maternal duties—moral educators frequently cited the mothers of famous men.

❖

Many advice writers dwelt long and graphically on the general evils that sprang from poor mothering. An 1841 issue of *Parents Magazine* contained a case study of a convict, whose life of crime was analyzed in the following terms: 'His mother, although hopefully pious, never prayed with him in private. . . . There was no maternal association in the place of their residence.' Then a warning was issued: 'Reader, are you a parent? . . . *Train up a child in the way he should go*.' Even such cataclysms as the French Revolution, with its 'atheism, licentiousness, and intemperance', could be avoided by 'seizing upon the infant mind and training it up under moral and religious influence', suggested another author in the same magazine. Mrs Elizabeth Hall, writing in *The Mother's Assistant*, made the point succinctly: 'Perhaps there is no proposition that is so hackneyed, and at the same time so little understood, as that women are the prime cause of all the good and evil in human actions. . . . Yes, mothers, in a certain sense the destiny of a redeemed world is put into your hands' (Hall 1849: 25; quoted in Kuhn 1947: 67; emphasis in original). Mothers were given a strong message. They were the potential source of *both* evil and good in the world, so that they had best be mindful of the proper performance of their maternal duties.

Many authors pointed out that while women should not go out into the world, the mother role, because of its far-reaching influence, still gave women a lofty position in society. 'Though she may not teach from the portico nor thunder from the forum . . . she may form and send forth the sages that shall govern and renovate the world', wrote Catherine Beecher, the popular domestic educator. 'The patriotism of women', Mrs Sigourney agreed, 'is not to thunder in senates'—it is to be expressed in the 'office of maternal teacher'. A writer in *Ladies' Magazine* noted that a mother's influence is 'unseen, unfelt', but through it 'she is forming the future patriot, statesman, or enemy of his country; more than this she is sowing the seeds of virtue or vice which will fit him for Heaven or for eternal misery' (Beecher 1829: 54; Sigourney 1838: 13, 16; *Ladies' Magazine* 1840: 246).

The rewards of motherhood were extravagantly described by the advice givers. To wit: 'My friends,' wrote Mrs Sigourney, 'if in becoming a mother, you have reached the climax of your happiness, you have also taken a higher place on the scale of being.' Since children have the power to change their mothers for the better and bring them joy, no matter how difficult the tasks of motherhood, a mother 'would willingly have endured a thousandfold for such a payment'. Children also could provide their mothers with eternal salvation. 'Does not the little cherub in his way guide you to heaven, marking the pathway by the flowers he scatters as he goes?' queried Mrs Child. There was no doubt that children were the keys to feminine fulfillment. The love of children, proclaimed an editorial in *Godey's Lady's Book*, 'is as necessary to a woman's perfect development, as the sunshine and the rain are to the health and beauty of the flowers'. Not only was a woman's entire happiness dependent on her civilizing task, her very identity was derived from it. 'A woman is nobody. A wife is everything . . . and a mother is, next to God, all powerful', trumpeted a writer in a Philadelphia newspaper at mid-century (quoted in Calhoun [1918] 1960: 84–5; Child [1831] 1972: 9; Sigourney 1838: 2, 24; *Godey's Lady's Book* 1860: 272).

This preoccupation with motherhood is baffling unless firmly set within its larger social and economic context. The demise of the self-contained household economy, the isolation of a much reduced living unit, the segregation of the home from the workplace, and the resultant segregation of daily life into male and female spheres were all elements in the stage setting in which this ideology emerged. These factors, rather than any strong domestic propensity in women, explain the overweening emphasis on the mother role. On this point I take issue with the historian Carl Degler, who writes that since only women bore and could feed children in the early years, it is not surprising that 'the ideology of domesticity stressed that women's destiny was motherhood'. But hadn't women always borne and nursed children? Why does this ideology appear in full strength only after 1820? In the words of another historian, Mary Ryan, why for the first time was 'childhood socialization, and not merely the physical care of infants . . . subsumed under the category of motherhood'? Why, asks another student of the subject, if there had always been mothers, had motherhood just been invented? The answer lies in the structural changes occurring in nineteenth-century society, changes that led to the increased seclusion of women and children in the home, the decreasing burden of household manufacture, the need for 'high quality' children, and the growing concern with the declining birth rate of the white middle class. These changes more than adequately explain why motherhood, as never before, 'stood out as a discrete task' (Ryan 1975: 84; Cott 1977: 84; Degler 1980; Dally 1982: 17).

Notes

1. This study does not measure the actual amount of time mothers spent with their infants, only whether mothers had primary or exclusive care of them.
2. This is what has been called 'the most important confidence trick that society plays on the individual—to make appear as necessary what is in fact a bundle of contingencies'.
3. I am indebted to Bloch's two articles for the sources contained in this and the next section of the chapter. They are the most thorough research on the prescriptive literature of the colonial period and early nineteenth century that I have found.
4. Although the fear of 'race suicide' is usually associated with the very late nineteenth and early twentieth centuries and with the figure of Theodore Roosevelt, there were in fact references to it prior to the Civil War. See L. Gordon, *Woman's Body, Woman's Right* (New York, 1977), Ch. 7, and A.W. Calhoun, *A Social History of the American Family: Since the Civil War* (New York, [1919] 1960), Ch. 11.
5. Somewhat later the British sociologist Herbert Spencer, who was widely read in the United States, propounded a similar idea when he wrote that 'Children . . . had to be long nurtured by female parents' for 'social progress' to take place (quoted in L. Duffin, 'Prisoners of Progress: Women and Evolution', in *The Nineteenth Century Woman*, eds S. Delmot and L. Duffin [New York, 1978], 78).

References

Abbott, Rev. J.S.C. 1833. *The Mother at Home* (New York: American Tract Society).

Ariès, P. 1965. *Centuries of Childhood* (New York: Vintage).

Beckwith, G.C. 1850. 'The Fate of Nations Dependent on Mothers', *The Mother's Assistant* 15: 4.

Beecher, C. 1829. *Suggestions Respecting Improvements in Education* (New York: Hartford, Packard, and Butler).

———. [1841] 1977. *A Treatise on Domestic Economy* (New York: Schocken).

Berger, P.L., and T. Luckmann. 1966. *The Social Construction of Reality* (New York: Doubleday).

Bernard, J. 1974. *The Future of Motherhood* (New York: Penguin).

Bloch, R.H. 1978a. 'American Feminine Ideals in Transition: The Rise of the Moral Mother, 1785–1815', *Feminist Studies* 4: 106.

———. 1978b. 'Untangling the Roots of Modern Sex Roles: A Survey of Four Centuries of Change', *Signs* 4: 242.

Brown, J.K. 1970. 'A Note on the Division of Labor by Sex', *American Anthropologist* 72: 1073–8.

Brownlee, W.E. 1974. *Dynamics of Ascent: A History of the American Economy* (New York: Alfred A. Knopf).

Buchan, W. [1809] 1972. *Advice to Mothers*, reprinted in *The American Physician and Child Rearing: Two Guides 1809–1894* (New York: Arno Press).

Calhoun, A.W. [1917] 1960. *A Social History of the American Family: The Colonial Period* (New York: Barnes and Noble).

———. [1918] 1960. *A Social History of the American Family: From Independence through the Civil War* (New York: Barnes and Noble).

Child, L.M. [1831] 1972. *The Mother's Book* (New York: Arno Press).

Cott, N.F. 1977. *The Bonds of Womanhood: 'Woman's Sphere' in New England, 1780–1835* (New Haven: Yale University Press).

Dally, A. 1982. *Inventing Motherhood* (London: Burnett Books Ltd.).

Degler, C.N. 1980. *At Odds: Women and the Family in America from the Revolution to the Present* (New York: Oxford University Press).

Demos, J. 1970. *A Little Commonwealth: Family Life in Plymouth Colony* (New York: Oxford University Press).

Dewees, W. 1847. *A Treatise on the Physical and Medical Treatment of Children*, 10th edn (Philadelphia: Blanchard and Lea).

Ehrenreich, B., and D. English. 1978. *For Her Own Good: 150 Years of the Experts' Advice to Women* (New York: Anchor).

Frost, J.W. 1973. *The Quaker Family in Colonial America: A Portrait of the Society of Friends* (New York: St Martin's Press).

Gordon, L. 1977. *Woman's Body, Woman's Right* (New York: Penguin).

Greven, Jr, P.J. 1970. *Four Generations: Population, Land, and Family in Colonial Andover, Massachusetts* (Ithaca, NY: Cornell University Press).

———. 1973. *Child Rearing Concepts, 1628–1861* (Itasca, IL: Peacock).

Hall, E.S. 1849. 'A Mother's Influence', *The Mother's Assistant* 1: 25.

Harris, M. 1981. *America Now: The Anthropology of a Changing Culture* (New York: Simon and Schuster).

Kessler-Harris, A. 1981. *Women Have Always Worked* (Westbury, NY: The Feminist Press).

Klevana, W.M. 1980. 'Does Labor Time Increase with Industrialization? A Survey of Time Allocation Studies', *Current Anthropology* 21: 279–98.

Kuhn, A.L. 1947. *The Mother's Role in Childhood Education: New England Concepts 1830–1860* (New Haven: Yale University Press).

Ladies' Literary Cabinet. 1822. 5 (Jan.): 5.

Ladies' Magazine. 1840. 'Influence of Women—Past and Present', 13: 246.

The Ladies' Museum. 1825. 'Maternity' 1 (Sept.): 31.

Lamber, W.E., J.F. Hamers, and N. Frasure-Smith. 1979. *Child Rearing Values: A Cross-national Study* (New York).

Mansfield, E. 1845. *The Legal Rights, Liabilities, and Duties of Women* (Salem, MA: John P. Jewett).

Masson, M.W. 1976. 'The Typology of the Female as a Model for the Regenerate: Puritan Teaching, 1690–1730', *Signs* 2: 304–15.

Mather, C. [1741] 1978. *Ornaments of the Daughters of Zion*, 3rd edn (Delmar, NY: Scholars Facsimiles and Reprints).

Minturn, L., and W.W. Lambert. 1964. *Mothers of Six Cultures* (New York: John Wiley).

Mohr, J.C. 1978. *Abortion in America: The Origins and Evolution of National Policy 1800–1900* (New York: Oxford University Press).

Norton, M.B. 1980. *Liberty's Daughters: The Revolutionary Experience of American Women* (Boston: Houghton Mifflin).

Parents Magazine. 1841. 'The Responsibility of Mothers', 1 (Mar.): 156.

Ryan, M.P. 1975. *Womanhood in America: From Colonial Times to the Present* (New York: New Viewpoints).

Sicherman, B. 1975. 'American History', *Signs* 1: 461–85.

Sigourney. 1838. *Letters to Mothers* (Hartford: Hudson and Skinner).

Sklar, K.K. [1841] 1977. 'Introduction', in C.E. Beecher, *A Treatise on Domestic Economy* (New York: Schocken).

Slater, P.G. 1977. *Children in the New England Mind* (Hamden, CN: Archon).

Smith, H. 1796. *Letters to Married Women on Nursing and the Management of Children*, 2nd edn (Philadelphia: Mathew Carey).

Stewart, A.J., D.G. Winter, and A.D. Jones. 1975. 'Coding Categories for the Study of Child Rearing from Historical Sources', *Journal of Interdisciplinary History* 5: 701.

Sunley, R. 1963. 'Early Nineteenth Century American Literature on Child Rearing', in *Childhood in Contemporary Cultures*, eds M. Mead and M. Wolfenstein (Chicago: University of Chicago Press).

Thompson, R. 1974. *Women in Stuart England and America* (Boston: Routledge & Kegan Paul).

Ulrich, L.T. 1979. 'Virtuous Women Found: New England Ministerial Literature, 1668–1735', in *A Heritage of Her Own*, eds N.F. Cott and E.H. Pleck (New York: Touchstone).

Wadsworth, B. [1712] 1972. 'The Well-ordered Family, or, Relative Duties', in *The Colonial American Family: Collected Essays* (New York: Arno).

Weisner, T., and R. Gallimore. 1977. 'My Brother's Keeper: Child and Sibling Caretaking', *Current Anthropology* 18.

Wishy, B. 1968. *The Child and the Republic: The Dawn of Modern American Child Nurture* (Philadelphia: University of Philadelphia Press).

Section 4 From 1950s Breadwinner–Homemaker Families to Twenty-first Century Diversity

While some social trends that developed in the nineteenth century continued into the twentieth century (e.g., declining birth rates, women's struggle for equality), new trends began as well. In the early part of the century, marriage was increasingly equated with heterosexual romance and sexual pleasure—for women as well as for men. But not until the 1950s did nearly all adults marry. The decade of the 1950s witnessed a reversal of many long-term trends—a rise in birth rates and a decline in divorce, for example. It became the most familistic period in Canadian and American history. It was an unusual period, and myths about its character have been the source of nostalgia in recent times.

In Chapter 10, Mary Louise Adams describes the social construction (in the 1950s) of ideas about heterosexuality, which was seen as natural, and the only 'normal' sexual expression. The next chapter contains a selection from Meg Luxton's study of working-class families in the 1970s in Flin Flon. Her findings reveal some of the consequences of full-time homemaking and the associated economic dependence of women on their male partners. Both chapters explore issues of power in nuclear families. Chapter 12 reviews demographic trends that have shaped family life over the years in Canada. The discussion situates current family diversity in the context of long-term changes, and explores the key factors behind important demographic trends.

Chapter 10

This is a chapter from Mary Louise Adams's book *The Trouble with Normal*, which explores the ways heterosexuality was constructed as 'normal'—the only normal sexuality—in the post-war period in Canada. Adams examines popular post-war discourses that aimed to define what constituted normal sexual expression, and thus (indirectly) normal sexual identity. Her work is informed by the work of Michel Foucault, who argued that public discourses about sexuality exert power over individuals. Discourse in the public arena is powerful when it so firmly establishes what is 'normal' that individuals take measures to regulate their behaviour in order to conform. While Adams's book is mostly about sexuality, this chapter highlights the tremendous symbolic importance that the heterosexual nuclear-family pattern assumed during the Cold War.

Sexuality and the Post-war Domestic 'Revival'

Mary Louise Adams

In present-day popular culture, the post-war period is routinely depicted by a predictable mix of Ozzie and Harriet, suburban bungalows, and rock 'n' roll teen culture. On the one hand, the period has come to represent a lost era of family values for which many now yearn; on the other hand, it is seen as a time of unceasing conformity, repression, and blandness, broken only by the tyrannies of McCarthyist anti-Communism. In Canada, any of a number of recent studies—Doug Owram's *Born at the Right Time*, Franca Iacovetta's *Such Hardworking People*, and Reg Whitaker and Gary Marcuse's *Cold War Canada*, among others—is capable of shattering these simplistic views.[1] While the post-war period was a time when social conformity was valued by many and when popular culture frequently traded in images of smiling suburban housewives, it was also a period that saw tremendous changes on the social landscape—such as a steady increase in the numbers of working women and huge increases in the numbers of immigrants coming to Canada from southern and eastern European countries.

Canadian sociologists and historians have dealt constructively with this contradictory image, avoiding the false polarization that has characterized some post-war scholarship in the United States: Was the period a time of repression or a time of social change? In her recent anthology *Not June Cleaver*, American historian Joanne Meyerowitz takes other feminist historians to task for focusing too much attention on the conservatism of the post-war years and not enough on women's resistance. Her argument seems to be directed primarily at Elaine Tyler May's book, *Homeward Bound*, which discusses the links between United States foreign policy during the Cold War and prevailing ideologies of gender and domesticity. While recognizing the era's conservatism, Meyerowitz claims that the emphasis on the constraints women encountered in the period 'tends to downplay women's agency and to portray women primarily as victims. It obscures the complexity of post-war culture and the significant social and economic changes of the post-war era . . . the sustained focus on the white middle-class domestic ideal . . . sometimes renders other ideals and other women invisible.'[2] But surely it is not a matter of either/or, or that researchers need to give priority to one of these projects over the other. The point of studying dominant cultural discourses—mainstream ideals—as May has done, is that we all have to negotiate them, whether we subscribe to them, are marginalized by them, or actively resist them. There can be no understanding of agency—the resistance Meyerowitz wants to reclaim—without an understanding of the context within which it occurs.

Domesticity and Security in Post-war Canada

While the term *post-war* is a convenient way of marking a time period, it cannot be emphasized enough that it refers to the specific social configurations that arose as six years of war came to an end. So, for instance, when we talk about post-war prosperity we need to remember that this prosperity arose in the wake of tremendous loss and disruption.

In 1945, the Canadian domestic economy underwent substantial change as both public and private sectors shifted production and services away from military requirements. While peace was obviously welcomed, many Canadians feared the type of economic downturn that had followed the First World War: Would the economy collapse with the end of military production? Such post-war concerns about economic security were complicated by the emotional and social upheavals that resulted from attempts to reintegrate into civilian life the million men and women who had been in the armed forces. More than 40,000 Canadians had been killed during the war, and thousands more had been injured either physically or mentally.[3] It is not surprising, then, that homecomings did not always provide a happy ending to long and difficult separations.

As victory celebrations subsided, Canadians struggled with the changes the war had brought to the home front. War work had introduced thousands of women and teenagers to relatively lucrative industrial jobs. Many children and teenagers had been free of adult supervision, with fathers in the military and mothers doing war work. Workers of all ages who had migrated to cities in search of wartime jobs experienced for the first time the freedom of living in communities away from their relatives. Further demographic changes occurred as tens of thousands of immigrants and refugees arrived from Europe, many from countries and ethnic/religious backgrounds not widely represented (or forcefully kept out) in previous waves of immigration: Jews, Czechs, Poles, Hungarians, Ukrainians, Russians, Yugoslavians, Italians. The degree to which these and other social changes would, or could, be integrated into the fabric of post-war life was open to considerable debate—as, for instance, in the widespread discussions about the place and acceptability of married women workers in the peacetime labour market, or those about the desirability of having Jews and southern and eastern Europeans enter the country.[4]

According to historian Doug Owram, the physical and emotional disruptions caused by the war, and the significant social changes it motivated, oriented Canadians toward home, family, and stability to a degree unparalleled in other historical periods in this country. Owram suggests that giving precedence to home and family was a primary value of the post-war era and is central to any understanding of the economy, gender relations, politics, or other aspects of those years.[5] As represented by married, middle-class, heterosexual couples and their legitimate offspring, the ideal family was at once seen as a source of affectional relationships, the basis of a consumer economy, a defence against Communism, and a salient metaphor for various forms of social organization, from the nation to the high-school class. In the 1940s and 1950s, writes Joy Parr, 'Domestic metaphors . . . proclaimed the promise of peace.'[6]

During the Depression of the 1930s, fears about security and the future were easily attributed to material deprivation and the social disruptions that followed from it. But after the Second World War, discourses about an uncertain future existed in spite of considerably improved material circumstances across North America. While 25 per cent of the Canadian population continued to live in poverty into the 1960s, this figure was down substantially from the 50 per cent that had been the average during the interwar years.[7] During the post-war period, the United States and Canada had the highest and second-highest standards of living in the world. Total industrial output rose by 50 per cent in the 1950s. Canadian manufacturing wages doubled between 1945 and 1956 while prices rose only slightly. Unemployment remained between 2.8 and 5.9 per cent, depending on the region, until the mid-1950s.[8] In contrast, the 1933 national unemployment rate had been 20 per cent.[9] Between 1948 and 1961, a decades-old housing crisis began to reverse as building boomed and home ownership jumped from just over 30 per cent to 60 per cent. Clearly, many Canadians were better off than they had been. Still, speech-makers and journalists referred to a collective distrust of the future.

In a 1952 editorial, *Chatelaine* editor Lotta Dempsey tried to put this unease into words. Writing of a cross-Canada train trip, she noted prosperous-looking people at 'every station' and found herself remarking on the difference a single decade could make:

> I listen to conversations of well-fed, well-dressed people enjoying the ease and luxury of modern trains and planes. They seem to have everything . . . everything except some indefinable inner security . . . and faith. Some sense of certain strength to hold and maintain this largesse.
>
> Perhaps we know that the borders of our peaceful land grow thinner as the turmoil of the outside world increases.[10]

After 15 years of domestic uncertainty, Canadians were confronted with the Cold War and they were nervous about 'the outside world', the unknown, the other. In the face of such a nebulous threat, there seemed little that an individual could do, and Dempsey counselled her readers to have faith in God.

In the 1950s, Christianity remained a profoundly important discourse in both popular and official media. Certainly, Christian values underlay recurring arguments that placed the heterosexual nuclear family at the centre of a secure future for both individuals and the nation.[11] In 1946, for instance, a Toronto mayor promoted good citizenship by declaring 'Christian Family Week'. An ad in the *Toronto Daily Star* read: 'If our country is to fulfill its destiny, family life, founded on Christian ideals and principles, must be preserved.'[12]

Domesticity as Cold War Strategy

In magazines, school board curricula, and instructional films, an idealized image of the nuclear family was promoted as the first line of defence against the perceived insecurity of the Cold War years.[13] Family life would shield Canada from the threat of 'outside turmoil'. As both Canadian and American historians have shown, in this age of prosperity both international and domestic affairs were suffused by familial discourse and, thus, contributed to the need North Americans expressed for control on a personal level. As American historian Elaine May puts it, the post-war family was located firmly 'within the larger political culture, not outside it',[14] although contemporary representations of the family usually portrayed the opposite.

Cold War rhetoric and the activities that followed from it were not the same in Canada as they were in the States, as Reg Whitaker and Gary Marcuse have shown.[15] Nevertheless, few Canadians could have escaped the American Cold

War hype that infused the popular culture of the era—from the predominantly US films and television shows that came across the border to the US magazines that, by 1954, occupied 80 per cent of Canadian newsstand space.[16] At the very least, Canadians and Americans shared both a fear of and a fascination with the bomb. In 1946, the Toronto Board of Education proclaimed the theme of Education Week to be 'Education for the Atomic Age',[17] marking the bomb and nuclear energy as the harbingers of a new era. Four years later, a *Chatelaine* editorial identified the bomb as the 'biggest thing in our new half-century'. Noting the fear that the bomb inspired in many people, the editorial carefully refrained from mentioning the potential of such an invention to cause mind-boggling harm, referring instead to that fear as 'man's [*sic*] reaction to his own creative powers'. *Chatelaine* readers were encouraged to focus on the good that could come of this creativity, to 'help abolish those Atom Bomb blues!'[18] *Chatelaine* was nothing if not optimistic; hence the claim that atomic energy might one day provide for 'a fantastic new way of life', one with 'luxury and security for all'.[19] Ironically, a feature on the same page acknowledged that most nuclear research at the time was going into 'making bigger and better bombs', not domestic innovations.[20] And while the feature writer didn't mention it, her readers knew what stood in the way of the hoped-for luxury and security, knew why military rather than other forms of research were necessary: Western democracies were on the alert against the threat of Communism.

In Canada, the East–West conflict that eventually came to be known as the Cold War started in 1945 when Igor Gouzenko, a cipher clerk in the Soviet embassy in Ottawa, defected and claimed that the Soviets had been running a spy ring in Canada.[21] Investigations into his allegations focused national attention on the need for internal defences against Communism. According to Len Scher, in his book on the Canadian Cold War, an unsuccessful search for spy rings gave way to efforts to track 'domestic dissidents'.[22] Between October 1950 and June 1951, the Royal Canadian Mounted Police (RCMP) dealt with 54,000 requests to screen both civil servants and private-sector workers.[23] Those who were most likely to be put under surveillance included labour organizers, members of Communist and socialist organizations, peace activists, and homosexuals. Deviance from any number of mainstream norms, writes Philip Girard, 'represented an independence of mind that could no longer be tolerated' during the Cold War. In such a climate, 'the unknown'—homosexuals, for instance—'represented a triune denial of God, family, and (implicitly or potentially) country at a time when departing from any one of these norms was immediately suspect'.[24] Deviance also precluded the homogenization that was seen to be central to Canada's strength as a nation. The conformity that is so often identified as a primary aspect of post-war social life wasn't simply a characteristic of increased consumerism and/or the centralization of popular culture and entertainment industries. It was also produced by an approach to citizenship that demanded a willingness to participate in social consensus, to adopt a shared set of behavioural standards and mores.

Democracy and Moral Standards

In 1946, an interdepartmental Security Panel (National Defence, External Affairs, and the RCMP) was established to check on federal civil servants who had been identified by the RCMP as security risks. As Larry Hannant writes, this was not the first time the RCMP had initiated security screening; however, it was the first time the effort had received formal government approval.[25] In the first three months of the panel's operation, the RCMP offered panel officials 5,466 names. Checks on these individuals resulted in 213 'adverse reports', although only 27 of the people in question were determined to be bona fide security risks—possible spies. The remainder had been included on the original list because of 'moral' failings or 'character' weaknesses, a category that included homosexuals, and parents of illegitimate children, among others.[26] To security officials, these character weaknesses suggested an inability to do the right thing, a tendency to compromise, an impairment of moral fibre. These were the characteristics of someone who might be influenced by Communists or, worse, who might be a Communist. Normal sexual and moral development signalled maturity and an ability to assume responsibility. By contrast, those who transgressed sexual and moral norms were assumed to be immature, trapped in adolescence. How could they be counted on to safeguard their country?

Despite the overenthusiasm of RCMP security checks, writer John Sawatsky claims that Canadian officials abhorred the McCarthyism that swept through the American military and the government bureaucracy.[27] In Canada, the search for the red menace was conducted more quietly, was more 'gentlemanly', says Erich Koch, who worked with the CBC International Service in Montreal after the war.[28] There were no televised proceedings, and there was little publicity. People were either fired quickly or were never hired in the first place. Communist sympathies were the original source of concern, but this quickly translated into a fear of anyone who could potentially be blackmailed by a Communist spy: alcoholics, gamblers, and people who visited prostitutes or who had affairs. Also on this list were homosexuals, and though they were no more blackmailable than any of the others, the RCMP formed a special unit, A-3, to root out homosexuals from the civil service. Eventually, writes Sawatsky, the Mounties had files on 3,000 people, including members not only of the civil service but of the general public as well.[29]

In 1952, Canada's immigration law was quietly changed to keep homosexuals out of the country.[30] In the late 1950s and early 1960s, attempts to construct homosexuals as security risks led the RCMP and the Security Panel to recruit psychologists and psychiatrists to assist in the ousting of 'perverts' from the civil service. The experts' co-operation culminated in a research project to develop what they called the Fruit Machine, an instrument that would confirm an individual's homosexuality by measuring his reaction to homoerotic imagery. (Men were the primary target of the purge. Lesbians, according to Sawatsky, refused to disclose the names of friends and colleagues, thus limiting the investigations of their networks by the mostly male Mounties.) The effort was, not surprisingly, unsuccessful, and stands as a stunning example of the use of science to support moral regulatory practices.[31]

That homosexuals were identified as particularly dangerous by the guardians of national security suggests the importance of normative sexuality in the social and political landscape of post-war Canada. Certainly the vilification of sexual deviants did much to shore up the primary position of the heterosexual nuclear family as the only legitimate site of sexual expression. But the links made between sexuality and national security also suggest the way that sexuality worked as a site for the displacement of general social and political anxieties. In official discourses, homosexuality was constructed not simply as the tragic fate of particular individuals but as a force so menacing it carried the potential to undermine the strength of the nation. In the face of the Cold War, Communists and spies and those with mysterious and questionable sex habits or morals were almost equal threats to the security of the Dominion.

In this context, having a family became an important marker of social belonging, of conformity to prevailing standards. It was a sign of maturity and adulthood, of one's ability to take on responsibility. The social positions of mother/wife and father/husband defined individuals as contributors to their community and their country. As a psychiatrist argued in *Chatelaine*, the formation of families and the raising of children was, at root, a patriotic obligation. In becoming parents, men and women were 'giving to the best of their ability'.[32] Thus, the nuclear family came to operate as a symbol of safety—not just on the individual level but on the national level as well.

Discourses about shared values, common goals, and mutual goodwill among Canada's citizens helped to construct an image of the Dominion itself as a family, as Annalee Gölz has argued.[33] In this frame, Communists and sex deviates were disruptions to the larger domestic order. By protecting the borders against perverts, the state was protecting the 'home', safeguarding those under its charge. After the war, with the expansion of the welfare state, the government was increasingly positioned as concerned parent of its citizens. Attempts to purge the country of 'perverts' and 'Commies' suggest that the state, as 'head of the family', was attending to more than the material well-being of Canadians. Policies and practices that targeted deviants were an effort to protect and foster moral standards, a primary task of any 'concerned parent'.

The Family

In a Canadian Youth Commission pamphlet called 'Speak Your Peace', the family was identified as 'the chief support of the new world'.[34] Certainly, as the crucible of consumption, the middle-class family was the chief support of the post-war economy. Essential to the nurturing of workers and the buying of goods, the nuclear family was also understood to be the primary site of moral education and the training ground for the democracy that, in part, was thought to define the age.[35] Hence the anxiety created when various expert voices claimed that 'the family' was threatened in the post-war world. If the family failed, would democracy—and, by implication, Canada—fail too? The fact that families were being formed by more people more often than at any other time in this century did little to counter a pervasive sense that 'the family' as a social institution was under threat.

As evidence of the family's decline, social critics were most likely to cite figures about divorce rates. At the end of the Second World War, the divorce rate in Canada tripled, 'from 56.2 divorces per 100,000 married persons 15 years of age and over in 1941 to 131.9 in 1946'. After 1946, the rate fell off, but then it 'rose steadily from 1951 to 1968 (88.9 to 124.3)'.[36] Most of the early rise was attributable to hastily considered wartime weddings, although increasing opportunities for women to achieve some measure of economic independence may also have been an important factor. The divorce rate served to bolster a protectionist stance toward the family and to justify its ideological fortification by way of, for instance, television programs, school health curricula, and moral panics over sex crime. The state of the family was a central—if not *the* central—concern of post-war life.

For the most part, the image of 'the family' that was used to represent the ideal was drawn from urban, white, Anglo-Saxon, middle-class and upper-middle-class communities. The authors of the massive *Crestwood Heights*, a 1956 study of Toronto's 'internal suburb' of Forest Hill, offered the following description:

> In infinite variety, yet with an eternal sameness, [such a community] flashes on the movie screen, in one of those neat comedies about the upper-middle-class family which Hollywood delights to repeat again and again as nurture for the American Dream. It fills the pages of glossy magazines devoted to the current best in architecture, house decoration, food, dress, and social behaviour. The innumerable service occupations bred of an urban culture will think anxiously about people in such a community in terms of what

> 'they' will buy or use this year. Any authority in the field of art, literature, or science, probably at some time has had, or will have, its name on a lecture itinerary. A teacher will consider it a privilege to serve in its schools. For those thousands of North Americans who struggle to translate the promise of America into a concrete reality for themselves, and even more important, for their children, it is in some sense a Mecca.[37]

The authors of *Crestwood Heights* argued that upper-middle-class families were a marker of 'what life is *coming to be* more and more like in North America—at least in the middle classes'. In this sense, they wrote, a community like Crestwood Heights 'is normative, or "typical", not in the sense of the average of an aggregate of such communities but in the sense of representing the norm to which middle-class community life tends now to move'.[38] While I agree with their point, that society tends 'to move' in such a direction, it bears remembering that it does not necessarily arrive. The experience of the 'ideal family'—breadwinner father, stay-at-home mother, and well-adjusted children—was not available to everyone.

If divorce was considered to be the main threat to this idealized image of the nuclear family, working mothers and immigrant families were also serious—and related—challenges to its claim on the Canadian imagination. As many historians have noted, the numbers of married women in the workforce increased rapidly in the post-war period. In the early 1940s, one in 20 women worked outside the home; in 1951 that figure had risen to one in 10, only to rise again, to one in five, by 1961. As Joan Sangster writes, concerns about increases in the numbers of married women working for pay masked class and race biases; the labour participation rates of recent immigrants, women in some ethnic and racial communities, and women who were poor had not changed.[39]

Between 1946 and 1954, Canada admitted almost a million immigrants.[40] That not all of the new arrivals organized their families in accordance with Canadian middle-class norms led to concerns that 'New Canadians' would disrupt post-war efforts to shore up the family as an institution. Settlement services and advocacy groups encouraged immigrants to abandon their own family structures in favour of those thought to be essential to the moral strength of the nation: single-family households presided over by breadwinner fathers and stay-at-home mothers. Franca Iacovetta says that the Cold War gave social workers an opportunity to frame such assimilationist rhetoric as a matter of national urgency 'by equating the predominance of respectable, middle-class family values with the superiority of Western democracies such as Canada'.[41] That Canadian family norms were neither desirable for many immigrants, who had their own ways of doing things, nor attainable for those facing the hardship of arrival in a new country, did not deter Canadian experts from labelling immigrant families as 'deviant' and a threat to both 'Canadianization' and the institution of the family itself.[42]

An emphasis on the family was not a new phenomenon in Canada. However, this emphasis took a new shape in the post-war period. Whereas the primary focus of many earlier family discourses had been on women, motherhood, and the development of proper femininity,[43] post-war discourses about the family tended to show (and construct) most concern for the development of properly adjusted—normal—children. Certainly these strands of concern are closely tied together, but what is important here is the way their relationship was characterized. In post-war discourses the construction of appropriate forms of femininity—and masculinity—were seen as the means to the nobler goal of child rearing. In *Crestwood Heights*, the production of the future Crestwood adult was *the* focus of the community's institutions.[44]

According to the *Crestwood* authors, the upper-middle-class families they studied were relatively isolated social units with limited connection to a wider network of kin. In contrast to 'the usual Victorian family', or, presumably, working-class or immigrant families, Crestwood families were units of consumption, rather than production. And, importantly, they allowed 'more individuality and freedom' to their members than had earlier forms.[45] These modern families, though not as religious as their predecessors, drew heavily on Judaeo-Christian ethics, 'democratic practice', and the advice of 'child-rearing experts'. Deviation from prevailing norms could result in a family's being defined by such experts as malfunctioning and likely to produce 'disturbed' children.[46]

Present-day writers have also noted this tendency of post-war, middle-class families to be relatively self-contained.[47] While 1990s conservatives nostalgically recall the post-war family as a link to earlier times, and as exemplifying enduring 'traditional' values, Elaine May claims that 'the legendary family of the 1950s . . . represented something new. It was not, as common wisdom tells us, the last gasp of traditional family life with roots deep in the past. Rather, it was the first wholehearted effort to create a home that would fulfill virtually all its members' personal needs through an energized and expressive personal life.'[48]

The extent to which the ideal family had come to be constructed in popular discourse as a set of relationships, a source of affectional and material needs, is evident in a 1950s educational film for adolescents called *A Date with Your Family.* In the film, a teenaged boy and girl arrive home from school full of excitement because they have 'an important date . . . dinner with the family', which to them 'is a special occasion'. Sister changes her clothes to 'something more festive' because 'the women in this family seem to feel that they owe it to the men of the family to look relaxed, rested, and attractive at dinner-time'. Brother studies while sister sets the table. Then he gets Junior ready for dinner. Sister makes a centrepiece of flowers for the dining table. Father comes through the door, and the boys greet him enthusiastically, before Mother calls them all to the dining room where 'they converse pleasantly' over their meal. Brother compliments Mother 'and maybe sis' on the food because 'it makes them want to continue pleasing you'. The whole event is a 'time of pleasure, charm, relaxation . . . '.[49] For the non-cinematic families who failed to meet this ideal of civility and gratification, it was, nevertheless, a modern standard by which they would be measured, one that took material comforts for granted. It assumed a strict sexual division of labour and a public life in which troubles were manageable enough to be either left at the door or assuaged by family harmony. Certainly this picture of the 'united, happy family'[50] was distinct from earlier versions in which affectional needs came second to economic ones and expectations for emotional fulfillment were considerably lower.

In part, idealized images of the post-war family were a consequence of the economic changes and prosperity that favoured consumerism over mutual dependence, suburban bungalows over farms and crowded downtown apartments. But the constitution of the notion of nuclear-family-as-island was also related to post-war desires for individual satisfaction and needs for social stability. Middle-class families were frequently portrayed as offering refuge from the turmoil of the outside world. That they could actually engender isolation and alienation, as we now know from numerous articles in *Chatelaine* and from books like Betty Friedan's *The Feminine Mystique*, was not widely discussed.[51] Nor was the fact that many Canadians, by choice or circumstance, lived in families that bore little resemblance to the middle-class nuclear ideal.

In 1956, *Maclean's* published a special report on 'the family' by Eric Hutton. Noting 'the comeback of the Canadian family', Hutton characterized it as a resilient but basically unchanging entity, although he also told his readers 'the family way of life has changed out of recognition in half a century'.[52] It had taken on a particularly modern guise as Canadian young people married at younger ages, gave birth to more children, and, like the parents in *A Date with Your Family*, had more expectations of the whole package than had the generations before them. As Doug Owram writes, 'the young adults of the 1940s were the most domestically oriented generation of the twentieth century'.[53]

In 1941, the average age of first marriage for women was 25.4 years of age. By 1961 that figure had dropped to 22 years of age. Between 1937 and 1954, the marriage rate for women between the ages of 15 and 19 doubled from 30 per 1,000 to 62 per 1,000.[54] Once married, these women had more children, more quickly, than their mothers did. Between 1937 and 1947, the number of births per 1,000 of the population rose from 20.1 to 28.9, and it continued to rise until 1956. Much of this increase was accounted for by mothers under 25 years of age and by families with three or more children. In 1956, almost 50 per cent of live births in Canada were third or later children.[55]

Maclean's accounted for the popularity of babies and families in a number of ways: large families, Hutton said, provided security in an insecure world; the baby bonus (established in 1945) and an overall prosperity made them easier to afford; maternal and child health had improved; television encouraged families to spend their leisure time together at home; Princess Elizabeth and Princess Grace of Monaco had made maternity fashionable; and parents—even fathers—had come to realize that children could be fun. According to the provost of Trinity College at the University of Toronto, 'the family is returning to favour because so many men are making the discovery that it's the pleasantest company they're ever likely to have in a world that is full of competition and unpleasant episodes'.[56] That fathers were under heavy pressure from psychological experts to participate to a greater extent in the life of their children, especially to prevent the abnormal sexual and emotional development of their sons, is not discussed in Hutton's article. Without adequate fathering, some experts said, a boy might become delinquent, turn into a homosexual, or suffer 'untold mental distress'.[57]

What is also not mentioned in Hutton's article about the comeback of the family is that there was tremendous pressure applied to anyone who failed to follow the trend, as evidenced by the RCMP crackdown on homosexuals. But that episode was only the most obvious aspect of a more widespread trend. In an American survey conducted after the war, only 9 per cent of those questioned believed that single people could be happy.[58] Toronto gynaecologist and author Marion Hilliard (who was herself not married) counterpoised single women and married women in ways that made them seem almost like different species. Single women, she said, could only be 'out of place at a gathering of married couples'. And single women and married women could 'only, unwittingly, hurt one another'.[59] Even young divorcees and widows, Hilliard wrote pityingly, 'fit in nowhere'.[60] Single men, in the 1950s, risked being seen as homosexuals, a group whose social currency was non-existent. From her reading of post-war American sociology, Barbara Ehrenreich says that experts claimed a number of reasons why men might not marry: 'Some were simply misfortunes, such as "poor health or deviant physical characteristics", "unattractiveness", and extreme geographical isolation. But high on the list for men were homosexuality, emotional fixation on parent(s), and unwillingness to assume responsibility.'[61]

But simply getting married was not enough to satisfy post-war social expectations. Married couples without children were also subject to disapproval and admonishments for not doing their duty to their country.[62] A *Chatelaine* article featured an infertile couple who received constant ribbing from their friends: 'How come you two are leading such selfish lives?'; 'Aren't you going to prove yourself a man? What are we supposed to think, eh?'[63] Another *Chatelaine* story, a first-person account by a woman who chose not to have children, was roundly denounced in the letters column of two subsequent issues.[64] A reader from Ontario wrote: 'That writer who is "not going to have any" [children] has aroused my indignation to such a point that I must answer, in the face of such malformed humanity . . . I am mother of nine . . . Such a woman is denying herself the greatest of all love and satisfaction, that of mothering a child, and giving life the purpose of your being, the purpose of your Creator, great and true.' After a number of similar comments, *Chatelaine* editors intervened on the letters page to set things right: 'One moment please! The editors are happy to announce, for all such readers' peace of mind, that the anonymous writer in question has just telephoned to say "Hurray", she *is* going to have one!'[65]

While this particular exchange can be read as little more than a rally of individual opinions, the importance of post-war professionals in constructing this kind of discussion cannot be overstated. In magazines, on the radio, and in newspapers, experts were increasingly evident as mediators of everyday life and as primary participants in the construction of boundaries between normality and deviance. For instance, the *Chatelaine* letters about the woman's decision not to have a baby appeared exactly one year after the magazine published an article by a psychiatrist criticizing those who chose not to have children, suggesting that they were immature and unpatriotic.[66] The point is not that the letter writers were directly influenced by the earlier article; rather, their comments were part of a larger discourse that was, in part, constructed via expert commentary.

While the middle class often consulted experts voluntarily, or sought out their ideas in print, working-class and immigrant families were likely to encounter these professionals in any number of institutional settings—such as schools, the courts, or social service offices.[67] But even as the general category of 'the expert' was gaining prominence, some experts were more revered than others. Psychologists and psychiatrists had a particular appeal in a social system that was based more and more on individualism. Part of the appeal of the mental health professionals stemmed from the influence they had wielded during the war. Their contribution to the screening and rehabilitation of the troops had increased public awareness of their work,[68] and widely circulating discourses about the importance of mental hygiene validated their concerns. But sociologists and medical doctors were also routinely called upon to diagnose social trends, to make pronouncements on behaviours or identities, and to lend legitimacy to certain positions.

It was the increasing influence of psychiatry in post-war North America that constituted babies as evidence of their parents' 'normal', gendered, sexual, and emotional development—of their having achieved maturity. Babies were a public sign of married sexuality and, in theory, of marital harmony. Babies could also be seen to signal acceptance of community norms and to confirm that men and women were performing their respective normative gender roles (whether, in fact, they were or not) and assuming the responsibility that came with them.

Those seen to be outside the family, from runaway youths to homosexuals, were anomalies. Hard to classify, they were often the objects of scorn or pity. Discourses about life in the middle-class nuclear family made available a variety of subject positions (albeit gendered and restrictive ones)—parent, sexual being, responsible citizen, consumer—that either were not available or were available in limited ways to adults who were single. Families, narrowly defined—monogamous, heterosexual marriages and the children produced within them—provided an important way of making sense of one's position in the post-war social structure.

Marriage: Site of Legitimate Sex

One of the primary defining factors of the post-war nuclear family was an emphasis on the sexual compatibility between husband and wife and the importance of sex in a conjugal union. According to Steven Seidman, the eroticization of romantic relationships was a trend that had been building throughout the twentieth century.[69] Certainly, reproduction continued to be a primary goal of marital sexual activity, but sex had come to be understood as entailing more than this. In the post-war period, sex was meant to be a source of pleasure and emotional fulfillment for both men and women.[70] In this framework, women's sexuality was, in theory if not in practice, as important as men's.[71] Sex was also perceived to be a 'natural' part of a healthy life, even if it wasn't engaged in for the sole purpose of producing babies.

Isolated within their families, away from kin or other members of the community, the ideal post-war couple were meant to draw their support primarily from each other. In some popular constructions of marriage, even close friends were to be shunned in order to protect the sanctity and privacy of the heterosexual bond. One article in *Chatelaine* goes so far as to suggest that 'The [wife's] girlfriend is a danger signal, a clear alarm that the marriage is sick and in need of loving attention . . . '.[72] In the same article, a psychiatrist argues that the 'primary rule of married life' was 'that nothing of intimate consequence be discussed with friends'. Marriage was drawn as the most important, indeed as the only important, relationship between adults. Husbands and wives were to gain their 'basic sense of belonging, of well-being, of fulfillment' from each other. Sex was the glue that would hold them together. As Steven Seidman argues, sex was *the* sphere upon which rested the success of the marital bond.[73]

While the role of sex within marriage may have been clear, the role of men and women in that same relationship was seen to be in an incredible state of flux. Once glued together by their sexual attraction, it was not always clear how men and women were to perform their non-sexual conjugal duties. The presence of married women in the labour force—rates rose from 12.7 per cent of all women in paid employment in 1941, to 30 per cent in 1951, to 49.8 per cent in 1961[74]—suggested to some people that the difference between gender roles was diminishing. While this could have been looked upon as a positive gain for women, it was interpreted by many as a demasculinization of men. It was also seen to spell trouble for heterosexual relationships, based as they were on an assumption of essential difference between men and women. In 1954, *Chatelaine* printed this advice to young brides from a Protestant minister:

> Wives you can unman your husband by taking his place. If you are going to go to work, you should work only for a few years . . . While working you should still live on your husband's income . . . Within one or two years, depending upon your ages, you should quit work and let him support you and live on what he can make . . .
>
> The wife should also take pride in being good at her wifely job. In our day it is sometimes difficult for women to adjust themselves to this fact . . .
>
> . . . Make the man act his part. Do not start to be the man yourself.[75]

Women's advances in the workplace, slim as they were, and new forms of corporate organization contributed to what some contemporary writers have called a post-war crisis of middle-class masculinity.[76] Corporate culture demanded a personality concerned with the thoughts of others, tuned to the needs of others. It was the antithesis of the 'rugged individualism' that grounded the versions of white, middle-class masculinity available in popular culture. In his study of conformity in (male) middle-class America, sociologist David Riesman, author of *The Lonely Crowd*, called this the 'other-directed' personality.[77] Its characteristics, he said, were more closely matched to a traditional feminine identity than to a traditional masculine one. In robbing men of their 'individuality', 'other-direction' feminized men.

On top of this, changes in the structure of the economy and the increasing importance of consumption as a family-based activity shifted men's place of importance in the household. As Barbara Ehrenreich points out in her study of (male and female) middle-class America, men might have earned the money, but women were the ones who spent the bulk of it. Consumption was women's work. Men's paid employment certainly made it possible, but it did not necessarily give men control over it: 'In the temple of consumption which was the suburban home, women were priestesses and men mere altar boys.'[78]

These transformations in the organization of gender contributed to a stressful negotiation of the relationship between husband and wife. Both women and men were under a tremendous strain to build what *Chatelaine* called 'modern marriages': 'a new kind of joint-ownership marriage . . . which may beat any earlier model back to Adam and Eve'. As one psychologist put it, 'We are moving from dictatorship to equality in marriage, from the day when the husband's word was law to a time when the wife shares equally in the family decisions. And the working wife is probably doing more for the partnership idea than anything else.'[79] Indeed, it was middle-class assumptions about the lack of equality in the marriages of some working-class immigrants that led social workers to label those marriages deviant and in need of 'Canadianizing'.[80] The popular assumption was that gender roles in marriage were relaxing, but not too far. Expectations remained that women would be responsible for domestic life and men for 'breadwinning'. In a 1955 investigation of marriage, *Chatelaine* encouraged women to give more rather than less to their homes and families: 'And the siren–wife–mother who realizes the once simple business of being a married woman has become a complex and full-time career in itself is at least halfway to licking these [aforementioned] problems'[81]—problems like confusion over roles, loneliness, and boredom.

As Wini Breines writes, despite discourses about 'modern marriages' and the 'age of equality', men and women continued to experience gender as a deep-rooted site of social difference. While there were more options for white, Anglo-Saxon, middle-class women than there had been in previous decades, few women were encouraged to pursue them. Middle-class women's social worth continued to be measured by their success in raising children and providing a comfortable home for their husbands. Marriage continued to be an inevitability rather than a choice. At the same time, middle-class men were being told to participate more in the affectional life of the family while having to give themselves over to a corporate culture that was constructed on the assumption of their freedom from domestic responsibilities. For both men and women, frustration seemed an inevitable consequence of a relationship that was supposed to reflect 'new' forms of gender organization without giving up the old ones. That this package of contradictions was supposed both to inspire and to sustain sexual attraction and pleasure was just one more strain on a relationship that, nevertheless, maintained remarkable levels of popularity right up until the late 1950s.

The Kinsey Reports and the Sexual Climate

Although marriage remained the only legitimate site of sexual activity between adults throughout the late 1940s and the 1950s, post-war sexual discourses did preserve some of the liberalization that had been fostered by the war.[82] Popular culture, especially, became increasingly sexualized by way of sexy movie stars, the so-called 'sex appeal' of advertisements, and sexually explicit books and magazines. Divorce rates increased.[83] Some Protestant churches supported the need for sex education and were even prepared to accept its limited introduction into the schools.[84] And, though the birth control movement was hardly at its peak in the 1950s, interest in the pill, which would be released in 1961, was high.[85] Lesbians and gay men in urban centres gained access to limited but important public spaces.[86] Single mothers in Ontario were eligible for the first time to receive mother's allowance. While these and other changes were significant, they existed alongside a more familiar reticence about matters pertaining to sexuality. Thus, even the mention of sex in the public realm continued to elicit reactions of strong disapproval from some people. *Chatelaine* readers, for instance, regularly chastised the editors for succumbing to so-called prurient interests. Questionable material included an article about menstruation for teenage girls, cover illustrations that showed too much leg, and self-help-type features that focused on psychiatric explanations (perceived to be inherently sexual explanations) for emotional and relationship problems.[87]

Nothing crystallizes the various strains of post-war sexual discourse like public response to the Kinsey reports, *Sexual Behavior in the Human Male* (*SBHM* 1948) and *Sexual Behavior in the Human Female* (*SBHF* 1953). When the first volume appeared, in an 800-page, hardcover edition, published by a little-known scientific publishing house, it sold a total of 200,000 copies in its first six months. Even the publishers were unaware of the impact the book would have and originally planned to print only 10,000 copies, 'one of the more spectacular publishing mistakes of the decade', says Kinsey's associate Wardell Pomeroy.[88] Within a month, Kinsey had received more than 1,000 letters, only six of which, Pomeroy claims, were negative.[89] When the female volume was about to come out in 1953, more than 150 magazines and major newspapers wanted pre-release access to the text. That same year, *Time* declared the sex researcher their man of the year, and Kinsey was, by all accounts, a household name.

In general, reaction to the two books was mixed, and perhaps therefore suggestive of the various ways that sex was understood to fit into North American culture. According to Pomeroy, reaction to the male volume was largely favourable, with most of the criticism it received focusing on the method of the study. In contrast, reaction to the female volume was significantly more negative and tended to focus on the morality of the findings and on the moral basis of the project itself. Clearly, it was one thing to talk about men's sexual activity and quite another to talk of women's. The uproar over the second book eventually led to the termination of funding (from the Rockefeller Foundation) for Kinsey's research.[90] Still, there were many who appreciated the work that Kinsey had done and the impact it could make, even if they weren't particularly thrilled with what the doctor had found. At the very least, reviewers were impressed by the sheer size of Kinsey's sample. The male volume was based on interviews with 5,300 men, the female volume on interviews with 5,940 women. Both samples were diversified in terms of class background, age, region, and religion, but they dealt almost exclusively with white people, a fact not noted in any of the Canadian commentaries. Reviews in liberal Canadian magazines like *Saturday Night*, *Canadian Forum*, and *Canadian Welfare* were largely positive and took seriously the implications of the research for sexual standards.[91] Even *Chatelaine* sent a reporter to Indiana to interview Kinsey at work.[92] In her article, *Chatelaine* writer Lotta Dempsey took pride in being the first Canadian woman to be part of the sex doctor's sample—as a rule, Kinsey only granted press interviews to those who would agree to be interviewed for his study.

Canadian reviewers made little of the fact that Kinsey's material was American. B.K. Sandwell, in a piece for *Saturday Night*, criticized Kinsey's first volume for succumbing to the familiar American habit of not openly identifying itself as American. But Sandwell also concluded that the difference between Canadian and American males was so slight that the absence of Canadians from the study was of little importance.[93] That Kinsey had identified numerous social factors as having an influence on sexual behaviour (education, religion, class, region) was certainly an opportunity for Canadian critics to speculate on the possible sexual implications of Canadianness. But it was an opportunity that seems not to have been taken up.

Before Kinsey, public discussions of sex had taken place in the context of related issues such as birth control, divorce, sexual crime, and venereal disease. While marriage manuals with explicit descriptions of sexual activities had been published throughout the first half of the century, these were not the subject of mainstream, everyday discussion. Certainly, such material was unlikely to find its way into newspapers and magazines. One of Kinsey's main achievements, then, was packaging information about sex in a fashion that could be widely disseminated. In his books, sex was reduced to a series of clean statistics. Kinsey's emphasis on his own scientific background and on the scientific integrity of his study made sex more acceptable as a topic of conversation. In a period when North Americans were enamoured of scientists and experts of all kinds, and were concerned about wartime changes in sexual mores, Kinsey's timing was perfect.

In publishing his findings, Kinsey not only brought sex into public discussion, he brought a lot of different kinds of sex into public discussion: homosexual acts, premarital sex, oral sex, anal sex, and masturbation. In his description of sexual behaviour, heterosexual intercourse was just one of many possible activities in which North Americans engaged to satisfy what Kinsey understood to be a natural need for orgasm. It was this challenge to normative standards of sexual behaviour—to the definition of normal sexuality—that most concerned Kinsey's critics and supporters alike. As Janice Irvine has written, homosexuals and others who wanted to liberalize moral standards used the reports' statistics about sexual diversity to back demands for social tolerance for sexual minorities. On the other hand, 'vigilantes' against such changes used the same figures to show the extent of a moral breakdown, 'to fuel the post-war backlash' against relaxing sexual mores.[94]

A reviewer in *Canadian Forum* wrote that 'what this [diversity of sexual behaviours] does to our concepts of "normal", "excessive", and the like needs no emphasis . . . '.[95] An editor at *Saturday Night* wrote that there was no problem in the statistics themselves (remarkable as they were); rather, the danger lay in the conclusions people might draw from them. Some people might decide, he said, that 'anything that is done by seven-tenths of the population cannot possibly be wrong—a conclusion which reduces morality to a sort of popular plebiscite'.[96] In another *Saturday Night* article, Perry Hughes questioned even the ethics of applying statistics to sex. Sex, he wrote, is a 'subject that cannot be divorced from its moral and spiritual associations, and which therefore is not a proper subject for statistics at all . . . the obligation to behave oneself in a certain manner is not affected by the question whether 90 per cent, or 50 per cent, or only 20 per cent of one's fellow citizens behave in that manner'.[97] Not everyone was as willing as Kinsey was to base moral norms on statistical ones.

In the years following the Second World War, the heterosexual nuclear family was valued as the 'traditional' foundation of the Canadian social structure. The family was reified as a primary stabilizing influence on both individuals and the nation as a whole. Metaphorically and practically, it was assumed to be the basis of the social consensus that was a central part of Cold War discourse and practice. Mainstream discourses suggested that dissent and difference could weaken the face of democracy in the ideological fight against Communism. Canadians were called upon to show an impressive social cohesiveness as evidence of their dedication to the superiority of the Western way of life. A commitment to the family was central to the social homogeneity necessitated by this display.

Inherent in the post-war definition of 'the family' was its basis in a sexually charged heterosexual marriage. Elaine May argues that marriage operated to 'contain' sexuality, to protect against the social disorder that was thought to be the inevitable result of sex out-of-control.[98] Certainly, this type of anxiety was evident in the vilification of homosexuals practised by agencies of the Dominion government. As a form of social organization and the only site of legitimate sexual behaviour, the family was integral to the definition of deviance. Those who found themselves on the outside of the family existed beyond the bounds of social legitimacy, and so were denied claim to one of the defining features of normality. It was a lesson that adults would emphasize over and over again in their dealings with post-war youth.

Notes

1. Owram, *Born at the Right Time*; Iacovetta, *Such Hardworking People*; Whitaker and Marcuse, *Cold War Canada*.
2. Meyerowitz, 'Introduction', in *Not June Cleaver*, 4; May, *Homeward Bound*.
3. Finkel, Conrad, and Strong-Boag, *History of the Canadian Peoples*, 384.
4. For a discussion of women war workers, see Pierson, *'They're Still Women after All'*; and Joan Sangster, 'Doing Two Jobs'. For a discussion of Canadians' reluctance to accept non-northern European immigrants and refugees, see Iacovetta, *Such Hardworking People*.
5. Owram, *Born at the Right Time*.
6. Parr, ed., 'Introduction', *A Diversity of Women*, 5.
7. Finkel, Conrad, and Strong-Boag, *History of the Canadian Peoples*, 429–30.
8. Francis, Jones, and Smith, *Destinies: Canadian History since Confederation*, 338–9, 353.
9. Finkel, Conrad, and Strong-Boag, *History of the Canadian Peoples*, 331.
10. Dempsey, *Chatelaine* editorial, 1.
11. See, for example: Canadian Youth Commission, *Youth, Marriage and the Family*; Franks, 'A Note to Brides', 29ff; *Marriage Today*, a film produced by McGraw-Hill Book Company, 1950.
12. Advertisement for Christian Family Week, *Toronto Daily Star*, 2 May 1947.
13. The idea that strong families are the root of social stability has been a recurring theme in the face of capitalism's rise and evolution. For a discussion of this, see Ursel, *Private Lives, Public Policy*; Dehli, 'Women and Class'.
14. May, *Homeward Bound*, 10.
15. Whitaker and Marcuse, *Cold War Canada*.
16. Finkel, Conrad, and Strong-Boag, *History of the Canadian Peoples*, 426–7.
17. Advertisement for Education Week, *Telegram*, 11 Apr. 1946.
18. Sanders, 'What's the Biggest Thing in Our New Half Century?', 6.
19. Ibid., 53.

20. Adele White, 'Let's Abolish Those Atom Bomb Blues', 6–7ff.
21. Whitaker and Marcuse, *Cold War Canada*, Chs 2–4.
22. Scher, *The Un-Canadians*, 8.
23. Ibid., 9.
24. Girard, 'From Subversion to Liberation', 3.
25. Hannant, *The Infernal Machine*, 144. For discussion of the Security Panel, also see Whitaker and Marcuse, *Cold War Canada*, Ch. 7.
26. Girard, 'From Subversion to Liberation', 4. Also see Kinsman, '"Character Weaknesses" and "Fruit Machines"'.
27. Sawatsky, *Men in the Shadows*, 116.
28. Cited in Scher, *The Un-Canadians*, 81.
29. Sawatsky, *Men in the Shadows*, 126.
30. See Girard, 'From Subversion to Liberation'.
31. Kinsman, '"Character Weaknesses" and "Fruit Machines"'; Robinson and Kimmel, 'The Queer Career of Homosexual Security Vetting in Cold War Canada'.
32. Franks, 'A Note to Brides', 29.
33. Gölz, 'Family Matters'.
34. The quotation is from a pamphlet produced by the Canadian Youth Commission, 'Speak Your Peace: Suggestions for Discussion by Youth', Bulletin No. 2—Youth and Family Life, NAC, MG 28 I 11, Vol. 64 (Ontario Committee).
35. For an example of discussions about the family as a site of democracy, see the National Film Board films *Family Circles*, produced in 1949, and *Making a Decision in the Family* (1957); Osborne, 'Democracy Begins in the Home'. For discussions about the family as the primary site of moral education, see newspaper debates about the introduction of sex education into school classrooms: 'Board of Education Considers Courses in Sex Education'; 'No Need for Haste'.
36. Alison Prentice et al., *Canadian Women: A History*, 323.
37. Seeley, Sim, and Loosley, *Crestwood Heights*, 3.
38. Ibid., 20 (emphasis in original).
39. Joan Sangster, 'Doing Two Jobs', 99–100.
40. Li, *The Making of Post-war Canada*, 97.
41. Iacovetta, 'Remaking Their Lives', 143.
42. Iacovetta, 'Making "New Canadians"'.
43. See, for example, Arnup, *Education for Motherhood*; Comacchio, *Nations Are Built of Babies*.
44. Seeley, Sim, and Loosley, *Crestwood Heights*, 4. See also, Owram, *Born at the Right Time*.
45. Seeley, Sim, and Loosley, *Crestwood Heights*, 161.
46. Ibid., 165.
47. See, for example, Owram, *Born at the Right Time*; or May, *Homeward Bound*.
48. May, *Homeward Bound*, 11.
49. *A Date with Your Family*, a Simmel-Meservey Release, produced by Edward C. Simmel and written by Arthur V. Jones (no date, appears to be mid-1950s).
50. Gölz talks about how discursive constructions of the 'happy united family' were 'interlinked with an idealized notion of the "Canadian family" as both the social foundation and the metaphorical microcosm of Canadian nationhood'. See her 'Family Matters', 49.
51. Starting in the late 1940s, *Chatelaine* published numerous articles about women's fate in the suburban middle-class family. Features and editorials mentioned the 'something missing' in women's lives, a sense of unease and dissatisfaction. See, for instance, 'Unhappy Wives', 2. For discussion of *Chatelaine* as a source of material that challenged prevailing ideologies, see Korinek, 'Roughing It in Suburbia'; also, Friedan, *The Feminine Mystique*.
52. Hutton, 'The Future of the Family: A *Maclean's* Report', 74.
53. Owram, *Born at the Right Time*, 12.
54. Alison Prentice et al., *Canadian Women*, 311.
55. Ibid.
56. Cited by Hutton, 'The Future of the Family', 76.
57. Nash, 'It's Time Father Got Back in the Family', 28.
58. Cited in May, *Homeward Bound*, 80.
59. Hilliard, *A Woman Doctor Looks at Love and Life*, 94.
60. Ibid., 99.
61. Ehrenreich, *The Hearts of Men*, 20.
62. Franks, 'A Note to Brides', 29ff.
63. Morris, 'Give the Childless Couple a Break', 11ff.
64. Anonymous, 'I'm Not Having Any', 14.
65. *Chatelaine* (June 1947): 6.
66. The article was 'A Note to Brides' by Ruth MacLachlan Franks, MD (see above, nn11, 62).
67. Iacovetta, 'Making "New Canadians"'.

68. Seeley, Sim, and Loosley, *Crestwood Heights*, 426.
69. Seidman, *Romantic Longings*, 118.
70. Marion Hilliard's book and her regular columns in *Chatelaine* frequently espoused the importance of sexual happiness in marriage.
71. For discussions of North American women's sexual dissatisfactions during the 1950s, see Breines, *Young, White, and Miserable*; and Harvey, *The Fifties: A Women's Oral History*.
72. Morris, 'Don't Let Your Girl Friends Ruin Your Marriage', 26.
73. Seidman, *Romantic Longings*, 94.
74. Strong-Boag, 'Home Dreams', 479.
75. Lautenslager, 'A Minister's Frank Talk to Brides and Grooms', 98–9.
76. See, especially, Ehrenreich, *The Hearts of Men*.
77. Riesman, *The Lonely Crowd*.
78. Ehrenreich, *Fear of Falling*, 34.
79. Anglin, 'Who Has Won the War between the Sexes?', 12.
80. Iacovetta, 'Making "New Canadians"', 276.
81. Ibid., 70.
82. Costello, *Love, Sex and War*, 9.
83. In the year after the war, the divorce rate tripled as hastily constructed wartime marriages withered under more prolonged consideration. But between 1947 and 1951 rates were relatively stable. Between 1951 and 1968, the divorce rate rose steadily from 88.9 to 124.3 divorces per 100,000 married persons (Alison Prentice et al., *Canadian Women: A History*, 323).
84. 'Church Group Would Study Sex Education'.
85. For a discussion of the Canadian birth control movement, see McLaren and McLaren, *The Bedroom and the State*. On excitement about the pill, see Anglin, 'The Pill That Could Shake the World', 16–17. Letters for and against Anglin's article appear in *Chatelaine* (Dec. 1953), 3.
86. See Kinsman, *The Regulation of Desire*, and the National Film Board film *Forbidden Love*, directed by Aerlyn Weissman and Lynne Fernie, 1992.
87. The menstruation article, 'High School Huddle', was written by Adele White, 26–7. It was followed by both positive and negative letters. The letter complaining about 'the ungainly display of limbs' appeared in *Chatelaine* (Nov. 1952): 2. And the complaint about psychiatry, from a reader wondering why 'every issue *has* to have an article about sex', appeared in *Chatelaine* (Oct. 1949): 14.
88. Pomeroy, *Dr Kinsey and the Institute for Sex Research*, 265.
89. Ibid., 273.
90. Ibid., 360, 363.
91. Ketchum, 'Turning New Leaves', 44–5; Sandwell, 'Statistical Method Applied to Sex Shows New and Surprising Results', 12; Seeley and Griffin, 'The Kinsey Report', 40–2; Rumming, 'Dr Kinsey and the Human Female', 7–8; Kidd, Review of *Sexual Behavior in the Human Male*, 45–6. For a less positive critique, see Hughes, 'Kinsey Again: Leers or Cheers?', 10ff. For a bona fide anti-Kinsey rant, see the review by 'E.J.M.', 50ff.
92. Dempsey, 'Dr Kinsey Talks about Women to Lotta Dempsey', 10–11.
93. Sandwell, 'Statistical Method Applied to Sex', 12.
94. Irvine, *Disorders of Desire*, 54.
95. Ketchum, 'Turning New Leaves', 45.
96. Sandwell, 'Statistical Method Applied to Sex'.
97. Hughes, 'Kinsey Again: Leers or Cheers?', 10.
98. May, *Homeward Bound*, Ch. 4.

References

Anglin, Gerald. 1953. 'The Pill That Could Shake the World', *Chatelaine* (Oct.): 16–17, 99–103.

———. 1955. 'Who Has Won the War between the Sexes?', *Chatelaine* (June): 11–13, 66–70.

Anonymous. 1947. 'I'm Not Having Any', *Chatelaine* (Apr.): 14, 64, 78.

Arnup, Katherine. 1994. *Education for Motherhood* (Toronto: University of Toronto Press).

Breines, Wini. 1992. *Young, White, and Miserable: Growing Up Female in the Fifties* (Boston: Beacon).

Canadian Youth Commission. 1948. *Youth, Marriage and the Family* (Toronto: Ryerson).

Comacchio, Cynthia R. 1993. *Nations Are Built of Babies* (Montreal and Kingston: McGill-Queen's University Press).

Corrigan, Philip, and Derek Sayer. 1985. *The Great*

Arch: English State Formation as Cultural Revolution (Oxford: Blackwell).

Costello, John. 1985. *Love, Sex and War: Changing Values, 1939–1945* (London: Collins).

Dehli, Kari. 1988. 'Women and Class: The Social Organization of Mothers' Relations to Schools in Toronto, 1915–1940', PhD diss., University of Toronto, Ontario Institute for Studies in Education.

Dempsey, Lotta. 1949. 'Dr Kinsey Talks about Women to Lotta Dempsey', *Chatelaine* (Aug.): 10–11, 59–60.

———. 1952. Editorial. *Chatelaine* (Aug.): 1.

Ehrenreich, Barbara. 1983. *The Hearts of Men: American Dreams and the Flight from Commitment* (New York: Anchor/Doubleday).

———. 1989. *Fear of Falling: The Inner Life of the Middle Class* (New York: HarperCollins).

'E.J.M.' 1948. 'Review of *Sexual Behavior in the Human Male*', *Canadian Doctor* (July): 50–6.

Finkel, Alvin, and Margaret Conrad, with Veronica Strong-Boag. 1993. *History of the Canadian Peoples, 1867–Present,* Vol. II (Toronto: Copp Clark Pitman).

Foucault, Michel. 1979. *Discipline and Punish: The Birth of the Prison* (New York: Vintage).

———. 1981. *The History of Sexuality,* Vol. I, trans. Robert Hurley (New York: Pelican).

Francis, R. Douglas, Richard Jones, and Donald B. Smith. 1992. *Destinies: Canadian History since Confederation*, 2nd edn (Toronto: Holt, Rinehart and Winston).

Franks, Ruth MacLachlan. 1946. 'A Note to Brides: Don't Delay Parenthood', *Chatelaine* (May): 29, 44, 100.

Friedan, Betty. 1963. *The Feminine Mystique* (New York: Dell).

Girard, Philip. 1987. 'From Subversion to Liberation: Homosexuals and the Immigration Act 1952–1977', *Canadian Journal of Law and Society* 2: 1–27.

Gölz, Annalee. 1993. 'Family Matters: The Canadian Family and the State in the Post-war Period', *Left History* 1, 2 (Fall): 9–49.

Hacking, Ian. 1993. 'Normal', a discussion paper prepared for the 'Modes of Thought' Workshop (Sept.), Toronto.

Hannant, Larry. 1995. *The Infernal Machine* (Toronto: University of Toronto Press).

Harvey, Brett. 1993. *The Fifties: A Women's Oral History* (New York: HarperCollins).

Henriques, Julian, et al. 1984. *Changing the Subject: Psychology, Social Regulation and Subjectivity* (London: Methuen).

Hilliard, Marion. 1956. *A Woman Doctor Looks at Love and Life* (New York: Doubleday).

Hughes, Perry. 1950. 'Kinsey Again: Leers or Cheers?', *Saturday Night* (20 June): 10, 15.

Hutton, Eric. 1956. 'The Future of the Family: A *Maclean's* Report', *Maclean's* (26 May): 12–15, 74–9.

Iacovetta, Franca. 1992. 'Making "New Canadians": Social Workers, Women and the Reshaping of Immigrant Families', in *Gender Conflicts*, eds Iacovetta and Valverde, 261–303.

———. 1992. *Such Hardworking People: Italian Immigrants in Postwar Toronto* (Montreal and Kingston: McGill-Queen's University Press).

———. 1995. 'Remaking Their Lives: Women Immigrants, Survivors and Refugees', in *A Diversity of Women*, ed. Parr, 136–67.

———, and Mariana Valverde, eds. 1992. *Gender Conflicts: New Essays in Women's History* (Toronto: University of Toronto Press).

Irvine, Janice. 1990. *Disorders of Desire* (Philadelphia: Temple University Press).

Johnson, Richard. 1983. 'What Is Cultural Studies Anyway?', *Anglistica* 26, 1, 2: 1–81.

Ketchum, J.D. 1948. 'Turning New Leaves', *Canadian Forum* (May): 44–5.

Kidd, J.R. 1949. 'Review of *Sexual Behavior in the Human Male*', *Food for Thought* (Feb.): 45–6.

Kinsman, Gary. 1995. '"Character Weaknesses" and "Fruit Machines": Towards an Analysis of the Anti-homosexual Security Campaign in the Canadian Civil Service', *Labour/Le Travail* 35 (Spring): 133–61.

———. 1996. *The Regulation of Desire*, rev. edn (Montreal: Black Rose).

Korinek, Valerie. 1996. 'Roughing It in Suburbia: Reading *Chatelaine* Magazine, 1950–1969', PhD diss., University of Toronto.

Lautenslager, E.S. 1954. 'A Minister's Frank Talk to Brides and Grooms', *Chatelaine* (May): 18–19, 96, 98–100.

Li, Peter S. 1996. *The Making of Post-war Canada*

(Toronto: Oxford University Press).

McLaren, Angus, and Arlene Tigar McLaren. 1986. *The Bedroom and the State* (Toronto: McClelland and Stewart).

May, Elaine Tyler. 1988. *Homeward Bound: American Families in the Cold War Era* (New York: Basic Books).

Meyerowitz, Joanne. 1994. *Not June Cleaver: Women and Gender in Postwar America, 1945–1960* (Philadelphia: Temple University Press).

Morris, Eileen. 1954. 'Don't Let Your Girl Friends Ruin Your Marriage', *Chatelaine* (Oct.): 26, 50–1, 55, 58–9.

———. 1955. 'Give the Childless Couple a Break', *Chatelaine* (May): 11, 76, 78, 80–1.

Nash, John. 1956. 'It's Time Father Got Back in the Family', *Maclean's* (12 May): 28–9, 82–5.

Owram, Doug. 1996. *Born at the Right Time: A History of the Baby Boom Generation* (Toronto: University of Toronto Press).

Parr, Joy, ed. 1995. *A Diversity of Women: Ontario, 1945–1980* (Toronto: University of Toronto Press).

Pierson, Ruth Roach. 1986. *'They're Still Women after All': The Second World War and Canadian Womanhood* (Toronto: McClelland and Stewart).

Pomeroy, Wardell B. 1972. *Dr Kinsey and the Institute for Sex Research* (New York: Harper & Row).

Prentice, Alison, et al. 1988. *Canadian Women: A History* (Toronto: Harcourt, Brace Jovanovich).

Prentice, Susan. 1993. 'Militant Mothers in Domestic Times: Toronto's Postwar Childcare Struggles', PhD diss., York University.

Riesman, David. 1950. *The Lonely Crowd* (New Haven: Yale University Press).

Robinson, Daniel J., and David Kimmel. 1994. 'The Queer Career of Homosexual Security Vetting in Cold War Canada', *Canadian Historical Review* 75, 3 (Sept.): 319–45.

Rumming, Eleanor. 1953. 'Dr Kinsey and the Human Female', *Saturday Night* (15 Aug.): 7–8.

Sandwell, B.K. 1948. 'Statistical Method Applied to Sex Shows New and Surprising Results', *Saturday Night* (21 Feb.): 12.

Sangster, Joan. 'Doing Two Jobs: The Wage-earning Mother, 1945–1970', in *A Diversity of Women*, ed. Parr, 98–134.

Sanders, Byrne Hope. 1950. 'What's the Biggest Thing in Our New Half Century?', editorial *Chatelaine* (Jan.): 6.

Sawatsky, John. 1980. *Men in the Shadows: The RCMP Security Service* (Toronto: Doubleday).

Scher, Len. 1992. *The Un-Canadians* (Toronto: Lester).

Seeley, John R., and J.D.M. Griffin. 1948. 'The Kinsey Report', *Canadian Welfare* (15 Oct.): 40–2.

———, R. Alexander Sim, and Elizabeth W. Loosley. 1956. *Crestwood Heights: A Study of the Culture of Suburban Life* (Toronto: University of Toronto Press).

Seidman, Steven. 1991. *Romantic Longings: Love in America, 1830–1980* (New York: Routledge).

Strong-Boag, Veronica. 1991. 'Home Dreams: Women and the Suburban Experiment in Canada, 1945–1960', *Canadian Historical Review* 72, 4: 471–504.

Ursel, Jane. 1992. *Private Lives, Public Policy: 100 Years of State Intervention in the Family* (Toronto: Women's Press).

Urwin, Cathy. 1985. 'Constructing Motherhood: The Persuasion of Normal Development', in *Language, Gender and Childhood*, eds Steedman, Urwin, and Walkerdine, 164–202.

Whitaker, Reg, and Gary Marcuse. 1994. *Cold War Canada: The Making of a National Insecurity State, 1945–1957* (Toronto: University of Toronto Press).

White, Adele. 1947. 'High School Huddle', *Chatelaine* (Sept.): 26–7, 48.

———. 1950. 'Let's Abolish Those Atom Bomb Blues', *Chatelaine* (Jan.): 6–7, 53.

Chapter 11

In 1976–77, Meg Luxton studied full-time homemakers in working-class families in Flin Flon, Manitoba. She chose Flin Flon because the oldest generation of women living there had raised their families in the most primitive of housing conditions—without running water, electricity, or household appliances. Interviewing three generations of Flin Flon women meant that Luxton was able to learn about how their household work changed as their households modernized. *More Than a Labour of Love*, the book in which Luxton reported her findings, examines how family life—and especially the relationships between women and their husbands and women and their children—is affected by the larger capitalist economy. In this chapter from the book, Luxton explores the gender relations typical of nuclear families in which women are full-time homemakers and men are breadwinners. In so doing, she describes the power and privilege that a single male breadwinner is likely to have in his family.

Wives and Husbands

Meg Luxton

I [woman] take thee [man]
To my wedded husband
To have and to hold
From this day forward
For better for worse
For richer for poorer
In sickness and in health
To love, cherish, and to obey
Till death do us part

Solemnization of Matrimony

In her marriage vows, a woman promises 'to love, cherish, and to obey' her husband. While couples appear to marry on the basis of free choice and love, their dependence on the wage imposes structural imperatives which undermine their freedom and love. The daily requirements of household survival mean that both adults must subject themselves and each other to dictates which, for the most part, are beyond their control and which are not particularly in their interests.

Consequently, marriage is indeed 'for better for worse'. While some aspects of marriage are good and women often mention the pleasure and happiness they derive from their marriages, the underlying imperatives create all sorts of tensions which diminish the marital relationship, binding people to each other not by choice based on love but by dependency and a lack of alternatives.[1]

Wage Labour and Domestic Labour

For many working-class women, supporting themselves independently by wage labour is not an inevitable or even a realistic alternative. The sex segregation of the labour market restricts women to the lowest paid, least secure, and most monotonous jobs. Women's wages are so low that it is virtually impossible, especially if they have children, for women to survive.[2] Often in periods of high unemployment or in small towns like Flin Flon, there are simply not enough jobs available for those women who want to work. For these women marriage becomes a primary option—it appears to be the only viable life strategy available to them.

In this way there is a basic economic compulsion to marriage and women's low wages help to keep the nuclear family together. Though women marry on the basis of free choice, they have very few real alternatives because of how those alternatives are structured. By associating themselves with men who are earning relatively higher wages, women probably have a higher standard of living than they might have if they depended on their own wage labour.

This economic dependency permeates and threatens female/male relationships. For family households to survive, the husband must sell his labour power in exchange for wages to an employer on an ongoing, regular basis. Once the men enter the bosses' employ, they are no longer free but come under the direct control of their employer.

The employer's primary objective is to extract from his employees as much of their ability to work as possible, to maximize the product of their labour by the end of the shift. Once workers are employees, they become part of capitalist production and how they work depends on how the capitalist organizes production—his control over his labour force, his capacity to coordinate and rationalize the various operations of his enterprise—in other words, his capacity to harness labour in the production process and to utilize his workers' labour power to the hilt.

Marx described this type of labour, showing vividly its implications for the (male) worker's state of being:

> Labour is external to the worker—that is, it is not part of his nature—and the worker does not affirm himself in his work but denies himself, feels miserable and unhappy, develops no free physical and mental energy but mortifies his flesh and ruins his mind. The worker therefore feels at ease only outside work, and during work he is outside himself. . . . The external nature of work for the worker appears in the fact that it is not his own but another person's, that in work he does not belong to himself but to someone else. (Easton and Guddat 1967: 292)

From the perspective of the worker, the labour process is not for the satisfaction of needs. Rather it demands the denial of needs. Time spent at work is segregated from 'real life'; it is time spent for, controlled by, and at the service of another. The man returning after a day of work comes home tired. His capacity to labour has been consumed, so he is spent and depleted. He considers his time off work to be his own, to do with as he pleases. He demands the right to spend his time away from wage work in voluntary activities.

But the experiences of wage work are not so easily shaken. His experiences at work usually leave him tired, frustrated, and irritable. The worker bears the social residue of this alienating labour process and of the oppressive social relations of capitalist production. He needs to find ways of releasing those feelings of tension, of assuaging the dissatisfaction. He wants his leisure time to be free of conflict and to be refreshing, restful, and personally satisfying. He needs the opportunity and the means to re-energize—to reproduce his labour power—before he goes back to work the next day.

A miner who had worked for the Company for 41 years explained how he experienced this process:

> I work hard, see. And it's not great work. And when I gets home I'm tired and fed up and I want to just rest till I feel better. I come home feeling sort of worn down and I need to loosen up and feel human again. At work there is always someone standing over me telling me I have to do this or that. Well, I don't want any more of that at home. I want to do what I want for a change. I want a chance to live when I'm off work.
>
> (Generation II, b. 1920)[3]

Despite the social relations of production, or perhaps because of them, a man is usually proud of his skill, strength, and intelligence in performing his job. This pride focuses on the wages he receives; a good wage is an expression of his ability as a worker.

For the man the importance of the wage is represented by his home, for it is his wage that buys the house he lives in and provides for his needs and those of his wife and children. A male worker measures his worth by his ability to provide for his family. He is proud to be able to support a wife who can devote all her time and energy to maintaining their household. His self-esteem is derived from his ability to provide and maintain his side of the sexual division of labour. This helps motivate him to continue working. And for his labour he expects that the home will be his castle. For the man there is a distinct separation between his workplace and his home, between work time and leisure time. He usually assumes that his wage labour fulfills his obligations within the division of labour of the family household. When a man comes home he is finished work:

> He is at home when he is not working and when he is working he is not at home. His work, therefore, is not voluntary, but coerced, forced labour. It is not the satisfaction of a need but only a means to satisfy other needs. Its alien character is obvious from the fact that as soon as no physical or other pressure exists, labour is avoided like the plague. (Easton and Guddat 1967: 292)

No such separation exists for the woman. Her workplace is her home, and for her, work time and leisure time are indistinguishable. She discharges her obligations within the division of labour by doing all those things that are necessary to ensure that the adult members of the household are available for work every day—able and relatively willing to work. In this way she ensures, as far as possible, the regular continuance of the wage on which she depends in order to meet her own physical and social needs. Because the labour power of her husband is exchanged for a wage, while hers is not, the needs of the husband and the requirements of his wage labour always take precedence over other household considerations. Part of the woman's work includes caring for her husband, creating a well-ordered and restorative home for him to come back to. In the process her work becomes less visible and its importance is less acknowledged. The wife is subordinated to the husband.

The sexual division of labour, although inherently hierarchical, makes the participants mutually dependent. While the dependency of women is greater economically and socially, men are dependent on their wives not only for the physical aspect of domestic labour but also for important psycho-emotional support. Within the household division of labour, it falls to the woman to provide for the immediate needs of the wage worker. All aspects of women's work, from its schedules and rhythms to the most subtle personal interactions, are touched and coloured by the type of wage work the men are doing, by the particular ways in which their labour power is consumed by capital.

If the man is engaged in shift work, the household then operates around two, or sometimes three, often contradictory schedules. It is the woman's task to service each routine and to prevent each of them from coming into conflict. This process is well illustrated by one housewife's day. The woman gets up at 7 a.m., feeds the baby, then gets the three older children up, fed, and off to school by 8:45 a.m. Meanwhile, her husband who is on the graveyard shift (midnight to 8 a.m.) comes in from work and wants a meal, so once the children are fed she prepares his dinner. Then he goes to bed and sleeps until about 6 p.m. During the day she must care for the toddler, do her housework, feed and visit with the older children who come home for lunch from noon to 1:30 p.m. and return again at 4 p.m. All of this occurs while 'daddy is sleeping' and the noise level must be controlled to prevent him from being disturbed. At 5 p.m. she makes supper for the children and at 6 p.m. she makes breakfast for him. By 8:30 p.m., when the children are in bed, he is rested and ready to socialize while she is tired and ready to sleep. Another woman in a similar position described it this way:

> It totally disrupts my life, his shift work. I have to keep the kids quiet—I'm forever telling them to shut up—and I can't do my work, because the noise wakes him. It makes my life very difficult.
>
> (Generation II, b. 1941)

The impact of shift work on family life is subtle and difficult to pin down. Workers on weekly rotating shifts cannot sleep properly and their eating patterns are disrupted. The result is general irritability, headaches, constipation, and a host of other physical ailments. The social and psychic effects are more elusive.[4] Flin Flon women generally maintained that the graveyard shift was the hardest for them. Some of them did not like being alone with small children at night. Others said they never had time with their husbands, who went to bed as the women were getting up:

> Those changing shifts are awful. It's a constant reminder that his work comes first, over any other needs his family might have. We can never get ourselves organized into any regular pattern because our lives are always being turned upside down.
>
> (Generation III, b. 1947)

The requirements of the husband's wage work affect the women's work in a variety of other ways. Women usually have to pack a lunch for their husbands. They may have to wash and repair work clothes. Most significantly, they have to organize their time around their husband's time. All of the women interviewed said that they got up before their husbands in the morning because it was their responsibility to wake them and get their breakfast ready in time for them to leave for work.

A song from a play about mining towns illustrates how women have to organize their time around the Company's schedules:

> 'Who says we don't work to the whistle?
> With us it just don't show.
> We got to have dinner on the table before
> that whistle blow.'
>
> (Winnipeg Women's Liberation 1978)

Or, as a Flin Flon housewife described it:

> Lots of people say what a housewife does isn't work. Well, it is work, and it's just like men's work only it isn't paid and it isn't supervised. But I have things I have to do at certain times. The main difference is, my work is regulated by his work. And whatever I have to do is somehow always overshadowed by the requirements of his work.
>
> (Generation II, b. 1934)

Beyond doing these immediate tasks, the housewife must enter into a far more complex and profound relationship with her husband, for she must also ensure his general psycho-emotional well-being.

The types of demands placed on domestic labour in trying to meet the husband's needs are partly a function of the specific way in which the husband's labour power has been consumed by capital. For example, levels of mental or physical fatigue vary according to the job as do the types of stress, kinds of injuries, size of appetite, and so on. What restoring his ability to work actually involves depends to a large extent on the personality and personal preferences of the individuals in the marriage. These various constraints and possibilities account for some of the differences between households.

In many cases the men develop their own ways of dealing with their work-related tensions. Their wives simply have to recognize their patterns and allow them to do what they want. Some men want to be left alone for a while when they get home. Others insist on going to the pub for a few drinks before coming home. Three of the women interviewed said their husbands insisted that supper be on the table when they walked in the door. These men refused to talk to anyone until they had eaten.[5] In some households the wife and children had to be home waiting for him when he arrived home from work:

> Bill likes to play with the kids when he comes in, so I always make sure we're home and the kids are washed and changed.
>
> (Generation III, b. 1955)

In others the children had to be neither seen nor heard when their fathers first returned from work:

> When Mike comes in he likes a quiet time with a beer and no kids, so I have to make sure the kids keep quiet and don't bug him in any way.
>
> (Generation III, b. 1950)

Men who do heavy physical labour such as shovelling muck (broken rock) or very noisy work, such as drilling, may need a quiet time alone to relax when they first get off work. Those working under the direct supervision of a boss may choose to release the tensions generated by drinking, playing with their children, or yelling at their families. Some men like to spend their free time at home watching television. Others like to go visiting or have friends over. Some prefer to go off with their male friends to the bush for hunting or fishing or to the pub for drinking. Others like to be very active in voluntary organizations, municipal politics, union politics, or other activities that take them out of the home and away from their families. Whatever their choice, the women's task is to facilitate.

This is a subtle process. Though the tendency for women is to do things 'his way' women are not powerless within marriage. They do have a certain amount of leeway and considerable influence, and they regularly exercise discretion about how much they let their husbands' needs structure their lives. When the man is not present, the housewife can do things 'her way'. She can sometimes expand and alter his tastes. Depending on the quality of their relationship, she can even get him to do things her way.

If the relationship is poor, the wife may do all she can to make her husband's life miserable by regularly asserting her own will in deliberate opposition to his. When there is no conflict between them, she may do things his way because she loves him and wants to make him happy. Finally, many women will say that they do things their husband's way because they believe that is the way a household should function. In fact, the events they describe suggest that what is often designated 'his way' is often really 'their way'.

On some level all of the woman's work takes into account her husband's preferences. This was reflected repeatedly in the decisions Flin Flon women made about what to buy, what to cook, what to wear. When asked why they prepared the foods they did, most women replied that they made what their husbands liked. Often women mentioned that they liked certain foods or were interested in trying a different type of cooking but they refrained because their husbands' tastes had priority. They also bought clothes with their husbands' tastes in mind. A friend and I were shopping for shoes. She tried on a pair that she liked very much. After much indecision she rejected them because 'Henry just wouldn't like them.' In another instance a woman spent several hours preparing her dress and getting ready for a formal party. When her husband came in he took one look at her and commented that he had never liked that dress. She immediately went to change her clothes.

An older woman recalled moving into a new house from a two-room cabin in 1940. The new house was completely modern, and they had enough money to furnish it as they liked:

> We settled in slowly. We did one room at a time. We would sit down and discuss the room and what we wanted to do with it. We would talk it out together, then I would go and buy the things we needed and set it up. I always did it the way he wanted. After all, it was his money what bought it and he should have his house as he likes.
>
> (Generation II, b. 1915)

This woman described a co-operative process of decision-making and then, without mentioning any conflict or deferral, she said it was his way. How much this suggests that her preferences are guided by him and how much it reflects her notion of how things should be is impossible to determine.

Love and Affection

All of these types of interactions have an impact on the social relations of marriage. One of the striking features of marital relations in Flin Flon over the last three generations is that, as soon as limitations imposed by their working conditions were modified, Flin Flon residents altered their marital arrangements. Love, affection, and caring have changed considerably over the last 50 years. Largely because of their respective work patterns, women and men in the early period had little time to spend socializing together. Sometimes men had to work away from home for months at a time. Even when they lived at home, they often worked for 12 and 14 hours each day six days a week. The woman's housework required long, uninterrupted days.

Older women described their expectations of marriage as 'making a family'. For them the sexual division of labour was explicitly embodied in their interpersonal relations as well. A couple co-operated to form a household and to have children. They recognized very distinct women's and men's spheres in their leisure activities. As working time decreased for both women and men, the quality of their relationships changed. The shortened workweek and the improvements in housework meant that men could be at home more often and that women had more opportunities to take a few hours 'off'.[6]

Younger women described their marriages as 'partnerships'. While they adhered to the traditional division of labour based on work, they seemed to share more activities with their husbands and they expected to be 'friends' with them. Over the last 50 years wives and husbands have increasingly spent more time together. Couples seem to expect more demonstrated affection, intimacy, friendship from each other. A young woman described how her marriage differed from her mother's:

> They didn't seem to expect much of each other. They lived together and I know they cared, but they each went their own ways. I don't think that's right. I want to have more closeness with my husband. I think husbands and wives should be each other's best friends.
>
> (Generation III, b. 1952)

Comparing observations of an older woman recalling her past and a young woman describing her present confirms this changed perspective:

> When we was married [1926] and moved here we knew we each had our own harness to pull. Jake worked for the railway and

later for the Company and he worked long hours for most of the week. I recollect he worked 12 to 14 hours each day Monday to Saturday and on Sunday he slept or went out for a drink with his mates. He brought home the wages; that were his job. Me, I looked after the house and took care of the kids and made sure his clothes were clean and his meals were on the table. That were my job.

(Generation I, b. 1895)

Jim's my best friend in the world. I don't like to do anything unless he can too. Well he works for the Company, eh, and I take care of the house and the kids but all the time he's home we do things together.

(Generation III, b. 1949)

Besides changing work patterns, other social forces, such as the increasing isolation of the family, have affected marital relationships. In the early period in Flin Flon social life involved regular collective activities. Large groups of people held dances, floating card games, berry-picking outings, and socials organized by groups of individuals who came together for a specific event. Women were central to organizing these get-togethers.

Over the years there has been a shift from community-based entertainment to smaller family events. The number of communal activities has decreased and are organized either by businesses or formal organizations. Women are still active, but the scope of their decision-making and authority has been reduced. Where women once organized for both the community and their families, they now organize primarily for their families.

This shift has reduced women's social horizons and increased their orientation toward the family. An older woman described her experience:

When we first came here the town was small and there weren't no Trout Festival Association or Rotary or whatnot to organize things. So we did it. Oh I remember lovely times, big dances and lots of fun. The men were all working odd hours so we women would do it and everybody would go. . . . Now it seems everything is done for us. There's this or that event, all organized in advance for you, and families go to them or not. It's not the same somehow.

(Generation I, b. 1901)

As she suggests, this change is partly as a result of the municipal infrastructure. However, other factors have also contributed to the changing social patterns.

Before people in Flin Flon owned cars, groups of people sometimes got rides in horse-drawn wagons into the bush to collect berries or to go hunting, picnicking, or exploring:

Before we had the car we often used to go in groups for a wagon ride somewhere. Now we just all go off separately in our own cars.

(Generation II, b. 1923)

Another source of major social change was the development of television:

Before the TV come we used to have a regular, floating card game with the people on the street. We'd go from house to house playing cards and having a whale of a time.

(Generation I, b. 1898)

Used to be, we'd go visiting. Folks would go out for a walk and drop in and chat, have a beer. Nowadays we just all stay home and watch telly.

(Generation II, b. 1931)

The result of these changes is that families have become more dependent on their own leisure activities. When female and male spheres were quite separate, women were less concerned with entertaining their husbands and more involved with the community at large. Their increased isolation within the family, coupled with the modern expectation of friendship and companionship, has meant that wives and husbands are more dependent on each other and therefore more vulnerable to personal whim:

> I don't like to go out visiting without Mike. It just doesn't seem right. We like to do things together. But he hasn't been feeling like going out since he started working the night shift, so I haven't been going out either. I miss it.
>
> (Generation III, b. 1951)

Sexuality

> I don't know what sex is all about. Sometimes I wish you could just do it because it feels good. But of course you can't. You're not supposed to do it till you're married. You might get pregnant. He wants it and you don't. There's all these different things happening all at once. And you don't know what's right or wrong or why it's all happening. Oh sex! Who would have thought anything so simple could be so complex?
>
> (Generation III, b. 1950)

The 'long arm of the job' stretches from the workplace into the bedroom and exerts its grip on the most intimate part of marriage. Sexuality is so complex that it operates on many levels and has different meanings in different situations. In some ways it is an expression of human need, of pleasure, and of the social togetherness of lovers. In other ways it is an oppressive and repressive relationship which grinds the tenderness and love out of people, leaving behind the frustration, bitterness, and violence. From the perspective of domestic labour, there is an aspect of sexuality that is work. On one level marriage can be understood as an exchange between wife and husband—her domestic work, including sexual access, for his economic support.[7]

This underlying exchange becomes apparent in the prelude to marriage, the period in which women are recruited for domestic labour. The process of dating—of selecting a mate for marriage—is, of course, not experienced as an exchange by the people participating in it. The economic necessity for women and the sexual motivation for men are hidden under massive layers of ideology, propaganda, and confusion. People date and marry for many reasons, often because 'that is the way things work'. They are usually so caught up in the process that they do not have time to reflect on it. Although very few Flin Flon women and men had analyzed the forces that underpin their lives, they did experience the power of those forces. In dating practices, for example, women generally dated men their own age or older. Men rarely dated older women. While a couple may have agreed to share the costs on a date, men were generally expected to pay. Most significantly, women were not supposed to initiate a relationship. They had to wait until a suitable man approached them.

This means that the balance of forces in any female/male relationship is likely to be unequal. Men tend to have the advantage of being older, having economic power and social authority. Women rarely have access to as much money and they cannot act forthrightly. They are forced to manipulate and insinuate—to set things up so that men will ask them out and, ultimately, ask them to marry.

This inequality permeates sexual activities. Whatever their real feelings (and often they do not know what their real feelings are), both women and men get involved in the process of serious dating where women trade sexual 'favours' for a 'good time' and economic rewards. On some level the participants are aware of this underlying exchange.

The women know that if they hold out too long, they risk losing the man to someone who is less resistant. Three young women were evaluating their relationships with their current, steady boyfriends. All three men were working. One woman, age 16, had been out with her 17-year-old boyfriend six times. She commented:

> Tomorrow will be our seventh date. Last time he really wanted me to neck with him but I wouldn't. I only let him kiss me goodnight when he took me home. I don't think I can get away with that again this date. I'm going to have to let him go further or he'll never take me out again.

Her boyfriend had been working for the Company for two years. He owned a car and had sizeable savings. He had also stated publicly that when he married, as a wedding present he would give his wife the down payment for the house of her choice. Because of his resources he was considered a 'good catch'.

Her 15-year-old friend replied:

> Yeh, John [age 16] and me were necking last weekend and we got real close. He wants to go all the way but I said no way. Not till I get married. But he laughed and said I'd be an old maid if I never made out till then. I'm afraid that if I give in, I'll get pregnant, but if I don't, then I'll lose him.

The third woman, 16 years old, agreed:

> Yeh! Boys always expect you to go all the way. And if you won't, then they go find someone else who will. Andy [her 18-year-old boyfriend of six months] said that it wasn't worth his while taking me out all the time, spending his money on me, if I didn't come across.

The men had a similar understanding. One 17-year-old man returned from a date in a foul mood. He complained bitterly that he had had a 'lousy time' because:

> Jesus, I took her out for supper and we went to a show, and when I took her home she would do nothing but peck my face and say, 'Thank you for the nice time.' I spent all that money on her, and was real nice to her too and that's all the thanks I get.

Men try to cajole and coerce women 'to go all the way'. Women resist, give in a bit, resist some more. Everyone knows the risks involved and when a woman finally 'gives in' and 'allows' the man to go all the way, two related but opposed social expectations come into play. The first is the assumption that pregnancy is the woman's responsibility. If she does not take precautions to prevent conception, she must face the consequences alone. The second is that men do have responsibilities. If a couple have sexual relations and the woman gets pregnant, then they will probably marry.

Once a woman is pregnant, the man is not bound by the same constraints in the situation. Unlike the woman, he can decide or choose whether or not to accept some of the responsibility for her pregnancy. If he does not accept it, then she has been 'knocked up' and as a single woman she is subject to material and social hardships. If the man does accept some responsibility, they get married. For the woman this is clearly the preferred choice. It indicates to her as well as to others that he thinks enough of her to want to marry. It makes her a 'good woman'. However, her dependency on him establishes yet another tension in their relationship.

Many Flin Flon women expressed feelings of gratitude because their husbands had married them. Some spoke of feeling indebted to men who offered to marry them:

> Bob is my honey. When I told him I was pregnant he didn't give me no hassle. He just said right off, 'Why then we'll get us married and I'll be a daddy.' He was so good to me.
>
> (Generation III, b. 1955)

> I owe him so much. You know, I got that way and I wasn't going to tell him, only my sister said she would if I didn't. At first he was mad. But he agreed we'd get married.
>
> (Generation III, b. 1956)

Many women expressed anxiety that their husbands had married them only because they were pregnant. These women talked about how they and their children were burdens that the man had 'nobly' taken on. One woman, married for over 30 years and the mother of five children, described her fears:

> I think maybe he hates me deep down. We had to get married and then I had four more after that one. So he didn't want to marry me. I don't think he ever loved me. But he stuck with us. It was a sort of noble gesture on his part back then. I don't think he knew what it would mean.
>
> (Generation II, b. 1924)

After the first child is born couples are confronted with a series of problems and decisions that focus on sex, children, and domestic work. Here, more than anywhere else perhaps, the different interests of women and men are illuminated. For men the issue seems relatively straightforward. They have an acknowledged and socially recognized desire for sexual intercourse. They tend to assume both that birth control is the responsibility of the woman and that having children is part of marriage. They also generally favour having several children.

For women the question is far more complex. While a few women have come to terms with their sexuality and have apparently satisfying and active sex lives, most young women find sexuality problematic. They say that they rarely enjoy sex except as an indication that their husbands still love them. They are ignorant about their own sexual needs and are terrified of getting pregnant. A standard complaint raised by women of all ages was that their husbands wanted sex 'too often':

> He's forever wanting it. Never a weekend goes by but he isn't after me to sleep with him. I don't understand why men want it so often.
>
> (Generation II, b. 1929)

This discrepancy between the experiences of women and men is reflected in interactions between friends or cohorts of the same sex. Men at work joke about making it or 'scoring' with their wives on a regular basis. Older men comment regularly on younger men's work patterns by assuring them that the reputed laziness of the younger men occurs because they have such active sex lives. Older men caution younger men to wait until they have been married for 10 years; then they will not have sex so often and will be able to get a good day's work done.

Women regularly console each other for having 'over-sexed' husbands who constantly make demands on them. Older women reassure younger women that after they have been married for 10 years or so their husbands will not want sex so much. It will then happen only a couple of times a year and the younger women will not have to worry any more. A young woman who had been married for three years commented:

> My husband wants sex too much. I think he is oversexed. If he had his way, we'd make out every day!
>
> (Generation III, b. 1950)

Her older neighbour reassured her:

> My man used to be that way too, but he got over it. Just wait a few more years and yours will slow down too. It's hard on you now, but it gets better.
>
> (Generation II, b. 1925)

While the primary reason women give for avoiding sex is the fear of pregnancy, the contradictions they experience are compounded by the fact that their work is continuous and tiring. When a man gets home from work he expects to relax. For a woman home *is* work and she can rarely relax. Relaxing and concentrating on sex may be almost impossible for the woman if she is listening for the children, or has just finished cleaning up and is trying to organize herself for the next day:

> Then he wants to make out, but I just can't. My head is racing, thinking of all the stuff to be done tomorrow morning, and I'm tired and just want to collapse asleep. And part of me is always listening for the baby.
>
> (Generation III, b. 1954)

In general, their tension about pregnancy and the nature of their work combine to make women reluctant sexually. Just as patterns of love, affection, and caring have changed over the last 50 years, so too have patterns of sexuality. In her analysis of 'the marriage bed', Lillian Rubin (1976: 44) found that in the last 50 years American sexual practices have changed tremendously. 'The revolution in American sexual behaviour is profound.' She also found that while working-class couples were having sex more frequently and with greater variation, it was at the man's initiative. The women felt great ambivalence and insecurity about sex.

In Flin Flon it also appears that women of the third generation experienced greater confusion, bewilderment, and pressure about sexuality than their mothers and grandmothers did before them. One explanation is that as sexuality is increasingly identified with leisure activities, popularity, and personal expression, it acquires increased significance for both women and men. Another explanation emerges from an analysis developed by Michael Schneider (1975) regarding the dynamic between wage work and male sexuality. Schneider notes the oppressive characteristics of wage work, where the work processes and the machines take over the worker. The body of the worker moves in response to predetermined patterns. His mind has to obey the logic of work processes determined by someone else. Fundamentally, he is denied his humanity.

One area that capitalism does not directly control at work is his sexuality. Because this is one area left to the man, it becomes an important one for him to develop and express. Schneider also notes that as labour has been steadily degraded by capitalism, sex has become increasingly important as a focus of survival for the individual. In sex, male workers have increasingly sought solace and release and an assertion of power, which means there is now more sexual pressure on women.

Older Flin Flon women described sex as a duty a woman is obliged to provide for her man. Because they believed that male sexual needs are direct and urgent, they said it was the responsibility of women to meet them. They rarely referred to any sexual drive on the part of women:

> A woman doesn't need that like a man. Men need it regular or they go a bit nutty. So women have to give it to them. You just leave it up to them; just let them do what they want.
>
> (Generation I, b. 1894)

These women received no direct sexual education. Instead they received extremely contradictory messages. Sex was 'not nice' and something to be avoided. Sex was a duty that a woman performed willingly and passively for her husband. They learned to repress and deny their sexual feelings while submitting to men. Older Flin Flon women said that their usual sexual experience was limited to the missionary position, which maximizes the passivity of women. Younger women described a considerably wider range of sexual activities. The sexual revolution of the 1960s expanded knowledge about sexual physiology and sexual practices. As various studies have shown, more people are practising more variations in their sexual behaviour now than in the 1940s.[8]

Rubin found that men were interested in changing their sexual behaviour and pushed women to experiment. She also found that women viewed men's attitudes, including their concern for female orgasm and gratification, as a mixed blessing. She concluded:

> As long as women's sexuality is subjected to capricious demands and treated as if regulated by an 'on–off' switch, expected to surge forth vigorously at the flick of the 'on' switch or to subside at the flick of the 'off', most women will continue to seek the safest path and remain quietly some place between 'on' and 'off'. (Rubin 1976: 92)

'Quietly somewhere between on and off' is an apt description of the way most younger Flin Flon women talked about their sexuality:

> Sometimes I get real excited and I really want it but what we do doesn't really do it to me so then I feel frustrated and irritable. So it's better if I never get turned on.
>
> (Generation III, b. 1952)

> I usually don't get turned on very much but sometimes he's just so nice and he loves me so much that I feel sort of like it.
>
> (Generation III, b. 1951)

> Mostly I don't think about sex, but if I get too turned off then it's awful when he wants it, so I can't shut myself off completely.
>
> (Generation III, b. 1954)

The passive lover is a natural extension of the 'good girl'. Women who for years learned to deny their sexual needs cannot suddenly reverse those years and 'turn on'. But for younger men sexuality is an important part of the way they have learned to express their feelings. As one man explained:

> I love her and I want her to know how deeply I feel and I can't understand why she won't let me show her [by having sex].
>
> (Generation III, b. 1945)

His bewilderment was genuine; so was his affection. Rubin (1976: 47) describes the uncertainty that women and men experience when they confront each other's sexual expectations:

> The cry for understanding from both men and women is real. Each wishes to make the other understand, yet, given the widely different socialization practices around male and female sexuality, the wish is fantasy. As a result, he asks; she gives. And neither is satisfied.

For women the recent sexual patterns that men have introduced are bound up in contradictions. Men want women to be more active, to participate more energetically in sex, to initiate it more often. They want greater variety, particularly oral sex. They also want to feel that women are enjoying sex. But women and men have not generally learned how to share mutual pleasure. Instead men tend to exert even more pressure on women and then appropriate women's pleasure for themselves.

So women become more active, take the initiative, and either have orgasms or fake them, still mostly to satisfy the men:

> He keeps telling me he wishes I'd start things off sometimes. But when I do he's always busy or too tired or I'm interrupting him. I think he wants me to start things when he wants them to start.
>
> (Generation III, b. 1945)

For some women, sex is still a duty, but a duty that now includes being active:

> He wants me to be real turned on and excited. He sort of likes it when I pant and moan and wiggle around.
>
> (Generation III, b. 1941)

Some women do what their husbands want out of resignation or fear:

> I don't care any more. I just let him do what he wants, and if he wants me to do something I do it. So what?
>
> (Generation III, b. 1946)

> When he wants it he has to get it or he gets mad and beats me up, so I always do as he wants.
>
> (Generation III, b. 1957)

Just as women are afraid when dating that if they hold back they may lose the men, some wives are afraid that if they do not participate in sex, they will lose their husbands to other women, to the pub, or to male friends:

> I do whatever he wants. Otherwise I figure he'll run off with other women—ladies of the night types.
>
> (Generation III, b. 1945)

> I try to act real interested and sexy just as he's leaving for work so he'll be interested and come straight home after work.
>
> (Generation II, b. 1935)

> I always seduce him just before we go to a party. That way I figure he won't be interested in other women. He'll be too pooped.
>
> (Generation III, b. 1946)

For some women sexual co-operation is a way of inducing or rewarding good behaviour. Some even recognize the sexual–economic exchange that underlies marriage:

> If I want something, I just get all sexy and loving, and after I tell him what I want.
>
> (Generation III, b. 1956)

> If he does something really nice, like help me with the dishes or take me out somewhere to something special, then I always try to make love to him so he'll know I liked what he did.
>
> (Generation II, b. 1933)

> When I want something for the house, like a new washing machine or something, then I just make love like crazy for a while and then stop. Then I tell him what I want and say that if he wants more loving he has to buy it.
>
> (Generation III, b. 1949)

For many other women, however, sex is a way of expressing their feelings of affection and caring. For them 'making love' is literally that. Sex both expresses and reinforces the love they feel for their husbands:

> I love that guy. So I try to show him.
>
> (Generation III, b. 1947)

> He's a sweetie. I love him so I make love with him lots.
>
> (Generation III, b. 1948)

> He's a wonderful man. I love him. It's the best way I can let him know.
>
> (Generation III, b. 1953)

Love and affection can hold women back sexually. Some women decide that there is no percentage in 'turning on'. To turn on is to assert one's own needs. Sex traditionally revolves around the man's advances, his schedules, his rhythms, his climax—*his* needs. For a woman to be turned on seems to contest this one-sidedness. Women often subordinate their needs and wants to ensure family harmony. Sublimating their sexuality to their husbands' may be an expression of this pattern, an attempt on the part of the wife to express her love for her husband.

> Sometimes I'd like to say stop when he is pounding away at me. Then I'd tell him to slow down, to touch me the way I dream about. And I imagine us making love beautifully. And I like it and I love him. But if I did, I know he'd feel hurt. It's important to him that he thinks I like the way he makes love. If I started suggesting things he'd feel bad. So I don't.
>
> (Generation III, b. 1948)

The sublimation of sexuality in the interests of marital harmony may be one reason sexual activity apparently decreases as the marriage ages. Sixty of the women interviewed reported that as their marriages progressed, their level of sexual activity decreased. It may be that, faced with their inability to resolve all the contradictions that surround sexuality, many couples give up. They minimize their sexual activities rather than continue to confront the tensions:

> When we were first married, sex was really difficult. I never liked it and he knew that and it made him feel bad. Gradually it just didn't seem worth it to go on. So we don't do it much any more.
>
> (Generation II, b. 1931)

Family Violence Is a Hateful Thing

Men and women come to marriage from very different positions and their experiences of work and marriage create different understandings. At best these contrary positions are barriers which must be struggled against. For most couples they become sources of tension and all too frequently the tension leads to hostility and conflict.

At work men are powerless, so in their leisure time they want to have a feeling that they control their own lives. Because they are responsible for the household's subsistence, men often feel that they have the right to control the arrangements of the household and the people who live there. As the wage *earner*, the man is the wage *owner*. He is the property owner in the family; his power is rooted in real property relations. This property prerogative is the basis of the unequal relations of the family. Structured into household relations therefore is a 'petty tyranny' which allows the man to dominate his wife and children. Such male domination derives partly from the fact that domestic labour is predicated on wage labour and therefore caters to the needs of the wage worker. It is reinforced partly by societal norms of male dominance and superiority. Male chauvinism easily flourishes in such a setting. Some men exercise their 'petty tyranny' by demanding that their wives be at home when they get off work. The reason men give for making this demand is partly a reflection of their desire to assert their authority:

> She's my wife and she should be there when I get off.
>
> (Generation II, b. 1919)

> You [to wife] be home when I get off. That's where you belong.
>
> (Generation III, b. 1946)

Knowing that they can demand that their wives be at home waiting for them is a mechanism for releasing some of the feelings of powerlessness the wage work engenders:

> It makes me feel good to know she is at home waiting for me, like there's a place where I'm a man. I think about that when I'm at work.
>
> (Generation III, b. 1953)

One result of the economic relationship between women and their husbands is to bind the men to their jobs. While divorce from the means of production structurally compels men to do wage work, once a man has a dependent wife and children he incurs responsibilities and debts, which means that he cannot afford to stop working. While a single man can choose to quit a particular job when it becomes too unpleasant, a married man cannot. Objectively the woman becomes a force in keeping the man tied to his job. From her position of economic dependency, a wife adds more pressure to the structural compulsion to work.

Historically the Company has hired married men precisely because they create a more stable workforce. Sometimes women themselves recognize this aspect of their relationship:

> I know he hates his job. It's a terrible job. But he can't quit 'cause of me and the kids. We need his wages.
>
> (Generation III, b. 1953)

Subjectively, women act as pressure to keep their husbands not only at work but working regularly and responsibly. Many men deal with their dislike of work by quitting periodically, or less drastically, by going late, taking time off, or slacking on the job. Such behaviour is directly threatening to the household standard of living as it affects the amount of money the men bring home. It is in the women's interests to try to prevent the men from taking time off. When a man considers doing so, his wife may point out that they are in debt and need his money. Thus some men see their wives as constantly nagging, forcing them to work when they hate it. This induces tensions between the needs of women as domestic workers and the response of the men to wage work, tensions which are often expressed as hostilities between the sexes. A woman whose husband regularly skipped shifts expressed her sense of frustration and anger at men:

> Men. They're just no good. They are lazy and irresponsible and selfish. Look at Jim, he just skipped another shift and how are we going to make do?
>
> (Generation II, b. 1929)

On the other hand, the responsibility of being breadwinners generates in men all sorts of pressure and fear, which in turn are often projected onto women (Guettel 1974: 14). This hostility is reinforced by women's work as tension managers for their husbands.

When men express their work-related tensions, anxieties, and hostilities at work, it is economically threatening to the employer. When their protest is collectively expressed, for example in a general strike, the results are politically threatening to the capitalist state. Therefore, both employers and the state employ sophisticated means to minimize this potential.

The threat of firing is the most significant means of repressing outbursts in the workplace. Labour legislation, especially laws against wildcat strikes, and the armed force of the police protect the interests of the state.

On the other hand, family violence is not directed against either employers or the state. While in recent years, primarily because of pressures from the women's liberation movement, family violence has gradually come to be considered socially deviant, it is still not recognized as a major social problem. Very little is done by either employers or the state to prevent family violence.

If no mechanisms are available by which workers can channel their work-related tensions into forms of struggle at the workplace, they carry those tensions and angers home with them. Part of reproducing the worker's labour power must therefore include ways of displacing those work-related fears and hostilities:

> When he comes home from work, I really think it's up to me to help him relax and feel good. If he's grumpy and tired, I cheer him up.
>
> (Generation II, b. 1926)

This part of women's work in reproducing labour power is the most hidden and profound. It is also of vital importance for her work and her life. While part of this tension management is done for the sake of the man, another part is for herself and the children. Women do not want to live with fights and the threat of violence every day. They defuse tension, refrain from a certain argument, or protect their husbands from things that will upset them in order to maintain peace:

> I remember how I always used to try and meet him at the door with a cup of tea. He liked his tea. If I made him feel better after work, then our home was a happy one.
>
> (Generation I, b. 1900)

In some instances, women are the recipients of overt anger and rage. Some examples will illustrate what this means in practice. A 32-year-old man had worked for the Company for 16 years. His current supervisor did not like him and they had regular clashes at work. He came home almost every night tense and irritable. His wife described what happened at night:

> We go to sleep and then sometimes in the middle of the night I wake up because he is groaning and punching me and crying out angry stuff at his boss. Sometimes he punches me real hard and once he broke my nose. Course he didn't mean to and it wasn't me he was mad at. It was his boss, but still. So I get out of bed and go make tea and wake him up and talk to him, then he settles down and we go back to sleep. It happens maybe two or three times a week.
>
> (Generation III, b. 1949)

The wife received the brunt of the rage and violence that her husband bottled up and repressed at work. She considered it her duty to get up and make him tea and comfort him, even though she had an infant to feed at 6 a.m. She was constantly tired and sometimes dozed off in the middle of a conversation. She apologized for doing so by explaining:

> See Joe has a hard time at work so I have to get up with him in the night, so I don't get too much sleep these days.

In another case, a 28-year-old man had worked for the Company for 12 years. He too had a supervisor with whom he fought regularly. His solution to his work-related tensions was to get drunk or stoned on marijuana every night after work. His wife was concerned for his health and worried that he drank or smoked 'all that hard-earned cash'. When he was 'ripped' he tended to think that she was the hated boss and he lashed out at her:

> Once he came at me with the kitchen knife saying I was [the boss] and he wasn't going to take no more shit from me. Another time he took a swipe at me and broke my glasses. Usually though he just yells at me that I can take my fucking job and shove it or something like that. I just keep out of reach till he calms down.
>
> (Generation III, b. 1951)

Growing out of the various power struggles that occur between men and their work and between wives and husbands is sex-based hostility where male contempt for women is expressed through physical violence.

Wife beating is one of the hidden crimes in this society. In recent years the women's liberation movement has pointed out how widespread it is. The few studies that have been done show unequivocally that wife beating is a phenomenon that occurs with equal frequency among families of all classes (Eekelaar and Katz 1975; Borland 1976; D'Oyley 1978; Martin 1978; Renvoize 1978; MacLeod 1980). It is part of the larger problem of generalized violence against women and must be understood in that context. For working-class families, it is compounded by the pressures and dependency generated by the proletarian condition:

> My husband beats me, usually on payday. He gets mad and hates me. His violence is a really hateful thing.
>
> (Generation II, b. 1935)

Why do women put up with such treatment? They do so partly because there are no resources to give them the support necessary to deal with the abuse. Flin Flon has no hostels for women; the police will not interfere in what they term 'domestic squabbles'; and economically the women have no resources to leave. Equally important is the fact that most women feel it is their responsibility to 'stick it out' because marriage is 'till death do us part' and tension managing is part of their work. Of the hundred women interviewed, only three were divorced. Most women, when male violence erupts, 'just keep out of reach' until it subsides.

One woman who was beaten regularly by her husband was recovering after a particularly bad attack in which her arm was broken. What she said explains in part why so many women accept the abuse they receive from their husbands:

> He puts up with shit every day at work and he only works because he has me and the kids to support. Weren't for us he'd be off trapping on his own, with no boss breathing down his neck. He hates his job. He's got all that mad locked up inside with nowhere for it to go. So sometimes he takes it out on me and the kids. Well I sort of don't blame him I guess.
>
> (Generation II, b. 1935)

Thus a terrible but logical and extreme extension of their roles as tension managers is for women, as the victims, to blame themselves and to feel guilty for having induced male hostility and aggression.

Meeting Women's Needs

Domestic violence is the most extreme form of women's oppression within the family. However, in a myriad of other less obvious ways the subordinate character of domestic labour denies women their full humanity.

Domestic labour is responsible for reproducing the labour power of all the adults of the household. In other words, the woman is responsible for reproducing not only her husband's capacity to work each day but her own as well. In some ways, domestic labour is similar to wage work. It is frequently physically and mentally exhausting and monotonous. While it is not alienated in the sense that wage labour is alienated, it is the epitome of self-sacrificing labour. Because it is unpaid, women can justify it as reasonable and honourable work only by considering it a 'labour of love'. This definition reinforces its self-sacrificing quality and encourages women themselves to underplay the extent to which it is much more than a labour of love. In daily life this means that women's needs are not always met.

When household resources are scarce, it is the women who cut back their consumption first. There is a working-class tradition of women eating less than their husbands and children, denying themselves sustenance they badly need so that other household members can have more.[9]

In many Flin Flon households, on the day before payday there was very little food in the house. A number of women regularly did not eat that day because there was only enough for one or two people.

> He's got to eat or he can't do his work and the baby needs food to grow, but it won't hurt me to skip a meal for once.
>
> (Generation III, b. 1958)

Women's sleeping time is also vulnerable to demands from other household members. In some households where men worked the night shift, their wives got up at 3 a.m. either to greet them coming off shift or to send them off to work. When those women had school-aged children, they also had to get up at 7:30 a.m. so their sleep was disrupted and inadequate. When other household members were sick or frightened or simply unable to sleep at night, the women got up with them to comfort, feed, and care for them. A number of women talked about how tired they felt all the time. They attributed this 'housewife's fatigue' to regularly interrupted sleep.

Even when women were ill, they had to carry on with their work. Those women who were actively engaged in domestic labour reported that their husbands were sick enough to stay in bed an average of four days each year. Their husbands went to bed when they got sick, and the women took care of them in addition to doing their regular work. The women themselves were sick enough to warrant staying in bed an average of eight days each year. However, they unanimously agreed that, no matter how sick they were, they could not take time off to go to bed. They continued with their regular work despite their illness. In every case, women took time off work only when they were hospitalized—for a major illness or having a baby. Women said they enjoyed their stays in hospital when their babies were born. They relished the rest and being catered to.

The 22 women who were retired said that a similar pattern continued even when the couple was older and nearing retirement. In older people, illness was compounded by the fact that many of the men had work-related injuries or illnesses, which meant they required constant nursing. Even though the women were also often ill or crippled by age-related diseases, such as arthritis and rheumatism, they still continued to nurse the men. A number of women said that dealing with an ill spouse finally forced them to retire:

> I kept on managing my house for 20 years after my husband retired. He had bad lungs [from working underground] and at last he took to bed and needed regular nursing. Well I kept at it for about a year, but I wasn't strong enough so I finally had to give it up.
>
> (Generation I, b. 1888)

Reproducing labour power also involved ensuring that workers have a chance to recuperate, relax, and engage in leisure activities that are not related to their regular work. For domestic workers, especially with young children, meeting this need is almost impossible. There is no time when the woman is totally free from work-related responsibilities. Even when she is relaxing, she is on call. Women recognize that their situation differs from their husbands':

> I guess I have to take care of all of them and then I have to take care of myself too.
> (Generation III, b. 1955)

> How come there's no one to take care of me?
> (Generation II, b. 1934)

> When they are tired, or can't find something or they want something, I do it for them. When I want something I get it for myself.
> (Generation III, b. 1945)

When women described their activities during a typical day, they frequently mentioned periods when they took time 'off' to visit with friends, watch TV, or just sit down for a cup of tea and a cigarette. However, even during these breaks, those with young children must be alert to their activities. And all too often, women described their breaks as time not only to relax but also to 'do a bit of mending or sewing'.

The responsibility of constantly caring for the needs of others means that it is often difficult for women to determine what their own needs are:

> When I wake up early I like to lie in bed and have a think about my life. It's the only time I have to myself and what I need, you know, to get me through my day. Like I know what he needs—his lunch box and a hot supper—and what they need—clean clothes and their lunch. And they all need love I guess. But what do I need?
> (Generation II, b. 1936)

Sometimes the work women do becomes so merged with their identity that they have trouble distinguishing them. They confuse their own needs with those of their families. This confusion is reflected in the way women sometimes describe family needs. A woman buying a jacket for her six-year-old child remarked: 'I need this jacket. It's getting cold these days.'

The lack of clarity that women have about their own needs as domestic workers begins with marriage when most couples set up households and the women establish the social relations of their work based on inexperience and lack of knowledge. The first few years of household formation are critical, for it is during this period that patterns of work, personal interactions, and the particular expression of the division of labour within the household are established. Once established they are extremely difficult to change.

A woman with three children under 10 years of age observed that when her first baby was born she was so interested and excited by the new baby that she wanted to take care of it herself. She never asked her husband to help out with childcare. When the second and third children were born, the novelty had worn off, her energy was dissipated, and she wanted him to become involved:

> But he just wouldn't. He said he'd never changed a nappy and he wasn't about to start. In fact, he used to point out regularly that I had insisted on doing it alone with the first one and why had I suddenly changed my tune now?
> (Generation III, b. 1948)

Because of their initial experience and lack of knowledge, women frequently flounder around for several years trying to understand what is happening to them and trying to get some control over the situation.

At the same time, they are caught up in the demands of young children, keeping a house, and relating to their husbands. Many of them end up in the same situation as the Red Queen in Lewis Carroll's *Through the Looking Glass*, having to run as fast as they can simply to stay in one place.[10] An older woman recalled her feelings of bewilderment and confusion during this early period of her marriage:

> I never quite got on top of things. I kept thinking that if I could just get a week of peace I could think things through and then I'd be okay. But everything was always rushing here and there and I didn't ever catch up. Now I sort of have a routine and a pattern of work. But I never chose it. It just happened by default.
>
> (Generation I, b. 1907)

Most women are not deliberate martyrs; they make a concerted effort to ensure that their own needs for relaxation and support are met at some level. They develop strategies, such as organizing their workplace and the social relations of their work in the most convenient and convivial ways possible. This means that women are interested in adopting any new developments in household technology, in the organization of their work or in new products and materials.

Another strategy involves organizing their work so that they can assert themselves as they choose when their husbands are not around. Most women organize this part of their time around their own interests:

> When he's not here I do things how I want. I scrub my floors or do my wash or go visit or play with the kids—whatever I want to do and how I want to do it. When he gets off, I have to make sure I'm on time for work, I have to be home waiting for him and I do what he wants while he's there. That way he feels good, we have a good time together and I get my own time too.
>
> (Generation III, b. 1947)

As a third strategy women establish and maintain networks of co-workers, friends, and neighbours to provide a milieu in which they can pool their knowledge about their work and share information, goods, and services. All of the women interviewed described these networks as vitally important to them. On an average, women spent three to four hours each day visiting, either in person or on the phone, with friends and neighbours. During these visits women combine a number of activities. They enjoy each other's company while exchanging information about their work and their lives. Simultaneously they care for their children and continue doing some aspect of their housework, such as ironing or cooking:

> I try to visit with my friends as often as possible. It helps me get through my day. We sit and chat about this and that. We watch the kids. I help do the laundry or whatever.
>
> (Generation III, b. 1949)

They also rely a great deal on assistance and support from female relatives. Of the 20 women interviewed who had mothers living in Flin Flon, 19 said that they saw their mothers at least twice a week. Of the 88 active domestic workers interviewed, 72 said they relied on a close female relative, mother, mother-in-law, daughter, or sister to help out in crisis situations. Women in 63 households said they visited with a close female relative at least once each week and that those women provided assistance, information, and affection:

> My sister and my husband's mother are just always there when I need them. If I want to pop out to the store, one of them will mind the baby. If I'm feeling low, I go for a visit.
>
> (Generation III, b. 1951)

Through their women friends and relatives, housewives can improve the social relations of their work and meet some of their own needs for work-related tension managing. Even women who considered their husbands to be their best friends asserted that women friends were special and important:

> Well, my husband, he's my husband and I love him, and he knows me better than anyone and he's my best friend. But Sarah is something else. I see her every day and we chat and when I'm down she cheers me up and when I'm in a muddle she sorts me out and when things aren't good with my husband, she hugs me.
>
> (Generation III, b. 1948)

Frequently, several women got together to do some part of their work collectively. Two or three women went shopping in one car, and as they shopped they pooled ideas about good deals and menu suggestions. They looked out for each other's children and borrowed money from each other. On occasion, several women assembled in one house to spend the day cooking. They usually did this when the food such as pierogies, cabbage rolls, or preserves required lots of chopping or a long cooking time and constant watching. The women prepared a large quantity of food to be shared among all of them. I participated in two collective cooking activities. One day three of us worked from 9 a.m. to 5:30 p.m. and made 435 pierogies. On another day, four of us worked from 10:30 a.m. to 4:30 p.m. and made 193 cabbage rolls. Working together turned an onerous job into an interesting social occasion.

Most of the women interviewed said that periodically when their children were young they arranged with another woman to exchange childcare services. Two women with children of similar ages took turns looking after each other's children for a number of hours each week. This gave each of the mothers some time 'off' to spend as they wished.

Because individual women work most of the time in the isolation of their own home, these relations with other women combine both the need for co-workers with whom to share information and advice and the need for friends with common interests. It is these relationships that provide much of the tension managing that domestic workers need. Women pointed out that their husbands rarely did domestic work and consistently undervalued both its difficulty and its worth. Other women, who from their own experience understood the requirements and rigours of the work, were more helpful in providing support, reassurance, and comfort for work-related problems:

> Sometimes I feel so tired and out of sorts with my family. I can't really talk to David about it. He tries but he really doesn't understand, and anyway sometimes he's part of the problem, if you know what I mean. My mother or my sister or my neighbour next door, I just go and have a good cry with them and then I feel better.
>
> (Generation III, b. 1942)

Women's efforts to improve the conditions of their work, and their families' lives, and all the contradictions inherent in that, have an impact beyond their immediate household and friendship networks.

The tension between women's short- and long-term interests as domestic labourers and as members of their class was illustrated during the period of contract negotiations between the union and the Company in 1976. A number of women noted that the negotiations directly affected them and their ability to do their work. One woman pointed out the contradictions between the immediate objective conditions of her work, the long-term interests of that work, and her subjective understanding of her class interests. Her immediate interests were the regularity of the wage, ensuring that money kept coming into the household purse. Her long-term interests as a domestic labourer were concerned with the magnitude of the wage and its increase. As a member of her class she had to grapple with the short-term/long-term trade-offs that are always part of class struggle:

> I don't want a strike because I can't live on strike pay. I just can't feed my kids on strike pay. But I think we should strike because that company makes so much money off those men and it thinks it can get away with murder. We need to stand up to the Company and show them that they can't go on trashing us workers any more.
>
> (Generation II, b. 1926)

There is a long tradition of miners' wives acting militantly in support of the miners in class-struggle situations.[11] In both strikes in Flin Flon, in 1934 and 1971, the wives of strikers played an important role in the union struggles. They organized strike support committees, went on the picket lines, and regularly indicated both their support for the men and their own interests in winning the strike.

A woman who was active in the 1971 strike described her experiences and noted the connections between her work in the home and her husband's wage work:

> The men were on strike and their families were hurting. A bunch of us women were talking. Some of them wanted to end the strike—they were scared and just wanted life to be normal again. But others understood better that it was our strike too. We needed more money and better conditions for our men, [and this] meant better conditions at home. Miserable angry workers make rotten husbands. . . . So we went on the picket line and did what we could.
>
> (Generation II, b. 1929)

By seizing the initiative, women begin to gain some control over their working conditions and their lives. This gives them strength to struggle against the inequalities of their marriages. It undermines their subordination and helps to make better, rather than worse, the position of wife in industrial-capitalist society.

Notes

1. The most important lack of alternatives is the fact that heterosexual, monogamous marriage is generally considered to be the only normal life choice for everyone. People who choose to be single, to have children alone, to have no children, to live with several people, lesbians, homosexuals, and bisexuals, even couples who live together without marrying—all are subjected to some degree of social sanction and disapproval. As long as this is so people cannot 'choose' freely to marry.
2. The situation of women wage earners with respect to the sex-segregated job market and the unequal pay differentials between women and men was well documented in 1970 by the *Report of the Royal Commission on the Status of Women in Canada* (Ottawa: Information Canada, 1970). More up-to-date figures from the Department of Labour, Women's Bureau, are summarized by Pat Armstrong and Hugh Armstrong in *The Double Ghetto* (Toronto: McClelland & Stewart, 1978). These more recent figures confirm that the pay differential between women and men is, if anything, increasing.
3. Luxton interviewed 60 women who had set up their households between the 1920s and 1970s: five did so in the 1920s, 15 in the 1930s, and 10 from each of the later decades. (She interviewed

other women as well, but this was her initial sample.) She divided these 60 women into three 'generations' (which she signified with I, II, and III). The first generation established their households in the most primitive of conditions, and the last had houses that were equipped with modern services and technology. Whenever she quotes them, Luxton indicates the birth date (b.) of each woman.

4. For a study of the impact of shift work on the social relations of the family, see P.E. Mott, *Shift Work: The Social, Psychological, and Physical Consequences* (Ann Arbor: University of Michigan Press, 1965), 18.
5. This is a typical pattern for working-class families. Denis et al. cite the example of the man who threw his supper into the fire even though he admitted that it was particularly good food. His wife had gone out and arranged for another woman to prepare his meals for him. They quoted him when he explained that he threw out the dinner because it was his wife's job to prepare his meal and she could not allocate her work to someone else. N. Denis, F. Henriques, and C. Slaughter, *Coal Is Our Life: An Analysis of a Yorkshire Mining Community* (London: Tavistock Publications, 1969), 182.
6. Michael Young and Peter Willmott in *The Symmetrical Family: A Study of Work and Leisure in the London Region* (London: Routledge & Kegan Paul, 1973) suggest that the shorter workweek for wage workers and the improved situation for domestic workers created by household technology have resulted in a new type of family relations where the sexual division of labour is breaking down. They note that men have begun to spend a bit more time around the house helping out with domestic work and that women are increasingly taking on wage work. They hypothesize from these observations that a basic equality is evolving within the family. They are able to make such a statement only because they have never stopped to investigate what actually does constitute domestic labour. While it is true that men are helping out more around the house, they are still 'helping out'. The internal household labour is still the primary responsibility of women.
7. While marriage laws vary, one universal feature is the recognition that legal marriage must be 'consummated'; that is, sexual intercourse must take place. If it does not, the marriage may be annulled, which essentially means that the marriage never occurred.
8. For a summary of the major studies on North American sexuality since Kinsey, see Ruth Brecker and E. Brecker, *An Analysis of Human Sexual Response* (New York: Signet, 1966); M. Hunt, *Sexual Behavior in the 1970s* (Chicago: Playboy Press, 1974); Shere Hite, *The Hite Report* (New York: Dell Books, 1976).
9. For a good discussion on how and why women subordinate their needs to those of their husbands, see Laura Oren, 'The Welfare of Women in Labouring Families: England 1860–1950', in M. Hartman and L.W. Banner, eds, *Clio's Consciousness Raised: New Perspectives on the History of Women* (New York: Harper and Row, 1974); M.L. McDougall, 'Working Class Women During the Industrial Revolution, 1780–1860' (Houghton Mifflin, 1977); Jane Humphries, 'The Working Class Family, Women's Liberation, and Class Struggle: The Case of Nineteenth-century British History', *The Review of Radical Political Economics: Women, Class, and the Family* 9, 3 (Fall 1977).
10. In Lewis Carroll's *Through the Looking Glass* (London: Penguin Books, 1971), Alice meets the Red Queen and they begin to run just as fast as they can because they want to stay in the same place. Alice suggests that this is unusual but the Queen assures her: 'Now here you see, it takes all the running you can do to keep in the same place. If you want to get somewhere else, you must run at least twice as fast as that.' A number of women who had read this story saw a similar pattern in their own lives.
11. For information on the role of women in miners' strikes in North America, see M.E. Parton, ed., *The Autobiography of Mother Jones* (Chicago: Charles H. Kerr, 1974); and Kathy Kahn, *Hillbilly Women* (New York: Avon Books, 1973). The important part that women play in primary resource strike situations was graphically portrayed by Barbara Kopple in her film *Harlan County*, USA (1975). For a sketchy

outline of the role of women in the Flin Flon strikes, see Valerie Hedman, Loretta Yauck, and Joyce Henderson, *Flin Flon* (Flin Flon, MB: Flin Flon Historical Society, 1974). *The Wives Tale/L'histoire des femmes* is a film about the 1978 strike against Inco in Sudbury, Ontario.

References

Borland, M., ed. 1976. *Violence in the Family* (Manchester: Manchester University Press).

Denis, N., F. Henriques, and C. Slaughter. 1969. *Coal Is Our Life: An Analysis of a Yorkshire Mining Community* (London: Tavistock Publications).

D'Oyley, V., ed. 1978. *Domestic Violence* (Toronto: Ontario Institute for Studies in Education).

Easton, L.D., and K.H. Guddat, eds and trans. 1967. *Writings of the Young Marx on Philosophy and Society* (New York: Doubleday).

Eekelaar, J.M., and S.N. Katz. 1975. *Family Violence* (Toronto: Butterworths).

Guettel, C. 1974. *Marxism and Feminism* (Toronto: The Women's Press).

MacLeod, L. 1980. *Wife Battering in Canada: The Vicious Circle* (Ottawa: Canadian Advisory Council on the Status of Women).

Martin, J.P., ed. 1978. *Violence and the Family* (New York: John Wiley).

Renvoize, J., ed. 1978. *Wed of Violence* (London: Routledge & Kegan Paul).

Rubin, L. 1976. 'The Marriage Bed', *Psychology Today* (Aug.): 44.

Schneider, M. 1975. *Neurosis and Civilization* (New York: The Seabury Press).

Winnipeg Women's Liberation. 1978. *Newsletter* (Feb.).

Chapter 12

At any point in time, there is considerable diversity in family patterns. Family organization also changes through time, with shifts in the conditions under which people acquire their livelihood and build their intimate relationships. This chapter reviews demographic trends that have shaped families for over a century. It also explores the larger social changes that are behind these trends.

As Times Change: A Review of Trends in Family Life

Bonnie Fox with Jessica Yiu

On 13 September 2007, Canadians awoke to the news that 'the family' was being 'redefined' in this country (Alphonso 2007). According to the results of the 2006 census, fewer than half of the adult population had ever been married, common-law families were growing in number more than five times faster than married-couple families, and same-sex couple relationships were increasing five times faster than any type of heterosexual union. As well, a slightly higher proportion of couples (married and common-law) were living without any children (24 years of age and under) than with them—in spite of a significant increase in the percentage of children in their twenties who live with their parents (i.e., about 44 per cent of Canadians 20 to 29 were living with their parents) (Statistics Canada 2007).

That Canadian families are changing, and have been for some time, is undisputed. Declining rates of marriage, large and increasing numbers of common-law relationships, substantial numbers of lone-parent families, significant numbers of lesbian and gay families, low birth rates, and high rates of divorce signify changes in an important institution. Advocates of a return to 'family values' see cause for alarm in these changes. Assuming the imminent demise of the nuclear family, they typically propose that society itself is threatened. For example, conservative merican sociologist David Popenoe (1993: 539) has argued that 'today's family decline . . . [is] both unique and alarming' because it is about [the] decline of the 'nuclear unit [which is] the fundamental and most basic unit of the family [and, he implies, society]'.

Popenoe's reasoning resonates strongly with popular wisdom. Repeating the argument that Talcott Parsons developed in the early post-World War II period, Popenoe states that the nuclear family performs two critical functions—good quality child rearing and the satisfaction of adults' needs for affection. He argues further that 'there is strong reason to *believe*, in fact, that the [nuclear] family is by far the best institution to carry out these functions' (Popenoe 1993: 539; emphasis added). Like Parsons before him, Popenoe's primary concern is that these functions must be fulfilled for the sake of social order. Although the heads of corporations and many politicians are concerned to preserve the status quo, for most of us there is a larger concern—that the needs of children, women, and men be met, whether they live in nuclear families or in some other arrangement.

Taking issue with the notion of a crisis in 'the family', American social historian Stephanie Coontz (1997: 2) reviewed the history of family life in the United States to show that 'there never was a golden age in family life, a time when all families were capable of meeting the needs of their members and protecting them from poverty, violence, or sexual exploitation'. Instead, her book *The Way We Never Were* shows:

> the tremendous variety of family types that have worked—or not worked—in American history. When families succeeded, it was often for reasons quite different than stereotypes about the past suggest—because they were flexible in their living arrangements, for example, or could call on people and institutions beyond the family for assistance or support. (1997: 2)

While Popenoe blames individuals, and their increasing selfishness, for 'rejecting the family', Coontz argues that the problems people are experiencing in these times of change stem from the absence of public supports to changing families. This is the conclusion of Canadian sociologist John Conway as well. Conway believes (like Popenoe) that there is a 'crisis' in 'the family' in Canada, but argues that 'the obvious conclusion is to support emerging family forms at both personal and policy levels' ([1990] 1993: 39).

In order to assess the merits of the different arguments in any debate about family change, one has to understand something of the nature and extent of the changes that are occurring in people's personal and family lives, as well as the economic, social, and cultural factors promoting those changes. This chapter reviews the key changes in family patterns. In order to provide some perspective on these changes, I examine long-term trends and argue that these trends, and the changes in them, are shaped by economic and social factors. Changing family patterns especially reflect changes in the economy and the adjustments adults must make to earn a livelihood. As the ways people earn their livelihoods change so too will the probability that people will form families and the nature of the families they create. Moreover, because families have been organized around a division of work and responsibility based on gender, changes in gender relations and the relative positions of women and men also affect family patterns.

In this chapter, I describe long-term and recent changes in family patterns. I also offer explanations of these changes. In so doing, I assume that changes in the economy, and thus what adults must do to earn a livelihood sufficient to support a household, has a fundamental impact on how families are organized. My explanations of change, then, focus on the economy. I assume as well that a division of labour based on gender, in which men have wages sufficient to support a family and women take responsibility for childcare and essential housework, is the basic organizing principle in conventional nuclear families. Thus, I assume that changes in gender will affect families. After reviewing trends affecting families, I discuss the diverse family patterns common today.

Long-term Trends

There are many ways to measure changes in family life. We will ask first what the average ages have been when women and men typically experience the key life events that are central to family—like marriage and parenthood. Second, we will ask how likely it has been that women and men actually experience such life-changing events as marriage, parenthood, and divorce.

We begin our review of long-term trends by examining the typical life course for successive birth cohorts[1] between the mid-nineteenth century and 1970. Table 12.1 shows estimates of the median ages[2] for each major life event, for 10-year birth cohorts, starting with people born between 1831 and 1840, and ending with people born between 1961 and 1970. For each birth cohort, the table presents our best guess of the average ages at which important events in women's and men's life cycles typically

Table 12.1 Median Ages at Family Life-course Events

	Approximate Birth Cohorts:												
	1831–40	1841–50	1851–60	1861–70	1881–90	1891–1900	1901–10	1911–20	1921–30	1931–40	1941–50	1951–60	1961–70
Females													
Median Age at:													
First Marriage	25.1	26.0	24.9	24.3	25.1	23.4	23.3	23.0	22.0	21.1	21.3	22.5	25.0
First Birth	27.1	28.0	26.9	26.3	27.1	25.4	25.0	25.4	23.5	22.9	23.3	24.5	26.0
Last Birth	41.0	40.0	38.2	36.2	36.2	33.9	29.1	28.8	29.5	29.1	26.7	26.3	27.8
Empty Nest*	61.0	60.1	58.2	56.2	56.2	53.9	49.1	48.8	49.5	49.1	46.7	46.3	47.8
Widowhood	58.2	59.5	58.9	58.3	60.1	59.4	61.3	63.0	67.0	67.2	68.8	69.9	70.0
Males													
Median Age at:													
First Marriage	27.9	29.1	29.2	28.0	28.5	28.4	27.0	26.3	24.3	24.0	23.5	24.6	27.0
First Birth	29.9	31.1	31.2	30.0	30.5	30.4	28.7	28.7	25.8	25.8	25.5	26.6	28.0
Last Birth	43.8	43.1	42.5	39.9	39.6	38.9	32.8	32.1	31.8	32.0	28.9	28.4	29.8
Empty Nest*	63.8	63.1	62.5	59.9	59.6	58.9	52.9	52.1	51.8	52.0	48.9	48.4	49.8

* Age at which last child is 20 years old.

Sources: Gee 1987: 278. For 1961–70 birth cohort: 1991 Census of Canada, Cat. No. 84-212, Table 1; 1991 Census, Cat. No. 84-210, Tables 11 and 15; and DBS, Vital Statistics, Cat. No. 84-802. (See Gee 1987: Appendix, for methods used to derive estimates.)

occurred—first marriage, first and last birth (and thus the period in women's lives taken up with pregnancy and the care of infants), the start of the 'empty nest' (when the last child is 20 years old and presumably leaves home) and (for women) widowhood. This kind of estimate of the typical family life cycle of different birth cohorts seems a satisfying kind of summary, but resulting figures should be taken as only crude indicators of trends and changes. Moreover, an average is just that: it does not tell us about the extent of variation around the average. Other demographic analyses have shown that, at least for the 1911–20 birth cohort (but likely others), the lives of the majority of people have not followed what is assumed to be the 'typical' sequence for adults (leaving home, then getting married, then having children and raising them, and then seeing them leave home) (Ravanera and Rajulton 1996: 145). There has been considerable diversity in the paths constituting different people's life cycles; the diversity common in recent decades is therefore not unusual.

Nevertheless, the figures in Table 12.1 show some interesting trends and changes. The largest change over time is a product of the decline in birth rates. While women born before the mid-nineteenth century likely spent between 12 and 14 years pregnant and bearing their five or six (live) children (Gee 1987: 275), the period women spent having babies shrank over the course of the twentieth century as the birth rate declined. It increased slightly for the women who had their children during the post-World War II 'baby boom': women born in the 1920s and 1930s (and having children in the 1940s and 1950s) spent about six years in the child-bearing stage of life. Nevertheless, women born between 1901 and 1910 (and having babies in the 1920s and 1930s) spent only four years pregnant and having their babies; and, when the decline in the birth rate continued after the baby boom, women born in the 1950s and 1960s (and having babies in the 1970s and 1980s) spent only about two years in this stage of life, usually having one or two children. In other words, the small period women spent having babies in the late twentieth century was similar to the experience of women born at the beginning of the century.

The age when women and men typically first married also declined over time, until the 1970s. Together with the decline in birth rates, earlier marriage meant that women were younger when they finished child-bearing. It is worth noting as well that the period following World War II, affecting 1921–30 and 1931–40 male and female birth cohorts, brought a substantial decline in age at first marriage. In fact, the notable drop in age of marriage in the post-World War II period through 1960—occurring in the 1950s, essentially—is just one indicator of a period significantly different from that preceding it (as we will see). Note that women born in or before 1890 and men born in or before 1920 married when they were in their mid- to late twenties, as has been the case recently, and beginning with the 1961–70 birth cohort.

Before asking why these changes occurred, we should note one other related long-term trend that is clear in Table 12.1. The 'empty nest' period—the time couples live together after their youngest child has moved out of the home—developed in the twentieth century. With extensions in life expectancy and declining numbers of children, this stage in life expanded over the course of the twentieth century (until, perhaps, near the end, as children left home at later and later ages). In short, adults', and especially women's, lives involve much less time caring for young and dependent children than they did in earlier centuries.

Why have women had fewer and fewer children? The long-term decline in the birth rate reflects changes over time in women's position and in the economic situation of families. Starting in the mid-nineteenth century, women had fewer children despite considerable odds. Until well into the twentieth century, women apparently knew almost nothing about the biology of reproduction and, until the 1930s at least, Canadian doctors were typically unwilling to help patients anxious to reduce the number of their pregnancies (McLaren and McLaren 1986). There was reason for doctors' reluctance. Abortion, which was fairly commonly resorted to—and a principal means by which birth rates were lowered—was illegal in Canada (from the moment of conception) after 1837 (McLaren and McLaren 1986: 39).[3] Even the dissemination of information about contraception—as well as its use—was illegal after 1892 (McLaren and McLaren 1986).[4]

Nevertheless, by the nineteenth century many women had developed a conviction that the dangers attached to childbirth were unacceptable (Arnup, Levesque, and Pierson 1990; Leavitt 1986; Wertz and Wertz 1979).[5] Apparently men's interest in limiting family size grew as well, whether out of concern about their wives' health and well-being or because of the financial burdens of parenthood. Women might resort to abortion without their husbands' help or even knowledge, but *coitus interruptus*, or withdrawal—which was apparently the chief means of contraception well into the twentieth century—required the man's co-operation (McLaren and McLaren 1986). So the decline over time in the birth rate represents both women's and men's desires for fewer children.

Central to couples' desire to have fewer children was, no doubt, their changing economic situation. Through the nineteenth century, a 'family economy' in which husbands and wives had the resources they needed (land or trade skills) to support themselves and their children—and in which women contributed to subsistence—eroded (Coontz 1988; Ryan 1983).[6] This kind of economy was, of course, replaced by a capitalist economy in which people had to do waged work (or sell their products or services in the marketplace) in order to survive. [At] least in the United States, middle-class men began to identify themselves as 'breadwinners' by the middle of the nineteenth century (Kimmel 1996). As men's work moved outside the household, wives became economically more marginal, even though middle-class women in Canada and the US continued to contribute to their families' subsistence—gardening and keeping cows or pigs even in cities, until the latter practices were outlawed toward the end of the century (Bradbury 1984; Stansell 1987).

The erosion of an economy located in households was important. Not only had women done essential productive work when married couples had access to the necessary means of production but also fathers had provided for their children's future, passing on land or ensuring an apprenticeship in a skilled trade for their sons, and ensuring their daughters' dowries. The long-standing tradition of apprenticeship—whereby youth lived in the household of a man and a woman who trained them in a trade or other skills essential to adulthood—eroded in the first half of the nineteenth century in urban Canada, according to historian Michael Katz (1975). Until an institutional framework in which to 'contain young adolescents' developed, there was thus a 'crisis of youth' (Katz 1975: 307).

Social historian Mary Ryan (1981) describes a similar problem in upstate New York in the early decades of the nineteenth century, largely because of the fact that numbers of young men were moving from rural areas into towns, and beyond their parents' control, to find work.[7] According to Ryan, middle-class women in these towns addressed the 'youth problem' by assuming the role of educators, and specifically by setting up activities that would help instill in the young men important civic values—in addition to housing them. They advocated the 'Protestant Ethic', with its emphasis on hard work and thrift, for example. Within decades, these same women realized that the values they were promoting were critical to their own sons' survival and success in a quickly changing economy. Accordingly, they began keeping their sons and daughters home through their teens, allowing them to get more formal education. Katz (1975) found that in Hamilton between 1851 and 1871 the length of time boys (and girls, to a lesser extent) remained in their parents' homes, and the amount of education they received, increased. In short, parental responsibilities—which shifted from fathers to mothers in the nineteenth century—became more labour intensive, requiring long years of women's attention. Having a child became a heavier responsibility than in earlier eras. And having fewer children meant that women could devote 'less of their lives to infant care, freeing them to attend to growing children' (Vinovskis and Frank 1997: 55). Over the course of the century, middle-class womanhood was increasingly equated with motherhood (Margolis 1984; see Chapter 9).

Thus a 'separate-spheres' ideology developed in the middle class in the nineteenth century: women and men were said to be different in ways that made domestic roles 'natural' to women and market-oriented work 'natural' for men (Cott 1977; Davidoff and Hall 1987; Welter 1966). This ideology was not simply imposed on women; middle-class women themselves (as Ryan argues) had a hand in creating ideals that equated womanhood with motherhood. Hindsight tells us that such ideas were central to women's subordination, but at the time they were associated with a sentimentalization of domesticity, the home, and childhood, and, at least for American women, involved a critique of the capitalist economy that allowed women to claim a kind of moral superiority over men (Cott 1977; Stansell 1987: 22). In the short term, amidst dramatic changes in the nature of households, such ideas likely helped women increase their bargaining power in marriage, as well as to make claims for a larger role in the public sphere (e.g., the right to vote) (Laslett and Brenner 1989; Prentice et al. 1988).

Middle-class women also embraced an image of physical frailty (Wood 1974). This identity seems ironic until its utility in excusing sexual inactivity, and thus reducing the risk of pregnancy, is recognized (Laslett and Brenner 1989). By the end of the nineteenth century, many middle-class women were arguing for 'voluntary motherhood', and thus women's right to refuse to submit to men's sexual demands (Gordon 1974). So, as the weight of child rearing shifted to women's shoulders, and the responsibility it entailed increased, women took action to enable the successful fulfillment of a role that increasingly defined their lives and to reduce the weight of the responsibility it entailed. One way they did that was by having fewer children.

The economics of nineteenth-century working-class households suggest that they too had an incentive to reduce their number of children. Except for skilled workers, working-class men were very unlikely to be earning a 'family wage' until as late as the 1950s or 1960s (Fox 1980; Bradbury 1993). Not only did men earn too little to support their families through the nineteenth century (and the first half of the twentieth century) but working-class women were also less able than their middle-class counterparts to contribute to family subsistence by extending their household work (gardening, keeping animals, taking in boarders), as was common for middle-class women. They typically could supplement their husbands' earnings only by doing waged work (Bradbury 1993; Bullen 1992). Children earned money also and, in fact, were more important secondary earners than women until well into the twentieth century. Too much can be made of children's economic value, however. The added cost of each new mouth to feed must have been as salient to parents as whatever added wages a child would eventually bring home. That many working-class families maintained a precarious balance between destitution and subsistence indicates how significant another dependant could be to a family (Bradbury 1982).

Of course, more than economic considerations influence the number of children couples have. Power dynamics in marriage and men's attitudes toward women also matter. The financial interest that middle-class husbands and wives had in limiting family size was unlikely for a working-class population without much prospect of improving their lot. In fact, working-class status eroded men's authority in the household, and seems to have fuelled misogynist attitudes and struggles by men to reassert control over their households (Stansell 1987; Gordon 1988). Negotiations around sexuality were no doubt shaped by a feeling of entitlement that apparently characterized many working-class men's attitudes toward their wives (Stansell 1987). There is evidence that working-class women were battling with their husbands over definitions of gender, domestic roles and responsibilities, and decent treatment in marriage (Gordon 1988; Laslett and Brenner 1989). But the reduction in the birth rate occurred largely with middle-class couples.

By the twentieth century, rising expectations about marriage added to the issues of the cost of raising children and the dangers of childbirth to increase women's desires for small families. Newly won legal rights and improved educational and employment opportunities (especially for single women) raised new hopes for personal autonomy, at least for middle-class women (Strong-Boag 1988). Nevertheless, the demands of homemaking and childcare, as well as 'marriage bars' prohibiting the employment of married women, produced a huge discrepancy between the opportunities middle-class women faced before marriage and the financial dependence and social constraints they experienced once married. This reality must have made the love and companionship that women were coming to hope for, and sometimes experienced, in marriage in the late nineteenth century increasingly important in the twentieth century (Brenner and Laslett [illegible]1, Noel 2003). Indeed, the consumer culture that developed in the early decades of the century featured a recurring message that heterosexual romance and marriage were the routes to personal happiness (Rapp and Ross 1986). The prominence of this message in advertisements at the time underscores its appeal to women (and perhaps to men as well). And the drop in the age of marriage for women, beginning with the 1891–1900 birth cohort, partly reflects the power of that message. Yet, women had to negotiate a contradiction—between romance and sexual excitement, on the one hand, and motherhood and devotion to children, on the other. Thus, women who took the roles of wife and mother seriously needed to have manageable numbers of children. McLaren and McLaren (1986) found evidence that the Canadian women who were desperate for help with contraception in the early decades of the century were typically married, already raising several children, and wanting ongoing companionship in their marriage. Of course, in reducing the number of children they raised, women encountered another contradiction, since their role in life was defined (culturally and often personally) in terms of having and raising children. This contradiction in married women's lives is one reason why the trend of declining birth rates was reversed, and a 'baby boom' occurred, in the economically prosperous and highly domestic years of the 1950s and early 1960s.

The 1950s was an unusual decade. It was a brief period in which most of the adult population seemed to expect complete personal fulfillment from life-long heterosexual relationships and, in the case of women, domestic roles (Coontz 1992). The popularity of this investment in nuclear family is reflected in the changes that occurred: the age of marriage dropped, a very high percentage of people married, teen pregnancy became common (and was seen as unproblematic because it was usually within marriage), birth rates rose after a long decline, divorce became rarer, and the number of lone-parent families decreased (Adams 1997; Bradbury 2005; Coontz 1992; May 1988). In this period (extending into the 1960s), the vast majority of the adult population lived in breadwinner–homemaker families—a pattern that was short-lived because married women flooded into the paid labour force and men's real earnings began a long decline in the early 1970s (Fox 1993; Hobson and Morgan 2002: 15). What was long-lasting was the belief that this family pattern was 'traditional'.

Long-term trends converged with a supportive short-term environment to make breadwinner–homemaker families common in the 1950s. Campaigns by unions to secure a 'family wage' for their members, which began in the nineteenth century (May 1985); gender ideology from that century that held 'women's place' to be in the home (Cott 1977) and labour-market barriers to women that put them there (Parr 1990); a vilification of same-sex relationships by 'sex experts' and a glorification of heterosexual romance in films and advertisements that originated early in the twentieth century (Rapp and Ross 1986) all fostered this family pattern. Some immediate factors shaped this period as well. The men and women who entered adulthood in the 1950s, and set the patterns that characterized the post-war period, grew up during times of economic depression and war, and were likely driven by desires for material security and social/emotional tranquility (May 1988).[8] American historian Elaine May has argued that nuclear-family life represented a kind of cocoon that offered peace in a world where peace seemed fragile. Of course, there were individuals who were not eager to marry and embrace domestic roles, but as Mary Louise Adams (1997; see Chapter 10) argues, the social pressures to conform, by marrying and having children, were also pervasive and unsubtle in the post-war period.

As well, the period featured a booming economy and generous government spending on infrastructure, social services, and 'welfare-state' policies, as well as policies that assumed the single-earner family. Steady rises in real earnings—the product of strong labour unions—meant that most men were able to earn a wage or salary sufficient to support a family (that is, a 'family wage') (Bradbury 2005) and that families had at least an expectation of continuing improvement in their economic position, even if sizeable numbers still were not prosperous. Meanwhile, a generation of women who had earned good wages during the war faced very limited job opportunities in the post-war labour force (Sugiman 1994). At the same time, the development of a 'welfare state' meant increased government support of families: Unemployment Insurance, universal Family Allowances, and Old Age Pensions all provided financial support that families were previously without (Bradbury 2005). And, some laws and policies assumed and reinforced the breadwinner family (e.g., income-tax law, social-security programs) (Eichler 1988). In short, a number of factors came together to produce the so-called conventional family (Fox 1993).

By the time people born between 1941 and 1960 were adults, the economic boom of the 1950s was over and a retrenchment in government services had begun—and the birth rate fell. These cohorts of women had fewer children, and they had them well before they were 30 years old. Before they reached 50 years of age their children typically were grown and living away from their parents' home. The period in which the generation of women born in the 1960s gave birth was short as well, and they too had raised their children before they turned 50, even though they married later and began child-bearing later. As in the nineteenth century, the declining birth rate corresponded with heightened responsibility associated with motherhood (see Chapter 9). The period after the 1950s featured weakened support of families by the state and the economy, including shortages of good, affordable daycare facilities. Simultaneously, the labour requirements involved in mothering inflated as 'intensive-mothering' ideals fostered very child-centred care, which adds to the weight of women's daily responsibility for their children (Hays 1996). But, in large part, the reduction in the birth rate and the time these cohorts of women spent focused exclusively on motherhood had to do with their increasing, and often necessary, involvement in the paid labour force, as well as the limitations of full-time domesticity.

Another Long-term Trend

Throughout the twentieth century—and even in the 1950s—women increasingly did paid work. Barriers to women's involvement in the paid labour force meant only a slow rise in their participation until the 1970s, but once the demand for women workers rose there followed tremendous increases in women's—and especially married women's—paid employment. While only 11.2 per cent of married women were in the paid labour force in 1951, by 1971, 37 per cent were; and in 1991, 61.4 per cent of married women were in the labour force (Statistics Canada 1953; 1974; 1994). Indeed, by 2006, 72.9 per cent of women with children under 16 were employed, and 64.3 per cent of women with children under the age of three were employed (Statistics Canada 2006a). Most employed women work full-time, but their involvement in part-time work increased with the mass influx into the labour force: the proportion of women working part-time rose steadily from about 11 per cent in 1953 to 24.9 per cent in 1970; 26 per cent of women worked part-time in 2006 (Leacy et al. 1983; Statistics Canada 1998; 2006a).

By 1971, an interesting change had occurred in women's involvement in the labour force. See Figure 12.1,[9] which shows the labour-force participation rates of 'synthetic cohorts', or ups of women who entered the labour force at me time.[10] For the first time, in 1971 the labour-force participation rate of women 25 to 34—that is, women in their prime child-bearing years—was not lower than it was 10 years earlier, when the women were 15 to 24 years old. That is, beginning with the cohort of women who reached adulthood (ages 15 to 24) in 1961, the earlier life-cycle pattern of reduced labour-force involvement during the child-bearing years (ages 25 to 34) ended. For this cohort of women, and those who came after them, labour-force involvement actually *increased* during the period in which women were also having their children. While motherhood used to entail withdrawal from the labour force, women now attempt to accommodate its demands by an increase in part-time work (Duffy, Mandell, and Pupo 1989: 81), and delaying marriage and child-bearing (as we will see).

Behind the rise in women's labour-force involvement were changes in the economy,

Figure 12.1 Women's Age-specific Labour-force Participation Rates for Synthetic Cohorts

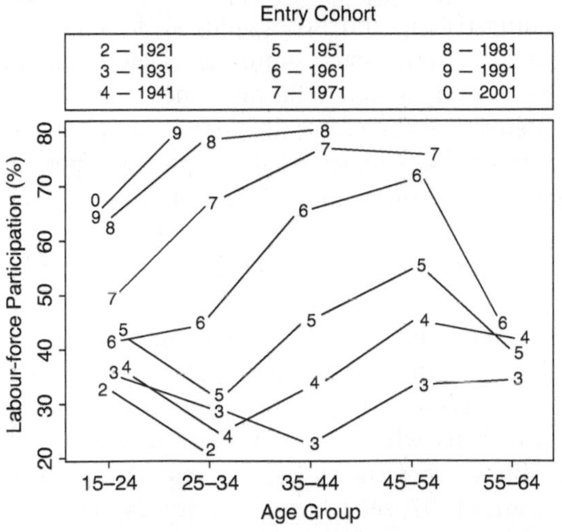

Sources: Leacy et al. 1983, *Historical Statistics of Canada*, 2nd edn (series D107–123); 1971 Census, Cat. No. 94-702, Table 2; 1981 Census, Cat. No. 92-915, Table 1; 1991 Census, Cat. No. 93-324, Table 1; 2001 Census, Cat. No. 97F0012XCB200 1003.

families, and women. In the labour market, there was increasing demand for clerical workers for much of the twentieth century, and there was also a shift away from manufacturing jobs and toward service jobs after World War II. Accordingly, 'marriage bars' and other barriers to women's involvement in wage work broke down, especially in the post-World War II period. From the vantage point of families, about half of Canadian households were in need of a second income throughout the twentieth century (Fox 1980). Until after World War II, teenagers, especially boys, were the preferred second earners, but as school requirements rose women became the main second earners in families.[11] Also prompting the movement of homemakers into waged work was a post-war economy in which it increasingly made more economic sense for women to earn money than to produce subsistence goods (like clothing) at home; in fact, it became less possible to substitute home production for the purchase of necessary goods once commodities such as cars became essential. Social factors pushed and pulled women into the labour force as well. Women's increased levels of education (and therefore expectations), coupled with the limitations women experienced being home full-time (and economically dependent on their husbands), meant that most women were eager to work outside the home (Luxton 1980).

Since the 1980s, systematic restructuring of the economy has meant a decline in real hourly wages for men under 35 years of age, and a drop in the purchasing power of all men's earnings (Armstrong and Armstrong 1994; Picot and Heisz 2000; Yalnizyan 1998: 19, 25). Consequently, many Canadian families have maintained their standard of living only because of women's employment. The economic restructuring that is ongoing means a drastic and progressive drop in the numbers of men earning a family wage, and thus able to support a family (Bakker 1996). Two incomes will therefore remain a necessity for most Canadian households. And as men have been less likely to earn a family wage marriage has become less likely and less stable.

To the extent that economic restructuring has meant not only lower individual earnings but also unemployment and the threat of job loss, especially for men, it directly undermines marriage and nuclear families. Research on families in the 1930s Depression, and on male–female relations in poor African-American communities, indicates that the damage to men's identity when they fail at breadwinning directly undermines stable male–female relationships (Elder 1974; Stack 1974; Sullivan 1998). Moreover, to the extent that women are no longer fully dependent on men for access to a decent standard of living, they have been able to leave unhappy marriages and choose not to marry in the first place. Higher rates of divorce, lower birth rates, a decline in marriage, and even a rise in common-law relationships, make sense given the changes occurring in the economy—and that is indeed what has occurred.

Recent Changes

Getting married and having children are central to many people's definition of family. But in recent years, both have become less essential to the creation of family, or at least to committed long-term couple relationships. Table 12.1 gives some indication of the substantial change that has occurred recently with respect to marriage. The 1961–70 female and male birth cohorts—who married mostly in the 1980s and 1990s—typically married for the first time about two-and-a-half years later than did the cohort before them. This is a large change given how stable the average age of marriage has been through the years. Moreover, the increase in the age at first marriage has continued. The median age for the 1970–79 female birth cohort was estimated (in 2000) to be 26 years of age (Beaujot and Kerr 2004: 212). The estimated age of first marriage for that cohort of men was 28 years of age

(Beaujot and Kerr 2004: 212). Similarly, the cohort of women born between 1961 and 1970 gave birth to their first child about a year and a half later than did women born between 1951 and 1960. And women born between 1971 and 1980 typically gave birth to their first child about a year later than the cohort preceding them—at an average (mean) age of 27 years (Statistics Canada 2006b: 41). These figures indicate significant change in people's life cycles, involving a postponement of marriage and child-bearing—and more than that.

Table 12.2 gives an indication of some important changes in adult relationships. Here we see age-specific percentages of people between the ages of 15 and 55 who are currently married, people in unions (both marriages and common-law relationships), people who are separated (and, for those over 30, separated, divorced, or widowed), and people never married, for 1981 and 2001. Over these three decades, the percentage of women and men who are married has gone down in all age groups, while the percentage of people living in common-law relationships has increased—but not so much as to compensate for the decline in marriage. The percentage of people living in either kind of union has decreased between 1981 and 2001. Of course, gay and lesbian unions have become more common, although the official tally of their numbers indicates that they are a small portion of all couples—0.5 per cent of all couples in 2001, 0.6 per cent in 2006 (Statistics Canada 2007: 12). According to the census data shown in Table 12.2, more than one in four women between the ages of 30 and 55 were not living in intimate relationships in 2001, and that was true for over one in four men 30 to 45 years of age and over one in five men 45 to 55 years of age. Yet, by 2001, nearly every woman and man had married at some point before age 45, and a majority of the women over 35 and n over 40 who were not living with a partner eparated, divorced, or widowed. That a high percentage of people are living alone is not a new phenomenon. Through the nineteenth century, about 15 per cent of women in Canada stayed single through adulthood—whether because of obligations to care for parents or siblings, or simply in preference to marriage (Bradbury 2005: 94). As well, a substantial percentage of women were widowed at a relatively early age (though often to become lone parents). What is new to the twentieth century is that large numbers of people live alone because of divorce or separation. Overall, then, marriage has been declining as a life-long involvement for adults, common-law unions have become a popular pattern, and increasing percentages of adults at all ages live outside of any kind of intimate partnership.

The postponement of marriage and general decline in the popularity of marriage are both in evidence here. The percentage of people who have never married increased between 1981 and 1991 for all age groups except those 50 to 54 years of age, and continued to increase to 2001 for women under 35 years of age and men under 45 years of age. Looking at a couple of key age groups highlights the change. Of women in their mid- to late twenties, the decline in the percentage currently married was from 82 per cent of women in 1971 (not shown in Table 12.2) to 65.9 per cent in 1981, 50.9 per cent in 1991 (not shown) and 37.3 per cent in 2001. Even after inclusion of the portion of this age group living in common-law relationships, there was still a decline in the percentage living in intimate relationships—from 73 per cent in 1981 to 65.1 per cent in 1991 to 57.3 per cent in 2001. For men 25 to 29 years of age, there was a decline in the percentage currently married from 74 per cent in 1971 to 55.6 per cent in 1981 to 37.6 per cent in 1991 to 25.6 per cent in 2001—from the vast majority being married to a minority in that state. Indeed, while 63.7 per cent of men 25 to 29 were in an intimate heterosexual union in 1981, fewer than half were in 2001. Marriage has

Table 12.2 Per Cent of Women and Men Presently Married, in a Union (Married or Cohabiting), Separated, or Never Married—1981 and 2001

	1981				2001			
	Married	Total in Union	Separated	Never Married	Married	Total in Union	Separated	Never Married
Women								
15–19	3.6	6.5	0.1	93.4	0.6	3.0	0.2	96.8
20–24	36.5	45.9	2.1	52.0	10.2	25.6	1.3	73.1
25–29	65.9	73.0	3.8	23.2	37.3	57.3	5.1	37.6
30–34	75.5	80.2	9.4	10.5	55.1	71.4	10.4	18.2
35–39	78.1	81.7	11.0	7.3	60.7	74.4	15.2	10.3
40–44	79.2	82.0	11.9	6.1	63.3	74.7	19.2	6.1
45–49	78.8	80.9	13.3	5.8	65.0	74.3	22.5	3.2
50–54	76.4	78.1	15.8	6.0	66.4	73.6	24.6	1.8
Men								
15–19	0.7	1.4	0.1	98.5	0.3	1.0	0.2	99.6
20–24	19.8	26.9	0.9	72.2	4.5	14.2	0.6	85.2
25–29	55.6	63.7	2.6	33.7	25.6	44.7	2.7	52.6
30–34	73.1	79.1	6.0	15.0	47.3	64.7	6.5	28.8
35–39	79.1	83.8	6.8	9.3	56.8	71.6	10.5	17.9
40–44	81.2	84.8	7.4	7.8	62.2	74.5	14.5	11.0
45–49	81.8	84.6	7.9	7.5	66.2	76.5	17.5	6.0
50–54	81.6	83.7	8.4	7.8	70.2	78.8	18.8	2.4

Sources: Beaujot, R., et al. 1995: 10, 41; 2001 Census, Cat. Nos 95F0405XCB2001004 and 95F0407XCB2001004.

become a minority status for Canadian men and women in their twenties. Many enter common-law relationships (some of which end in marriage) in their twenties, but it is more common for men and nearly as common for women to remain single through their twenties.

The decline in marriage is evident even for men and women in their mid- to late thirties. The percentage of women that age who were currently married declined from 89 per cent in 1971 to 78.1 per cent in 1981, 69.5 per cent in 1991 and 60.7 per cent in 2001. Moreover, the percentage of women that age in some kind of intimate heterosexual union fell from 81.7 per cent in 1981 to 77.5 per cent in 1991 and 74.4 per cent in 2001. For men 35 to 39 years of age, the decline in percentage married was from 88 per cent in 1971 to 79.1 per cent in 1981, 68.4 per cent in 1991 and 56.8 per cent in 2001. The percentage of men that age in an intimate heterosexual union fell from 83.8 per cent in 1981 to 77.3 per cent in 1991 and 71.6 per cent in 2001.

Common-law relationships have, however, become increasingly popular: in 2001, of men and women 20 to 24 years of age, slightly over 60 per cent of women and 68 per cent of men who were in a union were cohabiting; in 1991, 42 per cent of women and 51 per cent of men in their early twenties who were in a union were cohabiting, and that was about double the proportion in 1981. Among those 25 to 29 years of age, 35 per cent of women and 43 per cent of men in unions were cohabiting in 2001, and about a quarter of women and men in unions were cohabiting in 1991, which was twice the 1981 figure (Beaujot et al. 1995: 12). Apparently, for the majority of women and men born between 1966 and 1985 a common-law relationship has been the first form of union (Ravanera, Rajulton, and Burch 2005: 4)—and this was not the case for earlier cohorts. Of course, these statistics vary across provinces, such that common-law unions are significantly more typical, and marriage less typical, in Quebec than elsewhere (Nault and Belanger 1996). In 2001, 25 per cent of couples (in all ages) in Quebec were in common-law unions, which was considerably higher than the national average (14 per cent) (Statistics Canada 2007: 36). Common-law relationships are also prevalent in the territories: in 2002, over 30 per cent of couples in Nunavut, 26 per cent of couples in the Northwest Territories, and 23 per cent of couples in the Yukon were living common law (Statistics Canada 2007: 36). In 1991, it was estimated that as many as 25 per cent of Canadian women and 30 per cent of Canadian men would never marry, if patterns typical then continued (Nault and Belanger 1996).[12]

Common-law unions are significant for more than their numbers. On the one hand, they are connected with the pattern of later marriage, given that many cohabiters eventually marry each other: according to the 1990 General Social Survey, 37 per cent of married people aged 18 to 29 had previously cohabited. The estimate from that study is that about 40 per cent of common-[illegible] relationships end in marriage within five [illegible] (Beaujot et al. 1995: 12). Many others that do not lead to marriage are nevertheless stable, and the couples involved have children. In 2001, 46 per cent of common-law couples had children living with them (and born from this or another union) (Statistics Canada 2003b: 11). On the other hand, common-law relationships are considerably less stable than marriages. One estimate is that about a third of them end within five years, which is more than double the rate of marriage breakdown (Beaujot et al. 1995: 12; Wu 1999). Moreover, although many of these relationships are stable, there is some evidence to suggest that they are somewhat different than marriages. For example, heterosexual common-law couples tend to more evenly divide the household work than married couples, and women and men living common law are also more likely to keep separate bank accounts than are married couples—patterns that indicate an intention to avoid conventional gendered patterns and dynamics, and/or maintain greater autonomy of the individuals in these relationships (Blumenstein and Schwartz 1983; South and Spitze 1994). We might conclude that common-law relationships reflect the difficulty that young adults have getting established in the labour force—and thus marrying—but it is also likely that their popularity signifies changes in gender relations precipitated by declines in young men's labour-market position and improvement in women's position in the labour market.

The decreased likelihood of marrying has meant increased rates of childlessness. As Table 12.3 indicates, rates of childlessness were especially high, rising to over 15 per cent, for those women born between 1907 and 1911, who were of child-bearing age between 1927 and 1946[13]—in other words, during the 1930s Depression and World War II. For women born after 1922, who entered child-bearing years (mostly) during the post-war period, childlessness declined; for those who came of age during the 1950s and 1960s (and born between 1932 and 1941), rates of childlessness were very low. The rate of childlessness started to climb again for women born after 1941. These women were less subject to the 'feminine mystique' of the 1950s and faced more options—especially in the form of jobs—than did women entering adulthood in the 1950s.[14] Additionally, many of them came of age in the 1970s, when women's earnings were becoming essential to couples. Finally, as more women remain single, that too has an impact on child-bearing, even though sizeable numbers of never-married women are now having children. In 1991, of all women, those who have and have not been married, the rates of childlessness were fairly high, and probably rising. In 1991, over 16 per cent of all women 40 to 45 years of age, 14 per cent of all women 45 to 49 years of age, and over 12 per cent of all women 50 to 54 years of age were childless (Statistics Canada 1993).

Table 12.3 Per Cent of Never-married Women Who Are Childless

Census Year	Age	Birth Cohort	% Childless
1941	55–64	1877–86	13.2
1941	45–54	1887–96	12.3
1961	50–54	1907–11	15.3
1961	45–49	1912–16	13.1
1971	50–54	1917–21	11.8
1971	45–49	1922–26	9.6
1971	40–44	1927–31	8.2
1981	50–54	1927–31	8.4
1981	45–49	1932–36	7.2
1981	40–44	1937–41	7.3
1991	50–54	1937–41	8.0
1991	45–49	1942–46	9.4
1991	40–44	1947–51	10.7

Sources: Gee 1987: 273; 1971 Census, Cat. No. 92-718, Table 24; 1981 Census, Cat. No. 92-906, Table 7; 1991 Census, Cat. No. 93-321, Table 2.

Women are also postponing motherhood (as is clear in Table 12.1). In 1961, nearly 90 per cent of women 25 to 29 years of age had children; in 1991, only slightly more than 60 per cent did (Beaujot et al. 1995: 17). Increases in the rates of childlessness and the trend toward a postponement of motherhood attest to both changes in women's lives and increased differences among women. Postponing marriage and motherhood is clearly related to women's increasing education and combined need and desire to establish themselves first in a labour market where jobs and especially careers are still incompatible with family responsibilities. The continuing reality that women pay a price in the labour market for marriage and motherhood (Budig and England 2001; Waldfogel 1997), and continue to shoulder more responsibility for housework and childcare at home than men, likely indicates why many women are postponing and even avoiding marriage and long-term commitments to men. Rod Beaujot and colleagues (1995: 2) summarized the labour-market costs of marriage for women in the 1990s: the employment income of single women was 94 per cent of men's, and while 72 per cent of single women were in part-time work, so were 66 per cent of single men; in contrast, for women 30 to 34 who were married and had children, employment income was 49 per cent of men's, and only 35 per cent of them (as opposed to 81 per cent of men) worked full-time. Marie Drolet (2003: 20) has estimated that in 1998 'the average hourly wages of mothers were 2 per cent less, overall, than those of women who did not have children'. She also found that women who delay having children have substantially higher hourly earnings than women who do not (Drolet 2003: 20).

As many writers have pointed out, the place women now have in the labour force has allowed them choice about whether or not to marry; it has eroded a structural imperative that women marry in order to have the possibility of a decent standard of living.[15] Moreover, the fact that so many jobs no longer pay a family wage has undermined men's breadwinner role, and thus inhibited the formation of conventional families. The erosion of men's ability to support their families also underscores the injustice of relationships in which men claim privileges that women do not have—especially that of taking on less responsibility in the home (Hochschild 1989; Frederick 1995). This privilege, which appeared to be deserved when men earned a family wage (Luxton 1980; see Chapter 11) no longer seems so when two people together support their family. The likelihood that women are choosing inequality when they choose to marry may be a significant deterrent of marriage for women.

The absence of significant change in many (though not all) men and the decline of the family wage, coupled with the failure of state policies and programs to support working mothers (e.g., good, affordable daycare) and most employers' failure to accommodate family responsibilities (e.g., with shorter workweeks, flexible schedules, good part-time jobs), explain why many women increasingly have felt that they must choose between family and career. As well, the thorough questioning of conventional gender roles and nuclear-family organization that flourished in the late 1960s under the influence of the Women's Liberation Movement permeated popular culture in a way that enabled people to make different choices than their parents. The rise of common-law relationships provided a middle ground between marriage and the single state—an intimate heterosexual relationship where sexual activity does not entail having children, and intimacy does not mean 'forever'. And the fact that sizeable numbers of women are now able to have careers means that a fulfilling adult life is possible without children for more women now than in older generations.

For men as well, marriage and parenthood involve personal costs as well as benefits. An American study of men's life choices found that young adult men did not hold marriage and fatherhood to be their priorities in life; occupational success was a more important personal goal (Gerson 1993). Changes in the labour market that have greatly increased the educational credentials necessary for success and also greatly reduced the chances of finding secure, well-paid jobs have no doubt made commitment to long-term relationships even less appealing to young men. The increased likelihood that women will expect their partners to share housework and childcare as well as breadwinning has also probably diminished the appeal of marriage and commitment to men.

That women and men are postponing marriage, entering it not only when they are older but also more educated and employed than earlier generations, that they are likely to live in common-law relationships first and even instead of marriage, and that women are spending only a small fraction of adulthood in the early years of motherhood, should promote greater gender equality in heterosexual relationships. Arguably, the relative ease with which both men and women are able to separate and divorce also enhances the chances that the unions people stay in will be satisfying for both parties.

Divorce

Increasing rates of divorce have established another trend shaping family. Divorce rates rose slowly over the course of the twentieth century until the late 1960s when federal legislation making divorce easier[16] was passed, and there followed a major increase in the rate of divorce. Increases in divorce continued through the late 1980s, after which divorce rates have fluctuated. Figure 12.2 shows the rates of divorce the cohorts of men and women born between 1911 and 1960 have experienced with each year of marriage. Clearly, each birth cohort was significantly more likely than the one before it to divorce. For example, after 10 years of marriage, fewer than 2 per cent of women born between

1911 and 1920 were divorced but nearly 20 per cent of women born between 1951 and 1960 were. The increase is similar for men, except that about 17 per cent of men born between 1951 and 1960 were divorced after 10 years of marriage. While slightly over 3 per cent of men and women born between 1911 and 1920 were divorced after 20 years of marriage, almost 35 per cent of women and about 30 per cent of men born between 1951 and 1960 were divorced after two decades of marriage.

In the late 1990s, it was estimated that if current patterns continued into the future, 31 per cent of marriages contracted in 1991 would end in divorce (Nault and Belanger 1996: 17). Although many people remarry, it is also the case that the propensity to remarry following divorce decreased between the 1980s and the 1990s (and even more so than the decline in the propensity to marry for the first time) (Nault and Belanger 1996: 7).[17]

It is common to attribute the increasing instability of marriage to people's 'selfishness'. Mostly, this means *women's* selfishness, as it is women who typically do more of the emotional work in heterosexual relationships, as well as the housework and childcare (Hochschild 1989). That there are two experiences of any marriage—'his' and 'her' experiences[18]—is overlooked in this glib explanation, which assumes that people should remain in relationships that are problematic. An American study of divorced women found that most of their marriages had ended precisely because of the negative gender dynamics in them (Kurz 1995).[19] Demie Kurz (1995: 45) found, in her representative sample of divorced American women, that almost one-fifth of them (especially the middle-class women) had divorced for reasons involving conventional male behaviour—the man's failure to share housework, childcare, and even emotional work, and/or his need to be in control.[20] Another one-fifth of the women in the study (especially working-class and poor women) ended their marriage because of their partner's violence. Altogether, the majority of reasons for divorce in this study had to do with men's problematic behaviour, since another 19 per cent of the women referred to an 'other woman' as the reason for the breakup, and 17 per cent cited drug/alcohol abuse by the man, and his absence

Figure 12.2 Cumulative Percentages Separated or Divorced by Sex and Birth Cohort, 1911 to 1960

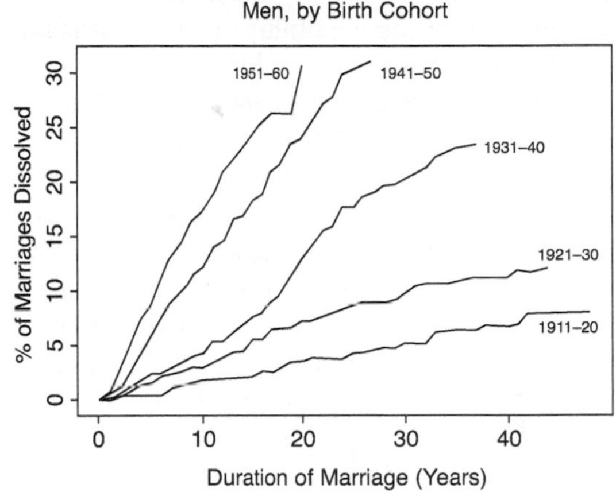

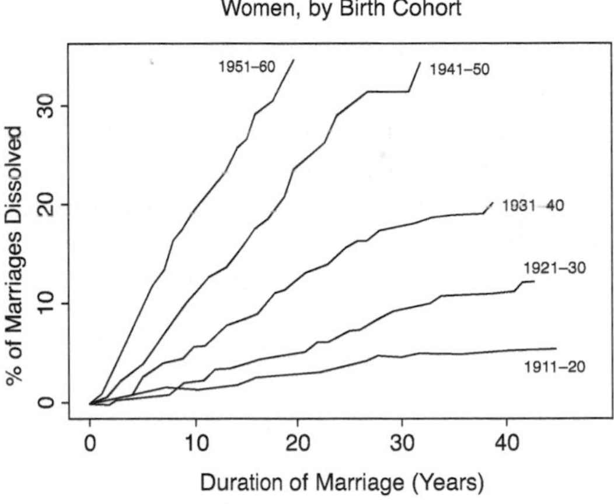

Source: Beaujot et al. 1995: Figure 4.5, 133. Data provided by Z. Ravanera.

from home, as the key reasons for the divorce (Kurz 1995: 45). Kurz's study suggests that marriages that end in divorce are not providing what we all expect of marriage—love and support. Given the possibility of choice, it is not surprising that women would opt to leave such relationships. Of course, there are many causes of the rise in divorce; and men as well as women (though less so) initiate divorce. Supporting all the individual decisions is a changed cultural climate that makes divorce easier.

For the adults and children who experience it, the emotional and social consequences of divorce are varied. Moreover, it is not at all easy to separate the effects of divorce from the effects of the conflict that caused the divorce (Furstenberg and Cherlin 1991; see Chapter 32). What is clearly a major problem affecting most women who experience divorce, however, is the drop in income that typically occurs. Using longitudinal data tracing the impact of divorce on a representative sample of Canadians, between 1982 and 1986, Ross Finnie (1993: 228) found that as a result of divorce, women 'experience a steep decline in economic well-being while men enjoy moderate increases'. Using income-to-needs ratios (which adjust for family size) to measure well-being, Finnie (1993: 225) found the ratio of women's well-being to men's well-being to be about 0.59 a year after divorce. It improved only slowly over the subsequent years. He also found that over a third of women who were not poor before their divorce became poor in the year following it (compared with about 10 per cent of men) (Finnie 1993: 219).

The aftermath of divorce, for women and children, makes clear the contradictions in the current environment of family life. The old exchange between men and women—involving his financial support for her domestic and sexual services (Kronby 1981)—that was the foundation of nuclear families has broken-down, and yet social arrangements predicated on that old pattern remain. So, for example, women's position in the labour force has not changed dramatically: the gender gap in earnings persists, and many women still do not earn enough to support themselves and their children (Drolet 2001). At the same time, provincial family laws governing divorce assume that society has changed in such a way that individual women can now support themselves, whatever their labour-force history. Since the late 1970s, most provinces stipulate a division of 'family property' into two equal parts, so that the man and woman who are separating can go on with their lives without continuing dependence on each other. A man's ongoing support of a former wife who stayed home full-time is to be short term only, and a woman with any source of income is not expected to need ongoing support. So, women face a dramatic drop in income, and children—who typically live with their mothers—experience a similar drop in their standard of living. They may also lose their home (in the split of the family assets), which means a loss of friends, a move to a new school and neighbourhood, etc. Thus, family law, in the absence of societal changes—in employment and government policy—that would support families headed by women contributes to child poverty.

For many children, divorce also means the loss of their father, since fathers often lose contact with children not living with them (Conway [1990] 1993). Research suggests that the reasons have to do with the centrality of family life to fatherhood and even manhood. Thus, fathering is difficult in a situation that is removed from normal, daily family life and the presence (and facilitation) of the mother (e.g., contact restricted to eight-hour visits every Sunday). As well, though, men who withdraw from contact with their children may do so as a result of an ongoing battle with their ex-wives—a battle often about men feeling that they have lost the 'rights' due them as fathers and household heads (Arendell 1992). For some men, divorce means loss of the control and authority that was central to their marriage; and the need to reaffirm their sense of manhood may mean battling over 'rights' (seen as due them by payment of child support) rather than investing energy in sustaining relationships with the children. For some, their last vestige of manliness may depend upon maintaining control of their emotions, which means avoiding the stress of visitation (Arendell 1992).

Whatever the reasons why many fathers find it hard to maintain close relations with their children after divorce, many even fail to follow through on their financial obligations to them. Somehow, not living with their children means, for many men, no longer being responsible for them (Eichler 1997). In the 1980s, a majority of men defaulted on court-ordered child-support payments (which were already set at levels below half the cost of raising children); there is no reason to believe that matters have improved significantly since then (Conway [1990] 1993: 122). The economic consequences for children are dire: in 1997, the poverty rate for children in lone-parent families headed by women was 60.4 per cent, which was tremendously higher than the rate of 12.7 per cent for children in two-parent families (National Council of Welfare 1999: 90). Given the difficulty of combining childcare and employment, in the absence of state commitment to affordable childcare facilities, and given the relatively low levels of earnings attached to many of the jobs women are in, it is still the case that women attempting to raise children outside a live-in relationship with a man often have a hard time. In one important sense at least—the financial support of children—this society still assumes the nuclear family, with one adult who does the earning and another responsible for childcare.

It is also the case that, despite the changes in family patterns, the majority of women 25 years of age and older and men 30 years of age and older were living with an intimate partner in 2001 in Canada. Indeed, a majority of women 30 and older and men 35 and older were married. The continuing attraction of living with a partner should not be surprising. Aside from the emotional and sexual satisfactions that intimate unions promise, adults who wish to have children find it far easier to live as a couple than as lone parents. Indeed, the organization of paid jobs and careers, the content of state policies and the law, the physical structure of housing, the demands of good parenting, and many other aspects of life in Canada today promote nuclear-family living with one adult prioritizing income earning and the other the responsibility for children. Common-law relationships and gay and lesbian relationships—especially those involving children—typically produce nuclear families, with many characteristics similar to families based on heterosexual marriage. In many ways, the 'path of least resistance' in this society leads to this pattern. But, arguably, what most directly shapes that path is the economy, and the way we earn our livelihood—and the economy has been changing for some time.

Diversity, but an Ongoing Pattern

Because jobs in the economy today pay only a minority of men a family wage and thus two earners are essential, because jobs are less secure than they used to be, and because work days are longer, the breadwinner–homemaker family is unusual. That conventional family pattern rested on men earning a family wage. Now that so many families need two incomes, family patterns have become much more diverse. Whether we consider family in Canada at one point in time, or think of the patterns that develop across people's life cycles, we see considerable diversity—as well as some common arrangements. In 2006, only 34.6 per cent of all 'census families' (i.e., married or common-law couples or lone parents living with at least one child) consisted of married couples with children 24 years of age or under living at home (Statistics Canada 2007: 11). (See Table 12.4.) Given that over 70 per cent of women with children under 16 years of age were employed that year, we can estimate that fewer than 10 per cent of all Canadian families consisted of a married couple, a full-time homemaker, and dependent children at home (Statistics Canada 2006b: 121). In short, in 2006, fewer than one in 10 Canadian families fit the pattern we have seen as conventional since the 1950s. Additionally, only 68.6 per cent of families involved a married couple. Moreover, couples living with children were outnumbered by couples living without children: there were 41.4 per cent of the former and 42.7 per cent of the latter.

Children are definitely growing up in a variety of different types of families. In 2006, slightly fewer than two-thirds (65.7 per cent) of children aged 14 and under lived with married parents. And some of these children were living with a step-parent—nearly 7 per cent of children under 15 years of age in 1998–99—and thus in families that had more fluid boundaries than most nuclear families, given the likely involvement of a non-residential parent and/or members of his extended family (Ahrons and Rodgers 1997; Statistics Canada 2003b: 13). As well, significant percentages of young children have parents who are in common-law unions—14.6 per cent of children 14 years of age and under in 2006. And 18.3 per cent of children aged 14 and under lived with a lone parent that year. Additionally, a small percentage (but sizeable number) of children are growing up in the homes of same-sex partners. This diversity indicates that many children will live in more than one type of family before they grow up and leave home; having to adjust to changed families is not an uncommon part of childhood today. Children in lone-parent families likely have experienced their parents' divorce (and the marital conflict related to breakup), and many will need to adjust to a step-parent. Some children will experience the death of a parent—but far fewer than in times past. Additionally, children being raised by same-sex parents face daily challenges in a heteronormative world in which both children and adults, and the institutions around them, can make their lives difficult (Nelson 1996). At the same time, most children today live with at least one parent, and that stands in sharp contrast with the large numbers of children who spent all or part of their childhood in orphanages in the late nineteenth and early twentieth centuries, whether because of their parents' death or poverty (Bradbury 1982; Coontz 1992).

Statistics summarizing a single point in time underestimate the diversity over a person's life cycle, but because of life-cycle changes they also overestimate diversity. For example, decline over time in the number of married couples with dependent children was largely a life-cycle effect, not something more dramatic. That is, many married couples without children at home have grown children: the median age of married couples without children at home (in 2006) was nearly 61 years (as opposed to slightly over 43 years for those with children at home and only slightly over 40 years of age for common-law couples without children at home) (Statistics Canada 2007: 11). So, the significance of families composed of a married couple with children is under-represented in the static picture presented in Table 12.4. Assuming the 1950s to be a good comparison point also emphasizes change over continuity. For example, according to historian Bettina Bradbury (2005: 94), 13 to 15 per cent of all Canadian families were headed by a single parent—usually a widow—through the nineteenth century and up to 1931. The large numbers of common-law couples with children—unmarried by choice and not by circumstance—is a new phenomenon, but these are nuclear families and not necessarily much different from families in which the adult couple is married.

There is another family pattern that is not usually considered in discussions of family

Table 12.4 Type of Family of Adults and Children Aged 14 Years and Under, 1986 and 2006

Family Structure	% of Families		% of Children 14 Years and Under	
	1986	2006	1986	2006
Married Couples	80.2	68.6	81.2	65.7
With children 24 and under living at home	49.4	34.6		
Without children 24 and under living at home	30.8	34.0		
Common-law Couples	7.2	15.5	4.5	14.6
With children 24 and under living at home	2.7	6.8		
Without children 24 and under living at home	4.5	8.7		
Lone-parent Families	12.6	15.9	12.4	18.3
With children 24 and under living at home	10.5	12.4		
All children 25 and older	2.1	3.5		

Sources: Statistics Canada 2007, Cat. No. 97-553-XIE, Figures 1 and 13.

patterns, but likely has been enduring and important—that involving extended-family relationships spanning two or more households. Only a small percentage of Canadian families involve three generations living in the same house, but for immigrant families, especially, help from extended kin often figures in their migration to and adjustment in Canada. In 2006, over a hundred students in my undergraduate course on families conducted interviews with an adult who had experienced the migration of his or her family of origin. A common theme in those interviews was the assistance given to people's families by their kin. Aside from the help they received in the immigration process, families (and members of families who migrated before the rest of their families) often lived with a sibling, aunt, uncle, or even cousin, for example, when they first came to Canada. Kin often helped them find jobs as well. Once whole families were here, elder parents sometimes came to live with their adult sons or daughters in order to care for their young children while they worked outside the home. In short, the support of extended kin was central to the process of immigration and often remained central to the daily lives of these immigrant families.

Kin helping kin in the process of immigrating is not the only kind of help that extends across households. Many families in Canada, whether formed here or in another country, and of whatever social class, depend on help from people outside the nuclear unit—relatives, friends, and paid employees. As Karen Hansen (2005) argues with respect to American families, nuclear families are often 'not-so-nuclear', in fact. Many middle-class families, and certainly most upper-class families, fully depend on paid employees—nannies to care for their children for much of the day and women to clean their homes (see Arat-Koc 1989; see Chapter 26; Bakan and Stasiulis 1997). Middle-class and working-class couples who are dual earners often depend upon parents or siblings to care for their children during the hours women are employed; or they depend on paid babysitters or the staff of a daycare facility. Many Canadians also depend on friends and neighbours to help them out occasionally but in important ways. For example, Luxton (2006) found that people needing help of various sorts during their recovery after a medical emergency got it surprisingly often from friends and neighbours. For a long time, social scientists assumed that reciprocal exchanges of help of various kinds, and even of daily necessities, across households were 'survival strategies' unique to working-class neighbourhoods (like East London in the 1950s, as studied by Michael Young and Peter Willmott, 1957) or poor African-American neighbourhoods (Stack 1974; Collins 1990). In these cases, it was recognized that 'family' consisted of extended kin spread across more than one household, or personal networks of kin and fictive kin living in several households. Now, there is growing evidence that the maintenance (or social reproduction) of many nuclear families across all social classes depends upon the unpaid work of people living outside them (Hansen 2005; Roschelle 1997). And it has been apparent for some time that sizeable numbers of middle- and upper-class families are dependent upon the paid labour of women who are typically ethnic-/racial-minority women from Third World countries. While not new in comparison with the nineteenth century, the shift in childcare and housework to the shoulders of paid domestic workers has happened relatively recently if the 1950s is the point of comparison; it has happened as paid work has become a central part of the lives of women with families.

The question who does the housework and childcare must be considered alongside that of household and family composition when exploring changes in family patterns, and the extent to which there has been change. Most sociologists see women's high levels of labour-force involvement as the major change in families in recent times, because the division of work and responsibility based on gender has been so central to family organization. The mass movement of women into paid employment has the potential to disrupt that gendered division. Researchers in both Canada and the US have recently proclaimed the 'convergence' of gender roles (Marshall 2006) and equality in the hours of paid plus unpaid work that husbands and wives do each week (Bianchi, Robinson, and Milkie 2006). Because men are participating more in housework and childcare than they used to, and even spending more time doing that unpaid work, the impression is that gender divisions of work in the household are also declining rapidly, if not already negligible. Indeed, over the last two decades men are doing somewhat more housework, while women are doing considerably less (Marshall 2006). But even though the gap has shrunk, married women in Canada, especially women with children, are still doing significantly more housework than married men (Marshall 2006: 10). Moreover, while men's housework and childcare have increased, the other unpaid work they do (e.g., shopping) has declined—leaving men's total unpaid work unchanged over 20 years (while women's has gone down a bit, because they are doing less housework). Perhaps the most revealing finding in the Canadian data is that when a comparison is made among men living alone, men who are married but childless, and married men who have children, the average time men spend doing housework increases only a bit (i.e., a fraction of an hour per day) as men marry and become fathers. In contrast, when women who live alone are compared with married but childless women and married women with children, the time spent doing housework increases substantially (i.e., by about an hour per day) as women marry and then become mothers. The difference between the hours that women living alone and women who are married spend doing housework is especially large (Marshall 2006: 8). As well, American researchers are still finding that in dual-earner couples women work more hours (of paid plus unpaid work) every week than men do (Bianchi, Robinson, and Milkie 2006: 56). And finally, when couples have children they tend to divide their work by gender more than before they became parents: men typically increase their participation and time in paid work and women cut back on their hours of employment and take on more housework (Marshall 2006).

Change is occurring in heterosexual nuclear families, then, as women's commitment to paid work—and thus their bargaining power—has grown. Indeed, a sizeable proportion of women earn more money than their male spouses. Men are doing more housework and childcare than they used to, and increasing (though small) numbers of men are staying home with young children while their wives are earning the money (Doucet 2006). Yet, the gendered divisions of work that have been the chief organizing principle of family in this culture have a decided persistence. Even when men are involved in doing childcare and housework, women usually retain the responsibility for the children and management of the household (Daly 2001; 2004; Doucet 2006). Moreover, as significant as the increase in men's housework and childcare has been the shifting of this work to the shoulders of working-class, ethnic-minority women who are paid to do the work (Arat-Koc 1989; see Chapter 26; Bakan and Stasiulis 1997). The change that has occurred in families involves reallocation of the work inside families—and only partially from women to men—more than it does the shifting of the work from the household to the community.

The continuing privatization of responsibility for children means that women especially, but also men who are involved in the care of their children, are pulled in two directions, between two incompatible sets of responsibilities (Jacobs and Gerson 2004; see Chapter 27) On the one hand, the terms of employment continue to assume an employee who is unencumbered by family responsibilities. On the other hand, the definition of what children need for healthy development has inflated over the decades while the responsibility for their well-being remains squarely on the shoulders of parents. As a result, the expectations that mothers bear are tremendous (Hays 1996). Mothers of babies and young children are now expected to focus their energy and time on their children, whose physical, mental, emotional, and cognitive development they are responsible for (Fox 2006; Hays 1996; Wall 2001; 2004). At the same time, community support for mothers is still meagre. Most important, there is still no national commitment to providing state-funded, affordable, high-quality daycare. And the outrage that such stingy public support warrants has been inhibited by the persistence of old beliefs about mothers' natural abilities and babies and toddlers being better off at home full-time (see Eyer 1992).

Stress is clearly an outcome of the 'juggling act' that many women must do daily (Hochschild 1989; see Chapter 27). It is also the case, however, that women's mental and physical health benefits from combining employment and family (Coontz 1997). Nor do children suffer from having mothers in the labour force (Coontz 1997). Indeed, parents—fathers and mothers—now spend more time with their children than they did decades ago (Marshall 2006: 11). What seems to be affected the most when both adults are in the labour force is marriage: when men fail to share the load, tensions in the relationship are common, and divorce more likely (Hochschild 1989; Kurz 1995).

That parenting in dual-earner families is difficult highlights the problems faced by lone-parent families. In 2006, almost 16 per cent of families were lone-parent families, and over 18 per cent of dependent children lived in them (see Table 12.4). Produced chiefly by divorce, lone-parent families are handicapped by living in a society organized around nuclear families. When one adult is responsible for both childcare and financial support, poverty is likely: in 1997, 57.1 per cent of lone-parent mothers were living below the poverty line (compared with 11.9 per cent of couples with children) (National Council of Welfare 1999: 36). In 2001, over 45 per cent of people living in female-headed lone-parent households were poor (Statistics Canada 2003a). With very few supportive social policies and programs, the material support of extended kin (e.g., grandparents of the children) is likely the main way many of these families survive. Probably a sizeable portion of them live in extended-family households.[21]

Lone parenthood is just one condition that may move young adults back to live in their parents' home (Boyd and Pryor 1989). While the percentage of young, unmarried adults living at home declined in the 1970s, it has risen dramatically since then. Young adults are both leaving their parents' home later than in previous decades (though about the same time as they did in the early part of the twentieth century) and returning home in greater numbers. This state of semi-dependence is prompted, no doubt, by the rising costs of post-secondary education and the difficulty young people have finding a good job, as well as rising rates of divorce and motherhood outside marriage. What the return of young adults to their parents' home means is that the stresses of living in a society that is only minimally supportive of families not only weigh on parents while they are raising their children but also extend over a longer stretch of the life course. Families of origin have become 'a type of social safety net for young adults in times of need' (Mitchell 1998: 41). In turn, this type of private social safety net may serve to reproduce inequalities of wealth: how well young adults do is even more dependent on the financial resources of their parents now than it was before.

The elderly also sometimes rely on their families, especially their daughters, to care for them, although support and care are more likely to flow from parents to their children (Martin-Mathews 2000). People over the age of 65 are most likely to be living with a partner, and next most likely to be living alone. But they are also more likely living with their children than in an institution. In 2001, 13 per cent of older men and 12 per cent of older women lived with an adult child, while only 5 per cent of senior men and 9 per cent of senior women lived in health-care institutions (Statistics Canada 2003b: 12).

In sum, there is considerable diversity in the way Canadians live today. Economic changes that have eroded the family wage and brought most women into the paid labour force for much of their adult lives have shaken the gendered division of work that structured the nuclear family so common to the 1950s. This material change, which accompanied cultural changes pushed by the Women's Liberation Movement, promoted changes in the organization of heterosexual nuclear families—more housework and childcare by men, greater instability (given women's increased financial independence), and an increased popularity of common-law unions (featuring more individual autonomy). Current family diversity also includes large numbers of lone-parent families and the enduring importance of extended families (which often do not involve co-residence). And this diversity includes sizeable numbers of women who will live their lives without becoming mothers and men who avoid the responsibilities of social fatherhood. These personal trends are important: parenthood is, arguably, the linchpin of family. Couples often marry in order to have children, and the mother–child relationship at least is a binding one. Parenthood also continues to promote conventional family: when heterosexual couples become parents they typically divide the work and responsibility on gender lines.

Conclusion

These are times of change in family life. Family patterns frequently change, however. Whenever the material (or economic) foundations of families shift, the adjustments that people have to make are reflected in changing family patterns.

This brief overview highlights key changes in family patterns. The long-term decline in birth rates that has had profound effects on family relationships—most important, a heightening of the emotional intensity of parent–child relationships—began with a reconfiguration of families in the nineteenth century. Then, as household economies were undermined, raising children became a more privatized and demanding responsibility. Women assumed the responsibilities of parenting and homemaking while men became primary breadwinners, and this gendered division of labour between spouses provided the organizational scaffolding of families for decades afterwards. Recently, as women have come to share the responsibilities of financial support, that scaffolding has been shaken. An argument can be made that high rates of separation, divorce, and avoidance of marriage have resulted because all else has not significantly changed—except women's move into the labour force. In short, mothers who are also in the labour force have not been supported—by necessary changes in social policy (especially state provision of good, affordable daycare facilities), employment practices (especially shorter workweeks, flexible schedules, and good part-time jobs), and men's sharing of household responsibilities. And as the cost of family has risen for women, they have pushed changes in family patterns.

Women's labour-market earnings allow them more choice about how they will live. Thus, the formation of heterosexual unions has declined, rates of divorce have increased, and childlessness has increased; at minimum, marriage and childbearing are postponed. Nevertheless, while women are both choosing and/or compelled to live in a diversity of family types these days, we still live in a society organized around nuclear families. With very meagre support of family in general, those families that deviate from the nuclear pattern often are especially likely to suffer materially. Thus, family patterns are entangled in the social inequality that characterizes this society.

The fact that economic restructuring is producing bad jobs and a variety of non-standard jobs, and that more people are self-employed, also promotes increasing diversity of family arrangements. At the same time, the economic instability of many jobs and employment contracts today means that people increasingly need the kind of sharing and collective support that families can offer. This means that families—however configured—are likely to persist.

Notes

1. This table (except for the last column) was composed by the late Canadian demographer, Ellen Gee. Note that 'birth cohorts' are groups of people who were born in the same year (or decade, in this case).
2. The median age is the age that divides the population evenly—into half below and half above.
3. Abortion was decriminalized in Canada only in 1988.

4. It remained technically illegal here until 1969, in fact.
5. This conviction would, toward the end of the nineteenth century, lead them to seek medical doctors to attend childbirth, instead of female midwives who were seen as less well trained (Leavitt 1986).
6. Social historian Michael Katz (1975: 293) found that by the mid-nineteenth century women were working alongside their husbands in fewer than half of all households in Hamilton. This gives us some indication of the decline in the family economy in urban Canada.
7. That the same kind of migration was happening in at least Hamilton in mid-nineteenth century is clear from the high numbers of young boarders that Katz (1975) found in evidence.
8. There is even evidence that children of the Great Depression reacted to the upheaval in family life and gender roles that followed men's unemployment, and especially women's assumption of the role of financial provider (which was a common pattern), by aiming to create families characterized by conventional gender roles (Coontz 1992).
9. I thank John Fox for turning my pencil drawings into very clear computer-generated figures, and both Rod Beaujot and Zenaida Ravanera for help in my search for demographic sources.
10. These 'synthetic' (or constructed) cohorts, represented by the different lines in the figure, were constructed by taking the age-specific labour-force participation rates for each ascending age category from one census to the next—for example, the rate for 15 to 24 year olds in the 1921 census, the rate for 25 to 34 year olds from the 1931 census, etc. Essentially, we have a picture of participation in the labour force over the life course for people coming of age at different times.
11. In 1931, while only about 3 per cent of married women worked for wages, over 54 per cent of teens 15 years and older, living in families with both husband and wife present, earned money during the year (Dominion Bureau of Statistics 1933).
12. These average figures were, however, pulled up by the very high estimates for Quebec: it was estimated that 44 per cent of women and 50 per cent of men in Quebec would never marry. The estimate for Ontario was 18 per cent of women and 22 per cent of men (Nault and Belanger 1996).
13. This assumes that women have children between 20 and 35 years of age.
14. This is Betty Friedan's (1965) term. Her best-selling book, *The Feminine Mystique*, argued that women in the 1950s had a 'problem that has no name', because they were subject to a heavy message that personal fulfillment could be found in full-time motherhood and homemaking.
15. While the majority of women in the labour force do not earn as much as men, in about 25 per cent of marriages women earn more than their male partners.
16. In 1968, the first federal legislation on divorce was passed, in the Divorce Act, which specified eight grounds for divorce involving fault, and seven ways of establishing marital breakdown (e.g., three years of separation). Apparently the adversarial process the legislation established was cumbersome and time-consuming, however (Richardson 1996). Then, the 1985 Divorce Act made divorce considerably easier: instead of establishing fault, parties simply have to give evidence of marriage breakdown—separation for one year, adultery, or mental and physical cruelty (Richardson 1996: 227).
17. As with the pattern for common-law unions, divorce is considerably higher in Quebec than in the other provinces, and the likelihood of remarrying is lower (Nault and Belanger 1996).
18. The idea of 'his' and 'her' marriage is Jessie Bernard's (1972).
19. Not many researchers have systematically examined why couples divorce. The bulk of research effort has gone to examine the effects of divorce.
20. In the majority of cases, women are the ones who file for divorce; so studying women makes sense.
21. In the United States in 1991, children living with one parent were four times more likely to live in an extended family than children living with two parents (30 per cent vs. 7 per cent) (Taylor 1997: 79).

References

Adams, Mary Louise. 1997. *The Trouble with Normal: Post-war Youth and the Making of Heterosexuality* (Toronto: University of Toronto Press).

Ahrons, C., and R. Rodgers. 1997. 'The Remarriage Transition', in *Family in Transition*, 9th edn, eds A.S. Skolnick and J.H. Skolnick (New York: Longman), 185–97.

Alphonso, C. 2007. 'Canadians Redefine the Family', *The Globe and Mail* (13 Sept.).

Arat-Koc, S. 1989. 'In the Privacy of Our Own Home', *Studies in Political Economy* 28.

Arendell, T. 1992. 'After Divorce: Investigations into Father Absence', *Gender & Society* 6, 4: 562–87.

Armstrong, P., and H. Armstrong. 1994. *The Double Ghetto: Canadian Women & Their Segregated Work*, 3rd edn (Toronto: McClelland & Stewart).

Arnup, Katherine, Andree Levesque, and Ruth Roach Pierson. 1990. *Delivering Motherhood: Maternal Ideologies and Practices in the 19th and 20th Centuries* (London: Routledge).

Bakan, A., and D. Stasiulis. 1997. *Not One of the Family: Foreign Domestic Workers in Canada* (Toronto: University of Toronto Press).

Bakker, I., ed. 1996. *Rethinking Restructuring: Gender and Change in Canada* (Toronto: University of Toronto Press).

Beaujot, R., et al. 1995. *Family over the Life Course: Current Demographic Analysis*, Cat. No. 91-543E (Ottawa: Industry).

———, and D. Kerr. 2004. *Population Change in Canada*, 2nd edn (Toronto: Oxford University Press).

Bernard, J. 1972. *The Future of Marriage* (New Haven: Yale University Press).

Bianchi, S., J. Robinson, and M. Milkie. 2006. *Changing Rhythms of American Family Life* (New York: Russell Sage Foundation).

Blumenstein, P., and P. Schwartz. 1983. *American Couples* (New York: The Free Press).

Boyd, M., and E.T. Pryor. 1989. 'The Cluttered Nest: The Living Arrangements of Young Canadian Adults', *The Canadian Journal of Sociology* 14, 4: 461–79.

Bradbury, B. 1982. 'The Fragmented Family: Family Strategies in the Face of Death, Illness, and Poverty, Montreal, 1860–1885', in *Childhood and Family in Canadian History*, ed. J. Parr (Toronto: McClelland & Stewart), 93–109.

———. 1984. 'Pigs, Cows, and Boarders: Non-wage Forms of Survival among Montreal Families, 1861–91', *Labour/Le Travail* 14: 9–46.

———. 1993. *Working Families: Age, Gender, and Daily Survival in Industrializing Montreal* (Toronto: McClelland & Stewart).

______. 2005. 'Social, Economic, and Cultural Origins of Contemporary Families', in *Families: Changing Trends in Canada*, 5th edn, ed. M. Baker (Toronto: McGraw-Hill Ryerson), 69–98.

Brenner, J., and B. Laslett. 1991. 'Gender, Social Reproduction, and Women's Self Organization: Considering the US Welfare State', *Gender & Society* 5, 3: 311–33.

Budig, M., and P. England. 2001. 'The Wage Penalty for Motherhood', *American Sociological Review* 66, 2: 204–25.

Bullen, J. 1992. 'Hidden Workers: Child Labour and the Family Economy in Late Nineteenth-century Urban Ontario', in *Canadian Family History*, ed. B. Bradbury (Toronto: Copp Clark), 199–220.

Collins, P.H. 1990. *Black Feminist Thought: Knowledge, Consciousness, and the Politics of Empowerment* (London: Unwin Hyman).

Conway, J. [1990] 1993. *The Canadian Family in Crisis* (Toronto: James Lorimer).

Coontz, S. 1988. *The Social Origins of Private Family Life* (London: Verso).

______. 1992. *The Way We Never Were: American Families and the Nostalgia Trap* (New York: Basic Books).

———. 1997. *The Way We Really Are: Coming to Terms with America's Changing Families* (New York: Basic Books).

Cott, N. 1977. *The Bonds of Womanhood: 'Woman's Sphere' in New England, 1780–1835* (New Haven: Yale University Press).

Daly, K. 2001. 'Controlling Time in Families: Patterns that Sustain Gendered Work in the Home', in *Minding the Time in Family Experience*, ed. K. Daly (New York: JAI, Elsevier Science), 227–49.

______. 2004. 'The Changing Culture of Parenting', Contemporary Family Trends Series (Ottawa: The Vanier Institute of the Family).

Davidoff, L., and C. Hall. 1987. *Family Fortunes: Men and Women of the English Middle Class, 1780–1850* (Chicago: University of Chicago Press).

Dominion Bureau of Statistics. 1933. 1931 Census, Vol. 5: 686–7.

Doucet, A. 2006. *Do Men Mother? Fathering, Care, and Domestic Responsibility* (Toronto: University of Toronto Press).

Drolet, M. 2001. 'The Persistent Gap', Research Paper Series 157 (Ottawa: Statistics Canada, Analytic Studies Branch).

———. 2003. 'Motherhood and Paycheques', *Canadian Social Trends* No. 68: 19–21, Cat. No. 11-008.

Duffy, A., N. Mandell, and N. Pupo. 1989. *Few Choices: Women, Work, and Family* (Toronto: Garamond Press).

Eichler, M. 1988. *Families in Canada Today* (Toronto: Gage).

———. 1997. *Family Shifts: Families, Policies, and Gender Equality* (Toronto: Oxford University Press).

Elder Jr, G.H. 1974. *Children of the Great Depression: Social Change in Life Experience* (Chicago: University of Chicago Press).

Eyer, D. 1992. *Mother Infant Bonding: A Scientific Fiction* (New Haven: Yale University Press).

Finnie, R. 1993. 'Women, Men, and the Economic Consequences of Divorce: Evidence from Canadian Longitudinal Data', *Canadian Review of Sociology and Anthropology* 30, 2: 205–43.

Fox, B. 1980. 'Women's Domestic Labour and Their Involvement in Wage Work: Twentieth-century Changes in the Reproduction of Daily Life', PhD diss., University of Alberta.

______. 1993. 'The Rise and Fall of the Breadwinner–Homemaker Family', in *Family Patterns, Gender Relations*, ed. B. Fox (Don Mills: Oxford University Press).

______. 2006. 'Motherhood as a Class Act: The Many Ways in Which Intensive Mothering is Entangled with Social Class', in *Social Reproduction: Feminist Political Economy Challenges Neo-liberalism* (Montreal and Kingston: McGill-Queen's University Press), 231–62.

Frederick, J. 1995. 'As Time Goes By . . . Time Use of Canadians', Cat. No. 89-544 (Ottawa: Industry).

Friedan, B. 1965. *The Feminine Mystique* (New York: Dell).

Furstenberg, F.F., and A.J. Cherlin. 1991. *Divided Families: What Happens to Children When Parents Part* (Cambridge, MA: Harvard University Press).

Gee, E. 1987. 'Historical Changes in the Family Life Course of Canadian Men and Women', in *Aging in Canada: Social Perspectives*, ed. V. Marshall (Markham: Fitzhenry and Whiteside), 265–87.

Gerson, K. 1993. *No Man's Land: Men's Changing Commitments to Family and Work* (New York: Basic).

Gordon, L. 1974. *Woman's Body, Woman's Right: A Social History of Birth Control in America* (New York: Penguin).

———. 1988. *Heroes of Their Own Lives: The Politics and History of Family Violence* (New York: Viking).

Hays, S. 1996. *The Cultural Contradictions of Motherhood* (New Haven: Yale University Press).

Hansen, K. 2005. *Not-so-nuclear Families: Class, Gender, and Networks of Care* (New Brunswick, NJ: Rutgers University Press).

Hobson, B., and D. Morgan. 2002. 'Introduction: Making Men into Fathers', in *Making Men into Fathers: Men, Masculinities, and the Social Politics of Fatherhood*, ed. B. Hobson (Cambridge, UK: Cambridge University Press).

Hochschild, A. 1989. *The Second Shift: Working Parents and the Revolution of Home* (New York: Viking).

Jacobs, J., and K. Gerson. 2004. *The Time Divide: Work, Family and Gender Inequality* (Cambridge, MA: Harvard University Press).

Katz, M.B. 1975. *The People of Hamilton, Canada West: Family and Class in a Mid-nineteenth-century City* (Cambridge, MA: Harvard University Press).

Kimmel, M. 1996. *Manhood in America: A Cultural History* (New York: The Free Press).

Kronby, M.C. 1981. *Canadian Family Law* (Don Mills, ON: General).

Kurz, D. 1995. *For Richer, For Poorer: Mothers Confront Divorce* (New York: Routledge).

Laslett, B., and J. Brenner. 1989. 'Gender and Social Reproduction: Historical Perspectives', *Annual Review of Sociology* 15: 381–404.

Leacy, F.H., et al., eds. 1983. *Historical Statistics of Canada*, 2nd edn (Ottawa: Supply and Services).

Leavitt, J.W. 1986. *Brought to Bed: Child-bearing in America, 1750 to 1950* (New York: Oxford University Press).

Luxton, M. 1980. *More Than a Labour of Love: Three Generations of Women's Work in the Home* (Toronto: Women's Press).

______. 2006. 'Friends, Neighbours, and the Community: A Case Study in the Role of Informal Caregiving in Social Reproduction', in *Social Reproduction* (Montreal and Kingston: McGill-Queen's University Press), 263–92.

McLaren, A., and A.T. McLaren. 1986. *The Bedroom and the State: The Changing Practices and Politics of Contraception and Abortion in Canada, 1880–1980* (Toronto: McClelland & Stewart).

Margolis, M. 1984. *Mothers and Such: Views of American Women and Why They Changed* (Berkeley: University of California Press).

Marshall, K. 2006. 'Converging Gender Roles', *Perspectives on Labour and Income* (Ottawa: Statistics Canada).

Martin-Mathews, A. 2000. 'Change and Diversity in Aging Families and Intergenerational Relations', in *Canadian Families: Diversity, Conflict, and Change* (Toronto: Harcourt Brace Canada), 323–60.

May, E.T. 1988. *Homeward Bound: American Families in the Cold War Era* (New York: Basic Books).

May, M. 1985. 'Bread Before Roses: American Workingmen, Labor Unions, and the Family Wage', in *Women, Work, and Protest: A Century of US Women's Labor History* (Boston: Routledge & Kegan Paul), 1–21.

Mitchell, B. 1998. 'Too Close for Comfort? Parental Assessments of "Boomerang Lid" Living Arrangements', *The Canadian Journal of Sociology* 23, 1: 21–46.

National Council of Welfare. 1999. *Poverty Profile 1997* (Ottawa: Public Works and Government Services).

Nault, F., and A. Belanger. 1996. 'The Decline in Marriage in Canada, 1981 to 1991', Cat. No. 84-536 (Ottawa: Statistics Canada, Health Statistics Division).

Nelson, F. 1996. *Lesbian Motherhood: An Exploration of Canadian Lesbian Families* (Toronto: University of Toronto Press).

Noel, Francoise. 2003. *Family Life and Sociability in Upper and Lower Canada, 1780–1870* (Kingston and Montreal: McGill-Queen's Press).

Parr, Joy. 1990. *The Gender of Breadwinners: Women, Men and Change in Two Industrial Towns, 1880–1950* (Toronto: University of Toronto Press).

Picot, G., and A. Heisz. 2000. 'The Performance of the 1990s Canadian Labour Market', Business and Labour Market Analysis Division, No. 148 (Ottawa: Statistics Canada).

Popenoe, D. 1993. 'American Family Decline, 1960–1990: A Review and Appraisal', *Journal of Marriage and the Family* 55: 527–55.

Prentice, A., et al. 1988. *Canadian Women: A History* (Toronto: Harcourt, Brace, and Jovanovich).

Rapp, R., and E. Ross. 1986. 'The 1920s: Feminism, Consumerism, and Political Backlash in the United States', in *Women in Culture and Politics: A Century of Change*, eds J. Friedlander, B.W. Cook, A. Kessler-Harris, and C. Smith-Rosenberg (Bloomington: Indiana University Press).

Ravanera, Z., and F. Rajulton. 1996. 'Stability and Crisis in the Family Life Course—Findings from the 1990 General Social Survey', *Canadian Studies in Population* 23, 2: 165–84.

———, and T. Burch. 2005. 'Cohort and Social Status Differentials in Union Dissolution: Analysis Using the 2001 General Social Survey', paper presented at the 2005 Annual Meeting of the Canadian Sociology and Anthropology Association.

Richardson, C.J. 1996. 'Divorce and Remarriage', in *Families: Changing Trends in Canada*, 3rd edn, ed. M. Baker (Toronto: McGraw-Hill Ryerson), 315–49.

Roschelle, A. 1997. *No More Kin: Exploring Race, Class, and Gender in Family Networks* (Thousand Oaks: Sage).

Ryan, M. 1981. *Cradle of the Middle Class: The Family in Oneida County, New York, 1790–1865* (Cambridge: Cambridge University Press).

_______. 1983. *Womanhood in America: From Colonial Times to the Present* (New York: Franklin Watts).

South, S., and G. Spitze. 1994. 'Housework in Marital and Non-marital Households', *American Sociological Review* 59, 3: 327–47.

Stack, C. 1974. *All Our Kin: Strategies for Survival in a Black Community* (New York: Harper & Row).

Stansell, C. 1987. *City of Women: Sex and Class in New York, 1789–1860* (Urbana: University of Illinois Press).

Statistics Canada. 1953. 1951 Census, Vol. 4, Table 11, Cat. No. 98-1951.

———. 1974. 1971 Census, Vol. 3, Pt. 7, Table 6, Cat. No. 94-776.

———. 1993. 1991 Census, Vol. 1, Table 2, Cat. No. 93-321.

———. 1994. *Women in the Labour Force*, Table 6.3, Cat. No. 75-507E.

———. 1998. *Historical Labour Force Statistics*, Cat. No. 71-201XBP, p. 18.

______. 2003a. *Income in Canada*, Cat. No. 75-202-XIE.

______. 2003b. Update on Families, *Canadian Social Trends*, No. 69, Cat. No. 11-008.

______. 2006a. *Women in Canada: Work Chapter Update*, Cat. No. 89FO133XIE.

______. 2006b. *Women in Canada*, 5th edn, Cat. No. 89-503-XPE.

______. 2007. *Family Portrait: Continuity and Change in Canadian Families and Households in 2006*, 2006 Census, Cat. No. 97-553-XIE.

Strong-Boag, V. 1988. *The New Day Recalled: Lives of Girls and Women in English Canada, 1919–1939* (Markham: Penguin).

Sugiman, Pamela. 1994. *Labour's Dilemma: the Gender Politics of Auto Workers in Canada, 1937–1979* (Toronto: University of Toronto Press).

Sullivan, M. 1998. 'Absent Fathers in the Inner City', in *Public and Private Families*, ed. A. Cherlin (Boston: McGraw-Hill), 100–8.

Taylor, R. 1997. 'Who's Parenting? Trends and Patterns', in *Contemporary Parenting: Challenges and Issues*, ed. T. Arendell (Thousand Oaks, CA: Sage), 68–92.

Vinovskis, M., and S.M. Frank. 1997. 'Parenting in American Society: A Historical Overview of the Colonial Period through the 19th Century', in *Contemporary Parenting: Challenges and Issues*, ed. T. Arendell (Thousand Oaks, CA: Sage), 45–67.

Waldfogel, J. 1997. 'The Effect of Children on Women's Wages', *American Sociological Review* 62, 2: 209–17.

Wall, G. 2001. 'Moral Constructions of Motherhood in Breastfeeding Discourse', *Gender & Society* 15, 4: 590–608.

______. 2004. 'Is Your Child's Brain Potential Maximized? Mothering in an Age of New Brain Research', *Atlantis* 28, 2: 41–50.

Welter, B. 1966. 'The Cult of True Womanhood: 1820–1860', *American Quarterly* 18, 2, Pt. 1: 151–74.

Wertz, R., and D.C. Wertz. 1979. *Lying In: A History of Childbirth in America* (New York: Schocken Books).

Wood, A.D. 1974. '"The Fashionable Diseases": Women's Complaints and Their Treatment in Nineteenth-century America', in *Clio's Consciousness Raised*, eds M. Hartman and L.W. Banner (New York: Harper & Row), 1–22.

Wu, Z. 1999. 'Premarital Cohabitation and the Time of First Marriage', *Canadian Review of Sociology and Anthropology* 36, 1: 109–28.

Yalnizyan, A. 1998. *The Growing Gap: A Report on Growing Inequality between the Rich and Poor in Canada* (Centre for Social Justice).

Young, M., and P. Willmott. 1957. *Family and Kinship in East London* (London: Routledge & Kegan Paul).

PART THREE

Elements of Family

Section 1 Sexuality: Negotiating Adult Intimacy

Social scientists who study sexuality—Steven Seidman, Julia Ericksen, John D'Emilio, and Jonathon Katz, among others—have uncovered the history of ideas about sexuality. These ideas have changed considerably through time. In the nineteenth century, only reproductive sexuality was seen as proper. The middle class was advised to control their lust even in the marital bed. Sexual acts that did not involve reproductive sex were criminalized. Apparently, it was assumed that anyone was capable of a variety of non-reproductive sexual acts. In short, there was no notion that sexual behaviour signified a type of person.

Ideas about sexuality changed with the development of industrial capitalism and the erosion of a family economy in which teens and young adults worked and lived under the authority and supervision of a male household head until they were able to marry. Declines in the availability of land for farming and increasing numbers of jobs in towns and cities meant that young, single adults flooded into towns and cities, where they worked and lived outside the scrutiny of their parents or guardians. In this context, sexual exploration—involving both heterosexual and same-sex sexuality—became more possible and more likely to occur. Accordingly, self-identified gay male communities developed in the late nineteenth century, as did 'sexologists' who labelled them and their sexuality deviant. At the same time, white-collar jobs, urban life, and increases in the rights accorded to women raised popular fears about societal threats to 'manliness'. It seems that partly in response to anxieties about manhood, heterosexuality came to be seen as a marker of white men's gender identity (and homosexuality the opposite and the deviant). Sigmund Freud's work also significantly shaped popular assumptions about sexuality. He argued that a social process, involving repression, was responsible for people's sexual orientation and their gender identity. For Freud, personal histories produce heterosexual and homosexual people. It seems, then, that a number of factors played a role in creating the modern idea that heterosexuality was 'normal' and that people's sexuality expressed something basic about them as types of people.

Social change in the early twentieth century produced a number of changes in the meaning of sexuality in popular culture. The development of a consumer culture, for example, meant that the advertising industry 'sold' heterosexual romance as it sold its products. Meanwhile, increases in women's autonomy, rises in divorce, and decreases in birth rates in the white middle class fuelled fears about the stability of 'the family'—seen as the bedrock of the social order. In response, experts developed and promoted the argument that marriage was grounded in romantic love and sexuality that fulfilled both partners. Of course, in promising sexual pleasure to women as well as men, this new discourse co-opted middle-class women's new-found sense of autonomy, and defined marriage as the sole source of their fulfillment. Moreover, that fulfillment was contingent upon women's sexuality meeting their partners' needs: only then would marriage last. Moral authorities worked to tie sexuality to marriage for much of the twentieth century—as long as it was heterosexuality. In the post-World War II period, teen sexuality—unhinged from marriage and carrying the threat of homosexuality—prompted an educational campaign to regulate 'dating behaviour and, ultimately, to promote marriage as the only arena suitable for women's sexuality' (see Mary Louise Adams, The Trouble with Normal*).*

Throughout the twentieth century, sexuality has been a marker of difference and privilege in another way, as gays and lesbians in committed relationships were denied the rights and benefits accorded to married heterosexual couples. Only after protracted legal challenges to the law did same-sex partners win the rights given to other types of couples. During their battle to win the right to marry, conservative politicians and religious groups continually argued that gay and lesbian relationships posed a 'threat' to 'the family'. The assumption that their sexuality was unnatural was also clear in those debates. The chapter by Mariana Valverde examines popular assumptions behind the notion that heterosexuality is natural and 'normal'. And the short essay by Chrys Ingraham raises provocative questions about the relationship between heterosexuality and gender inequality.

Amidst divided opinion in the gay and lesbian communities about the merits of embracing marriage, with its legacy of gender inequality, the campaign for the right to marry was won. Since July 2005, gay and lesbian couples have been marrying (legally) in Canada. The divide in popular culture between heterosexuality and homosexuality, however, is only beginning to weaken. And the regulatory function of conservative religion persists, and thus influences how many people think about sexuality. Tish Langlois explores this matter, in her look at the sexual histories of a group of French-Canadian women.

Chapter 13

In this brief selection from her book *Sex, Power and Pleasure*, Mariana Valverde pushes us to question our assumptions about sexuality. She especially challenges all notions that heterosexuality is somehow natural rather than socially created—as both an ideal in our culture and a set of desires on the part of the individual. The idea of heterosexuality, or the attraction of 'opposite sexes', is, of course, central to the popular meaning of gender as differences between men and women. It is also central to the belief in this culture that heterosexual nuclear families are 'natural'.

Heterosexuality: Contested Ground

Mariana Valverde

It is not easy to write generally about heterosexuality. Relations between men and women have been subject to much scrutiny over the past 20 years and although traditional ideas and practices continue to hold sway in some quarters, there are other circles in which little can be taken for granted any more. These different perspectives do not merely coexist in peaceful détente. Even if there are some 'islands' of both traditionalism and feminism where people live without many direct, personal challenges to their beliefs, by and large we are all living in an ideological battlefield. The combined effect of skyrocketing divorce rates and feminist ideas has produced a counterattack by the traditionalists, who have become increasingly shrill about the divine rights of husbands. This right-wing backlash is a desperate reaction to a situation in which the breadwinner husband/ dependent wife model has become economically unfeasible for the vast majority of couples as well as emotionally unsatisfying for many women.

We live therefore in a very polarized situation, with different groups contending for the power to define heterosexuality and the family. Within each camp people strategize about how to strengthen their forces and how to improve their position on the field; they react to one another's ideology and on occasion are influenced by ideas from the 'enemy' camp. All this means that, reassurances of sex and family experts notwithstanding, we cannot speak confidently about heterosexuality in general. Both the ideas about it and the corresponding sexual and social practices are quite diverse and we are in a process of struggle and change.

Furthermore, we see many gaps between theory and practice. Some women have embraced the idea of an egalitarian heterosexuality that stresses choice and creativity, but in their own lives fall into traditional gender roles which they experience as 'natural'. On the other hand, many women who have sincerely believed in traditional concepts of marriage are finding themselves by design or by accident in unorthodox situations that are not part of the plan. Faced with such realities as an unwanted pregnancy, a daughter who comes out as a lesbian, or a divorce, women who have led 'traditional' lives sometimes show a remarkable degree of flexibility and inventiveness. So we cannot assume that all women with feminist beliefs have what one might describe as feminist relationships, or that women who are married and go to church on Sundays necessarily restrict themselves to monogamous heterosexuality in the missionary position.

It might be useful first to pause and consider one of the most prevalent myths used by the anti-feminists in the ideological struggle to define heterosexuality. It is a myth that often lingers in the hearts if not the minds of feminists, and so must be explicitly refuted if we are to make a fresh start. This myth comes in many guises but the common denominator is an appeal to Nature to legitimize a certain traditional definition of heterosexuality as 'natural' and therefore inevitable, good, and not to be argued about or criticized. Arguments for Nature try to remove heterosexuality from the realm of politics and history and put it safely away on a high shelf marked 'Mother Nature: things that just are'.

An influential exponent of this argument for Nature is 'America's number one counsellor', Dr Joyce Brothers. In her 1981 book entitled *What Every Woman Should Know About Men*, she blithely 'deduces' the traditional nuclear family from her perception of 'primitive' human life. Appealing to our stereotype of 'cavemen', she writes:

> It is as if way back in prehistory Mother Nature had searched for the most effective way of protecting mothers and children. Without someone to provide food for and defend the mother and child, they were at the mercy of wild beasts and predatory males. . . . The obvious source of protection and provisions was the male. But how to keep him around?
>
> Mother Nature's solution was sex. Sex on tap, so to speak. The day-in, day-out sexual availability of the human female created what scientists call a pair bond and most of us call love. The nuclear family was born. (Brothers 1981: 178)

Let us unpack the assumptions and values contained in this unfortunately typical piece of popular 'scientific' writing.

- 'Mother' Nature is portrayed as a manipulative mother-in-law. This is anthropomorphism at its worst, where Nature is not only a human female but an 'old hag' who manipulates people for her own purposes.
- Men are portrayed as naturally predatory and obsessed with sex. Dr Brothers is apparently relying here on some now-discredited anthropological studies that claimed to show it was the aggressiveness and sexual jealousy of the male that pushed us along the evolutionary path and made us into a civilized species. The myth of 'Man the Hunter' has been successfully challenged by feminist anthropologists and primatologists. Male anthropologists have tended to assume that, for example, a social system could be understood by looking at the *men* in the system, and that competition and aggression were 'natural' and beneficial to the species. Without going into details about how this traditional view was challenged, suffice it to say that now only the die-hards in the anthropological profession would see even a grain of truth in Dr Brothers's description.[1]
- Further, even if her description were accurate there is a logical error in her argument. If males were so predatory, why would women turn to them as the 'obvious source' of protection? . . .
- The women in Dr Brothers's prehistory appear to have not sexual feelings but only sexual 'availability'. Now, given that many female primates show clear signs of sexual pleasure, and some species even exhibit what can be interpreted as female orgasms, one wonders why women in prehistory would have such a passive sexuality. But the myth is that women do not really want sex, and exchange sexual favours only for male protection, while men do not really want to nurture but will reluctantly provide protection for the sake of sex. There is a lapse here in the logic of how the nuclear family can emerge from this coming together of such vastly different beings with such completely different purposes in mind.

- Finally, it seems clear that according to Dr Brothers the only 'natural' expression of human sexuality is monogamous heterosexuality within a nuclear family. By trying to ground her view of heterosexuality in 'Mother Nature' she confines all other possibilities to the obscurity of non-natural or anti-natural human behaviour. In the rest of her book she downplays the family and does not insist on children the way the Pope does. But she certainly believes that real sex is heterosexual sex, and real love is heterosexual love.

This belief in the naturalness of heterosexuality is so commonly accepted that we do not even notice it. . . . These days it is seldom articulated in its most blatant forms. But in its more sophisticated and subtle versions, which de-emphasize reproduction and stress sex itself, it continues to exercise a great deal of influence not just over our thoughts but over our very feelings. We feel it is somehow right for men and women to be attracted to one another precisely because they are men or women. We smile on young, happy heterosexual couples and we attend wedding celebrations regardless of the actual interactions of the two people in question. By contrast, we feel uncomfortable when rules about monogamy and exclusive heterosexuality are broken, and feel compelled to find explanations for why woman *A* has so many lovers or why man *B* is attracted to men. But if *A* and *B* join up as a stable, monogamous couple, then we cease to ask questions. Their relationship, like Dr Brothers's primitive society, simply is.

One of the most crucial building blocks of the traditional view of natural heterosexuality is the idea that penises and vaginas 'go together' or 'are meant for each', and that erotic attraction between men and women is only the psychological manifestation of the physiological urge to engage in intercourse. There are several problems with this view. First it portrays men and women as the dupes of their own physiology and considers eroticism as a mere cover-up for Nature's reproductive aims. People are thus dehumanized, first by being reduced to one sexual organ and then by having those sexual organs reduced to the status of reproductive tools. Secondly, it ignores the specificity of sex by collapsing it into reproduction. This implicitly devalues not only homosexuality but all non-reproductive sexual practices. It is true that if one wants to have a child, intercourse is one of the best means. But sex research has shown that if female sexual pleasure is the aim then intercourse is a poor choice, since masturbation and lesbian sex are both much more effective. (Shere Hite [1976] for example found that only 30 per cent of a large sample of women regularly achieved orgasm from intercourse, while 99 per cent of the women could easily achieve orgasm by masturbating.) Men, for their part, often prefer fellatio to intercourse.

This sex research ought to have demolished once and for all the myth that sexual pleasure is maximized by intercourse. And the increasing availability of birth control ought also to have helped break the bond between sex and reproduction. But people still cling to the theory that the vagina is women's 'real' sex organ and the 'natural' receptacle for the penis and for sperm.

Why is this?

Well, perhaps the sexual revolution happened a bit too fast for us all. Despite our experiments in sexual practices we still keep alive the notion of intercourse as the most 'natural' kind of sex, providing ourselves with a fixed point or home to which we can return. It is genuinely unsettling to watch old ideas and values go out the window. We are more comfortable adding diversions and 'deserts' (as *The Joy of Sex* calls them) to our sexual repertoire than questioning the underlying assumptions of a hierarchy of sexual acts that puts regular intercourse in the role of 'main dish' and everything else in the role of hors d'oeuvre. It is very important to question the division of sexual acts into 'basic' or 'natural' and 'frills'. Only after we have shaken the foundations of the old edifice will we be able to look honestly at our own sexual desires and decide what really pleases us. *The Joy of Sex* approach appears very liberated, but the way sexual acts are classified suggests that one would not want to make a whole meal out of 'just' oral sex. The equation of intercourse with protein in a meal is simply an ideological construct. This argument for intercourse as the real thing is based on assumptions about penises and vaginas 'fitting' together. Indeed, if a woman has to be told she is 'infantile' and 'immature' if she doesn't experience intercourse as the most natural and pleasurable form of sex, or if her privileging of the vagina is achieved only after a lengthy process of indoctrination and internalization of what being an adult woman is all about, then one must wonder how well penises and vaginas do fit together. The tired clichés used to convince us that our sexuality can be reduced to the vagina (the 'lock' or the 'glove') and the vagina in turn to a place for the penis (the 'key' or the 'hand') reveal a crucial logical fallacy, a phallocentric fallacy. The lock was made so that a key would fit into it, and has no purpose in and of itself; ditto for gloves which make no sense if considered apart from hands. But vaginas have all sorts of purposes such as allowing menstrual blood out, and most importantly giving birth to children—that have nothing to do with the phallus. One is tempted to understand the clichés about the vagina as nothing but male jealousy and defensiveness around female reproduction.

The myth of intercourse is also sustained by the idea that all eroticism depends in an essential way on *difference*, and specifically *genital difference*. Now, this idea is not necessarily patriarchal in its form and intent, for difference does not necessarily imply subordination. There can be amiable, egalitarian difference, which is presumably what fuels eroticism among enlightened heterosexuals.

The idea of difference as erotic is so common sense and commonplace that we do not usually pause to criticize it. We merrily proceed to examine our own erotic attraction to individual X or type Y and come up with the 'differences' that are significant. But we could just as well analyze our own attractions and non-attractions by reference to similarities.

Let me give an example. A friend of mine once said 'I like men because they're so different!', so I envisaged her with a tall, muscular hunk with a masculine beard and a masculine personality. But when I met her lover he turned out to be neither tall nor muscular nor aggressive; rather he was androgynous both in physique and personality. So where was the big difference? (My friend, incidentally, also looks more androgynous than feminine.) Was the difference that he had a penis? But other men who were much more 'different' than this guy also had penises, and my friend was not interested in them. Was it really difference that attracted her to him?

There are many criteria one could use to measure human differences: size, weight, skin colour, hair colour, race, language, age, intelligence, physical fitness, beliefs, talents, etc. If a heterosexual couple is composed of two individuals who are remarkably similar in, for example, their class backgrounds, interests, and ethnicity (as is usually the case), and who are different primarily in their gender, then one cannot claim with any certainty that the key to their erotic attraction is difference. In their case gender difference has been eroticized, but so have their much more numerous non-gender similarities.

It is not my intention to argue for the intrinsic erotic appeal of similarity or difference. Some people can only get interested in partners who are basically similar to them, while others need sharp differences in order to have their erotic interest sparked. To each her own, as far as I'm concerned. The point is that I do not see any valid reason for privileging gender above all else, and then *assuming* that gender difference is essentially erotic while other differences are not. In ancient Athenian culture for instance, adult men saw adult women primarily as reproductive partners and reserved their odes to eroticism for adolescent boys. There, age differences were eroticized as a matter of course, whereas the gender difference might or might not have been erotic.

By understanding eroticism as a force which pivots around sex and gender differences, we separate the erotic realm from other aspects of human existence. Activities and relationships in which sex and gender are not major factors are perceived as non-erotic. Now, to some extent there is clearly something specific about erotic interaction that makes it distinct from the pleasure of working together with others, or of having shared family roots. However, to take this distinction for granted and to absolutize it is a mistake that reinforces certain philosophical beliefs that are simply myths. First, the separation of the erotic—as the sexual, the mysterious, the irrational, the dialectic of difference—from other aspects of human interaction fosters a view of the human self as essentially and eternally divided between Reason and Passion. Secondly, because eroticism is exiled beyond the pale of reason, the everyday life of rational interaction is de-eroticized. And finally, separating Reason from Passion constructs a realm of the instinctual to which women are largely confined.

Women have suffered from this ideological division of the passionate and the rational, as many feminists have noted and criticized. . . . Because erotic play is thought to depend on sexual difference and on the contrast between reason and passion, erotic relations have been largely confined to relations between unequals. Reason and Passion as the male and female principles are not simply different. They are unequal within the hierarchy that prevails between them. On the other hand, relations among equals as 'thinking persons' have been a priori de-eroticized because they hinge not on difference but on a sameness in what the philosophers have called 'the common light of reason'. Western philosophers have argued that this commonality is the basis both of thinking itself and of democratic society. Most of them also believed women did not share fully in the light of reason and therefore could not enter into the world of politics or philosophy. But even those few who argued that women did indeed have the prerequisite rationality and personhood to enter into the realm and be participants in the social contract still left untouched the basic division between the erotic and the rational. Even if women had an element of rationality, they still had to represent Mother Earth and the dark instincts. And much popular culture since the nineteenth century hinges on women's *internal* struggle between their personhood, as the desire for example to learn or succeed, and their womanhood. This struggle is often tragic because the claims of the feminine are considered to be contradictory to the claims of personhood.

Thus whether or not women were allowed some access to the realm of reason and public life, there was still a sharp separation between 'human' interactions (based on male-defined equality among rational human beings as conceived on the male model) and erotic interactions based on sexual difference. The equality prevailing in the intellectual world and the marketplace was considered to be inherently non-erotic, even anti-erotic, while the unequal struggle between Reason and Passion was understood as inherently sexy. Women's confinement to the realm of the semi-rational went hand in hand with a desexualization of the world of men, politics, work, and culture. One of the reasons for this was the age-old desire to use Reason as a tool to dominate Nature, subjugate the passions, and not coincidentally to put women, as those closest to Nature, in their place. But certainly another reason was that to admit sexuality and eroticism into the public world would have necessarily entailed recognizing homosexuality, or at the very least homoeroticism. Thus, insofar as men and women were defined as being divided by sexual difference and so fundamentally unequal, society could not afford to eroticize equality.

A further result of this has been to create a much larger gap than necessary between heterosexuality and homosexuality. Just as we have exaggerated the role of difference in heterosexuality eroticism, so too have we exaggerated the role of similarity in homosexuality. A gay man does not necessarily eroticize only his partner's masculinity. And two lesbians might have certain commonalities in bodily parts and psychological traits, but can otherwise be as different as night and day. So my point is not so much that one has to 'make room for' homosexuality as an eroticism of sameness, but more fundamentally to question the very separation of sameness and difference, and the process by which we overvalue difference when theorizing about sexual attraction.

Heterosexuality is too complicated and too unpredictable to be reduced to such a simple formula as 'boy meets girl', 'like meets unlike', 'opposites attract'. Men and women are clearly different, but their attraction to one another does not necessarily depend only on that difference. And in any case they are not *opposites*. Because there happen to be only two sexes, we absolutize this fact and assume that the two sexes are opposites. But why? What if there were three or four sexes created through some miracle of modern science? Or if we only had two senses instead of five, would we assume that those two—sight and hearing, let's say—were 'opposites'? If I have two daughters, or a daughter and a son, are they opposites of one another?

Heterosexuality cannot be free until we stop thinking in terms of 'opposites' that are 'drawn' to one another. Men and women are not like iron filings and magnets, keys and locks, or any object in those functionalist and fatalistic metaphors that try to legitimize heterosexuality as the norm by presenting it as a fate imposed on us by Nature. Heterosexuality is not our fate. It is a *choice* that we can make—or, more accurately, it *would be* a choice if our society were more pluralistic and less rigid in its construction of sexual choices. After all, choice implies the existence of several valid options, and as long as we continue to see eroticism between the sexes as fated by some inevitable sexiness inherent in genital differences, we will have a rather impoverished experience of heterosexuality. . . .

In all our erotic desires and activities there is an interplay of sameness and difference, of recognition and fascination, of familiarity and strangeness. Neither difference nor sameness are *per se* erotic; rather it is the playful movement of and between them which creates erotic exchange. . . . What we need to work toward and begin imagining is an eroticism where sameness and difference are both eroticized and valued. This can help us to both break down the walls of the ego and recognize the other as our equal while maintaining the 'admiration' for otherness and difference. Perhaps the most important thing to remember is that men and women were not made for heterosexuality but rather heterosexuality exists for men and women. . . .

Note

1. See for instance Ruth Bleier, *Science and Gender* (New York: Pergamon, 1984), especially Chapter 5 on human evolution. See also Eleanor Leacock, 'Women in Egalitarian Societies', in *Becoming Visible*, eds R. Bridenthal and C. Koonz (Boston: Houghton Mifflin, 1977).

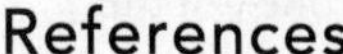

References

Brothers, J. 1981. *What Every Woman Should Know About Men* (New York: Ballantine).

Hite, S. 1976. *The Hite Report* (New York: Dell).

Chapter 14

If our sexuality is not given at birth, then we need to develop some explanation of how we come to be the way we are sexually. American sociologist Pepper Schwartz has argued that our personal histories, our traditions, the circumstances we live in, the opportunities we face, the ideas and ideals in popular culture—and thus our expectations—all affect our sexuality. In the selection below, Tish Langlois explores the complex sets of social factors that have influenced the sexual behaviour and history of a group of French-Canadian women. Based on interviews Langlois carried out between 2003 and 2005, she describes how these women have negotiated their paths into adult sexuality amidst powerful competing ideas about sexual behaviour and marriage.

Navigating Sexual Terrain: Legacies of the Sacred and the Secular in the Lives of French-Canadian Women[1]

Tish Langlois

Introduction

In the midst of popular images of sexually liberated women, sexuality continues to be a complicated negotiation for many girls and women. It is true that, following the introduction of the 'birth control pill' and the 'sexual revolution' of the 1960s, when the connection sexuality had to reproduction was undone, women began to experience more choice in their sexual lives (Vance 1984). With marriage occurring at later ages—and increasingly optional [see Chapter 12]—sexuality has become separated from marriage for many women. Yet, many girls and women continue to face restrictions of one kind or another. For some girls, the message that sexuality should be confined to marriage retains its power because of the influence of religion. Catholics' ideal model of family life, for example—one in which the husband is the breadwinner and the wife is responsible for childcare and the home—entails the belief that sexuality should be confined to heterosexual marriage. By contrast, a 'secular postmodern' approach to sexuality breaks with conventional heterosexual norms and makes room for sexual innovations that are free of religious moralizing (Stacey 2002).

We can see, then, that in the sexual lives of many women, there are opposing sets of forces at work. Secularization and the sexual revolution have made it relatively easy, in contemporary Western societies, for unmarried girls and women to be sexually active. In Canada, the state has played a role in this by passing legislation that makes contraception and abortion legal. Another contributing factor is Canada's 'culture of individualism', which celebrates personal freedom and presupposes that individuals should not be unduly bound by the demands of their families, their religious traditions, or the state (see Bellah et al. 1996; Isajiw 1999). Thus, like the citizens of other industrial-capitalist countries, Canadians experience only limited pressure to conform to rigid and conventional sexual scripts. Yet, as mentioned above, the sexual terrain also remains a site of danger and restriction, especially for women. The 'sexual double standard'—so much the legacy of earlier historical periods (Sangster 1996)—continues to create anxiety for girls because of potential damage to their reputations should they end up labelled 'sluts' or 'bad girls' (Maglin and Perry 1996; Tanenbaum 1999). And our society is undeniably heteronormative (Gamson and Moon 2003; Ingraham 1999)—that is, organized around the assumption that women should marry men and establish nuclear-family households—which imposes real limits on people's ability to pursue unconventional sexual options. As well, there is a growing recognition among scholars that, along with religion, ethnicity also strongly conditions people's—and especially women's—sexual options.

To examine how these many *entangled* forces influence people's lives, sexuality scholars often use a mode of analysis called 'intersectional theorizing' (Gamson and Moon 2003; Stasilius 1999). An intersectional approach might consider, for instance, how sexual conduct is conditioned *simultaneously* by prevailing gender norms (such as notions about how 'good girls' should behave), ethnic traditions (such as beliefs about marrying within one's own ethnic group), and religious dictates (such as Catholic doctrine condoning sexual activity only within heterosexual marriage). Intersectional theorizing thus extends one of Michel Foucault's (1976: 103) key insights—that sexuality, far from being simply a personal affair, is rather a 'dense transfer point' for all sorts of relations of power. Taken together, insights about these intersecting areas of social life have prompted sexuality scholars to complicate the overly tidy traditional-to-modern (or religious-to-secular) 'master narrative' that is often used to describe sexuality in postmodern societies.

One way of developing a deeper understanding of the complexity of the sexual landscape is by asking people to describe their *lived experiences* of sexuality. To date, however, surprisingly little scholarly attention has been paid to women's sexual journeys—that is, to the ways in which women navigate this complicated terrain (the work of Gloria González-López is a clear exception). The focus of the present chapter, which has been adapted from a study based on in-depth interviews with a sample of French-Canadian[2] women, is women's transitions to adult sexuality in contemporary Canadian society.

The Study

The interviews I conducted were with 33 French-Canadian women living in Toronto, and took place between the fall of 2003 and the spring of 2005. The study's participants were born after 1960 and raised in various locales throughout Ontario, including rural and small-town settings as well as cities—such as Timmins, Welland, and Sudbury—that have prominent French-speaking quarters. Most of these women were raised in family and community settings in which French-Canadian culture was fragile and existed in a clearly demarcated *minority* relationship to Anglo-dominant Ontario.

I settled on the phrase 'transition to adulthood' as a means of capturing the stages these women passed through as they developed into adults: first, their teenage years, when they lived with their families of origin, and found themselves sorting through a variety of messages about sexuality; second, the leaving-home phase, when they entered college or university or moved away from home in search of better paid work; and, finally, the settling-in phase, during which they established themselves as full-fledged adults.

When I interviewed these women, I was eager to find out what the transition to adulthood had been like for them, since they had experienced a broad cultural spectrum, from traditional Catholic French-Canadian milieus to the secular 'big city' life of Toronto. In order to understand the context for their sexual journeys, I asked them to speak candidly about their families of origin—their religious practices, whether they had used French regularly at home, and their parents' educational and work histories. I asked them about their dating histories and the kinds of messages they had received from their parents about sexuality. Then I asked about the circumstances surrounding their leaving home, whether they had attended post-secondary institutions, what kinds of paid work they had done, and, in general, what their lives were like as they made this transition, including the kinds of sexual practices they had engaged in along the way. In particular, I sought to understand how these women negotiated competing loyalties to Catholicism on the one hand (especially the Catholic dictate that sexuality belongs only in marriage) and to personal sexual freedom on the other. I wanted to know how much latitude these women actually *experienced* in the realm of sexuality. What I found, in a nutshell, is that the conflicting forces of religious traditionalism and secular postmodernity were very much at play in their lives. The analysis presented in this chapter draws from the general patterns in the narratives to construct a composite picture of the women's transitions to adulthood.

Why did I choose to focus on French Canadians living in Ontario? The main reason is that members of this ethnic group are positioned squarely between the forces of religious traditionalism and secular postmodernity.[3] French Canadians are a decidedly Catholic ethnic group, and their strategy for cultural survival has historically drawn on a dogmatic form of Catholicism (see Heller and Labrie 2004). Historically, religion has played a dominant role in the definition and control of women's sexuality, and it is fair to say that for Catholic women the sexual terrain has been unambiguously gendered by Catholic theology's morally elevated archetypes of the virgin, wife, and mother, and their opposing denigrated archetype of the whore. However, processes related to secularization—that is, declining respect for religious authority—have liberalized sexual practices, even among Catholics (Greeley 2004), including the French Canadians I learned about in my study. And so I felt that a study about Catholic (or formerly Catholic) women would provide a revealing window into how, in their sexual lives, women negotiate between religious and secular meanings.

At the same time, ethnicity more generally was also relevant. When ethnic migrants leave their homeland, they frequently transport cultural practices that become museumized—or frozen in time—and thus end up 'out of sync' with changes occurring in their places of origin (Anderson 1992). This is certainly true for French Canadians in Ontario, especially when we consider, by contrast, the more secularized and sexually permissive culture of Quebec (Wu 2000). Gender scholars have also begun to document how preoccupations with retaining ethnic identity place special pressures on ethnic women to remain sexually pure, to be keepers of their culture, and to adopt conventional roles as wives and mothers (Yuval-Davis and Anthias 1989). This is partially because women's sexuality is central to the kinds of *moral* boundaries that ethnic groups seek to maintain. Traditional family values and premarital virginity, for example, can be used as vehicles for establishing a sense of cultural or moral superiority in relation to the dominant ethnic group. Among Filipinos in the United States, for example, the narrative of the virtuous Filipina stands in contrast to that of the 'immoral' white American woman (Espiritu 2001). They say their women 'don't sleep around like white girls do'. This places enormous pressure on Filipino daughters to exhibit sexual restraint. A similar dynamic is at work among the French-Canadian women I interviewed. Interestingly, though, many ethnic parents—including Franco-Ontarians—are beginning to redefine sexual morality due to a strong desire for their daughters to become educated and thus avoid the pitfalls associated with conventional gender roles (see also González-López 2005).

Complicated Terrain: Sacred and Secular Codes Governing Sexual Conduct

For these women, the most salient feature of their sexual journeys was the complexity of the terrain. They were often expected by devout and ethnic-minded family members to uphold Catholicism's 'no-sex-outside-marriage' rule. Yet, because the circumstances of their lives permitted it, they did not adhere to the hardline letter of Catholic sexual doctrine. By the time I interviewed them, in fact, most had had several consecutive sexual partners, and in this respect they appeared firmly ensconced within secular Canadian society. Whereas they typically described their parents as devout believers—with the no-sex-outside-marriage mantra retaining a powerful hold on their consciousness[4]—they themselves disregarded the moral imperative to save sex for marriage. At the same time, however, these women retained an attachment to Catholic notions of respectability because 'good Catholic girl' conduct offered a range of benefits, including the fact that it pulled them into the core of ethnic membership and helped them to turn precarious sexual liaisons into stable romantic partnerships. Further, despite their anxieties over their daughters' sexual practices, many parents—and especially mothers—became collaborators with their daughters in carving out an alternative to the conventional Catholic ideals that privilege marriage and motherhood.

My analysis of these women's sexual journeys draws on *practice theory*—an approach anchored in culturally oriented sociology that gives attention to how people navigate the various constraints and opportunities in their lives (see Bourdieu 1990; DiMaggio 1997; Ortner 2005; Sewell 1992). Practice theory also focuses on the 'rules' that govern daily life. Applied to women's sexual lives, practice theory enabled me to make sense of what I was seeing in the narratives: that as these women made their transitions to adulthood, they found themselves negotiating between two distinct cultural codes[5] or sets of guidelines for sexual conduct, each of which served as social organizers both at the level of women's personal subjectivity and at the level of everyday social practices. Each had its own set of 'rules' (whether stated or tacit) with respect to how sexuality ought to be expressed, the kinds of sexual practices that confer honour and shame, and the sorts of privileges that people ought to have in the sexual realm. Given that these women were positioned between conflicting social forces—forces favouring religious traditionalism on the one hand and secularization and the sexual revolution on the other—it was not surprising to uncover the existence of these two competing codes. I have designated these as the 'sacred code' and the 'secular code'.

The sacred code is rooted in obedience to Catholic religiosity and represents an elevation of sexuality when it occurs within the sanctified form of marriage. It holds that sex outside marriage is morally wrong. Indeed, because sexual intercourse between spouses is considered a sacred act, unmarried Catholics are admonished to 'avoid occasions of sin'—occasions in which they might be tempted to 'go too far'. Under this code, a person's respectability is heightened through conformity to marriage, and religious authority is expected to prevail over the desires of individuals. According to the logic of the sacred code, parents are not only entitled but also *expected* to regulate their unmarried children's sexuality. The secular code, by contrast, privileges personal freedom and treats sexuality as a matter of individual choice. According to its logic, religious moralism has no place in people's sexual lives, and it is considered inappropriate for parents—indeed anyone at all—to intervene in a person's sexual life. Pleasure is, in effect, the governing principle under the secular code, rather than any notion of morality. The secular code thus disrupts the Catholic world view, and democratizes sexuality by recasting it as something beyond the exclusive preserve of married, heterosexual couples.

As guidelines for sexual conduct, these cultural codes coexisted in an uneasy and ambiguous state of tension. They produced considerable conflict within the women's families and communities of origin—and within the women themselves—over the ground rules for dating, 'how far to go' in their sexual encounters, and the extent to which it was seen as appropriate for parents to interfere in a daughter's romantic pursuits.

Families of Origin: A Dialectic of Constraint and Freedom

The first phase in the transition to adulthood was the period during which these women, as teenage girls, negotiated with their parents over sexual freedom and began to develop a sense of their own sexual subjectivity. Parents played prominent roles as gatekeepers around sexuality, and daughters often fought long and hard with them over curfews, dating ground rules, and their sense of entitlement to regulate their daughters' romantic relationships. Parent/daughter negotiations were thus a contentious and highly charged area of life, in part because the two cultural codes—both very much alive on the cultural terrain—offered opposing sets of guidelines with respect to daughters' sexual conduct.

For one thing, within these families of origin, marriage—especially its consecrated Catholic form—operated as a powerful indicator of ethnocultural belonging, identity, and honour, reinforcing the pressure many of these women felt from their parents to conform to Catholic sexual dictates. The majority described at least one of their parents as devout Catholics whose religious identities were tightly bound up with their sense of duty as good French Canadians.[6] In fact, I found that devout Catholic religiosity, while apparently on the decline, still constitutes a dominant element in the symbolic universe of Franco-Ontarians (see also Boudreau 1995).

Consider the account provided by one of the participants, Céline: 'My hometown [a village close to Sudbury] was very francophone, very homogeneous, very white, and extremely Catholic. I mean, doctors who came to practise there, if they weren't Catholic [and were perhaps willing to perform abortions] then there was always the behind-the-scenes stuff going on to push them out. It was just a highly, highly Catholic area.' (Note that Céline was born in 1979, so this is a recent memory rather than one from many decades ago.)

Blanche, who was born in 1964 and raised in a tiny francophone village close to North Bay, views her family as hermetically sealed off from the secular world by a particularly dogmatic form of Catholicism: 'My parents are very, very Catholic. If 13 kids was what God meant for you to have, you just accepted it, no questions. We'd have containers of Holy Water in every room so every time we entered a room we blessed ourselves. If you walk into their house today, it's got more religious statues than a church.' I also frequently heard words like Cécile's, for whose parents 'finding someone French Canadian was a prerequisite! [I]t was so old-school that [the children were told], "You've gotta find someone French [to marry] and you've gotta find someone Catholic."'

Lynn, whose family settled in Kingston—and whose genealogy has been carefully traced back several generations to Quebec—described her family as preoccupied with ethnic traditions that revolved around the Catholic Church:

> We were really traditional, like we went to church all the time, and, uh, like, Christmas Eve was always the midnight mass and then *le Réveillon* [the traditional French-Canadian Christmas party afterward] and my uncle

was the, like—the father figure, so we'd have it there and then on Christmas Day, we'd go on my Mom's side. And, like, New Year's Day was always at my Aunt Francine's, like it was very specific. And you didn't question it—that was part of the tradition.

It is apparent, then, that religious traditionalism was part of the social landscape and deeply intertwined with anxiety over the preservation of ethnic identity. Yet at the same time, the messages parents delivered were almost always deeply mixed. Only a handful of parents were described as holding fast to a genuinely hardline religious world view, while the majority engaged (albeit some very cautiously) with secular postmodern practices that facilitated their daughters' sexual autonomy. Thus, while a basic distinction held between the generations—with daughters oriented principally, but not exclusively, toward the secular code, and parents oriented principally, but not exclusively, toward the sacred code—this distinction was far from clear-cut. Parents were deeply ambivalent about their daughters' conformity to Catholic sexual ideals. They were especially concerned about the socio-economic vulnerability entailed in women's conformity to the sacred code. This did not mean that parents were not anxious about their daughters becoming sexually active outside of marriage; but it did mean that their hopes that daughters would not end up economically dependent on a man functioned as a trump card. In particular, they viewed their daughters' education as a crucial step to achieving socio-economic independence and the possession of a form of insurance against the insecurity of contemporary married life. Part of this picture was the recognition, on the part of parents and daughters alike, that premarital virginity has lost its 'exchange value' in secular Canadian society—and that, as a result, the traditional sacred code (according to which sexuality is reserved for marriage) has limited social currency. Nearly all of these women therefore received the blessing and encouragement of their families to move away from home. Their parents usually communicated the hope that their daughters would be moderate and restrained in their sexual practices. Along with that, parents hoped that they would avoid the pain of sexual exploitation or the possibility of bringing shame upon themselves or their family members.

This homegrown ambivalence about conventional Catholic gender ideals was expressed particularly by mothers, for whom the dangers associated with sexual freedom—the risk of pregnancy or the probability of committing a mortal sin (the gravest kind for devout Catholics)—seemed to constitute the lesser of possible evils. It was as if the worse evil would be to allow their daughters' lives to be constrained in the ways that their own had been.

Cécile's dilemma offers an illustration of this ambivalence. Born in 1983 to working-class parents in a substantial francophone enclave in Timmins, Cécile left her hometown, with her parents' blessing, and moved to Toronto to attend university. Shortly after arriving in Toronto, she fell (for the first time) deeply in love. But this experience created enormous anxiety for Cécile, who tied her anxiety directly to the fierce brand of sexual 'abstinence' that her mother had taught her four children. According to Cécile's mother, sexual intercourse is a sacred act, and good unmarried Catholics abstain from sexual activity. Her mother also took the liberty of expressing strong disapproval of Cécile's anglophone boyfriend (of atheist upbringing, no less), and had even managed to secure a promise from Cécile never to 'live with' him. Cécile declared unambiguously: 'My dating history? Non-existent. . . . A big reason? My mother. A big reason? Catholicism. Big reason. Um, my mother taught us abstinence, like she believes in, like, you only have sex when you're married. . . . When I visit at [my boyfriend's] place, his parents let us sleep together, it's never an issue.

But when he comes to Timmins, it's like separate beds! Separate floors even!' As a result, Cécile felt confused about how to proceed—about whether she was entitled to make her own decisions about sexuality (that is, free to follow the secular code) or was obliged to feel anxious about the consequences of transgressing the sacred code. She said, for example: 'I ended up telling [my mother when I went on the pill] because I felt that she needed to know. She hates secrets, and I guess it's sort of like I *owe* it to her. She's a big part of my life and we're very, very close, so [I told her] out of respect . . . She's got such a strong hold on my life that I sort of need that clearance.' At the same time, Cécile felt deeply pained—indeed, deeply wronged—by her mother's harsh criticism because, by Toronto standards, she felt herself to be exceedingly restrained in her sexual conduct.

However, Cécile's mother's objections seemed grounded not only in anxiety over her daughter's possible descent into immoral sexual activity but also in her equally profound fear that Cécile would not pursue the many options the wide world made available to her—that she would fail to do something 'more' with her life than become a wife and mother. Cécile was thus receiving mixed messages: she was expected, on one hand, not to transgress the sacrosanct beliefs about premarital chastity that were woven into the fabric of life in her family and community of origin, while being told, on the other hand, to make something of herself in this new world of possibilities for women. 'Women of [my mother's] generation didn't have much chance', Cécile recounted.

> They could be secretaries, teachers, or nurses. And now it's, like, I have *opportunities*. [My mother] always says, '*Broaden* your horizons, *broaden* your horizons.' So that's why she doesn't want me to settle down [too early] and she's worried that I'll end up just serving [my boyfriend], or not doing the things I want to do. . . . She's just worried the same thing will happen to *me* that happened to *her*.

In fact, mothers' efforts to facilitate daughters' opportunities were a resounding theme of the narratives. Marcèle put it this way: 'My mother was hell-bent on making sure [my sisters and I] made something of ourselves. She started university and never finished so it seemed like a sore spot in her life [but] it was also just this super-strong message, like this assumption that us girls should go to university and push to become more than she'd been able to do.' And the words of Marie Pierre were strikingly similar to those expressed by Cécile and Marcèle.

> My Mom would always say, 'It's better to wait till you're married kind of thing but if you really, really can't wait, and, you know, you find someone serious and the whole thing, then we'll go to the doctor and [get a prescription for the birth control pill]. It's better to take precautions than to be, like—well, 'cause stuff happens, right? But, you know, you need to have a good job. You can't depend on a man, you know, and things can happen very quickly. Like if a marriage doesn't work, then you need to move on but, you know, you'll be able to take care of yourself and your kids.' So that was her rationale.

Thus, even while harbouring anxiety about their daughters becoming sexually active, parents—even devout parents—often assisted daughters, with the aim of insulating them from the harshest aspects of conventional marriage and motherhood. This pattern was further reinforced by parents' own compromises with secular postmodernity, which at times gave daughters tacit psychic permission to engage in their own. Some parents got divorced, for instance; others stopped attending mass; still others, through the particular circumstances of their lives, began to engage with feminist ideas or with the gay rights movement.

However, conflicts between these sacred and secular value systems were not only waged between daughters and their parents; they were also waged *internally*, as women described themselves as ambivalently attached to both possible approaches to sexual conduct. In other words, the dialectic of constraint and freedom was operating not only at the level of familial interactions but also at the level of their personal subjectivity. In the course of constructing their own sexual subjectivity, these women worked hard to redefine and update traditional Catholic dictates around sexuality. Though they did not typically encounter ridicule from sexual partners over the loss of their virginity or suffer any real material penalties on that account, and though virginity *per se* was not experienced as a sacred or a deeply meaningful boundary, they were nevertheless aware of a culturally pervasive distinction between 'good' and 'bad' girls.

Lillian told me, 'there were about eight of us who were fairly outgoing girls [in high school], we all dated a lot of guys, you know, we were active in the school—like, popular girls—and we were all *virgins*.' She went on to explain that while other girls in the school would 'sleep around' and 'tell about their little escapades', she and her clique of virgin friends would never sleep with a guy outside the context of a committed relationship. In fact, these women were often explicit about the measures they took to ensure that they never fell into the category of the 'slut' or the 'high-school tramp'. Rachèle recalled her earliest experience with dating:

> When I first dated someone in Grade 12, I'd never kissed anyone before, I'd never done *anything* [sexual]. I feel so bad looking back because that must have sucked, three or four months being with this, like, totally prudish girl who, like—I, like, made him wait a month, like, just to *kiss* me! 'Cause I was just so nervous about everything. . . . I probably was just having, like, conflict between [pause]—like, I wanted to be, like, a *good* girl.

Being 'good' was also described as having less to do with whether a girl was *actually* a virgin than with whether she *acted* like a 'good girl'—that is, displayed virginal conduct. During the data analysis, I struggled to make sense of a pattern of conduct that I came to designate as 'symbolic abstinence'.[7] Symbolic abstinence entails disingenuous displays intended to create the illusion of sexual purity, modesty, and restraint. As a strategy, symbolic abstinence worked to blunt the harsh discrepancies between the (unrealistic) Catholic ideal of premarital chastity and the reality of their lives (i.e., that women these days are sexually active outside of marriage). Interestingly, receiving Holy Communion was an opportunity to practise symbolic abstinence. Because Catholic doctrine requires both premarital chastity and abstention from receiving Holy Communion while in a 'state of sin', a number of women explained, receiving Holy Communion is the equivalent of a public statement about sexual purity. Lillian, for example, described making a point of attending mass and receiving Holy Communion when she and her boyfriend (who is also Catholic and half French Canadian) would visit their families. This served to ease family tension by giving the impression that she and her boyfriend weren't actually sleeping together. It also allowed her to maintain a 'good-girl' form of sexual subjectivity. Thus, haunted by the prospect of being perceived as a 'bad girl', Lillian played on the religious meanings that Holy Communion had for her family members.

Practising symbolic abstinence—deliberately cultivating a posture of sexual innocence—also enabled these women to construct themselves as 'good girls' by conceptualizing their own sexual practices as comparatively restrained and well inside the boundaries of today's 'good-girl' standards. They also rationalized their sexual activity by noting that their parents (and grandparents) had been held to comparatively stricter standards. As well, in family contexts where heightened attention was given to daughters' sexual purity, appearing to be good served to pull these young women into the core of ethnic and familial membership. Retaining a sense of belonging—a sense of being in the 'good graces' of one's family—was a seductive and not insignificant by-product of conformity (even if only ostensible) to the script of the 'good Catholic girl'. As a strategy, then, symbolic abstinence allowed these women to have similar sorts of sexual experiences as their Canadian sisters while simultaneously allowing them to maintain 'good-girl' standing—both within their families and within themselves.

Leaving Home for the Big City: Broadening the Parameters of 'Good-girl' Conduct

During the leaving-home phase, a range of new circumstances had the effect of broadening the parameters of women's sexual options. It is true that parent–daughter conflict over daughters' sexual conduct tended to carry on long after most daughters had left home. Even from a distance, parents were described as keeping vigilant eyes on their daughters, and often gravely expressing the hope that they would never 'play house' or 'live in sin'. For instance, when a daughter's boyfriend visited over Christmas, parents routinely insisted on separate sleeping quarters. Daughters typically experienced this as an embarrassing and frustrating imposition on their freedom. And a daughter's decision to cohabit usually represented an occasion for family discord, as did decisions favouring a civil over a Catholic Church wedding. Cécile's father threatened, 'Weddings are supposed to take place in a *church*—if you get married at City Hall, we won't come!' When Blanche first left her francophone village in the mid-1980s to find work in Toronto, she was faced with many 'surprise visits' from her father. A true French-Canadian patriarch, he was thoroughly shaken when she left as he was convinced that her real reason for moving to Toronto was to become a prostitute. For Blanche, asserting her right to personal freedom was a mighty struggle as her father sought to assert his own self-perceived rights—grounded, as they were, in a firm sense of entitlement to impose the rules of the sacred code. She told me:

> When I [first left home], my Dad's thinking was that, until I got married, he was the primary male in my life and when he entered my home, he became the boss. And I had to tell him, 'No, my home doesn't have a *king* right now, but it has a *queen* and she pays the rent. So *she's* the boss.' And I remember I was just shaking in my boots when I said that.

And so, in Blanche's case (as in many others), fledgling economic autonomy gave her a sense of entitlement to lead her life as she saw fit. This is a prime example of the many new circumstances that had the effect of expanding the parameters of women's sexual conduct. The main point here is that, in light of these new circumstances, parents' wishes tended to recede into the background. Occasionally, too, parents and other tradition-minded family members offered surprising gestures of accommodation to secular postmodern realities, expressing a resigned acceptance of the fact that the 'rules of the game' have changed for the younger generation.

So what were the other new circumstances? For one thing, Toronto exhibited a secular climate in which traditional forms of religious authority simply lacked credibility. It also fostered a climate in which it was taken for granted that people will be sexually active outside the context of marriage. In turn, Toronto's cosmopolitan setting seemed to nurture in these women a deep disenchantment with Catholic dictates. Cécile, for example, characterized the Catholic rulebook as arbitrary, artificial, and outmoded, as something thrust upon [her] by her schoolteachers and parents—in other words, as a code for which she had no genuine cognitive foundation. She told me:

> Myself, I don't feel comfortable in church. I'm really against any form of organized religion. . . . This one time I was visiting Montreal and I went into this church and took a bunch of pictures . . . When I was inside I was thinking about my mother and I felt compelled, I just, you know, lit a candle for her. So when I was showing her the pictures I told my mother, 'You know, I lit a candle for you in this church.' And she started *crying*! And she was like, 'Ohhh, Cécile, you *do* have faith!' And I was, like, '*Whoa!* This is really powerful stuff.' Like for *her*, but not for *me*.

And so, when push came to shove, big-city life encouraged in these women a profound feeling of entitlement to place their sense of personal authority ahead of parental and religious dictates. City life nurtured their sense of entitlement to 'find their own way'—to carve out lives of their own. Drawing on a range of influences, from feminism to their experiences of multicultural and ethno-religious diversity (including their observation that many Canadians today espouse no religious affiliation at all), they explained that Catholic beliefs gradually lost their meaning. Institutional Catholicism was also widely and uncharitably characterized as corrupt and morally vacuous. Blanche expressed it this way: 'No, I'm not going to follow what I've been told my entire life. Like, "You must do this and you must follow this path and you must follow that." No, you do what feels good for you, which is how I live my life.' Danièle was perhaps the most clear of all: 'Do I share any of the political stands of the Catholic Church? Absolutely not. Do I share their viewpoint about marriage? No. Do I share their viewpoint about women? No. Do I share how they act in the Third World? No. Do I believe any of the crap that comes out of the mouth of the Pope? No.'

On this front, consider Monique's story. The daughter of 'old-fashioned' parents who were born in Quebec during the late 1930s and who migrated to St Catharines during the 1950s, Monique is haunted by a mixture of pride and resentment, the former for her Québécois roots, the latter over her parents' efforts to instill Catholic values in their four daughters. As the youngest, Monique adopted a co-operative, dutiful-daughter role that did not, however, translate into blind conformity to Catholic precepts. Rather, she expressed contempt toward the dogmatic and non-negotiable nature of her parents' imposition on her of the same religious standards to which they held themselves. This violated her sense of personal freedom. While she certainly desired to become a wife and mother, doing so did not require, in her estimation, the 'blessing' of a religious institution that presumed to impose on her morally. Monique chose to have a decidedly secular wedding ceremony and her message to her parents seemed to be: 'The choice is *mine*; I'm not obliged to conform to your demands.' Like many of the women, Monique felt it was inappropriate, even undignified, for her parents to attempt to dictate their wishes, highlighting the extent to which personal authority has eclipsed traditional forms of authority. The sheer weight—one might even say hegemony—of socio-cultural ideas about personal freedom (along with the perceived irrelevance of religious authority) gave these women a powerful psychic licence to contravene the tenets of the sacred code. The message was, in effect, 'If others are not obliged to obey religious dictates, why should I be?'

Contrasting experiences of small-town and big-city life were also striking, and figured prominently in women's accounts of the leaving-home phase. Because Toronto seemed to place virtually no constraints on these women becoming sexually active outside of marriage, it provided a form of escape and refuge from the constricting worlds in which they'd been raised. They described taking delicious pleasure in being able to have sexual experiences without fear of reprisals, scrutiny, or surveillance. Where the small-town, face-to-face structure of hometown life had virtually ensured that others would know their business, they revelled in the covert opportunities afforded by city life—such as life in unmonitored university residences or in private rental accommodations—to date and 'try things out' without having to worry about the potential damage to family honour or the consternation of family members anxious about the perils of urban living. Euphrosine described it this way: 'Once I got to university it was, like, woo-hoo! Freedom! People! And I'm not related to any of them!' In describing the contrast between life in her hometown and life in Toronto, Cécile relayed that in Timmins she was 'reserved' and 'prudish' but that by living in Toronto she has begun to feel freer to express herself. 'Physically, I wore baggy clothes. I'm very reserved, very prudish like that, like I'm not going to wear like a tight sweater or whatever, like show off my boobs . . . But I've gotten a little more girly now, like a little more girly clothes and I feel a bit more confident with that, so—like I can wear . . . clothes that I never would have worn in high school. . . . I have a bit more courage [in Toronto].'

For many, in fact, the 'narrow-mindedness' of hometown culture had been a strong motivation for leaving. Blanche put it bluntly: 'I had to leave [home], for my mental sanity. I had to go. [There's] a narrow-mindedness there and they were trying to push it on you and any growth or change that you were trying to express was snuffed right out.' Gena's queer/bisexual orientation, in conjunction with her clear desire to stretch beyond the confines of small-town life, made her decision to leave Welland an easy one. She told me, 'I've moved into a big city but all my cousins are still [in Welland] and they've gotten married and the narrow-mindedness continues! Which is shocking! So amongst my cousins . . . I'm sort of the outsider.' Gena has anchored a sense of belonging within Toronto's queer community—a community that to some extent has served as a substitute for her family and community of origin. In Gena's case (as in a handful of others), city life was especially attractive because it supported practices that deviated sharply from a conventional script. As for Danièle, the transition out of a narrow small-town mentality toward a secular postmodern world view as a gradual one: 'The process was gradual . . . I just found that university meant I was confronted with a whole bunch of cultural diversity and differences in world views than I'd had when I was growing up. My upbringing was white, middle-class Ottawa, mostly Catholic and very narrow. . . . And also, I was training in journalism so I just had to step outside that narrow world view.'

Educational and professional opportunities—opportunities to become economically self-sufficient—also encouraged these women to apply 'new metrics' (González-López 2005) in their sexual relationships. Such alternative 'metrics' entailed evaluating sexuality in terms of pleasure and self-expression rather than in terms of what seemed an outmoded contractual arrangement in which women avoid exploitation by securing a man's commitment and economic support. This rationale was most clearly expressed by those on a professional track—Rachèle and Mélodie as medical students, Danièle as a journalist, Marcèle as a high-school teacher, to give a few examples—and was based in the fact that a professional career trajectory insulates women from the economic vulnerabilities associated with conventional wife and mother roles.

For example, Rachèle's decision to live with her boyfriend was predicated in part on the fact that she is going through medical school. And while her tradition-minded parents raised her never to 'live in sin', they also gradually came to see that by living with her fiancé Rachèle was not being sexually exploited; they came to discover that a woman living with a man could be commensurate with respectability. 'It's probably not their ideal situation where I'm living with my [fiancé] but I think, on the other side of the coin, if I said, "Mom, Dad, I'm 22 and I'm going to get married", right? I think they'd be equally be like, "Oh, well, what's the rush?"' And so, despite Rachèle's knowledge that she is, technically speaking, violating the code that, in a basic way, her parents still deeply cherish, she can nevertheless rest assured that her parents 'totally respect' her choices.

But, for some of these women, veering too far from a sacred traditional path amounted to alienation from the core of familial membership. Marcèle confessed to feeling humiliated and excluded within her family because of the 'string of bad boyfriends' she'd had during her early adult years. She recalled: 'When I was 20 I brought my first boyfriend home to meet the family. My grandmother found him totally charming and she just assumed we'd be getting married, like she talked about [it with] all my relatives [as if] we were engaged. . . . So after I broke up with that boyfriend, and all the boyfriends after that, I felt so ashamed about my love life that I just avoided her. . . . I know she's really disappointed in me.' Blanche's path is the best illustration of how an unconventional path can translate into a sense of alienation from the core of familial membership. By the time we met, Blanche was in her early forties and, although she had had several long-term relationships, she had never married; she was in fact the only unmarried adult child among her parents' brood of 13. As a result, her path to adulthood has been fraught with a sense of exile from her family; her parents accuse her of having brought all her personal troubles upon herself because she left the Catholic Church. 'For them it all comes back to, "Well, if she went to *church* this wouldn't have happened!" Like, according to them, if I went to church I would fit in their box.' Taking a secular path and resisting conventional forms of womanhood has thus for Blanche exacted some hefty emotional costs, rendering relations with her family members threatening to her sense of well-being.

As for these women's *internal* deliberations over sexual conduct during this leaving-home phase, not being devout Catholic believers did not render them automatically immune to 'Catholic guilt' or a nagging sense that it was 'slutty' to be involved in casual (i.e., uncommitted) sexual relationships. In Monique's case, despite her feminist leanings (she had taken a couple of women's studies courses in university) and defiant stance against Catholicism, she felt deeply inhibited during her first years as a sexually active adult. She struggled with indecision and then guilt when she slept with a man she barely knew and had no intention of being with long-term. And Lillian's deliberations over whether, when and with whom to lose her virginity involved carefully weighing the meaning of sexuality in light of both sacred and secular value systems. She concluded (as did many others) that an approach to sexuality that was too liberal cheapens the gift of a woman's sexuality:

> I was 20 [when I lost my virginity and afterward] I thought, 'Okay, [having sex] is not as big of a deal as I thought it was, but it's also not—like, it's worth more than just [pause] sleeping around.' . . . One of the things about [my university] was that there was a lot of sleeping around. And I realized I could get caught up in that and I didn't want to. I had to restrain myself to wait that long—like I was a partier, I partied a lot, stayed out late,

smoked up, did whatever, hung out with all these different guys, and the desire to go beyond, like, just kissing was there. But I didn't. And then when I gave in, I wished I hadn't. Like [the guy] was casual—like most guys in university, and girls for that matter, he was just looking to have fun, not looking for anything beyond the end of the night.

Settling in: Returning to the Sacred Code

Questions about how to evaluate sexuality pervaded the third and final phase, the 'settling in'—shorthand for the period in which these women established themselves as full-fledged autonomous adults. In women's descriptions of this phase, an interesting pattern emerged. On the one hand, as already stated, these women relished the ways in which city life freed them from parental surveillance; they celebrated the opportunities that education and good paid work afforded them; they resented any imposition of rigid Catholic sexual dictates; and in all of these things they voiced a sense of unease about applying harsh moral/religious judgment in the realm of sexuality. But, on the other hand, because life in Toronto was frequently experienced as cold, lonely, and isolating—especially during periods of prolonged singleness—they began to rethink the Catholic messages they might once have been eager to reject. In particular, Toronto's culture of casual sex—sexual encounters guided by a no-strings-attached logic—frustrated their efforts to turn precarious sexual liaisons into stable romantic partnerships. In short, these women sought ways to creatively resist a newer and more secular brand of patriarchal privilege: men's sense of entitlement to obligation-free sexual access.

And so, in this settling-in phase, they tended to return to the sacred code that had operated within their families of origin as a way of negotiating better deals with their sexual partners. While these Toronto-based women seemed decidedly ensconced in an urban, secular milieu, the contours of their personal value structures manifested a lingering attachment to gendered Catholic messages. Even when they explicitly rejected *official* Catholic sexual doctrine, they nevertheless dug into a deeply gendered reservoir of Catholic messages that in turn provided some sort of foundation for interpreting their sexual experiences. Certainly there was diversity with respect to the extent to which (or how deeply) these women returned to the sacred code. Seven of the 33 women remained fairly strongly attached to a devout form of Catholic religiosity that elevates married, monogamous sexuality above less committed, less socially respectable forms of sexual expression. They were of the opinion that women deserve the sort of reverence and respect from their sexual partners that a sanctified marriage confers. Yet these seven were at the same time also drawn toward secular postmodern values and not immune from ambivalence about institutional Catholicism. The remaining women—26 of the 33—distanced themselves from devout Catholic religiosity, but nevertheless felt drawn to select features of the sacred code.[8] For example, the vast majority were attracted to the prospect of being in an unconditionally loving sexual relationship and to experiencing forms of belonging and honour that often accompany long-term and deeply committed sexual unions. And so they tapped into the sacred code as a package of traditionally gendered expectations to bolster their bargaining power. 'Because sexuality is *somehow* sacred', they seemed to be saying, 'I'm *entitled* to monogamy and lifelong commitment.'

For instance, Cécile told me: 'The whole *moral* aspect of [sexuality], like I just, the whole thing about sex is very important, like there has to be *love* involved. I still, like, I think it's the Catholicism issue, like [casual sex] just makes no sense to me. It would be a violation. It's so like that with Catholicism, it's so embedded in your brain.' Lucie said: 'When I was dating, my strategy was to say, "My body is my temple, and not just anybody is going to sleep with me." I had this way of testing guys to see if they were going to stick around. I'd say, "Can you wait three months [to have sex with me]?" So a lot of guys fell by the wayside.' Hélène was unequivocal in her view that men who are unwilling to commit are communicating profound disrespect for women. She recounted one failed relationship this way: 'I've realized that [my ex-boyfriend] is the worst person I've ever met. Like, I've never met anyone in my life who's treated me with such disrespect. . . . He knew where I stood on relationships, that I'm a very passionate person, and that, you know, you're white or you're black, there's no walking on the grey line.' Chantal recalled with a sense of anguish the fact that a liberalized sexual culture compromised her ability to say no to sexual intercourse within her teenage dating relationships. She recalled: 'I never had the strength to say, like, "If you go out with me, we won't do that.". . . There was no negotiation or no asking. . . . It's a very sore spot in my whole life—I was pleasing the *guy*, I wasn't pleasing *myself*.' And Anique recounted the utter devastation she felt when she discovered that her brother was having an affair.

> When my brother left his wife—and he was having an affair and was even doing it while his wife was pregnant!—that shook my whole idea of what men are. I used to idolize my brother [and] now he's cheated on his wife and she's pregnant and he doesn't love her any more and he's started this whole sordid [affair]. So it's like, does this mean the man I'm gonna marry will just get tired of me and move on to some other chick?

These narrative excerpts point to a lingering nostalgia for Catholic traditionalism that is bound up with women's desire for stable and secure romantic unions.

Conforming to the sacred code (even if only in partial ways) had other benefits too. It also served to pull these women closer to the core of ethnic and familial membership. This became clear in several accounts of the settling-in phase, where a surprising dynamic was at play among tradition-minded parents who nonetheless engaged with the new secular realities and respected their daughters' sexual autonomy. In those cases, daughters were often willing to give their parents the gift of conformity to Catholic precepts. For example, Rachèle's parents are traditional but nonetheless careful to respect their daughter's autonomy. Rachèle was planning to have a Catholic wedding in her hometown parish, despite the fact that neither she nor her fiancé are practising Catholics. She described the rigamarole of a Catholic Church wedding as a small price to pay for the joy it would bring to her parents—whom she described as deeply anxious about the demise of their beloved French-Canadian culture. So Rachèle seemed to be rewarding her parents for the fact that they never actively interfered in her personal life, and this dynamic shows how conventional gender ideals can be reproduced for surprising, even counterintuitive, reasons. It is perhaps also the case that Rachèle's desire for a Catholic wedding reflects her desire for belonging, both to their families of origin and to the families of their imagined futures—a feeling that was described as a powerful and seductive force in the lives of many of these women.

Conclusion

These descriptions of women's lived experiences of sexuality help to concretize the claim that sexuality is a complicated domain of daily life. The accounts provided by these French-Canadian women invite us to be attuned to the subtleties and contradictions at play on the sexual terrain. Through its use of an 'intersectional lens', this study also sheds light on many of the entangled forces—including gender, ethnicity, religion, and locale—that shape contemporary women's sexual journeys.

More specifically, I have argued that these women are ambivalently positioned between 'secular' and 'sacred' approaches to sexual conduct—and that, as a result, they selectively evaluate their sexual practices through both secular and sacred meaning systems. Certainly, on the 'secular' side of things, they have discarded the harsh and judgmental elements of Catholic religiosity (e.g., the belief that sex outside marriage is a mortal sin) and they are ill at ease with the prospect of moral/religious judgment being imposed upon their sexual lives. Indeed, their experiences mirror today's secular postmodern realities since nearly all of them have had several consecutive sexual partners outside (or prior to) marriage. They also see themselves as their own authorities on sexual matters and resent the imposition of parental or religious dictates. Furthermore, educational and professional opportunities (frequently enabled by their parents) insulate them from the prospect of economic dependency within marriage and encourage them to think about sexual exchange more in terms of pleasure, companionship, and self-expression than in terms of an outmoded sex-for-economic-security bargain.

At the same time, however, I have shown that these women are ill at ease with Toronto's climate of casual sex, a climate that diminishes women's bargaining power and frustrates their desire for durable sexual unions. In turn, these women tend to express a nostalgic attachment to Catholic notions about the sanctity and respectability of sexuality—notions that work to offset the cheapening effects of a liberalized sexual climate and nurture their sense of entitlement to long-lasting sexual/romantic partnerships. I have also argued that because Catholic religiosity still constitutes a dominant element in Franco-Ontarian life, religion mediates these women's experiences of sexuality; even partial conformity to the 'good Catholic girl' script rewards these women by securing their place at the core of ethnic and familial membership. The preceding analysis lends weight to the claim that we need to complicate prevailing images of today's unfettered, sexually liberated women, since the conflicting forces of secularization and the sexual revolution, on the one hand, and religious traditionalism, on the other, are, for these women at least, very much alive on the social landscape.

Notes

1. I am very grateful to Bonnie Fox, Judy Taylor, Diana Worts, Simeon Alev, Russell Field, and Derek Brown for comments on earlier versions of this paper.
2. I use 'French Canadian' here to capture not only those who identified as 'Franco-Ontarians' (a modernized ethno-nationalist label that came into use among many francophone Ontarians during the 1970s) but also those who identified in a more traditional sense as members (or descendents) of the 'French-Canadian nation'. For the purposes of this chapter, I use the terms somewhat interchangeably.
3. There was of course diversity in the participants' experiences of traditional French-Canadian life. Participants raised in ethnically embedded small-town settings within Ontario experienced its most extreme forms, while participants raised in large urban centres or in close proximity to the culture of post-Quiet Revolution Quebec (where language has eclipsed religion as the pivotal indicator of ethnic identity) experienced less traditional forms of French-Canadian life. My focus in this paper is mainly on the women (about two-thirds of the sample) who were raised within these tradition-bound small-town settings.

4. It is worth mentioning, though, that in sharp contrast to devout parents who upheld the sacred code, a handful of parents were described as having wholeheartedly secular views about sexuality—cherishing absolutely no expectations or illusions about their daughters' premarital chastity. These parents privileged a secular—even permissive, in some cases—approach to sexuality, and their daughters felt comparatively free to pursue sexual relationships outside the confines of marriage. For these parents, Catholic morality seems not to provide a meaningful template for evaluating sexual conduct.
5. My use of the term 'cultural code' is shorthand for 'semiotic code'—that is, a set of relationally defined meanings. By way of illustration, consider the practice of giving gifts at Christmas. In spite of the fact that middle-class Americans consider gift-giving to be a burdensome waste of time and money, they nevertheless persist in it because it constitutes a semiotic code in which the value of the gift signals the relative importance the giver holds for the recipient (Swidler 1995: 33, citing Caplow 1984). What governs action in this case is people's knowledge of the meanings their actions have for others. My analysis of the social relations of sexuality is developed in these terms—that religious and secular meaning systems constitute distinct semiotic codes.
6. This pattern contrasts with Quebecers' decidedly post-Catholic approach to sexuality since they more or less reject the traditional template regarding the sanctity of married sexuality. This is not to say, however, that all of these Ontario-based French-Canadian parents were described as devout Catholics. Two general patterns were significant: first, a family's connections to the liberalized culture of post-1960/Quiet Revolution Quebec had a corresponding liberalizing influence in the domain of sexuality; and second, competence in French allowed family members to anchor their sense of ethnic identity in language rather than religion (much as Quebecers have done in the post-1960 period). For anglicized French Canadians, then, Catholic religiosity, rather than language, is more likely to serve as a basis for ethnic identity.
7. As I developed this concept, I benefited from Sally Gallagher and Christian Smith's (1999) analysis of 'symbolic traditionalism' and 'pragmatic egalitarianism' among a sample of evangelical Christians in the United States.
8. For these 26 women, then, conformity (such as it was) to the sacred code was always partial and much more a reflection of the fact that it occasionally bolstered their bargaining power than their authentic devotion to Catholic dictates.

References

Anderson, Benedict. 1992. 'The New World Disorder', *New Left Review* I/193: 1–13.

Bellah, Robert N., et al. 1985/1996. *Habits of the Heart: Individualism and Commitment in American Life* (Berkeley: University of California Press).

Boudreau, Françoise. 1995. 'La francophonie ontarienne au passe, au présent et au futur: Un Bilan sociologie', in *La francophonie ontarienne: Bilan et perspectives de recherche*, eds Jacques Cotnam, Yves Frenette, and Agnès Whitfield (Hearst, ON: Les Éditions du Nordir).

Bourdieu, Pierre. 1990. *The Logic of Practice* (Cambridge: Polity Press).

DiMaggio, Paul. 1997. 'Culture and Cognition', *Annual Review of Sociology* 23: 263–87.

Espiritu, Yen Le. 2001. '"We Don't Sleep around Like White Girls Do": Family, Culture, and Gender', in 'Filipina American Lives', *Signs: Journal of Women in Culture and Society* 26: 415–40.

Foucault, Michel. 1976. *The History of Sexuality*, Vol. I (New York: Random House).

Gallagher, Sally K., and Christian Smith. 1999. 'Symbolic Traditionalism and Pragmatic Egalitarianism: Contemporary Evangelicals, Families, and Gender', *Gender & Society* 13: 211–33.

Gamson, Joshua, and Dawne Moon. 2004. 'The Sociology of Sexualities: Queer and beyond', *Annual Review of Sociology* 30: 47–64.

González-López, Gloria. 2005. *Erotic Journeys: Mexican Immigrants and Their Sex Lives* (Berkeley: University of California Press).

Greeley, Andrew. 2004. *The Catholic Revolution* (Berkeley: University of California Press).

Heller, Monica, and Normand Labrie, eds. 2004. *Discours et identités: La francité canadienne entre modernité et mondialisation* (Bruxelles, Belgium: Éditions Modulaires Européennes).

Ingraham, Chrys. 1999. *White Weddings: Romancing Heterosexuality in Popular Culture* (New York: Routledge).

Isajiw, Wsevolod W. 1999. *Understanding Diversity: Ethnicity and Race in the Canadian Context* (Toronto: Thompson Educational).

Maglin, Nan Bauer, and Donna Perry, eds. 1996. *"Bad Girls"/"Good Girls": Women, Sex, and Power in the Nineties* (New Brunswick, NJ: Rutgers University Press).

Ortner, Sherry B. 2005. 'Subjectivity and Cultural Critique', *Anthropological Theory* 5: 31–52.

Sangster, Joan. 1996. 'Incarcerating "Bad Girls": The Regulation of Sexuality through the Female Refuges Act in Ontario, 1920–1945', *Journal of the History of Sexuality* 7: 239–75.

Sewell, William. 1992. 'A Theory of Structure: Duality, Agency, and Transformation', *American Journal of Sociology* 98: 1–29.

Stacey Judith. 2002. 'Gay and Lesbian Families Are Here', in *Sexuality and Gender*, eds Christine L. Williams and Arlene Stein (Malden, MA: Blackwell).

Stasilius, Daiva. 1999. 'Feminist Intersectional Theorizing', in *Ethnic Relations in Canada*, ed. Peter Li (Toronto: Oxford University Press).

Swidler, Ann. 1995. 'Cultural Power and Social Movements', in *Social Movements and Culture*, eds Hank Johnston and Bert Klandermans (Minneapolis: University of Minnesota Press).

Tanenbaum, Leora. 1999. *Slut! Growing up Female with a Bad Reputation* (New York: Seven Stories Press).

Vance, Carole S. 1984. 'Pleasure and Danger: Toward a Politics of Sexuality', in *Pleasure and Danger: Exploring Female Sexuality*, ed. Carole S. Vance (Boston: Routledge & Kegan Paul).

Yuval-Davis, Nira, and Floya Anthias, eds. 1989. *Women, Nation, State* (London: Macmillan).

Wu, Zheng. 2000. *Cohabitation* (Toronto: Oxford University Press).

Chapter 15

Apparently, readers of personal advice columns in women's magazines frequently want to know if they are 'normal' with respect to their sexual practices and experiences. Because our sexuality is private and personal, popular ideas and discourses about sexuality likely have a very powerful impact on us—especially because in this culture our sexuality is considered to be central to our identity. In this provocative piece, Chrys Ingraham argues that heterosexuality is an 'institution' that underlies gender and gender inequality.

One Is Not Born a Bride: How Weddings Regulate Heterosexuality

Chrys Ingraham

All aspects of our social world—natural or otherwise—are given meaning. Culture installs meaning in our lives from the very first moment we enter the social world. Our sexual orientation or sexual identity—or even the notion that there is such a thing—is defined by the symbolic order of that world through the use of verbal as well as non-verbal language and images. Heterosexuality as a *social* category is much more than the fact of one's sexual or affectional attractions. What we think of when we talk about heterosexuality or refer to ourselves as heterosexual is a product of a society's meaning-making processes. In reality, heterosexuality operates as a highly organized social institution that varies across nations, social groups, culture, history, region, religion, ethnicity, nationality, race, lifespan, social class, and ability. In America and elsewhere, the wedding ritual represents a major site for the installation and maintenance of the institution of heterosexuality.

The title of this chapter pays homage to French feminist Monique Wittig whose classic and provocative essay 'One Is Not Born a Woman' examines what she calls the political regime of heterosexuality and its requisite categories of man and woman. She argues that the category of woman and all of the meaning attached to that category would not exist were it not necessary for the political regime of (patriarchal) heterosexuality. For the purpose of this chapter, the same holds true of the taken-for-granted category of bride. While it may seem obvious to most that one is not born a bride, in reality many women see themselves as following a naturalized path toward heterosexual womanhood.

But how did this contrived and constructed social practice become naturalized? The task of examining this taken-for-granted social arrangement requires a conceptual framework capable of revealing how heterosexuality has become institutionalized, naturalized, and normalized. Any attempt to examine the institution of heterosexuality requires a theory capable of understanding how this institution with all its social practices, such as dating, proms, and Valentine's Day, is often viewed by many of us as natural.

The Heterosexual Imaginary

French psychoanalyst Jacques Lacan's concept of the 'imaginary' is especially useful for this purpose. According to Lacan, the imaginary is the unmediated contact an infant has to its own image and its connection with its mother. Instead of facing a complicated, conflictual, and contradictory world, the infant experiences the illusion of tranquility, plenitude, and fullness. In other words, infants experience a sense of oneness with their primary caretaker. Louis Althusser, the French philosopher, borrowed Lacan's notion of the imagery for his neo-Marxist theory of ideology, defining ideology as 'the imaginary relationship of individuals to their real conditions of existence'. The 'imaginary' here does not mean 'false' or 'pretend' but, rather, an imagined or illusory relationship between an individual and their social world. Applied to a social theory of heterosexuality, the *heterosexual imaginary* is that way of thinking that relies on romantic and sacred notions of heterosexuality in order to create and maintain the illusion of well-being and oneness. This romantic view prevents us from seeing how institutionalized heterosexuality actually works to organize gender while preserving racial, class, and sexual hierarchies. The effect of this illusory depiction of reality is that heterosexuality is taken for granted and unquestioned, while gender is understood as something people are socialized into or learn. The heterosexual imaginary naturalizes male to female social relations, rituals, and organized practices and conceals the operation of heterosexuality in structuring gender across race, class, and sexuality. This way of seeing closes off any critical analysis of heterosexuality as an organizing institution and for the ends it serves (Ingraham 1994; 1999). By leaving heterosexuality unexamined as an institution we do not explore how it is learned, how it may control us and contribute to social inequalities. Through the use of the heterosexual imaginary, we hold up the institution of heterosexuality as fixed in time as though it has always operated the same as it does today. This imaginary presents a view of heterosexuality as 'just the way it is' while creating obligatory social practices that reinforce the illusion that, as long as one complies with this naturalized structure, all will be right in the world. This illusion is commonly known as romance. Romancing heterosexuality is creating an illusory heterosexuality for which wedding culture plays a central role.

The lived reality of institutionalized heterosexuality is, however, not typically tranquil or safe. The consequences the heterosexual imaginary produces include, for example, marital rape, domestic violence, pay inequities, racism, gay bashing, femicide, and sexual harassment. Institutionalized heterosexuality and its organizing ideology—the heterosexual imaginary—establishes those behaviours we ascribe to men and women—gender—while keeping in place or producing a history of contradictory and unequal social relations. The production of a division of labour that results in unpaid domestic work, inequalities of pay and opportunity, or the privileging of married couples in the dissemination of insurance benefits, are examples of this.

Above all, the heterosexual imaginary naturalizes the regulation of sexuality through the institution of marriage, ritual practices such as weddings, and state domestic relations laws. These laws, among others, set the terms for taxation, health care, and housing benefits on the basis of marital status. Rarely challenged—except by nineteenth-century marriage reformers and early second-wave feminists—laws and public- and private-sector policies use marriage as the primary requirement for social and economic benefits and access rather than distributing resources on some other basis such as citizenship or ability to breathe, for example. Heterosexuality is much more than a biological given or whether or not someone is attracted to someone of another sex. Rules on everything from who pays for the date or wedding rehearsal dinner to who leads while dancing, drives the car, cooks dinner, or initiates sex, all serve to regulate heterosexual practice. What circulates as a given in Western societies is, in fact, a highly structured arrangement. As is the case with most institutions, people who participate in these practices must be socialized to do so. In other words, women were not born with a wedding gown gene or a neo-natal craving for a diamond engagement ring! They were taught to want these things. Women didn't enter the world with a desire to practise something called dating or a desire to play with a 'My Size Bride Barbie'; they were rewarded for desiring these things. Likewise, men did not exit the womb knowing they would one day buy a date a bunch of flowers or spend two months income to buy an engagement ring. These are all products that have been sold to consumers interested in taking part in a culturally established ritual that works to organize and institutionalize heterosexuality and reward those who participate.

Heteronormativity

A related concept useful for the study of the heterosexual imaginary and of institutionalized heterosexuality is heteronormativity. This is the view that institutionalized heterosexuality constitutes the standard for legitimate and expected social and sexual relations. Heteronormativity represents one of the main premises underlying the heterosexual imaginary, again ensuring that the organization of heterosexuality in everything from gender to weddings to marital status is held up both as a model and as 'normal'. Consider, for instance, the ways many surveys or intake questionnaires ask respondents to check off their marital status as either married, divorced, separated, widowed, single, or, in some cases, never married. Not only are these categories presented as significant indices of social identity, they are offered as the only options, implying that the organization of identity in relation to marriage is universal and not in need of explanation. Or try to imagine entering a committed relationship without benefit of legalized marriage. We find it difficult to think that we can share commitment with someone without a state-sponsored licence. People will frequently comment that someone is afraid to 'make a commitment' if they choose not to get married even when they have been in a relationship with someone for years! Our ability to imagine possibilities or to understand what counts as commitment is itself impaired by heteronormative assumptions. We even find ourselves challenged to consider how to marry without an elaborate white wedding. Gays and lesbians have maintained long-term committed relationships yet find themselves desiring state sanctioning of their union in order to feel legitimate. Heteronormativity works in all of these instances to naturalize the institution of heterosexuality while rendering real people's relationships and commitments irrelevant and illegitimate.

For those who view questions concerning marital status as benign, one need only consider the social and economic consequences for those who do not participate in these arrangements or the cross-cultural variations that are at odds with some of the Anglocentric or Eurocentric assumptions regarding marriage. All people are required to situate themselves in relation to marriage or heterosexuality, including those who *regardless of sexual (or asexual) affiliation* do not consider themselves 'single', heterosexual, or who do not participate in normative heterosexuality and its structures.

One is not born a bride, and yet to imagine oneself outside of this category is to live a life outside of the boundaries of normality and social convention. To live outside the contrived and constructed social practice is to live on the margins of society, excluded from the social, legal, and economic rewards and benefits participation brings. To resist membership in the heteronormative social order—as bride or as groom—is to live with the penalties and challenges to all those who resist. It means living a life where you have to defend your sexual loyalties on a daily basis—are you straight or are you gay?

Weddings

To demonstrate the degree to which the heteronormative wedding ritual regulates sexuality we must begin with an investigation into the ways various practices, arrangements, relations, and rituals standardize and conceal the operation of institutionalized heterosexuality. It means to ask how practices such as weddings become naturalized and prevent us from seeing what is at stake, what is kept in place, and what consequences are produced. To employ this approach is to seek out those instances when the illusion of tranquility is created and at what cost. Weddings, like many other rituals of heterosexual celebration such as anniversaries, showers, and Valentine's Day, become synonymous with heterosexuality and provide illusions of reality that conceal the operation of heterosexuality both historically and materially. When used in professional settings, for example, weddings work as a form of ideological control to signal membership in relations of ruling as well as to signify that the couple is normal, moral, productive, family-centred, upstanding citizens, and, most importantly, appropriately gendered and sexual.

To study weddings means to interrupt the ways the heterosexual imaginary naturalizes heterosexuality and prevents us from seeing how its organization depends on the production of the belief or ideology that heterosexuality is normative and the same for everyone—that the fairy-tale romance is universal. It is this assumption that allows for the development and growth in America of a $35 billion per year wedding industry. This multi-billion dollar industry includes the sale of a diverse range of products, many of which are produced outside of the USA—wedding gowns, diamonds, honeymoon travel and apparel, and household equipment. Ironically, the production of these goods frequently occurs under dismal labour conditions where manufacturers rely on a non-traditional female workforce, indirectly altering cultural norms in relation to heterosexuality and family. In Mexico, Guatemala, and China, for example, the effect has been to shift the job opportunities away from men with the consequence of significant levels of domestic violence and femicide. Sexual regulation in these locations is directly related to the gendered division of labour working to produce goods that support the American heterosexual imaginary. Veiled in the guise of romance and the sacred, these social relations conceal from view the troublesome conditions underlying the production of the white wedding.

When you think of weddings as 'only natural', think again! This process of naturalization begins with children. By targeting girls and young women, toy manufacturers have seized on the wedding market and the opportunity to develop future consumers by producing a whole variety of wedding toys, featuring the 'classic' white wedding, and sold during Saturday morning children's television shows. Toy companies, generally part of large multinational conglomerates that also own related commodities such as travel or cosmetics, work to secure future markets for all their products through the selling of wedding toys. Mattel, the world's largest toymaker and a major multinational corporation, has offices and facilities in 36 countries and sells products in 150 nations. Their major toy brand, accounting for 40 per cent of their sales, is the Barbie doll—all 120 different versions of her. Mattel's primary manufacturing facilities are located in China, Indonesia, Italy, Malaysia, and Mexico, employing mostly women of colour and at substandard wages. Annually, Mattel makes about 100 million Barbie dolls and earns revenues of $1.9 billion for the California-based company. The average young Chinese female worker whose job it is to assemble Barbie dolls lives in a dormitory, sometimes works with dangerous chemicals, works long hours, and earns $1.81 a day.

The staging of weddings in television shows, weekly reporting on weddings in the press, magazine reports on celebrity weddings, advertising, and popular adult and children's movies with wedding themes or weddings inserted all work together to teach us how to think about weddings, marriage, heterosexuality, race, gender, and labour. Through the application of the heterosexual imaginary, the media cloak most representations of weddings in signifiers of romance, purity, morality, promise, affluence or accumulation, and whiteness. Many newlyweds today experience their weddings as the stars of a fairytale movie in which they are scripted, videotaped, and photographed by paparazzi wedding-goers, not as an event that regulates their sexual lives and identities along with those of the labourers who make their wedding possible.

The contemporary white wedding under multinational capitalism is, in effect, a mass-marketed, homogeneous, assembly-line production with little resemblance to the utopian vision many participants hold. The engine driving the wedding market has mostly to do with the romancing of heterosexuality in the interests of capitalism. The social relations at stake—love, community, commitment, and family—come to be viewed as secondary to the production of the wedding spectacle.

The heterosexual imaginary circulating throughout the wedding industry masks the ways it secures racial, class, and sexual hierarchies. Women are taught from early childhood to plan for the 'happiest day of their lives'. (Everything after that day pales by comparison!) Men are taught, by the absence of these socializing mechanisms, that their work is 'other' than that. If they are interested in the wedding it is for reasons other than what women have learned. The possibilities children learn to imagine are only as broad as their culture allows. They are socialized to understand the importance of appropriate coupling, what counts as beauty, as appropriate sexuality, what counts as women's work and men's work, and how to become 'good' consumers by participating in those heterosexual practices and rituals that stimulate their interests and emotions and reap the most rewards.

One is not born a bride. One learns to comply with the social and cultural messages that flow to and through the wedding ritual. It is the rite of passage for appropriate heterosexual identity and membership. It is everything but natural.

References

Ingraham, Chrys. 1994. 'The Heterosexual Imaginary', *Sociological Theory* 12, 2: 203–19.

———. 1999. *White Weddings: Romancing Heterosexuality in Popular Culture* (New York: Routledge).

Section 2 Marriage and Domesticity: Becoming Family

For decades, sociologists have focused on socialization (or learning) to explain why women and men typically end up with somewhat different work and responsibilities as adults. Problems with these explanations have been apparent for some time, however. On the one hand, children still grow up in a culture that is thoroughly saturated with the idea of gender difference; and there is evidence that boys and girls are still subject to different treatment, expectations, and experiences. On the other hand, it is not at all clear—according to the evidence—that men and women are different in ways that would account for the different work they do, and the responsibilities they bear, as adults. We have to find answers to questions about gender differences in work, responsibility, and social position somewhere other than in the notion of stable individual personality characteristics created by childhood socialization.

The next three chapters shed some light on the processes by which many women come to take on family responsibilities conventionally seen as 'women's'. In Chapter 16, Dawn Currie examines wedding preparations and finds differences based on gender at this early stage of family formation. Chapter 17 is from a study by Kathleen Gerson, which addresses the question whether socialization or other social processes are responsible for the different responsibilities assumed by women and men in long-term relationships. In Chapter 18, Gillian Ranson explores factors that affect women's decision to have a child. Both Gerson's and Ranson's findings indicate that the way society is organized is a key cause of gender divisions in families.

Chapter 16

Getting married represents a very meaningful passage for many couples. Thus, weddings hold powerful significance for those couples who decide to marry. As students of sociology, then, we might try to uncover the meaning of these ceremonies for the people who engage in them. One way of doing so is to examine the rituals and symbols in the ceremonies—the father 'giving away' the bride, the ring exchange, the bride's white gown. We might also ask people who follow such 'traditions' in their ceremonies why they do so.

Sociologist Dawn Currie takes a different approach. She examines not only what their marriages meant to the women and men she interviewed but also how they planned and arranged their wedding ceremonies. Currie's interviews were done in the 1990s, yet this article retains its relevance: expensive 'traditional' weddings continue to be popular. The interviews occurred years after legal definitions of marriage in Canada changed to reflect ideals of greater gender equality in marriage. In the late 1970s and early 1980s, English-speaking provinces across the country changed their family laws in a way that omitted old assumptions about women's and men's different rights and responsibilities in marriage. But what Currie finds in this small study raises questions about the extent to which gender relations have changed.

'Here Comes the Bride': The Making of a 'Modern Traditional' Wedding in Western Culture

Dawn H. Currie

Changes in marriage and family dynamics during the past 25 years have given rise to new questions for sociologists of the family. Following legislative changes in the 1960s, the divorce rate in Canada has increased steadily, so that up to one-third of marriages today are likely to end in divorce.[1] As indicators of marital instability rose in most Western industrialized societies, commentators declared a 'crisis in the family' (see Gittins 1985). However, against trends of family breakdown the vast majority of Canadians continue to marry, and also to remarry after divorce. On this basis some writers claim that marriage and the family are 'alive and well', or even 'getting better'. In support of the latter interpretation, writers note that Canadians continue to value family life: between 1984 and 1986, 86 per cent of women and 83 per cent of men were, or had been, married, supporting *Maclean's* (1987) poll that 81 per cent of Canadians rate the family as becoming a more important part of their lives (in Nett 1988: 2). These types of data have been used to advance the claim that marriage remains popular because it is more possible now, than before, for individuals to seek out fulfilling relationships. On the other hand, feminists draw attention to the frequency of violence against wives by husbands and the unequal division of domestic labour which characterizes most heterosexual households. For these writers, the modern nuclear family is interpreted as a central factor in women's continued oppression in the West, and thus as being in need of further dismantling (see Burt, Code, and Dorney 1988; Boulton 1983; Thorne 1982; Barrett and McIntosh 1982). Given the public documentation of trends which underlie this latter claim, and a rising consciousness about gender parity among Canadians, feminists are beginning to ask why the traditional nuclear family persists.

The answer to this question is complex, and thus is the matter of ongoing academic debate. Here, one enduring aspect of traditional family life is explored: the everyday activity of 'getting married'. While the past few decades have seen growth in alternatives to marriage (Wilson 1990; see Chapter 12), Canadians continue to perceive legal marriage as an indicator of greater commitment, even when they are already living in common-law unions. Baker (1990: 48) notes that the wedding ceremony itself is frequently seen as a 'rite of passage' to adult status. Many families save for years and spend considerable sums on wedding clothing and receptions, even though the event itself is short-lived. For those marrying, church weddings remain important. Although they declined from 91 per cent of marriages in 1972 to 70 per cent in 1982, this figure has levelled off (Nett 1988: 211).[2] At the same time, Nett (1988: 211) notes that conventional wedding ceremonies and receptions are filled with customs which are unambiguously patriarchal and that much of the symbolism in church weddings is sexist. The bride is the object of attention, the exchange occurs between the [bride's father] and the man to be her husband, the ring is a remnant of bride price, the white gown symbolizes virginity, and the throwing of rice fertility. She interprets the persistence of these customs as a reminder that emotions, and not fact-based knowledge, surround the activity of the wedding. This emphasis upon the emotional aspects of weddings is characteristic of the work appearing in most textbooks on the sociology of the family, and it is quite likely that this view of wedding customs as 'irrational' accounts for the lack of research interest in weddings.

While sociologists generally refer to these unions as 'conventional weddings', during my research I came to call these occurrences 'modern traditional' weddings, a term which captures the notion of paradox. Participants in my study acknowledged that marriage as a union 'for life' is a now outdated view, and few brides promised to 'love, honour, and obey' their spouses. Despite slight modifications of wedding vows, however, participants consciously followed 'tradition', and in so doing acted out rituals with not entirely progressive meanings. My primary interests therefore were to explore why traditional weddings remain popular and to examine the role which the wedding itself plays in the reproduction of gendered family relations.

The Study

This paper is based on interviews with a small non-random sample of 13 brides and three grooms.[3] Criteria for participation in the study were simply that respondents were either planning a wedding or had been recently married with a conventional wedding. Brides and grooms participating in the weddings included in this study ranged from 21 to 44 years of age. The occupational and economic status of the brides varied, and included 'pink collar' work in sales and clerical positions as well as professional and managerial employment. All women interviewed intended to continue working after marriage, and many planned to combine marriage, employment, and motherhood. The majority of couples had been living together prior to their wedding, and a small number of prospective grooms had been previously married. Interviews, which were unstructured and open-ended, focused on the meaning of weddings to respondents and documented the activities involved in making weddings happen.

With one exception, the weddings in this study occurred in a church.[4] Receptions which followed included anywhere from 25 to over 300 participants, although most involved at least 100 guests. Brides wore white, full-length gowns, and for many respondents the choice of the bridal gown was among the most important decisions.

Despite that fact that all weddings were planned as religious ceremonies, however, religious beliefs emerged as important to only three couples. More typically, respondents spoke of the symbolic importance of 'following tradition':

> We did want to have a church wedding. . . . Neither of us have any feelings, I guess, against the Church or for the Church. I was brought up more-or-less Lutheran. I'm not really a strong frequenter, but still I did want to get married in a church. (Elizabeth, 27-year-old sales representative)

> There's nothing the way a tradition is for a wedding that I would really want different. That was really strong for me. For me, it was the best to go along with the traditional wedding. (Christine, 27-year-old nurse)

> For some reason I didn't think it would be a proper wedding if I didn't have the traditional. (Margie, 23-year-old employee of Parks and Recreation)

> I think it's a reflection of the tradition that I like. . . .When I hear the word 'tradition', . . . I think along the lines of something solid, something quality. Something's traditional, or has been a tradition because it has stood the test of time, and that's the whole idea about marriage. (Brian, 28-year-old jewelry designer)

While the notion of following tradition may seem deceptively simple, what this entails proved to be much more extensive than what I had anticipated. More surprisingly, perhaps, in most cases wedding preparations entailed more work (and expense) than even respondents themselves had anticipated or actually desired. This could result in a sense of wedding plans being out of the control of respondents, or of the wedding excluding them:

> If I'd had my way, it would have just been really small and simple, and that was what we initially intended. . . . I just felt caught up in this big thing that I didn't have any control over, and people just kept pressing me to do this or that. . . . I was under a lot of stress. (Helen, 21-year-old student)

> We never initially intended to have a big deal. I think, maybe I wanted to wear a nice dress or something, but I didn't have this idea—and neither did Bill—of a great big wedding. It just kind of happened. . . . We kind of conceded to the fact that this was more for other people than for us, which is really ironic. (Michelle, 22-year-old student)

As researcher, therefore, I could not assume that as social agents, respondents were either fully aware, or in control, of events which made their wedding. However, this did not mean that respondents were simply acting on their emotions: indeed, weddings required many months of research and rational planning on the part of participants. Thus I was curious as to how weddings came to take on 'a life of their own'.

The Symbolism of Getting Married: Wedding as Commitment

As sociologists have noted elsewhere, although social actors generally view themselves as behaving in a rational manner, they can seldom tell researchers why they engage in specific behaviours. This proved to be true in the case of getting married. Jane and Brian, for example, had lived together off-and-on for over six years. In thinking about why they decided to marry, Jane, a 26-year-old nurse, reflected that:

> I don't know—I feel quite married right now, but there's something that's not there. It's not a negative thing, and it's not 'Oh god,

> I have to have this thing', but it's not there and I have no idea what it is. I've looked elsewhere for it. I think the actual 'I do' is the end of something and the beginning of something [else], although it really is the same thing. . . . I guess it really boils down to [the fact that] it seems like the right thing to do for all sorts of reasons.

While the bride in this case obviously couldn't really say what marriage meant to her, her husband-to-be articulated the associations which many of the other respondents made between marriage and a commitment which would lend their relationship a new sense of stability. In response to the same question, Brian maintained that the wedding signified:

> We're going to stick together through thick and thin. We commit ourselves to each other before God. It's holy. It has an aura about it. We're saying that we're going to be together till the day we die.

Overall, this sense of commitment and stability was the most common theme concerning the meaning of the marriage to respondents. Patty, a 22-year-old clerk at Eaton's who had been engaged for nine months prior to the wedding, maintained that:

> I think there is still a sense of confidence and—what's the word? Confidence, I guess, that you are together and even though it is a piece of paper, in a sense, in a more important sense there is that bond. . . . I don't know. I think just the fact that you've made the decision and made it clear that commitment is significant.

Similarly:

> I think it's the 'for better or for worse' thing. . . . If things get really bad and you're living together, you think, 'OK, I'll split.' But if you're married, and you know that you are both really committed, then it means that you can work through that thing together. I could see in Dick that he had that kind of intent, just from our conversations and stuff. We both had this similar idea about marriage. (Helen)

> Just living together just seems—there's no commitment then to stick around, to really work at it. I guess this silly piece of paper and this ceremony just enforced that we are committed to each other to spend a life together and we were really going to make a good stab at it, if that makes any sense. (Faye, 23-year-old nurse)

Since commitment can be signalled in any number of ways, it is interesting to ask how the wedding ceremony, in particular, communicates this meaning to participants. Here the attendance of the wedding by extended family members is important. Like many other celebrations, a wedding may be the time during which family membership and ties are affirmed and renewed:

> I think I'll feel a little more part of the family. I'll be the 'son-in-law'—there's a title right there, not just a boyfriend, not quite a son. (Brian)

> It's more of, to us it's going to be like a family reunion rather than a wedding because I haven't seen a lot of my aunts and uncles. I don't know his aunts and uncles, so it'll be a big get-together. (Heather, 28-year-old secretary finishing BA)

> I see it as a celebration of friends and family. In other words, a celebration of people who are important for us from our past and our present, who are suggesting something nice

> for our future by being there. (Larry, 30-year-old computer operator)

For many respondents, including extended family members meant that planning the wedding was driven by the need to include appropriate relatives:

> I talked to my parents and my mom went through her address book which she's had since she probably got married and found all the relatives that had to be invited. . . . So we just went to our parents and our parents told us who we were supposed to invite from our families and then we added to that. (Rachael, 23-year-old university graduate)

The pressure to include relatives often determined the planning of the wedding:

> It was kind of important for me to have people there like my mother and my father, and my brother and close family. The same with Jim. Anything above and beyond that was, well initially we had this idea that we were just going to have this very small wedding. We were to invite our parents and our siblings, and it turned into more than that . . . there were aunts and uncles, and relatives who were close enough to come, so [trails off]. (Helen)

> We didn't want a large wedding in the first place. I had originally said it would be nice with about 75 people, but with all my relatives and Rob's relatives and friends we couldn't pick out—it was just impossible to cut it back that much. (Elizabeth)

Patty had 450 people on their guest list:

> The guest list, I think, is probably always hard. When I look over the list, when it came almost time for the wedding I kept thinking, 'Well, why did we invite them and not these people?' I'm sure if I did it differently there'd be a lot of people that I probably wouldn't put on the list that I did. . . . I felt that there were people we could leave off, yet I wondered why we invited these people.

Christine managed to keep their guest list down to 130 people, although they were 'having a tough time of it':

> Well, we talked about it. And we figured we didn't really want more than 100 people because it was fairly expensive. Then, my parents—they said that—well, the caterer's giving us a little bit of a deal. My dad's a fisherman and he's giving them some fish. So we're getting a good deal there. . . . But we really felt a little uncomfortable. We don't want to have that many people because it does get expensive.

Initially, it appeared that this need to include more participants than intended accounted for the amount of planning and preparations. Joan, a 30-year-old dental assistant who emphasized the religious importance of her marriage over all other aspects, remarked:

> There's so much preparation that you're excited about it, but you want it to be over, too . . . It's just—the caterers, the church, the florist, the photographer, and—you don't just visit these people once, it's a couple of times. Check the flowers, see whether they're okay, and talk to the photographer and go over details, you know. It's just like—it was a lot of work.

'Going All the Way': The Work of Getting Married

On the surface, it might appear that the work and expense of weddings were simply a function of the size of events. During interviews, however, it became evident that this was not the case. For the large part, both the amount of planning and expense were the results of paying attention to details which, although often seen as 'not really necessary', were important to respondents. A case in point is Patty and Eric, who had a relatively small wedding with 100 guests. Although Patty had just relocated to Vancouver from Toronto, and as a consequence had also been recently unemployed, her wedding cost $8,500 ('not counting the wedding bands'). In explaining their expenditures, she noted that they 'did a few things that you wouldn't have to do':

> A lot of little things. Like we rented a limousine for four hours which is fairly expensive, and rented a car for our parents to drive in. They could of used their own, but we wanted them to have a nicer sleek white [car]. And we put the fathers in tuxedos, the ushers in tuxedos—we paid for all of that. The ring bearer, we paid for his tuxedo. The two flower girls, we bought their dresses and accessories. We had real flowers, too.

Respondents referred to this as 'going all the way':

> I figure that if we're going to do the ceremony in a traditional way, that we might as well do it all the way. I just feel like why do part of it? Might as well just do it all. (Michelle)

Going all the way meant taking care of the minutest details. In the final analysis, it was the drive to have things 'picture perfect' that determined the amount of work and expense:

> The issue for us was what looked good in the church. I wanted a kind of rosy colour, but Sharla said 'It'll look awful in the church, because the church is orange.' . . . So we even went so far as to get swatches of different colours and take them to the church. We hadn't chosen this exact colour, but knew that maybe this was what would look the best [shows interviewer wedding photos]. (Patty)

> You're so vulnerable because you want to look your best. It's important that you look nice. And they [salespeople] say, 'Well, it really would make your dress just look that much better if you have the right bra under it.' . . . And nylons. I did notice at all the bridal shops you'll get—of course, your dress—but they've got necklaces and some even sell, not so much makeup, just things that would really add to it all. (Faye)

Getting things perfect required careful planning:

> We also had to make an appointment to see the photographer within two weeks, just to get our last minute checklist. . . . That kind of thing. Buy a guest list and pen, organize my girlfriends—I didn't want them wondering what to do so I typed out lists for all of them. Phoned the organ music at the church, call Purdy's to confirm the chocolates were ready and available for picking up, and I bought yards and yards of fabric, of ribbon, because I was going to tie little royal blue bows around each box of chocolates. I purchased candles for the wedding. I purchased car decorations—I bought tons of these little plastic pompom kits two weeks before—not even thinking it was going to take me about three hours a box, and I had eight boxes. I was working full-time right up to the end. (Faye)

Looking back, it seemed to respondents that 'one thing just led to the next':

> You know about the basic steps. You have to have a place to get married, and you have to have a place to have the reception. You need a cake, you need a dress, you need flowers, and then, of course—oh yes, there's the car, and then there's decorations for the car, and then there's choosing the wine, and the menu, and then there's this and that. . . . One thing just leads to the next. (Joan and Brian)

> I did feel that there was a lot of unnecessary pressure to have the wedding this way or you have to have this. . . . One example I'll give you was shoes for my bridesmaids. I was originally going to have them wear white shoes so they could wear them again, you know, practical pumps. But then after awhile I said 'No. These dresses would really look much nicer if they had dyed satin shoes.' And so, even while they were being dyed I thought 'Oh, this is a waste. This is so unnecessary, both for the girls and overall.' (Patty)

> I had an image in my mind, like a pretty wedding, so I wanted to have a nice dress. Then it seemed to me that there was a lot of things that went along with having a nice dress. . . . If you're spending a lot of money on your dress then you've got to invite people to come and see it. So, we started getting relatives coming. Then you've got to have some place for them to go after the wedding, for food and stuff like that. As it turned out, we had a reception, which we weren't planning on. (Helen)

Joan and Brian found planning so complex that they used a professional wedding consultant:

> I just got so fed up and I said 'I don't want to do this any more.' So I phoned a wedding consultant, and she said 'Well, what are you having problems with?' . . . The woman who helped us was most helpful, very helpful, asking 'Have you done this yet?'

Unlike Joan and Brian, however, most respondents could not afford to hire a consultant, who usually charges an hourly fee. Heather and Larry, who had been living together for two years before deciding to get married, initially expected to have about 80 guests. As plans progressed, however, their guest list grew to 160. In order to keep the costs down, they decided to have the wedding in the small town where the bride's parents live rather than in Vancouver, the groom's home. They had been planning their wedding for the past year, and Larry estimated that for the last six months they were 'putting in at least two hours a day'. Larry explained how he kept track of planning:

> We have our schedule already organized for the week before and up to the date. We have all our costs put on a spreadsheet so we can see various things. We have a database for the invitations and the reply cards, and the gifts. It's the only way of keeping track of so many people and so many little things.

Heather put her commuting time to good use:

> I spend a lot of time on the SkyTrain making notes. My big fear is 'What am I forgetting?' So I read the magazines and if I see something I make a note. So I've got an hour to get to work and I just make notes. But the problem is I get home and I'm so tired.

Although Larry's active involvement in planning was not typical of all interviews, Heather's reliance on bridal magazines to be sure that she was 'doing the right thing' was shared by other brides. Even though wedding traditions appealed to respondents because they symbolize generational ties, respondents in this study did not rely on the knowledge of mothers or other relatives who had been married. In fact, it was typical for respondents to minimize the role of their mothers, either avoiding them altogether or including them in a token way:

> I'd organized it so well in the first place, as I say, right down to the flowers and my flower arrangements so I would say things—because of course I didn't want her [mother] to feel excluded at all—I would ask her advice about something, or a suggestion, or whatever, but it was just to make her feel that she was involved in it. (Sara, 34-year-old secretary)

> She [mother] was just there for practical advice and helping, and things like that—I actually did it more so that she feels involved. (Rachael)

Almost without exception, respondents used books and magazines to find out how to plan their wedding:

> I got library books out. I did that because I wanted to make sure I covered all the details. I knew the basics for planning a wedding, I think, but I didn't want to miss anything out. That's where a book came in handy, because then I had everything there. I knew I wasn't missing anything. I had a little list of things to do. (Margie)

> I bought a book—a bride magazine. It had what to do the first six months, what you should do three months before the wedding, one month before. So that's what I did. . . . I just checked it off every time I accomplished or got something done. It really worked good because otherwise, without that list I'd be a mess [Joan shows an appointment calendar—one month showed 11 of 27 days on which there were notations for wedding chores—next two months were busier].

> I was so excited when I first found a wedding planner! . . . This actually has been an extension of my body for the whole engagement, this dear old red book [points to her wedding planner]. . . . I had pages marked. At four months, things I needed to do, at two months, and one week. *Modern Bride* made it all so neat and uncomplicated. You could just make a phone call and check it off. (Faye)

> Mom was really helpful. Then I bought a wedding planner book. It's just a small book from Coles for $4.95. It just gives you an idea of things to do, like three months ahead of time, and two months ahead of time, as a guideline. (Christine)

The problem is, however, that bridal magazines and planners did not always simply make the wedding plans easier. In many cases, women wanted their weddings to match what they saw in bridal magazines. The most typical example was in choosing a wedding gown:

> I bought *Modern Bride* and got an idea for what kind of dress I wanted. . . . I wanted to spend a week just looking for a wedding dress. I was up early every day on my own and must have hit 90 per cent of the wedding dress stores in Vancouver and the lower mainland. . . . I went to that many stores because I'd feel better if I could say I'd been really thorough. It was important to me that I didn't buy something that I liked and then was wondering 'Oh, did I miss a dress that was even nicer somewhere else?' But at the same time, I kept saying 'I'll know when I find it' and 'It is just taking me that many places to find it.' (Faye)

I was looking through a magazine—a small BC magazine—and there was a dress designer that had some really wild dresses. I saw one which really struck me, so I played with her design and changed a few things, and did this and that. . . . I showed her [dressmaker] my idea, and she wasn't really sure about it at first, . . . but it's turned out much better than I even expected. (Jane)

However helpful bridal planners were, they also added to the sense of what needed to be done:

I bought these two bridal magazines. That's when I really started to realize how much work it was going to be. Those books are full of 'this month you have to do this', and 'this month you have to do that', and 'make sure you've gone here'. (Rachael)

In this way, although respondents bought wedding planners to be reassured that plans would proceed smoothly, these planners could precipitate worry about things going right:

I haven't been officially using that [the above-mentioned bridal planner]. I just sort of write stuff down for myself, and I guess I cross my fingers that we do everything. (Rachael)

I had eight months to plan. I sort of laid out what I had to do each month, I was pretty organized. About two weeks before the wedding I panicked, I just felt 'all this stuff to do'. Two weeks before, I panicked. So I just rushed for those two weeks and got everything done. (Elizabeth)

As well, following wedding planners and bridal magazines could add to the expense:

What we did say was 'Let's spend as little as possible for the wedding, but don't—uhm, don't not buy something because we don't feel that we have the money.' I mean, if it's important, go for it, just maybe try to get it on sale or the cheapest one of them. (Faye, whose wedding cost $15,000)

During interviews, respondents often spontaneously suggested that they had spent far more than they thought was reasonable, or even stated that weddings themselves were a 'waste of money':

I think it's a waste of money, and I don't think that's what a wedding—forget the marriage part—is about. I don't think it's about mortgaging your house. (Rachael)

It's a trap. They just want you to spend money. I wanted to make it simple and low cost—like my shoes were $29. I really cut corners. My dress was half-price, even though it was still expensive. (Joan)

That was the dress [shows wedding photos], and it just happened to be on sale, too. It was regularly $880 and I got it for $580, so I was really happy with it. I mean, I wasn't trying on dresses, as much as I would have loved them, that were over $800 or $900. That to me, I mean that's ludicrous. I mean, $580 is ludicrous actually, but I could justify that, [pause] still. (Faye)

One result was that many couples began their newlywed life in debt:

We haven't paid them all yet. . . . [we made] a lot of down payments. (Patty)

There'll be—what we did was we just 'balanced' it—tried to put as much as possible on credit cards. That way we deferred it for another month until we did

> have some more money in the bank account. (Elizabeth)

However, debt was not the only strain which wedding preparations could place on the new couple. While purchasing products may appear to decrease the amount of work associated with weddings compared to the past when gowns were hand-sewn and receptions prepared by the bride's family rather than catered, shopping itself is work. Bridal magazines emphasize the importance for the prospective couple to be well informed about competing products. For example:

> Now that you and your fiancé will be shopping for wedding bands, it's to your advantage to walk into the store as educated consumers. With so many beautiful rings to choose from, you'll want to know what distinguishes one from the other. (*Modern Bride*, Apr./May: 194)

As with any major purchase, consumers are advised to 'do their homework'. For those trying to minimize expenditures, this meant shopping around for bargains:

> I think the trick is to make the effort and take the time to really shop around and ask a lot of questions. You know this is your day and you want it exactly how you want it. Don't compromise because what you want is out there and you can find it, and you can get it at a reasonable price. You just have to be willing to do some footwork. (Jane, targeted $4,000 but thought that $5,000 would be more realistic)

> I looked for the cheapest things. I really wanted to keep it inexpensive. . . . I checked around all the local places and checked out prices. I mean, I must have gone to about four different places checking invitations, and I must have gone to about four different photographers to check out prices. (Margie)

Probably aware of the frustration which shopping might entail, magazines reassured readers that it will be worth the extra work:

> Be patient, shop wisely and most of all, have faith. In the end you'll find the perfect gown. After all, didn't you find the perfect guy? (*Today's Bride*, Summer 1989: 14)

Ironically, avoiding these pressures by making rather than buying things had the effect of increasing the amount of work:

> A lot of the rest of the stuff we're doing ourselves—that's why we spend so much time doing it [preparing]. . . . It just makes you a bit tired. Some days you'd rather just go home and go to sleep, but you know you have to go and do this. (Heather)

In this way, debt is not the only strain placed upon the newlywed couple. Reflected above but also in most of the interviews, consumption is primarily 'women's work'. Like many brides, Sara assumed most of the responsibility for the actual work of the wedding:

> Because I was doing so much of the wedding it annoyed me to be organizing right down to the minute—who was saying what, what speeches were going to be made, who I wanted to have a speech made to. That annoyed me because I felt that it was the groom's thing, but he said 'No. No, I want you to do it.' . . . Obviously, all this is not going to be a man's job, I guess.

Although Sara initially saw this division of labour as a source of conflict, she came to accept the wedding as her work:

> At first I thought, 'Why am I doing it?' I thought he was being, uhm—lazy was actually how I first termed it, lazy. And then, knowing him, you know, his integrity and how he is a super-organized man himself, I thought 'No, no, no. This is great. In fact, if anything it was a compliment to me.' But at the beginning, you won't see it at all, because I certainly couldn't see it [that way].

As did most brides and grooms:

> He affirmed or vetoed decisions! No, I shouldn't say it like that. He wasn't involved a lot in the planning. I planned most of it because I had the time. I checked things out with him and we talked about certain things, like the wedding vows, for instance, things like that. . . . He's the type that gets distracted very easily and if has too many things on his mind, he gets distressed. (Patty)

Larry referred to a lot of the work as 'girls' stuff', especially taking care of details:

> I think she spends more hours a day thinking about the conscious little details which I would miss, than I do.

Brian quite agreed with Joan's comment that 'He really is quite useless':

> For some reason my mind goes blank. She asks how things should happen on the day of the wedding—'We need cars. Who's going to ride with whom to the wedding?' I couldn't figure it out to save my life. And I don't know why. I have a feeling that it's not in men's genes.

Interestingly, Joan commented that 'he just has better and more pressing things to think about'. Overall, for most couples the groom's role involved the final say or right to veto:[5]

> I was always running ideas past him. He had a lot of input. It's just when it came to actually doing the stuff, he wasn't around. But one time he came over and we picked out the invitations together. (Margie)

> He's just playing right along with it. I'd just as soon take responsibility, one way or the other, you know. I'm willing to do it, not because I think I have to, but because it feels better if I just take care of the whole thing. You know, then it's no hassle. But things we want, we decide together. (Michelle)

> What we had not agreed upon, for one reason or another, we would discuss. . . . If I went over the limit on something he would certainly pull me up on it and say 'Listen, that's not the way to do it.' . . . So, he let me go on my own merry way, but when he knew something was 'out' he would stop me and say 'Now look, I don't want to do that', 'I absolutely refuse', or whatever. (Sara)

Reflected poignantly in these quotes, the notion of a 'modern traditional' wedding is more than a literary oxymoron: it expresses quite well the contradictory outcome of establishing 'modern' relationships in the name of 'tradition'.

The Quest for Meaning: Re-writing Tradition

As a ritual symbol, the wedding signifies commitment and shared love. Indeed, we have seen that this meaning is stated by respondents as the 'reason' to be married rather than to cohabit. However, focusing on weddings as rituals obscures the way in which gender relations are reproduced through this everyday search for stability and personal fulfillment. It is not simply that wedding ceremonies are couched in patriarchal symbolism, as Nett notes: indeed, here we have seen that changing the language and content of wedding vows to convey an egalitarian commitment stands in direct contrast to the way in which the women assumed responsibility for the work of weddings as symbolic of this commitment. For the large part, men participated primarily in decision-making, where they often 'had the final say'. Thus, although respondents did not vow to 'obey' their husbands, the brides-to-be very often avoided conflict by deferring to their partner's wishes. As an extreme example, Rachael radically broke with tradition in choosing her wedding gown—one decision which has been historically the bride's to make:

> Then the dress I had in mind, exactly what I wanted and what I found in a magazine,—he hated it. He hated it. He thought it looked stupid. . . . I couldn't buy it if he didn't like it. I couldn't make the decision myself. I figured if he thinks I'm going to look terrible in it, there's not much use in wearing it, right? (Rachael)

In this research it became important to explain how the actions of respondents came to unintentionally contradict their stated expectations for egalitarian marital relations.

As we have seen, wedding planners and bridal magazines were a major contributing factor to the amount of work involved and to the subsequent feeling that respondents were 'out of control' of the events which unfolded. In the final analysis, the commercialized nature of wedding planning accounted for much of the financial stress, as well as the ambivalence, which respondents expressed. Virtually every couple interviewed after their wedding had spent more than anticipated, and respondents were frequently quite critical about their unanticipated level of conspicuous consumption. To point out ways in which wedding planning is about consumption is not to argue simply that respondents were 'dupes' of capitalism, however. Here, commodification is interesting as a process through which 'modern traditional' weddings appeal to consumers and become primarily women's work. Weddings are a good example of the increasing commodification of ritual elements of social life in Western cultures. Despite widespread economic recession, weddings are 'big business': in 1988, the year in which this project was initiated, weddings were a $3.8 billion industry in Canada (*Wedding Bells*, Spring/Summer 1989: 76).

Specialized books and magazines are the major vehicle of wedding commodification.[6] While it would be overly simplistic to attribute wedding plans entirely to the bridal magazines mentioned by respondents, it is clear that they contributed to women's dilemmas. For this reason, wedding magazines became the subject of further ongoing textual analysis. Of relevance here are the 'wedding planners' which respondents universally referred to. In total, 28 such planners appeared in seven magazines purchased during the time that interviews were conducted. Given that bridal magazines are published seasonally and that there is a small, identifiable selection, it is safe to speculate that these lists are the ones referred to by respondents. At any rate, analysis reveals a great deal of similarity and repetition from magazine to magazine, with identical photo-spreads appearing in more than one issue, for example.

As reported by the brides in this study, wedding tasks on each checklist began anywhere from one year to a minimum of six months before the wedding. Reflecting the almost military precision implied in wedding planning, 'Wedding Countdown' (*Wedding Bells*, Spring/Summer 1989) identified 54 tasks, while a 'Wedding Day Schedule' presented in *Today's Bride* (Winter 1988: 120) listed the same number of items, reminding readers that:

> Your wedding can run smoothly if you take the time to make up your itinerary beforehand. Plan your day from start to finish. Write everything down in proper sequence

> and, if possible, appoint a close friend to make sure you get to the church on time without forgetting anything.

Separate checklists are usually provided for the groom and the bride. *Today's Bride* (Summer 1989) itemizes 20 tasks for the groom, followed by a list of nine expenditures for which he is responsible. The same magazine carries a companion list of 42 tasks for the bride, which include choosing the groom's attire; ordering, addressing, and mailing all invitations; and visiting the cosmetician for skin-care and makeup tips. Only a few tasks are included on both lists. Feature articles further added to this bare minimum: *Bride's* (Feb./Mar. 1989), for example, suggests that learning how to dance will add to the success of the wedding day, while *Wedding Bells* (Spring/Summer 1989: 292) features a 'Bridal Beauty Countdown' which advises brides to 'start early (six months prior) to face your big day beautifully'. In this way, the use of bridal magazines is likely to increase the amount of work and planning by drawing attention to extra, additional things that help to make a 'perfect' wedding.

Although the necessary tasks in making a wedding prove to be relatively easy to identify in bridal magazines, the reader is likely to be overwhelmed by choices of how to accomplish these tasks: content analysis revealed that 91 per cent of feature articles about the wedding day presented differing options on how to do things. While tasks itemized on the bride's inventory may include, for example, a notation to pick up flowers, order invitations, or remember to have a final dress fitting, each item presupposes a complex series of decisions concerning a seemingly endless array of choices. In part, these choices are guided by etiquette or tradition, which are regularly discussed in magazines. However, articles which discussed wedding etiquette or tradition account for only 3.5 per cent and 2.9 per cent, respectively, of subjects covered in feature articles. In contrast, 33.8 per cent of feature materials concerned how to coordinate wedding details or choose between competing wedding options according to latest trends and fashions. In fact, the emphasis on being 'up-to-date' overrides what tradition and etiquette have dictated in the past. An editorial in *Today's Bride* (Winter 1988: 6) declares that 'brides should feel free to do away with any tradition or all of them'. Within the discourses of bridal magazines, 'tradition' refers to a carefully coordinated wedding 'theme' rather than an actual wedding practice, reflected in the comment that 'fortunately, tradition is honoured when most brides indulge in the luxury of a lavish white ensemble!' (*Bridal Guide*, 1989: 26). While this appeal to tradition imparts historical credentials to white weddings, it is interesting to note that not so long ago *Vogue*—a leading commentator on Western fashion—admonished brides that 'there must be no exaggerated décolletage, for *Vogue* considers the wedding in its traditional light as a religious ceremony' (from the 1920s, quoted in Probert 1984: 16). Here modesty is a remnant of the time when bridal etiquette concerned one's proper sense of social status:

> Extravagance in any of the appointments of the wedding is in extremely bad taste. It is sometimes well to remember the delightful logic of the old lady who said that she did not dress better than she could afford to at home because everybody knew her there . . . and she did not dress better than she could afford when she went to the city because nobody knew her . . . magnificent ornamentation is out of place in a simple chapel or church, and in every place profusion beyond one's means is not only ill-bred but foolish. (Eichler 1921: 49–50)

Lansdell (1983: 81) notes that the element of 'fancy dress' began to appear in wedding fashion in the late 1960s, with a noticeable appeal to 'tradition' emerging only in the mid-1970s. Thus bridal magazines do not act to simply preserve, or even to restore, old customs, but rather to re-write tradition:

> Whether you are being married for the second, third, or fourth time, your wedding day is still a 'first', the beginning of a new partnership, the sharing of joy that this commitment represents. . . . The *old myth* that only a first-time bride may wear white has been replaced with the understanding that white symbolizes the wedding itself rather than the purity of the bride. . . . All of these decisions are strictly personal ones. (Piccione 1982: 130, 134; emphasis mine)

In this way, while white weddings appealed to respondents because they signify tradition, brides are being advised that a traditional wedding is a matter of personal preference, tempered by what experts suggest is in 'good taste'. Judy Siblin-Rakoff, quoted in *Wedding Bells* as author of a well-known bridal planning book, encourages couples to update wedding customs according to their personalities and taste:

> Despite the allure and integrity of many wedding traditions, today's couples feel that it is important to personalize the event. Bridal consultants point out a host of small details that, when considered together, show how the ceremony, and especially the reception, are changing with the times. . . . 'Today's young couples are bright, they have their own careers, they're independent. Their wedding should be their own.' (*Wedding Bells*, Spring/Summer 1989: 68)

Similarly, *Today's Bride* exhorts readers that:

> Today's bride is looking for something more than just the essentials. She's looking for something new and interesting, something out of the ordinary, something exciting. She demands creativity. (*Today's Bride*, Winter 1988: 78)

During interviews, items which respondents referred to as giving their wedding a 'personal touch' ironically recurred in other weddings: although commodification promises 'consumer magic', it is a contradictory process in that it must appeal to what consumers have in common while addressing their search for individuality (see Fiske 1989a). In this way, because commodification and mass consumption act to standardize products, a personalized wedding can only be achieved through giving attention to a myriad of individual details. In the final analysis, this 'attention to details' is what created the work of wedding planning. Perhaps ironically, the stress led some respondents to maintain that:

> At that time I remember feeling 'I'll just be glad when it's all over.' . . . I did want it how I had it, but I was just feeling tired. I was tired. I was tired of thinking of it. (Faye)

As the 'big day' drew closer, Helen maintained:

> I never really wanted to call off the marriage, the idea of marriage. The wedding, I really wanted to call [it] off.

Conclusion

As a small exploratory study, generalizations about how, or why, traditional weddings remain popular in Canada cannot be made. However, this in-depth investigation illustrates how traditional weddings reproduced relations of the patriarchal nuclear family for the couples in this study, despite claims by respondents to be establishing 'modern' partnerships. This paradox becomes apparent by exploring weddings as activities rather than as simply symbolic ritual. As rituals, weddings symbolize family ties: legally, the wedding acknowledges the couple as husband and wife and, publicly, it links the new couple to an extended network of kin relations. Hidden by this emphasis on the purely symbolic aspect of weddings, however, is the reproduction of unequal marital relations and women's wedding work which these relations reflect. Because respondents expected—or even claimed—to have egalitarian domestic relations, it is perhaps ironic that the couple's first public act already begins to establish a traditional, unequal pattern of domestic labour. It also makes the persistence of traditional white weddings appear to be all the more perplexing. What does this study tell us, then, about the current popularity of the 'modern traditional' wedding?

Although it is tempting to simply dismiss the behaviours described in this study as 'irrational', such an approach would not help us understand the everyday activities through which dominant social relationships are reconstituted. Here, it is perhaps more fruitful to view traditional weddings as a rational pursuit of a pleasurable occasion to celebrate personal and familial relations.[7] The affirmation of kinship relations was a source of emotional fulfillment for both the women and men in this study. As 'the bride's day', weddings remain one of the few public occasions where women's roles in the family are celebrated. This public recognition appealed to many respondents:

> I understand now why people say: 'It's the bride's day.' It doesn't matter what anybody does, nothing really takes away from your being the centre of attention. (Sara)

> I get to get up in the morning, have a bubble bath, go and get my hair and makeup done, wear something that I would never ever on any other occasion wear. Just [pause] be absolutely pampered. This sounds really selfish, self-centred as well. But, to be the centre of attention for a while—and also be a reason why all these people we care about are all getting together—it feels good to be a catalyst for something like that to happen. (Jane)

This pleasure does not simply reflect 'false consciousness' on the part of women involved:

> Well, I'm a bit of a feminist and I see myself as having more important or more valid things to be thinking about, to concern myself with than what I'm going to look like on my wedding day. It just seems very trivial and insignificant to me, but [pause]. When the day comes, when you do have to think about it, it becomes, then [pause] you know, I loved doing it. (Patty)

As reflected above, despite the stresses associated with extensive planning and preparations, weddings provided respondents with one day of 'self-indulgence'. It remains to be seen whether the pattern of unequal domestic labour which emerged during wedding preparations is a better predictor of future relations than the premarital expectations of brides. However, the immediate appeal of weddings is in fact due to their transient nature: as a one-day event, the indulgence of a wedding does not require feminists, working wives, or other 'non-traditional' participants to compromise the ideals of their everyday, 'ordinary' lives. Thus Brian described their wedding day as a 'rented fantasy', while Jane maintained:

> One day in fairyland. It's going to be fun, no matter why or how! . . . It's a very 'me' day. We want this, and we want that, and it's going to last for the whole day. We're going to get everything out of it.

As a one-day event, they saw their wedding as being distinct from their relationship or marriage:

> You really do feel quite special, and that's nice. It is totally separate from actually getting married. There's the getting married and then there's the day of getting married, and all the stuff that goes with it—and I find that sort of thing is very separate. (Jane)

It is this separation which gave rise to their desire for a public celebration:

> There's just something about a wedding that stirs your soul. So if all these people we know can come to our wedding, somehow we can let them know that this is the best thing, and let them know that this is the right thing to do. (Brian)

As it did for other couples:

> The celebration is the public thing, but the commitment and even the whole building up to the wedding itself is a very private thing. . . . The whole idea of all the little things [wedding details] is because they're part of us making this making what happened in private between the two of us public. (Rachael)

As we have seen, this appeal of 'self expression' is kindled by a mass wedding culture that is perpetuated by bridal magazines. Here discourses address the reader's desire to feel connected to the tradition of weddings, albeit encouraging identifiably non-traditional practices. Thus the discourses of bridal magazines do not simply transmit wedding traditions, but in so doing actively re-write what is meant by 'tradition'. Writers of both bridal books and bridal magazines refer to 'tradition—*with a new twist*. From the proposal to the honeymoon pictures, their way is the Right Way.'[8] As we have seen, tradition is thus transformed into a wedding theme rather than being presented as a wedding practice, facilitating the sense that meanings associated with weddings are separate from those which respondents assigned to their marital relations. Perhaps ironically, therefore, however 'modern' the material, symbolic elements of their wedding, market processes led respondents to re-enact 'traditional' patterns of marital relations.

Notes

1. The incidence of divorce varies by region. Estimates range from fewer than one-quarter in the Atlantic provinces to almost one-third in British Columbia (*Canadian Social Trends*, No. 13, Summer 1989: 27).
2. As Nett (1988: 211) notes, since remarriages are more likely to involve a civil ceremony or home wedding, this initial decrease probably reflects increases in remarriages. By 1985, more than 20 per cent of marriages of both men and women were second or later marriages (*Canadian Social Trends*, Spring 1987: 3).
3. This study is a pilot study, and generalizations are not intended. Nevertheless, observations and analyses here have interesting implications for understanding aspects of our everyday life.
4. The exception is a Jewish couple, who held a religious ceremony and reception out-of-doors.
5. Here it may be important to note that it is not simply that the husbands-to-be assumed the traditional 'burden' of paying for their new wives' consumption. In most cases the new couple shared the cost of the wedding, and families of both the

bride and groom usually helped to cover some of the expenditure.

6. How to plan a wedding is discussed in both wedding guidebooks, available at most bookstores and at the local library, and bridal magazines. The tasks outlined in these guidebooks closely follow those presented in magazines. The most striking difference between guidebooks and magazines is the dominance of photographic layouts in the latter, provided in feature articles but more importantly in advertisements. Undoubtedly, this glossy format accounted for the appeal of magazines over guidebooks.
7. By describing these activities as pleasurable, I do not intend to imply that they are therefore desirable, beneficial, or that they are somehow acts of 'resistance', in the way that cultural studies often implies. (See Chapter 2, Fiske 1989b, for example.)
8. Comment by editor-in-chief of *Bride's*, Apr./May 1989: 22; emphasis in original.

References

Baker, Maureen, ed. 1990. 'Mate Selection and Marital Dynamics', in *Families: Changing Trends in Canada* (Toronto: McGraw-Hill Ryerson).

Barrett, Michele, and Mary McIntosh. 1982. *The Anti-social Family* (London: Verso).

Boulton, Mary Georgina. 1983. *On Being a Mother* (London: Tavistock).

Burt, Sandra, Lorraine Code, and Lindsay Dorney, eds. 1988. *Changing Patterns: Women in Canada* (Toronto: McClelland and Stewart).

Eichler, Lillian. 1921. *Book of Etiquette,* Vol. I (Oyster Bay, NY: Nelson Doubleday).

Fiske, John. 1989a. *Understanding Popular Culture* (Boston: Unwin Hyman).

———. 1989b. *Reading the Popular* (Boston: Unwin Hyman).

Gittins, Diana. 1985. *The Family in Question: Changing Households and Familiar Ideologies* (London: Macmillan).

Lansdell, Avril. 1983. *Wedding Fashions, 1860–1980* (London: Shire Publications).

Nett, Emily M. 1988. *Canadian Families: Past and Present* (Toronto: Butterworths).

Piccione, Nancy. 1982. *Your Wedding: A Complete Guide to Planning and Enjoying It* (Englewood Cliffs, NJ: Prentice Hall).

Probert, Christina. 1984. *Brides in Vogue since 1910* (London: Thames & Hudson).

Thorne, Barrie, with Marilyn Yalom, eds. 1982. *Rethinking the Family: Some Feminist Questions* (New York: Longman).

Wilson, Susannah J. 1990. 'Alternatives to Traditional Marriage', in *Families: Changing Trends in Canada*, ed. Maureen Baker (Toronto: McGraw-Hill Ryerson).

Chapter 17

This chapter addresses the important question how women come to prioritize family responsibilities and the work central to family. The chapter is from Kathleen Gerson's book *Hard Choices*, which reports on her study of American women who became adults in the 1970s. Gerson was interested in the life choices this cohort made, and she interviewed them in the 1980s, when they were in their thirties. Her focus was on the relationship between the priorities these women had when they were interviewed—whether family or paid employment/career—and the priorities they had when they were in their early twenties. She found that no matter which priority they held in early adulthood the majority of them switched priorities between then and their thirties. Women who abandoned a focus on domesticity, for a focus on their employment or careers, did so for a variety of reasons—dissatisfaction with full-time domesticity, an unstable marriage or relationship, a tight household budget, or good employment opportunities. The women who switched their focus from employment to family are described below.

Veering Toward Domesticity

Kathleen Gerson

The lives of the women analyzed in the first part of this chapter underwent significant change in adulthood. These women traded their earlier work ambitions and aversions to domesticity for motherhood and domestic orientations. They began adulthood with high aspirations and a strong ambivalence toward domestic pursuits, but adult events and experiences intervened to challenge their assumptions and redirect their lives. In contrast to their non-traditional counterparts, these women were exposed to forces in the home and on the job that loosened their psychological and actual ties to work and replaced them with children and domestic aspirations.

The backgrounds of this group's members were not substantially different from those of the other respondents. Indeed, taking socialization factors and starting points alone into account, these women were, if anything, more predisposed to seek out a non-domestic life pattern. Over 60 per cent of those whose early life orientations were non-domestic veered in a domestic direction. This chapter explains why this group veered toward domesticity and what distinguishes it from those who did not.

Declining Work Aspirations and the Home as a Haven

Like non-traditional women, women who veered toward domesticity experienced events that pushed them off their expected tracks. This group, however, was propelled down a different road. Unlike non-traditional women, they were subjected to the traditional package of incentives and constraints that have historically made domesticity attractive and other options difficult and costly for women to choose. Members of this group were more likely than those who veered toward non-traditional pursuits to become committed to traditional marriages that undermined efforts at career building, insulated them from economic squeezes, and allowed them to implement domestic choices. They were also more likely to encounter blocked work opportunities, which enhanced the pull of motherhood and domesticity. They were thus drawn toward domestic commitments despite the structural changes leading other women to eschew such choices. In this sense, their lives underscore the continuing forces of traditional arrangements, which have persisted even as new alternatives have gained growing numbers of adherents.

The Precedence of Personal Relationships

For those who veered toward domesticity, stable marriages and committed relationships with men provided the conditions that made the bearing and rearing of children possible. Committed heterosexual partnerships also promoted the development of the desire to do so.

Most in this group struck a traditional bargain with male partners. Through a negotiated process, they exchanged allegiance to their partner's career for emotional and financial support. This bargain exacted a sometimes subtle, sometimes obvious cost at the workplace because the male partner's job took precedence over the respondent's own. Long-term commitment to a heterosexual relationship thus gradually undermined these women's work commitments and directed them toward mothering and domesticity.

Developing commitment to marriage over work

Women who traded work accomplishments for a committed relationship confronted an intractable conflict between their public and private commitments. Either directly or circuitously, these women had to *choose between* a valued relationship and the promise of satisfying work. When a relationship was an accomplished fact and a career a risky possibility, the option of family was more compelling than the option of work. This married woman in her late twenties thus relinquished a promising job in a male-dominated occupation in order to preserve a relationship she valued more:

> Q: If you were so happy being a customs inspector, why didn't you stay with it?
>
> A: The customs thing was interesting, exciting to me, but at that point I got married and *that* became very important to me. So it was to keep that relationship. It was more desirable to live with Don than to be a customs inspector.

For women faced with a conflict between commitment to work and commitment to an intimate partner, a number of factors promoted the choice of love over work. First, these traditional partnerships were based, at least in part, on a mutual, if often unspoken, assumption that the male partner's work mattered more. Because women in this situation generally perceived that they benefited from their partners' success, they became enlisted in the process of male career building. When conflicts arose between two careers, as they often did, it was the woman who sacrificed job opportunities.

For example, career building often required geographic mobility. When the male partner's career took precedence, women in these relationships were forced to go along with their partners' work demands at the expense of their own. (Papanek 1973 and Kanter 1977a; 1977b discuss how middle-class male careers have historically required the efforts of two persons—a man at the office and a woman at home.) This need to follow where the male career led made it difficult to establish a solid base at the workplace or to take advantage of advancement opportunities when they arose. This homemaker and mother of two declined a promotion so that she could follow her spouse during the early years of their marriage:

> A: I did take a job with the telephone company and left when I had my first child and was offered a management position. I know a lot of people at the

phone company now, women who are making exorbitant salaries, and then I think, 'Gee, that would have been me if I had stuck with it.' [But] we were doing a lot of moving. . . . I couldn't really make a commitment to anyone, because Jeff was in a training program, and every time he got a promotion, we moved. I go with my husband wherever he goes; that was always a very clear thing.

The threat of losing a valued relationship also posed a powerful obstacle to female career development. When success could be purchased only at the expense of a relationship, women in traditional relationships chose to forgo long-standing dreams as well as real opportunities. This respondent chose to avoid competing with her spouse, for she feared a win at work would entail a greater loss at home:

Q: Why didn't you pursue your interest in retail merchandising?
A: I explored the field when we were first married, but it was a strange situation. We laugh about it now. My husband was at ——. I had an interview with ——, and I thought, 'Well, gee, what if I get to be a buyer and he doesn't? That could really blow a relationship.' So I guess you would say I deferred a little.

Some women translated the fear of losing a relationship into a fear that they lacked the ability to handle a more demanding position. It is difficult to distinguish between fear of success and fear of failure in these instances. Despite this 28-year-old, childless secretary's elaborate efforts to convince herself that she really did not want a promotion, she acknowledged that her partner wanted it less than she did. She thus perceived that a career could be purchased only at the expense of love, security, and motherhood. Faced with such potentially high costs, she declined to take advantage of advancement opportunities that arose:

A: I had a couple of opportunities to get into sales, and I passed them up. I don't know if that was wise, but anyway . . .
Q: Why did you pass them up?
A: I know the business and everything, but now I'm living with Bill. He's not a businessman; he's a country boy, and he likes me to spend my time with him. I think my main reason for turning it down was I was scared of it, too, you know. Bill expressed his opinion, although he would never say to me, 'Don't do it.' But I think deep down inside the idea scared me.
Q: Why did the idea scare you?
A: Bill wanted me to be a secretary. And I thought, why should I take on more responsibility and travel and entertain and get involved? So I just decided no. But I think deep down inside it just sounds like such a big challenge for me, and I think I'm scared about it. . . . I'm getting older, the family image. I really want to become a mother someday, and that's really on my mind, I think. And I guess I keep thinking, if I get into sales, that's going to get further and further away [from having a family]. . . . I'm really kind of split right down the middle, because you could eventually make a lot of money being in sales, and I like that part of it. But, like I say, my personal life means so much more to me. I'm really happy with Bill, and that means more to me than my job.

Although it may appear that these women behaved according to Matina Horner's 'motive to avoid success' syndrome (1972), their actions did not result from a psychological handicap peculiar to the female sex. Their choices were rooted in structural circumstances that forced them to choose between love and work and threatened to exact a great price if they chose work over love. In short, these women *did* have something to lose by succeeding. To the extent that they perceived their options correctly, they made sensible choices in an effort to preserve personal happiness. They did not respond in peculiarly 'feminine' and irrational ways.

We must look, therefore, to the decision-making context as a whole to understand when fear of success is experienced and why such fear is acted on rather than overcome or ignored. A psychological process may set up a tension, but it does not predetermine how an actor will resolve it, especially when she experiences a variety of conflicting emotions. Fear is only one of a number of potentially motivating emotions, and not necessarily the most influential on behaviour. We may fear the very goals we are motivated to seek, but fear will not in itself prevent us from seeking them.

Actual choices, as distinct from fears or hopes, thus depend on social circumstances and on how the social context sets up a balance of gains and losses. Because women face different sets of costs and benefits, they vary in the extent to which success at work threatens other valued life pursuits. They also vary in the degree to which they 'fear' success rather than embrace it unambivalently and in the degree to which such fear actually impedes their work mobility. For women in traditional partnerships, who were faced with a choice between love and work, the high cost of work success was simply not deemed worth the price.[1]

If subtler inducements failed to dampen their enthusiasm for work commitment, women sometimes faced more overt opposition from traditional husbands. In these instances, a male partner intervened directly to thwart a woman's work plans so that he might preserve some valued aspect of his life. Patriarchal authority prevailed when this mother of two sought to enter police work:

Q: What happened to your plans to become a policewoman?
A: I got married, and my husband said no. He didn't feel that was a position for his wife and the mother of his kids to be in. It's not an eight-to-five job, and sometimes it's an 18-hour job; so he didn't go for that.
Q: Were your plans for becoming a policewoman serious at that time?
A: They were at the point when I realized I had to make a choice, and they became less. I didn't particularly *like* it, but I didn't have much choice.

Men also intervened less directly to dampen women's chances for success at work. In some instances, simply caring for a man led to the loss of workplace opportunities. This homemaker's first husband required as much attention as a child, eventually reducing her career aspirations to the hope of mere economic survival:

A: [In my] early twenties I was very work-oriented. I did get married when I was 20, a previous marriage, and that sort of sidetracked it. Where before I think I'd been more career-oriented, marrying left it as 'work' rather than career.
Q: What happened?
A: It wasn't a decision. It happened that the man I married was more of a babysitting job; so to maintain the marriage was as much as I could handle. Work became just something I had to do to feed us without really having the energy to put myself into it, to consider it a career. In fact, at the time, I worked at a bank, and they had an opening. But because my personal life was so fouled up, it sort of shot down my possibilities of getting that, which was a bad move on my part.

Thus, through a variety of mechanisms, commitment to a traditional relationship directly and indirectly undermines a woman's work ties. Although the proportion of marriages (or heterosexual partnerships) that operate according to these traditional rules is on the decline, arrangements that grant precedence to the male's career and penalize a woman for having one persist and continue to provide powerful incentives for women's domestic orientations. When a husband has strong incentives to see his wife succeed at work—as in the case of the economically squeezed family—the advantages he gains through her success may offset the marginal power he loses at home. Supportive spouses are not unknown in many modern marriages, and a supportive partner fuels non-traditional aspirations just as surely as a non-supportive one undermines them. Recent studies show, however, that although husbands support a certain measure of success on the part of their wives, they tend to get uncomfortable when that success, especially as measured by income, equals or surpasses their own. (See, for example, Blumstein and Schwartz 1983; Huber and Spitze 1980.) Patriarchal marriage patterns persist, however, not simply because men continue to benefit from them. Many women, too, continue to uphold patriarchal marriage because they have interests of their own to protect. Income inequality between the sexes, for example, reinforces a traditional sexual division of labour and supports the priority of the male career on practical grounds.[2]

The financial and emotional benefits of traditional partnerships led respondents with declining work aspirations to overlook or minimize the price they were paying. Indeed, this gradual decrease in work commitment was not typically experienced as a cost. Rather, respondents in traditional marriages felt fortunate to retain a domestic foothold in the face of so much change around them. They did not experience 'patriarchy' as domination, but rather greeted it as their good fortune in securing spouses willing to care for them and support their preferences for domesticity. This ex-secretary regarded her dependence on her husband's paycheque not as domination but as liberation:

> A: There's this mystique about the charismatic man, who's not a decent and dependable sort of man. They're movie types. . . . [My husband] goes to work and comes home at five, and [people] say, 'Isn't that boring?' And I say, 'No, not at all', because it gives me time to [do what I want]. I'm not always struggling down at the bottom of the ladder. Once you get that and taste it, you never want to let that go.

A part-time nurse felt privileged to have an option her husband did not share:

> A: [My husband] thinks I'm getting my cake and eating it, too. I get to stay home and am enjoying it. And he has an ulcer.

Commitment to a traditional relationship thus tended to exact gradual, often imperceptible costs at the workplace. Whether or not these costs were perceived as costs, women in this situation faced a choice between a satisfying personal life and satisfying work. This set of options made their choices not a matter of whether they lost, but rather what they chose to lose. For those with declining work aspirations, forgone work opportunities were easier to bear than the loss of emotional ties and a secure family life.

Consequences of marital commitment

However it was evaluated, the sequence of events that led these women to choose commitment to a man over commitment to work had two interdependent consequences. First, pressures to maintain a valued relationship diminished the chances of securing satisfying work and ultimately made domesticity more attractive. This mother of two chose homemaking after the search for challenging work proved futile:

> A: Becoming a teacher was sort of a little dream I had. When I did meet my husband, right after graduation, we just hit it off so perfect, I didn't want to jeopardize any relationship we might have by running off to go to school. [So] I went to the business school instead. [But] I didn't like typing and taking shorthand that well, so I ended up as a keypunch operator. I really didn't like that either, but I didn't know what I wanted to do. I just finished that, and I went to work as a keypunch operator for an insurance company. If I work again, I want it to be something I really like.

Second, decisions that built a committed relationship with a man also created a context in which child-bearing became feasible and desirable. When the experience of intimacy was coupled with declining work opportunities, it sparked a new attitude toward children and motherhood. Work aspirations lessened, and children came to be seen as a natural expression of the relationship. Newly awakened desires for parenthood emerged to replace work goals, and old ambivalences toward child-bearing subsided. A deepening commitment to her spouse nurtured a new desire for a child as this pregnant ex-saleswoman wearied of work at 33:

> Q: Have there ever been times when you seriously considered having children before now?
>
> A: I think I'd make a good mother, but I've never yearned for motherhood *per se*. The only time I ever *really* felt a desire to have a baby was with my husband before we were married.
>
> Q: So it's very tied up with the man?
>
> A: With the loving. And the way it's going, because if it hadn't been going right and if it hadn't been unfolding as it was, we wouldn't have had children. There was a time when I felt I would never have children. Around five or six years ago I felt that way.

The desire for a child did not result from an abstract, generalized 'mothering need'. It arose in the context of a specific relationship and from the commitment, goals, and desires this relationship fostered. In this context, having a child became an expression of commitment and a means for establishing a permanent home, as this 36-year-old ex-nurse and mother of two explained:

> Q: Thinking back to when you first got pregnant, what were your main reasons for having a child at this time?
>
> A: Because I wanted one [laughter]. I don't know. I guess after you live together so long, you just want more, and a baby really does fill it. It doesn't make your house a place where you stop in to sleep. It kind of brings you closer.

Although the stereotype that women leap hungrily into motherhood, dragging their reluctant husbands along, persists in theory as well as in popular culture, many mothers reported a reverse process. This 34-year-old mother of three acquiesced to her husband's strong desire for children:

> A: Jim was the person of primary importance, and he wanted kids. If I had married a man who didn't want children, fine. I would have gone along with that, too. I didn't think much about it. Motherhood was no big thing to me. I took it very casually. I had no great

emotional interest in it. I didn't fight it or anything. [But I did it] to please my husband.

Indeed, some planned for or bore children despite their own reluctance. These reluctant mothers (most of whom are members of the non-domestic group) viewed child-bearing not as an end in itself but as a means of pleasing a valued partner and cementing a relationship that might not otherwise endure. This motivation also prevented some from pursuing more autonomous goals. Remarriage to a child-oriented man thus prompted this 33-year-old, childless teacher to suppress her ambivalence toward motherhood and trade her emerging independence for the security of home and family:

A: After my divorce, I first became fully aware of the choices that I had. I liked not being responsible to anyone, just being in charge of myself. I realized the limits that a marriage places on that, that you can't always do what you want; you have to reach a compromise. But Peter is very understanding and willing to listen and willing to sacrifice in my behalf. So I'll probably have children. I don't know if freedom is worth the loneliness. You have to give up something to get something. I don't want to lose Peter, and children are very important to him. He has definitely made the difference in my decision.

Finally, for some, marriage itself was a package deal. The decision to marry automatically implied the decision to have children. For this part-time saleswoman and mother of two, the choice to bear children did not involve a conscious process:

Q: Why did you decide to have children?
A: I was very naïve. You get married; you get pregnant. We were only married a month, and I got pregnant. I guess I wouldn't have thought of getting married and *not* having children; put it that way. For me, the way my family grew was natural for us. It just was not a conscious decision-making thing.

The packaging of marriage and children had a greater impact on work aspirations than did marriage alone. The early arrival of children in a marriage placed immediate pressures on the new wife to withdraw from school or work. This robbed her of the time postponers had to be exposed to alternative options and opportunities. Thus, the decision to marry, itself, was a crucial turning point when this 35-year-old mother of two chose family over career:

A: I was 21 when I got married. I was not planning on marrying at that age. I was sort of star-struck. He was a hero from Vietnam, a green beret. He was also trying to decide if he was going to . . . go back to Vietnam. He was set for another tour then. I guess it was a big decision: Am I getting married, or am I going ahead with my career? We decided on marriage instead. At that time, I was very unsure about wanting to get married. My husband had strong feelings about having his own family. And I was at that point beginning to think I could financially put myself through school. There were a lot of mixed emotions at that time.
Q: Why did you get pregnant right away?
A: My husband wanted children because he was adopted. As he put it, either we get married and we start our family, or we just end our courtship and he goes back into the service. . . . That was a very strong factor [in having a child]. Like I said, I was star-struck at the time.

The packaging of marriage and child-bearing thus led some previously ambitious women to forgo strong work commitments.

The structure of traditional (or patriarchal) marriage and the maintenance of a committed relationship within such a marriage promoted the choice of family over committed work. Over time, women in traditional relationships watched opportunities outside the home slip by and workplace aspirations erode. As this happened, mothering took on greater importance in their lives.

Even in the absence of marital pressure, however, the relatively flat mobility structure of 'women's work' promoted domesticity and the defusing of ambition. Blocked opportunities at the workplace not only reduced women's motivation to work; limited job mobility also changed their orientations toward mothering, child-bearing, and homemaking. The push *out* of the workplace was thus as important as the attraction of a traditional marriage in encouraging initially ambitious women to veer toward domesticity.

Blocked Mobility and the Lure of Domesticity

In contrast to those whose exposure to expanded opportunities sparked increased commitment to work, blocked mobility promoted disaffection from work among those who experienced declining aspirations. Unlike their counterparts who veered away from domesticity, this group did not gain access to the widening job opportunities for women in male-dominated occupations that opened to some during the 1970s. Instead, they remained ghettoized in female-dominated, pink-collar occupations with limited chance for advancement (Howe 1977), often despite their fondest wishes and best efforts.[3]

Consigned to occupations that failed to provide significant upward mobility over their work careers, these respondents experienced declining work aspirations. Although their jobs often appeared promising at the outset, this initial glow tended toward monotony and frustration as blocks to upward movement were encountered. The resulting demoralization at the workplace dampened their initial enthusiasm for paid work, eased their ambivalence toward motherhood, and turned them toward the home in spite of their earlier aversion to domesticity.

Routes to blocked mobility

Most who experienced declining aspirations entered the workforce with high hopes, only to find that the opportunities available to them did not measure up to their expectations. A 33-year-old full-time mother of two took a secretarial position that seemed to promise initiative, responsibility, and eventual status, only to find that it rapidly degenerated into busywork:

> A: In my early twenties, I knew I would get a job, and I knew what I needed. By this time, I was thinking career. I was on my own. I wanted a job that had responsibilities and no slack time. When I interviewed, I'd rather be adamant than get the wrong job.
>
> Q: Why did you take the job as secretary at ———?
>
> A: In the beginning, it was terrific. It was a brand new plant; they had to hire 200 people. I had the responsibility of setting up all the filing; the job of figuring out how to set up a lot of record-keeping systems was mine. They sent me back to Virginia to a seminar to pick up on that. The fact that they would send *me* to fly back instead of sending my boss—I thought that really showed promise. Then everybody *got* hired and all my systems were set up and worked very well, worked too well. I would finish my work on Tuesday morning and have to sit there until Friday afternoon. And that for me, personally, was as much agony as anyone could impose on me.

Others entered dead-end 'careers' not as the result of initial enthusiasm but because they possessed no better alternative. These respondents were unable to break out of traditionally female occupations despite their own desire to do so. This 33-year-old homemaker and mother of two found that even a college education did not open the door to occupational opportunities. Economic necessity and lack of parental and social support forced her to relinquish the hope of joining a male-dominated profession in favour of work in a female-dominated one—work she ultimately grew to detest:

Q: What did you do after college?

A: I was sort of ambitious at that point. I was thinking of law or business. It was pretty much put down by the family, who felt that was ridiculous; it was better to get the teaching credential, which was *their* thinking. It was woman's work, blah, blah, blah. I did *not* want to go into teaching. I was forced into that because I needed to get a job. So I went to get the credential to get a higher paying job than the secretarial shit. I wanted to get out of the house; I wanted independence. There were no other options for me at that point. I was desperately angry. I saw my brother get offered his job right from the placement centre and then they hired me to type.

Q: What happened after you got your credential?

A: Then the series of nightmares began. I can only think of teaching in terms of nightmares, I'm sorry to say. They gave me a permanent job teaching art. It was just gruesome. I made money, but it was awful. There was no way out. You can't go up in a job like that. You can't change it in any way. It's a war zone teaching in the public school system. I really didn't like it.

Thus, among both the high-school and the college educated, the route to blocked mobility involved a process of channelling women with initially high work aspirations into female-dominated occupations. Some entered these occupations enthusiastically; others were forced to opt for work they had hoped to avoid. Whatever their initial feelings and motives, however, the structure of opportunity they encountered was the same. Nurses, librarians, primary school teachers, and other female professionals generally faced the same low pay, circumscribed discretion, and limited advancement opportunities that their clerical counterparts confronted. Whether clerical or professional, these workers encountered poor working conditions and blocked mobility. In addition, female-dominated professions tend to cluster among those 'helping professions' where the gap between clients' needs and the limited resources available to help them leads to high rates of 'burnout' among workers (whom Lipsky, 1980, calls 'street-level bureaucrats'). Low status and an erratic work schedule left this ex-nurse disillusioned:

A: I liked working, but I just couldn't stand working at nights or on weekends. Things were getting worse and worse, and I couldn't stand being put down.

The route to blocked mobility began with the choice of a traditional female occupation. This choice, whether forced under protest or embraced enthusiastically, held unforeseen and unintentional consequences for both working-class and middle-class women with initially high work aspirations. Unlike their peers who experienced rising work aspirations, these women encountered blocked advancement and a host of attendant frustrations. Limited movement upward combined with low pay, low status, circumscribed control, and a lack of challenge to encourage a downward spiral of work commitment among this group of initially aspiring women.

The choice of a female occupation, however, does not inevitably lead to this conclusion. Among those who veered away from domesticity, some were given unanticipated chances to advance and others were able to switch occupations rather than forsake work commitment. Whatever the route, women who veered away from domesticity were generally able to break out of the female labour ghetto. In the process, they improved their position at the workplace as well as the conditions of their work.

Unlike their more fortunate peers, however, women with declining aspirations did not meet unanticipated opportunities at work and were unable to break out of traditional female jobs. What distinguishes these women from those whose disenchantment with their jobs sparked an occupational change rather than a rejection of work altogether?

Just as the time was not 'right' among members of the first group to opt for domesticity when workplace dissatisfaction mounted, the time was never quite 'right' for those with declining aspirations to make an occupational change that would have improved their work situation. Both groups were constrained, but in different ways. The first group lacked the means to opt for domesticity (for example, a willing partner); the second lacked the means, and especially the economic means, to escape from unrewarding work to pursue a new occupation. Even though events triggered the desire for change, the means were not available. At such critical points, women with declining aspirations were forced to stay in a bad situation that ultimately led to work disaffection.

Constraints other than commitment to a heterosexual relationship, especially economic constraints, also served as powerful inhibitors to career development. Financial pressures prevented this discouraged primary school teacher from pursuing a profession that promised greater social and personal reward:

A: I was separated in 1974. That was kind of a turning point because teaching just wasn't very gratifying. I felt I really needed something more for myself. I signed up for the LSAT and went through all the red tape, but I never took it.

Q: Why?

A: I seem to be unable to leave what I'm doing, because of the financial risk of losing the income and taking a chance on that, maybe not finding something else. I have felt trapped. I didn't feel that I had a choice to stop and quit and find another job because I've always had financial obligations. So here I am 11 years later, doing something I don't like doing. I feel overall my life has been wasted.

Thus, financial need kept some in jobs they disliked, which led to waning self-confidence as well as work disaffection. Because there is usually a delicate balance between economic need and how much a woman is motivated to work, job commitment persisted only for those who found satisfying employment that fed their egos as well as their bank accounts. When this search proved futile, a woman's outlook turned toward other pursuits, as in the case of this disillusioned government bureaucrat approaching 30:

Q: Has working affected your feelings about yourself in any way?

A: It has in terms of I'm really disappointed that I haven't changed before now, that it's taken me so long to get my rear end in motion and jolly well take the risk of change.

Q: Why do you think you haven't changed jobs?

A: Probably because it has been so economically unfeasible. But now I know the house will somehow get paid for. The relationship will go on; somehow we'll make it if I don't earn this many dollars. So if I don't like it, I'm really an unpleasant lady to live with, and I ought to be doing something else.

Q: So you think you'd prefer staying home and having children?

A: I think it would be better because the gratification I'm *not* getting from the job hopefully I would get from being a parent. I would get a lot more instant feedback and more control over the situation. My change in behaviour, attitude, activity, whatever, would have a direct effect, which I really don't feel now. The only reason I say that is that I have not achieved any goal in work.

As their hopes for work accomplishment dwindled in the face of blocked opportunities, these women veered toward the home. They looked to motherhood to provide the fulfillment work had failed to offer.

Consequences of blocked work opportunities

The consequences of blocked work opportunities reached beyond the confines of the workplace itself into the most private spheres of these women's lives. As their work expectations turned to disappointment and disaffection, women with declining aspirations began to look elsewhere for meaningful 'work'.

Two additional changes in outlook accompanied declining work aspirations. Previous ambivalences toward motherhood subsided, and domesticity became more attractive than it had earlier appeared. These changes were closely related, and one enhanced the pull of the other.

First, the decision to have a child typically coincided with mounting frustration at work. This 31-year-old full-time mother of two decided to have her first child at 27, when her secretarial job hit a dead end:

Q: Was secretary as high as you could go?

A: Apparently. The company was good about using young men; they had a lot of young male executives. I didn't see any young female executives.

Q: What happened next?

A: By this time I had married Jim, and we were talking about having a family; so it became a case of waiting it out. I wanted to have a baby. So the last six months was an extremely frustrating waiting period until I got pregnant. The career went down the drain, and it was extreme boredom.

As the experience of working soured, motherhood provided an enticing alternative, and doubts about child-bearing turned to curiosity and enthusiasm.

The experience of blocked work mobility, although not the only factor, was a major contributing factor in this group's decision to become mothers. It promoted declining work aspirations, which in turn lessened old ambivalences toward motherhood, gave child-bearing a more fulfilling aura, and halted the strategy of postponement. Although those who encountered unanticipated work opportunities found the child-bearing decision increasingly problematic, those who faced blocked mobility found motherhood an increasingly attractive option.

A second consequence of blocked work mobility and the declining aspirations it fostered is that the decision to bear a child became linked to and reinforced by the decision to withdraw from the paid workforce to rear a child. In the context of dissatisfaction with work, the meaning of motherhood changed: bearing a child became not simply an end in itself; it also furnished an alternative occupation. In other words, motherhood provided an avenue—in most cases, the only avenue—toward domesticity.

The linking of child-bearing with domesticity, which made child-bearing problematic for women with rising aspirations, had the reverse impact on those with declining aspirations. These women came to define motherhood as full-time mothering. This disillusioned teacher, for example, let go of earlier aversions and embraced motherhood as the only acceptable escape from work conditions she defined as oppressive:

Q: What changed your feelings about having children?
A: To be honest, what changed is that I reached a point in the job where I was just hating it daily, plus we were also moving into a new house. It's almost as stupid as saying, 'What colour do I paint the room? Yellow. We'll have a baby in there. Let's get pregnant.' We went and got pregnant. The time seemed right. It was a relief not working, the relief of not having that pressure. I was doing something I wanted to do.

This ex-teacher's aide wanted more than a child; she wanted the chance to stay at home as well:

Q: What were the main reasons you got pregnant when you did?
A: I'll tell you the truth. I wanted an excuse to stay home. I wanted an excuse to do my own thing—not to be a housewife, but to do my own thing. I loved having my own time. Being a woman is the neatest role. You can choose what you do with your time, whereas men still have that pressure. I was glad I quit [work]; I hated the nine-to-five drag.

A would-be mother did not typically see the link between the development of disaffection from the workplace and the decision to have a child, but this process was all the more powerful because it was hidden. The birth of a child seemed natural and unforced in these cases. As this ex-clerk who could 'hardly wait to stop' working explained:

Q: Why did you decide to have a baby?
A: We really loved each other, and we wanted to share in creating one. . . . We decided the time was right.

This ex-secretary, for whom work was becoming 'terrible', agreed:

Q: Why do you think you decided to have a child at that time?
A: I don't know. I never really enjoyed children. I don't know what it is you feel. You just want one.

The 'right' time to have a child was consistently linked to job dissatisfaction. This ex-teacher came to view child-bearing as a natural, inevitable choice, despite her earlier doubts:

A: I think there's a very ambivalent period, before you're married or just after when you *don't* have any children, and you look around and you see your friends and they are tied down and you say, 'Well, I'll put this off for a while.' And more and more of your friends do have children, and you sort of join the crowd and have a couple, and that's what happened. I don't think *anybody* is *desperate* to have children. Maybe there are cases, but I wasn't that desperate. I just did it one day.

Although not apparent to the person making the choice, the movement toward motherhood was rooted in the structure and experience of work itself. Blocked mobility triggered a downward spiral of aspirations and gave child-bearing a liberating aura by comparison. In this context, the choice to bear a child—and the choice to withdraw from the workplace to rear it—felt natural. In important respects, women's work is organized to promote this turn toward a home-centred life. The structure of blocked work opportunities thus encouraged a set of related responses in this group of initially aspiring women—the choice to bear a child, the choice of becoming a full-time mother, and the perception that both these choices were 'natural'. In some cases, blocked mobility and frustrating work were even judged to be good fortune. An ex-teacher and recent mother exclaimed:

> A: If my career had really taken off, it's conceivable to me that I could have come to a decision not to have children. But I don't think that would have been a good idea. I think I was meant to have children.

Domesticity as a Way of Life

For women veering in a traditional direction, the decision to bear a child involved two closely linked and mutually reinforcing choices. Becoming a mother and becoming a homemaker came to be defined as the same act. Unlike those who veered away from domesticity, respondents with declining work aspirations found this 'package' of choices all the more inviting because these two acts were united: each aspect of the choice enhanced the pull of the other. An ex-nurse favourably compared her position as a homemaker to the alternative she would face if child rearing did not consume her daytime hours:

> A: [If I didn't have children,] I'd probably still be working at the health department, and I would feel just awful. I don't know whether the tension [I felt at work] was because of the health department. I shouldn't say that the children make me *not* tense. Just being home is much more relaxing.
>
> Q: And you wouldn't be home if you didn't have children?
>
> A: I don't think so. I would probably want to be, but with society the way it is, everybody thinks you should be working if you don't have children. I don't know if I'd be strong enough to buck it.

Thus, even when a return to work had been planned, unpleasant work experiences and blocked mobility sent these new mothers into the home. One day back on the job convinced this ex-secretary that mothering was far more rewarding and challenging than the work she was paid to do:

> Q: How did you feel about the idea of quitting work to care for your child?
>
> A: I loved it. I hated my job. I didn't quit right away. I took a leave and then went back after he was born and worked one day and quit. I had people tell me, 'After you're off for a few months, you're going to get so bored; you're going to want to come back to work.' What they didn't realize was that there was no way I could be as bored. [I wouldn't go back] unless somebody wants to make me the boss, but I have doubts that that's ever going to happen.

The realization that staying home was preferable to working came as a surprise to those who saw themselves as committed workers. They made the decision to mother full-time only after the birth of the first child, when they were finally in a position to make a comparative assessment between the job of child rearing and paid work. An ex-clerk discovered unexpected pleasure in full-time mothering:

> A: I thought I could work and have a child, too. I was totally prepared [to return to work], and the only thing I hadn't prepared myself for was how I was going to feel the day she was born about going

back to work. I thought it would be easy; I thought I'd be able to do it. Then I realized that I couldn't stand being away from her. [And I was] frustrated on the job because I really didn't have the job I wanted. The best alternative seemed to be quit and stay home.

After a history of ill-rewarded jobs and thwarted aspirations these women chose domesticity as the better alternative, even though they could have pursued other avenues. They concluded that motherhood was the only occupation that did not threaten to disappoint. This ex-secretary decided to have a second child rather than return to work:

Q: What about the decision to have your second child?

A: I had intended to quit work when I got pregnant with Jenny, to wait until Jenny was in school, then go back to work. But when I went back, I wanted to go back as other than a secretary. I thought, would I like to be an electrician, a fireman? What is there in the world that I want to spend the rest of my life at? Then it came to me that I really enjoy what I'm doing now more than anything else I've done or anything I could think of doing. So I decided to have another baby. For a year I had been going back and forth. Yes, no, yes, no. Once I had eliminated the other [a career] and only that was left [a child], it sort of solved itself and then became a strong desire.

For these women, mothering became their 'career'. They concluded that domesticity offered them many of the things they had sought in the paid workforce and failed to find: self-control, self-expression, self-direction. An ex-clerical worker explained:

Q: And now you like staying home?

A: I don't have to have anybody bossing me around! I like being with my children most of the time. Sometimes I don't, but . . . I like taking care of my own house and being in charge of what goes on in my own household.

This choice of domesticity was not without its costs. The hardest cost to bear was the lurking fear that, by giving up earlier work aspirations, these women had disappointed themselves and others. Because many of their female friends and neighbours *did* work, they faced either overt or covert social disapproval as well as personal doubts. This ex-secretary absorbed the disapproval of her peers, but nevertheless contested its validity:

A: [Sometimes I think] 'What's wrong with you? You want to be home.' But I really don't have any need [to work] at this point in our lives.

For those whose work experiences were deflating and discouraging and whose future prospects at work promised more of the same, domesticity offered freedom from market work and its attendant ills. Motherhood provided the route out of the workplace and into a more fulfilling job. Like their non-traditional counterparts, these respondents did not greet the accompanying devaluing of homemaking with enthusiasm. Given their other alternatives, however, they saw these drawbacks as a necessary and acceptable price to pay for the chance to engage in the more personally rewarding (if less socially rewarded) work of caring for children.

The Traditionally Sexual Division of Labour

Implementing a domestic choice required more than motivation; it also required structural support. Domesticity depended on the presence of a breadwinner who was willing and able to provide the economic means for his partner's withdrawal from paid work.[4] Those who veered away from domesticity often lacked this structural support. In contrast, those who veered toward domesticity could do so only because their spouses' economic support allowed it to happen. This enabling circumstance was a necessary, if not sufficient, condition for domesticity. It was, however, a circumstance that many took for granted. This salesman's wife, for example, mentioned her spouse's financial support almost as an afterthought:

Q: Why did you decide not to return to work after your children were born?
A: It really wasn't a conscious decision to work or not to work. It was just my lifestyle. I never had any doubts about my husband's ability to support us; so I didn't look for work outside the home for financial reasons. We always had a place to live, and we enjoyed the way we lived; so there was no burning need to go out and work.

Remember, however, that assessment of need is a subjective process. It involves agreement between *both* spouses that the emotional benefits of female domesticity outweigh the economic costs. This homemaker, for example, looked to her husband, a trucker, for 'permission' to stay home:

Q: Did you consider working after your children were born?
A: I just knew when my babies were little that I wanted to be the one to take care of them, and I know my husband thought that was just fine. His mother worked a lot when he was growing up, but he didn't feel I had to work because he never depended on my income. We didn't have any money worries at all. My husband's job was adequate. He never made super big money, but we didn't have any bills.

This reliance on the male paycheque had important repercussions on the sexual division of labour within the home. Those who opted for domesticity 'earned' their economic security by performing the least desirable tasks associated with caring for a child. This homemaker took total responsibility for all-night vigils in order to avoid paid work:

Q: How did you make a decision about not working?
A: When Gail was born, it was sort of a joke. Charlie said, 'The first time I have to get up and change diapers in the middle of the night, you go back to work', because he was working and I wasn't. If he had to get up in the middle of the night, there was something wrong with the arrangement. So I made sure I got up in the middle of the night.

The inequality in the income commanded by each partner reinforced this traditional exchange and made role reversal an option in name only. Trading places with her husband, a businessman, was unthinkable to this ex-nurse:

Q: Did you ever consider working and having your husband stay home to look after the baby?
A: That would have to be an economic question. Work is not a hobby. You work primarily to make money. It becomes a trade-off. If I could make more money than him, that's another thing.

In this context, it became difficult to distinguish preferences from real options. When a respondent realized that she would have to add paid employment to the work performed at home, her motivation to work outside the home decreased. Faced with the complications of combining home and market work, this ex-secretary concluded it was easier to stay home:

> A: Our understanding was, if I wanted to work, I could work—as long as I made adequate provisions for the children. Well, the pieces didn't fit. It was a very strung-out kind of puzzle thing; it just didn't all fit right.

In the face of mounting duties at home, work for pay became increasingly less attractive, and the pride of earning a paycheque was replaced by the pride of caring for others in less strictly economic ways. This eased the acceptance of economic dependency, even among ex-workers, such as this 33-year-old ex-secretary who had been accustomed to supporting herself for many years:

> Q: Was it difficult for you to adjust to not earning money?
> A: No. I liked it. My husband gives me money. It's not hard for me.

Once committed to domesticity, moreover, these women perceived events forcing others into the workplace as threats to a preferred way of life. Having relinquished occupational aspirations, this 27-year-old ex-clerk feared the loss, especially through divorce, of her construction worker husband's earnings and the way of life it permitted her to have:

> Q: Has having a child changed your feelings about yourself in any way?
> A: It made me very dependent, which is just the reverse of what I used to be. . . . I think [my husband] was attracted to me because I was very independent, and now I'm very dependent. I don't know what I would do if things didn't work out between him and me and we had to separate and I had to go to work to support my child. . . . I just don't know if I could handle that, taking her to some lady's house and saying, 'Here. Take care of my child while I'm at work.' It's scary to me.

In opting for motherhood, women with declining work aspirations traded what they had come to define as a bad job for what, in comparison, came to be seen as a good one. Disenchantment with work created the context that made mothering attractive; it also reinforced a traditional structure of marriage and parenting. This process involved gradual changes in orientation that were generally not experienced on a conscious level. Because breadwinning is a historic male responsibility and not working for pay a historical female 'right', the balance of male economic responsibility and female economic dependency was rarely noticed unless it was threatened or upset. For this group, disruptions in the traditional sexual division of labour did not occur. Rather, a set of interrelated and reinforcing circumstances made traditional arrangements the preferred alternative.

Notes

1. Gilligan (1982) argues that women tend to stress a morality of intimacy and interconnectedness over a morality of autonomy, objectivity, and independent accomplishment. This female morality, she suggests, contrasts with a male morality that affirms independence, rationality, and personal success at the expense of connectedness. She concludes that the male stress on accomplishment

at the expense of intimacy is as skewed as, or even more skewed than, the female stress on interpersonal connection at the expense of individual autonomy.

A morality that excludes connectedness is surely as suspect as a morality that excludes autonomy. Gilligan thus provides an important corrective to prevailing and one-sided theories of moral development. However, her characterization of the first perspective as distinctively male and the second as distinctively female is questionable. There is nothing inherently masculine or feminine about stressing independence versus interdependence. Many women place success before interpersonal commitment. Moreover, some women's concern with interpersonal relationships and some men's concern with success reflect and emerge from the structural constraints each group faces. The fundamental problem for both sexes stems from structural arrangements that force people to choose between the equally important pursuits of love and work.

2. Despite a dramatic rise in the ratio of employed women to employed men, large earning differentials persist according to sex. According to Masnick and Bane (1980: 100), 'The mean earnings of female workers stand at about 56 per cent of those of males, a rate that has been surprisingly constant over time. In 1955, the median earnings of year-round, full-time female workers were about 64 per cent of males, 60 per cent in 1965, and 59 per cent in 1975. The ratio of female to male earnings has, if anything, declined slightly over time.' This earnings gap persists even when age, educational level, prior work experience, and number of hours worked are controlled (Barrett 1979).
3. Although unprecedented job opportunities in male-dominated occupations opened to women during the 1970s, most women workers remain in overwhelmingly female occupations with relatively blocked advancement ladders (Howe 1977). Clerical, service, and private household jobs account for almost 55 per cent of all women workers. These female-dominated occupations are rarely structured to provide significant upward mobility over a work career. Moreover, whether an occupation is male-dominated or female-dominated, men tend to occupy a disproportionate share of the positions at the top. In sum, although growing, the percentage of female clerical workers, secretaries, bank tellers, saleswomen, nurses, and the like, able to rise into the ranks of management or into the better rewarded occupations still dominated by men remains small.
4. Despite the rise of the dual-income family, a significant number of women retain the social and psychological option of economic dependency. In contrast, men who feel trapped at the workplace are rarely able to muster similar material, social, and emotional support for *not* earning a wage—for themselves and their families. Even among the non-traditional respondents in this sample, who placed great importance on their own economic self-sufficiency, few expressed a willingness to provide full economic support for their partners or to indulge male partners who might prefer total domesticity to paid work.

References

Barrett, N.S. 1979. 'Women in the Job Market: Occupations, Earnings, and Career Opportunities', in *The Subtle Revolution: Women at Work*, ed. Ralph E. Smith (Washington, DC: Urban Institute).

Blumstein, P., and P.W. Schwartz. 1983. *American Couples: Money, Work, Sex* (New York: Morrow).

Gilligan, C. 1982. *In a Different Voice: Psychological Theory and Women's Development* (Cambridge: Harvard University Press).

Horner, M. 1972. 'Toward an Understanding of Achievement-related Conflicts in Women', *Journal of Social Issues* 28: 157–75.

Howe, L.K. 1977. *Pink-collar Workers: Inside the World of Women's Work* (New York: Putnam's).

Huber, J., and G. Spitze. 1980. 'Considering Divorce: An Expansion of Becker's Theory of Marital Instability', *American Journal of Sociology* 86 (July): 75–89.

Kanter, R.M. 1977a. *Men and Women of the Corporation* (New York: Basic Books).

———. 1977b. *Work and Family in the United States: A Critical Review and Agenda for Research and Policy* (New York: Russell Sage Foundation).

Lipsky, M. 1980. *Street Level Bureaucracy: Dilemmas of the Individual in Public Services* (New York: Russell Sage Foundation).

Masnick, G., and M.J. Bane. 1980. *The Nation's Families: 1960–1990* (Cambridge: Joint Center for Urban Studies of MIT and Harvard University).

Papanek, H. 1973. 'Men, Women, and Work: Reflections on the Two Person Career', in *Changing Women in a Changing Society*, ed. Joan Huber (Chicago: University of Chicago Press).

Chapter 18

Kathleen Gerson's findings indicate that the experiences women have in the paid workforce significantly shape their decisions as adults about whether to devote their time and energy more to family or to their careers/jobs. In a smaller study, Gillian Ranson explores a more specific question that follows from Gerson's work—that of the relationship between whether and when women have children, on the one hand, and their field of academic concentration and job choices, on the other. At a time when motherhood is often planned and thus (to a large extent) under women's control, many of us likely continue to think of women's life cycles as shaped mostly by their decisions about whether and when to have children. Yet, paid work has become increasingly essential for women, and women's jobs and careers increasingly monopolize their time and energy. Women's lives have become more like men's, in that respect. Meanwhile, social policies and programs have not changed significantly over time, in ways that would enable Canadian women to balance more easily the responsibilities of motherhood and employment. Thus, the decision about if and when to have children is a difficult one for many women. And Gillian Ranson's findings suggest that paid work may be a major factor shaping women's life cycles, including if and when they become mothers.

Education, Work, and Family Decision-making: Finding the 'Right Time' to Have a Baby[1]

Gillian Ranson

The challenges of combining family responsibilities and paid employment have been extensively documented, as has the fact that the combination has a different effect on women than on men. Becoming a parent has a more profound impact on women, because motherhood is much more difficult to synchronize with paid work than is the case with fatherhood. Women's exclusive biological capacity to bear children has come to be generalized to an exclusive capacity to care for them. Ideologies of motherhood which call into question women's commitment to paid employment underlie public policy-making which downplays the importance of providing quality public childcare. Women compelled either by economic necessity or their personal aspirations to build a career at work may either defer the transition to motherhood, or face considerable conflict and struggle as they attempt to synchronize motherhood and a paying job. They may also find that some jobs make the balance of paid work and motherhood much more manageable than do others.

The research described here is part of a larger study of the effect of educational and occupational choices on the transition to motherhood among university-educated women. Specifically, this research examines the *timing* of the transition, and the influence that different educational and occupational choices may exert on the decision to have—or not to have—a baby. The first proposition to be addressed is that the *kind* of university education has an effect on the timing of first childbirth among university-educated women (assuming that it is likely to be through access to particular labour markets and kinds of jobs that the influence of particular degree choices will be most clearly felt).

Evidence that such a link exists comes from a longitudinal study of 185 female university graduates who were first surveyed after their graduation from the University of Alberta in 1985 (Krahn and Lowe 1993).[2] Between 1985 and 1992 they were part of an ongoing panel study which generated a detailed record of their work experiences after graduation, and also their changing family circumstances. In 1986, 25 per cent were married and 5 per cent were raising children. When last surveyed, in the spring of 1992, 70 per cent were married and 31 per cent were raising children. The fact that some 70 per cent were *not* raising children—in 1992, when their average age was 30—was not surprising given the evidence of delayed child-bearing on the part of educated women noted below. But since all of these women were 'educated', and 31 per cent of them had not postponed having children, the question of the *timing* of the transition to motherhood in this apparently fairly homogeneous group became relevant. Comparing graduates from the five university faculties included in the study—arts, business, education, engineering, and science—it became clear that the women who were most likely to be mothers by 1992 were the education graduates, most of whom went on to become elementary schoolteachers.

More persuasive support for the link between educational choice, occupation, and fertility comes from a preliminary analysis of the 1991 public use microdata files for the 1991 census. Table 18.1 compares a sample of women aged 28–38 with university degrees in education, business, engineering, and nursing, in terms of whether or not they have children.

As Table 18.1 suggests, women in this age group with education and nursing degrees—both linked to traditionally female occupations—are much more likely to have children than are women with degrees in business and engineering—which link to traditionally male-dominated occupations.

Table 18.1 Presence of Children by Major Field of Study: 1991 Census (Public Use Microdata Files)

	Education	Business	Engineering	Nursing
No children	39.1%	52.6%	47.9%	38.4%
Children	60.9%	47.4%	52.1%	61.6%
n	2,954	1,560	307	698
	(100%)	(100%)	(100%)	(100%)
(Total = 5,519)				

$X^2 = 85.62$

$p < .001$

These findings clearly invite further investigation. For example, is it something about education graduates that makes them so much more likely than business graduates or engineering graduates to have children sooner rather than later? Or is [it] something about the way their work is organized, compared to the work of engineers or business graduates, that facilitates (if it does not actually promote) earlier child-bearing? The longitudinal study, with its small sample, could not ordinarily be expected to supply generalizable answers. But given the similarity of its findings to census data findings[3] on the relationship between educational background and fertility, interpretive research aimed at exploring the relationship among a sub-sample of the study participants could be considered a legitimate first step toward understanding the relationship in the much larger census sample. It is as a first step, then, that the present research is intended.

Literature Review

The nature of women's decision-making in relation to both fertility and occupation is relevant to the current discussion. But the literature tends to bracket off each area; few researchers explore both dimensions fully. Several studies of reproductive decision-making (e.g., Daniels and Weingarten 1982; Soloway and Smith 1987; Currie 1988) report the perceived importance of meeting educational and career goals before starting a family. But they fail to address material differences in work experience, and the differences between careers in terms of how easily goals *can* be met.

Studies of women's occupational aspirations and choices are similarly oblique in their attention to reproductive decision-making. In general, much tends to be assumed. Studies from the 1970s and early 1980s (e.g., Trigg and Perlman 1976; Lemkau 1979; 1983) typically focused on individual background and personality characteristics, or the inventory of feminine and masculine traits that accompanied traditional and non-traditional career choices. But this focus has given way to research which explores the social context of individual career choices. Notable here is the work of Eccles and her colleagues (Eccles 1987; 1994). This research addresses the extent to which gender socialization mediates people's subjective values—which in turn influence educational and occupational choices. Implicit in this work is the assumption that women are more likely than men to 'value' family over paid employment, with obvious consequences for their employment choices.

But Eccles and her colleagues also note the 'multiple roles and multiple goals' which increasingly characterize women's lives (Eccles 1994: 603). Assumptions from a human capital perspective that women's higher subjective valuation of family life may reduce their commitment and attachment to paid employment, or lead them to make traditional rather than non-traditional career choices are now being challenged (see also Moen and Smith 1986; Bielby and Bielby 1988; Desai and Waite 1991). Also under question is the assumption that work aspirations, whatever the motives behind them, actually do influence employment outcomes. Levine and Zimmerman (1995) replicated and built on the work of Jacobs (1987) and found, as he did, a 'very weak relationship' between traditional or non-traditional work aspirations and actual achievement (Levine and Zimmerman 1995: 82). In other words, labour-market and workplace forces may influence employment outcomes at least as much as family intentions and aspirations. Indeed, as Gerson (1985) points out, women's labour-force experiences may significantly shape the employment choices they make as mothers, sometimes challenging long-held beliefs and intentions. In her research on women's family and employment choices, Gerson found women who intended to pursue careers after having children, but who later changed their minds, often because of blocked mobility or other unsatisfactory work experiences. She also found women who intended to stay home with their children, but instead returned to the paid labour force—often because they found their jobs unexpectedly satisfying and fulfilling. A similar confounding of assumptions about women's career choices and their child-bearing intentions appears in research on female college students by Baber and Monaghan (1988). Comparisons between students planning traditional and non-traditional ('innovative') careers found that the groups differed little in their intention to have children. Even though innovators anticipated delaying child-bearing, the groups did not significantly differ in their intention to establish a career before having children, and most of the women were highly career-oriented. The researchers conclude: '[W]hile these young women have been rethinking their career options and expanding their occupational horizons, there has not been a reciprocal rethinking of their child-bearing expectations. Their career orientation seems to exist in a separate sphere from marriage and fertility expectations' (Baber and Monaghan 1988: 201).

Theoretical Framework

In attempting to account for the fact that women in traditional female occupations have children sooner than women in non-traditional occupations, the powerful effects of gender socialization must be considered. Clearly some women choose to become elementary schoolteachers, for example, because they intend to have children and anticipate that teaching will more readily accommodate their family responsibilities than a less traditional career. But this explanation takes no account of the women who become teachers because they want to become teachers, not because they want to become mothers. Nor does it account for the women who want to be engineers and accountants and *also* mothers.

As the literature review suggests, the link between occupational choices and family decision-making is complex; intentions are often confounded by the material circumstances of particular jobs and particular family relationships. If the first proposition of this research, noted earlier, is that there *is* a link between occupation and fertility, the second proposition must be that, whatever directs a woman to a particular traditional or non-traditional career choice, the organization of the work she does will materially influence her family decision-making. It is this second proposition that organizes what follows.

Data and Methods

The Youth Employment Study which impelled the present research was designed as a multi-sample, comparative, longitudinal panel survey, initially in three cities (Edmonton, Sudbury, and Toronto). The university sub-sample was a one-in-three systematic sample of all graduates from five faculties (arts, business, education, engineering, and science). An initial response rate of 64 per cent to the first mailed survey, combined with a decision to omit from the study students born before 1955, yielded a sample of 589 graduates, 289 of them women (Krahn and Mosher 1992). The present research focuses on the female university graduates in the Edmonton sample.

Of the 289 women first sampled in 1985, 185 women (64 per cent of the original sample) remained with the study through all five waves of the survey (1985, 1986, 1987, 1989, and 1992). Of particular interest were the numbers of women who were raising children by 1992, and the faculties from which they graduated. A description of the sample on the basis of these variables is found in Table 18.2. Briefly, as Table 18.2 shows, only 31 per cent of the women (n = 57) were raising children. Of these, 68 per cent (n = 39) were education graduates. In fact, 47 per cent of all the education graduates in the sample had children by 1992, compared to 18 per cent of graduates from other faculties.

Table 18.2 Presence of Children by Faculty of Graduation: Youth Employment Study (1992)

	Education	Arts	Business	Engineering	Science	All
No	44	42	23	5	14	128
	(53%)	(82%)	(85%)	(83%)	(78%)	(69%)
Yes	39	9	4	1	4	57
	(47%)	(18%)	(15%)	(17%)	(22%)	(31%)
	83	51	27	6	18	185
	(100%)	(100%)	(100%)	(100%)	(100%)	(100%)

The characteristics of the 1992 respondents, as described above, raised important questions. Even allowing for concerns about attrition from the original panel study (see Ranson 1995 for details), there seemed to be clear educational and occupational differences between women with children and women who had no children—differences which, as noted earlier, seemed to echo the most recent census findings on educational background and fertility among this age group. In order to explore this relationship, in-depth interviews were conducted between November 1993 and March 1994, with 45 of the 1992 respondents. In order to make the interview sample as representative as possible, prospective interviewees were drawn roughly equally from two categories of educational background (education graduates, and all others); within those two main groups, women with children and childless women were almost equally represented; and for purposes of the larger study, women in full-time paid employment, part-time paid employment, and those not in the paid labour force were also represented. The sampling strategy included a decision to over-sample mothers from faculties other than education; given that there were so few of them in 1992, *all* these women were approached, and an equivalent number of education graduate mothers were also chosen for comparison purposes. In the interests of making the study as comprehensive as possible, in view of the small number of women from other faculties who had had children by 1992, an attempt was made to conduct telephone interviews with as many as could be reached of the 31 women from *all* faculties who were married and childless in 1992. Nineteen telephone interviews were conducted through the summer of 1994.

The method chosen for the research was a semi-structured, open-ended interview which sought information on each woman's work and family history, the decisions she had made (or was in the process of making) about work and family, and the circumstances surrounding each decision. The women interviewees represented a wide range of domestic situations: there were women who were married or in relationships and who had children, married women who were pregnant for the first time, married women who had no children, and single or separated and divorced women who had no children. The line of questioning had to change to fit these different situations. The interviews, both face-to-face and by telephone, were informal. The 45 face-to-face interviews lasted from about 45 minutes to more than two hours; the 19 telephone interviews lasted on average about half an hour.

Table 18.3 Family Status of In-person Interviews at Interview Date

	Education Graduates	Other Graduates
Married with children	11	13
Married, pregnant	3	1
Married, no children	4	5
Engaged	1	–
Single	3	4

Findings

The women in the sample, who were well educated and predominantly middle-class, would be expected to have access to, and be knowledgeable about, effective contraception. Since assumptions about ability to control conception are fundamental to any discussion of reproductive decision-making, it is necessary to address first the extent to which these assumptions are justified in the present sample. Of the 36 women who either had children, or were pregnant for the first time when interviewed, six described their first pregnancies as unplanned. The first pregnancies of five other women could best be described as 'semi-planned': either a child was clearly anticipated, but arrived a little earlier than intended; or a pregnancy, while not being actively sought, was not being actively prevented either. Of these 11 women, six were teachers, and five were in other occupations. In other words, to the extent that unplanned pregnancies might undermine the argument of a link between fertility and occupation, in this group at least the effect is evenly distributed between traditional and non-traditional occupations. A further point worth making is that whether a baby was 'planned', and what the motivation was for the planning, are probably not questions that can be reliably answered once the baby has arrived. Original intentions and motivations are subverted to the reality of the child's presence, and quickly become irrelevant in most cases. That said, the tenor of the interviews strongly suggested that the 'semi-planned' pregnancies were experienced by women who were clearly intending to have children in the near future, and for whom the pregnancy was not an unwelcome experience. And the fact remains that more than two-thirds of the women who had been pregnant at least once (25 out of 36) described their pregnancies as planned. In these cases, planning seemed to involve the achievement of a pregnancy at a time which, for various reasons, seemed to be 'right'.

Reaching the 'Right Time': Women with Children

In most cases, several reasons for the 'rightness' of the timing were cited in combination. The most common were age, financial security (variously defined, but often including the purchase of a house), job security, and the achievement of professional goals on the part of either or both partners. For example, Siobhan,[4] an urban planner with a master's degree, had wanted to have children sooner than she did, but described how she was delayed by career constraints:

> School took too long, and we had sort of an agreement that I was going to work for at least three years, two or three years after I graduated—partly because I wanted to get my professional status, and you have to work for two years in the field. . . . That was part of the agreement that we had, and, after I'd worked two years I . . . started working on my husband.

According to Gail, a speech pathologist, having a baby 'just seemed like the next logical step':

> I guess because we had been married for a while and things were going OK there. We had our jobs . . . so both of us were kind of working on getting further than where we were at the time. It just seemed like the right thing to do. I think the other thing was, I mean age certainly is a factor. And I didn't want to start having kids at 35.

Tania, a bank manager, cited comfort with her marriage, and the ticking biological clock, as reasons for wanting her first child. But she also noted:

> I didn't want to have kids before I became manager because I felt it would limit my chances of becoming one. And once I'd become one then they'd have to give me the same level of job back.

For the women who were teachers, this ongoing job security was achieved by a permanent teaching certificate and a permanent contract with a school board. For most teachers, both were acquired after two years of full-time employment with a board. Sandra, an elementary schoolteacher, described the part her permanent contract played in her decision to have children:

> I have it [a permanent contract], yeah. And I am so thankful for that. I think I knew I wanted that before I even considered having kids. I needed that. That was my security blanket in a sense. And I know now, I think you can take up to a two-year leave with your permanent, then they have to place you. Not necessarily at the school that you left but they do have to place you.

Of the women in the sample who were pregnant or had children, 18 had worked as teachers (or were education graduates trying to get work as teachers). Eleven of these women had permanent, full-time teaching jobs at the time they first became pregnant. All but one of them took maternity leave and returned to teaching, either full- or part-time, under the provisions of their teaching contracts. The eleventh took a two-year maternity leave, at the end of which she gave birth to her second child. She was entering her third year of maternity leave, and was still technically an employee of the board holding her contract. Of the remaining seven teachers, one had her first child before she got a permanent teaching job, but was able to take maternity leave and return to teaching after the births of her second and third children. Five had not yet started full-time teaching jobs and so were outside the system. Only one resigned from a full-time teaching position, but after her second child, not her first. In fact, she resigned only because she thought that working as a full-time babysitter would earn her more money than part-time teaching, as well as allowing her to be home with her own children.

All of this suggests that education graduates enter a specific labour market in which the organization of the work greatly facilitates its combination with child-bearing. As Sarah, a teacher pregnant with her first child, commented, it's not that teachers are 'naturally' fond of or more knowledgeable about children, and therefore predisposed to earlier motherhood:

> We have a really good union. We have very good benefits. A lot of those things make it very safe to have kids. You get time away, you get to go back, you get paid while you're off. . . . All your different benefit packages, they'll carry your packages, you can still pay into your packages. That's pretty nice. You get the six months [leave] if you want it. You can't say that if you're in engineering or science. Some other . . . of those degree areas don't necessarily make for a continuous job.

Another advantage available to teachers—and other women working in predominantly female workplaces—is the support of a community of women with wide experience in the balancing of work and family responsibilities. Barbara, an elementary schoolteacher six months pregnant with her first child, commented:

> The other night I had to go to a meeting and . . . the Grade 3 teacher said to me, 'Well, I'll go and you don't have to, and you can stay home and relax.' And I thought, isn't that neat? . . . Or, 'I'll do your supervision for you, you must be tired.' Or, just talking about, you know, they get together and they talk about my little one cried all night or whatever and they're bouncing ideas off each other and things like that. And I don't see that sharing in other [professions].

Gail, the speech pathologist quoted earlier, had similar experiences in her mainly female workplace. When she was expecting her first child, she took a six-month maternity leave, then returned to her old job three days a week. In a department of more than 40 people, most of them speech pathologists, she estimated that about 90 per cent were women, and 'a very high number' were in the 25- to 35-year age group. Seven other women were pregnant at the same time she was.

> So the natural thing is you know you're going to be hiring people, knowing full well they're going to be having families. So they're really good that way, in being able to come back. We've got a high, high number of part-time staff. . . . They've been really accommodating. My job was there to come back to.

One source of satisfaction for Gail, from her ongoing professional work, was being able to turn to other people for information 'both about your job, but about your kids as well'.

Another category of women who had not deferred having children were those who were either not working at the time of their first pregnancy, or who gave up formal paid employment when they had their children. For example, Annette, formerly an engineer, had given up her job to accommodate her husband's job transfer. 'I wasn't working and we were fairly settled', she said. Linda, a nurse, said she and her husband started to think about a baby 'after I got laid off from my full-time position'.

For five of the women, however, their desire for a pregnancy coincided with a dissatisfaction with the work they were doing, and/or a conviction that it could not be combined with family life. Jessica, a former childcare counsellor, had been working in a treatment centre for disturbed adolescents. The high level of stress under which she worked, and the constant risk of violence, persuaded her that she could not keep on with the job if she also wanted to have children. Jennifer, a lawyer three months pregnant when interviewed, had been working as a crown prosecutor:

> In this job, in this particular job, I don't think I could do justice to the child and I've made the decision that . . . either after maternity leave or in the near future, I'm quitting, because it's not fair. I come home, I can't even talk to my husband because I'm so wound up, stressed out.

Even teaching was viewed by some of its practitioners as less than family friendly. One elementary schoolteacher who chose to leave her job on the birth of her first child commented:

> In any other kind of profession, if you do really well . . . you either get a promotion, or a special bonus, or extra holidays, or you're rewarded in some sense. And in teaching it sort of works backwards, that if you prove yourself competent in any measure they give you more to do, or you get the more difficult class or the more difficult load . . . So in that sense I was in a bit of a bind because I was getting burnt out, and didn't have the perspective to see that.

Women without Children: Voluntary Postponement of Pregnancy

The conclusion that their jobs would be incompatible with family life was the reason why some of the married women were still childless at the time they were interviewed. Dana, aged almost 30, was an arts graduate who had worked as a social worker. Though her husband had wanted children, she had felt unready for a pregnancy at least partly because of the stress and exhaustion which were by-products of her job.

But what else could be said to characterize the women who were childless when they were interviewed? For some women, delays and difficulties in getting a career established also contributed to the postponement of motherhood. Karen, aged 31, had left her science-related job to enter medicine. With several more years of study and residency ahead of her, and a husband still working to launch his own career, children were not an option. Anna, a 30-year-old engineering graduate, wanted to defer having children until she had gained more work experience. She had graduated as a petroleum engineer at a time when the labour market for her skills was extremely tight, and had re-qualified as a computer programmer in order to get a job.

Though education graduates tend to have their children sooner than other graduates, teachers who had difficulty getting their careers established were also postponing having children. Claire, a teacher working in a rural community, was fired by the separate school board when she converted on marriage to her husband's religious denomination. The couple moved to the city, where for nearly five years she was unable to find a permanent teaching job. There was no question that she and her husband wanted children—but not without the security of a full-time teaching job. 'Once I get tenure, I'll take a year off [maternity leave] and then maybe come back full-time', she said. Kim, whose teaching career was punctuated by moves to accommodate her husband's work, said that for the first five years she 'hated' the job. In her sixth year, she became one of 14 people teaching English as a second language in a large inner-city school. It was, she said 'fantastic—the first time I ever enjoyed going to work'. Having taken so long to establish her career, she was not willing to compromise it in a hurry. 'I've only had my niche for two years', she said. 'And I don't want to just . . . cash it in'.

Other childless women in the sample had successfully established careers, but in workplaces and occupational fields that gave them few models and little incentive for combining work and family life. For example, Leslie, a 30-year-old business graduate working in a provincial government department, was exploring work options when she was interviewed. Having worked for seven years (almost her whole working life) in the same department branch, she had just started a two-year secondment to another branch. In her previous branch, work had become 'very stressful'. The branch was a high-profile branch, high performance standards were set, overtime was routine, and 'you were expected to be giving 150 per cent at all times'.

> I think I consider work to be very important. I believe in coming in and doing a good job . . . but I do have a tendency to probably let it weigh me down some days. When I go away I don't actually leave the job once I've walked out of the building. I think I've become much more dedicated to work in the last few years, and I think you can slip into that very easily once you start to take on more responsibilities. . . . And I have questioned, when you talk about your personal life, I find that to be conflicting at times. . . . I felt like I was giving up a lot of personal things and just kind of, just taking on work as being, you know, the number one thing. And that becomes too hard on you in terms of your home life.

In neither her former branch nor the area where she was currently working did Leslie have models of professional women successfully combining work and family responsibilities. In fact, in her former job, there were examples of mothers at her professional level or above either leaving the branch or considering doing so because of the workload. In the job to which she was seconded, she was, at age 30, 'in the youngest age group', and none of the women working with her had children.

Leanne, a 30-year-old business graduate and accountant, had worked continuously since graduation for two companies, and had been promoted steadily. Now, 'I like it, but I'm not sure if I'm cut out to be a behind-the-desk accountant.' Asked if having a baby might be a welcome break, she answered:

> It's funny. I thought of that. We had a meeting this morning, and I thought of that. I thought, I was just really tired, I didn't want to be at this meeting, and I thought as I was sitting there, I could decide to have a baby and that would get me out! [But] that's not the right reason!

Leanne considered that her company would provide a supportive working environment if she did have a baby and decided to keep working full-time—even though a co-worker who was then pregnant was the first pregnancy in the company since Leanne started there. What that said, according to Leanne, was that 'we have a lot of males, or females, who have already had their children'. She also stated her belief that companies in general, and her company in particular, were 'becoming more flexible in that they're allowing you to work part-time, they're allowing you to work from your home if you have a computer'. Her dilemma was rather in deciding what she really wanted to do.

> Actually I've thought, would I work or would I stay home? . . . I've spent a lot of time going to school. I've worked my way up. Like, do I want to give all that up? [Because] if you come back to the workforce in five years you're not going to work where you left off. Then the other part of me thinks, well, you have to make that choice, it's one or the other.

Permanent Childlessness?

Examples of permanent childlessness, voluntarily chosen, were more difficult to find among the childless women interviewed. Given that pregnancy can be achieved, albeit with increasing difficulty and risk, until a woman reaches menopause, a decision at 30 or 31 to remain permanently childless can be revoked (unless of course either partner in the case decides to be sterilized). None of the voluntarily childless women interviewed had permanently closed the door on motherhood, but in any case all were simply too young to make a permanent decision *not* to have children.[5]

Involuntarily Childlessness

Several of the 28 childless women interviewed had not chosen to defer pregnancy, but were forced by circumstances beyond their control to remain childless. One was undergoing treatment for infertility. Nine were not in stable, long-term, committed relationships, a fact that for all of them mitigated against having children. But for some, work also played a role. For example, Amy, a librarian with two master's degrees, was in a live-in relationship and wanted 'marriage and then babies'. But a more pressing issue than marriage was a permanent job. Although she had a solid work history in reputable academic libraries, Amy's career was a series of short-term contracts. Of her present priorities, she commented:

> Probably having a permanent position is more current, more of a worry. You know, when I see cute babies . . . oh, it'd be great to have a baby. And, I don't know if being married would be much different. My parents would approve a bit more. But I think probably getting settled in [a] career, so I *can* partake of maternity benefits . . . and have something to go back to, you know.

Several of these women felt that their educational and occupational choices had led to jobs which seriously affected their personal lives—and ultimately, their chances of establishing relationships and having children. Rosemary, 30, an arts graduate unable to find long-term stable employment, eventually joined her parents selling real estate. She commented:

> You really don't have a personal life in this business if you want to do well. Nights and

weekends, long weekends, holidays, you have to be available 24 hours a day. So I really don't have a social life, don't have weekends I go out, don't go out evenings, which is when everybody goes out. And really, you don't meet anybody single in the business because you're dealing with married people and couples who are buying or selling houses. . . . If I had to do it all over again, I would have done it much differently. Just because I always wanted kids, always wanted a family.

Discussion and Conclusions

For the women interviewed in this study, educational choices and the occupational opportunities which followed seemed to exert a considerable influence on the timing of the transition to motherhood. The successful establishment of a career appeared to be an important prerequisite. This was most clearly demonstrated by the education graduates in the group, most of whom became elementary schoolteachers. Women whose career paths were less straightforward, and women whose careers took longer to establish, were generally the ones to prolong the postponement of motherhood—and this was true of some of the teachers too. In some cases, difficulties experienced in establishing careers, or the need to accommodate further education or career shifts, resulted not only in postponed pregnancies but also in prolonged singlehood, which all those involved saw as a further barrier to having children.

Women whose training took them into more male-dominated occupations and workplaces, or into workplaces which they perceived as being unsupportive of families, seemed in this study at least to take one of two very different paths: either to have children and leave the job, or remain in the job, and continue childless.

What these findings particularly illustrate is what happens at the point where paid employment and family choices become material for women who, in the terms of Baber and Monaghan (1988), may have kept them in separate ideological spheres. Most of the college women in the Baber and Monaghan study anticipated that they would 'have it all', and expressed the belief that if they 'handled their responsibilities properly, could stay on top of things, and were organized and flexible enough' they should have little difficulty combining careers and motherhood (Baber and Monaghan 1988: 200). But as the present study suggests, the reality is different from the anticipation—particularly, but not exclusively, for women whose career choice is non-traditional.

The irony here is clear. Traditional career choices expose women to serious practical disadvantages, including generally lower pay and fewer promotion prospects. But these may be the jobs (with occupationally based, rather than organizationally based, internal labour markets) that are far more responsive to the needs of women with children. Women who make non-traditional career choices may enjoy many of the benefits of increased pay and promotion prospects—but at the price of prolonged postponement of pregnancy, and/or much more of a struggle to combine paid work and children.

The answer is clearly not to confine women to traditional occupations so that they will be able to combine paid work and family responsibilities. But the prospect of women in non-traditional occupations being prevented by the work they do from having children when they too are ready to have them, is equally unpalatable. The deeper dilemma is that anything done, in a structural or policy sense, to 'help' women combine paid work and family responsibilities only entrenches the belief that children are women's work. In fact, women can only be 'helped' by structural change which will allow men to share equitably in the work of and the responsibility for their families.

The interpretive findings reported here are based on a small sample, and should be treated with caution. But, as a first step in understanding a relationship which, in the census data, is much more generalizable, they may raise some important new questions.

Notes

1. The author would like to thank Harvey Krahn and the CRSA reviewers for their helpful comments on an earlier draft of this paper. Harvey Krahn and Graham Lowe offered encouragement and generous access to data, and a SSHRC doctoral fellowship provided financial support for the duration of the research. Funders for the Youth Employment Study which was the basis of this research included the Social Sciences and Humanities Research Council, Alberta Advanced Education and Career Development, and Alberta Education. . . .
2. The Youth Employment Study was conducted by Dr Harvey Krahn and Dr Graham Lowe through the Population Research Laboratory in the Department of Sociology at the University of Alberta. Its purpose was to examine the school-to-work transitions of a panel of university and high-school graduates. Panel members were surveyed in 1985, 1986, 1987, 1989, and 1992.
3. The longitudinal study sample, consisting as it does almost entirely of white women from middle-class family backgrounds, is much more homogeneous than the census sample. Its similarity to the census sample in terms of respondents' age, and level and kind of education, however, are the rationale for the present comparison.
4. Names of interviewees, and certain other identifying details, have been changed to preserve confidentiality.
5. This is not to deny that a proportion of the women in the sample will choose never to have children. Neither is it to suggest that everyone *ought* to have them. Nevertheless the fact is that most women do have children. Most postponements of pregnancy, however prolonged, are not permanent.

References

Baber, K., and P. Monaghan. 1988. 'College Women's Career and Motherhood Expectations: New Options, Old Dilemmas', *Sex Roles* 19, 3, 4: 189–203.

Bielby, D., and W. Bielby. 1988. 'She Works Hard for the Money: Household Responsibilities and the Allocation of Work Effort', *American Journal of Sociology* 93, 5: 1031–59.

Currie, D.H. 1988. 'Re-thinking What We Do and How We Do It: A Study of Reproductive Decisions', *The Canadian Review of Sociology and Anthropology* 25, 2: 231–53.

Daniels, P., and K. Weingarten. 1982. *Sooner or Later: The Timing of Parenthood in Adult Lives* (New York: W.W. Norton & Co).

Desai, S., and L.J. Waite. 1991. 'Women's Employment during Pregnancy and after the First Birth: Occupational Characteristics and Work Commitment', *American Sociological Review* No. 56: 551–66.

Eccles, J. 1987. 'Gender Roles and Women's Achievement-related Decisions', *Psychology of Women Quarterly* No. 11: 135–72.

———. 1994. 'Understanding Women's Educational and Occupational Choices', *Psychology of Women Quarterly* No. 18: 585–609.

Gerson, K. 1985. *Hard Choices: How Women Decide about Work, Career, and Motherhood* (Berkeley: University of California Press).

Jacobs, J. 1987. 'The Sex Typing of Aspirations and Occupations: Instability during the Careers of

Young Women', *Social Science Quarterly* No. 68: 122–37.

Krahn H., and G.S. Lowe. 1993. *The School-to-work Transition in Edmonton, 1985–1992*. Population Research Laboratory, Department of Sociology, University of Alberta.

———, and C. Mosher. 1992. *The Transition from School to Work in Three Canadian Cities, 1985–1989: Research Design and Methodological Issues*. Population Research Laboratory, Department of Sociology, University of Alberta.

Lemkau, J. 1979. 'Personality and Background Characteristics of Women in Male-dominated Occupations: A Review', *Psychology of Women Quarterly* 4, 2: 221–40.

———. 1983. 'Women in Male-dominated Professions: Distinguishing Personality and Background Characteristics', *Psychology of Women Quarterly* 8, 2: 144–65.

Levine, P., and D. Zimmerman. 1995. 'A Comparison of the Sex Type of Occupational Aspirations and Subsequent Achievement', *Work and Occupations* 22, 1: 73–84.

Moen, P., and K. Smith. 1986. 'Women at Work: Commitment and Behaviour over the Life Course', *Sociological Forum* 1, 3: 450–75.

Ranson, G. 1995. 'The Transition to Motherhood: Occupational Choices and Family Decisions in the Life Course of University-educated Women', PhD diss., University of Alberta, Edmonton.

Soloway, N., and R. Smith. 1987. 'Antecedents of Late Birth-timing Decisions of Men and Women in Dual-career Marriages', *Family Relations* No. 36: 258–62.

Trigg, L., and D. Perlman. 1976. 'Social Influences on Women's Pursuit of a Non-traditional Career', *Psychology of Women Quarterly* 1, 2: 138–50.

Section 3 Parenthood and Childcare: Taking on Gendered Responsibilities

When heterosexual couples marry, the way they allocate household work and responsibility typically changes: divisions based on gender usually become stronger. Parenthood means taking on considerably more work and responsibility, which entails significant pressure on people's time. As a result, the 'path of least resistance' involves dividing the work between the woman and her male partner. Because men have tended to make more money in the paid labour force than women and because popular beliefs have assumed that babies are best cared for by a full-time mother, parenthood often has produced more conventional family patterns in heterosexual couples.

Associated with the division of work based on gender are a number of problematic outcomes. In Chapter 19, Bonnie Fox looks beneath gendered divisions to describe something of the interpersonal dynamics that can develop in heterosexual couples' relationships when they become parents—dynamics that entail gender inequality. In the next chapter, Harriet Rosenberg describes the problems that mothers who are at home full-time with babies often face, which produce serious depression in some women.

It is usually assumed that if partners share the care of their children these problems will disappear. The conditions that would promote the sharing of parenting are not developing very quickly, however. For example, granting new parents extended leave from paid work (some of it 'parental' leave, available to either women or men)—as the Canadian government has done—allows couples flexibility but goes only a short way to promote shared parenting. Moreover, expectations that young children will receive 'intensive mothering'—or child-centred mothering—persist (Hays 1996). Indeed, women who stay home full-time and adopt fully child-centred lives are likely to accept very conventional household patterns with respect to gender (Bobel 2002).

We might question the common assumption that nuclear families provide the best arrangement for ensuring the care of babies and children. Alternative ways of having and caring for children are difficult to imagine in this society, however. Of course, many immigrants to Canada come from countries in which members of their extended families provide daily support to couples when they become parents, and ongoing help with child-care. Because most of us do not have the option of surrounding ourselves with family who are eager and able to help, we (as a society) must look to more creative solutions. Alternative designs of housing and local communities are one such possibility, as are increased social services. Chapter 21, by Diana Worts, describes the benefits that mothers of young children can experience when they live in housing co-operatives—benefits that address the problems described in Rosenberg's chapter.

Of course, family patterns are increasingly diverse; couples are increasingly organizing their families in unconventional ways. Growing numbers of men are involved in the care of their babies, and even staying home with them. Moreover, the growing numbers of same-sex partners who become parents do not typically divide their work and responsibilities between partners; instead, they tend to share them. In Chapter 22, Gillian Dunne describes the very different pattern of parenting that she and other researchers have found when they examine lesbian parents.

Chapter 19

In the discussion below, Bonnie Fox describes some findings from a study based on interviews with heterosexual couples making the transition to parenthood. Most of these couples became more conventional with parenthood, but not all of them did. The focus below is on subtle dynamics that unfolded in some of the couples' relationships.

When the Baby Comes Home: The Dynamics of Gender in the Making of Family

Bonnie Fox

Couples have babies for all sorts of reasons.[1] For many women and men, the attraction of parenthood is the promise of a special relationship with a precious child and a life that includes nurturing. Having a child is a project that couples ideally take on together, as an extension of their love for each other. And they anticipate that when they become parents they will become a family: couples expect to enrich their lives, hope to deepen their relationship, and imagine living in a more family-centred way than is likely without children.

Indeed, people's lives change when they become parents, and couples often feel more like a family when they become parents. But they typically experience something else with parenthood that they might not have fully anticipated or understood: heterosexual couples usually become more conventional when they become parents, as they handle the weight of their new responsibilities by dividing them between partners. As a result, it seems that, for heterosexual couples, gendered divisions of work and responsibility, and related gender inequalities, are inherent in the making of family—unless women and men resist that development.[2] A key reason why heterosexual couples' lives often become more gender-divided when they become parents is that it takes work to make 'family', and women often do more of that work than men.

Many researchers have reported that heterosexual couples typically experience a strengthening of gendered divisions of work and responsibility when they become parents (Cowan and Cowan 1992; Feeney et al. 2001; Fox 2001; Lewis 1986; MacDermid et al. 1990; Rexroat and Shehan 1987; Sanchez and Thomson 1997; Walzer 1996; 1998). Women tend to take on the bulk of the caring for and thinking about their babies, and a greater proportion of the housework than before they were mothers, while men tend to concentrate more on financial providing while also becoming their babies' playmates and their wives' helpers. Some research indicates that this gendered division of work and responsibility in early parenthood establishes the template for a more lasting division of household work based on gender in families formed by heterosexual couples (MacDermid et al. 1990; Perkins and DeMeis 1996; Rexroat and Shehan 1987). These gendered divisions are central to the gender inequality that is characteristic of many Canadian and American families (Bianchi et al. 2006; DeVault 1991; Hartmann 1981; Hochschild 1989; Luxton 1980; see Chapters 11 and 27; A. McMahon 1999).

Of course, not all women have children in the context of a lasting couple relationship: marriage has become far from universal, increasingly predicated on educational, occupational, and financial accomplishment and thus optional (Furstenberg 1996). Lone motherhood is on the increase, though it has been common for poor African Americans and, to a lesser extent, African Canadians for some time (Calliste 2001; Hill 2005). But images of parenthood in this culture assume the heterosexual couple and nuclear families (Richardson 1993; Wall and Arnold 2007). Indeed, the 'experts' on infant care prescribe a kind of child-centred care that requires 'intensive mothering' by a full-time mother (at least when children are babies) (Hays 1996). Such mothering assumes a breadwinning partner, as well as middle-class circumstances (Blum 1999; Bobel 2002; Fox 2006).

Gendered divisions of work are not the only products of parenthood that entail gender inequalities. The message that women should devote themselves to intensive mothering defines motherhood in terms of self-sacrifice. In accord with a neo-liberal political climate, and policies that move responsibility for care from state-funded agencies and institutions to individuals, mothers' responsibility for their infants has increased in scope over the years (Brodie 1996). Coupled with messages about the need to 'bond' with their babies, and to breast-feed them, are those on the importance of the 'early years' to children's cognitive development (Wall 2001; 2004). These increases in mothers' responsibilities no doubt raise the anxiety associated with mothering a helpless infant. Some evidence shows that for white middle-class women at least, the prescriptions in authoritative discourses on mothering are a persistent point of reference and regulation of behaviour (Miller 2007). Moreover, Martha McMahon (1995) has argued that the emotional intensity with which women experience motherhood produces a transformation such that women identify more with femininity (that is, more with caring, nurturance, etc.).

But popular expectations of parenthood have been changing. Partners today often embark on their journey into parenthood with intentions of greater sharing than was common in the past: men often intend to be involved in the care of their babies, and women often insist on that involvement (Backett 1987; Coltrane 1996; see Chapter 23). Women have more bargaining power and sense of entitlement in their relationships now that they are earning sizeable proportions of household income. Yet, a number of social changes have made parental ties more voluntary for men (Gerson 1997). As a result, the changes that occur in couples' relationships when they become parents are varied and unpredictable.

This chapter discusses two interpersonal dynamics entailing gender inequality that developed in the couple relationships of some first-time parents who were interviewed several times before and after the birth of their babies. These dynamics involve women protecting their partners and catering to them in the first few months following the birth of their babies (Fox 2001; Kelleher and Fox 2002). Examining these dynamics reveals something about the subtleties of gender in families and how the project of making family can promote interpersonal dynamics that involve gender inequality. It also indicates how couples' social context and their material and social resources—which are shaped by their social class and their race—affect the ways they handle the challenges of caring for an infant.

A Study of First-time Parents

This discussion is based on a study of the social relations of parenthood, which involved in-depth interviews with couples who were making the transition to parenthood. The women and men who participated in this study volunteered following brief presentations during their prenatal classes on childbirth—including both hospital classes and Lamaze classes (with sizeable fees) and classes sponsored by the Public Health Department (free of charge). The hospitals and classes were located in diverse neighbourhoods, with populations that substantially varied in terms of social class. I interviewed 10 women and their male partners between 1992 and 1994, in a pilot project; and Diana Worts, Sherry Bartram and I interviewed 30 more heterosexual couples between 1995 and 1998, in a larger project involving a very similar set of questions. We interviewed these women and men separately, late in the pregnancy and then at two months and again one year after the birth of their babies. Shortly after the births—all in a hospital—we interviewed the women alone; six months after the births, we interviewed the women and men together. The interviews were recorded and lasted between one and two-and-a-half hours. The interview guide consisted of a set of semi-structured questions that directed the inquiry but allowed participants considerable scope for response. And we encouraged people to talk about any relevant matters not raised by our questions. Of course, interviews are a poor substitute for 24/7 observation. Interviewing the women five times and the men four times, however, promoted the development of trust and familiarity between them and us. It also meant that we had repeated opportunities to witness daily activities and interactions, as the interviews nearly always took place in people's homes.

Analysis of the interview material involved making summaries of key themes in the experiences of each woman, man, and couple, and of the changes in their lives over the course of the year. To derive tentative answers to my questions, examine hypotheses, and derive general arguments, I developed inductive and deductive codes of interview transcripts, categorized the people and their behaviour, and made systematic comparisons across couples to uncover relationships and patterns. I read all interviews several times, over several years, in a process that moved back and forth between the interview material and tentative findings.

The couples in the study are likely not representative of the population of first-time parents in Toronto in the 1990s, even though the problems and patterns they developed with parenthood seemed typical. The fact that they volunteered for the study while participating in childbirth classes meant, however, that the traits distinguishing them from any other cross-section of parents served the study well. They likely undertook parenthood with more than the usual thoughtfulness and commitment to being 'good parents'. That distinction no doubt contributed to the diversity of gender arrangements these couples created as they became parents. Thus, several couples shared the baby care and housework, and thus avoided the conventional patterns that usually develop—an unusual outcome, and one unlikely to appear in a small sample representative of the general population.

These 40 couples were similar in some ways and different in others. All except five couples were married when the study began. Two more were married and a third couple was planning their wedding before the study ended; only two couples intended to remain common-law. The sample was also mostly white and middle-class. Only two couples were immigrants from non-English speaking countries, and only one of them (an East Indian couple) was a visible minority. Four people (two women, two men) were black Canadians—all of them married to white Canadians. While fairly similar ethnically and racially, these couples differed significantly with respect to education, occupation, and income.[3] Considering both the women's and the men's educational attainment, jobs, income, and whether or not they owned a home, nine couples were working-class and 31 couples were middle-class (and two of these upper-middle-class). Most of the working-class participants had high-school educations, while most of the middle-class people had college or university degrees, and many had post-graduate degrees. Most of the working-class couples had low incomes: six had household incomes below \$40,000. Only two middle-class couples had incomes this low; 20 had incomes over $60,000 and 10 had incomes over $100,000. And the differences in occupational status between the two groups were significant.

Most of these couples were dual earners. When the study began, all except four of the men were employed full-time, though three of them were self-employed and working at home. The other four men had part-time jobs. As well, 36 of the 40 women were employed, most of them full-time. After their babies were born, all except two of the women (both working-class) stayed home for at least six months.[4] Twenty-five women returned to paid work before the end of the year, usually at the end of maternity leaves that lasted about six months. Fifteen women were home for the entire year, although five of them spent some time away from baby care (writing, taking classes, or doing some paid work). Three of the men—only one of whom had been working full-time—stayed home full-time with their babies when their partners returned to work.

In spite of the fact that this was mostly a white middle-class group of couples, the patterns they developed were diverse. Circumstances and ideologies of motherhood and gender pushed many couples along 'paths of least resistance' involving gendered divisions. But other couples resisted those forces and developed more shared arrangements.

After briefly exploring why the couples in the study wanted to be parents and how the women and men initially reacted to parenthood, this chapter describes two dynamics that developed in their relationships as they coped with the demands of parenthood. One of those dynamics involved the women protecting their partners—who were usually more focused on breadwinning than ever before—from much of the demand and disruption that living with an infant can entail. The other dynamic consisted of the women's strategies for pulling their men into involvement in the care of their baby. Both dynamics give us some insight into the nature of the gender inequalities that often develop when heterosexual couples become parents.

Becoming Parents

While these couples became parents for a variety of reasons, and out of a variety of circumstances, parenthood for them was usually intimately connected with their relationship and the desire to become 'a family' (or more of a family). As is common, pregnancy was not the result of a rational decision-making process by these women (Currie 1988; M. McMahon 1995). In fact, when we first interviewed them (late in the women's pregnancy), both women and men struggled to tell us why they wanted to be parents. They usually settled on talking about parenthood as a normal part of adulthood, the next stage in life, and the 'natural' product of a loving relationship. For many of the women and men, the answer to our question why they were having a child was simply that 'it was time' (see also Ranson 1998; Chapter 18). Of course, there were eight couples for whom the pregnancy was *un*timely—unexpected and indeed a shock.

Although these couples saw parenthood as a normal life-cycle stage, they also usually saw it as intimately entangled in their relationship with their partner. Many people referred to parenthood as a normal extension of their loving relationship. Caitlin[5] said just that: 'I think it's the natural culmination of two people who love one another.' Helen also described her pregnancy as an extension of her relationship with her partner: 'it's an extension of my love for [Gary] and wanting to have a child we created together'. Gary felt the same way: he said that parenthood had 'something to do with us as a couple'. Parenthood was seen as a joint enterprise, firmly situated in these couples' relationships, and often so intimately bound together with the relationship that it could not be imagined independently of it. The women especially saw it that way. While many women said that they had 'always' wanted to have a child, they also made clear that doing so required a stable relationship. As Jane said, 'it wasn't as though I'd have had one if I weren't in this situation with [Tom]'.

Highlighting the entanglement of parenthood and marriage was the fact that pregnancy closely followed marriage for a large number of the women in the study, many of whom had been living with their partners in common-law relationships for several years (see also Beaujot 2000). Nineteen of the 35 women who were married (54 per cent of them) were pregnant within two years of marrying (and at least one other woman had a miscarriage within two years of marriage); another six women (25 altogether, or 71 per cent of the 35) were pregnant within three years of marriage; and another five women (30 altogether, or 86 per cent of the 35) were pregnant within four years of marriage. Vic summed up the connection that many made between marriage and parenthood when he commented, 'marriage is something that you do if you want to have a family'. Of the five unmarried couples in the study, two had unplanned pregnancies and, as mentioned above, three married or made wedding plans near the time their babies were born.

Even though parenthood was not the product of a reasoned decision, these women and men were clear about what parenthood meant. At one time or another, all of the women and nearly all of the men indicated that parenthood primarily meant assuming responsibility. For example, when she was pregnant, Jane commented, 'I see myself as a mother, as taking responsibility.' After two months of motherhood, Esther described what being a mother meant to her as follows: 'It's a huge responsibility; it's being responsible for unconditional love.' Similarly, Andrea explained that for her motherhood meant 'an overwhelming sense of responsibility'. Keith, like many of the men, had the same definition of parenthood: 'I think fatherhood is really responsibility. You're responsible to yourself to bring a person into this world, you're responsible to the other person you're bringing this child into the world with, and you're responsible to the child.' And Adam said, 'responsibility is the main issue . . . I mean, it's the ultimate step into adulthood, in some ways'.

For these couples, parenthood not only meant assuming responsibility; it also involved an expectation of greater personal fulfillment. Participating in the development of a precious child and having a relationship with that child were central to this vision of fulfillment. But so was an image of family. In fact, our everyday language commonly equates having a baby with 'having a family'. So, like others, Jane explained that '[Tom] wants to have a family. I want to have a family' when she talked about why she decided to get pregnant. Some people talked about their desire to have a 'family lifestyle' as a reason for wanting to become parents. Many other couples indicated anticipating a more family-oriented life, focused on their relationship with each other and with their child and the simple pleasures of being together. Robin, for example, expressed this goal in terms of her hope that parenthood would help her avoid becoming 'a workaholic' and live a more 'reasonable' life. Caitlin explained why she and her husband wanted to be parents by saying, 'both of us believe that family life is a good life'. And Robert's explanation of Emma's and his decision to have a child was that 'it's family. It's the next progression in life. It feels like creating a family, which is very important.' Overall, then, parenthood was premised on the couple relationship and it held the promise of family.

When the Baby Comes Home

These women and men typically expected that when their babies came home the women would take on the infant care but that the men would be involved in their care as well. Many of the women were quite adamant, while pregnant, about how important it was to them that their partners be involved in the care of the baby. Moreover, in their responses on a short questionnaire, many of the women and men indicated that they did not think that women were better able than men to care for babies.[6]

Nevertheless, most of these women and men thought that mothers should be the primary people to care for their babies. Social-organizational factors also promoted women's primary, full-time caregiving and men's prioritization of breadwinning. In a majority of the couples the men made more money than the women did. As well, a majority of the women were entitled to paid maternity leaves of about six months, while whatever paternity leaves the men could get involved days or weeks—and most men felt they would be wise to take vacation time instead, to avoid jeopardizing their positions at work. Accordingly, a slight majority of the women were home on maternity leave for approximately six months, and 15 women were home full-time all year. Only two of the women returned to their paid work before six months: limited finances pushed them to return to work before their babies were three months old. In contrast, a (slight) majority of the men stayed home for only a week, or less, after the birth of their babies. Nearly all of the other men were home for two weeks only, although a few were home for three weeks and a couple of men worked at home.[7]

More subtle divisions between women's and men's roles and responsibilities unfolded very soon after their babies were born. The shape the women were in following birth varied significantly, but only a few of them felt able to resume normal activities right away. Nevertheless, the women felt compelled to learn to care for their babies without delay, in part because they were breast-feeding[8] but also because they were the ones who would be home caring for their infants. In contrast, many of the men seemed to feel they had a choice about learning to care for their babies. And once the women acquired some skills the men often were quick to perceive the differences in skills, and to decide that their wives were 'naturals' at mothering.

Jill, for example, went through a very long labour and delivery, during which her husband, Adam, was at a loss to help her—while her birth coach provided considerable support and assistance. The birth left her absolutely exhausted and in need of recovery. Nevertheless, Jill felt that she needed to learn to care for her baby: Adam—though thrilled to be a father—was not stepping forward to do the learning. Two months later, when Jill was discussing the limited amount of baby care that Adam did, she commented, 'women aren't born knowing how to look after babies. It's a learning experience for both of us [women and men].' In a similar comment that denied any 'natural' maternal instinct, Joanne noted that active mothering 'is one of those things where until you're sort of forced to do it you don't jump right into it'. The men's reluctance to take the lead in learning to care for their babies, coupled with the fact that the women knew they would have to manage infant care virtually alone once the men returned to work, pushed the women to quickly learn how to care for their babies.

Nevertheless, some of these new fathers had partners who simply could not or would not—because of their physical condition—take on the baby care by themselves immediately after giving birth. In these cases, the men learned with their wives how to soothe their babies, change their diapers, and even bathe them. One man in the study—Sam, who was the only man who stayed home nearly full-time all year—learned these things before his partner, Rosa, and he remained the parent most able to intuit what his baby needed over the course of the year. The dominant pattern for these couples, however, was that the women quickly became the more skilled parents while the men developed varying degrees of comfort doing infant care. This pattern developed in spite of the fact that it would be months before the women felt even somewhat confident about how they were caring for their babies.

In the weeks and months following the birth of their babies, the women's reactions to the infants, and their feelings about full-time motherhood, were extremely varied. Many of the women were clearly spellbound by their babies, and in love with them from the beginning. When her baby was two months old, Esther noted, 'I didn't really expect to sort of fall in love with her as much, as completely, as I have.' In contrast, many of the women clearly did not 'bond' with their babies for quite some time.[9] They were overwhelmed by the weight of their new responsibility, and struggling with both sleep deprivation and anxiety about whether they were providing adequate care for their baby. A few women were clearly depressed. Following a drug-free labour and delivery, Lara's first reaction to her baby was, 'I don't know quite what to do with it!' Lara described her first two months of motherhood—in which her husband (who was beginning a professional career) was away for about 12 hours every day—as a 'vast pit of exhaustion'. She explained that, 'my body was just totally off kilter for quite a while. I was zonked, and I think mentally unstable for a bit because of the sleep issue and the exhaustion.' Six months after her baby was born, Lara was very distressed about the fact that she was still not 'bonded' with her baby.

The men also had a range of reactions to their babies and to fatherhood. A few men commented about how unequipped and inadequate they felt when faced with their tiny infants (see also Kelleher 2003; Lupton and Barclay 1997). Greg, for example, talked about how a baby seemed 'so fragile it could break in two'. Some men mentioned how rough and large their hands suddenly seemed when they were with their babies. More generally, in the weeks that followed there was a range in the men's reactions to being fathers. Some men were clearly enthralled by their babies, and talked about how they 'love[d] being a father'. Caleb's comment about fatherhood was, 'I think it's great. It just feels good.' In contrast, some men continued to feel very marginal. Lance commented, at two months postpartum, 'I don't feel very fatherly.'

The degree to which the men became involved in the care of their infants in the early period after the birth varied tremendously. The men's varying involvement was related to differences in their partners' needs (given their physical condition), the women's expectations of the men, the degree to which the men wanted to be involved in baby care or wanted to help their partners, whether or not the men had a history of sharing the housework, and the amount of time they were home. Some of the men devoted their time at home to doing as much baby care as they could, as well as doing housework. Sam's case was unusual: he learned to comfort and care for his baby before his partner did because he defined fatherhood as the priority in his life once his baby was born and because Rosa felt unable to function for some time after giving birth. Some other men learned to care for their babies alongside their partners, did a fair amount of infant care in the period when they were home full-time, and took the babies for much of the time in the evenings, after they returned to work. Some men provided good help to their wives, taking their turn giving care through the first few months of parenthood. But fully half of the men in the study gave their partners only limited help: they could and would do some of the tasks involved in infant care but not others, and they helped only when asked. A few of the men were very marginal to their babies' lives, and mostly restricted their involvement to holding them and playing with them for a brief period every day, as well as keeping their wives company while the women cared for the baby. While many factors affected the men's involvement in the care of their babies, chief among them was the nature of a couple's relationship, as well as the circumstances of their lives.[10] A pattern that developed for a number of the couples highlights some of these causal factors.

Caring for the Baby, Protecting Dad[11]

Whatever the men's early reactions were to fatherhood, a common reaction the women had to motherhood was a sense of heightened dependence on their partners (Fox 2001). What they expected of the men varied, from just 'being there' physically and emotionally, to recognizing how hard the women were working to provide good care for the baby, to being fully involved in the baby's care whenever they were home. Only a few women gave no indication that they felt more dependent on their partner. Nearly all of the women commented on this sense of dependence by noting that they could 'never' make it as a single mother. Jeanne, for example, mentioned what many women clearly felt, that 'strong support from her partner is like the number one need [of a mother]'. At the same time, the women's full absorption in infant care meant that they were unable to provide the men with the attention and care they usually gave them (A. McMahon 1999). This redirection of the women's emotional energy and caregiving meant a contradiction of sorts: while the women felt more dependent on their partners they were unable to nurture them or the relationship.

The stresses characterizing the weeks and months following birth were an obvious reason why the women were so sure they were dependent on their partners. Most of the women felt overwhelmed by the new demands on them, and the weight of their new responsibility (Rosenberg 1987; see Chapter 20). Susan described how stunned she was by . . .

> how completely and utterly all-consuming and overwhelming the whole thing is . . . It is the most overwhelming thing. I can see why people go back to work because it's easier, because you can have your coffee when you want to, and go to the bathroom when you want to. I'm not putting down work at all. But as far as having control goes, you do have control at work and you just don't here, until you know what you're doing, which you don't until after the fact, I think.

Having to learn to care for their babies under the pressure of their crying and their generally unpredictable demands, and amidst anxiety about whether they were adequately caring for them, the women were left feeling both overwhelmed and stretched to their physical and emotional limits. Only a few women—those with tremendous amounts of support from their partners and other close family—did not feel overwhelmed by their new responsibility.

Many of the women had a surprising reaction to their sense of increased dependence on their partners: they acted to protect the men from the very demands that the women themselves were finding so stressful (Kelleher and Fox 2002). A majority of the women in the study—though not all of them—worried about and acted to protect their partners in the weeks and even months following the birth of their babies. When they were recovering from childbirth, they worried about how tired the men looked, and even how hard the birth experience had been for them. In spite of sleep deprivation and physical exhaustion, these women protected their husbands' sleep. After being home all day and getting no 'break' from their responsibilities, they urged the men to play with the baby instead of cleaning the dirty dishes. They cleaned the dishes while the men played with the baby. In short, many of the women in the study often sacrificed their own needs—especially their need for rest—to safeguard the men's well-being.

There were several reasons why these women acted to protect their partners in the early months of parenthood. One of them is ideological. It has to do with an equation of individual 'choice' with individual responsibility that is common to this culture (M. McMahon 1995; Wall 2001). For most of the women in the study, choosing to have a baby meant accepting full responsibility for that baby. Helen, for example, answered a question about who held the daily responsibility for her two-month-old son by saying that she 'definitely' was the one responsible for the baby. When asked how that responsibility felt she said,

> Most of the time it feels, it's wonderful, and it's, you know, I, I think like 'this is my child' and, you know, I brought him into the world and he's my responsibility. But other times, some days you just feel sort of overwhelmed, like, who decided to have this baby, you know? Ha ha.

In a later interview, Helen again explained, 'I *chose* to have this baby . . . It's my responsibility . . . This is my job now.' Helen was not the only woman who equated 'choice' with responsibility. The understanding that 'it takes an entire village to raise a child' may be folk wisdom in societies where kinship plays a strong role in social organization, but not in ours, where nuclear families are assumed to be the best arrangement for raising children.

Of course, the equation of 'choice' with responsibility rests on the assumption that biological mothers are responsible for their children (Eyer 1996). This assumption is ironic given that women are rarely aware of the implications of the decision to become a mother. Once their baby is born, women commonly feel remarkably unprepared for motherhood (Miller 2007). In this study, the middle-class women especially felt that they were ready to be parents: they had a good relationship with their spouse, both they and their partners had good incomes and some security in the labour force, they usually owned a home, and they had taken a prenatal class and read about childbirth, if not parenting.[12] Yet, as is common, they typically felt incredibly unprepared once their babies were born.

But these women were right about responsibility: there are remarkably few social supports for new parents; the responsibility for a child rests solely with them, and especially mothers. One of the chief consequences of the dearth of social support is women's heightened sense of dependence on their partners. The women in the study who most obviously protected their partners were women who were completely financially dependent on them—and the working-class women were more likely to be so dependent. Beth, for example, had only a high-school degree and some experience working part-time as a sales clerk. She came from a dysfunctional family and expressed gratitude about 'finding' her husband, Albert, who had a full-time, though low-paid, job. Unable to cook when she got married, Beth was taught by her husband, just before their baby was born. Even though she had no help caring for her baby during the day, she worked hard over the year to cook dinner every evening, and generally 'made sacrifices to make sure he's happy, as much as I can'. One of the other working-class women in the study, Nancy, was in a position like Beth's, having only minimal job credentials and thus clearly financially dependent on her partner who was a skilled tradesman. Additionally, Nancy was grateful that Simon had agreed to her wishes to have a baby. Even in the early months after the birth of her baby, Nancy got up at dawn every day to prepare breakfast for Simon, who worked very long hours; and before the baby was six months old, she started putting him to bed at 9 p.m. every evening so that she could spend the evenings with Simon (as he insisted).

The working-class women seemed not only more dependent on their partners but also more conscious of and concerned about the men's position as financial providers—and the need to protect that position. Fatherhood intensifies the pressures on men to succeed as breadwinners, and many men in the study reacted to their partners' pregnancy by increasing their hours at work and becoming more determined to improve their position there (Fox 2001). But for some of the working-class men—five of the nine men—the increased responsibility as breadwinner meant approximately 60 hours of work every week. In response, the women felt they could not ask much of the men. Sophia, whose husband worked long hours, often on the night shift, commented, 'I can't very well expect him to do work around here when he's working 60-hour weeks.'

Just as social class affected the dynamic of women protecting men, race also had an impact. For three of the four African Canadians in the study, the absence of any social support from their extended families (who were unable to provide any) affected how they coped with the challenges of parenthood. Rachel, the daughter of a woman who had worked as a nanny, had only a cousin in the city and no friends she felt comfortable visiting (because their apartments were not 'safe enough' for a baby, she said). Socially isolated, she seemed to feel more dependent on her husband, and more grateful to him for supporting her financially, than most of the other women in the study. She did all the housework in their apartment, and battled her sense of isolation. One of the two black men in the study was among a small number of men who contested their partners' absorption in infant care, and clearly did so because they had trouble handling the withdrawal of their partners' attention (as we will see below).

White middle-class women who were financially dependent on their partners also acted to protect their male partners. Ruth, who had just graduated from university and was only beginning to plan her career, was a full-time homemaker when she got pregnant. She was clear about her calculations behind protecting her husband's sleep:

> I can't have him not sleeping when he has to go to work. That's number one. Even though I think he could do with a little less sleep . . . I'd much rather—it's sort of a strategy I have—I'd much rather have him be stable and healthy so he can help me when I really need it . . . Before I wake him up, I weigh the pros and cons. It's funny how strategic I have to be.

Ruth continued, 'so on the weekend, he'd better help—a lot!'

Dave *helped* Ruth, but she struggled through the year to find time and energy to train for the career she wanted. As Ruth's determination to develop a career waned, she explained what was happening as follows: 'He [Dave] really likes family—family being the most important thing in his life. And we've sort of committed to that as an ideal.' Dave wanted Ruth home when he was home, which meant there was no time for her training. Ruth explained that 'having a baby changes my perspective. I'm not the most important thing any more. You learn to sacrifice so much.'

A third reason why many women protected their partners' sleep and a few other privileges was that they saw the men as their primary support and help with infant care. Ruth consciously calculated whether she needed Dave more as breadwinner or as her backup caregiver and chief helper, and when one need outweighed the other. She saw her husband as a breadwinner from Monday morning until he came home on Friday. Other women seemed to be doing the same, and some of them were as clear about it as Ruth. But still other women simply felt that it 'made no sense' to have two tired parents rather than one. They wanted the certainty that when they could no longer handle the baby in the middle of the night they could call on someone who could. What is interesting about this reasoning by the women is that they were conceding that the men were only marginal caregivers, that they were *helpers* (Kelleher and Fox 2002; Wall and Arnold 2007). These women accepted the men's limited caregiving.

Another assumption at play in this dynamic involved women feeling that the work they did all day was less valuable than the work the men did, and therefore that the men's needs took precedence over their own. In part, that feeling was because the women were doing *unpaid* work. But it also had to do with their economic dependence on their partners—albeit, often temporary dependence. Sally, for example, said she went through two weeks of worrying about money when her baby was about two months old. Jake, her husband, had a full-time job, but she had earned about as much as he did before getting pregnant. Now that she was home, Sally said, 'I just feel like I am not contributing. I feel that a lot.' Similarly, Jane, who quit a good job to stay home for a year, talked about going through 'a period where it hit me that [baby] and I are more or less dependent on him [her husband] . . . I spent a lot of time thinking . . . It occurred to me and it was frightening when it occurred to me because I've never been dependent, you know, as an adult.' Sally's husband, Jake, wanted to do more baby care than Sally allowed him. Jane's husband, Tom, said that he would do whatever Jane asked him to do, but interestingly she rarely asked him to do much baby care. For many of these women, who were used to supporting themselves—and to deriving a sense of their own worth, or at least contribution, from money-making—their sudden financial dependence weakened their sense of their own entitlement in their relationships.

Needless to say, these women's feelings also reflected a cultural devaluation of the work that mothers do: somehow the men's need to be wide-eyed in the morning was more important than their own. Indeed, many of the women seemed to feel that they owed something to their partners for 'putting up with' the fact that the women had drastically reduced time and energy for giving the men the kind of attention and care that was usual in their relationships. Because the women's caregiving was redirected from the men to the babies, the women seemed to feel indebted to their spouses.

A final, less apparent, cause seemed to be behind the tendency for many women to protect their male partners from the disruption and stress of living with a newborn. Many of these women seemed to be protecting their partners not only because they were breadwinners but also because the men—as husbands and fathers—were central to their developing families. This concern was evidenced by the ways many of the women made efforts to build their partners' relationships with their babies. Most of the women were more concerned that their babies have a good relationship with their fathers—that the men and babies 'bond'—than that the men help them with baby care. To nurture the father–child relationship, these women regularly encouraged the men to play with their baby rather than do housework. They also were strategic about how they involved the men in baby-care tasks. As well, some of the women made an effort to create the kind of home environment that the men were happy to come home to.

Jane, for example, told me when her baby was two months old that

> my priorities are totally different, you know, totally different. [Baby] and [Tom] are the first priorities, and then everything after that fits in whenever. Maybe because of me identifying with [baby's] needs, I'm more conscious of [Tom's] needs.

Having spent little time at home before she got pregnant, Jane was not only making her apartment more home-like, she was also cultivating Tom's bond with his baby. To that end, she urged Tom to play with the baby whenever he asked how he might help. She did the housework while he was with the baby, and in fact ended up doing all of the housework over the year she was home (even though Tom had done some of it before the baby was born).

Other women also promoted the relationship between father and baby by taking on extra work themselves. Some women strategized about when to give the baby to their husbands—and chose times when the infant was clean, fed, and not crying or upset. Apparently, they aimed to ensure a good experience for the men. One of the women was explicit about protecting her partner this way. Carla explained, 'I don't want to put him through that [dealing with a fussy baby]. It's not fair. It makes him feel like he's not a competent father.' Other women set aside an activity or time for their spouses to be with the baby. Some had their partners feed the baby, with a bottle of 'expressed' breast milk; some had them bathe the baby. In short, some of the women worked to create the men's relationships with their babies, and their involvement in their care, and did so by protecting them from the more stressful and difficult aspects of infant care. They were working to ensure the development of the men's relationships with their babies, and thus their fledgling families.

The men's reactions to the women's attempts to protect them from the stresses of life with a newborn varied. Most of the men who benefited from this ongoing care by their wives seemed to be oblivious to it. Apparently, they were used to their wives giving them a certain amount of care and privileging their needs. In fact, some of the men told us that because they were the ones who were 'working' it was only fair that their partners did the housework and infant care. Justin, for example, commented that, 'If I could stop working I'd do all the housework . . . If she wanted to go out working all day long, I'd take it over.' Yet, there was also a hint in Justin's comments that he did not feel completely entitled to the privilege he was given at home; he also said, 'I like living in a clean place, and she does it well and, you know, she does it. So I get very selfish.' A few men, however, were uncomfortable with the women's sacrifices. Gary, for example, commented on Helen's efforts to spare him as follows: 'I just thought she worked too hard to insulate me from the problems.' And Carla's husband felt that he was marginalized as a parent. Both of these men wanted to, and expected to, be involved in the care of their babies. As well, there were quite a few men who had no expectation that the women should work any longer over the course of the day than they did, or that they should relax while their wives were busy.

In contrast, a few men whose partners were protective—and some whose partners were not—clearly felt that they needed more of their wives' attention, company, and care than they were getting. These men had a hard time dealing with the women's absorption with the baby, the dramatic changes in daily life, and the women's inability to spend relaxed time with them. They wanted more protection against the disruption to their lives. Joe, for example, struggled with the loss of his wife's attention and time, even though he was thrilled with his baby. At one point, he commented that with fatherhood men 'sort of get displaced' when couples become parents.

The men's different reactions to the demands on them and to the redirection of the women's emotional energy are not easily explained. But the men who were both involved in the care of their babies and successful as providers seemed to be much better able to make the adjustment to life with an infant. The men who seemed in need of their wives' ongoing attention were typically marginal to the babies' care and, in most cases, stressed by their financial responsibilities—and not successful providers. Nicholas Townsend (2002) has argued that successful breadwinning is central to men's sense of masculine identity. He also argues that marriage, fatherhood, and employment are a 'package deal', and that successful breadwinning is often considered by men to be central to fulfilling the responsibilities of fatherhood (Townsend 2002; Coltrane 1996). The men in the study who did not feel good about themselves as men struggled the hardest to adjust to fatherhood and the loss of their partners' attention.

While women's protection of the men was the most common pattern in the postpartum period, some (13) women in the study gave no indication that they were protecting their partners in any way. Indeed, some of these women insisted that their partners pay attention to their own needs as well as to the babies' needs. Susan, for example, was determined that her husband, Charles, be as involved with the baby as she was during his two (vacation) weeks at home. She felt that he had broken a virtual 'marriage vow' to do some of the cooking, and she was determined that something similar did not happen with respect to parenthood. Charles did all of the housework (including the cooking) and much of the infant care in the weeks following the birth, when he was home. All but two of the women who did not try somehow to protect their partners were employed when they got pregnant, with jobs and earnings comparable to or better than their partners' (and one of the two women who were exceptions to this rule was working on a doctoral degree). What nearly all of these women had in common (Susan was the other exception) was an absence of financial dependence on their male partners. They also typically had advanced educational credentials, an orientation influenced (to varying degrees) by feminism, and often a partner who shared the household work before the couple became parents.

Making Dads

Protecting their partners became an increasingly contradictory strategy for the women as the year wore on because those men who remained marginal to the care of their babies were less committed to their families. Thus, the women's concerns about their developing families and desires that the men be actively involved in the care of their babies moved those who had protected their partners to adopt a new strategy. Especially when the men were not very involved in the care of their infants, the women took action to construct the men's active caregiving (see also Coltrane 1996: 60; Gerson 1993). Helen—whose partner, Gary, commented that she had protected him—noted that, 'it takes work to bring the man into the picture and into the, you know, care. Through the care of the baby you can do that, and through, like I say, giving him more responsibility.' For Helen, Gary's care of the baby was not her main concern; there was a larger 'picture'—their evolving family.

Like Helen, many of the women took action to create the men's involvement with their babies. In the process, they usually created more work for themselves—work that the men did not have to do. Often women set aside a baby-care task for the men to carry out (as mentioned above). A few of the women 'expressed' milk into a bottle, and had the men feed the baby once a day; more women drew the men into a daily feeding after they moved their babies onto formula. It was also common for the women to save the baby's bath for the men. Marie noted, 'I usually try to keep certain things for [Bill], like bathing the baby . . . I figure those are his special moments.' Interestingly, this typically meant that the women prepared everything before they turned the job over to the dad—pouring the bath water and ensuring its temperature was right; and lining up the soap, towel, washcloth, baby seat, and clean clothes (Kelleher and Fox 2002). Even less ambitiously, some of the women stuck to the strategy of encouraging the men to play with the baby. In more extreme cases, the women tended to hand over the baby only when s/he was fed, clean, and contented. But invariably, having the man play with the baby meant that the women were doing housework while the men were so engaged. All of these strategies involved the women in more work.

Less obviously, women worked to create a comfortable home and pleasant 'family' experiences. Many women cooked dinner every night, and many did housework during the day so that evenings were free for spending time as a threesome, or during the week so that weekends were free for family activities. Some women did this because they felt that it was part of 'the bargain' when they were home and the men were making the money, but others did so even though they felt it was not quite fair, and in spite of growing resentment about the allocation of the work. Susan, for example, talked about making especially appealing dinners, and even eating by candlelight after the early months of parenthood because, 'I'm trying to make it a little bit nicer.' Having good food and a pleasant dinner was important to her: 'We both eat a lot and we didn't want to skip dinner or order pizza—seems so transient and temporary. Awful. You can't have a sense of home.' Susan also did housework during the week so that she, Charles, and their baby could spend weekends together. And when asked at six months postpartum what had changed in her life, Susan said,

> I think the most significant thing, and as far as our lives go, what's changed? I think we're probably, we're more of a, we've realized that we're more of a family unit, I think. And it's kind of, we're all willingly one big happy family—more so than just, 'oh gosh, there's the baby.'

And after a year of motherhood, Susan commented,

> I love the little threesome, the little home scene. I love weekends. They drive me nuts. On Sunday night I'm furious half the time because the joint's a wreck and we didn't get anything done. But we manage to go out for walks together and we play together. And that's so fantastic.

Clearly, making home life pleasant suited Susan's needs, but it also pulled her husband into the project of making family as well: while he had abrogated his 'vow' to cook meals before their baby was born, he cooked when Susan was unable to and was very involved in baby care when he was home from work, for the entire year.[13] Nevertheless, Susan struggled with resentment about doing all of the housework.

A majority of the women in the study did more housework than they had before becoming mothers. While few of them explained their increased domesticity with direct claims about making family, many more talked about making the time their partners were home pleasant. Still other women noted that they regularly complimented, indeed praised, their partners' parenting skills—and often in spite of seeing problems with what the men were doing. Sophia said she often had to 'bite her tongue' when she watched her husband with their baby, but she nevertheless noted, 'I tell [Max] all the time how wonderful he is with her [the baby], and how lucky she is to have a dad like him.' Ensuring that the men were developing solid relationships with their babies seemed to be a priority for these women.

Providing a contrast with the women who did extra work to pull their partners into active parenting were the women who took an entirely different strategy: they made sure that they left the men alone with their babies for regular periods of time (after the first several months). Unlike the other women, this strategy did not involve any catering to the men, and instead evidenced the women's sense that they were entitled to some time to themselves. After about four months of motherhood, Emma, for example, made arrangements to go out with friends one night every week, in order to give her husband time with their baby—and while the baby was awake. Some other women did the same, though less regularly, but usually at least partly to put their partners in the position of having to care for the baby. Claire returned to her paid job before her baby was two months old, partly out of financial need, partly 'to get out of the house', but also partly to push Jaime (who worked only part-time) to do more infant care while she was gone. The women who adopted this strategy, and gave no indication of catering to their partners to pull them into involvement with the baby, were women with as much bargaining power as the men they lived with—bargaining power that accrued because they earned as much money as the men, and had jobs of equal status to the men's jobs.

In general, the women in the study were more concerned that their partners form a relationship with their babies than that they do significant amounts of infant care. The middle-class women were more determined that the men be involved in infant care. But both middle- and working-class women took measures to draw the men into active parenting involvement of whatever kind. The type of strategy they used, and thus the extent to which it involved catering to the men, was largely a product of the women's relative bargaining power in the relationship: women who were financially dependent on their partners were more likely to cater to the men in some way in their effort to draw them into active involvement. Many women also seemed to be concerned about sustaining their own relationships with their partners, through a period when they could give the men little attention and when couples' sexual relationships were changed and sometimes non-existent.

Wrapping Up

Motherhood is a source of profound meaning and pleasure in the lives of many women. It is also an experience that positions women differently in this society, making them subject to all of the handicaps associated with being women (Crittenden 2001). It is significant that parenthood enforces and even produces divisions of work and responsibility in the lives of heterosexual couples. There is a long-standing conviction among those who study gender that the fact that women do more childcare and housework than men provides one of the main bases of gender inequality in this society, at least in the white population. The low status of this unpaid work, the social isolation it often entails, the service nature of the work, the monetary cost it entails, and the longer hours of work it has meant are all identified as central to that inequality (Budig and England 2001; Hartmann 1981; Luxton 1980; Waldfogel 1997). This chapter examined two relational dynamics that developed for many of the couples in a study of couples becoming parents. These dynamics may represent another dimension of the increased gender inequality in families that often accompanies the transition to parenthood.

This study of first-time parents revealed a relational dynamic in which many of the new mothers catered to their partners for the short-term goal of protecting the men from the disruption of life with an infant and the long-term goal of creating 'family'. Many of the women in the study protected their partners in the early weeks and months after their babies were born, out of a strong sense of dependence on the men as breadwinners and as central to the development of their babies' families. Even when women changed their approach in later months, and worked to pull the men into active involvement in infant care, that effort often involved extra work for the women, which again entailed some catering to the men (see also Fox 2001).

Before these dynamics were established, the initial gender divisions that developed for most of these couples—whereby the women became the main caregivers—were the product of both gender ideologies and social circumstances—especially the fact that the women knew they would be home caring for their infants—and not women's natural ability for mothering or even the bond they established with their baby. Yet, there were differences among the women in the study, and among the men. Some men did not need to be pulled into baby care or protected from the demands of an infant; some men were quite involved with the baby, and committed to their families from the beginning. This variation among couples and the importance of circumstances—and not 'nature'—in establishing the patterns common among these couples make clear the possibility for egalitarian parenting.

Notes

1. I thank the 40 couples who generously allowed me to interview them at a time in their lives when they were incredibly busy. I am also grateful to Diana Worts and Christa Kelleher for their invaluable insights over the course of this project; to Judith Taylor, Josee Johnston, Anna Korteweg, Cynthia Cranford, Barrie Thorne, Ester Reiter, Meg Luxton, Kate Bezanson, and other colleagues for comments on various pieces of my forthcoming book; and to Bonnie Erickson for the title of this chapter. Also, thanks go to Sherry Bartram and Diana Worts for excellent research assistance, and to Sheila Martineau, Evangeline Davis, Elizabeth Walker, Rebecca Fulton, Ann Bernardo, Sharon Saunders, David Guetter, and Jennifer Bates for careful transcribing. The research on which this chapter is based was made possible by a grant from the Social Sciences and Humanities Research Council, # 410-94-0453.
2. This is not so for lesbian couples. Research on lesbian couples shows that when they make the transition to parenthood they typically do not divide their work and responsibilities between the two adults, in the way that is common to heterosexual couples (Dunne 2000; Nelson 1996).
3. Also, the people participating in the study varied widely in age. Age proved not to be an important predictor of experience, but the 'age' of the marriage did have an impact on a number of things.
4. In the 1990s, women living in Ontario who had been employed full-time for at least six months were eligible for 17 weeks of maternity leave, 15 of which were paid; they could also take 10 weeks of paid parental leave. They applied for money through Unemploy-ment Insurance, and could receive up to 60 per cent of their usual wages/ salaries in replacement earnings. Additionally, employers often 'topped up' the money to varying percentages of women's usual earnings. Women typically took the full 27 weeks.
5. All of the names are fictitious.
6. We asked some of the participants a battery of questions that measured attitudes toward gender. We did so during the first interview.
7. In an unusual case, one man (Sam) was home nearly full-time for the entire year: he was still in school, and clearly giving priority to things other than occupational success; his unusual position was possible because he and his partner owned a house and the latter had credentials that enabled her to find high-paying contract work.
8. See Glenda Wall (2001) on the promotion of breast-feeding by various authoritative sources. Only one woman in the study did not breast-feed her baby; another woman stopped after several weeks of trying.
9. See Diane Eyer's (1992) *Mother–Infant Bonding: A Scientific Fiction* for a discussion of the myths around the notion of 'bonding'.
10. Many researchers have made the point that men's involvement in infant care is related to what is going on in their relationships with their partners (Backett 1987; Lamb and Lewis 2004; Walzer 1998).
11. This section is based on Christa Kelleher's observation that the women were often protecting their husbands, in the days and weeks after the birth.
12. See Martha McMahon (1995) on how middle-class women typically feel they have to accomplish certain things before they are ready to be mothers. A good relationship is the most important requisite, but financial stability is also important.
13. Charles remained involved in infant care for the next year as well. I interviewed this couple when their first baby was two years old, and indeed they had two children.

References

Backett, Kathryn. 1987. 'The Negotiation of Fatherhood', in *Reassessing Fatherhood*, eds Charlie Lewis and Margaret O'Brien (London: Sage), 74–90.

Beaujot, Rod. 2000. *Earning & Caring in Canadian Families* (Peterborough: Broadview Press).

Bianchi, Suzanne M., John Robinson, and Melissa A. Milkie. 2006. *Changing Rhythms of American Family Life* (New York: Russell Sage Foundation).

Blum, Linda. 1999. *At the Breast: Ideologies of Breastfeeding and Motherhood in the Contemporary United States* (Boston: Beacon Books).

Bobel, Chris. 2002. *The Paradox of Natural Mothering* (Philadelphia: Temple University Press).

Brodie, Janine. 1996. 'Restructuring and the New Citizenship', in *Rethinking Restructuring: Gender and Change in Canada*, ed. Isabella Bakker (Toronto: University of Toronto Press), 126–40.

Budig, Michelle, and Paula England. 2001. 'The Wage Penalty for Motherhood', *American Sociological Review* 66, 2: 204–25.

Calliste, Agnes. 2001. 'Black Families in Canada: Exploring the Interconnections of Race, Class, and Gender', in *Family Patterns, Gender Relations*, 2nd edn (Toronto: Oxford University Press), 401–19.

Coltrane, Scott. 1996. *Family Man: Fatherhood, Housework, and Gender Equity* (New York: Oxford University Press).

Cowan, Carolyn, and Philip Cowan. 1992. *When Partners Become Parents: The Big Life Change for Couples* (New York: Basic).

Crittenden, Ann. 2001. *The Price of Motherhood: Why the Most Important Job in the World Is Still the Least Valued* (New York: Metropolitan Books).

Currie, Dawn. 1988. 'Rethinking What We Do and How We Do It: A Study of Reproductive Decisions', *Canadian Review of Sociology and Anthropology* 25, 2: 231–53.

DeVault, Marjorie. 1991. *Feeding the Family: The Social Organization of Caring as Gendered Work* (Chicago: The University of Chicago Press).

Dunne, Gillian. 2000. 'Opting Into Motherhood: Lesbians Blurring the Boundaries and Transforming the Meaning of Parenthood and Kinship', *Gender & Society* 14, 1: 11–35.

Eyer, Diane. 1992. *Mother–Infant Bonding: A Scientific Fiction* (New Haven: Yale University Press).

———. 1996. *Motherguilt: How Our Culture Blames Mothers for What's Wrong with Society* (New York: Random House).

Feeney, Judith, Lydia Hohaus, Patricia Noller, and Richard Alexander. 2001. *Becoming Parents: Exploring the Bonds between Mothers, Fathers, and Their Infants* (Cambridge: Cambridge University Press).

Fox, Bonnie. 2001. 'The Formative Years: How Parenthood Creates Gender', *Gender & Society* 38, 4: 373–90.

———. 2006. 'Motherhood as a Class Act: The Many Ways in Which "Intensive Mothering" Is Entangled with Social Change', in *Social Reproduction: Feminist Political Economy Challenges Neo-liberalism*, eds Kate Bezanson and Meg Luxton (Montreal & Kingston: McGill-Queen's University Press).

Furstenberg, Frank. 1996. 'The Future of Marriage', *American Demographics* 18.

Gerson, Kathleen. 1993. *No Man's Land: Men's Changing Commitments to Family and Work* (New York: Basic).

———. 1997. 'The Social Construction of Fatherhood', in *Contemporary Parenting: Challenges and Issues*, ed. Terry Arendell (Thousand Oaks: Sage).

Hartmann, Heidi. 1981. 'The Family as the Locus of Gender, Class, and Political Struggle: The Example of Housework', *Signs* 6, 3: 366–94.

Hays, Sharon. 1996. *The Cultural Contradictions of Motherhood* (New Haven: Yale University Press).

Hill, Shirley. 2005. *Black Intimacies* (CA: Altamira Press).

Hochschild, Arlie. 1989. *The Second Shift: Working Parents and the Revolution at Home* (New York: Viking).

Kelleher, Christa. 2003. 'Postpartum Matters: Women's Experiences of Medical Surveillance: Time and Support after Birth', unpublished doctoral dissertation, Sociology, Brandeis University.

———, and Bonnie Fox. 2002. 'Nurturing Babies, Protecting Men: The Unequal Dynamics of Women's Postpartum Caregiving Practices', in *Childcare and Inequality: Rethinking Care Work for Children & Youth* (New York: Routledge), 51–64.

Lamb, Michael, and Charlie Lewis. 2004. 'The Development and Significance of Father–Child Relationships in Two-parent Families', in *The Role of the Father in Child Development*, 4th edn (New York: John Wiley), 272–306.

Lewis, Charlie. 1986. *Becoming A Father* (Milton Keynes: Open University Press).

Lupton, Deborah, and Lesley Barclay. 1997. *Constructing Fatherhood: Discourses and Experiences* (London: Sage).

Luxton, Meg. 1980. *More Than a Labour of Love: Three Generations of Women's Work in the Home* (Toronto: The Women's Press).

MacDermid, S., T. Huston, and S. McHale. 1990. 'Changes in Marriage Associated with the Transition to Parenthood: Individual Differences as a Function of Sex-role Attitudes and Changes in the Division of Household Labor', *Journal of Marriage and the Family* 52: 475–86.

McMahon, Anthony. 1999. *Taking Care of Men: Sexual Politics in the Public Mind* (Cambridge: Cambridge University Press).

McMahon, Martha. 1995. *Engendering Motherhood: Identity and Self-transformation in Women's Lives* (New York: Guilford Press).

Miller, Tina. 2007. '"Is This What Motherhood Is All About?" Weaving Experiences and Discourse through Transition to First-time Motherhood', *Gender & Society* 21, 3: 337–58.

Nelson, Fiona. 1996. *Lesbian Motherhood: An Exploration of Canadian Lesbian Families* (Toronto: University of Toronto Press).

Perkins, Wesley, and Debra DeMeis. 1996. 'Gender and Family Effects on "Second-shift" Domestic Activity of College-educated Young Adults', *Gender & Society* 10: 78–93.

Ranson, Gillian. 1998. 'Education, Work, and Family Decision-making: Finding the "Right Time" to Have a Baby', *Canadian Review of Sociology and Anthropology* 35, 4: 517–34.

Rexroat, Cynthia, and Constance Shehan. 1987. 'The Family Life Cycle and Spouses' Time in Housework', *Journal of Marriage and the Family* 49: 737–50.

Richardson, Diane. 1993. *Women, Motherhood, and Child Rearing* (New York: Macmillan).

Rosenberg, Harriet. 1987. 'Motherwork, Stress, and Depression: The Costs of Privatized Social Reproduction', in *Feminism and Political Economy: Women's Work, Women's Struggles*, eds Heather Jon Maroney and Meg Luxton (Toronto: Methuen), 181–96.

Sanchez, Laura, and Elizabeth Thomson. 1997. 'Becoming Mothers and Fathers: Parenthood, Gender, and the Division of Labor', *Gender & Society* 11, 6: 747–72.

Townsend, Nicholas. 2002. *The Package Deal: Marriage, Work, and Fatherhood in Men's Lives* (Philadelphia: Temple University Press).

Waldfogel, Jane. 1997. 'The Effects of Children on Women's Wages', *American Sociological Review* 62: 209–17.

Wall, Glenda. 2001. 'Moral Constructions of Motherhood in Breast-feeding Discourse', *Gender & Society* 15, 4: 590–608.

———. 2004. 'Is Your Child's Brain Potential Maximized? Mothering in an Age of New Brain Research', *Atlantis* 28, 2: 41–50.

———, and Stephanie Arnold. 2007. 'How Involved Is Involved Fathering? An Exploration of the Contemporary Culture of Fatherhood', *Gender & Society* 21, 4: 508–27.

Walzer, Susan. 1996. 'Thinking about the Baby: Gender and Divisions of Infant Care', *Social Problems*: 43, 2: 219–34.

———. 1998. *Thinking about the Baby: Gender and Transitions into Parenthood* (Philadelphia: Temple University Press).

Chapter 20

Below, Harriet Rosenberg discusses the responses new mothers commonly had to their experience of motherhood in the 1980s. Canadian women are now often able to take leaves of nearly a year from their paid work, but the problems that Rosenberg describes have not changed significantly. In order to understand these problems, Rosenberg presents an analysis of the social relations in which full-time mothering occurs, and its general social organization. She discusses the isolation of 'motherwork' from other work, and the lack of social supports for mothers. She also carefully considers the nature of this very important work as it is done in our society.

Motherwork, Stress, and Depression: The Costs of Privatized Social Reproduction

Harriet Rosenberg

The Political Economy of Pain

'Mother who killed two sons says she's paid price', announced a front-page headline. In 1970 a woman smothered her six-week-old son; two years later she smothered a second infant. Both deaths were recorded at the time as crib deaths. In 1984, 'frayed for more than a decade of struggling for her sanity', she said that she wanted to warn other women about the postpartum depression that led to the killings. 'At the first sign of that, don't hesitate to. . . . For God's sake, ask for help', she said. 'I just wouldn't want any woman to go through what I went through' (*Toronto Star*, 3 Mar. 1984).

Why did this happen? Such violence is usually explained in individual psychological terms: people go crazy and do violent things. Yet other violent crimes such as rape, murder, and suicide have been linked to underlying social causes. The correlation between increases in suicide rates, for example, and rising levels of unemployment (Brenner 1973; 1977; 1979) established a link between crisis in individual lives and crisis in an economic system. But, because childbirth and child rearing are widely considered to be a 'natural' female condition, the possibility of social structural origins of 'postpartum depression' has rarely been investigated (Friedan 1963; Oakley 1972). Rather, the dominant contemporary explanatory model, constructed and maintained by a powerful medical establishment, is explicitly asocial. It defines the emotional distress of mothers as an exclusively individual problem called 'postpartum depression' and has developed a variety of individual therapies including psychoanalysis, drugs, and vitamins to deal with it. To combat the tendencies which constantly push analysis of motherhood and depression in a personalistic direction, we must start with a fresh perspective—one that has both feminist and political economy underpinnings.

Producing or not producing human beings is part of the political discourse of most societies. Historically, as nation-states developed, debates about population grew with them. From the mercantilists to Malthus, demography, taxation, and militarization all became intertwined problematics (Davin 1978; Seccombe 1983). Furthermore, the institutions which turned children into soldiers, taxpayers, and workers have always been part of the public debate on how societies organize to reproduce themselves.

Public funds are now seen as being legitimately allocated to these tasks, through school systems and the armed forces, for example. It is the proportions which are debated, not the appropriateness of the undertaking.

And yet the daily work of child rearing within the household/family is almost entirely eclipsed from political discussion and considered to be a private matter. The fact that the motherwork is integral to social reproduction and not a personal pastime is obscured. In the public domain debates rage about sexuality, abortion, and birth control, but not about the social condition of motherwork.

This radical separation of motherwork from social reproduction has a variety of consequences, including depression, anxiety, and violence. But if we start with the premise that the personal is political and that political economy is a significant component of even the most seemingly personal experience, we can analyze motherwork as an integral part of social reproduction. Such an approach enables us to view postpartum depression not just as an issue of private medicine but as one of public health, and to explore the consequences of the denial of parenting as a form of social labour under capitalism. . . .

Emotional Pain after Birth or Adoption

> When they say to me, 'Oh, what a wonderful baby. How lucky you are', I look around in a daze to see who they're talking to. I'm in a fog all the time. I'm so tired I can't think straight. I hate it. I want my life back.

In Western societies between 60 per cent and 80 per cent of mothers have emotional problems after childbirth (Hamilton 1962; Yalom 1968; Dalton 1971; Davidson 1972; Balchin 1975; Kruckman 1980). Depression and anxiety are also experienced by women who adopt[1] and by men (Bucove 1964). About 20 per cent of women continue to experience depression for many months after birth or adoption, or even occasionally throughout life (Kruckman 1980; Welburn 1980; Rosenberg 1980).

In the medical and popular literature the terms 'postpartum depression', 'baby blues', and 'postpartum psychosis' are often used interchangeably. 'Baby blues' is frequently applied to all forms of postnatal psychological problems. Ideologically dismissive, it is akin to the blame-the-victim connotation of 'blue-collar blues'. However, more precise medical usage distinguishes different forms of the depressed experience. More carefully defined, the term 'blues' is restricted to a depressed mood and transitory tearfulness that is experienced by about 80 per cent of mothers on the third or fourth day after birth. This mild postpartum depression lasts for a few hours only. Although some explanations have associated it with hormonal changes at the onset of lactation (Dalton 1971), others have pointed out that there is little cross-cultural evidence for such a claim and have argued that there is a historical link in North America between the medicalization of birth and the appearance of mild postpartum depression (Catano and Catano 1981).

At the other extreme, 'postpartum psychosis' is also frequently conflated with postpartum depression, especially in medical literature. This confusion results from the fact that medical studies are frequently based on hospitalized populations. Actual psychosis is relatively rare, occurring in one in a thousand cases. It is treated by psychiatric intervention, hospitalization, and electroconvulsive therapy (ECT).

There is also a 'mid-range' depression which may be expressed as slow, tired, hopeless behaviour, eyes filling with unshed tears or a constant crying, or by intense anxiety and frantic behaviour. In this form, feelings of anger and conflict with children or mates is common. About 65 per cent of the 1,000 women who sought the services of the Post Partum Counselling Services (see note 1) expressed fears of harming their children, although very few actually did so. Physiological symptoms like constant colds and rashes, as well as frequent accidents and alcohol and drug abuse, are all associated with this form of postpartum depression (PPCS files). It is a terrifying and debilitating experience, made all the more frightening by the fact that it is rarely mentioned. 'You never hear about this', said one woman. 'No one ever talks about it. Are they all lying?'

It is this mid-range form of postpartum depression which will be discussed in this paper. It is this type of depression which can be clearly seen to have social structural causes. . . .

Treatment: Medical Models, Feminist Models

> My doctor is very squelching. He says 'It's just cabin fever, dearie. Don't worry.'

> Sometimes I think my volunteer [at Post Partum Counselling Services] is the only person in the world who puts the mother first.

There are two competing general models for the treatment of postpartum depression. The medical model stems from an analysis of depression as an individual problem; the feminist model identifies it as a problem related to the oppressed social position of women.

Although there have been different explanations of the etiology of postpartum depression and consequently different fashions in its treatment, the medical model has consistently tried to 'cure' the individual. Treatment has included the use of drugs, sleep cures, and prolonged hospitalization in the nineteenth century and electroconvulsive, insulin shock, and psychoanalytic therapies in the twentieth century (Kruckman 1980). One practitioner in the 1940s was so fond of shock therapy that he claimed a 75 per cent recovery rate and was not at all alarmed by the 5 per cent death rate resulting from it (Kruckman 1980). By the mid-1950s, a new psychopharmacological approach had come to dominate in research and treatment. Psychoactive drugs, often coupled with hormonal injections, were widely used by doctors claiming phenomenal success rates.

The psychoanalytic theories of postpartum depression which developed in the 1930s rested upon the normative conception that biological mothering was the essential mark of femininity. A pioneer of this approach, Zilboorg, stated that depression after childbirth was related to 'symbolic castration' and was common 'in narcissistic, frigid, latent homosexual women' (cited in Kruckman 1980: 8). The psychiatric literature still characterizes women with postpartum depression as infantile, immature, having unresolved conflicts with their mothers, failing to adjust to the feminine role, and having penis envy. And contemporary medical analyses continue to rely heavily on theories of biological causality (Karacan and Williams 1970; Seltzer 1980).

> Therapy is usually directed at the conflictual areas—helping the patient accept the feminine role or express jealous feelings toward the child, occasioned by thwarted dependency needs. . . . (Seltzer 1980: 2549)

However, the studies of hormonal and genetic causes of depression tend to be poorly designed and yield insufficient and even contradictory results (Livingston 1976; Weissman and Klerman 1977; Parlee 1980). The poor quality of research on the physiological causes of postpartum depression should not cause us to discount this line of inquiry, but should alert us to the inadequacy of relying on the simplistic, unicausal models which medical research tends to favour.

A path-breaking alternative feminist model has been developed by the Vancouver Post

Partum Counselling Services (PPCS) after over a decade of experience in working with more than a thousand women (Robertson 1980; Robertson with Howard 1980). The PPCS model is explicitly woman-centred, and looks to find the causes of depression in the structure of society rather than solely in individual pathology or hormonal imbalance. This perspective has informed the PPCS definition of depression, the population at risk, and the organization of treatment.

> Basically we redefine the term. We invented a definition separate from blues and psychosis.

A social perspective has enabled them to identify situations likely to generate postpartum depression. Since they do not see the causes of postpartum depression to be either exclusively physiological or a manifestation of failed femininity, the counsellors and volunteers at PPCS are able to respond to symptoms of depression in all new parents, including men and adoptive parents. It has also enabled them to draw a profile of the person who is most likely to get postpartum depression. The most striking feature of the profile is that the woman who is expected to make the most trouble-free transition to motherhood is the one who is most at risk.

The average woman seen by PPCS is 27, married, middle class (in terms of occupation and income),[2] and has had at least two years of post-secondary education. She has held responsible paying jobs (e.g., nurse, teller, social worker, hairdresser, secretary, teacher). The pregnancy was planned. Both parents attended prenatal classes. The father was present at the delivery. The woman chose to breast-feed. No significant prior incidents of depression were found among these women. PPCS also found that there was no significant correlation between Caesarean sections and depression, although many of the mothers had negative hospital experiences.[3] Nor have they found that the supposed closeness or bonding said to be inherent in non-medical childbirth and in breast-feeding has been a mitigating factor (Robertson 1976; Arney 1980).

The societal model used by PPCS has identified loss, isolation, and lack of social support as significant factors contributing to depression. Women who have lost their connection with their paid workplace are particularly vulnerable to depression. Some women keenly feel the loss of status as a 'girl' in this youth-oriented culture, an ironic situation when we consider that many societies count motherhood to be the resolution of a crisis period and the onset of social adulthood for women (Silverman 1975). Other feelings of loss stem from the very real experience of many women who report feeling deserted by their friends and family members after the first few weeks of their child's life (Saulnier 1988). They have few sources of reassurance, advice, or assistance in their work as mothers. They feel their husbands do not understand the pressures of 'full-time mothering'. And even men who 'help' can be undermining because they define the problem solely as the woman's. They do not seem to be able to offer emotional support ('I want a hug and he vacuums the living room'). Past miscarriages, the recent or past death of a parent, or loss of emotional contact with a significant person because of illness or alcoholism can also contribute to feelings of depression.

In an overall sense, postpartum depression is an expression of social isolation accompanied by loss of personal identity, loss of confidence in one's ability to cope. To understand why this should be so, we need to look at how motherhood and motherwork are structured in our society.

Mothering as Social and Personal Work

Defining mothering as work is crucial to the PPCS strategy for postpartum depression.

> It is very important for women to realize that what they are doing is work. When I talk to women, I consciously change the language I use. I talk about the job and the fact that the woman is the manager. That's one of the hardest parts about the job and it usually isn't even recognized as work—even by husbands who are 'nice guys' and 'help' [with housework and childcare]. They don't seem to realize that helping is not the same thing as carrying the weight of responsibility that mothers carry.

This redefinition is also a prerequisite for a feminist analysis of the political economic determinants of mothering as an aspect of social reproduction under capitalism. The overlapping organization of gender relations and the division between what are called 'the public' and 'the private' (or the domestic household and the economy) effectively assigns the major responsibility for the social work of reproduction to women without any social recognition or social support. Geographical mobility and segmented households, combined with the ideology of family privacy, mean that women with babies get very little on-the-job training from experienced workers.

For many women, becoming a parent is often devastating and confusing because they suddenly find themselves in unfamiliar work situations. Although they have prepared for childbirth by taking classes and reading books, they suddenly find that they have not just given birth to a baby but to an endlessly demanding human being. The care of that human being is not defined as work: it is seen as a private, natural, and essentialist enterprise. When women complain or despair they are frequently told, 'Well, you were the one who wanted this baby. . . .' But raising a baby is not a personal hobby like raising begonias; it is an undertaking which reproduces society as well as expressing the individual need to love and cherish children.

Examples from kin-ordered societies demonstrate that child rearing is usually viewed as being both social and personal, and most cultures have provided very rich systems of social support to new parents (Dawson 1929; Bettelheim 1954; Lewis 1958; Mead 1962; Metraux 1963; Kupferer 1965; Newman 1966; Oakley 1976). While postpartum customs and rituals may seem obscure or unusual to Western eyes, they serve the very concrete social function of making a public statement that a new birth is significant to the community as a whole and that social attention must be focused on care for the new child. In industrial-capitalist societies the spotlight tends to be on the fetus, the doctor, and the technology of hospital births (Arms 1977; Jordan 1978). After a mother leaves the hospital, the thousands and thousands of socially approved dollars and hours and hours of work energy crystallized in the hospital setting evaporate. The woman is on her own: she moves from the public realm of hospital medicine to the private world of her household.

In contrast, in kin-based communities mothers can usually command social support as their right in custom and ritual. Mothers can expect kin to cook, clean, protect, and advise. A new mother may be ritually prohibited from preparing food, thus placing the onus of meal preparation on her kin (Solway 1984). In such settings new mothers are not expected to know or do everything for themselves. They are seen to be at the centre of a social drama and are understood to be entitled to help with caregiving and household tasks. The existence of amulets, special foods, and behavioural taboos constantly reinforce the sensibility that mothering is a public concern and not a private pastime.

In part these social concerns reflect fears for the health of mother and child in societies with high rates of infant and maternal mortality. Postpartum ritual is at one level of a communal attempt to deal with a time of real danger for babies and mothers. But such cultural supports can persist and have other effects even when mortality rates are not obviously at issue. By maintaining these rituals communities symbolically testify to their collective responsibility for children and mothers. In one study, Mexican-American women in Chicago who adhered to customary rituals in the postpartum period had no incidence of depression (Kruckman 1980). The confidence these mothers had in the social importance of child rearing was revealed in their attitude toward the evil eye. Mothers felt that if a stranger were to look at a baby he or she must immediately touch the child to ward off the evil eye. One woman recounted how when she spied a man looking at her baby, she crossed a crowded restaurant and insisted that he touch the infant. This belief, which defines uninvolved onlookers as dangerous, presses incorporating claims which prohibit looking without touching. What may look like 'superstition' to those outside the culture is actually a cultural safety net which asserts community responsibility for infant and maternal well-being. The women in this study, unlike those that PPCS found to be vulnerable in their isolation, did not find that they had to solve all problems by themselves.

For most women in North America and western Europe, however, the capacity to override claims of social non-involvement in childcare is quite limited. Unwaged caregiving in the household is rarely recognized as either a contribution to social reproduction or as real work; rather, it is seen in essentialist biological terms for women and as a private and personal reward for waged work for men. Mothers are not supposed to need, nor have the right to need, social services or social funds. Public funding for social services to alleviate the work done by mothers in households is identified as a 'frill'—an unnecessary expenditure which is unwarranted, especially in times of economic decline.

Furthermore, for women who do the work of caregiving there are contradictions between the low status of the work they do and the seemingly high status of the role.[4] 'Mother', 'motherhood', and 'mothering' are words that bring forth flamboyant, extravagant, romantic images. In contrast, the work itself includes many tasks which are not socially respected. Motherwork involves dealing with infant bodily functions: people who clean up human wastes have low status (Luxton 1983). Few jobs have this contradiction so deeply ingrained.

Equally significant to the stress of mothering tasks is the fact that many women do not really know what motherwork involves until they are faced with doing it. They have only a series of platitudes to go on, about it being 'the most important job in the world'. It is as if one were hired for a new job with the understanding that the job description would be so vast and so vague as to be undoable, that little assistance would be provided, and that any errors would be the employee's sole responsibility. Motherwork, like any other job, must be learned. Books and courses have become the major means of learning: for most it is an inadequate method, because it is not based on experience. There is no apprenticeship period in our society as there is in small-scale, kin-ordered societies where young girls learn the ropes as caregivers to younger children. In industrialized societies, a falling birth rate has resulted in small families in which girls (and boys) grow up playing in peer-oriented, age-segregated groups. Many leave home having experienced little or no contact with newborns and infants. Said one North American mother, 'When the baby was born, I knew I wasn't ready. I hadn't got through the reading list.'

One should add that the experts, the writers of child-rearing guides, are often men who in fact rarely do the daily work of caregiving themselves.[5] ('Provide a stimulating environment for the infant but don't overstimulate him', says one TV advice giver.) Advice givers define the job goals, and they judge the outcome. They garner wealth, prestige, and status by explaining three-month colic, thumb-sucking, and toilet training without experiencing the day-to-day working conditions of mothers. This separation between expert and worker can lead to condescending attitudes on the part of the expert. For example, Dr Frederick W. Rutherford, in *You and Your Baby*, has some inkling that all may not go well for mothers. He had no index entry under depression but does mention 'baby blues'. His advice:

> If you are feeling blue, pour out your troubles to someone who will make no moral judgments, someone who will understand that *no matter how little real basis there is for your depression* you nevertheless feel it strongly, but who also knows that with a little help you will manage nicely before very long. Try not to wallow in the blues, but don't be ashamed to express your feelings. You don't have to act like a cheerful cherub when you feel like Pitiful Pearl. (Rutherford 1971: 167; emphasis added)

To the non-worker, the pain of the worker is not quite real.

Contradictory, guilt-inducing 'how-to' books, magazines, and TV talk shows cater to the isolated model of caregiving and miss the social context—people with whom to talk, ask questions, share experiences. Some doctors fill this role, but the medicalization of parenting has been a risky business for mothers. Visits to the doctor can further reinforce the isolated and individuated nature of child rearing. Medical consultations are usually brief and centre on the health of the child, not the work of child rearing or the mental health of the mother. Simple-minded measures like weight gain can become an index for whether the mother is doing a good job. The fact that the child may be gaining and the mother falling apart may not be perceived by the doctor. Furthermore, family doctors may be reluctant to raise the issue of postpartum depression because they feel that women are suggestible and will get the symptoms if the issue is discussed.

Yet women are very dependent on advice from the medical establishment. Mothers may be labelled over-involved or hysterical, but since they so rarely have alternative methods of assessing health and nutrition matters, they must rely on their doctors. If they go outside the doctor–patient dyad, women risk criticism for listening to 'old wives' tales' (i.e., other women) or for negligence (e.g., attacks on home birth). Thus the privatized, asocial model of child rearing is constantly reinforced.

Stress, Depression, Burnout

> This is a very scattered job. I can't think any thoughts more than halfway. At least when my husband goes to work he gets silence.

> I work 24 hours a day. He [her husband] doesn't. At night when the baby cries, he never wakes up first. I have to wake him and he goes to the baby. Then he's so proud because he let me sleep!

> I wish I could remember what it felt like not to have a knot in my stomach.

If we step back from the issue of mothers learning a new job, to the larger context of workplace stress, we gain some useful insights into the predicament in which many women find themselves.

The effects of stress (Selye 1956; 1974; 1980; Holmes and Rahe 1967; Lumsden 1981) on mental health are now being widely studied. Unions representing police, firefighters, public employees, and teachers in Canada and the USA have become very concerned with psychosocial stress in the workplace. Unions, employers, and courts are increasingly reading symptoms like chronic anxiety, depression, fatigue, and substance abuse (alcohol, drugs, overeating) as signals of strain produced on the job (Ellison and Genz 1978).

Some extreme forms of mental strain and emotional exhaustion have been called 'burnout' (Freudenberger and Richelson 1980). It has been argued that 'any kind of front-line person—teacher, social worker, therapist, nurse—who is at the beck and call of needy individuals is prone to burnout' (Murdoch 1981: 6). The literature on burnout among professionals offers some important insights into what unwaged mothers experience in the home. Burned-out front-line workers complain of unrelenting demands, little time away from intense personal interaction with clients or patients, shift work, and constant responsibility for two or more things at once (Maslach and Pines 1977). Burned-out professional childcare workers are reported to experience feelings of 'inarticulated personal distress' and fatigue as do lawyers, psychiatrists, nurses, and clinical psychologists when faced with the tense conditions of their jobs (Maslach 1976; Mattingly 1977; Maslach and Pines 1977; Pines and Kafry 1978).

If they are not alerted to burnout as a potential response to these stressors, professionals may respond by blaming themselves and seeking psychiatric help for what they perceive to be personal deficiencies. Those who have studied this process among daycare workers, for example, argue that it is the structure and intensity of the job, and not personal idiosyncrasies, that cause some workers to develop feelings of worthlessness. Psychiatric intervention, according to this research, rarely succeeds unless the work situation is taken into account (Maslach and Pines 1977).

These stressful job conditions are also true of motherwork. Most of the psychological and physical symptoms associated with burnout are the same as those reported by mothers diagnosed as having postpartum depression. Thus I would argue that postpartum depression, like burnout, is actually a syndrome in response to the organization of work.

Not all professionals have emotional problems; nor do all mothers. But there are times in any worker's life when job demands deplete, exhaust, and undermine. Motherwork, especially in relation to an infant, is a job of high demands. For many women it is a job of perpetual shift work—of always being on call (see Stellman and Daum 1973 on health and shift work). In that respect it is like policing or nursing, with the exception that in motherwork there are rarely shifts off. Furthermore, unlike other workers, mothers are not encouraged to separate home and work life. Since mothering is seen as a role, and not as work, mothers are supposed to always remain in character. They rarely get restorative 'time outs', let alone extended vacations or sick leave. The disorientation caused by lack of sleep and the disappearance of predictable routines of eating, sleeping, and waking contribute to a 'twilight zone' atmosphere. In addition, women who do motherwork also do housework and frequently must combine both jobs in a space like the kitchen that can be unsafe for infants and young children (Rosenberg 1984). Time–budget studies (Meissner et al. 1975; Proulx 1978) and case studies (Luxton 1980; 1983) tell us just how unrelenting these jobs are.

Low Control and High Demands

Those who study industrial workers argue that the most stressful job situations are not caused by high demand levels alone. Multiple demands, under the right circumstances, can create positive work experiences. It is situations of high demand combined with low levels of control in decision-making that cause the highest levels of worker stress, measured in terms of exhaustion and depression (Karasek 1979). Daycare workers who feel that they have high levels of participation in their centres, or social workers who feel they participate in agency decision-making, express high levels of job satisfaction (Maslach and Pines 1977; Pines and Kafry 1978).

Mental strain from high demands and low control occurs more commonly among assembly-line workers, whose movements are often rigidly contained, than it does among executives, who can set hours and control working conditions (Karasek 1979). Mothering is usually thought to be more similar to an executive job than to assembly-line work. But for many women,

> It's a myth that we are our bosses or that we can have a cigarette and a coffee when we want. You can't plan a thing, especially when they are young. You are lucky if you can find time to go to the bathroom. And even then, you don't go alone.

Women as mothers are like women in many other work situations: they have the appearance of wide 'decision-making latitude' or control, but in reality they have little power to define their work situations.[6] Typically, women's waged work (nursing, teaching, social work, working as bank tellers, as well as pink-collar jobs) is structured by institutionalized gender hierarchies. Female teachers have responsibilities within classrooms, but major decisions are usually made by predominantly male administrators. Men supervise women in social service agencies, banks, department stores, and beauty shops (Howe 1975; Tepperman 1976; Bank Book Collective 1979; Armstrong and Armstrong 1984). Women who quit underpaid, undervalued jobs for the 'freedom' of domestic work and child rearing may find themselves escaping into more of the same. They may make trivial consumer choices between brands of detergent, but ultimately they can be very dependent. Women who give up waged work become financially dependent on mates; they become dependent on 'expert' advice givers; and they are tied to infant-defined schedules, the schedules of other children, and the schedule of the wage earner.

In motherwork, one of the most devastating aspects of lack of control is the absence of feedback. The isolation of the job severely limits the feedback which is so essential to decision-making. Daycare workers who work with under-two year olds argued that isolation from adult company is what they felt most distinguished motherwork from daycare work. As one teacher said,

> Even though the job description is sometimes vague, I know I will get support and feedback from other [teachers] on how I am doing and how a child is doing. That's the big difference between us and mothers.

Some mothers have compared their isolation to being a prisoner of war. Said the nursing mother of a two month old whose mate was frequently absent because of job commitments,

> It's pure torture. Your street clothes are taken away and you wear a bathrobe, since all you do all day is [breast-]feed the baby. Just as you fall asleep, you are woken again. You're afraid to fall asleep anyway. What's the point? But God, the worst is that there is no one to talk to.

Strategies for Job Redesign

Occupational health and safety research on stress and social science studies of burnout situate the problems of exhaustion and depression in the workplace. They argue that solutions are social and structural, and lie in redesigning the job to lessen demands and increase control.[7] This is also true for motherwork stress and burnout, and is a solution that was first suggested by nineteenth-century feminists.

Over one hundred years ago, feminist economist Charlotte Perkins Gilman wrote a short story called 'The Yellow Wallpaper' ([1899] 1973). It is a nightmarish account of postpartum depression based on Gilman's own experience. Gilman's pioneering economic and architectural writings go further. They outline plans for job redesign which take up the whole question of how housework and motherwork should be socially structured, albeit from a somewhat elitist perspective (Hayden 1979). Other thinkers and activists struggled to bring housework and motherwork overtly into the public sphere through daycares and producers' and consumers' co-operatives (Hayden 1981). But by the 1930s these movements were defeated. Housework and motherwork became thoroughly identified as women's individual, private projects and as 'natural' expressions of femininity.

The reawakened women's movement of the 1960s once again introduced housework and mothering as social issues. Such a task is not easy and has led to reassessments of stereotyped patterns of the division of labour. With the exception of breast-feeding, motherwork is not sex-typed labour. Caregiving can be performed by other adults, including men, or by older children, within and outside the nuclear-family unit. This work is not 'help', which still pins organizational responsibility on a supposedly all-knowing mother, but rather inclines toward the development of strategies for sharing responsibility, which may require women to relinquish some of the pleasures of feeling indispensable. Said one woman:

> When it was his shift with the baby, I had to leave the house. Otherwise, I just hovered over him the whole time. He got anxious and insecure and then I'd take over. It took me a long time to let go and let him be really in charge.

Such a restructuring of jobs and responsibilities forces women and men to face very deep currents of internalized socialization about what mothers and fathers should do and how they should act. It may require constant struggle with previously unacknowledged feelings and fears. At times it may seem that the struggle to assign tasks fairly is just too difficult. But discussions within the household and actions which aim to deliberately involve community members (e.g., drop-in centres, paid maternity/paternity leave or paid leave for a designated caregiver, flexible work hours, choice of workplace or community daycare, babysitting exchanges, co-operative non-profit daycare, and political pressure groups that lobby for the maintenance and enhancement of locally controlled social services for parents) all ultimately serve to create dense networks of involvement which can lessen the ambivalences, stresses, and burnout of motherwork.

At the level of political practice, the women's movement has provided the context for this kind of debate. Local self-help groups, such as the Vancouver Post Partum Counselling Service, have provided immediate crisis support and have helped to reduce women's dependency on experts, enhanced self-perceptions of competence, and enabled women to break down the tendency to personalize domestic problems. Since the 1960s, the lesson of consciousness-raising groups has always been that groups of women who have shared experiences begin to see that their private pain has social roots. This type of collective experience has often served as a prelude to the formation of a variety of helping organizations, from rape crisis centres to shelters for battered wives to groups like PPCS.

However, attempts to socialize childcare outside the household—a project crucial to the redesign of motherwork and parenting—continue to meet with enormous resistance. In North America there is still much popular and official hostility to 'institutionalized' daycare. While it may be tolerated for 'working mothers', the idea that women who do not work for wages should have access to publicly funded childcare arrangements raises even stronger negative reactions.[8] The intensity of the 'fight for good daycare', defined as top-quality, universally accessible,

24-hour-a-day and community controlled (Ross 1979), illustrates that redesigning the job of parenting is deeply ideological, because it challenges the essentialist ideologies of 'the nuclear family' and 'motherhood', and the allocation of resources and funds. But such struggles—economic, ideological, and political—are necessary to dismantle the crazy-making structure of privatized motherwork and in its place to create the social job of caregiving.

Notes

Data for this paper were collected during visits to the Post Partum Counselling Service (PPCS), Ministry of Human Resources, Vancouver, British Columbia, in 1980, 1981, and 1982. PPCS was founded in 1971 and has served over 1,000 women. Despite the efforts of hundreds of people, PPCS was closed by the Social Credit government of British Columbia in 1983. This paper is dedicated to Joann, Jim, Penny, Allison, and Fran, former counsellors who truly fought the good fight.

I would like to thank the men, women, and children whom I interviewed in New York, Toronto, and Vancouver for their time and the effort they made to share their understanding of parenting with me.

Thanks, too, to Gloria Gordon, Jeanne Stellman, Lawrence Kruckman, Jan Schneider, Rayna Rapp, Joan Jacobson, Don Hale, Meg Luxton, and Richard Lee for their encouragement and suggestions.

1. Based on interviews with Post Partum Counselling Service (PPCS) counsellors and interviews with adoptive parents in Toronto.
2. Most of the women who went to PPCS are middle class in terms of income level, lifestyle, and education. The counsellors have assumed that this self-selection was an artifact of a class-based society in which middle-class people have better access to services. However, some poor women do come to PPCS. They tend to be young (late teens or early twenties) single parents on welfare. PPCS counsellors concluded that their depressions were so concretely rooted in economic and social deprivation ('Dealing with the welfare system is automatically depression') that their situation was not technically postpartum depression.

   Over the years PPCS has received letters from women across Canada in response to various radio and television broadcasts they have done. This admittedly informal and unscientific survey seems to indicate that postnatal depression does cut across geographic, occupational, and ethnic lines.

   Since so little research has been done on the question of postpartum depression and class, we cannot make any assumptions about differential rates between working-class, upper-class, and middle-class women. One community study in London on depression and marriage (i.e., not specifically the postnatal period) found that, subject to equivalent levels of stress, working-class women were five times more likely to become depressed than middle-class women. Working-class married women with young children living at home had the highest rate of depression (Rice 1937; Brown, Bhrolchain, and Harris 1975).

   This data should caution one against assuming that working-class women are automatically plugged into networks of support that mitigate the effects of stress and depression.
3. J. Croke, *Postpartum Depression* (Master's thesis, School of Social Work, Carleton University, Ottawa, 1982), shows that women who have had home births are less likely to experience depression after birth. However, her sample is small and further research is needed to obtain more significant data.
4. There exists a body of literature (reviewed by Parlee 1980) which links postpartum depression to a woman's difficulty in her *role* as a mother. With the exception of Luxton (1980), however, there has been little discussion of the actual work that women do as mothers on a day-to-day basis.

Since mothering is constantly defined as a role, women who don't like to do some parts of the job may be considered crazy. See Boszormenyi-Nagy and Spark (1973) for family therapists who criticize women who do not fulfill the female domestic role, and Ehrenreich and English (1979) for criticism of the experts.

5. See Bloom (1976) for a short summary of the vagaries of childcare advice from the mid-nineteenth century to the late 1960s, as well as Ehrenreich and English (1979).
6. The terms 'control', 'decision-making latitude', and 'discretion' as used in Karasek's study deserve a closer look. Karasek based his data on male labour-force statistics in the USA and Sweden. 'Control' was defined through the questions in the questionnaire that received a yes answer to whether the job was at a high skill level; one learned new things; the job was non-repetitious, creative; allowed freedom; permitted one to make decisions; and to have a say on the job. These were collapsed into the definition of 'control' over tasks and conduct during the day. Two measures—'decision authority' and 'intellectual discretion'—were selected for the study because of their similarity to other measures in the literature. Karasek argues that the literature shows that 'decision authority' and 'intellectual discretion' are highly correlated. He argued that highly skilled work rarely combined with low decision-making authority.

   This combination may be rare in male jobs, but it is more common in female jobs, where the contradiction of high skill but low authority is built into a sex-segregated labour force. Thus female nurses, teachers, tellers, and social workers are usually in the position of knowing that male authority can override their decisions. This sexist structure, coupled with the fact that women are more vulnerable to layoffs than men, argues for more sensitive measures in aggregate data studies to pick up the special stressors to which women are subject. Furthermore, in relation to (unwaged) domestic labour like motherwork, we find the contradiction between high skill levels and low authority levels to be important. The popular myth that housewives/mothers are autonomous and have high degrees of decision-making power in their jobs is belied by their economic dependence on a male breadwinner (Smith 1973; Zaretsky 1976; Luxton 1980).
7. Karasek (1979) argues for work teams rather than single-task assembly lines. Maslach and Pines (1977), Pines and Kafry (1978), Freudenberger and Richelson (1980), and Mattingly (1977) all include mention of techniques which can give professionals more control in their workplace, including rotations and times off from constant face-to-face patient or client contact. Collegial support, awareness sessions, and variation in tasks are considered useful ways of restructuring work situations.

   Other stress-reducing techniques operate on an individual level. They include strenuous exercise (Freudenberger 1977) and biofeedback (Greenspan 1978). These individual solutions are frequently difficult for mothers of new infants, who may be overwhelmed by lack of energy, time and money, and by the difficulty of finding babysitters to take over while they go out.

   The mother of an infant said in this regard, 'I know exactly why I didn't get postpartum depression. I bought my way out. We hired a housekeeper to come in five days a week, make meals, clean, and babysit. I went out and just sat in the library. Eventually, I got a job and felt less guilty about the housekeeper.'
8. When I proposed this solution to a group of previously quite sympathetic upper-middle-class women, they balked. Said one woman, 'Sure, it sounds like a good idea, but our husbands would never give us the money. It'll never work.'

References

Arms, S. 1977. *Immaculate Deception* (New York: Bantam).

Armstrong, P., and H. Armstrong. 1984. *The Double Ghetto: Canadian Women and Their Segregated Work*, rev. edn (Toronto: McClelland & Stewart).

Arney, W.R. 1980. 'Maternal Infant Bonding: The Politics of Falling in Love with Your Child', *Feminist Studies* 6, 3.

Balchin, P. 1975. 'The Midwife and Puerperal Psychosis', *Midwife Health Visitor* 11, 2.

Bank Book Collective. 1979. *An Account to Settle: The Story of the United Bank Workers (SORWUC)* (Vancouver: Press Gang).

Bettelheim, B. 1954. *Symbolic Wounds: Puberty Rites and the Envious Male* (New York: Free Press).

Bloom, L.Z. 1976. 'It's All for Your Own Good: Parent–Child Relationships in Popular American Child Rearing Literature, 1820–1970', *Journal of Popular Culture* 10.

Boszormenyi-Nagy, I., and G.M. Spark. 1973. *Invisible Loyalties: Intergenerational Family Therapy* (New York: Harper & Row).

Brenner, M.H. 1973. *Mental Illness and the Economy* (Cambridge, MA: Harvard University Press).

———. 1977. 'Health Costs and Benefits of Economic Policy', *International Journal of Health Services* 7, 4.

———. 1979. 'Unemployment and Economic Growth and Mortality', *Lancet* 24 (Mar.).

Brown, G., M. Bhrolchain, and T. Harris. 1975. 'Social Class and Psychiatric Disturbances among Women in an Urban Population', *Sociology* 9.

Bucove, A. 1964. 'Postpartum Psychosis in the Male', *Bulletin of the New York Academy of Medicine* 40.

Catano, J., and V. Catano. 1981. 'Mild Post-partum Depression: Learned Helplessness and the Medicalization of Obstetrics', unpublished manuscript (St Mary's University, Halifax).

Dalton, K. 1971. 'Puerperal and Premenstrual Depression', *Proceedings of the Royal Society of Medicine* 64, 12: 1249–52.

Davidson, J.R. 1972. 'Postpartum Mood Change in Jamaican Women: A Description and Discussion of Its Significance', *British Journal of Psychiatry* 121: 659–63.

Davin, A. 1978. 'Imperialism and Motherhood', *History Workshop* 5 (Spring): 9–65.

Dawson, W.R. 1929. *The Custom of Couvade* (Manchester: Manchester University Press).

Ehrenreich, B., and D. English. 1979. *For Her Own Good: 150 Years of Experts' Advice to Women* (Garden City, NY: Anchor/Doubleday).

Ellison, K., and J.L. Genz. 1978. 'The Police Officer as Burned Out Samaritan', *FBI Law Enforcement Bulletin* 47, 3 (Mar.).

Freudenberger, H.J. 1977. 'Burn-out: Occupational Hazard of Child Care Workers', *Child Care Quarterly* 6, 2.

———, and G. Richelson. 1980. *Burn-out* (New York: Doubleday).

Friedan, B. 1963. *The Feminine Mystique* (New York: Dell).

Gilman, C.P. [1899] 1973. *The Yellow Wallpaper* (Old Westbury, NY: Feminist Press).

Greenspan, K. 1978. 'Biologic Feedback and Cardiovascular Disease', *Psychosomatics* 19, 11.

Hamilton, J.A. 1962. *Postpartum Psychiatric Problems* (St Louis, MO: C.V. Mosby).

Hayden, D. 1979. 'Charlotte Perkins Gilman and the Kitchenless House', *Radical History Review* 21: 225–47.

———. 1981. *The Grand Domestic Revolution: A History of Feminist Designs for American Homes, Neighbourhoods, and Cities* (Cambridge, MA: MIT Press).

Holmes, T., and R. Rahe. 1967. 'The Social Adjustment Rating Scale', *Journal of Psychosomatic Research* 1, 2.

Howe, L.K. 1975. *Pink Collar Workers* (New York: Avon Books).

Jordan, B. 1978. *Birth in Four Cultures: A Cross-cultural Investigation of Childbirth in Yucatan, Holland, Sweden, and the United States* (Montreal: Eden Press).

Karacan, I., and R.L. Williams. 1970. 'Current Advances in Theory and Practice Relating to Postpartum Syndromes', *Psychiatry in Medicine* 1: 307–28.

Karasek, R.A. 1979. 'Job Demands, Job Decision Latitude, and Mental Strain: Implication for Job

Redesign', *Administration Science Quarterly* 24: 285–308.

Kruckman, L. 1980. 'From Institutionalization to Self-help: A Review of Postpartum Depression Treatment' (Chicago: School of Public Health, University of Illinois Medical Center).

Kupferer, H.J.K. 1965. 'Couvade: Ritual or Illness?' *American Anthropologist* 67d: 99–102.

Lewis, O. 1958. *Village Life in North India* (Urbana: University of Illinois Press).

Livingston, J.E. 1976. *'An Assessment of Vitamin* B_6 *Status in Women with Postpartum Depression'*, MSc thesis, Department of Medical Generics, University of British Columbia.

Lumsden, D.P. 1981. 'Is the Concept of "Stress" of any Use, Anymore?', in *Contributions to Primary Prevention in Mental Health*, ed. D. Randall (Toronto: Canadian Mental Health Association).

Luxton, M. 1980. *More Than a Labour of Love: Three Generations of Women's Work in the Home* (Toronto: The Women's Press).

———. 1983. 'Two Hands for the Clock: Changing Patterns in the Domestic Division of Labour', *Studies in Political Economy* 12.

Maslach, C. 1976. 'Burned-out', *Human Behaviour* (Sept.).

———, and A. Pines. 1977. 'The Burn-out Syndrome in the Day Care Setting', *Child Care Quarterly* 6, 2 (Summer): 100–13.

Mattingly, M.A. 1977. 'Sources of Stress and Burnout in Professional Child Care Work', *Child Care Quarterly* 6, 2.

Mead, M. 1962. 'A Cultural Anthropological Approach to Maternal Deprivation', in *Deprivation of Maternal Health Care: A Reassessment of Its Effects*, ed. World Health Organization (Geneva: WHO).

Meissner, M., et al. 1975. 'No Exit for Wives: Sexual Division of Labour and the Cumulation of Household Demands', *Canadian Review of Sociology and Anthropology* 12, 4, Pt. 1 (Nov.).

Metraux, A. 1963. 'The Couvade', in *Handbook of South American Indians, Vol. 5*, ed. J.H. Stewart (New York: Cooper Square).

Newman, L. 1966. 'The Couvade: A Reply to Kupferer', *American Anthropologist* 68.

Oakley, A. 1972. *Sex, Gender and Society* (London: Temple-Smith).

———. 1976. *Housewife* (Harmondsworth, UK: Penguin).

Parlee, M.B. 1980. 'Psychological Aspects of Menstruation, Childbirth, and Menopause', in *Psychology of Women: Future Directions Research*, eds J.A. Sherman and F.L. Denmark (New York: Psychological Dimensions).

Pines, A., and B. Kafry. 1978. 'Occupational Tedium in the Social Services', *Social Work* (Nov.): 499–508.

Proulx, M. 1978. *Five Million Women: A Study of the Canadian Housewife* (Ottawa: Advisory Council on the Status of Women).

Rice, M.S. 1937. *Working Class Wives: Their Health and Conditions* (Harmondsworth, UK: Penguin).

Robertson, J. 1976. 'The Abusive Parent: A Different Perspective', *Canada's Mental Health* 24, 4 (Dec.): 18–19.

———. 1980. 'A Treatment Model for Post-partum Depression', *Canada's Mental Health* (Summer).

———, with A. Howard. 1980. *The Post-partum Counselling Service Manual* (British Columbia: Ministry of Human Resources).

Rosenberg, H. 1980. 'After Birth Blues', *Healthsharing* (Winter): 18–20.

———. 1984. 'The Home is the Workplace', in *Double Exposure: Women's Health Hazards on the Job and at Home*, ed. W. Chavkin (New York: Monthly Review Press).

Ross, K.G. 1979. *Good Day Care: Fighting for It, Getting It, Keeping It* (Toronto: The Women's Press).

Rutherford, F.W. 1971. *You and Your Baby: From Conception through to the First Year* (New York: Signet).

Saulnier, K.M. 1988. 'Social Networks and the Transition to Motherhood', in *Families and Social Networks*, ed. R. Milardo.

Seccombe, W. 1983. 'Marxism and Demography', *New Left Review* 137.

Seltzer, A. 1980. 'Postpartum Mental Syndrome', *Canadian Family Physician* 26 (Nov.): 1546–50.

Selye, H. 1956. *The Stress of Life* (New York: McGraw-Hill).

———. 1974. *Stress without Distress* (Toronto: McClelland & Stewart).

———. 1980. Preface to *Selye's Guide to Stress Research*, Vol. 1 (New York: McGraw-Hill).

Silverman, S. 1975. 'The Life Crisis as a Social Function', in *Toward an Anthropology of Women*, ed. R. Reiter (New York: Monthly Review Press).

Smith, D.E. 1973. 'Women, the Family, and Corporate Capitalism', in *Women in Canada*, ed. M. Stephenson (Toronto: New Press).

Solway, J. 1984. 'Women and Work among the Bakgalagiadi of Botswana', paper presented at the Canadian Ethnology Society, Montreal.

Stellman, J.M., and S. Daum. 1973. *Work Is Dangerous to Your Health* (New York: Vintage).

Tepperman, J. 1976. *Not Servants, Not Machines* (Boston: Beacon Press).

Weissman, M.M., and G. Klerman. 1977. 'Sex Differences and the Epidemiology of Depression', *Archives of General Psychiatry* 34 (Jan.): 98–111.

Welburn, V. 1980. *Postnatal Depression* (Glasgow: Fontana).

Yalom, D.I. 1968. 'Postpartum Blues Syndrome', *Archives of General Psychiatry* 18: 16–27.

Zaretsky, E. 1976. *Capitalism, the Family and Personal Life* (New York: Harper & Row).

Chapter 21

Like Harriet Rosenberg, a number of researchers have examined why so many women who are home full-time with babies or young children feel stressed, isolated, and sometimes depressed. They have concluded that the fact that mothers almost single-handedly hold the responsibility for their children for most of the day is key to these problems. This conclusion is not a new one. Early in the twentieth century, a number of feminists (such as Charlotte Perkins Gilman) argued that private nuclear-family living was a problem, and especially that it was a chief source of women's subordination to men. As well, they thought, the position of homemakers was problematic because they did housework and childcare alone. Some of those feminists proposed the design of multi-family housing that would include communal kitchens, dining rooms, laundries, and childcare centres, as well as private dwelling units. The proposals these visionary women had were never realized. But today co-operative housing in Canada involves some communal space, as well as collective management. As a result, such housing has the potential to create less private definitions and experiences of family life and the work that sustains family. In this chapter, Diana Worts reports on her research involving in-depth interviews, done in 2000–2001, with women living in co-ops in Toronto. She describes the differences that living in co-operative housing can make for women raising children.

'Like a Family': Reproductive Work in a Co-operative Setting

Diana Worts

> There's a bond with the people across the street because they're also in the co-op. . . . It's ki-i-ind of like a little bit of [an] extended family community. And sometimes it's really made a big difference. (Karen)

Introduction

Nuclear families raise a number of concerns for gender scholars. One of these is that this family pattern goes hand in hand with the *privatization* of 'reproductive work'—or the myriad everyday tasks involved in tending to the health and well-being of others.[1] Moreover, privatization combines with a gendered division of labour in marriage that assigns this work *to women*. Thus, while caregiving work benefits society as a whole, privatization ensures that the bulk of it is performed by individual women, as an unpaid 'labour of love' for family members. Privatization also establishes a less-than-optimal context for family work—a context that virtually guarantees its isolation, invisibility, and devaluation. As a result, those who carry responsibility for these tasks risk a variety of problems, including depression, physical exhaustion, and family violence—and if they choose to leave, poverty (Dobash and Dobash 1979; Goldberg and Kremen 1990; Oakley 1974; Rosenberg 1987). Importantly, the difficulties associated with the organization of caregiving work are magnified if and when women become parents, as the workload in the home increases dramatically at this time while the gendered division of labour loses much of its flexibility. Indeed, studies have found that parenthood can transform a marriage in which roles are relatively fluid to one in which the woman is the primary caregiver and the man the primary breadwinner (Cowan and Cowan 1992; Fox 1997). Thus, it is to *women raising children* that the critique of the privatization of family life in Western societies most obviously applies.

But the organization of caregiving work is not uniform across Western nations. Research comparing social policies in different countries demonstrates that governments vary widely in their approach to childcare and other reproductive work. While policies and programs in the US and most of Canada are organized around the assumption that this work is a private family responsibility, those in many European nations (and to some extent, Quebec) are based on the notion that the work should be *socialized*—or that *society as a whole* should bear a large share of the costs. Thus, in Sweden, for example, state-funded childcare, extended parental leaves, and high-quality part-time work are readily available; and as a result, women do not suffer the same consequences as their North American counterparts, despite the fact that they do the bulk of the reproductive work in their families (Daly 1994; Sainsbury 1994).

Moreover, research on poor American communities also identifies alternative ways of organizing caregiving tasks. For example, studies highlight the fluid boundaries of poor black women's households in past decades, showing the variety of ways 'family' may be constructed, and—for better or for worse—the lack of economic dependency on a single (male) partner these relationships often entail (Collins 1990; Stack 1973). This research directs attention beyond a focus on the division of labour in marriage, and suggests, instead, a need to look at how 'domestic' tasks may become the concern of the *entire local community*.

In the US and Canada, as well as many other countries, the organization of caregiving work bears a direct connection to the organization of *housing*. The home is the material and symbolic base of family life; and domestic work is typically carried out within private households or on behalf of individuals who live (or have lived) under the same roof. In a nation where few institutional means exist for socializing the burden of care, settings where housing is organized collectively are of interest. They offer an opportunity to examine whether alternative ways of organizing shelter can foster alternative ways of carrying out family work.

In Canada, *co-operative housing* is such an alternative. A form of social housing (i.e., government-owned, non-equity), it is funded in part by the Canadian welfare state. While the primary aim is affordability, one means by which affordability is achieved is a unique organizational structure known as 'collective self-management'; and this feature distinguishes the co-operative model from other social and rental housing. Co-ops are like private rental or ownership accommodation in that they consist of single-family houses and apartments and each unit is self-contained; however, they are not individually owned or rented but are leased at cost from the co-operative corporation. More important, in contrast to both private housing and other forms of social housing, decisions about their operation and maintenance are made and carried out *collectively* by the *community of residents*. Thus this form of housing introduces an element of collectivism into the very basis of family life—the home.

In large part because they are affordable, co-ops are attractive to women (and men) raising children. As a result, they are more likely to house children than the private housing market (Burke 1994). Co-ops are especially appealing to women parenting alone. A primary reason is affordability, but secondary reasons include central location, reliable maintenance, security of tenure, protection and mutual support, and control over the housing environment (Selby and Wilson 1988; Spector and Klodawsky 1993; Weckerle and Novac 1989). At least some of these drawing cards can be seen to 'substitute' for the advantages that might accompany marriage and home ownership. Co-ops are also attractive to women raising families in two-parent households. In many cases the economic and social advantages are less obvious than they are for women raising children alone. However, housing costs are often considerably lower than they would be in the rental market, and there is the added benefit of having access to rent-geared-to-income (RGI) should the need arise (Cooper and Rodman 1992).[2] Moreover, the advantages of community support, and of gaining some control over housing costs and the local environment (particularly in cases where the alternative is long-term renting), can make co-ops attractive to partnered women as well (Cooper and Rodman 1992; Selby and Wilson 1988).

This study makes use of in-depth interview material to investigate the organization of caregiving work in co-operative settings. It draws on the experiences of 25 women living in housing co-ops in and around the city of Toronto. The women represent a total of 18 different co-ops, and at the time of interview they had been co-op residents for anywhere from three to 25 years. All the women interviewed were parents. All had at least one child who had spent a substantial part of their growing-up years living in co-op housing. In addition, three of the women had spent a part of their own childhood in a co-op. At the time of interview, 11 of the women were living with a male partner, while 14 were raising children alone.

The analysis is organized around the notion that, as members of housing co-ops, these women gained access to a variety of resources *beyond the household* that assisted them in carrying out family work. Access to these resources was, moreover, structured in unique ways by the setting itself. The analysis identifies and describes two broad 'channels' through which community-level resources flowed to members of co-op communities: (1) *affordability* in housing, and (2) *ties to other members*. The discussion focuses on the kinds of resources the women in this study received through each of these channels. It shows that affordability delivered a variety of more or less tangible resources that helped them provide adequately for their children's physical and socio-emotional needs. The ties to other members offered a wide range of both tangible *and* intangible support. This support assisted women, on both the practical and the socio-emotional level, with the work of raising a family.[3] The conclusion draws out the consequences of each resource channel for the organization of family life. It suggests that the first channel, by itself, served primarily to shore up the privatized family household—and (women's) personal responsibility for caregiving work. The second channel, on the other hand, challenged the private nature of family life and began, in small ways, to shift the burden of responsibility for child rearing away from the household and toward the local community.

Affordability as a Resource Channel

Affordability served as a resource channel for these women in several ways. It was important in itself because it gave them *access* to an essential resource—housing. But beyond this, it often improved both the *quality* of their accommodation and its *location*. These affordability outcomes had quality-of-life implications for the women and their families.

Housing Access

The most obvious product of affordability was the housing itself. In fact, the majority of women in the study cited their need for affordable housing as the primary reason they had originally chosen to live in a co-op. The significance of affordability was, moreover, linked to personal (i.e., privatized) responsibility for children. Especially among the single women, responsibility for children was both the reason their living arrangements mattered, and the reason their financial resources were strained. Marilyn explained: 'On your own . . . you can live with a friend or do something [temporary]. But not with two kids.' Similarly, Anne-Marie described herself as having been a 'free spirit' prior to becoming a parent, but observed that, 'Everything's different now that I've had my daughter, because of financial needs and realities [that have] just taken a role in my life that they never did before.'

For many of these women, the problem was that the time and energy required to care for their families limited their ability to generate income, and so pushed them into the realm of need. Karen, whose older child was chronically ill, explained that, 'There's no way [I could work full-time]. I would be stressed out of my mind . . . at work and at home. And there's no way I'd be able to look after my kids.' Irene added that, 'I've lived on a housing subsidy for many years. . . . And I'm *very* grateful for that opportunity to do so. It's meant that I could raise my kids, you know, in the way that I wanted to raise them.' So, the state support that makes this type of housing affordable was a major means by which women with limited means managed to keep a roof over their families' heads while *also* continuing to care for their children. As Karen observed, 'It's made all the difference in the world. . . . It kind of ameliorates the effects of poverty, being there. Just softens it.'

Affordability was most important to the low-income single mothers in this study. For these women, rent-geared-to-income programs were a critical component of affordability, and several had been paying RGI for extended periods of time. However, both single and married women also used RGI as a 'backup' system in the event that personal or household incomes dropped unexpectedly for a short period of time. Indeed, several women with moderate household incomes had initially chosen co-op housing because it offered this kind of safety net to members. Elizabeth, for example, worked part-time while her partner worked short-term contract positions. She commented that,

> I guess when we moved in we knew [my husband's] income . . . there were no guarantees when it would come in. . . . And I was at home with [my older child] at the time. So . . . we really needed a place that was affordable. And we had that security [of RGI] if we needed it. So that seemed like a good thing for us.

Thus, for women (both married and single) whose household-level resources were limited or uncertain, the knowledge that RGI was there provided a sense of security they would not otherwise have had. As Elaine put it, 'Yeah, there've been times when I've used the subsidy pool. It's been great! It's got me through.'

RGI also served as a kind of safety net for women whose marriages were unstable. Julia reported that the possibility of getting a subsidy gave her 'the security of knowing if . . . something happened [to my marriage] and I couldn't make it on my own I'd be able to get some kind of assistance'. And Barbara recalled that RGI had enabled her to keep a roof over her own and her children's heads, while also getting back on her feet and caring for her children, after her first marriage dissolved.

> I mean it was bad enough being separated; and it was bad enough, you know, having very low income. But I can't *imagine* doing it in a regular rental market. . . . [With RGI] I was able to stay in university. [And because I was working at home] I was able to be more accessible to my kids when they were young and [I was] going through a divorce.

So RGI meant women, single or married, were less dependent on the economic protection marriage can provide. Thus they were in a stronger position to provide care for their children both within a financially insecure marriage and, if necessary, on their own.

Regardless of how they used it, though, a major benefit of RGI was that it gave women and their families *stability* in housing. When household incomes changed, whether through the loss of a partner or the loss of employment, housing costs were adjusted accordingly. Thus families were spared the search for less expensive accommodation at a time when they were already under considerable strain. The single women interviewed were especially aware of how important this kind of protection was to their families' well-being. Anne-Marie commented that the stability RGI had brought to her daughter's life was '*totally* important; it's the most important thing in my life, basically.' And Hannah echoed the sentiment. 'At this point I think [living outside the co-op with my kids] would be quite difficult, just because of the financial situation. . . . I don't have the confidence that I could set up something that would feel, you know, really stable.'

Affordability was also important to women not receiving RGI. The combined effects of co-op housing's non-profit status and members' volunteer labour ensured that even the non-subsidized costs were lower than those in the surrounding private rental or ownership markets. This was sometimes a factor, both in the choice to move into co-op housing, and in the decision to remain there over the long-term. As was the case for many of the women who relied on RGI, affordability was important to women paying unsubsidized rents, not only as a means of keeping a roof over their families' heads but also for its impact on their ability to care for their children.

> Affordability gives you . . . some freedom to have a family life. . . . I can work three days a week, or three and a half days a week, and still pay my rent and . . . have a little bit of money leftover. So that's important—'cause I'd rather be with [my baby and toddler] than at work all the time. (Monica)

For Victoria, affordable housing left enough in the budget to enrich her daughter's life. 'Even though my income didn't allow it . . . my kid had the advantages. She had the classes. She had the trips. She had all the same things as her [middle-class] friends.' Thus, for these women, too, affordability served not only to keep a roof over their own and their families' heads but also to let them raise their children in a way that made sense to them.

Housing Quality

Another resource available through affordability was better *quality* housing. Women who were, or had been, lone parents were most likely to observe that their co-op home was an improvement over the private housing they had been able to afford. And housing quality, like access, was linked to the ability to care for their children. Alice, who had a long history of living in 'slummy households all over the city', recalled that her first reaction to finding her co-op was a huge sense of relief because, in contrast to her previous arrangements, 'it look[ed] neat—nice, neat and clean', and 'like a nice place for a kid to grow up in'.

Equally important to low-income women was the fact that their home was not readily identifiable as 'social housing'. Thus they escaped the stigma so often attached to other forms of affordable accommodation. Once again, this was important largely for its impact on their children's well-being.

> I don't think my daughter thinks of it as a single mother's ghetto or anything like that. . . . See, living in [identifiable social housing] you can't fail to feel some kind of stigma, right? . . . Whereas we live in a little enclave, you know, and we're not really very identifiable as anything. I think that's really quite important. Yeah. Really, *really* important, in fact. . . . We just blend in. We're not very noticeable. (Anne-Marie)

> I get . . . a lot of really positive responses about living in [my co-op]. . . . So I'm hoping that, because of that, [my son's] going to have more of a positive experience with growing up. And not have that stigma attached to him, of, 'You live in low-income housing', and stuff like that. 'Cause . . . it's really hard for a kid to hear that. (Norma)

So, affordability helped these women meet the needs of their children. Moreover, it helped them do so in ways that went beyond the basic requirement for shelter. The quality of housing it delivered also meant their children had a better chance of growing up with a healthy sense of self-worth.

Housing Location

Affordability also connected these women to resources available outside the co-op. This was especially important for women raising families alone, as they were able to live closer to the downtown core, and/or in a better quality neighbourhood than they otherwise could. Central location was important because it placed households within easy reach of facilities and services not available in outlying areas. Most single mothers in this study relied on public transit, so proximity to high-quality daycares, schools, medical services, and their place of employment was often crucial to their ability to juggle multiple responsibilities. For Lucy, location was the primary reason for moving into her co-op. It put her within easy reach of a high-quality daycare and school, a large park and playground, and her place of employment. This, she said, made juggling her daily tasks 'much more manageable' than it had been in her previous suburban apartment.

Location not only simplified these women's lives; it also helped them provide opportunities for their children. For example, living downtown could mean children were exposed to a broader range of experiences than they would have been in other similarly priced housing.

> On the weekend I don't have to range far with my kids to find something interesting that's happening. . . . And 'specially, being a person with limited income and no car, I find that tremendously beneficial for my kids. . . . Because the reality of Toronto is that, like I said, for [what I pay here], where am I going to live? The edges of Scarborough? . . . I mean, just the reality, I think, for a lot of, especially single moms, is when you have to live in the middle of nowhere and you're an hour-and-a-half bus ride away from anything enjoyable, or especially [anything] free [of charge], you're not going to go do it. (Monica)

For single women who had lived downtown even before moving into a co-op, the significance of location was less that it gave them access to facilities and services than that it improved the quality of the surrounding neighbourhood. These women had often lived in areas that were unsafe and/or otherwise not 'family friendly', simply because this was all they could afford. By improving the quality of their neighbourhood, affordability made parenting a less risky undertaking for these women. Karen recalled that the rental units she had lived in with her older son 'were places where I would have to escort my son to the door, they were so unsafe'. Her younger son had grown up in a co-op, and this, she said, had 'made all the difference in the world, between . . . life for my [older] son and life for my [younger] son'.

For these single women, affordability did not, in itself, challenge the notion of maternal responsibility for their children's well-being. For the most part, they drew on the resources available to them through their housing to sustain their personal responsibility for child rearing. In fact, a significant minority of women who had received RGI over the long-term remained quite isolated from their local community. From this perspective, then, affordability *per se* served to shore up privatization and not to redistribute the burden of care beyond the household.

Ties to Other Members as a Resource Channel

The same is not true, however, of the second channel through which these women gained access to the resources needed to raise a family—their ties to other members of the community. Ties to neighbours gave the women in this study various types of practical help with the work of raising a family. But they also provided another resource that could be equally, or sometimes more, important—the socio-emotional support that nourished them on a more personal level and at times made the local community come to resemble an extended family.

Practical Support

Many women received small, but important, assistance with general household tasks through their ties to other co-op members. So, for example, members sometimes picked up groceries or emergency items, or ran errands, for each other; or they borrowed or loaned vehicles, equipment, or supplies. Several women also exchanged clothes and/or toys with neighbours; and in at least one co-op, members had organized a more formal clothing exchange that operated out of their laundry facility. Meal preparation was sometimes shared, most often in emergency situations such as a serious illness or injury, or following a birth or death in the family; occasionally, though, members who were especially close engaged in this type of exchange on a more regular basis. Skills exchanges (e.g., haircutting, sewing, gardening, or providing 'alternative' health care) were important in a few cases; and childcare exchanges—mostly on an irregular basis, but occasionally more formally organized—also occurred between women who were close, or whose children were close. All these exchanges took some of the work of raising a family beyond the boundaries of the household, and therefore off the shoulders of individual women.

One of the most frequently mentioned forms of practical support, however, indicates something unique about this kind of setting. Especially in co-ops with shared outdoor space, women described being able to spontaneously call on other members to watch preschool-aged or young school-aged children in the co-op yard while they 'r[a]n into the house to start dinner' or did other small tasks or errands. In fact, 16 of the 25 women made spontaneous reference to this kind of exchange being (or having been) a regular part of their life. This includes nearly all of those who lived in co-ops with shared yards, and a few other women as well. As Fiona explained, 'There's a community of moms. And we watch each other's kids.' Elizabeth echoed the sentiment. 'You know your neighbours' children; they know your children; so we tend to look out for each other that way.'

Similarly, women with older school-aged children, while not feeling their children needed full-time supervision, nevertheless found relief in the knowledge that they lived in a community with 'many eyes watching' as their children played outside on co-op property. These women's experiences suggest that a kind of *collective responsibility for children* can and does develop in this setting. Monica put it this way: 'After school and on the weekends and stuff, people keep their eyes on all the kids around here. You don't see kids messing around without some adult going, "Hey", you know, "I know your parents."' This aspect of co-op life stands in contrast to the notion of personal/familial responsibility associated with the privatization of family life.

Where it existed, the sense of collective responsibility for children was especially important to women (generally single women) whose household-level resources were strained, or women whose children were unusually vulnerable for any reason. Carmen, a single mother of two, had serious health challenges that placed her at risk of being unable to care for her children. Living in a co-op she found, to her great surprise and relief, that other members treated her children like their own, and so eased some of the frightening burden of sole responsibility.

> When I didn't live in the co-op I was constantly very scared. . . . I realized, what happens if something happen[s] to me? What happens with my kids? . . . So when I came here . . . I immediately became more relaxed about it, knowing that my kids could go any place, any neighbour's, because they knew them, they talked to them. . . . They knew my situation.

Kathleen, whose son had a learning disability, took comfort in the knowledge that he was surrounded by people who understood him and were therefore more inclined to treat him with compassion.

> It's been really good to know that the kids that he plays with on the street, that their parents know him. They know that he's a lot younger [mentally] than he appears to be. They know, they just know the situation, and I don't have to, sort of, worry.

The sense of collective responsibility for children came to Gillian's aid when her older daughter suffered a serious illness that permanently changed the child's life. Neighbours 'watch[ed] out for her' because they cared about her well-being. Moreover, this caring was important to Gillian because it signified their ability to see 'beyond' the young woman's difficulties, and affirmed her daughter's continuing value in the eyes of others. 'People knew her before. And they still know her now. And that's really important for me.' The kind of ongoing commitment in the face of challenges that Carmen, Kathleen, and Gillian described is akin to what *family* members are typically expected to provide for one another.

For all these women, then, the sense of collective responsibility for children that developed in this setting resembled the kind of 'caring' generally associated with family. Because this attitude extended to the entire local community on some level, their children were better cared for, and/or the women themselves were less overworked, than would have been the case in a privatized setting where children have only their parent(s) to turn to.

Socio-emotional Support

Ties to other members of the co-op also provided a more personal form of support to women engaged in family work. They were the source of ongoing socio-emotional exchanges that helped these women face the challenges of raising children. These exchanges consisted primarily of talking, but sometimes included 'just being there' in times of need. They grew directly out of the fact that these women had regular contact with one another in the course of their daily activities. Moreover, this contact was especially likely to occur when the women's daily activities were based in the home—the very circumstance that leads to isolation in a more privatized setting.

For example, Fiona commented that living in a collective setting kept her from feeling alone while she was at home with an infant.

> When she was really little and I'd be feeling a little stir-crazy I would just walk out into the courtyard, go around the block. I'd run into someone, have a nice conversation about something, and I'd go back home feeling a lot better. And that's been really important, for sure. . . . It saved me, a few times, from . . . feeling overwhelmed or sad.

Likewise, some women who had lived outside their co-op during at least one child's infancy regretted not having moved in sooner for just this kind of reason. Elaine described the first two years of her daughter's life, living in a suburban townhouse, as a time of feeling 'disconnected' and 'very isolated'. And Victoria recalled a similar experience during her daughter's infancy in a suburban apartment building. 'It was the most horrendous year, probably, of my entire life—well, *definitely*, of my entire life. . . . I was *so* isolated. I was *so* lonely. . . . The next move was basically because I was so unhappy there.' Hannah, who had spent her first two children's infancy in private housing and her third child's infancy in a co-op, remarked on the difference between the two settings. 'You know, when you have a baby, and the kind of isolation that can go on when you have a baby. You don't have that here. Or you're less likely to have that here, because you can just step outside [and find someone to talk to].' So, having others nearby for social contact and emotional support was especially important for women at home with an infant. During this period of heavy demands these women did not feel they coped alone; and this stood in contrast to their experiences in private housing.

The socio-emotional support they received through their ties to other members was also important to women at home with preschool-aged and young school-aged children. The reasons were similar to, though less pronounced than, those of women with infants. Julia, whose partner worked very long hours, had sole responsibility for her school-aged children. She had been at home with them until her youngest entered school; and with little money and no car, leaving the house had been difficult. She explained how living in a collective setting had allowed her to connect with other mothers of young children without really having to leave home.

> Living in a co-op brings people together. . . . Whereas if you weren't living in a co-op . . . you'd have to go out and join something to get that. . . . But when you're in a co-op . . . the whole point is that you're *supposed* to be doing things together. . . . So, even if you don't consciously plan it that way, you're setting up a situation where you're in a group of other parents who are in the same situation.

Women with teenaged children often continued to value the socio-emotional support of other members as their children entered adolescence. This was especially true of single women who had lived in the co-op through their children's younger years. Marilyn, a lone parent with a teenager and a grown child, had gone through a difficult period with her daughter during the young woman's early teens. She explained, after a long pause that suggested it was painful to recall, what living in a co-op community had meant to her during this emotionally trying time.

> And then, of course, when [my daughter] left home for that period of time, I had a *lot* of support. And there were people I knew I could just phone. And people . . . —two in particular—I became very close friends with. We would sit over coffee after [co-op] meetings and just *talk*. . . . It was great. . . . It was a *lifesaver*.

Similarly, Alice, a single parent of a grown child, had turned to fellow co-op members for moral support during her daughter's teenage years.

> [Living in a co-op has made being a single parent] easier because there are more people. There are more people who have either been there [or can offer] moral support. . . . I mean, what do I do with my horrible [teenager], you know? And you find out . . .

> other people have lived through it. . . . And you don't feel quite so bad.

Once again, the ties between neighbours that developed in this setting expanded the boundaries of home and family, so that women felt less alone in the challenges of raising children.

The feeling that a shared concern for children's well-being existed among members of the local community was, however, much less common for women with teenagers than it was for women with younger children. In fact, several women stated that their older children were somewhat alienated from the co-op community. Patti, for example, commented that her co-op was very supportive of young children, but that it often failed to address the needs and concerns of teenagers. 'It's a wonderful, wonderful place for raising kids. . . . People take care of the kids. People really do. It's just the youth and up they get a little stitchy about.' This suggests that the socio-emotional support women with teenaged children received in this setting was most often directed toward the women themselves, not toward their children.

Sometimes, however, socio-emotional support did come through older children's contact with other adult members of the community. Women who referred to this phenomenon all had children who at the time of interview were in their early twenties, but who had grown up in the co-op. These women described feeling validated as parents because other members, having been a part of their children's growing up, were genuinely interested in these young adults as individuals in their own right.

> As [my daughter] goes through the courtyard, people stop and ask how she is, what she's doing. They are . . . genuinely interested in her life. . . . It's a really nice feeling to hear from someone else that they've talked with your child. . . . That's a very affirming thing as a parent, to have other people interested in your child separately from you. (Victoria)

Gillian echoed the sentiment: 'There is, for me, a sense of validation in that [experience] . . . as a parent. And also . . . there's a really nice sense that other people have been part of [my children's] growing up.' Once more, these women's comments suggest that they did not feel alone in an aspect of parenting that generally follows from being a close family member—the genuine valuing of the child that develops in the context of regular ongoing contact.

The socio-emotional support women received from fellow members was also important during the sometimes lengthy process of getting back on their feet following a marital breakup.

> I guess the one thing that stood out [during my early time as a single parent] is . . . there were a couple of women who were in the same situation as me, who were staying focused. You know, they weren't falling apart. . . . We would touch base from time to time, you know, call on the phone, get together, maybe go out for a drink or something like that. And that was a real, sort of, solidarity. . . . That was comforting. (Barbara)

> [When my first marriage broke up] I knew . . . other single moms in the co-op, and was able to get some support from them. [That] was a really great source of comfort to me in all those questions—you know, 'Have I done the wrong thing? It's better to stay together for the kids', and all that stuff. (Kathleen)

So, these women drew on the socio-emotional support of members of the local community to help them sustain their families during periods of high demand, in which supports within the household were absent or in short supply.

On the most general level, the practical and socio-emotional support women received through their ties to other co-op members led to a sense of being supported in their child rearing at a level beyond the household. As Victoria said, '[The co-op community] has been the underpinning, in some ways, of my parenting, for the last [18] years. . . . [It's given me] a feeling that there was a constant that I could depend on.' For Hannah, it was 'a really good feeling to know that there are people—and quite a few of them, actually—who would be there for you. And for your kids. . . . [It's a] sort of safety net, actually.' Carmen added that, '[I feel that] I'm not the only mother. There's also the mothers of the others, looking [out] for all the children. So that [is] something I find amazing. You know, I don't have to take care of my children alone.' In other words, for these women, raising a family was in some respects a community rather than a private household concern. Although as mothers they retained primary responsibility for their children's well-being, they clearly felt they had strong 'backing' in their role as a parent through their ties to other members of the local community. The result, as Julia explained, was that living in a supportive community 'makes me a better mother'.

One final form of socio-emotional support women gained through their ties to members of the local community was a sense of physical safety, for themselves and their children, in the knowledge that they were surrounded by 'familiar' others. Several women contrasted this feeling with the fear and insecurity they had experienced in previous housing.

> I've had a couple of pretty lousy incidents with men when I was little, and as an adult, when I was [in our previous apartment]. So I'm pretty sensitive about that. [But] I always felt safe here, being surrounded by people who, you know, know me and would hear if something strange was going on. (Gwen)

> It's safer. It's absolutely safer for my kids [here]. . . . There's a bond with the people across the street because they're also in the co op. . . . It's ki-i-ind of like a little bit of [an] extended family community. And sometimes it's really made a big difference. Safer. My younger son [raised in the co-op] feels more secure. (Karen)

As Karen's comments suggest, the ties to neighbours that developed in this setting could create the kind of comfort normally associated, at least on the ideological level, with family. Thus this sense of physical safety is another measure of the extent to which the boundaries around the family household were expanded in this setting, to incorporate the local community.

Co-op Networks as Extended Family

Indeed, women raising families in co-op housing often indicated that they thought of their ties to other members as constituting a kind of *extended family*. Ten of the 25 women in the study spontaneously named other co-op members as part of what Gillian called 'chosen family', or 'spiritual family'—that is, people who were not related by blood or marriage, but who could be counted on to 'be there' in times of need.

> I always think there's your blood family . . . and the ones that you choose as well. And I think of them as more my spiritual family. And there are people in the co-op that I would say that of. I just know that, you know, even if one of us moves, that we'll always be a part of each other's lives. (Gillian)

Similarly, Hannah thought of members of her co-op as 'family' 'in the sense that . . . I could rely on them . . . if I needed anything for my kids'. Kathleen also experienced her co-op as something of an 'extended family'. In part, this feeling grew out of her personal history. She had first lived in the co-op as a teenager in her parents' household, and later had moved to her own unit in the same co-op where both her parents and brother had separate residences. The blood relatives had since moved away, but Kathleen felt the co-op community as a whole had '*become* a family'. Similarly, Carmen commented that '[When] you are 18 years in the same place and with the same people, it's your family, and you create a family.' Other women used family terminology to refer to specific neighbours with whom they were especially close. Monica, for example, spoke of three of her neighbours as being 'like a sister'. And Victoria described how one of her neighbours, 'just sort of walks in [to my place]. She goes through the cupboards and gets what she wants. And I think she feels like she's part of our family here.' Elizabeth talked about a teenaged neighbour who felt 'like an adopted daughter, or a niece, maybe', and who was 'like a big sister to my kids'. Julia referred to a neighbouring couple as 'my kids' honorary grandparents', while Gillian thought of one of her neighbours as her daughter's 'guardian angel'. Still other women described a kind of pride in association generally reserved for family or very close friends. Irene, for example, referred to the 'family pride' she and many of her fellow members felt in connection with several well-known former co-op residents—writers, artists, and political figures who had made a name for themselves in the world at large. 'We always feel when somebody's sort of getting their name out there, apart from the co-op, there is a family sort of feeling here.' And Freda, Hannah, and Gillian all talked about the connections they felt to children from other co-op households they had watched grow from babyhood or childhood into young adulthood.

> I know all the kids here. I know all the teenagers. You know? All of the kids that have grown up here. If I see them on the street in another part of the city they say hello. . . . I think that's big. (Freda)

> Not only do you have your own kids, but you have all these other children out there. And you're just watching this whole community grow. You watch these kids grow up. (Hannah)

> [With a couple of young women in the co-op I've] had conversations that don't have to do with [their] parents' concerns. [It's] just between the two of us. And that is . . . for me, a real privilege, to have the opportunity of being able to talk with, you know, a young woman [I've watched grow up]. (Gillian)

All of these examples suggest that the meaning these women attached to their ties to members of the local community resembles the meaning attached to 'family'. Thus, for many women living in this setting, the boundaries of family life were, in this less tangible but still very real sense, expanded to include the local community.

The sense of belonging to a unit larger than the family household was most important to the women who needed more resources than their own households could supply. Single women, for example, were especially inclined to see the community as extended family. Victoria talked about how, living in the same community for many years, she had become 'part of the web'. And Hannah referred to the general sense she had, in her co-op, that other members were 'there for you', and that there was always a 'safety net' to fall back on in times of need. The sense of being surrounded by extended family was also very important to women who had weathered a crisis during their time in the co-op. Freda, whose youngest child had been born with a physical disability, put it matter-of-factly: 'I don't think I would have been able to raise my [youngest child] without the support I've found here.' And Carmen described how, during and following her own near-fatal illness, her neighbours had come through for her. She said, 'The neighbours, you should see the neighbours. The solidarity. . . . It's a family. It was like a family. They . . . came forward; they [looked after everything]. It was incredible. My neighbours—what they did!' Victoria had weathered three separate health crises with the help of neighbours. During this time she had received everything from in-home medical attention, through personal care, to care for her daughter. And when Gillian's daughter had suffered a permanently crippling illness, the family had received support from neighbours ranging from financial aid, through assistance with day-to-day tasks, to emotional support. In every case, these women felt they had received aid that went far beyond what they would have expected from neighbours. Instead, they felt it mimicked what they would have expected from family members.

Women not only experienced this extended family feeling directly; they also experienced it through their children. That is, many of them felt that their children also 'belonged' to a unit larger than their own household. Membership in such a unit is implied by the sense of collective responsibility for children that often developed in this setting, and the way other adults often took an interest in grown-up co-op children as individuals. But beyond this, many women also felt their children had developed special bonds with other children in the co-op. As Karen explained, 'You know, it's a co-op, and the kids share that bond.' Indeed, these women sometimes maintained that their children's ongoing contact with other co-op children came to resemble sibling interactions.

> There's also kids a little older, a little younger so, you know, [my daughter] can get a range of experience. . . . She has the experience of a brother through [one of those] relationship[s]. . . . Because we've done so much back and forth . . . they are that close. (Freda)

> You go out there [into the shared yard], and whoever's out there is the person you play with. If they're four, if they're nine, if they're 16 . . . It's a great thing because, you know, if you don't have older brothers and sisters—and there's a lot of only kids—they have a tremendous benefit of getting close to both boys and girls who are older and younger. (Gillian)

There is an obvious link between viewing the co-op community as extended family and feeling that some measure of collective responsibility for children exists in this setting. Given that the sense of collective responsibility was the source of such important benefits, it is no surprise to find that women sometimes fostered the sense of extended family in their children. One of the ways they did this was by encouraging their children to think of the entire co-op as 'home'. Fiona recounted a conversation between her daughter and the mother of her daughter's friend (who lived in private housing), in which this approach is evident. The child's friend had recited her street address and the friend's mother had then asked Fiona's daughter, 'Do you know where you live?' As Fiona recalled, '[My daughter] said, "Yeah, I live at [the co-op]." And so [the mother] said, "But what number?"' Her daughter had had no answer because, as Fiona had explained to the other woman, '*It doesn't matter*. If she turned up at the co-op someone would bring her home.' Fiona interpreted this incident as evidence of her daughter's sense that the co-op community was a kind of extended family—a unique 'social set' that reached beyond the family household, and one to which the little friend did not have access.

> [My daughter] has a sense of something that a lot of other kids don't, which is her community—her immediate community. And so when you say to her 'the co-op' it *means* something to her. . . . It's a whole other, sort of, social set that most people

> don't have. . . . And she sometimes feels sad for people who don't live in co-ops. That's what she says.

Freda described an incident that demonstrated that her daughter, too, had learned to think of the entire co-op as 'home'. Although the child had misunderstood the location of its boundaries, she had *not* misunderstood the message that the co-op as a whole was her 'home turf'.

> A couple of weeks ago we had a funny thing. We couldn't find the kids.[4]. . . And then my one friend said, 'Well, I found . . . my granddaughter two doors up from the co-op, with a little friend there.' . . . And I went and got [my daughter] and I brought her back, and I was very upset, and [told her], 'You can't leave the co-op.' And she says, 'Well, I didn't know that wasn't part of the co-op.'

Encouraging their children to think of the entire co-op as 'home' (and the community as 'family') released both parents and children from an overly tight grip on each other's time and energies. It gave children a freedom of movement they might not otherwise have had, and at the same time relieved parents of some of the pressure associated with being 'on duty' at all times.

> [My daughter] comes home and has a snack after school, and goes out. And, you know, I don't see her until suppertime. . . . And because we . . . have the fencing along the streets and so on, the property is very well defined. And, you know, as long as they stay within its boundaries, I can make two phone calls and find her. (Freda)

Patti described feeling similarly released from perpetual vigilance when the children from her first marriage were young. '[Living in a co-op with a shared yard], I could keep the kids sort of "corralled", and I wouldn't have to be looking at them every two minutes of the day.'

The freedom of movement that came from living in a community where everyone knew each other, and where people looked out for each other's children, relieved women in another sense. It meant children always had easy access to playmates, which took some of the pressure off their parent(s) to plan social activities for them. As Gwen put it, 'I think the advantages [to living in a co-op] are the kids. They have direct access to a whole group of other children out there. You know, you don't have to go looking for it.' Freda and Fiona both made similar comments:

> We didn't do kindergarten with [my daughter]. . . . I never felt that there was difficulty with that, because there were so many other children here—so that she could gain the experience of peer group. (Freda)

> [The courtyard is] a really great, giant front yard full of kids [my daughter's] age. And so they all just toddle out there. (Fiona)

So, the sense that the local community was a kind of extended family released both women and children from some of the constraints that accompany a more privatized approach to family life.

Shared Values

There was an important underpinning to this extended family feeling—the sense that members, or at least a core group of them, shared a similar set of values. The content of these shared values was not necessarily explicit, and likely varied from one group to another; but the sense that they were among 'like-minded others' was a theme that ran through the interviews of women with strong ties to other members. Carmen felt 'at home' in her community because, 'In terms of . . . the philosophy of the co-op, it was great [to move here], to understand that, in a way, I was really in a place close to my values that I came with.' And Freda, who had raised her older children mostly in private housing, described her early parenting as a time that 'really pushed me over the edge' because there was no support for the kind of 'left-wing politics' she had been involved in before having a family. By contrast, she felt comfortable in her current environment because it was what she referred to as 'an *alternative* co-op'. She explained that, 'because we're an alternative kind of housing . . . then alternative people tend to situate themselves here'. As a result, Freda found support for her own political activism and involvement in alternative health care.

The significance of shared values was not only that it validated women personally; it also created an environment in which they felt that their children would be nourished in much the same way as they were at home. Usually, the values cited in this connection were linked in some way to a sense of collective responsibility for people and/or the environment. Women felt that living in a collective setting encouraged their children to practise those ideals in their daily lives in a way that living in private housing could not. For example, several women spoke with pride of how their children participated in collective clean-up days, or shovelled snow or picked up garbage in the co-op on a regular basis. They felt that this fostered in their children a sense of responsibility toward a unit larger than their own household—a sense that would not have developed as easily and naturally in a private rental or ownership situation. Barbara described it this way: 'Because we live in a co-op, they can get the sense of the bigger picture that, you know, you don't just stop at the edge of your grass. You know, if there's a piece of garbage on the road, that you pick it up. . . . You know, this belongs to *all* of us.' Carmen echoed the sentiment. '[Being involved in shared activities meant] they grew up feeling that we have a responsibility, you know. And this is wonderful. . . . So they grew up with different values about the place they live. They have to share more.' Likewise, several women were pleased to see their children learning to think and act collectively as they shared a play area with other children in the co-op. As Carmen noted, '[All the] children play together, and they're very caring [toward] each other.' Gillian elaborated on children's experience growing up in a co-operative setting.

> Kids who've grown up here, they [teach] the younger kids. . . . So there is a modelling on that level as well. . . . [And] the sense of who gets to play is very different [from private housing]. It's not 'who's in, who's out'. [If] you're here, you're in.

At least as important as the *content* of the values to which children were exposed in this environment, though, was the feeling that members of the community *shared* them. This was important because it meant parents' belief systems were reinforced outside the household. Hannah explained that living in a co-op underscored for her children 'life values that, you know, you hope would be passed on to your children'. As a result, the job of raising a family fell less heavily on the shoulders of parents themselves. As Gillian put it, '[When kids] see their parents' values lived out in other households, among other adults, it bears much more weight.' Thus, living in a community where values were shared gave these women a feeling that there was support beyond the household for their children's social development.[5] This, in turn, laid the foundation for a shift in the way they conceptualized reproductive tasks. Rather than seeing this work as only a private matter, women living on co-op housing were able to turn often to the local community, and to find a surprising range of supports for child rearing located there.

Conclusion

This study has highlighted the phenomenon of access to community-level resources in a co-operative setting. It has identified and described the range of resources available, and shown how that access was structured. It has argued that the resources available to women raising families in this setting were both tangible (material and practical) and intangible (socio-emotional). It has argued, further, that women's access to resources in this environment could be seen as a system comprising two distinct channels—affordability and ties to other members. The distinction between the two resource channels corresponds in some ways to the distinction between the two resource types; however, the correspondence is not absolute. Although one channel (affordability) ostensibly provided only a material resource and the other (ties between members) was rooted in socio-emotional resources, the interview material demonstrates that at least the second channel actually delivered a range of tangible and intangible resources. The goal of conceptualizing access to resources in this manner is, however, more than descriptive. Ultimately the aim is to tease out the consequences for the organization of family life and caregiving work. With that in mind, several general points can be drawn from the analysis.

Regarding affordability, two points can be made. First, this resource had a number of quality-of-life implications for these women that went beyond the basic problem of securing shelter. Whether by freeing up parental time and money or by reducing family members' exposure to risk or stigma, affordability made the challenges these women faced raising their children more manageable. The second general point that can be made about affordability is that it bore a mixed relationship to the organization of family life. On the one hand, it decreased economic dependency on marriage. In this respect it seemed to challenge the assumed (nuclear family) context for child rearing. Yet, the provision of affordable housing did not, by itself, challenge the notion of women's *personal responsibility for children*. Access to affordable housing may have made the job more manageable but it did not fundamentally change the nature of the work.

With regard to the second resource channel, again, two general points can be drawn from the analysis of the interview material. First, like affordability, ties to other members delivered a variety of types of support. And like affordability, too, the significance of this support was often that it enabled women to better fulfill family roles and responsibilities. So, for example, members may have exchanged services and thereby simplified their daily routines; but they remained ultimately responsible for seeing to their family members' needs. Yet the second point that can be made about ties to other members is that the resources available through this channel did differ in important ways from those available through affordability; and where they differed there were important ramifications for the organization of family work. These ties could involve shared values, a sense of extended family, and perhaps most important of all, a sense of *collective responsibility for children*. To the extent that they involved these elements, ties to other members began to dissolve the boundaries of the family household. In this respect, they went some distance toward remaking reproductive work as a community rather than only a private familial matter.

Notes

1. The terms 'family work', 'caregiving work', 'domestic tasks', 'reproductive work', or simply 'family life', are used interchangeably here to describe this form of labour.
2. RGI is the term for a group of government-funded programs that provide housing charge assistance to co-op households, based on need and availability. They are administered at the co-op level, but in accordance with government regulations that determine eligibility. Charges are set as a proportion of total household income, and the difference between the cost to the household and the actual cost of the unit is covered by government funds.
3. For the purposes of this discussion, practical support refers to help with family-related tasks and with meeting material needs, while socio-emotional support refers to talking, sharing experiences, and 'just being there' through tough times.
4. Notice that Freda referred to both parents and children in the collective sense ('we couldn't find *the kids*', not '*I* couldn't find *my daughter*'). She clearly saw herself as connected to, and in some sense jointly responsible for, individuals beyond her own household.
5. This chapter focuses on the advantages of collectivism for women with family responsibilities. These advantages were identified by the majority of the women interviewed for this study. However, a small minority of study participants (all of whom desperately needed the affordable housing) were quite alienated from their co-op communities and thus did not benefit from the collective aspect of their surroundings. Indeed, this feature of co-op life actually proved costly to such women. It added an additional layer to their family work—the tasks involved in 'defending' family privacy in a setting that supported fluid boundaries (Worts 2005).

References

Burke, M.A. 1994. 'People in Co-operative Housing', in *Canadian Social Trends* (Toronto: Thompson Educational Publishing).

Collins, P.H. 1990. *Black Feminist Thought: Knowledge, Consciousness, and the Politics of Empowerment* (New York: Routledge).

Cooper, M., and M.C. Rodman. 1992. *New Neighbours: A Case Study of Co-operative Housing in Toronto* (Toronto: University of Toronto Press).

Cowan, C.P., and P.A Cowan. 1992. *When Partners Become Parents: The Big Life Change for Couples* (New York: Basic Books).

Daly, M. 1994. 'Comparing Welfare States: Towards a Gender-friendly Approach', in *Gendering Welfare States*, ed. D. Sainsbury (Thousand Oaks, CA: Sage Publications).

Dobash, R.E., and R. Dobash. 1979. *Violence against Wives: A Case against the Patriarchy* (London: Open Books).

Fox, B.J. 1997. 'Reproducing Difference: Changes in the Lives of Partners Becoming Parents', in *Feminism and Families: Critical Policies and Changing Practices*, ed. M. Luxton (Halifax, NS: Fernwood).

Goldberg, G., and E. Kremen. 1990. *The Feminization of Poverty: Only in America?* (New York: Praeger).

Oakley, A. 1974. *The Sociology of Housework* (London: Martin Robertson).

Rosenberg, H. 1987. 'Motherwork, Stress, and Depression: The Costs of Privatized Social Reproduction', in *Feminism and Political Economy*, eds H.J. Maroney and M. Luxton (Toronto: Methuen).

Sainsbury, D. 1994. *Gendering Welfare States* (Thousand Oaks, CA: Sage Publications).

Selby, J.L., and A. Wilson. 1988. *Canada's Housing Co-operatives: An Alternative Approach to Resolving Community Problems* (Vancouver: UBC School of Community and Regional Planning).

Spector, A.N., and F. Klodawsky. 1993. 'The Housing Needs of Single Parent Families in Canada: A Dilemma for the 1990s', in *Single Parent Families: Perspectives on Research and Policy*, eds J. Hudson and B. Galaway (Toronto: Thompson Educational Publishing).

Stack, C. 1973. *All Our Kin* (New York: Harper & Row).

Weckerle, G.R., and S. Novac. 1989. 'Developing Two Women's Housing Co-operatives', in *New Households, New Housing*, eds K.A. Franck and S. Ahrentzen (New York: Van Nostrand Reinhold).

Worts, D. 2005. '"It Just Doesn't Feel Like You're Obviously In": Housing Policy, Family Privacy, and the Reproduction of Social Inequality', *Canadian Review of Sociology and Anthropology* 42, 4: 445–65.

Chapter 22

As Kath Weston wrote years ago, lesbians' and gays' families are 'chosen' in a way that the families of heterosexual couples often are not. Weston was describing the fact that many lesbians and gays had been rejected by their families of origin when they 'came out', and that they worked hard to create new families based on friendship and caring. Because lesbian and gay couples must carefully plan and arrange to have children, their families are chosen in yet another sense. In this chapter, British sociologist Gillian Dunne describes the variety of ways in which lesbians organize their families and their childcare differently than heterosexual parents. In so doing, these couples provide all parents with guidelines for handling their responsibilities in ways that do not involve gender inequalities.

Opting into Motherhood: Lesbians Blurring the Boundaries and Transforming the Meaning of Parenthood and Kinship

Gillian A. Dunne

The extension of educational and employment opportunities for women, together with widening experience of the 'plastic' nature of sexualities (Giddens 1992: 57), has enabled increasing numbers of Western women to construct independent identities and lifestyles beyond traditional marriage, motherhood, and indeed, heterosexuality (Dunne 1997). As contemporary women's identities expand to incorporate the expectations and activities that have been traditionally associated with masculinity, there has not been an equivalent shift of male identity, let alone practice, into the traditional domains of women. Exceptions not withstanding (Blaisure and Allen 1995; Doucet 1995; Ehrensaft 1987; VanEvery 1995), a distinctly asymmetrical division of labour remains the majority pattern (Berk 1985; Brannen and Moss 1991; Ferri and Smith 1996; Gregson and Lowe 1995; Hochschild 1989). The intransigent nature of the gender division of labour means that women continue to perform the bulk of domestic work and that mothers bear the brunt of the social and economic penalties associated with caring for children. Men's relative freedom from the time constraints and labour associated with the home and parenting enables them to be more single-minded in the pursuit of employment opportunities and retain their labour-market advantages.

The perceived contradiction between employment success and motherhood has led to a growth in the numbers of women opting into a paid-working life and out of motherhood (Campbell 1985: 5–8; Morell 1994: 11). Changing patterns of household and family formation have stimulated debates in Europe and North America as to whether there has been a decline in the importance of kinship and family life (Popeno 1988; Scott 1997). Given the way that motherhood represents a core signifier of femininity, and the powerful social pressure on married couples to have children, academic interest is turning to voluntary childlessness (Campbell 1985; Abshoff and Hird 1998; McAllister and Clarke 1998; Morell 1994).

While women's decisions to remain child-free can be framed in terms of resistance in the context of heterosexuality (Abshoff and Hird 1998; Morell 1994), we need to remember that other groups of women are perceived to be excluded from the procreative equation (see Silva and Smart 1996). In common with gay men, lesbian women are popularly represented and viewed as barren (Weston 1991). At one level, lesbians, by virtue of their sexuality, represent a vanguard of women who escape social pressure to become parents. Indeed, this freedom to 'construct their own biographies' (Beck and Beck-Gernsheim 1995) without reference to children is understood by many as a major advantage of their sexuality (Dunne 1997). Differences in lesbian women's and gay men's relationship to reproduction and their families of origin have stimulated some fascinating North American (Weston 1991) and British (Weeks, Donovan, and Heaphy 1998) research on the recasting of kinship along lines of friendship.

While contemporary women begin to see the demands of motherhood as conflicting with their newly won bid for autonomy, there has been a recent shift in attitudes toward parenting among the lesbian population. A rising awareness of alternatives to heterosexual reproduction has led to the growing recognition that their sexuality does not preclude the possibility of lesbian and gay people having children. In Britain and in the United States, we are witnessing the early stages of a 'gayby' boom, a situation wherein lesbian women and gay men are opting into parenthood in increasing numbers. According to Lewin, 'The "lesbian baby boom" and the growing visibility of lesbians who became mothers through donor insemination constitute the most dramatic and provocative challenge to traditional notions of both family and of the non-procreative nature of homosexuality' (1993: 19). In this article, I want to address this apparent contradiction between childlessness as resistance and lesbian motherhood as provocative challenge by showing that the mothering experiences that lesbians are opting into are qualitatively different from those that some women seek to avoid.

I take the view that sexuality is socially and materially constructed and that heterosexuality plays a central role in reproducing gender inequality (Dunne 1997; 1998d; 2000). The dominance of heterosexuality is the outcome of institutional processes that render alternatives undesirable and/or unimaginable (Dunne 1997; Rich 1984) and that construct gender difference and gender hierarchies (Butler 1990: 17; Rubin 1975). Consequently, there is a crucial relationship between gender and sexuality. As Butler (1990: 17) and Rubin (1975) argue, social processes that construct gender as a meaningful category are deeply implicated in the construction of sexual preferences (Dunne 1997; 1998b). Gendered experience is mediated by sexuality in a number of other ways. For example, the existence of material constraints that usually limit women's ability to be financially self-reliant suggests that the capacity to lead a lesbian lifestyle is an economic achievement (see Dunne 1997; 2000). Additionally, we can extend the more interactive conceptions of gender formulated by Fenstermaker, West, and Zimmerman (1991) to show that the gender of the person who one does gender for and/or to and who does it to us makes a difference (see Dunne 1998b). The way that gendered action is mediated by sexual identity has important implications for the performance of household tasks and caretaking. For example, I argue (Dunne 1998b) that Berk's (1985) insightful observation about the domestic division of labour being about linking the 'musts' of work to be done with the 'shoulds' of gender ideals is somewhat dependent on the work being allocated between women and men. However, the unfortunate division of labour within the academy between those interested in sexuality and those interested in gender inequalities has meant that the implications of these important insights have not been fully developed in mainstream feminism (Dunne 2000).

I wish to support and extend Lewin's observations on single lesbian mothers by drawing on my work on lesbian couples who have become parents via donor insemination. I argue that an attentiveness to the gender dynamic of sexuality illuminates additional challenges that arise when women combine with women to rear children—the possibility of showing what can be achieved when gender difference as a fundamental structuring principle in interpersonal relationships is minimized (see Dunne 1997; 1998a). I suggest a complex and contradictory situation for lesbians who have opted into motherhood via donor insemination. By embracing motherhood, lesbians are making their lives 'intelligible' to others—their quest to become parents is often enthusiastically supported by family and heterosexual friends. However, their sexuality both necessitates and facilitates the redefinition of the boundaries, meaning, and content of parenthood. When women parent together, the absence of the logic of polarization to inform gender scripts, and their parity in the gender hierarchy, means that, to borrow Juliet's words, 'We have to make it up as we go along.' Their similarities as women insist on high levels of reflexivity and enable the construction of more egalitarian approaches to financing and caring for children. In this way, some of the more negative social consequences of motherhood can be transformed. Although not unique in their achievements, nor assured of their success, women parenting with women have a head start over heterosexual couples because of their structural similarities and the way that egalitarianism is in the interests of both partners.[1]

In an important study of divisions of labour, Berk concludes that gendered patterns of task allocation are so ingrained and taken for granted that they 'hamper our ability to imagine other ways of organizing work' (1985: 199). This leads her to suggest, in a footnote, that science fiction may represent a medium for the exploration of alternative arrangements. This conclusion, however, reflects the heterosexual framework that dominates mainstream theorizing about gender, work, and family life. I contend that beyond the constraints (gender, emotional, and sexual) of heterosexual relationships, there are spaces for creative thinking about the organization of work, parenting, and the involvement of men and extended kin in children's lives. A focus on lesbian experience offers a marvellous opportunity to explore the limits and possibilities of egalitarianism without recourse to science fiction (see Dunne 1998a; 1998b). The solutions women together find to solving the problem of finding time for children and time to earn a living may provide models for feminists regardless of how the women define their sexuality. Greater knowledge of how egalitarianism can be operationalized may also help raise people's expectations in relation to notions of fairness and encourage change.

I shall now introduce the study and summarize some findings in relation to the respondents' parenting circumstances. I will then focus on the stories of three couples to illustrate some of the ways that these women negotiate and transform the shifting boundaries of parenthood and kiship. I have chosen these couples because their experiences are not atypical and because their stories touch upon and bring to life many of the themes that emerged in the larger study of lesbian couples.[2]

The Lesbian Household Project

The Lesbian Household Project draws on the experience of 37 cohabiting lesbian couples with dependent children.[3] It is a detailed investigation of the allocation of work and parenting responsibilities between women that aims to provide empirically grounded theoretical insights into divisions of labour more generally. Using a snowball technique, the sample was recruited from across England through a wide range of different sources. The only selection criterion was that partners be living together with at least one dependent child: all who contacted me agreed to participate and were interviewed. The majority live in the inner-city neighbourhoods (usually with high ethnic-minority populations) of three northern cities and three southern cities. The sample includes several Irish women, a Greek, an Iranian, and at least five Jewish women; all are white. As anticipated, respondents tend to be educationally and/or occupationally advantaged.[4] The majority work for public-sector employers or are self-employed. They are usually professionals, managers, technicians, or administrators in 'female' occupations such as teaching, social work, local government, health, and counselling, and 70 per cent hold degrees or professional qualifications (see Dunne 1999). The sensitivity of the topic together with the invisibility of lesbians in the population means that no study of this nature can make claims of representativeness. However, there is no reason to assume that the sample is particularly unrepresentative, especially in relation to couples who have experienced donor insemination.

A number of methods, both qualitative and quantitative, innovative and conventional, were used to illuminate respondents' employment, domestic, and caring strategies (see Dunne 1999). After the completion of a background questionnaire, both joint and individual in-depth interviews were carried out, time-use diary data were collected, and participants were contacted again two years after first contact. To help establish context and to situate the couple within their wider social environment, the first interview began with a discussion of their pathways to parenting. Respondents were then asked to map out their social and kinship networks.

Parenting Circumstances

The sample includes eight households where children were from a previous marriage, one household where the children were adopted, and 28 (75 per cent) where they had been conceived by donor insemination. In the majority of households (60 per cent), there was at least one child younger than five; and in 40 per cent of households, co-parents were also biological mothers of older, dependent, or non-dependent children. The research revealed a fairly unique and important opportunity for women parenting together—the possibility of detaching motherhood from its biological roots through the experience of social motherhood. Interestingly, 15 women in the study expressed a long-standing desire to mother as a social experience but a strong reluctance to experience motherhood biologically. These women had often taken responsibility for siblings in their families of origin and for the children of others usually featured in their lives and occupational choices. This social–biological separation also meant that motherhood is not necessarily ruled out for women who have fertility problems. Parenting was depicted as jointly shared in 30 households (80 per cent). As we will see in the three case studies, in contrast to men who share mothering (Ehrensaft 1987) yet remain happy with the identity of father, the singularity and exclusivity of the identity of mother represented a major problem for women parenting together.

Contrary to media representation in Britain, almost all of the women who had experienced donor insemination organized this informally—they rarely used National Health or even private fertility services. Respondents tended to want to know the donor, and in 86 per cent of households, this was the case. A wide range of reasons was given for this preference. A common feeling related to wanting to know that a good man, in terms of personal qualities, had a role in creating their child. Sometimes more specific ideas about biogenetic inheritance came up in discussions, and for Jewish women there was a preference for Jewish donors. Some employed the metaphor of adoption—the idea that children should have the option of knowing their biological father at some stage in the future. Commonly, donors were located through friendship networks or by advertising. Occasionally, they made use of the informal women's donor networks that exist in many British cities. When organized informally, children were always conceived by self- or partner insemination, and the majority became mothers in their current lesbian relationship.

Lesbian motherhood undermines a core signifier of heterosexuality and challenges heterosexual monopoly of and norms for parenting. The social hostility toward those parents and children who transgress the sanctity of heterosexual reproduction is such that the decision to become a mother by donor insemination can never be easily made. Typically, respondents described a lengthy period of soul-searching and planning preceding the arrival of children. For some, this process lasted as long as seven years. Unlike most women, they had to question their motives for wanting children, to critique dominant ideas about what constitutes a 'good' mother and family, and to think about the implications of bringing up children in a wider society intolerant of difference. Informing this process was much research—reading the numerous self-help books that are available on lesbian parenting, watching videos on the topic, and attending discussion groups. I would suggest that lesbian parenting via donor insemination is the 'reflexive project' par excellence described by Giddens (1992: 30). For respondents in partnerships, a central part of this process was the exploration of expectations in relation to parenting, for example, attitudes to discipline, schooling, and if and how far responsibilities would be shared. Key considerations related to employment situations. Respondents did not expect or desire a traditional division of labour, and thus timing was often influenced by their preference to integrate childcare and income generation. In the meanwhile, potential donors were contacted. Respondents described a fairly lengthy process of negotiation with donors that focused on establishing a mutuality in parenting expectations and, if he was previously unknown to the couple, getting to know each other and developing confidence. While recognizing the generosity of potential donors, some were rejected because of personality clashes or concerns about motives, but more usually, rejection was because a donor wanted too much or too little involvement.

Men featured in the lives of most of the children, and it was not unusual for donors to have regular contact with their offspring (40 per cent of households); in three households, fathers were actively co-parenting. This involvement was usually justified in terms of providing children with the opportunity to 'normalize' their family arrangements by being able to talk to peers about doing things with father. Donors were usually gay men—and all male co-parents were gay. This preference appeared to be based on three main assumptions. First was the respondents' perceptions of gay men as representing more aware, acceptable, and positive forms of masculinity. Their desire to involve men (donors or other male friends) in the lives of children, particularly boys, was often described as being about counteracting dominant stereotypes of masculinity. Second, because of the particularities of gay men's lifestyles, respondents believed that they would be less likely to renege on agreements. Third, they thought that should a dispute arise, a heterosexual donor (particularly if he were married) had greater access to formal power to change arrangements in relation to access and custody. That none expressed any serious difficulties in relation to father and/or donor involvement attests to the value of the careful negotiation of expectations before the arrival of children. It also says much about the integrity and generosity of the men concerned, although it must be noted that most had preschool-aged children, and conflicts of interests may come as the children mature.

In situations where children had been conceived in a previous marriage or heterosexual relationship, there was more diversity and conflict regarding fathers' involvement. In several cases, the father had unsuccessfully contested custody on the grounds of the mother's lesbianism. Indeed, two had appeared on daytime television arguing that their ex-wives' sexuality conflicted with their capacity to be good mothers. There were also examples of good relations between mothers and ex-husbands. While there were several examples of fathers having lost contact with their children, in most cases, respondents suggested that the child or children had more quality time with their fathers after divorce than before. Despite tensions and possible conflict between mothers and ex-husbands, these respondents suggested that they worked hard to maintain their children's relationships with the fathers. Thus, ironically, in this group as well as in the donor insemination group of parents, there are examples of highly productive models of co-operation between women and men in parenting.

The role of fathers and/or donors and other male friends in children's lives reminds us that lesbian parenting does not occur in a social vacuum. While generally hostile to the idea of the privatized nuclear family, respondents were keen to establish more extended family networks of friends and kin. Often, respondents described the arrival of children as bringing them closer to or helping repair difficult relations with their families of origin. Typically, they described a wide circle of friends (lesbian 'aunties', gay 'uncles', and heterosexual friends) and kin supporting their parenting.

I now want to illustrate some of these themes by drawing on the voices of respondents in three partnerships where parenting was shared and where men were involved.

Vivien and Cay's Story

> We do feel lonely and unsupported and isolated at times, but we also feel very confident and excited about the way that we've carved out our family and the way that we go forward with it and the way that we parent. So although it's kind of a lonely path because there's not a lot of us to kind of reflect on each other, I don't see that as, oh, poor us. I see that more as, well, we're trying something out here and we've just got to get on with it. (Vivien)[5]

It was not uncommon to find a woman who had been married and had grown-up children who was starting over again with a partner who wanted to have children herself ($n = 4$). Women parenting together was understood as offering the opportunity to experience parenting in new and exciting ways that were tempered by the wisdom that comes from already having raised children. Cay and Vivien are fairly typical of these households. Vivien, age 44, has a grown-up son, Jo, who lives independently. Cay, age 32, is the biological mother of two boys, Frank, age four, and Steve, age two. When we first met, they had been living together for six years in a small terraced house in inner-city Birmingham. Cay, born in North America, is a self-employed illustrator of children's books who supplements her income by working as a cleaner. Vivien, of Irish-Greek descent, recently completed a degree and acquired her 'first real job' as a probation officer. Cay told me that she had always wanted to have children and that her sexuality had not changed this desire. Vivien was enthusiastically supportive of the idea although she did not want to go through a pregnancy herself.

Like the vast majority of respondents, Vivien and Cay organized donor insemination informally. They had little difficulty in locating a willing donor—John, an old friend of Vivien's.

> Vivien: It worked out well. He's my oldest friend, and we've known each other since we were teenagers, and he has the same kind of colouring and stuff, he could be my brother in terms of colouring and looks.

> Originally we asked one of my brothers to donate, and he felt he would maybe want more of an involvement, more of a say in the children's lives, and we wanted somebody who would let us have the responsibility and would take on a sort of a kindly uncle role. And John agreed to do that.

The description 'kindly uncle' was frequently used by respondents to describe what was a fairly limited yet enthusiastic relationship between a donor and his child or children. Respondents almost always wanted to retain responsibility for bringing up their children. Like most of the couples in the study, Vivien and Cay regard these responsibilities as shared.

> Cay: It can't be anything but joint I think. The way we've approached it is that if it's not totally agreeable between both of us, it couldn't have really gone forward, given the kind of relationship we have. We've seen other people, you know, where one parent has said, 'Well, I want a child and that's it.' But the other one says, 'Yes, you can have one, but I don't want to have lots of responsibility.' That's not our way.

When respondents described their parenting as jointly shared, they meant that each partner took an active role in the routine pleasures, stresses, and labour of childcare. In comparing current arrangements with her experience when married, Vivien described some of the advantages of the lack of demarcation around mothering:

> I can enjoy the mothering in a new and exciting way that I hadn't been able to before, because even though I was married I didn't have the freedom and sharing that I have in this relationship. I had the weight of the responsibility for the child squarely on my shoulders. So I felt I couldn't allow myself much time to actually enjoy just being a mother, which I can do now because I know that even if one—sometimes I just play with them, and Cay can come in and put them to bed or do something else. Whereas I wouldn't have expected that before.

Like Vivien, respondents took great pleasure in childcare, and this was reflected in their ordering of priorities. Cay suggested that because she and Vivien had joint responsibility for housework, they were less subject to the tyranny of maintaining high domestic standards—a sentiment reflected across the sample. This, together with their shared approach to doing tasks, she believed, gave them more fun time with their children—this was supported in the time-use data across the sample. For example, comparison of respondents' time use with trends for married parents with young children revealed that regardless of the employment status of married mothers, because they did the bulk of routine domestic work, it occupied far more of their time than childcare, while the reverse was the case for respondents (Dunne 1998a).

Vivien and Cay described their roles before and after the arrival of children as interchangeable; earlier, Cay had been the main earner when Vivien was a student. Routinely, birth mothers and co-parents alike spoke of seeking integrated lives—valuing time with children, an identity from the formal workplace, and the ability to contribute financially. Within reason, they were prepared to experience a reduced standard of living to achieve the kind of quality of life desired. Thus, there was an unusually wide range of partner–employment strategies in the sample. Like Vivien and Cay, some took turns in who was the main earner, while others (a quarter of the sample) opted for half-time employment for both parents. Rather than the polarization of employment responsibilities that characterizes married couples' parenting experiences, particularly when children are young,[6] few households had extreme partner differences in employment hours, and being the birth mother was a poor predictor of employment hours. Gartrell et al. (forthcoming), in their longitudinal study of donor insemination lesbian parents with young children in the United States, also note a tendency for both partners to reduce their hours of employment. Analysis of employment trends for married couples (even those with higher education) reveals that it is rare for partners to share care by both working part- or half-time (see Dunne 1998a; 1999). The experiences of women parenting together (and feminist-inspired, heterosexual couples) (Ehrensaft 1987; VanEvery 1995) raise thorny questions about the role of consumption in limiting egalitarianism in more affluent heterosexual partnerships. Increasingly, we are finding that a preferred solution for the achievement of equality is for both parents to prioritize their economic activities over mothering and pass caretaking and domestic work onto women with less power (Ehrensaft 1987; Gregson and Lowe 1995).

While Vivien and Cay describe themselves as the boys' mothers, in common with most respondents, they struggle over terminology to describe and symbolize that relationship. Because of the singularity and exclusivity of the label *mother* or *mum* and/or their feminist critique of the way the term can eclipse other important aspects of identity, respondents often preferred to encourage the use of first names, special nicknames, or the word *mother* borrowed from another language.

> Vivien: Yes, [we are the boys' mothers] absolutely, yes. Very much so.
>
> Interviewer: What do they call you?
>
> Vivien: By our names. . . . They very rarely use the word *mother*.
>
> Cay: In fact [Frank] never used the word *mother* until he started going to school, and then, hearing the other kids saying it, it was just a kind of copying thing.

Here we catch a glimpse of some of the everyday pressures toward social conformity and the dilemmas experienced by parents and children as they negotiate a world hostile to difference. Just as this motivated some to involve donors in their children's lives so that they had the option to pass as relatively 'normal' in school, many respondents relented and used the term *mother* to describe the biological mother.

Cay's parents live abroad and are described as proud grandparents. Because John, the boys' father, is not out about his sexuality to his parents, they have no knowledge about the boys. Vivien's parents are dead, but her immediate kin are actively involved in supporting them.

> Vivien: My brothers are thrilled, though. My brothers treat the children as if they were their own kids. They don't separate them, you know, they don't see them as any less their kids. And their cousins that they're totally unrelated to just are their cousins, and in fact Tom looks like one of my cousins in Ireland. He doesn't look like any of Cay's.

However, the very positioning outside conventionality that enables the construction of more creative approaches to organizing parenting brings also the problem of lack of recognition and validation from the outside world. Vivien speaks for many in the study:

> I think we have to acknowledge that within this house we can sit down and we can talk about the equality that we feel and the experiences that we have and the confidence that we have in our relationship and in our parenting. But very little outside of this house tells us that those things that we're talking about tonight are actually true. We don't get a lot of affirmation outside of our

own house that we are good parents, there is not that acknowledgement of the equality and negotiation that goes on within the relationship. And I think heterosexual friends that we have tend to probably see our relationship in their own terms. . . . I don't think they've got an insight into how much we really do work together. . . . You know, we have to work at it all the time, we have to forge links with the school, we have to forge links with this and forge links with that, we have to work hard at being good neighbours and making contact with the neighbours so that as the children come along they're not surprised and they can adjust. We're doing the work, we're doing the outreach, we're doing the education, and what we get back is the right to be ourselves, sort of, as long as we're careful.

Again, their experience underscores the difficulties associated with challenging the normative status of heterosexuality in relation to reproduction and the organization of parenting roles. Constantly, these pioneering women feel obliged to justify their alternative families and approaches to parenting to a wider society that cannot see beyond the constraints of heterosexuality and that is informed by media representations that vilify lesbian parents. Their struggle for validation was not confined to the heterosexual world.

> Vivien: Other lesbians I think may see us as trying to repeat some sort of heterosexual relationship, and that's not what we're trying to do. So we have to kind of justify it to our heterosexual friends and justify it to our lesbian friends.

The contradiction illuminated here between being a lesbian and being a mother serves to remind us that while it can be argued that assisted conception is an important expression of the ideologies supporting compulsory motherhood, it is less easy to apply this thinking to lesbian mothers. Within lesbian culture, the absence of children within a relationship does not constitute failure. In fact, research (Sullivan 1996) supports much of what respondents said about their decision to have children going against established societal norms, specifically those of the lesbian and gay community. Until recently, this community, particularly the radical or revolutionary wing, has been suspicious of motherhood because of fears of constraints on women's autonomy and the importation of oppressive family arrangements (see Green 1997).

Thelma and Louise's Story

> I think we go about things in our own way, we don't have the role definition. We get the best of both worlds really. We get to continue along the road with our careers and also to spend time as a family and to enjoy the time with the children. Disadvantages? We could earn more money I suppose if we worked full-time, but then it takes away the point of having children I would say. (Thelma)

It was not unusual for both partners to have experienced biological motherhood as the result of donor insemination while in their relationship. At the time of first contact, four couples were in this situation (this number had risen to seven at the follow-up stage two years later). In these households, children were brought up as siblings, and parenting was equally shared. The experiences of Thelma and Louise are not atypical of mothers in this situation. They have been living together for seven years in an apartment that they own in inner-city Manchester. They have two daughters, Polly, age four, and Stef, age two. Thelma works in desktop publishing, and Louise is a teacher. Like many in the sample, Thelma and Louise operationalize shared parenting by reducing their paid employment to half-time.

They both wanted to have children; their decisions about timing and who would go first were shaped by emotional and practical considerations. Thelma needed to build up sufficient clientele to enable self-employment from home, and Louise wanted to gain more secure employment.

> Louise: I was a year younger and I wasn't really sorted out work-wise and you were.
>
> Thelma: There were very pragmatic as well as emotional reasons for why I should go first. It was when I started freelancing at this place and then I ended up freelancing because I got pregnant. But that seemed okay anyway. . . . I mean it was all right to take a break. I knew that I could get work.
>
> Louise: And I hadn't got there. And there was time to save up as well. During that time we managed to save up quite a lot, to get over the small baby time. Before getting out to work again.

By the time Louise was pregnant, two years after Thelma, she was in a much stronger position at work, having undergone retraining. She had secured a permanent position in teaching and, after maternity leave, arranged a job share with a friend. Like women more generally, respondents' careers had rarely progressed in a planned linear manner. Instead, their job histories have a more organic quality (see Dunne 1997)—moving across occupations and in and out of education or training. However, in contrast to married women more generally, where the gender division of labour supports the anticipation of financial dependence on husbands when children are young (Mansfield and Collard 1988), an important consideration in the timing of the arrival of children for most biological mothers in this study was the achievement of certain employment aims that would enable greater financial security and allow time to enjoy the children. Their gender parity and this approach to paid employment meant that there were not major earning differentials between partners. This helps to explain why respondents have greater scope in operationalizing shared caregiving, as their options had not been foreclosed by earlier decisions. Although both partners working part-time brings a reduced standard of living, it also brings the advantage, as Thelma remarks, of enabling both to continue in their careers.

After several miscarriages with an earlier donor, Thelma finally got pregnant. Again, they used their friendship networks to locate a donor who then took on a 'kindly uncle' role.

> Louise: He was just living with a friend of ours, it was just brilliant.
>
> Thelma: Yeah, and ended up being a really good friend as well. . . . I got pregnant the first go really.
>
> Interviewer: And then did you have any views on how much involvement he should have?
>
> Thelma: I think we both wanted a known father and yes, if they wanted some involvement, that was fine. The clearly defined lines were, we're the parents of the children—or of the child at that time—and so any kind of parenting decisions would always be ours.
>
> Interviewer: And what will Polly call her donor?
>
> Thelma: His name—and she calls him Daddy Paul. So I mean she doesn't ever really call him Daddy. Either she calls him Paul or Daddy Paul.

Louise: He is a bit like an uncle [to them both] she'd see now and again, you know, he'd be like this kindly uncle figure, who'd take her to the pics and take her to the zoo and that kind of thing. Give her treats.

They originally planned that Paul would be the donor for Louise; however, there were difficulties in conception, so a new donor was found. Hugh, a gay friend of Thelma's brother, who was temporarily living in England, agreed. While Thelma and Louise both wanted to experience motherhood biologically, they viewed parenting as shared, and this situation was legally recognized in their gaining of a joint parental responsibility order.

Louise: We don't just happen to have a relationship and happen to have two children. We always thought joint, that's why the court thing was important to us. They are sisters and I defy anybody to question that. That's very important to us and we also made it clear that if we ever split up, if I depart with Stef into the horizon and Thelma with Polly, that we have joint care for them.

Again, their interpretation of shared parenting brought them up against the limitations of language to describe a social mother's relationship to a child.

Thelma: They both call us Mum.

Louise: It started off that you were going to be Mum and I was going to be Louise, and then coming up to me giving birth to Stef, it just got a bit kind of funny, so we thought it's not really going to work any more because if they're sisters how come?—it just all didn't work, so now we're both Mums. And they just call us Mum.

Thelma: Stef says Mummy Louise or Mummy Thelma.

Louise: And Polly mostly calls us Louise and Thelma doesn't she?

Thelma: Yeah she does. She calls us both Mum when she wants to, but mostly she calls us by our names.

Louise: The last couple of years she's started calling me Mum.

Some of the immensity of the creative project in which lesbians engage is revealed in the tensions in the last two extracts and in the next. While they describe the children as having two mothers, Louise reminds us of the contingent nature of this. The rule of biological connection is unquestioned in the assumption that in the event of a breakup each will depart into the horizon with her own child. This next extract illustrates other practical difficulties faced by the couple as they engage with the wider society.

Louise: It's a lot easier now because we've both had a child. I don't think I had any role models in terms of being a non-biological mum. There's a thing that if you want to be acknowledged as a parent, you just had to 'come out'. It's the only way to explain that you're a parent. And even that is a very hard way to explain you're a parent. My inner circle at work would know and it's funny—I nearly wrote it down one day—because it was just like some days I'd be a parent and some days I wasn't. So it would depend on what day of the week it was and who I was talking to. I think I made it harder for us by me not being called Mum [in the early stages]. Because as soon as people found out you weren't the mum, then they'd just—it was like 'who the hell are you then?'

Such is the power of ideas about the singularity and the exclusivity of the identity of 'Mum' in a social world structured by heterosexual norms that polarize parenting along lines of gender. Respondents had a store of both amusing and uncomfortable stories about other people's confusions about who was the mother of the child or children or the status of social mothers.

Again, the family has interesting and extensive kinship networks. The children have two fathers. Paul was not out to his elderly parents so they did not know about his child. However, Hugh, who comes to England several times a year to see them, had told his mother.

> Louise: I think Hugh was terrified of telling his mother—he's an only child—had a very close relationship with his mother and he was terrified of telling her. And she was absolutely delighted with it—'I'm the *children's* grandmother'—she's Stef's grandmother biologically, but she's also Polly's socially. So she's just been this incredible grandmother.
>
> Thelma: Paul's parents don't know. His parents are quite old, they're in their late eighties and they don't know he's gay and I don't think he'd ever tell them. So for him that one's a secret. But his sister knows.
>
> Louise: I think we'd be more worried by it, but I just guess by the time the kids are old enough—I think you've got to start coming out very confidently once you've kids, you can't be messing around really. And it would worry me I think if—if Paul explained to them [the children], that he's not been able to tell his parents. I'm just hoping that by the time it comes up, they won't be around any more.

This discussion illustrates several important themes that featured across the sample. First, respondents were keen to avoid keeping secrets from their children about their conception. Second, they articulated high levels of positivity about being lesbian[7]—this was seen as essential for supporting their children in their dealings with the outside world. Third, all expressed the desire to have their social bonds recognized by friends and kin as being equivalent to blood ties. Finally, kinship was calculated in a remarkable variety of ways. Kin appeared highly flexible in this, with countless examples like Hugh's mother. This next discussion illustrates respondents' strength of feelings with respect to recognition.

> Louise: And family that we see, all of them without exception treat both children equally. That's the deal basically, they're not allowed to pick and choose.
>
> Thelma: It was the same with Grandma. . . . Part of the deal was that Stef and Polly are sisters and if she took one of them, then she had to, by definition, take on the other.
>
> Louise: We were quite assertive with her—and that's why I'm not seeing my dad, it's because he's still kind of learning to do that, until he really gets his head around it. He can't just send one of them a present and not the other. Actually it looks like he's getting there, doesn't he? He's just about cracked it. . . . My sister, when Polly was born, my sister just said I'm auntie [name], without any—obviously she isn't biologically, but in all senses of the word, she is.
>
> Interviewer: And they wouldn't distinguish between the children?
>
> Louise: No. Nobody who we see regularly would. Even school and things like that—Stef is Polly's sister. . . . the kind of entry through schools is if you're a sibling and

that's kind of a high priority and Stef has entry into that school now, because she's Polly's sister. Although biologically they're nothing.

Without exception, respondents believed that they approached and experienced parenting in ways that were very different from the heterosexual norm. They were redefining the meaning and content of motherhood, extending its boundaries to incorporate the activities that are usually dichotomized as mother and father. Going against prevailing norms was never without difficulties and disappointments. In joint and individual interviews, respondents usually singled out the ability and commitment to communicate as crucial. They spoke of arrangements being constantly subject to negotiation and the need to check in regularly with each other so that routines that may lead to taking the other for granted could be rethought and sources of conflict discussed.

Bonnie and Claudia's Story

We've had a lot of interest and a certain amount of envy from a lot of heterosexual couples who had babies at the same time, because they just haven't had the breaks that we've had from the baby. They've had breaks, but they've felt guilty, whereas we don't particularly feel guilty because we know that Peter's with Philip and they both want to be together. (Claudia)

In three partnerships, donors were actively co-parenting from separate households—becoming a 'junior partner in the parenting team' as one father described himself. In two cases, the father's parenting was legally recognized in a joint residency order. Bonnie, Claudia, and Philip share the care of Peter, age two. Bonnie and Claudia have lived together for nine years in a terraced house in inner-city Bristol. Bonnie, Peter's biological mother, works full-time in adult education, and Claudia has a half-time teaching post. They describe and contrast their feelings about wanting to have children:

Claudia: Well, I think it was something that I was looking for when I was looking for a relationship. So I think it was a more immediate thing for me. You were interested in principle. And I knew the father—this is Philip—although not with the view to having children. So you got to know him after we met really. And then the subject came up.

Bonnie: I think for you it had always been like a lifelong thing.

Claudia: I always wanted a baby. I wanted us to have about two.

Bonnie: She was just obsessed with babies, weren't you? Whereas, I wasn't really like that, I come from a big family and I like having lots of people around me. It was more for me that I didn't want to have *not* had children. It's different, because I didn't want to look back and think, Oh Christ, I didn't have any children. But I tend to get very caught up in whatever I'm doing, and I was busy doing my job and having this relationship and our friends. So in a way it was Claudia's enthusiasm and sense of urgency about it that actually pushed us to making a decision, taking some action. And the only reason I ended up having the baby was that Claudia had a whole series of fertility problems. We just always decided, didn't we, that if one of us had a problem the other one would.

Their experience illustrates another fairly unique advantage for women who want to become mothers in a lesbian relationship—if one partner has fertility problems, the other may agree to go through the pregnancy instead. There were three other examples of partners swapping for this reason, and several others expressed their willingness to do so. As mentioned earlier, I was struck by the fact that many respondents desired to be mothers but felt reluctant to experience motherhood biologically. As there is no reason to believe that this feeling is confined to the lesbian population, it must pose a real dilemma for some heterosexual women. The advantage of the possibility of detaching motherhood from biology via social motherhood in lesbian relationships helps explain why co-parenting is so eagerly embraced—there were several examples of women who had advertised their desire to meet other lesbians, specifically mentioning a preference for women with children.

In their negotiations with Philip over the four years that preceded the birth of Peter, they came to the decision that he would be an actively involved father.

> Claudia: Philip wanted a child, and he, I think, was also looking for a kind of extended family relationship, wasn't he?—with us and the children. But he also wants his freedom, I suppose, his lifestyle, a lot of which he needs not to have children around for. Yes, so it fits in the sense that what we get is time without Peter, to have a relationship that needs its own sort of nurturing and stuff, and he gets special time with Peter and a real bonding. I mean he's seen Peter every day since he's been born. So he has become part of the family, hasn't he?—in a sense, or we've become part of his. But we live in two separate homes. People sometimes don't realize that.

Claudia's words alert us to another underlying reason for respondents' confidence in fathers and/or donors retaining a more minor role in children's lives—routine childcare does not usually fit in with the lifestyles of most men, gay or heterosexual. The masculine model of employment that governs ideas of job commitment and what constitutes a valuable worker is based on the assumption that employees are free from the constraints of childcare.

After extended maternity leave, Bonnie returned to her successful career in adult education. At this point, Claudia, despite being the higher earner, reduced her employment hours to half-time so that she could become Peter's main caregiver. Men's superior earnings are often described by egalitarian-minded heterosexual couples as ruling out opportunities for shared parenting (Doucet 1995; Ehrensaft 1987). However, women parenting together, without access to ideologies that polarize parenting responsibilities, bring fresh insights to this impasse, which supports gender inequalities.

> Bonnie: We started in a completely different place [from heterosexual couples]. I think we feel it's just much easier to be co-operative and to be more creative in the way that we share out paid work and domestic work, because that's how we look at it. We're constantly chatting about it, aren't we, over the weeks, and saying, 'How does it feel now? Are you still thinking about staying on part-time?' and we've talked about what it would be like if I went part-time as well, and could we manage on less money?

> Claudia: Yes, and I think the thing that's part of the advantage is that in a conventional setup, although it may be easier to start with, everyone knowing what they are supposed to be doing, but the men don't know their children so they miss out. . . . I'm having a balanced life really.

> Bonnie: I think that's why we've got the space to enjoy our child in a way that a lot of heterosexuals perhaps don't. It's so easy to fall in—the man earns slightly more so it makes sense for him to do the paid work,

and women have babies anyway. Because we could potentially each have had the child it's all in the melting pot. Nothing is fixed.

Claudia: And I don't think a lot of women [enjoy mothering]. They think they're going to, but they get isolated and devalued, and lose their self-confidence and self-esteem.

It was not unusual to find the higher earner in a partnership reducing her hours of employment to share care or become the main caregiver. In contradiction to the dictates of rational economic models, this was often justified on the grounds that a person in a higher paid or higher status occupation has more power and may be less penalized for time out than someone in a more marginal position (Dunne 1998a). I would argue that their rationale (like the part-time/part-time solution) can actually make good long-term financial sense. It also illuminates masculine assumptions in relation to value—the idea that market work is superior to caring.

As in the vast majority of households (Dunne 1998a), routine domestic work was fairly evenly divided between Claudia and Bonnie. Their guiding principle was that 'neither should be running around after the other'. Like most respondents, they spoke of the advantage of the absence of gender scripts guiding who should do what (see Dunne 1998b).

Bonnie: Well, I think one of the main advantages [of being in a lesbian relationship] for me is that unlike heterosexual couples there are no assumptions about how we are going to divide things up and how we're going to cope. Because I know that it's perfectly possible for heterosexuals to do things differently and some share tasks more than others and all the rest of it. But they're still all the time having to work against these kind of very dominant set of assumptions about how things should be done in heterosexual households, whereas we don't have that.

For heterosexual couples, gender difference not only shapes contributions but provides a lens through which they are judged (Baxter and Western 1998; Berk 1985; Dunne 1998b).

Peter goes to a private nursery three days a week (the costs are shared with Philip), and the rest of his care is divided between Claudia, Bonnie, and Philip.

Bonnie: Philip lives in the next street, and so he can just come round every day after work or pick Peter up from nursery and bring him back and do his tea, bath and things, and then we'll roll in about 6:30 or whenever, or sometimes one of us is here anyway.

Claudia: Yes, we try to work that one of us is always home, either with him or working at home. . . . He's the only one of us who works locally and he's got a bleep [beeper] as part of his job and it's ideal because the nursery can call at any time if there's an emergency.

Interviewer: It strikes me you've got the most ideal situation!

Bonnie: Yes, we think so! [laughing] We're the envy of the mother and toddler group.

Their experience with Philip provides a radical alternative model of co-operative parenting between women and men, based on a consensual non-sexual relationship with a father who is interested in being actively involved in his child's life. In effect, Philip is prepared to engage in mothering,[8] and in doing so, he shares some of the social penalties associated with this activity—all three parents collaborate in balancing the demands of employment and childcare, and the result is the lessening of its overall impact. While Bonnie and Claudia were aware that it was difficult to keep Philip abreast of everyday decision-making, they were keen to involve him in major ones. This seemed to work well in practice.

> Bonnie: [It's worked] extremely well. We keep being surprised. I mean we keep thinking . . . we're going to have a fundamental disagreement about something. But I don't think there has been really.

In this discussion, we can see some of the risks associated with involving biological fathers in children's lives—the potential for disagreement and conflict. While respondents generally seemed to have exercised high levels of control in relation to the terms and conditions of donor access to children, and arrangements were working well, the gradual extension of legal rights to biological fathers (see Smart and Neale 1999) increases the mothers' dependence on the integrity of these men.

Again, finding the right words to describe their parenting relationship was difficult. Bonnie expresses a common feminist critique of the label *mummy*, which is hostile to ways that it can be employed to subsume other aspects of a woman's identity.

> Bonnie: I've always been quite keen that Peter should know what our names are anyway. I think there's something completely depersonalizing about the way women sit around and talk about a child's mummy as if she's got no identity. It's fine if there's a baby in the room and it's your child, but everyone will say, 'Ask Mummy, tell Mummy.' But you become this amorphous mummy to everybody. All women are sort of mummy, they don't have their own identity. So I've been quite keen that he should grow up knowing that people have roles and names, and that you should be able to distinguish between the two.

Yet, her radicalism is tempered by her recognition and desire to celebrate her special connection with the child, and she becomes swayed by arguments for the best interests of the child.

> Bonnie: But I also feel completely contradictory, that there is something very special emotionally about having your own mummy.

> Claudia: And then Philip had very strong feelings about it all, didn't he? He'd always been clear that he wanted to be Daddy, and while we went on holiday together last summer, he made it very clear that he thought that in some sense you needed to be recognized as Peter's mother, that that was important, an important thing in terms of what the relationship meant, and that it would be wrong to deny Bonnie that. . . . Yes, he [also thought] that Peter would, if we started him calling both of us Mummy, sooner or later he'd be ridiculed by some of the other children, and then he would have a terrible conflict of loyalties—does he go with the crowd or does he protect us? And that we shouldn't put him in that position. So we went for Mummy, Daddy, and Claudia. And then he started calling me Mummy anyway. But now he calls me Addie. [laughter]

This Mummy, Daddy, and Claudia configuration that then evolved into Claudia being called Mummy or the nickname Addie is potentially very undermining of the co-mother. Other couples specifically avoided involving biological fathers to this extent because of such complications of status and role. Claudia's confidence in her relationship with Peter was affirmed through her experience of mothering as main caregiver and, hopefully, by their capacity to be aware of the issues, as the discussion above appears to indicate. Philip's desire for recognition as Daddy is at one level less problematic. He earns this validation through his active involvement in parenting, and because he is not attempting to share fatherhood with a partner, there are no additional complications in relation to exclusion. However, the gender dynamics of this are interesting. While much of the social aspect of Philip's parenting involves the activities of mothering, he is content with the identity of dad. Conversely, in common with the rest of the sample, rather than draw upon dominant polarized heterosexual frameworks—mother/father—respondents extend the meaning of motherhood to include so-called fathering activities such as breadwinning. This raises the wider question: What exactly is a father?

Once again, their parenting is supported by a complex network of kin who have been encouraged to recognize and act upon social as well as biological ties. As they map out the main people supporting their parenting, Bonnie and Claudia discuss the input of kin:

> Bonnie: That's my sister Holly and her partner Vickie, who is dyke as well, which is very nice, and they live round the corner as well. So in a sense they are part of our community, very much so, and Vickie was around for the birth. So they lead a different sort of lifestyle in the sense that they haven't got any children, so they're definitely sort of aunts that come in and do babysitting and things. They're sort of busy but they're important, and we promote the relationship actually, don't we?
>
> Interviewer: What about Philip's parents? Do they have any . . . ?
>
> Bonnie: Yes, there's Philip's mum and dad. They see him two or three times a year—it's only been a year and a half, but they've made a lot of effort. They came down just after his birth.

It is no simple act, however, for extended family to claim kinship ties in these non-traditional situations that require coming to terms with a relative's sexuality. While part of being lesbian and gay is about learning how to come out to self and others, I think we have given scant attention to the work involved when heterosexual family members, particularly elderly parents, claim kinship ties that require coming out on behalf of others. For Philip's parents, it was easier for them to explain his entry into fatherhood to other family members by inventing a complicated story about Philip and Bonnie being or having been lovers.

> Claudia: They told all their family that Bonnie and Philip have a kind of relationship.
>
> Bonnie: His parents lied, basically.
>
> Claudia: [The story being that] They're not living together any more because Bonnie is already living with this other woman who is a nurse and has got a mortgage and it would be too complicated to change things.
>
> Bonnie: They absolutely want Peter to be their grandson and they love that, and I think in their own head they're dealing with it, they're very nice to us both, aren't they? They send us joint cards and progress reports.
>
> Claudia: We even slept in a double bed in their house once.
>
> Bonnie: Yes, they accept it, you can see, on one level. But obviously they can't fully accept it, they can't tell their friends. So that's how that goes.

As Claudia had been adopted, her family was used to the complexity of kinship relations.

> Claudia: [My family is] all interested and very supportive but there's no one nearby to pop in. . . . They all only see him about twice a year. Family get-togethers, isn't it?
>
> Bonnie: And you made an effort to go and visit and show Peter off.

Claudia's biological parents were described as treating Peter similarly to their other grandchildren, all of whom receive scant attention. Interestingly, in the case of her adoptive parents, in common with many other respondents, the arrival of children helped rebuild bridges after earlier estrangement over issues of sexuality.

> Claudia: Well, [my adoptive parents] have much more difficulty with me being a lesbian than my parents do. And they've virtually rejected me really. Not immediately when I came out but later on. And then [my adoptive mother], since she found out that I was trying to get pregnant, has been completely supportive. I think [my adoptive father] finds it more difficult.
>
> Interviewer: And she thinks of Peter as your son?
>
> Claudia: Yes. And she describes herself as his adoptive grandmother.

Bonnie's mother could see distinct advantages in her daughter's parenting arrangements:

> My mum is Peter's grandmother. She's very, very involved with Peter, totally supportive of this relationship, and thinks that—why hadn't anyone ever mentioned it before? It seems a great way to bring up children. Having brought seven children up without the help of my father, she now thinks it's wonderful not only to have a supportive woman partner but a father involved who lives up the road. It's great. Peter sees more of his father than most children probably do. So she's good.

Aside from a wide circle of friends, Bonnie, Claudia, and Philip had support from parents and siblings, with their son Peter looking forward to presents from four sets of grandparents.

Conclusion

These three stories illustrate many common themes that emerged across the sample, particularly the creativity and co-operation that appear to characterize much of the parenting experience of lesbian couples. I have focused on the involvement of fathers and/or donors and on the complexity of kinship to show how like and unlike these families are to other sorts of family formations. I could equally have looked at the important friendship networks that supported their parenting, the presence of lesbian aunties and heterosexual friends. Lesbian families are usually extended families, supported by elaborate networks of friends and kin.

In common with single lesbian mothers in the United States (Lewin 1993: 9), kin occupy an important place in respondents' accounts of their social interaction. My focus on couples in shared parenting situations reveals other interesting dimensions of kinship: the complexity of these relations and the importance respondents placed on having non-biogenetic ties recognized and validated by family of origin. Demanding recognition of kinship ties in a same-sex context represents an extremely radical departure from the economy of sexual difference underpinning conceptions of kinship more generally (see Butler 1990: 38–43). Considerable effort was involved in achieving this end by all parties. One reason for their usual success in this respect, I believe, is that the presence of children helps make intelligible a lifestyle that can appear strange and 'other' to heterosexual observers.

This is supported, I think, by the way that often quite strained or difficult relationships between respondents and their parents were transformed as daughters became mothers and their parents became grandparents. Many respondents experienced high levels of enthusiastic support from heterosexual friends in their quest to become, and their experience of being, parents.

Regardless of whether parenting was shared, mothering was usually carried out in a context where mothers experienced a great deal of practical and emotional support from their partners, where routine domestic responsibilities were fairly evenly shared, and where there was a mutual recognition of a woman's right to an identity beyond the home. Beyond the confines of heterosexuality, they had greater scope to challenge the connections between biological and social motherhood and fatherhood. By deprivileging the biological as signifier of motherhood (although this appears to be contingent on the relationship remaining intact) and the capacity to mother, many were actively engaged in extending the meaning, content, and consequence of mothering to include both partners (or even fathers) on equal terms.

Lesbians opting into motherhood in a hostile world have to engage in an extended period of planning: nothing can be taken for granted. The pleasure they experienced in spending time with their children and the high value they attached to mothering are often reflected in the employment strategies of both parents. Thus, biological motherhood was a poor predictor of differences in income and employment hours within partnerships. They were advantaged by their structural similarities as women and their positioning outside conventionality. In resolving the contradiction between time for children and the need to generate income, their options had not usually been foreclosed by earlier employment choices shaped by the anticipation and/or experience of a gender division of labour (Dunne 1997; 2000). They consequently have greater scope to operationalize their egalitarian ideals in relation to parenting. The high value they attached to nurturing, together with their desire to be fair to each other, meant that within reason they were prepared to experience a reduced standard of living (see Dunne 1998a). Their views about what constitutes shared parenting were less distorted by ideologies that dichotomized parenting along lines of gender in such a way that men can be seen and see themselves as involved fathers when they are largely absent from the home (Baxter and Western 1998; Ferri and Smith 1996). Consequently, their solution to the contradiction was to integrate mothering and breadwinning.

In their everyday lives of nurturing, housework, and breadwinning, respondents provide viable alternative models for parenting beyond heterosexuality. While our focus is on lesbian partners, anecdotal evidence suggests that lesbians are also founding parenting partnerships on the basis of friendship—with gay men or other lesbians. By finding a way around the reproductive limitations of their sexuality, they experience their position as gatekeepers between children and biological fathers in an unusual way. Ironically, we find examples of highly productive models of co-operation between women and men in bringing up children. Unhampered by the constraints of heterosexuality, they can choose to include men on the basis of the qualities they can bring into children's lives. It is no accident, I believe, that respondents usually chose to involve gay men. These men were seen as representing more acceptable forms of masculinity, and their sexuality barred them from some of the legal rights that have been extended to heterosexual fathers.

Their positioning outside conventionality and the similarities they share as women enable and indeed insist upon the redefinition of the meaning and content of motherhood. Thus, when choosing to opt into motherhood, they are anticipating something very different from the heterosexual norm. Some felt that their gender parity and commitment to egalitarianism enabled a conscious recognition and articulation of the power that was perceived to derive from the actual bodily experience of creating another human being. Within the gender context that frames their arrangements, they felt safe to identify and celebrate this special biological and psychological connectedness with a child because it did not ultimately lead to polarization within the partnership in relation to access to other sources of social reward.

At one level, motherhood bridges the gap between the known and the unknown. It represents a common currency where we can predict the routines, pleasures, and concerns of parents, and sexuality can be sidelined. At another level, however, we have seen that their experience of motherhood seems quite different from that of most heterosexual mothers. Importantly, by building bridges in this way, friends, colleagues, and extended family bear witness to these differences, and their experience reflects back into the lives of others. These alternative reference points may help to reinforce women's confidence in their critique of conventional assumptions shaping heterosexual practice. Much recent scholarship on sexuality, for example, queer theory, sees a radical future in subverting gender categories through practices of parody (Butler 1990). To this end, the influential philosopher Judith Butler asks us to rethink the transformational potential of practices such as 'drag, cross-dressing, and the sexual stylization of butch/femme identities' (1990: 137). However, my concern is that in our contemporary preoccupation with these exotic and exciting aspects of sexual radicalism, we ignore the challenge that ordinary lesbian women and gay men pose to the status quo through their prioritization of egalitarian ideals. Central to the reproduction of the social order (institutional heterosexuality, gender inequality) are ideological processes that reify and legitimize current arrangements by rendering invisible or stigmatizing alternatives. The visibility of lesbian parents in the mainstream as they negotiate with schools, health workers, neighbours, employers and co-workers, and heterosexual parents helps to make intelligible the unimaginable to others. They create a cognitive dissonance that may enable others to evaluate and move beyond the taken-for-grantedness of heterosexuality. As women together, they renegotiate the boundaries, meaning, and content of parenthood. By doing so, they undermine much of the logic shaping conventional divisions of labour, for example, that specialization is the most efficient and effective way to finance and run a household and care for children, that prioritizing the career of the higher earner makes long-term financial sense, and that biological motherhood is the precursor of the capacity to mother. They challenge conventional wisdom by showing the viability of parenting beyond the confines of heterosexuality. Rather than being incorporated into the mainstream as honorary heterosexuals, by building bridges between the known and the unknown, their lives represent, I believe, a fundamental challenge to the foundation of the gender order.

Notes

I would like to dedicate this article to the memory of Linda Edwards, who graciously shared her story of mothering with me during the last few days of her struggle with breast cancer. Her courage and humanity was an inspiration throughout the study. My thanks to all participants in the Lesbian Household Project and to the following for their helpful comments on this article: Shirley Prendergast, Nina Hallowell, Ginny Morrow, Shelley Sclater, Beth Schneider, and the anonymous reviewers, particularly the one who raved!

1. Both VanEvery (1995) and Ehrensaft (1987: 20) mention that women are the driving force in the quest to achieve and maintain egalitarianism. Both comment on the extent to which structural factors, such as men's superior earnings, and wider social expectations mediate success in this respect.
2. See the extended version of this article for additional case studies (Dunne 1998c).
3. I am grateful to the Economic and Social Research Council for funding this recently completed three-year project (reference number R00023 4649).
4. See Dunne (1997; 2000) for exploration of the link between the capacity to move beyond heterosexuality and economic self-reliance.
5. To maintain confidentiality, the names of participants and their children and their geographical location and occupations have been changed. To give some sense of their employment circumstances, I have assigned similar kinds of occupations.
6. While British mothers are more likely now than in the past to be employed full-time, it is mothers rather than fathers who balance the demands of paid work and childcare. It is very unusual for mothers and fathers to have similar lengths of paid workweeks, even when mothers are employed full-time (Dunne 1998a; Ferri and Smith 1996).
7. I was struck by the almost unanimous confidence of the sample in their sexuality—respondents saw their lesbian identity as a great source of advantage. Their identification as lesbian rather than gay was also evidence of their usually feminist inclinations. In a previous life-history study of lesbians who were generally not mothers (Dunne 1997), there were more examples of ambiguity in this respect. I suspect respondents' self-assurance is related to a combination of factors including historical period, being in fulfilling relationships, their achievement of motherhood, and the process of soul-searching that preceded this.
8. Silva (1996) draws a useful distinction between motherhood, a uniquely female experience, and mothering, which, although usually a female practice, can be performed by either gender.

References

Abshoff, K., and M. Hird. 1998. 'Subverting the Feminine: The Case of Child-free Women', paper presented at the Annual Meeting of the British Sociological Association, University of Edinburgh.

Baxter, J., and M. Western. 1998. 'Satisfaction with Housework: Examining the Paradox', *Sociology* 1: 101–20.

Beck, U., and E. Beck-Gernsheim. 1995. *The Normal Chaos of Love* (Cambridge, MA: Polity).

Berk, S.F. 1985. *The Gender Factory: The Apportionment of Work in American Households* (New York: Plenum).

Blaisure, K., and K. Allen. 1995. 'Feminists and the Ideology and Practice of Marital Equality', *Journal of Marriage and the Family* 57: 5–19.

Brannen, J., and P. Moss. 1991. *Managing Mothers: Dual Earner Households after Maternity Leave* (London: Unwin Hyman).

Butler, J. 1990. *Gender Trouble: Feminism and the Subversion of Identity* (New York: Routledge).

Campbell, E. 1985. *The Childless Marriage* (London: Tavistock).

Doucet, A. 1995. 'Gender Equality, Gender Difference and Care', PhD diss., Cambridge University, Cambridge, UK.

Dunne, G.A. 1997. *Lesbian Lifestyles: Women's Work and the Politics of Sexuality* (London: Macmillan).

———. 1998a. '"Pioneers behind Our own Front Doors": Towards New Models in the Organization of Work in Partnerships', *Work Employment and Society* 12, 2: 273–95.

———. 1998b. 'A Passion for "Sameness"? Sexuality and Gender Accountability', in *The New Family?*, eds E. Silva and C. Smart (London: Sage).

———. 1998c. 'Opting into Motherhood: Lesbian Experience of Work and Family Life', London School of Economics, Gender Institute Discussion Paper Series 6.

———. 1998d. 'Add Sexuality and Stir: Towards a Broader Understanding of the Gender Dynamics of Work and Family Life', in *Living 'Difference': Lesbian Perspectives on Work and Family Life*, ed. G.A. Dunne (New York: Haworth).

———. 1999. 'Balancing Acts: On the Salience of Sexuality for Understanding the Gendering of Work and Family-life Opportunities', in *Women and Work: The Age of Post-feminism?*, eds L. Sperling and M. Owen (Aldershot, UK: Ashgate).

———. 2000. 'Lesbians as Authentic Workers? Institutional Heterosexuality and the Reproduction of Gender Inequalities', *Sexualities*.

Ehrensaft, D. 1987. *Parenting Together: Men and Women Sharing the Care of the Children* (New York: Free Press).

Fenstermaker, S., C. West, and D.H. Zimmerman. 1991. 'Gender Inequality: New Conceptual Terrain', in *Gender, Family and Economy, the Triple Overlap*, ed. R.L. Blumberg (London: Sage).

Ferri, E., and K. Smith. 1996. *Parenting in the 1990s* (London: Family Policy Studies Centre).

Gartrell, N., et al. Forthcoming. 'The National Lesbian Family Study 2: Interviews with Mothers of Toddlers', *American Journal of Psychiatry*.

Giddens, A. 1992. *The Transformation of Intimacy* (Cambridge, MA: Polity).

Green, S. 1997. *Urban Amazons: The Politics of Sexuality, Gender and Identity* (Basingstoke, UK: Macmillan).

Gregson, N., and M. Lowe. 1995. *Servicing the Middle-classes: Class, Gender and Waged Domestic Labour* (London: Routledge).

Hochschild, A.R. 1989. *The Second Shift* (New York: Avon).

Lewin, E. 1993. *Lesbian Mothers* (Ithaca, NY: Cornell University Press).

McAllister, F., and L. Clarke. 1998. *Childless by Choice: A Study of Childlessness in Britain* (London: Family Policy Studies Centre).

Mansfield, P., and J. Collard. 1988. *The Beginning of the Rest of Your Life: A Portrait of Newlywed Marriage* (London: Macmillan).

Morell, C. 1994. *Unwomanly Conduct* (London: Routledge).

Popeno, D. 1988. *Disturbing the Nest: Family Change and Decline in Modern Societies* (New York: Aldine).

Rich, A. 1984. 'On Compulsory Heterosexuality and Lesbian Existence', in *Desire: The Politics of Sexuality*, eds A. Snitow, C. Stansell, and S. Thompson (London: Virago).

Rubin, G. 1975. 'The Traffic in Women: Notes on the "Political Economy" of Sex', in *Towards an Anthropology of Women*, ed. R.R. Reiter (London: Monthly Review Press).

Scott, J. 1997. 'Changing Households in Britain: Do Families Still Matter?', *Sociological Review* 45, 4: 591–620.

Silva, E. 1996. 'The Transformation of Mothering', in *Good Enough Mothering?*, eds E. Silva and C. Smart (London: Routledge).

———, and C. Smart, eds. 1996. *Good Enough Mothering?* (London: Routledge).

Smart, C., and B. Neale. 1999. *Family Fragments* (Cambridge, MA: Polity).

Sullivan, M. 1996. 'Rozzie and Harriet? Gender and Family Patterns of Lesbian Co-parents', *Gender & Society* 10, 6: 747–67.

VanEvery, J. 1995. *Heterosexual Women Changing the Family: Refusing to Be a 'Wife'* (London: Taylor Francis).

Weeks, J., C. Donovan, and B. Heaphy. 1998. 'Everyday Experiments: Narratives of Non-heterosexual Relationships', in *The New Family?*, eds E. Silva and C. Smart (London: Sage).

Weston, K. 1991. *Families We Choose* (New York: Columbia University Press).

Section 4 The Gender-divided Work Involved in Maintaining Families

Divisions of work and responsibility between men and women have been basic to the organization of nuclear families in Canada for a long time. These gender-based divisions, in turn, are a chief source of inequality between women and men. But for decades women's involvement in the paid labour force has produced pressure on men to do more of the housework and childcare, and tension in relationships where that does not happen. Couples with high incomes can shift much of the work onto the shoulders of a paid employee, but a majority of couples cannot afford that (and some who can prefer that their children be cared for in a daycare facility with trained staff). In many couples, then, the issue of how the daily household work is handled is a source of strain.

For decades, researchers examining the allocation of work in households reported that despite a growing consensus that men should do their 'share' of the housework and childcare there was no significant change among men. Social-organizational factors (especially men's higher earnings) and cultural factors (e.g., masculinity as an ideology and identity) together helped explain this lack of change. The articles in this section were written after decades of research found no significant change in the division of work in the home. Indeed, Sandra Colavecchia's findings (in Chapter 25) on the allocation of 'money-work' indicate that even work that many assume to be handled by men might more often be the responsibility of women.

Yet, change is occurring. Recent research findings highlight increases in the amount of household work that men are doing, as well as declines in the amount of housework (though not childcare) done by their female partners. In Chapter 23, Scott Coltrane discusses some fathers who are doing significant amounts of childcare. Empirical evidence also indicates that lesbian partners have considerably more egalitarian patterns than heterosexual couples. Chapter 24, by Gillian Dunne, describes the arrangements of a sample of British lesbian couples. Their more equitable patterns highlight the significance of gender, and the power dynamics inherent in gender, in shaping the families of heterosexual couples.

The more immediate problem than inequality, for many dual-earner families with children, is the need to find childcare. Chapter 26, by Sedef Arat-Koc, examines the 'solution' that the Canadian government has promoted—hiring poor women from Third World countries as nannies. She outlines the problems that are inherent in families' hiring of another woman to provide care—including the fact that it fails to address Canada's 'childcare crisis'. In Chapter 27, Meg Luxton examines the more general question of the strategies families can use to handle the incompatible demands of employment and family.

Chapter 23

Scott Coltrane's approach to the study of gender is different from, but complementary to, one that focuses on social organization, or whether and how household work is divided between women and men. He is concerned with how people 'do gender' when they do childcare and housework. He adopts the 'doing gender' approach which sees gender as something people 'accomplish' in everyday work and interactions that are infused with gendered meaning. According to this approach, people 'do gender' because they are always held accountable to expectations that they act in accord with gender norms. And in so doing, their identities as women and men are confirmed. Few researchers working within this perspective ask how gender can be 'undone'. Coltrane does just that, as he explores some dual-earner couples' sharing of housework and childcare.

Household Labour and the Routine Production of Gender

Scott Coltrane

Motherhood is often perceived as the quintessence of womanhood. The everyday tasks of mothering are taken to be 'natural' expressions of femininity, and the routine care of home and children is seen to provide opportunities for women to express and reaffirm their gendered relation to men and to the world. The traditional tasks of fatherhood, in contrast, are limited to begetting, protecting, and providing for children. While fathers typically derive a gendered sense of self from these activities, their masculinity is even more dependent on not doing the things that mothers do. What happens, then, when fathers share with mothers those tasks that we define as expressing the true nature of womanhood?

This chapter describes how a sample of 20 dual-earner couples talk about sharing housework and childcare. Since marriage is one of the least scripted or most undefined interaction situations, the marital conversation is particularly important to a couple's shared sense of reality. I investigate these parents' construction of gender by examining their talk about negotiations over who does what around the house; how these divisions of labour influence their perceptions of self and other; how they conceive of gender-appropriate behaviour; and how they handle inconsistencies between their own views and those of the people around them. Drawing on the parents' accounts of the planning, allocation, and performance of childcare and housework, I illustrate how gender is produced through everyday practices and how adults are socialized by routine activity.

Gender as an Accomplishment

Candace West and Don Zimmerman (1987) suggest that gender is a routine, methodical, and recurring accomplishment. 'Doing gender' involves a complex of socially guided perceptual, interactional, and micropolitical activities that cast particular pursuits as expressions of masculine and feminine 'natures'. Rather than viewing gender as a property of individuals, West and Zimmerman conceive of it as an emergent feature of social situations that results from and legitimates gender inequality. Similarly, Sarah Fenstermaker Berk (1985: 204; emphasis in original) suggests that housework and childcare

> can become the occasion for producing commodities (e.g., clean children, clean laundry, and new light switches) and a reaffirmation of one's gendered relation to the work and to the world. In short, the 'shoulds' of gender ideals are fused with the 'musts' of efficient household production. The result may be something resembling a 'gendered' household-production function.

If appropriately doing gender serves to sustain and legitimate existing gender relations, would inappropriate gender activity challenge that legitimacy? Or, as West and Zimmerman (1987: 146) suggest, when people fail to do gender appropriately, are their individual characters, motives, and predispositions called into question? If doing gender is unavoidable and people are held accountable for its production, how might people initiate and sustain atypical gender behaviours?

By investigating how couples share childcare and housework, I explore (1) the sorts of dyadic and group interactions that facilitate the sharing of household labour; (2) how couples describe the requirements of parenting and how they evaluate men's developing capacities for nurturing; and (3) the impact of sharing domestic labour on conceptions of gender.

The Sample

To find couples who shared childcare, I initially contacted schools and daycare centres in several suburban California communities. Using snowball-sampling techniques, I selected 20 moderate- to middle-income dual-earner couples with children. To compensate for gaps in the existing literature and to enhance comparisons between sample families, I included couples if they were the biological parents of at least two school-aged children, they were both employed at least half-time, and both identified the father as assuming significant responsibility for routine childcare. I observed families in their homes and interviewed fathers and mothers separately at least once and as many as five times. I recorded the interviews and transcribed them for coding and constant comparative analysis.

The parents were primarily in their late thirties and had been living together for an average of 10 years. All wives and 17 of 20 husbands attended some college and most couples married later and had children later than others in their birth cohort. The median age at marriage for the mothers was 23; for fathers, 26. Median age at first birth for mothers was 27; for fathers, 30. Fifteen of 20 fathers were at least one year older than their wives. Median gross annual income was $40,000, with three families under $25,000 and three over $65,000. Sixteen of the couples had two children and four had three children. Over two-thirds of the families had both sons and daughters, but four families had two sons and no daughters, and two families had two daughters and no sons. The children's ages ranged from four to 14, with 80 per cent between the ages of five and 11 and with a median age of seven.

Mothers were more likely than fathers to hold professional or technical jobs, although most were employed in female-dominated occupations with relatively limited upward mobility and moderate pay. Over three-quarters held jobs in the 'helping' professions: seven mothers were nurses, five were teachers, and four were social workers or counsellors. Other occupations for the mothers were administrator, laboratory technician, filmmaker, and book-binder. Sample fathers held both blue-collar and white-collar jobs, with concentrations in construction (3), maintenance (2), sales (3), business (3), teaching (3), delivery (4), and computers (2). Like most dual-earner wives, sample mothers earned, on average, less than half of what their husband's did, and worked an average of eight fewer hours per week. Eleven mothers (55 per cent) but only five fathers (25 per cent) were employed less than 40 hours per week. In nine of 20 families, mothers were employed at least as many hours as fathers, but in only four families did the mother's earnings approach or exceed those of her husband.

Developing Shared Parenting

Two-thirds of the parents indicated that current divisions of labour were accomplished by making minor practical adjustments to what they perceived as an already fairly equal division of labour. A common sentiment was expressed by one father who commented:

> Since we've both always been working since we've been married, we've typically shared everything as far as all the working—I mean all the housework responsibilities as well as childcare responsibilities. So it's a pattern that was set up before the kids were even thought of.

Nevertheless, a full three-quarters of the couples reported that the mother performed much more of the early infant care. All of the mothers and only about half of the fathers reported that they initially reduced their hours of employment after having children. About a third of the fathers said they increased their employment hours to compensate for the loss of income that resulted from their wives taking time off work before or after the births of their children.

In talking about becoming parents, most of the fathers stressed the importance of their involvement in conception decisions, the birth process, and early infant care to later assumption of childcare duties. Most couples planned the births of their children jointly and intentionally. Eighty per cent reported that they mutually decided to have children, with two couples reporting that the wife desired children more than the husband and two reporting that the husband was more eager than the wife to become a parent. For many families, the husband's commitment to participate fully in child rearing was a precondition of the birth decision. One mother described how she and her husband decided to have children.

> Shared parenting was sort of part of the decision. When we decided to have children, we realized that we were both going to be involved with our work, so it was part of the plan from the very beginning. As a matter of fact, I thought that we only could have the one and he convinced me that we could handle two and promised to really help [laughs], which he really has, but two children is a lot more work than you realize [laughs].

By promising to assume partial responsibility for child rearing, most husbands influenced their wives' initial decision to have children, the subsequent decision to have another child, and the decision of whether and when to return to work. Almost all of the mothers indicated that they had always assumed that they would have children, and most also assumed that they would return to paid employment before the children were in school. Half of the mothers did return to work within six months of the birth of their first child.

All but one of the fathers were present at the births of their children and most talked about the importance of the birth experience, using terms like 'incredible', 'magical', 'moving', 'wonderful', and 'exciting'. While most claimed that they played an important part in the birth process by providing emotional support to their wives or acting as labour coaches, a few considered their involvement to be inconsequential. Comments included, 'I felt a little bit necessary and a lot unnecessary', and 'I didn't bug her too much and I might have helped a little.' Three quarters of the fathers reported that they were 'very involved' with their newborns, even though the mother provided most of the daily care for the first few months. Over two-thirds of the mothers breast-fed their infants. Half of the fathers reported that they got up in the night to soothe their babies, and many described their early infant care experience in terms that mothers typically use to describe 'bonding' with newborns. The intensity of father–infant interaction was discussed by fathers as enabling them to experience a new and different level of intimacy and was depicted as 'deep emotional trust', 'very interior', 'drawing me in', and 'making it difficult to deal with the outside world'.

About half of the fathers referred to the experience of being involved in the delivery and in early infant care as a necessary part of their assuming responsibility for later childcare. Many described a process in which the actual performance of caretaking duties provided them with the self-confidence and skills to feel that they knew what they were doing. They described their time alone with the baby as especially helpful in building their sense of competence as a shared primary caretaker. One man said,

> I felt I needed to start from the beginning. Then I learned how to walk them at night and not be totally p.o.'ed at them and not feel that it was an infringement. It was something I got to do in some sense, along with changing diapers and all these things. It was certainly not repulsive and in some ways I really liked it a lot. It was not something innate, it was something to be learned. I managed to start at the beginning. If you don't start at the beginning then you're sort of left behind.

This father, like almost all of the others, talked about having to learn how to nurture and care for his children. He also stressed how important it was to 'start at the beginning'. While all fathers intentionally shared routine childcare as the children approached school age, only half of the fathers attempted to assume a major share of daily infant care, and only five couples described the father as an equal caregiver for children under one year old. These early caregiving fathers described their involvement in infant care as explicitly planned:

> She nursed both of them completely, for at least five or six months. So, my role was—we agreed on this—my role was the other direct intervention, like changing, and getting them up and walking them, and putting them back to sleep. For instance, she would nurse them but I would bring them to the bed afterward and change them if necessary, and get them back to sleep. . . . I really initiated those other kinds of care aspects so that I could be involved. I continued that on through infant and toddler and preschool classes that we would go to, even though I would usually be the only father there.

This man's wife offered a similar account, commenting that 'except for breast-feeding, he always provided the same things that I did—the emotional closeness and the attention.'

Another early caregiving father described how he and his wife 'very consciously' attempted to equalize the amount of time they spent with their children when they were infants: 'In both cases we very consciously made the decision that we wanted it to be a mutual process, so that from the start we shared, and all I didn't do was breast-feed. And I really would say that was the only distinction.' His wife also described their infant care arrangements as 'equal', and commented that other people did not comprehend the extent of his participation:

> I think that nobody really understood that Jennifer had two mothers. The burden of proof was always on me that he was literally being a mother. He wasn't nursing, but he was

> getting up in the night to bring her to me, to change her poop, which is a lot more energy than nursing in the middle of the night. You have to get up and do all that, I mean get awake. So his sleep was interrupted, and yet within a week or two, at his work situation, it was expected that he was back to normal, and he never went back to normal. He was part of the same family that I was.

This was the only couple who talked about instituting, for a limited time, an explicit record-keeping system to ensure that they shared childcare equally.

> [Father]: We were committed to the principle of sharing and we would have schedules, keep hours, so that we had a pretty good sense that we were even, both in terms of the commitment to the principle as well as we wanted to in fact be equal. We would keep records in a log—one might say in a real compulsive way—so that we knew what had happened when the other person was on.
>
> [Mother]: When the second one came we tried to keep to the log of hours and very quickly we threw it out completely. It was too complex.

Practicality and Flexibility

Both early- and later-sharing families identified practical considerations and flexibility as keys to equitable divisions of household labour. Most did not have explicit records or schedules for childcare or housework. For example, one early-involved father reported that practical divisions of labour evolved 'naturally':

> Whoever cooks doesn't have to do the dishes. If for some reason she cooks and I don't do the dishes, she'll say something about it, certainly. Even though we never explicitly agreed that's how we do it, that's how we do it. The person who doesn't cook does the dishes. We don't even know who's going to cook a lot of the time. We just get it that we can do it. We act in good faith.

Couples who did not begin sharing routine childcare until after infancy were even more likely to describe their division of labour as practical solutions to shortages of time. For example, one mother described sharing household tasks as 'the only logical thing to do', and her husband said, 'It's the only practical way we could do it.' Other fathers describe practical and flexible arrangements based on the constraints of employment scheduling:

> Her work schedule is more demanding and takes up a lot of evening time, so I think I do a lot of the everyday routines, and she does a lot of the less frequent things. Like I might do more of the cooking and meal preparation, but she is the one that does the grocery shopping. An awful lot of what gets done gets done because the person is home first. That's been our standing rule for who fixes dinner. Typically, I get home before she does so I fix dinner, but that isn't a fixed rule. She gets home first, then she fixes dinner. Making the beds and doing the laundry just falls on me because I've got more time during the day to do it. And the yardwork and cuttin' all the wood, I do that. And so I'm endin' up doin' more around here than her just because I think I've got more time.

While mothers were more likely than fathers to report that talk was an important part of sharing household labour, most couples reported that they spent little time planning or arguing about who was going to do what around the house. Typical procedures for allocating domestic chores were described as 'ad hoc', illustrated by one mother's discussion of cooking:

> Things with us have happened pretty easily as far as what gets done by who. It happened without having to have a schedule or deciding—you know—like cooking. We never decided that he would do all the cooking; it just kind of ended up that way. Every once in a while when he doesn't feel like cooking he'll say, 'Would you cook tonight?' 'Sure, fine.' But normally I don't offer to cook. I say, 'What are we having for dinner?'

In general, divisions of labour in sample families were described as flexible and changing. One mother talked about how routine adjustments in task allocation were satisfying to her: 'Once you're comfortable in your roles and division of tasks for a few months then it seems like the needs change a little bit and you have to change a little bit and you have to regroup. That's what keeps it interesting. I think that's why it's satisfying.'

Underlying Ideology

While ad hoc divisions of labour were described as being practical solutions to time shortages, there were two major ideological underpinnings to the sharing of housework and childcare: child-centredness and equity ideals. While those who attempted to share infant care tended to have more elaborate vocabularies for talking about these issues, later-sharing couples also referred to them. For instance, all couples provided accounts that focused on the sanctity of childhood and most stressed the impossibility of mothers 'doing it all'.

Couples were child-centred in that they placed a high value on their children's well-being, defined parenting as an important and serious undertaking, and organized most of their non-employed hours around their children. For instance, one father described how his social life revolved around his children:

> Basically if the other people don't have kids and if they aren't involved with the kids, then we aren't involved with them. It's as simple as that. The guys I know at work that are single or don't have children my age don't come over because then we have nothing in common. They're kind of the central driving force in my life.

While about half of the couples (11 of 20) had paid for ongoing out-of-home childcare, and three-quarters had regularly used some form of paid childcare, most of the parents said that they spent more time with their children than the other dual-earner parents in their neighbourhoods. One father commented that he and his wife had structured their lives around personally taking care of their children:

> An awful lot of the way we've structured our lives has been based around our reluctance to have someone else raise our children. We just really didn't want the kids to be raised from 7:30 in the morning till 4:30 or 5:00 in the afternoon by somebody else. So we've structured the last 10 years around that issue.

Many parents also advocated treating children as inexperienced equals or 'little people', rather than as inferior beings in need of authoritarian training. For example, an ex-military father employed in computer research stated, 'We don't discipline much. Generally the way it works is kind of like bargaining. They know that there are consequences to whatever actions they take, and we try and make sure they know what the consequences are before they have a chance to take the action.' Another father described his moral stance concerning children's rights:

> I'm not assuming—when I'm talking about parent–child stuff—that there's an inequality. Yes, there are a lot of differences in terms of time spent in this world, but our assumption

has been, with both children, that we're peers. And so that's how we are with them. So, if they say something and they're holding fast to some position, we do not say, 'You do this because we're the parent and you're the child.'

About half of the parents talked directly about such equity ideals as applied to children.

Concerning women's rights, 80 per cent of fathers and 90 per cent of mothers agreed that women were disadvantaged in our society, but only two mothers and one father mentioned equal rights or the women's movement as motivators for sharing household labour. Most did not identify themselves as feminists, and a few offered derogatory comments about 'those women's libbers'. Nevertheless, almost all parents indicated that no one should be forced to perform a specific task because they were a man or a woman. This implicit equity ideal was evidenced by mothers and fathers using time availability, rather than gender, to assign most household tasks.

Divisions of Household Labour

Contributions to 64 household tasks were assessed by having fathers and mothers each sort cards on a five-point scale to indicate who most often performed them (see Table 23.1). Frequently performed tasks, such as meal preparation, laundry, sweeping, or putting children to bed, were judged for the two weeks preceding the interviews. Less frequently performed tasks, such as window washing, tax preparation, or car repair, were judged as to who typically performed them.

Some differences occurred between mothers' and fathers' accounts of household task allocation, but there was general agreement on who did what.

Table 23.1 shows that in the majority of families, most household tasks were seen as shared. Thirty-seven of 64 tasks (58 per cent), including all direct childcare, most household business, meal preparation, kitchen cleanup, and about half of other housecleaning tasks were reported to be shared about equally by fathers and mothers. Nevertheless, almost a quarter (15) of the tasks were performed principally by the mothers, including most clothes care, meal planning, kin-keeping, and some of the more onerous repetitive housecleaning. Just under one-fifth (12) of the tasks were performed principally by the fathers. These included the majority of the occasional outside chores such as home repair, car maintenance, lawn care, and taking out the trash. As a group, sample couples can thus be characterized as sharing an unusually high proportion of housework and childcare, but still partially conforming to a traditional division of household labour. The fathers and mothers in this study are pioneers in that they divided household tasks differently than their parents did, differently from most others in their age cohort, and from most families studied in time-use research.

Managing Versus Helping

Household divisions of labour in these families also can be described in terms of who takes responsibility for planning and initiating various tasks. In every family there were at least six frequently performed household chores over which the mother retained almost exclusive managerial control. That is, mothers noticed when the chore needed doing and made sure that someone adequately performed it. In general, mothers were more likely than fathers to act as managers for cooking, cleaning, and childcare, but over half of the couples shared responsibility in these areas. In all households the father was responsible for initiating and managing at least a few chores traditionally performed by mothers.

Based on participants' accounts of strategies for allocating household labour, I classified

Table 23.1 Household Tasks by Person Most Often Performing Them

	Mother More	Father and Mother Equally	Father More
Cleaning	Mopping Sweeping Dusting Cleaning bathroom sink Cleaning toilet	Vacuuming Cleaning tub/shower Making beds Picking up toys Tidying living room Hanging up clothes Washing windows Spring cleaning	Taking out trash Cleaning porch
Cooking	Planning menus Grocery shopping Baking	Preparing lunch Cooking dinner Making snacks Washing dishes Putting dishes away Wiping kitchen counters Putting food away	Preparing breakfast
Clothes	Laundry Hand laundry Ironing Sewing Buying clothes	Shoe care	
Household		Running errands Decorating Interior painting General yardwork Gardening	Household repairs Exterior painting Car maintenance Car repair Washing car Watering lawn Mowing lawn Cleaning rain gutters
Finance, Social	Writing or phoning relatives/friends	Deciding major purchases Paying bills Preparing taxes Handling insurance Planning couple dates	Investments
Children	Arranging babysitters	Waking children Helping children dress Helping children bathe Putting children to bed Supervising children Disciplining children Driving children Taking children to doctor Caring for sick children Playing with children Planning outings	

Note: Tasks were sorted separately by fathers and mothers according to relative frequency of performance: (1) Mother mostly or always, (2) Mother more than father, (3) Father and mother about equal, (4) Father more than mother, (5) Father mostly or always. For each task a mean ranking by couple was computed with 1.00–2.49 = Mother, 2.50–3.50 = Shared, 3.51–5.0 = Father. If over 50 per cent of families ranked a task as performed by one spouse more than the other, the task is listed under that spouse; otherwise tasks are listed as shared. n = 20 couples.

12 couples as sharing responsibility for household labour and eight couples as reflecting manager– helper dynamics. Helper husbands often waited to be told what to do, when to do it, and how it should be done. While they invariably expressed a desire to perform their 'fair share' of housekeeping and child rearing, they were less likely than the other fathers to assume responsibility for anticipating and planning these activities. Manager–helper couples sometimes referred to the fathers' contributions as 'helping' the mother.

When asked what they liked most about their husband's housework, about half of the mothers focused on their husband's self-responsibility: voluntarily doing work without being prodded. They commented, 'He does the everyday stuff' and 'I don't have to ask him.' The other mothers praised their husbands for particular skills with comments such as 'I love his spaghetti' or 'He's great at cleaning the bathroom.' In spite of such praise, three-fourths of the mothers said that what bothered them most about their husband's housework was the need to remind him to perform certain tasks, and some complained of having to 'train him' to correctly perform the chores. About a third of the fathers complained that their wives either didn't notice when things should be done or that their standards were too low. Although the extent of domestic task sharing varied considerably among couples, 90 per cent of both mothers and fathers independently reported that their divisions of labour were 'fair'.

Some mothers found it difficult to share authority for household management. For instance, one mother said, 'There's a certain control you have when you do the shopping and the cooking and I don't know if I'm ready to relinquish that control.' Another mother who shares most childcare and housework with her husband admitted that 'in general, household organization is something that I think I take over'. In discussing how they divide housework, she commented on how she notices more than her husband does:

> He does what he sees needs to be done. That would include basic cleaning kinds of things. However, there are some detailed kinds of things that he doesn't see that I feel need to be done, and in those cases I have to ask him to do things. He thinks some of the details are less important and I'm not sure, that might be a difference between men and women.

Like many of the mothers who maintained a managerial position in the household, this mother attributed an observed difference in domestic perceptiveness to an essential difference between women and men. By contrast, mothers who did not act as household managers were unlikely to link housecleaning styles to essential gender differences.

Many mothers talked about adjusting their housecleaning standards over the course of their marriage and trying to feel less responsible for being 'the perfect homemaker'. By partially relinquishing managerial duties and accepting their husband's housecleaning standards, some mothers reported that they were able to do less daily housework and focus more on occasional, thorough cleaning or adding 'finishing touches'. A mother with two nursing jobs whose husband delivered newspapers commented:

> He'll handle the surface things no problem, and I get down and do the nitty gritty. And I do it when it bugs me or when I have the time. It's not anything that we talk about usually. Sometimes if I feel like things are piling up, he'll say 'Well, make me a list', and I will. And he'll do it. There are some things that he just doesn't notice and that's fine: he handles the day-to-day stuff. He'll do things, like for me cleaning off the table—for him it's getting everything off it; for me it's

> putting the tablecloth on, putting the flowers on, putting the candles on. That's the kind of stuff I do and I like that; it's not that I want him to start.

This list-making mother illustrates that responsibility for managing housework sometimes remained in the mother's domain, even if the father performed more of the actual tasks.

Responsibility for managing childcare, on the other hand, was more likely to be shared. Planning and initiating 'direct' childcare, including supervision, discipline and play, was typically an equal enterprise. Sharing responsibility for 'indirect' childcare, including clothing, cleaning, and feeding, was less common, but was still shared in over half of the families. When they cooked, cleaned, or tended to the children, fathers in these families did not talk of 'helping' the mother; they spoke of fulfilling their responsibilities as equal partners and parents. For example, one father described how he and his wife divided both direct and indirect childcare:

> My philosophy is that they are my children and everything is my responsibility, and I think she approaches it the same way too. So when something needs to be done, it's whoever is close does it . . . whoever it is convenient for. And we do keep a sense of what the other's recent efforts are, and try to provide some balance, but without actually counting how many times you've done this and I've done that.

In spite of reported efforts to relinquish total control over managing home and children, mothers were more likely than fathers to report that they would be embarrassed if unexpected company came over and the house was a mess (80 per cent versus 60 per cent). When asked to compare themselves directly to their spouse, almost two-thirds of both mothers and fathers reported that the mother would be more embarrassed than the father. Some mothers reported emotional reactions to the house being a mess that were similar to those they experienced when their husbands 'dressed the kids funny'. The women were more likely to focus on the children 'looking nice', particularly when they were going to be seen in public. Mothers' greater embarrassment over the kemptness of home or children might reflect their sense of mothering as part of women's essential nature.

Adult Socialization through Child Rearing

Parents shared in creating and sustaining a world view through the performance and evaluation of child rearing. Most reported that parenting was their primary topic of conversation, exemplified by one father's comment: 'That's what we mostly discuss when we're not with our kids—either when we're going to sleep or when we have time alone—is how we feel about how we're taking care of them.' Others commented that their spouse helped them to recognize unwanted patterns of interaction by focusing on parenting practices. For instance, one father remarked,

> I'm not sure I could do it as a one-parent family, 'cause I wouldn't have the person, the other person saying, 'Hey, look at that, that's so much like what you do with your own family.' In a one-parent family, you don't have that, you don't have the other person putting out that stuff, you have to find it all out on your own and I'm not sure you can.

Usually the father was described as being transformed by the parenting experience and developing increased sensitivity. This was especially true of discourse between parents who were trying to convert a more traditional division of family labour into a more egalitarian one. A self-employed construction worker said his level of concern for child safety was heightened after he rearranged his work to do half of the parenting:

> There's a difference in being at the park with the kids since we went on the schedule. Before it was, like, 'Sure, jump off the jungle bars.' But when you're totally responsible for them, and you know that if they sprained an ankle or something you have to pick up the slack, it's like you have more investment in the kid and you don't want to see them hurt and you don't want to see them crying. I find myself being a lot more cautious.

Mothers also reported that their husbands began to notice subtle cues from the children as a result of being with them on a regular basis. The wife of the construction worker quoted above commented that she had not anticipated many of the changes that emerged from sharing routine childcare.

> I used to worry about the kids a lot more. I would say in the last year it's evened itself out quite a bit. That was an interesting kind of thing in sharing that started to happen that I hadn't anticipated. I suppose when you go into this your expectations about what will happen—that you won't take your kids to daycare, that they'll be with their dad, and they'll get certain things from their dad and won't that be nice, and he won't have to worry about his hours—but then it starts creeping into other areas that you didn't have any way of knowing it was going to have an impact. When he began to raise issues about the kids or check in on them at school when they were sick, I thought, 'Well, that's my job, what are you talking about that for?' or, 'Oh my god. I didn't notice that!' Where did he get the intuitive sense to know what needed to be done? It wasn't there before. A whole lot of visible things happened.

Increased sensitivity on the part of the fathers, and their enhanced competence as parents, was typically evaluated by adopting a vocabulary of motives and feelings similar to the mothers', created and sustained through an ongoing dialogue about the children: a dialogue that grew out of the routine childcare practices. Another mother described how her husband had 'the right temperament' for parenting, but had to learn how to notice the little things that she felt her daughters needed:

> When it comes to the two of us as parents, I feel that my husband's parenting skills are probably superior to mine, just because of his calm rationale. But maybe that's not what little girls need all the time. He doesn't tend to be the one that tells them how gorgeous they look when they dress up, which they really like, and I see these things, I see when they're putting in a little extra effort. He's getting better as we grow in our relationship, as the kids grow in their relationship with him.

Like many fathers in this study, this one was characterized as developing sensitivity to the children by relying on interactions with his wife. She 'sees things' which he has to learn to recognize. Thus, while he may have 'superior' parenting skills, he must learn something subtle from her. His reliance on her expertise suggests that his 'calm rationale' is insufficient to make him 'maternal' in the way that she is. Her ability to notice things, and his inattention to them, serves to render them both accountable: parenting remains an essential part of her nature, but is a learned capacity for him. Couples talked about fathers being socialized, as adults, to become nurturing parents. This talking with their wives about childcare helped husbands construct and sustain images of themselves as competent fathers.

Greater paternal competence was also reported to enhance marital interaction. Fathers were often characterized as paying increased attention to emotional cues from their wives and engaging in more reciprocal communication. Taking responsibility for routine household labour offered some men the opportunity to better understand their mother's lives as well. For instance, one involved father who did most of the housework suggested that he could sometimes derive pleasure from cleaning the bathroom or picking up a sock if he looked at it as an act of caring for his family:

> It makes it a different job, to place it in a context of being an expression of caring about a collective life together. It's at that moment that I'm maybe closest to understanding what my mother and other women of my mother's generation, and other women now, have felt about being housewives and being at home, being themselves. I think I emotionally understand the satisfaction and the gratification of being a homemaker.

More frequently, however, sharing childcare and housework helped fathers understand its drudgery. One father who is employed as a carpenter explained how assuming more responsibility for housework motivated him to encourage his wife to buy whatever she needs to make housework easier.

> It was real interesting when I started doing more housework. Being in construction, when I needed a tool, I bought the tool. And when I vacuum floors, I look at this piece of shit, I mean I can't vacuum the floor with this and feel good about it, it's not doing a good job. So I get a good vacuum system. So I have more appreciation for housecleaning. When I clean the tubs, I want something that is going to clean the tubs; I don't want to work extra hard. You know I have a kind of sponge to use for cleaning the tubs. So I have more of an appreciation for what she had to do. I tell her 'If you know of something that's going to make it easier, let's get it.'

Most sample fathers reported that performance of childcare, in and of itself, increased their commitment to both parenting and housework. All of the fathers had been involved in some housework before the birth of their children, but many indicated that their awareness and performance of housework increased in conjunction with their involvement in parenting. They reported that as they spent more time in the house alone with their children, they assumed more responsibility for cooking and cleaning. Fathers also noted that as they became more involved in the daily aspects of parenting, and in the face of their wives' absence and relinquishment of total responsibility for housekeeping, they became more aware that certain tasks needed doing and they were more likely to perform them. This was conditioned by the amount of time fathers spent on the job, but more than half reported that they increased their contributions to household labour when their children were under 10 years old. This did not always mean that fathers' relative proportion of household tasks increased, because mothers were also doing more in response to an expanding total household workload.

Gender Attributions

Approximately half of both mothers and fathers volunteered that men and women brought something unique to childcare, and many stressed that they did not consider their own parenting skills to be identical to those of their spouse. One mother whose husband had recently increased the amount of time he spent with their school-aged children commented: 'Anybody can slap together a cream cheese and cucumber sandwich and a glass of milk and a few chips and call it lunch, but the ability to see that your child is troubled about something, or to be able to help them work through a conflict with a friend, that is really much different.' A list-making mother who provided less childcare and did less housework than her husband described herself as 'more intimate and gentle', and her husband as 'rough and out there'. Like many others she emphasized that mothers and fathers provide 'a balance' for their children. She described how she had to come to terms with her expectations that her husband would 'mother' the way that she did:

> One of the things that I found I was expecting from him when he started doing so much here and I was gone so much, I was expecting him to mother the kids. And you know, I had to get over that one pretty quick and really accept him doing the things the way he did them as his way, and that being just fine with me. He wasn't mothering the kids, he was fathering the kids. It was just that he was [in] the role of the mother as far as the chores and all that stuff.

A mother who managed and performed most of the housework and childcare used different reasoning to make similar claims about essential differences between women and men. In contrast to the mothers quoted above, this mother suggested that men could nurture, but not perform daily childcare:

> Nurturance is one thing, actual care is another thing. I think if a father had to—like all of a sudden the wife was gone, he could nurture it with the love that it needed. But he might not change the diapers often enough, or he might not give 'em a bath often enough and he might not think of the perfect food to feed. But as far as nurturing, I think he's capable of caring . . . If the situation is the mother is there and he didn't have to, then he would trust the woman to.

This mother concluded, 'The woman has it more in her genes to be more equipped for nurturing.' Thus many of the manager–helper couples legitimated their divisions of labour and reaffirmed the 'naturalness' of essential gender differences.

Parents who equally shared the responsibility for direct and indirect childcare, on the other hand, were more likely to see similarities in their relationships with their children. They all reported that their children were emotionally 'close' to both parents. When asked who his children went to when they were hurt or upset, one early- and equal-sharing father commented: 'They'll go to either of us, that is pretty indistinguishable.' Mothers and fathers who equally shared most direct childcare reported that their children typically called for the parent with whom they had most recently spent time, and frequently called her mother 'daddy' or the father 'mommy,' using the gendered form to signify 'parent'. Most often, parents indicated that their children would turn to 'whoever's closest' or 'whoever they've been with', thus linking physical closeness with emotional closeness. In-home observations of family interactions confirmed such reports.

The central feature of these and other parental accounts is that shared activities formed an emotional connection between parent and child. Shared activities were also instrumental in constructing images of fathers as competent, nurturing caregivers. Two-thirds of both mothers and fathers expressed the belief that men could care for children's emotional needs as well as women. When asked whether men, in general, could nurture like women, mothers used their husbands as examples. One said, 'I don't necessarily think that that skill comes with a sex type. Some women nurture better than others, some men nurture better than other men. I think that those skills can come when either person is willing to have the confidence and commitment to prioritize them.'

However, the parents who were the most successful at sharing childcare were the most likely to claim that men could nurture like women. Those who sustained manager–helper dynamics in childcare tended to invoke the images of 'maternal instincts' and alluded to natural differences between men and women. In contrast, more equal divisions of household labour were typically accompanied by an ideology of gender similarity rather than gender difference. The direction of causality is twofold: (1) those who believed that men could nurture like women seriously attempted to share all aspects of childcare, and (2) the successful practice of sharing childcare facilitated the development of beliefs that men could nurture like women.

Normalizing Atypical Behaviour

Mothers and fathers reported that women friends, most of whom were in more traditional marriages or were single, idealized their shared-parenting arrangements. About two-thirds of sample mothers reported that their women friends told them that they were extremely fortunate, and labelled their husbands 'wonderful', 'fantastic', 'incredible', or otherwise out of the ordinary. Some mothers said that women friends were 'jealous', 'envious', or 'amazed', and that they 'admired' and 'supported' their efforts at sharing domestic chores.

Both mothers and fathers said that the father received more credit for his family involvement than the mother did, because it was expected that she would perform childcare and housework. Since parenting is assumed to be 'only natural' for women, fathers were frequently praised for performing a task that would go unnoticed if a mother had performed it:

> I think I get less praise because people automatically assume that, you know, the mother's supposed to do the childcare. And he gets a lot of praise because he's the visible one. Oh, I think that he gets far more praise. I can bust my butt at that school and all he has to do is show up in the parking lot and everybody's all gah gah over him. I don't get resentful about that—I think it's funny and I think it's sad.

While the fathers admitted that they enjoyed such praise, many indicated that they did not take these direct or implied compliments very seriously.

> I get more credit than she does, because it's so unusual that the father's at home and involved in the family. I realize what it is: it's prejudice. The strokes feel real nice, but I don't take them too seriously. I'm sort of proud of it in a way that I don't really like. It's nothing to be proud of, except that I'm glad to be doing it and I think it's kind of neat because it hasn't been the style traditionally. I kind of like that, but I know that it means nothing.

These comments reveal that fathers appreciated praise, but actively discounted compliments received from those in dissimilar situations. The fathers' everyday parenting experiences led them to view parenthood as drudgery as well as fulfillment. They described their sense of parental responsibility as taken-for-granted and did not consider it to be out of the ordinary or something worthy of special praise. Fathers sometimes reported being puzzled by compliments from their wives' acquaintances and judged them to be inappropriate. When I asked one what kinds of reactions he received when his children were infants, he said,

> They all thought it was really wonderful. They thought she'd really appreciate how wonderful it was and how different that was for her to father. They'd say, 'You ought to

know how lucky you are, he's doing so much.' I just felt like I'm doing what any person should do. Just like shouldn't anybody be this interested in their child? No big deal.

Another father said he resented all the special attention he received when he was out with his infant son:

> Constant going shopping and having women stop me and say 'Oh it's so good to see you fathers.' I was no longer an individual: I was this generic father who was now a liberated father who could take care of his child. I actually didn't like it. I felt after a while that I wanted the time and the quality of my relationship with my child at that point, what was visible in public, to simply be accepted as what you do. It didn't strike me as worthy of recognition, and it pissed me off a lot that women in particular would show this sort of appreciation, which I think is well-intentioned, but which also tended to put a frame around the whole thing as though somehow this was an experience that could be extracted from one's regular life. It wasn't. It was going shopping with my son in a snuggly or on the backpack was what I was doing. It wasn't somehow this event that always had to be called attention to.

Thus fathers discounted and normalized extreme reactions to their divisions of labour and interpreted them in a way that supported the 'natural' character of what they were doing.

One mother commented on a pattern that was typically mentioned by both parents: domestic divisions of labour were 'normal' to those who were attempting something similar, and 'amazing' to those who were not: 'All the local friends here think it's amazing. They call him "Mr Mom" and tell me how lucky I am. I'm waiting for someone to tell him how lucky he is. I have several friends at work who have very similar arrangements and they just feel that it's normal.'

Because fathers assumed traditional mothering functions, they often had more social contact with mothers than with other fathers. They talked about being the only fathers at children's lessons, parent classes and meetings, at the laundromat, or in the market. One father said it took mothers there a while before they believed he really shared a range of household tasks.

> At first they ask me, 'Is this your day off?' And I say, 'If it's the day off for me, why isn't it the day off for you?' 'Well, I work 24 hours a day!' And I say, 'Yeah, right. I got my wash done and hung out and the beds made.' It takes the mother a couple of times to realize that I really do that stuff.

In general, fathers resisted attempts by other people to compare them to traditional fathers, and often compared themselves directly to their wives, or to other mothers.

Fathers tended to be employed in occupations predominantly composed of men, and in those settings were often discouraged from talking about family or children. Several fathers reported that people at their place of employment could not understand why they did 'women's work', and a few mentioned that co-workers would be disappointed when they would repeatedly turn down invitations to go out 'with the boys' for a drink. One of three self-employed carpenters in the study said that he would sometimes conceal that he was leaving work to do something with his children because he worried about negative reactions from employers or co-workers:

> I would say reactions that we've got—in business, like if I leave a job somewhere that I'm on and mention that I'm going to coach

soccer, my son's soccer game, yeah. I have felt people kind of stiffen, like, I was more shirking my job, you know, such a small thing to leave work for, getting home, racing home for. I got to the point with some people where I didn't necessarily mention what I was leaving for, just because I didn't need for them to think that I was being irresponsible about their work, I mean, I just decided it wasn't their business. If I didn't know them well enough to feel that they were supportive. I would just say, 'I have to leave early today'—never lie, if they asked me a question. I'd tell them the answer—but not volunteer it. And, maybe in some cases, I feel like, you know, you really have to be a little careful about being too groovy too, that what it is that you're doing is just so wonderful. 'I'm a father, I'm going to go be with my children.' It isn't like that, you know. I don't do it for what people think of me; I do it because I enjoy it.

Some fathers said co-workers perceived their talk of spending time with their children as indications that they were not 'serious' about their work. They reported receiving indirect messages that providing for the family was primary and being with the family was secondary. Fathers avoided negative workplace sanctions by selectively revealing the extent of their family involvement.

Many fathers selected their current jobs because the work schedule was flexible, or so they could take time off to care for their children. For instance, even though most fathers worked full-time, two-thirds had some daytime hours off, as exemplified by teachers, mail carriers, and self-employed carpenters. Similarly, most fathers avoided extra work-related tasks or overtime hours in order to maximize time spent with their children. One computer technician said that he was prepared to accept possible imputations of non-seriousness:

I kind of tend to choose my jobs. When I go to a job interview, I explain to people that I have a family and the family's very important to me. Some companies expect you to work a lot of overtime or work weekends, and I told them that I don't have to accept that sort of thing. I may not have gotten all the jobs I ever might have had because of it, but it's something that I bring up at the job interview and let them know that my family comes first.

The same father admitted that it is sometimes a 'blessing' that his wife works evenings at a local hospital, because it allows him to justify leaving his job on time:

At five o'clock or five-thirty at night, when there are a lot of people that are still going to be at work for an hour or two more. I go 'Adios!' [laughs]. I mean, I can't stay. I've gotta pick up the kids. And there are times when I feel real guilty about leaving my fellow workers behind when I know they're gonna be there for another hour or so. About a block from work I go 'God, this is great!' [laughs].

Over half of the study participants also indicated that their own mothers or fathers reacted negatively to their divisions of labour. Parents were described as 'confused', 'bemused', and 'befuddled', and it was said that they 'lack understanding' or 'think it's a little strange'. One mother reported that her parents and in-laws wouldn't 'dare to criticize' their situation because 'times have changed', but she sensed their underlying worry and concern:

I think both sides of the family think it's fine because it's popular now. They don't dare—I mean if we were doing this 30 years ago, they would dare to criticize. In a way, now they don't. I think both sides feel it's a little

> strange. I thought my mom was totally sympathetic and no problem, but when I was going to go away for a week and my husband was going to take care of the kids, she said something to my sister about how she didn't think I should do it. There's a little underlying tension about it, I think.

Other study participants reported that disagreements with parents were common, particularly if they revolved around trying to change child-rearing practices their own parents had used.

Many couples reported that initial negative reactions from parents turned more positive over time as they saw that the children were 'turning out all right', that the couple was still together after an average of 10 years, and that the men were still employed. This last point, that parents were primarily concerned with their son's or son-in-law's provider responsibilities, highlights how observers typically evaluated the couple's task sharing. A number of study participants mentioned that they thought their parents wanted the wife to quit work and stay home with the children and that the husband should 'make up the difference'. Most mentioned, however, that parents were more concerned that the husband continue to be the provider than they were that the wife made 'extra money' or that the husband 'helped out' at home.

> In the beginning there was a real strong sense that I was in the space of my husband's duty. That came from his parents pretty strongly. The only way that they have been able to come to grips with this in any fashion is because he has also been financially successful. If he had decided, you know, 'Outside work is not for me, I'm going to stay home with the kids and she's going to work', I think there would have been a whole lot more talk than there was. I think it's because he did both and was successful that it was okay.

Another mother noted that parental acceptance of shared parenting did not necessarily entail acceptance of the woman as provider:

> There is a funny dynamic that happens. It's not really about childcare, where I don't think in our families—with our parents—I don't get enough credit for being the breadwinner. Well they're still critical of him for not earning as much money as I do. In a way they've accepted him as being an active parenting father more than they've accepted me being a breadwinner.

Here again, the 'essential nature' of men is taken to be that of provider. If the men remain providers, they are still accountable as men, even if they take an active part in childcare.

Discussion

This brief exploration into the social construction of shared parenting in 20 dual-earner families illustrates how more equal, domestic gender relations arise and under what conditions they flourish. All couples described flexible and practical task-allocation procedures that were responses to shortages of time. All families were child-centred in that they placed a high value on their children's well-being, defined parenting as an important and serious undertaking, and organized most of their non-employed time around their children. Besides being well-educated and delaying child-bearing until their late twenties or early thirties, couples who shared most of the responsibility for household labour tended to involve the father in routine childcare from the children's early infancy. As Sara Ruddick (1982) has noted, the everyday aspects of child-care and housework help share ways of thinking, feeling, and acting that become associated with what it means to be a mother. My findings suggest that when domestic activities are equally shared, 'maternal thinking' develops in fathers, too, and the social meaning of gender begins to change. This de-emphasizes notions of gender as personality and locates it in social interaction.

To treat gender as the 'cause' of household division of labour overlooks its emergent character and fails to acknowledge how it is in fact implicated in precisely such routine practices.

References

Berk, S.F. 1985. *The Gender Factory* (New York: Plenum).

Ruddick, S. 1982. 'Maternal Thinking', in *Rethinking the Family,* eds B. Thorne and M. Yalom (New York: Longman), 76–94.

West, C., and D.H. Zimmerman. 1987. 'Doing Gender', *Gender & Society* 1: 125–51.

Chapter 24

Gillian Dunne is one of a number of researchers who has examined the lives of lesbian couples. In this chapter from her book *Lesbian Lifestyles*, Dunne describes the patterns in the households of 60 lesbian women living with their partners in the 1990s. Dunne discusses the egalitarian relationships these women had, and explores the various factors that the women cited to explain the shared allocations of their household work. In so doing, she highlights characteristics of many heterosexual relationships that are related to the gender inequalities in them, especially those related to their division of work based on gender. Dunne's findings are rich with insight about the various factors that affect how couples organize their lives together—especially the material and emotional sources of power in many relationships.

Lesbians at Home: Why Can't a Man Be More Like a Woman?

Gillian A. Dunne

. . . Within the context of institutional heterosexuality, women and men are drawn into relationships with each other as socially, symbolically, and materially different persons. Their relationships are negotiated with reference to a framework of materially shaped, pre-existing gender scripts which guide interaction. Informing these differential scripts are dominant beliefs about the complementarity of feminine and masculine identities (Pateman 1988: 140; Connell 1987: 248; Rubin 1975: 178). Practices and ideologies which reinforce gender difference, for example, the undervaluing of women's occupational skills and an employment structure which denies the time and emotional component of men's home life and parental responsibilities, place constraints on the extent to which women and men can operationalize more egalitarian ideals. The analysis of lesbian partnerships is important because it provides visions of divisions of household and market labour which are not structured by dichotomous gender scripts.

This chapter will draw on respondents' accounts of their approaches to and experience of relationships. We are interested in ways that both *similarities* based upon their shared structural positioning within gender hierarchies and *differences*, derived from other sources of inequality, are manifested and managed between women. We begin by illustrating ways in which respondents perceived their partnerships with women differing from their experience and/or understandings of heterosexual relationships. The discussion will then move on to consider some potential sources of inequality and conflict, such as money, home ownership, and emotional commitment. This will be followed by an outline of divisions of labour in lesbian households. The chapter will conclude with a consideration of some employment consequences which respondents felt arose out of the context of their more egalitarian relationships which valued 'co-independence' rather than dependency.

Lesbianism and Egalitarianism

There is a small but growing body of North American research on lesbian relationships (for example, Weston 1991; Johnson 1990), some of which compares the experience of lesbian, gay, and heterosexual couples (Blumstein and Schwartz 1985; 1990; Caldwell and Peplau 1984; Peplau and Cochran 1990; Peplau et al. 1978). In her review of these relatively large-scale comparative studies, Lindsey (1990: 152) concludes that egalitarian arrangements are more likely to be valued and achieved in lesbian partnerships.

Peplau and Cochran's study (1990) found that lesbians, followed closely by heterosexual women, were much more likely to value egalitarianism than any of the men interviewed. In fact, 97 per cent of lesbians said that ideally partnerships should be 'exactly equal' in terms of power, and 59 per cent thought they had achieved this, which was the highest percentage of all the couple forms interviewed (339).[1] Lesbians also tended to be the least tolerant of inequalities in their partnerships, and this usually applied to both partners (Blumstein and Schwartz 1985: 61). When relationships were perceived as unequal they were more likely to report dissatisfaction (Caldwell and Peplau 1984: 598) and were less likely to be together for follow-up interviews (Peplau and Cochran 1990; Blumstein and Schwartz 1985: 310).

Feelings that relationships conform to a more egalitarian model appear to be a crucial dimension to enduring lesbian relationships. This is borne out in Johnson's (1990) excellent in-depth study of 108 long-term lesbian couples whose relationships ranged from 10 to 52 years in length. Johnson found that feelings of being in a partnership of equals were essential for most of her interviewees (120). A common belief was that their relationships allowed them to realize their egalitarian ideals in such a way as would not be possible in heterosexual relationships, which they tended to view as 'innately unequal' (120). Egalitarian ideals appeared to underpin couples' decision-making process, with 90 per cent reporting that they had an equal say (120–8). In terms of influence, Johnson found that 81 per cent of the sample felt that the balance of their partnerships was equally weighted (125).

These studies seem to indicate that lesbian women are comfortable neither with dominating nor with being dominated in their partnerships with each other. Longevity in relationships appears to be more usually contingent on partners having negotiated a satisfactory balance of power. Alternatively, sustained inequalities seem to give rise to high levels of dissatisfaction and contribute to the eventual downfall of a partnership.

An important question raised by this work is why issues of equality occupy such a central position in women's lesbian relationships. Peplau and Cochran (1990: 339) take us some distance toward understanding this when they suggest that many lesbians have access to feminist analyses and may therefore be more sensitive to the operation of power. We now turn to our own data to see if we can take this understanding a step further.

'Scripting' Gender Inequality

When respondents were asked if they could identify ways in which their relationships with women differed from heterosexual ones, the overwhelming response, volunteered in 53 cases, was that relationships with women were 'more equal'. The degree of certainty expressed was usually related to the amount of experience they had had of relationships with men, with those who had been married appearing the most confident in their assessment. What was actually meant by this was not immediately evident. However, as we will see in their commentaries, it is clear that respondents were sensitive to circumstances which supported relations of domination—between women and men, and among women. This was manifested through their adherence to an egalitarian perspective as an ideal or a political principle, which appeared to be constructed around notions of individual autonomy. Lesbian relationships, in contrast to their understandings of heterosexual relationships, were viewed as having the potential for realizing these objectives. We now briefly illustrate the main differentiating features they perceived between lesbian and heterosexual relationships, which together led them to this conclusion.

There were two main aspects of heterosexual relationships which were understood by respondents to pre-empt an egalitarian outcome. The first, and most obvious, was related to their belief that women and men do not share 'equality of conditions'. In other words, there exist structural inequalities between them. For example, men's access to greater economic power was seen to support and reinforce their ability to dominate their partners. Ursula explains:

> I just see that there is very little equality in heterosexual relationships in like the definition of a man and a woman, the man is the one with the power. There is no definition of who takes the lead or the power in a lesbian relationship . . . It is in 99 per cent of the cases the man that will earn more money, he will make all the decisions—well, most of the decisions . . . (19)

A second important differentiating feature was related to the gendered assumptions guiding the actual operation of heterosexual relationships. . . . [T]hose who had experienced relationships with men usually identified 'heterosexual role play' as a major medium of constraint on self-determination. This role play was perceived as a taken-for-granted practice whereby gender inequalities were intentionally or (most importantly) *unintentionally* translated into everyday actions, expectations, and outcomes.

When looking back on their relationships with men, heterosexual role play was understood by many respondents to have subtly controlled their behaviour. Valerie, a divorced woman who had recently 'come out', explains:

> Well [lesbian relationships] are just so much more relaxed, there's no obligation to fulfill a role, you make your own. You make your own position comfortable that fits round you, whereas, I mean in most heterosexual relationships, there's no way that people can ignore the set roles, the set expectations, and it's restricting. (43)

Sheila contrasts her lesbian relationship with her previous marriage, and highlights the consequences of adhering to heterosexual role play for decision-making:

> I feel more equal, I don't feel that I could leave all the decisions up to [my lover] or need to. Whereas with [my husband] I did, and I think in many ways I was happy to leave the decisions up to him, because that was what I saw as his role . . . [Relationships with women are] very much more fulfilling in that I feel like a person in my own right rather than an accessory. And I think I felt very much as an accessory when I was married. (45)

Roxanne describes some consequences of this 'role play' for women's and men's approaches to domestic tasks:

> I have never found that I am toeing the line with men . . . But I had been having to fight battles of role play. Like doing the dishes and just taking on those sorts of roles naturally. In my experience, if there are dishes there waiting to be done, it will occur to a woman to do it, but it won't occur to a man. So you would always be the one saying, 'Wash up.' I just couldn't cope with that side of things. Sounds a bit crazy, but it will just be too much for me. It will be the little 'niggly' things, which would become big, and then it gets out of hand . . . And they don't arise now. (27)

Women taking the bulk of responsibility for trying to break down gender boundaries and for constructing more egalitarian conditions in their relationships with men has been commented upon in research. For example, Statham's (1986: 168) study of 'non-sexist' couples, found that it was her female respondents who had to remind their husbands to do their share in the home. Gordon's (1990) study of feminist mothers in Finland echoes these problems. She makes an interesting point about the role of same-sex reference groups: her respondents' more egalitarian male partners compared themselves favourably with other men but their contributions often fell short of their partner's ideal (97). My respondents often spoke of the energy and disappointment involved in their attempts to expand gender roles in their relationships with men. For these women, being in a relationship with a woman with a similar agenda and view of the world was a major reason for their enthusiasm about lesbian relationships.

A central reason for respondents' sensitivity to heterosexual role play was their experience of entering relationships which simply lacked roles based on reciprocal gender expectations. The absence of scripts based on gender difference has been mentioned in other research on lesbian couples (Blumstein and Schwartz 1985: 153; Peplau and Cochran 1990: 342). Yvonne sums up the feelings of many of my respondents:

> Like I say before, it is more equal. There aren't any stereotypical images like in a man/woman relationship, it's something that is so dependent on the two different people. You just form the relationship that is between yourselves, if you know what I mean. There is nothing that [tells you]—this is what you should do, or this is what you shouldn't do and stuff. It's something that just clicks and every relationship is formed, and it is totally different from another one, 'cos it's just how the two people in the relationship make it. There is nothing there at the beginning to influence thoughts on how things should be done. (24)

Importantly, the absence of prescribed roles based on notions of gender difference was seen as emancipating, because this situation expanded choices and enabled greater creativity in the negotiation process between women. This is explained by Harriet:

> One of the things that struck me in my first lesbian relationship was the fact that there weren't any role models. I couldn't go and see a film on how to live. It meant that I was really free to do it the way I wanted to. I was uncluttered by images of how I should be doing it. I could more easily choose what I did want, in a way, without having to go against anything . . . If I had got married to [my boyfriend] there would have been loads of stuff telling me how I should have been behaving. [*Why do you think this is a positive situation?*] It may be easier to fit into prescribed roles, because they are there without you having to think and you can fall into them. I think they must oppress both people actually, because it is much better if you can have the confidence to do everything in a relationship. (35)

The lack of taken-for-granted guidelines for conducting relationships presented those involved with a 'problem to be solved'.[2] It seems that women negotiating lesbian relationships have to engage in an unusual amount of creativity, and this requires reflection upon and evaluation of what constitutes interpersonal relationships. The flexibility offered in lesbian relationships was understood to provide a context within which women could more easily operate on egalitarian ideals. This is not to say that respondents were unaware of the inequalities between women and the potential this had for creating power imbalances in the relationship. Daniella discusses this:

> Well, I mean I don't have any sort of romantic or idealized notions about relationships with

women. I think they are really hard. But I also think that there's obviously going to be power differences, and power imbalances, but I think there's a far greater chance of working them out. (25)

An important reason for the belief that power imbalances could be 'worked out' between women was that there was no clear overriding power dynamic shaping the relationship. This is discussed by Elspeth:

I think there are lots of power factors. She sometimes had power because she was older, I sometimes because I was younger. She sometimes had power because she had money, I because I was an academic. There were lots of power factors, none of which were overriding . . . Fluctuating power but no wild fluctuations, with a middle line of equality. (23)

In describing their relationships as 'more equal', respondents were talking about a range of features which were often constructed as the converse of their understandings of the operation of heterosexual relationships. They believed that within lesbian relationships they could exercise greater self-determination and experience relative freedom from domination.

The definition of power is a contested area in sociology.[3] Rather than entering into these sociological debates, my intention here is to consider my respondents' understandings of the different forms which they perceived power to take. The important point to make here is that these women were often conscious of potential power imbalances generated in interpersonal relationships. I therefore wish to place a focus on the ways that this awareness informed their approaches to relationships.

It has been implicit in respondents' accounts . . . in the remainder of this chapter that they were usually conscious of both the positive and negative effects of power. First, they were aware of the enabling aspects of power; ways that, for instance, access to economic power expanded their ability to be self-determining, to make choices over the conditions of their lives and in particular their relationships.[4] Second, they were aware of a range of negative ways in which power operated as a constraint upon themselves and others. They saw power expressed through structures of inequality. In terms of interpersonal relationships (heterosexual and lesbian), they associated, for example, excessive economic imbalances with providing a dependency context which allowed the higher-earning partner to exercise, intentionally or unintentionally, greater control over the conditions of that relationship.

Their recognition of the operation of power, however, extended beyond structural sources to include various 'belief systems' shaping everyday practices. One major source of this awareness was perhaps generated by their experience of simply being lesbians and having to face the contradiction between broader social definitions of them as sexual 'deviants' and 'unnatural', and their own positive experience of their sexuality. A main component of the often lengthy process of 'coming out' is coming to terms with this contradiction. To view one's sexuality positively requires the recognition that dominant beliefs can be fundamentally wrong, and for many respondents this insight was viewed as empowering. Gillian explains how coming to terms with her sexuality encouraged a more critical perspective:

[My sexuality] has been very empowering and it shook me out of my middle-class marriage slot into just thinking about the ways things worked and into thinking about power structures and conditioning. It just made me think, and I don't think you can be a real person without this. Certainly society is out to stick people into little boxes and that means keeping them heterosexual . . .

> Keeping the myths and brutalizing men in such a way as to make them 'men'. It gives you a sort of understanding . . . of what is going on. But you have to be on the wrong end of the power structure . . . So, yes, if you are a lesbian you notice the power structure against you and you have more understanding in an experiential way. (23)

Another aspect of being positioned outside 'institutionalized heterosexuality' was that they felt they became more aware of how power worked negatively (their value judgment) through taken-for-granted ideas about the ways that women and men should interact with each other. Eva discusses this:

> I think there's definitely a difference . . . I've had very equal relationships with women. When I see some of the relationships that straight female friends have had with men! But mostly, a lot of the time they don't see anything wrong with it, because it is what everyone around them is doing . . . [They are] accepting what to me appear to be horrendous imbalances . . . One friend goes home, a nine-hour day at work and, the usual thing, prepares the meal and looks after the house and everything, and he just sits there and tells all his friends what a slob she is, and all this kind of thing. But how, how, how . . . can we try to, to point this out to people, to other women? (25)

The inequalities that emerge through enacting heterosexual roles were often seen to be obscured from the view of participants (themselves included) because of the power of dominant ideologies which tend to naturalize and justify them. Here I am reminded of Lukes's (1974) 'three dimensional view of power'. He argues:

> [I]s it not the supreme and most insidious exercise of power to prevent people, to whatever degree, from having grievances by shaping their perceptions, cognitions, and preferences in such a way that they accept their role in the existing order of things, either because they can see or imagine no alternative to it, or because they see it as natural and unchangeable, or because they value it as divinely ordained and beneficial? (24)

There are no similar ideas that can be mobilized to naturalize and justify one woman's domination of her female partner, and so relations that involve domination will be more visible and perhaps less readily accepted. From respondents' discussions of their interpersonal relationships, it was apparent that their egalitarian position extended to include a general uneasiness about being in a situation of dominance over a partner. Déidre illustrates this:

> One thing I am, I'd say, I am one for equality. I don't believe anybody should dominate anyone in a relationship. The reason I like relationships with women is because the equality is there. You help each other. You know, one doesn't tell the other more, 'cos I don't like being dominated. (27)

This situation may be reinforced by the empathy derived from a lesbian's ability to place herself in the position of her partner, which is illustrated by Catherine in this next extract:

> I think there must be [a difference between lesbian and heterosexual relationships] because as a woman I would hate to be treated the way a man might treat a woman—this domineering thing. And I would never dream of doing to somebody what I would hate to have done to myself. (24)

Lesbians' sensitivity to the operation of power may provide a more conscious awareness of its abuse by self and others and, as we will see later, may lead to the development of 'damage limitation' strategies.

All these factors may inform the negotiation process between women and, because a more balanced outcome is likely to be in both their interests, their more flexible relationships make it easier to achieve.[5] Consequently, it is perfectly reasonable to assume that lesbians' home lives are more equal than the heterosexual norm, and this raises key questions. First, what impact do other sources of inequality have on their relationships? Second, what do divisions of labour look like in the absence of gender difference to shape task allocation and approaches to employment? The next two sections will explore these questions.

The Operation of an 'Egalitarian Ideal'

We now shift the discussion forward a little and explore respondents' accounts of their relationships with women to see how far their concerns about self-determination, egalitarianism as an ideal, and sensitivity to power were translated into practice. We will focus on some areas of potential inequality, such as economic inequality, unilateral home ownership, and emotional commitment, which may mediate the structural similarities women share with each other on the basis of gender.

Money Matters

Another point raised in the studies outlined earlier is that the ability to dominate a partner in relationships between women tends to be less contingent on access to economic and educational power than is the case for heterosexual partnerships. Peplau and Cochran (1990: 340) point out that economic factors may not be as relevant in lesbian relationships as access to other resources, such as status within the lesbian community. They suggest that domination in lesbian and gay relationships may be far more related to the degree of emotional commitment each partner invests in the relationship. A partner who feels greater emotional dependency will tend to have less power in a relationship. Johnson (1990: 127) suggests that, for her long-term couples, domination was more likely to be the result of the personality differences, rather than age or income differentials. Blumstein and Schwartz go as far as to say that 'lesbians do not use income to establish dominance in their relationship. They use it to avoid having one woman dependent on the other' (1985: 60). It is important to remember that most lesbian couples of employment age are and expect to be in 'dual-worker' relationships, and it is rare to find examples of one partner being financially dependent on another (Weston 1991: 149; Peplau and Cochran 1990: 344; Johnson 1990: 108; Blumstein and Schwartz 1985).

It is important not to dismiss the significance of economics in the power equation. If, as the above studies suggest, there is a tendency for money to be less important in establishing power relations then this is quite an accomplishment. My research and that of others would suggest that this is an outcome of a process whereby women have actively sought to avoid being in situations where financial imbalances are too extreme. This is implied by Blumstein and Schwartz's (1985) discussion of financial arrangements in lesbian households:

> sharing financial responsibilities equally, neither partner becoming dependent on the other, were common goals we heard from lesbians. When a relationship was seen as out of balance—with one woman contributing less to household bills than the other—it was disturbing to both partners. Each expressed a strong dislike of such a potential for power imbalance. (61)

Blumstein and Schwartz's observation suggests that the women interviewed were well aware of the *unintentional* consequences of economic imbalances. This is very much related to women's sensitivity to the power derived from money which may influence dealings between them. My respondents were well aware of the negative (constraining) and the positive (enabling) dimensions of economic power. They had often viewed the negative aspects of this power in their family of origin and/or experienced it in relationships with men. All recognized the positive aspects of economic power because it provided their independence. For these reasons, amongst others, respondents tended to value financial self-sufficiency and reject economic dependence. Thus, where possible, they actively avoided, or created strategies to offset the impact of, excessive economic inequality in their partnerships. We now briefly illustrate this argument with some examples of respondents' views on economic dependency, before moving on to explore ways that finances were organized between women.

The importance of financial independence

An emphasis on 'co-independence' was an important feature of lesbian partnerships amongst respondents interviewed. My respondents valued their financial independence and were very unwilling to become dependent on a partner for the maintenance of their standard of living. Respondents felt that economic dependency would tip the balance of power to an intolerable degree. As we will see, they thought that financial dependency would set up undesirable relations of reciprocity, for example sexual and/or domestic, and would lead to difficulties in terminating a relationship.

Nicola discusses the way she associates financial dependency with inequality and the need to repay in kind through sexual services:

> I couldn't handle [being financially dependent on a partner] at all . . . I just think that I really like to be autonomous and have my own money to spend as I want. And if the person I was with was supporting me, I really wouldn't like that . . . I'd feel too dependent . . . I think that I would feel that I owed them something, either sexually or I don't think it would be an equal partnership and I am not into that sort of thing. I would want it to be equal. (19)

For Elaine economic dependence was seen to foster an unequal division of labour:

> I think the price might be intellectual stagnation . . . and to, in fact, become the very kind of housewife that I have no wish to become. Because by virtue of being at home all day, it's very easy to slip into the old role models: 'You're at home all day, I am going out to work, where's my tea? Why isn't the house clean?' (37)

Even when a woman hated her job, she did not wish to exchange her economic independence for dependency. This was the case for Lillian, who worked all her life in a series of low-paid clerical jobs:

> [Once a woman offered to keep me] I was horrified that some person would keep me. I mean, I don't like work, but there is no way I would let anyone keep me. [*What do you think it would mean to be kept by someone?*] It would mean you would have to be there for them sort of, you know what I mean, you'd feel obliged to do things for them—whether it's doing washing up, or, you know, dropping your knickers. (45)

Importantly, financial dependency was seen to trap individuals in their relationship. Henrietta explains this:

> I would hate it, absolutely hate [being economically dependent on a partner].

> [*Why?*] I really think it would affect the power balance in the relationship, if I was spending somebody else's money. I would hate not to have my own money, or my means for leaving a relationship. Because I think a relationship can only be truly equal if both people can know they can get out of it. And it would be very difficult to get out of it if I was dependent financially on somebody. So I always have to be able to be alone in order to be happy with someone else. (35)

A similar feeling comes from Jocelyn, a professional woman, who has been in a relationship for five years with a partner in a manual occupation:

> [Financial independence is important]. I wouldn't give up my own bank account and I wouldn't want [my partner] to do that. And I also wouldn't want [my partner] to not work, and I wouldn't want me to not work. I think if ever it happens that either of us didn't work, say if we decided to have children or something like that, then I would think it was important that we would both get back to it. Largely because of economic independence, but also to do with [having] a feeling of contributing . . . My fear is—and it's not just for me, but from [my partner's] point of view too—I would hate to see one of us in a situation where I have seen a lot of [married] women, where they can't make the break and do what they really want to do because they don't have economic independence. (27)

Respondents who had been married were often the most fervent in their rejection of economic dependency, as is illustrated by Isabelle, a divorced clerical worker:

> [*Do you see yourself as a lifelong worker?*] Yes, I never want, I never ever want to be kept. I don't want to be a kept woman at all, no way! (29)

Overall, respondents believed that being totally or partially dependent on a partner for their standard of living would be difficult. Some had experienced this in their relationships with men and were unwilling to reproduce this kind of power dynamic unintentionally into their relationships with women. Importantly, respondents' sensitivity to the power derived from differences in income allowed many to anticipate this problem and develop strategies to mediate its impact. We now move on to explore ways in which respondents viewed and approached the tensions arising out of economic imbalances, and extend the discussion to include another source of tension, unilateral home ownership.

The organization of finances in lesbian households

Twenty-eight women in my sample were in long-term relationships ranging from one year to 19 years. Of these, 22 were living with their partners. Partnerships tended to be between women of similar ages and all but one respondent, who had given up waged work for health reasons, were in 'dual-earner' relationships. It must also be remembered that none of my respondents was currently responsible for children under school age.[6] Commuting at weekends to be with a partner because of job commitments was a quite common occurrence, with 16 respondents having experienced this in the past or at the time of interview. We now turn to respondents' accounts of the way household finances were organized in past and present relationships.

Cohabiting respondents usually held separate bank accounts. This seems to be a common practice amongst cohabiting couples who do not intend to marry (Blumstein and Schwartz 1985: 97; Pahl 1989: 106). The holding of separate accounts by respondents may have been motivated, at one level, by a desire to pre-empt haggling over money in the event of the relationship breaking up. It was also motivated by the desire to retain some control over their own income, so that, within reason, they could spend their money as they wished. Kathleen explains why this was important to her:

> Well, as you are handling your own money, that economic power is something, when you are deciding what you are spending your money on. If you are in a relationship, you are both earning equal wages, it's more equal. Whereas I think, when a woman goes out to work, when she is married, that money goes into the family, it's not really for her. They wouldn't think of going out and buying themselves a stereo system . . . The husband will buy that for the family, but he will have major use of it. (41)

This respondent has identified a problem faced by many married women. Pahl's (1989; 1991) British study exploring the links between money and power in marriage suggest that it is rare to find wives viewing their own earnings as personal spending money (129). Eileen, a childless, divorced woman, like most previously married respondents, found that her earnings had a different symbolic meaning during her marriage. Although she had pursued a career in a female profession, her salary was considerably lower than her husband's:

> I didn't realize how I felt about it, about being dependent, until I wasn't. And I realized now that I used to feel guilty about buying things for me, clothes and things, because it wasn't my money. It was our money, and therefore I ought to be buying things for the house. (45)

The most common way for respondents to organize household finances was to divide up household bills, rent or mortgage payments, and put this money into a joint account specifically for household bills. The paying of bills and keeping of accounts was usually carried out together, or taken in turns. None of the sample reported problems with this arrangement. An example of how this worked comes from May, a divorced woman with a teenage daughter:

> It was easy really, we divided the rent up and I paid more because I had [my daughter]. We just had a tin. It was really great, if either of us did shopping we just chucked the receipts in the tin and wrote our name on the back. And every month we did the accounts, and I paid a certain proportion and [my partner] paid the other, and we put so much into an account every month for bills. It was really good and it worked very well, it was never any problem. (49)

There was, however, one woman who delegated financial management to her partner. Veronica is a professional woman who has been living for almost three years with a previously married partner who had an administrative job. She earns more than her partner, and admits to being a poor manager of money:

> I am earning much more than [my partner] does. I don't think that is important. I am useless with money. I have been overdrawn since the age of 13 . . . I am a financial liability. I came [into the relationship] with £6,000 of debts, just for starters. She manages the money and she does it brilliantly. It's the only way to cope. I can't be trusted with money. I want to spend it . . . We have single bank accounts and we have a joint bank account, and [my partner] manages them all and balances the money between them; all I just do is sign the cheques. (37)

Coping with income differentials

Given the constraints on women's earnings and respondents' efforts to achieve living wages, the couples in my sample did not experience the large income differentials which appear to contribute to imbalances in power in heterosexual couples (Blumstein and Schwartz 1985: 146; Pahl 1989: 169). Most of the 10 couples where I know each partner's salary had income differentials of less than 20 per cent, and the highest was 44 per cent. In contrast, Pahl (1989) found substantial income differentials between wives and husbands, with 79 per cent of the men earning more than the highest-earning wife in the sample (65). Pahl concludes:

> Many couples wanted their marriage to be a relationship between equals and tried to express this equality in their financial arrangements. However, the results of this study showed that the greater earning power of husbands continues to be associated with greater control over finances and greater power in decision-making within the family. (169)

Pahl's conclusion reminds us that, despite the contrary intentions of individual actors, structural inequalities between women and men intervene to place limitations on the extent to which they may conduct 'equal' relationships. Couples who attempt 'equal' relationships usually do not take into account inequality of conditions, such as the lower earning power of women. Consequently, the pursuit of 'equality' which ignores the social and economic processes which construct women and men to be different serve to maintain the status quo.[7] For example, when each partner in a heterosexual relationship believes that s/he should contribute an equal share to the household finances this usually means that women contribute a greater proportion of their salaries than their male partners. When female partners fall short of parity in financial contribution (which they often do), they generally feel compelled to pay in kind, by taking on a greater share of domestic chores (Pahl 1989: 170; Blumstein and Schwartz 1985: 86).

As was noted earlier, although differentials in income were usually fairly narrow amongst my couples, larger differentials did sometimes exist. Many respondents appeared to be very sensitive to the potential power discrepancies generated by this situation. Although I was unable to pursue this in any great depth, some of the different strategies they followed in an attempt to neutralize the effects of economic imbalance are worth looking at.

When partners' financial conditions were markedly unequal, many took this into account so that feelings of dependency could be limited. In some cases, inequality of income was reflected in household contributions. Here, contributions were agreed according to the means of the respective partners, and this was perceived as the fair way of doing it. An example of this kind of financial arrangement comes from Theodora, a professional woman in a nine-year relationship:

> [The house is owned jointly] . . . she pays half the mortgage, as far as day-to-day things we split it down the middle, but for big purchases we split it according to our respective salaries; it works out at 12/17th or something silly like that [laughter]. (45)

A similar arrangement is reported by Suzanna who is in a 19-year relationship. Both she and her partner worked in female-dominated professions:

> [My partner] has always resented the fact that I have [earned] slightly more and she tends to think that I should pay for slightly more. So I pay slightly more of the mortgage, but it hasn't made a lot of difference . . . The salary difference has never been that important to me. (44)

Many respondents felt uncomfortable with the idea of living beyond their means. A solution offered by some couples was to live at the level of the lower-earning partner. Lotty, a professional woman, explains:

> [*Do you think there would be a problem if you had a partner who was earning a lot less than you?*] I would be very careful about [that] . . . Say someone was earning half my salary, I would choose things to do that she could afford, so that she could pay her half, rather than always pay for her—because I think that's 'yuckie'. Nobody likes to be bought, not too obviously anyway. (24)

The experience of being married to a higher-earning partner often provided empathy toward a partner in this situation. Heidi, a previously married woman in a senior administration job, explains how this experience has motivated her approaches to lesbian relationships. Her discussion also illustrates the contrasting options she saw as available for dealing with economic imbalances in heterosexual and lesbian relationships:

> [*You are in a well-paid job. What if your partner wasn't as well paid as you?*] Some have been better paid and some have been worse paid, but I have never found it to be a problem. [*How do you avoid the problem?*] Well possibly because I have been aware of the implications of it being a problem when I was married, I have actually worked hard at it not being a problem in relationships with women. [*How do you sort it out?*] We negotiate it. [*How do you sort out joint ventures like going on holidays that she can't afford?*] If she can't afford it we don't do it. That was never an acceptable option while I was married: we have to do it, we have the money. [*You wouldn't think of saying let's use some of my money?*] No, partly because I have been in the situation with a woman who earned more money than me and having to work quite hard at saying, 'Look, we are going to live within my means not yours.' And having to work quite hard to achieve that. (33)

Those respondents in well-paid employment often spoke of the power derived from their greater earnings as playing a negative role when it came to negotiating relationships with someone earning less. Norma, who has a high professional salary describes this:

> Well, speaking for myself, I can only say that sometimes I have been quite embarrassed about earning more than my partner. It's been an encumbrance rather than anything else. (52)

The examples above illustrate some of the strategies adopted by respondents for counteracting the effects of economic imbalances. My material is limited. The examples I have presented represent successful and thoughtful approaches to the problem. I do not suggest that all my sample utilized such diligence in approaching inequalities in income. Perhaps those who had abused their financial power were less willing to discuss the problem. However, although some did report situations where they had experienced power imbalances derived from money, none suggested that either they or a partner intentionally abused this power. None of the respondents was in a relationship at the point of interview which was seen as problematic in terms of economic imbalance. This may be because, when partners recognize an imbalance of economic power and are unable, or unwilling, to take steps to counter the problem, the relationship is short-lived.

Power and Unilateral Home Ownership

Another potential source of power imbalance related to income is unilateral house ownership. Often respondents suggested an awareness of difficulties associated with living in a house that was owned by a partner. This situation was understood to 'set the agenda' at a fundamental level of the decision-making process. In these situations, neither partner seemed particularly happy with the unintended power dynamics that resulted, because it constrained autonomy and supported feelings of dependency. However, with the best will in the world, some respondents experienced the unintentional power imbalances associated with unilateral home ownership and felt uneasy with this situation. Madelaine, a professional woman, describes how she felt that unilateral home ownership 'set the agenda' of decision-making in a previous relationship. In this case there was also an inequality in income and occupational status between herself and her partner:

> [The relationship] didn't involve role-playing, but unfortunately it also wasn't equal, because I had a better job and more money and the property was mine, which didn't lead to an equal relationship . . . I controlled where we lived, and that is never equal if you own a house and the other person doesn't. [*Did you abuse that power?*] Never! No. I didn't feel it to be a power, right, but had I been the other person I would have felt it as an unequal power, and ultimately it is, isn't it? But obviously it is, because if you fall out and part, that person's going to be the person who has to leave, hasn't she? [*What about decision-making?*] Decisions at a leisure level, definitely equal, but decision-making on what house and where we lived, where there were no choices. (45)

In this next extract from Charlotte we can see how it felt to be in the situation of living in a partner's home. Again imbalances came also from income differences and occupational status. She was employed at the time in factory work and her partner was a professional woman. Like the previous respondent, she experienced inequalities in power as the unintentional outcome of economic differentials:

> [*When you were involved with (this partner), you followed her job. Did you feel that because she earned more money it allowed her to make more decisions?*] Yes, yes. Well, I suppose the fact that it was her house and, as you say, the fact that she earned the biggest proportion of money, yes. I suppose towards the end, I suppose that was a lot of it, I felt that I was perhaps living in her shadow . . . [*Did you feel she was insisting on getting her way because she made more money?*] No, no there was never any pressure, it was just something I felt. (49)

I suggested to her that she may have been in a similar position to many married women. She did not agree:

> No I don't think so, not the same. Because I think men want women to feel that way, whereas this was just something that happened. I know in fact, I know [she] didn't think that way. It was just what I felt, but I think men want women to feel sort of beholden to them.

In this next extract, we can see how the discomfort of being dependent on a partner for housing can lead to a speedy renegotiation of the conditions of the relationship. This was the case for Michelle who had recently ended her marriage and had experienced a period of homelessness when she first left her husband. Despite earning a similar income to her female partner, she felt that living in her partner's house conflicted with her ardent desire never to be economically dependent again. As her partner was unwilling to sell the house and to co-own a home, Michelle decided to buy her own mobile home and move out. She works in a clerical occupation:

> [*Do you feel that you would be dependent on someone financially again?*] No! This is the trauma I am having with [my partner] now.

> This is why I can't remain living here. I can't actually stand the thought that if our relationship ends I am out on the street with nothing. I was given that choice before—I wasn't given a choice—but I walked away from it. This time I will not allow myself to even be given that choice, because I will own that mobile home, it will be mine. It doesn't matter who it is, but whenever you go into a relationship, even if it is shared, at the end of the day you end up with nothing. If I look at what I am getting from [my ex-husband], I have earned about £1,000 a year in 11 years of marriage. (29)

For those respondents who decided to remain in their lover's house, various strategies were developed to pre-empt feelings of alienation and dependency. Loraine has been living in her lover's house for four years. She is in management and earns a similar salary to her partner. She had just managed to achieve her ambition of buying her own flat when they met. Her partner did not wish to co-own a property as she had suffered financial loss in the break up of a previous relationship. Rather than feel overly dependent in the relationship, Loraine decided to keep on her own flat and rent it out:

> I have [a flat] but I rent it. I feel secure because I have that place, but I have been renting it out for three years. I don't intend to give it up and pool my resources with [my partner]. I want to keep my financial independence if nothing else. [*Why do you think that's important to you?*] I suppose because—having said I don't look to the future—I have begun in the last five or six years thinking about when I get older. And I know that relationships don't seem to last: the ideal is that you are going to be with someone for the rest of your life, but it doesn't work that way, with the best will in the world it doesn't always work that way. I am frightened of ending up on the street, or ending up in accommodation that I can't afford to pay for, so at least I know it's an investment. (32)

Even with having her own home to go to in the event of the relationship breaking up, Loraine still felt uncomfortable with the situation. The house furnishings and decor reflected the identity of her partner; living surrounded by her lover's choice of decor symbolically signified her externality. The solution she arrived at was to claim her own territory. She took over a room in the house, furnished and redecorated it to reflect her own identity:

> [*Do you ever feel it a problem living in someone else's house?*] I did at one stage. There are very few things in this house on display that are actually mine. The house shows [my partner's] personality rather than mine. She had just bought the house when I started to see her, and I got frustrated because nothing in the house is mine. When I moved in, a lot of my things were in my flat; whatever I brought over didn't seem to match or [my partner] didn't like, and that really worried me. I thought this is not going to work, I feel like a permanent lodger. It suddenly dawned on me one day, all I needed was one room to call my own, so I decorated it and put my things in it. And I don't ever really use it, but I know that I can. I like the garden too and a lot of that represents me.

Again decor represented a problem for Tierl, who has been living in her lover's home for the past year. In this case, a partial solution to the problem of feeling external in the relationship was to redecorate the whole house:

> [*You didn't experience power in the relationship in terms of your partner owning the house?*] No, we talked about that a lot. I expressed it was

> something I couldn't cope with, and it was something she didn't want. What we actually did, after a settling period of about six months, we redecorated, and we made it our house rather than her house, and we felt that was the way round it. That is one of the ideas behind moving, which we are considering . . . that was our way of overcoming the potential power—that neither of us wanted us to have—that was obviously there. So that was the way around it, to claim it for us. (27)

Respondents were usually uncomfortable with unilateral house ownership. They considered that this situation would undermine their own or their partner's sense of independence. Again, their discussions reflect their recognition of the unintentional consequences of power and, as a result, some attempted to construct strategies to defuse or avoid the situation. Co-ownership was the preferred option, for those respondents who could afford it. At the time of interview, 15 respondents were co-owners of their homes, and only three were in a unilateral home ownership situation.

Intimate Strangers Versus Intimate Friendships

People's experience of emotions is slowly becoming an area of interest to sociologists. Studies of couples in North America (Hochschild 1983; 1989) and Britain (Duncombe and Marsden 1993; Brannen and Moss 1991; Mansfield and Collard 1988) suggest that the gender division of labour includes 'emotional labour'. Women tend to do the bulk of this emotion work as they attempt to keep themselves and their families happy. Women and men appear to have very different understandings about emotional expression. Processes which construct gender difference seem also to place women and men in different *emotional cultures* (Duncombe and Marsden 1993). Mansfield and Collard (1988: 178–9) suggest that wives and husbands come together as *intimate strangers*, with very different emotional goals in marriage. Women desire intimacy and empathy, while most of the male partners interviewed wanted 'home life, a physical and psychological base'. Duncombe and Marsden (1993), whose study specifically explores the emotional worlds of heterosexual couples, suggest that men appear to find it difficult to articulate and express their emotions and feel threatened if encouraged to do so, while women feel disappointed and frustrated by the unwillingness of their male partners to participate emotionally in relationships with themselves or their children. They point out that women in long-term relationships with men usually have to work hard at constructing coping strategies to deal with their disappointment about the lack of partner intimacy and sharing they experience. They argue that the inequalities of women and men's perceived emotional needs should be seen as a form of intentional or unintentional power:

> Men's withholding from women the emotional validation which they seek through intimacy may become a source of male power, and indeed some women reported that they experienced men's unusual 'remoteness' as a form of power. In a mysterious way, the giving or withholding of emotion and intimacy thus becomes one kind of 'carrier' of gender power. (236)

Given the gendered nature of emotional expression, it is not surprising that my respondents did not usually experience their partners as *intimate strangers*. In fact, those who had had heterosexual experience as a reference point usually (n = 27) volunteered that the emotional content and quality of their relationships with women was a major differentiating feature. They commented on the high levels of intimacy and communication which characterized their lesbian relationships. Ginny describes her feelings about her partnership of two years:

> I think what I've got is a total trust, total understanding, and just a communication that I never thought I would ever have . . . It's almost like ESP . . . It's like strange things, like understanding, in the sense that I know what she is thinking, what she's feeling at certain moments, which is very important . . . there are so many traits that are attributed as being particularly female, but are nice, wonderful traits—softer, the kinder generosity—whether that's something that men try to hide about themselves that's really there or not, I don't know. (24)

Another example comes from Andrea, who has been in a lesbian relationship for the past eight years:

> [My relationship is] very much more in-depth as far as communication is concerned, and communication as distinct from chat. It's very much more fulfilling in that I feel a person in my own right. I didn't when I was married. (45)

However, lesbians are not immune to the negative operation of 'emotional power'. The research on lesbian couples discussed earlier suggests that, of all possible sources of power, differences in emotional involvement are the greatest source of inequality between women. A partner who is less involved in the relationship usually has more power. This may be self-evident and probably holds true for any emotional relationship. However, given that women may feel encouraged to invest greater emotional energy in their relationships with each other and expect this situation to be reciprocal, emotional imbalances may be experienced as a major source of power inequality.

Of all the different possibilities of inequality between women in a relationship, extreme emotional imbalances were reported by my sample as presenting the most difficulty. Imbalances involved different degrees of emotional manipulation. The fear of losing a partner inevitably led to allowing a partner to take greater control over the operation of the relationship. These emotional conflicts often temporarily affected the 'wronged' partner's ability to do her job as usual, and this sometimes led to having to 'come out' to an employer. The achievement of the high degree of closeness, so often described by respondents, generates a corresponding risk of vulnerability. In this situation a thoughtless, immature, or cruel partner can effectively wield considerable power (although these kinds of relationships were usually short-lived). Interestingly, none of my respondents admitted to being the 'abuser' in this domain, probably because it is easier to admit being wronged than having wronged.

It must be pointed out, however, that these abuses of emotional power were rare: taking all their relationships into account, only nine women reported having experienced this. In most cases women thought fondly of previous lovers. Because friendship is generally an important aspect of lesbian relationships they do not simply end in the conventional sense—they are transformed. In other words, usually after a period of (often very painful) adjustment, ex-lovers retain positions as close friends.[8] As one respondent commented with reference to her ex-lovers, 'as friends, they are the jewels in my life'.

Balancing Home and Employment Commitments

The division of labour within the home, and between the home and the workplace, has been identified as a major source of inequality between women and men. As lesbian couples do not have gender difference to guide their approach, it is interesting to see how respondents balance domestic and employment commitments in their relationships with women. This section first illustrates examples of their different approaches to household task allocation. We will then focus on the way waged work was negotiated in partnerships and outline some important employment consequences of their more balanced approach.

Gender Divisions of Household Labour

Research clearly demonstrates that, in the overwhelming majority of heterosexual partnerships, women take responsibility for, and perform the bulk of, domestic tasks, even when they are in full-time waged work (Mansfield and Collard 1988; Hochschild 1989; Brannen and Moss 1991). This situation holds for couples without children (Mansfield and Collard 1988; Blumstein and Schwartz 1985), for couples where wives have a higher occupational status (McRae 1986) or the man is unemployed (Morris 1990), as well as for cohabiting couples (Macklin 1983; Blumstein and Schwartz 1985) and those who see themselves as sharing household work (Doucet 1995). When the analysis is extended to include a broad range of household tasks, the very gendered nature of task allocation becomes clearly apparent (Pahl 1984; Seymour 1992). 'Male' household work includes activities such as car upkeep and house maintenance, improvements and repair, whereas women are responsible for routine and time-consuming housework, domestic production, and childcare (Pahl 1984). Gender boundaries exist between the two areas of responsibility, and change has generally taken the form of a slight increase in male participation in the wife's sphere rather than a rethinking of the boundaries of responsibility.[9] In consequence, it is women who generally find themselves balancing the responsibilities of home and paid work, so that it is their employment schedules that are adjusted to compensate, and it is they who experience the fatigue, strain, guilt, and anxiety because they 'choose' to be employed (Doucet 1991: 17).

Lesbian Approaches to Household Task Allocation

In the light of the above, it is interesting to look at the way the domestic division of labour is negotiated in households where there are no gender and differentiated guidelines upon which to base the allocation of tasks. The few North American studies that do consider task allocation in non-heterosexual households suggest that, contrary to popular stereotypes, homosexual couples rarely follow a traditional division of labour. Peplau and Cochran's (1990) comparative study of gay, lesbian, and heterosexual couples looked at household task allocation. They found that if there was any specialization in household tasks amongst lesbians, it was usually based on individual skills and interests (344). They noted that lesbians were less inclined toward role-playing than either gay men or heterosexual couples and it was rare to find one partner in a lesbian relationship performing mostly 'masculine' or mostly 'feminine' tasks. Blumstein and Schwartz's (1985: 149) large-scale comparative study of different couple forms found that, of all the couples, lesbians had the most equitable division of household labour. They also found that women in a lesbian relationship spent the least amount of time on household tasks of any of the other women interviewed.[10] Johnson (1990) also noted that, regardless of the job status of a partner, household tasks in lesbian homes were usually shared fairly evenly. Weston's study (1991: 149) of gays and lesbians in San Francisco found that both men and women felt that an equitable division of domestic labour was a crucial element in the construction of the egalitarian relationships they desired.

We now turn to my data to explore ways in which the allocation of household tasks were arranged. It must be pointed out, however, that my data are limited because the research did not specifically set out to investigate divisions of labour in lesbian households. The sample was not drawn with this aim in mind. I did not necessarily interview both partners or seek out couples with dependent children. My analysis of task allocation is based on their brief descriptions and in most cases their accounts could not be verified by their partners. However, where both partners were interviewed, I found little contradiction between their descriptions. My current research on the sharing arrangements of lesbian couples with dependent children does, however, suggest that we can be fairly confident about the findings outlined below.[11]

Overall, respondents' descriptions of divisions of household labour in lesbian partnerships past and present suggest that tasks were allocated in an even-handed way. Thirty-seven respondents commented on the importance to them of feeling relatively free from the *expectations* and *responsibilities* associated with a gender division of labour. They were aware of the 'double day' experienced by many of their heterosexual female colleagues and saw no reason to emulate this pattern in their own relationships. Home life was rarely ruled by the tyranny of being house-proud, perhaps because their identity and self-worth were not seen as being derived from a demonstration [of] domestic excellence. Consequently, some may have had low standards of household tidiness. Angela, a professional woman who has been living with her partner for the past three years, sums up a fairly typical approach to housework found amongst respondents:

> I do not consider housework and cooking the 'be all and end all of life'. I will hoover and clear up when friends come round, but I am not a fanatical housewife . . . I would rebel if it were expected of me. I mean, I had no objection this morning to belting around with the hoover, but nobody, neither [my partner] nor I, expects me to have to do it. It would have been impolite to you, I think, to have walked into the house in the mess it was in this morning [laughter]. But neither one of us expected 100 per cent that the house had to look clean and tidy, otherwise the interview could not go ahead. It's that absolute down-the-line expectation that I cannot understand. So [my partner] said she doesn't want to do the ironing, as she said just before you came—fine I'm not bothered. (37)

However, certain tasks ultimately have to be carried out and we now focus on some of their approaches to the allocation of these tasks, considering the three main styles of task organization which I have identified. I term these the 'symmetric shared approach', the 'symmetric specialized approach', and the 'asymmetric approach'.

The 'symmetric shared approach' to household tasks

A 'symmetric shared approach' to task allocation was very common and was particularly favoured amongst feminist respondents. Here tasks were performed together or taken in turns, and there was very little specialization. In fact, some went to great lengths to avoid specialization. Underlying this approach was a belief that each partner should feel competent in performing both 'male' and 'female' tasks. They generally viewed task specialization along gender lines, as supporting partner dependency and thus thwarting self-determination. Karen, working in a male-dominated manual occupation, describes this kind of approach and explains why she thinks it necessary. The relationship she is referring to began as a 'commuting relationship':

> The domestic thing worked out very well; we shared it. Shared the shopping, and the cooking, and the washing up, and all of that I really respect, that part of our relationship.

> I think if one of us was more stressed out, the other of us would like do it for a week at the most. Later on we lived together, because we bought a house together, and we lived together for 15 months in that house. [*Why do you think it is a positive thing not to have set roles?*] It is much better if you can have the confidence to do everything in a relationship. Although you might be better at doing something—so you might in the end always end up, say, doing the plugs. If you know how to mend a plug, then you are not going to give that power to someone else all the time. I think it is important for both people to know how to do things, like drive a car, cope with the running of the house; both people should be as competent as possible in all areas—to know that you both can do it, and you both know what it is like to do it, I think that must be the best way. (35)

In some cases a more formalized arrangement was devised for the allocation of household tasks. A rota would be drawn up to ensure that each did a fair share. In this next example, the rota was developed more as a way of introducing the young son of the respondent's partner to the responsibilities of household labour. Both partners are full-time employees and committed feminists. Rachel works in a 'Women's Movement' organization and has been living with Linda for a year:

> [*How do you work out roles and things?*] [laughter] We made out a rota at the weekend; how do we work it out? We share it, basically, the rota was merely to try and get [Linda's] son involved, rather than us. We both have very, very stressful jobs. We both work with people, we both do very emotionally draining work, so that means we are both very drained at the end of the day, so organization is of the essence to keep sanity, basically. So we are very organized about it. (26)

Usually those following a 'symmetric shared approach' were more flexible. Tasks were performed because they needed to be done, and whoever was available did them. Partners seemed to approach tasks on the basis of perceptions of fairness; they were happy to do more than their fair share at times, so long as this was not an *expectancy*. An example of this comes from Caroline who has been living with her partner for the past three years. She co-owns her house with her partner, and they renovated it together. She is in a male-dominated manual occupation; her partner is training to enter a male-dominated profession:

> No, there's no role play, things get done because they have to get done—if the washing has to be taken out of the washing machine and whoever's there at the time [does it]. The cooking has to be done, whoever is free cooks it. It may turn out that one of us does it three nights on the trot, and then the other one night, and then two nights on the trot, but then we don't really think about it like that, we do it because we want to do it. Generally speaking, we do most of the cooking together anyway, because we do enjoy doing it; we do most things together, quite honestly. It just happens if someone has to study for exams or something one of us covers and does both those sort of things a bit more often than normal. (29)

Importantly, underlying this shared approach was that neither partner held primary responsibility for the overall running of the household. The burden was shared and both partners were competent in performing 'male' and 'female' tasks. Doing tasks together was seen as an expression of love, making a relationship complete. Tasks performed together could become fun, rather than a drain on energy. Furthermore, this was seen to make sense, for two busy women performing tasks together was a speedy way to dispense with routine chores and provide more time for shared leisure.

The 'symmetric specialized approach' to household tasks

A strict sharing of tasks was not to everyone's liking. Dividing up tasks according to particular likes or dislikes was another favoured approach followed by respondents. This was particularly the case for older women, who had perhaps developed skills in previous relationships, or in marriage. It may also be associated with more long-term relationships where certain routines and patterns become established. Importantly, neither partner held overall responsibility for the domestic functioning of the household. Some tasks were shared, while others became the responsibility of one or the other. Sylvia contrasts her approach to household tasks in her current five-year partnership with a 'symmetric shared approach' she had experienced in an earlier lesbian relationship:

> [My ex-lover] was very much a feminist, would make a point of one week I would do the housework and the next week she would do it, and cooking the same. I found this very rigid. The way [Delia] and I work, which is much better—I hate ironing and she does all the ironing, we share the cooking, 'cos we both like cooking. I look after the kitchen, the bathroom and she looks after this room [living room] and the bedroom. She likes this and so do I. I think you should divide it up, and do it equally, but you do things you like, not things you hate. (38)

Her partner Delia describes the arrangements from her point of view:

> [Sylvia] does more of the day-to-day cooking, and I perhaps go mad if someone is coming to dinner, and throw myself into doing that. But we do things together which is very nice, we just seem to enjoy doing things together . . .

They are both enthusiastic gardeners and equally competent in household maintenance. One partner had been to night school to learn carpentry and she had made all the fitted cupboards in the house.

In this next example, we can see a greater degree of specialization in the relationship. Virginia, a divorced woman in professional management, has been living with her lover in their co-owned home for the past eight years. She and her partner mainly share out the tasks. However, as she has had more experience in cooking she tends to do more of that. Since she has injured her wrist and cannot lift heavy items, her partner performs more of the heavy work:

> [*Do you feel you have a double day?*] No, not at all. Simple things like doing the food shopping, if you do that on your own for a household it is really quite hard work on top of the day's work, but we do it together, all those sorts of things, like the ironing. All the stuff like that: the house the cleaning—not that we do very much cleaning [laughter]. No, it's much more equal. . . . As far as organizational things are concerned we split most things down the middle . . . shopping and cooking and housework and stuff, except that I tend to cook more because having been married for 10 years you get very used to cooking, and it's something I can do with my eyes closed, whereas [my partner] doesn't feel that she is very good at it, but she does from time to time. Other things we split down the middle. Except four years ago when we were on holiday I had a bike accident, and fractured my right

> wrist badly. It was mishandled here which means that my right hand is not good for heavy things like cutting the hedge, and mowing the lawn and shifting furniture, and so, because of that, a certain amount of the heavy work falls on [my partner], but I don't think it's a role thing, it's more out of necessity. (45)

Household labour involves tasks that have come to be socially defined as 'male' and 'female'. Unless women can afford to employ outside help, 'male' tasks must be learnt and carried out. If one partner, through developing a skill, or just by superior strength, performs certain 'male' tasks, is a traditional division of labour being replicated at some level? Do the gender labels that are attached to some tasks 'gender' the performance? The previous example and the next two are examples of this kind of specialization. My view, based on my impressions of these respondents, was that, contrary to examples that we will see later, these tasks were perceived as 'practical' tasks, rather than 'masculine' tasks. The women involved in doing these 'practical' tasks did not see them as expressing the more masculine side to their personality. Nor had they relinquished their more routine domestic responsibilities. This contrasts with the 'egalitarian' men in Pahl's study (1984) who 'helped out' substantially with the domestic routines, yet both partners still held to a gender division of *responsibility* within the two household spheres. This, I think, demonstrates the power of heterosexual gender scripts to impede the momentum of change toward egalitarianism.

Another example of task specialization in 'practical' areas comes from Ruth, who is in a 15-year relationship. She has shared in the care of her partner's two children. Domestic responsibilities and tasks are described as shared.

> No, we have always shared cooking, cleaning. The only thing [my partner] does that I can't do is woodwork, I really can't; I would if I could. Practical things, she does things like that, because I am not very practical. Whoever gets home first [cooks the dinner]. Sometimes both of us get home so late it's not worth starting faffing around, we just muck in together and get something quick and have the rest of the evening free . . . I certainly wouldn't want to fit into a wife role anyway, I don't want to fit into any role really, or have any label attached to me. I think I am just being me. (45)

For this next couple, there is more task specialization and less performing of tasks together. Shelly and Shirl divided up the domestic tasks; one did the cleaning and the other the catering. Again one partner appeared to specialize in the more 'male' areas of tasks that require physical strength. As in the previous example, neither partner saw this as being male/female role play; rather it was the result of one partner's greater strength. They are both in their early fifties; they have lived together for 19 years, and have recently retired from 'female' professions. They co-own a fairly large house, and have spent several years renovating it together. Shelly describes a fairly equitable division of domestic tasks, based on specialization and separate responsibilities:

> I do the housework and she does the cooking. I am a hopeless cook, and she is a very good cook, so it works out fairly evenly. [*And the shopping?*] She does all the catering.

Shirl's description reveals a greater degree of specialization, where she takes on more of the heavy tasks:

> Well, I think there is a great deal more giving and taking . . . in the 'housey' bit really. I don't do much of [the housework] now, [Shelly] does it. There is no great thing about who does what. We tend to do what we are

> better at, I suppose. I am stronger physically, so I have done the stronger things, she is not so strong physically, so I've done things like chopping logs, and gardening and things.

In none of these examples of specialization did one partner appear overburdened by household responsibilities. The division of labour appeared to be equitable and fair, and was perceived by each partner as such. It was the freedom from *expectations* regarding responsibility for, and the performance of, tasks that was perceived by respondents as essential. This they usually saw as differentiating their partnerships from past relationships with men or their observations of task allocation in most heterosexual households they knew. The flexibility in task allocation often extended to judgments about task execution: when both women were tired or busy with other activities, chores would just be left undone.

The 'asymmetric approach' to household tasks

Not all relationships, however, were free from inequalities in task allocation. When respondents took into account their experiences of living with female partners past and present there appeared to be a range of ways that inequalities in task allocation and execution could develop over the duration of a relationship. Sixteen respondents reported being familiar with this situation, although only a few were experiencing this in their current relationship. These inequalities were usually quantitative, where one partner did considerably more than the other, or they were occasionally gendered, insofar as the gender ideologies which shape task allocation between men and women were mirrored in relationships between women.

Just as some lesbian couples may find a solution to the demands of balancing domestic work and paid work by lowering their standard of household tidiness, inequalities can be introduced when partners have different dirt-threshold levels. As may be very familiar to people who have lived in shared accommodation, the one with the lowest 'dirt threshold' tends to do more of the domestic work. At least five respondents had experienced this in past relationships. Of these five, two women spoke of having taken on the main burden of domestic chores for this reason, while the others reported that their partners had done so. These kinds of relationships were more often between women with a fairly large age gap, and were generally short-lived. These inequalities were more usually understood as being the result of immaturity, or inexperience, than of adherence to role play.

Sometimes inequalities were related to unemployment or long-term illness; this was the case for three respondents. Rita explains how she fell into a more traditional division of labour when she was temporarily unemployed and her partner was in a well-paid professional occupation:

> I think I became quite a housewife at that point . . . it's so easy to fall into that. Someone has to get up in a rush—'That's OK, I'll do the washing up later'—and it just sort of goes on until you are no longer offering to do it, but it's assumed you will do it. (30)

For others a more traditional approach came about when their partnerships operated more along the lines of what I would call a 'mother/daughter' dynamic and, in a few cases, when their relationships attempted to mirror heterosexual relationships, that is, 'butch/femme'.[12] The 'mother/daughter' division of labour tended to be more like those with an imbalance of dirt threshold than those with 'butch/femme' relationships. They were often between a young woman, who had recently left home, and an older woman who had been previously married. The younger woman would be fairly incompetent at caring for herself and the older woman would take charge. Again these relationships tended to be short-lived and transitory.

The household division of labour in 'butch/femme' relationships tended to be fairly traditional, or at least began that way. Six respondents reported having experienced 'role play' with regard to household tasks. Bobbie discusses the approach to domestic work in a previous relationship. She was working in a supervisory position in the motor trade; her partner was doing factory work:

> [*In the eight-year relationship, how did you sort out the roles?*] I suppose it was very male/female. I was taking the 'male' role and she the 'female' role. [*What about in terms of roles around the home: were you coming home expecting the meal to be ready?*] No, no, I never ever did that. Very often I used to come home and cook the meal, especially if we were both working. I sort of mucked in with the housework; she did basically most of it—she complained that I didn't do it as well as her. I was prepared to muck in. It wasn't a partnership, certainly, she did probably most of the cooking. [*Were you earning the same money?*] Yes, about the same; in fact she was earning a bit more than me. Being a factory job, she was probably earning more than me.

Dot describes the evolution of the division of household labour in a previous long-term relationship, which began along the lines of 'butch/femme'. At that time she was in a management position in a male-dominated occupation and her partner was a successful business woman:

> In the beginning [my partner] did the cooking, and the bits and pieces and I did the garden and the painting and the decorating and things. But over the years, that's evolved round into us doing it together. The reason being that, if we did it together, we got the job done twice as quick, which meant we had more time to spend together. It did occur that I did the 'male' jobs more than [my partner], mainly because I was more competent at them than she was, but over the years I've learnt to cook better, iron . . . and things like this, but this was only to facilitate spending more free time together. [*Has (your partner) learnt how to do those more male tasks?*] Yes, she can decorate now; still can't put a plug on very well, but she has a bash—as she has tended to leave most of the male-oriented things to me: you do don't you? If you find that someone is good at a particular thing, you tend to leave them to do it, so that's what we tended to do really . . . At the end of the day, we would both get a meal, just fiddle around the kitchen, get the meal. She would dish up, I would wash up as we were going, sit down and eat it, finish up the washing up, and then go and have a bath together and talk, and that was the start of our evening. (43)

Interestingly, the women who took on the more 'feminine' tasks were often in their first lesbian relationship. Some of these women were described as unsure of their sexuality, and some had later returned to heterosexual relationships. However, for Meg, staying firmly within a traditional female role was seen as her way of affirming her femininity. She describes her reasons for filling a more traditional role in an earlier relationship. She reported that, in subsequent relationships, male and female tasks were slightly more shared:

> It was definitely a bit of a—she did the 'male-ish' things, but, having said that, I suppose it was a bit like that because I suppose I thought of her as in the 'male' role . . . I was determined that I was still going to be a woman; there was no way I was going to do

> mannish things. If I was in a situation where a 'man's' job needed doing, I'd either get a man to do it, or if I was with a woman I'd get the woman: if she wanted to do it and wanted to be like a man, let her do it. [*What sort of things did you see as a man's job?*] Well, making and mending things and painting, you know, 'men's' jobs. I still call it 'men's' jobs, I use it as a parody and I make a joke about it; at the same time I am not going to do these jobs. I can't, I can't even put a plug on. I am capable; I suppose I could do, but I don't want to know if it's a 'man's' job. I do gardening and I think that's very manly. (40)

The end result of these more 'butch/femme' divisions of household labour was more reminiscent of examples of Pahl's (1984: 288–308) egalitarian couples. In these cases husbands shared in the routine domestic tasks, while retaining responsibility for the male household tasks. Wives still viewed the routine domestic tasks as their responsibility, but welcomed the help given by their spouses. It must be pointed out that most of the women who had described these unequal divisions of labour had since developed a more equal approach. None of those aged under 30 had experienced 'butch/femme' relationships and they had no desire to do so.

Generally, respondents embraced an egalitarian approach to household labour. Part of the reason for this may be that contemporary lesbians, as has been argued earlier, lack an ideology that legitimizes the domination of one partner over another. Consequently, domination is more clearly perceived for what it is. It is probable that, for many, the egalitarian perspectives they held were a major underlying motivating factor in their previous dissatisfaction with and rejection of heterosexual relationships and their choosing to follow a lesbian lifestyle. While some strongly egalitarian women engage in the brave task of changing their male partners, others have discovered a different place to express these values. As a result, women who choose to share their lives with other women have no desire to subject themselves to the kind of power dynamic that they perceived as underpinning relationships with men.

Employment Advantages of Lesbian Home-life Circumstances

Finally, I would like to explore ways that respondents negotiated their careers in lesbian relationships. As we will see, most were aware that their relationships facilitated their ability to participate more fully in their jobs. First of all, the more equitable and flexible division of household labour experienced by most was seen as aiding them in the performance of their jobs. Fifteen women commented on this. This household situation was particularly valued by respondents in demanding and stressful employment. These women believed that they would have great difficulty in performing their jobs if they also had sole responsibility for the smooth running of the home. A second source of advantage, reported by 20 respondents, was the high levels of partner support, encouragement, and understanding of their work commitments that they received. These advantages were perceived as contrasting with their experience and/or understanding of married women's situation.

Importantly, a partner's right to be committed to her job was not challenged. This mutual support of careers is, it is suggested, very much linked with respondents' views on financial dependency, and their jobs represented, if nothing else, their independence. In general they expected mutual respect for the paid work component of life. Krish, who works in a male-dominated profession, illustrates this:

> I think we are both very good at valuing the other one's career and that even if that meant that we would have to work in different towns or we would have to work until eleven o'clock at night every night that

> would be OK. Her career's as important to me as mine is. (24)

Importantly, respondents did not seem to see themselves in competition with their partners in the way that Blumstein and Schwartz (1985) noted was the case for cohabiting men. Beth discusses ways that the encouragement she feels she receives in lesbian relationships differs from a previous heterosexual relationship. She works in a management position in transport:

> [He] was great . . . he encouraged me . . . He could only, and I think most men only encourage so far. If they think they are being shown up to be not as good, they don't like it, and they will pull back on the encouragement. There isn't the same genuine wanting to see you do well. Only if it suits them . . . I find that my relationships with women have been so different: it's encouragement all the way through, there are never any restrictions. (29)

This partner support was very much tied in with the more flexible roles that constituted relationships between women. There were no lines of demarcation regarding spheres of achievement. A woman doing well at work did not undermine her partner's gender identity, as appears to be the tendency in heterosexual relationships. . . . This held true even amongst 'butch/femme' couples, because employment status was independent of these roles. Poppy has been living with her partner for four years. She works in a management position in a male-dominated occupation. Poppy thought that the flexibility in the division of labour at home together with the understanding she received from her partner greatly facilitated her ability to do her job:

> [*How much time do you think you could devote to your job if you were in a heterosexual relationship?*] Probably not as much . . . My impression is that most men come home from work and expect things to be done for them, so I wouldn't be able to devote myself as much to my work. I would have to cut myself off from it. I would either have to have a less stressful job, or I think the relationship might suffer. I think a lot of men don't actually like to think that their wives are taken up with their jobs; they think it's just a means of getting some money. Perhaps I am wrong, because I haven't had any relationships with men for 12 years, but that was my impression then, and I still sort of get that sort of impression now. [*Have you found that in your relationship you have found encouragement towards your work?*] Yes, I have. She doesn't mind how much time I have spent at home doing work-related matters, not at all because any housework to do, you either leave it or she'll do it, or it can wait to another day. So, yes, I am not expected to do anything, I am not expected to have dinner on the table. I am not expected to hoover the floor . . . There is a certain amount I bring home; she's really good about it; but then she does a very similar thing, she brings home work from time to time, so it works both ways. I am not sure if a man or husband would put up with that; it depends on what sort of husband you have, I suppose. (32)

In this partnership there is 'give and take' between the demands made by a responsible job, the domestic demands, and the relationship. Each understood the other's need to bring work home from time to time. Both women are in fairly senior positions at work and they earn similar wages.

The same points are made by Mary-Jane. Her junior management position in agriculture makes considerable demands on her time and energy. Again she does not believe that she could devote as much energy to her job if she were married:

> [My sexuality has] enabled me to do the job I do . . . [In my line of work] there are a lot of gay people in it . . . I guess because the amount of time the job consumes you almost have to be gay. I couldn't hold down a marriage I don't think, to be honest, not if somebody wasn't, unless it was a gay marriage, because I don't think people would put up with it. I couldn't do it. I couldn't run a house, a family and do the job that I do, so it's probably just as well really. [*How does it help being in a gay relationship?*] Well [my partner] has her career and she's very definite what she wants to do . . . She actually knows I have to do work, I have to be there; if anyone else is working I want to be there, I want to be in the thick of it, and she understands that it takes a lot of my time, and gives me time to do it, and that then gives her time to do her job, so . . . We don't have a conflict with jobs really, she has a job that's very demanding. In the heterosexual relationships that I know, the man wants to be looked after, come home, dinner there. I might work till 10 p.m. I need to be able to know that I can, if necessary, work all night. (25)

Again the women in this partnership have jobs which make similar demands on their time and earn similar salaries.

In contrast to her experience of marriage, Mary-Rose was actively encouraged by her partner to move out of low-paid 'women's' work and start her own business. She is now employing 12 women and is the only woman in the region running such a business. She explains how other women see her lifestyle:

> Straight career women . . . say I am lucky not to have the restrictions of a man, and envy me. [*They see men holding them back?*] Yes, yes, but a necessary thing in their lives. I am often being told I am lucky, especially by single women in a heterosexual relationship. They say I have the support of someone but not the restrictions. [*It interferes with their careers how?*] I can't see how it doesn't, it has more effect. By choosing the sexuality I am, has made me more successful, work harder, and given me the freedom to work harder. [*What makes the difference?*] The role-playing. The male should be, in the world's opinion, a breadwinner; the woman can be successful provided the male is more successful. (35)

Indra felt that, if she were heterosexual, the time and mobility demands made by her traditionally male profession would preclude a relationship:

> If I was straight, I think it would be very difficult to find a man that could fit into my life. [*How so?*] Mainly the travelling and the hours that you spend at work, and the commitment you have: you have to work weekends; it's a type of thing that if you need to work late you do work late, and if you are posted you may be given two weeks' notice, but then you have to move, and I haven't yet met a man that would ever consider doing that for his girlfriend or wife. (24)

She is at present in a relationship which involves commuting to be with her partner who is in a similar occupation. This was seen as the best compromise until they could find satisfactory employment in the same location.

All these respondents quoted have something interesting in common. Both they and their partners were in occupations that are usually filled by men. Only the first and last couples were professional women. The rest had no further education and were almost all from intermediate or manual social backgrounds. Their jobs made similar kinds of demands to those faced by professional people. Their ability to do these demanding and well paid 'male' jobs was seen as greatly facilitated by the nature of their relationships. Here lies the great advantage experienced by many lesbians. They did not feel they had to sacrifice or forgo relationships for the sake of their careers, as may be the case for other women. Conversely, they do not have to subordinate their working lives to a relationship, as is the case for many married or cohabiting single women. It is by considering the experiences of these 'ordinary' working women that we can see the employment constraints imposed by gender dichotomies contained within institutional heterosexuality. . . .

The negotiation of career development within lesbian partnerships

. . . [R]espondents were usually highly committed to their jobs and often saw their occupational advancement as involving geographic mobility. Obviously, this can be a potential source of conflict between partners. Consequently, it is worth looking at the way partners negotiated employment opportunities which required relocation. Of the eight women in relationships of five years or more, five spoke of their career development involving relocation, and said that this had been carefully worked out as a joint venture, often with great difficulty. An example of this comes from Pru. Both she and her partner of 19 years rose to senior positions in female-dominated professions:

> [*Did you ever have a sense that one of your careers had priority?*] Not really, we worked very hard at making sure that we both got equal chances. We only ever looked for a situation where we were both going to get the job we wanted. We once applied to Worcester at one point and [my partner] got the job she wanted and I didn't get mine, so she had to go back and turn hers down. So there was no question of me taking on a lesser job. We have always worked so we could both get what we wanted. [*How easy has that been?*] Fairly difficult—not terribly, because we were prepared to go anywhere in the country as long as we could afford the property. Have been both fairly fortunate. (50)

This type of 'solution' was usually facilitated by the fact that the partners were in similar jobs. A different 'solution' was followed by a couple in a 15-year relationship who had brought up children together. Linda had devoted the early part of her life to the care of their children, and had consequently experienced fairly low-paid, part-time employment. When the children were older, she decided to return to full-time education. This involved moving home. Wilhemina, her partner, gave up a senior position by relocating, feeling that it was now Linda's turn to develop her career. Both considered this to be a fair compromise.

By partners not prioritizing one career over another, problems often arose when career opportunities could not be found in the same geographic location. One couple solved this by buying a house halfway between their two workplaces. However, commuting was the most common solution. At the time of interview, two respondents were in a commuting relationship because of job commitments and at least 14 had some experience of commuting relationships for this reason. Rather than giving up a good job to be with a partner, respondents spoke of the importance of taking time to find the right kind of job in the right location. This is discussed by Elizabeth, who works in the arts:

> it's got to be the career in a way, that is important. [My partner] can never be here just to be here, and I can never be there just to be there. I am perfectly prepared at this stage to look for a job in London, which would be convenient, because [she's] there, as long as it was the right job, I mean that's the thing. [*How important is work to you?*] It is

> very important to me but it is not as important as my relationship . . . but I am not just going to just, like, give it up, I've got to have a good reason to, I want to do it properly. (24)

Rebecca speaks of this dilemma. She is in a commuting relationship because she did not wish to jeopardize the career opportunities offered by her male-dominated profession. However, finding a compromise between the demands of her career and her desire to live with her partner was important to her:

> [*You said that with your kind of job you didn't think you could handle a relationship with a guy, how does it work out with a woman?*] With a lot of travelling, yes . . . I am going to Northampton most weekends or she is coming down here. I can see myself changing, changing jobs 'cos a relationship would mean a lot to me. I would not leave the industry, but I would change to a job that still gave me everything I wanted out of a job, but would mean that I wouldn't have to travel so much, so I could turn [the relationship] into a more permanent thing. (24)

. . . [R]espondents were often fairly ambitious. Unless a respondent was living in a large city such as London, career development often involved relocation. Clearly, the way that workplace opportunity is modelled on a 'traditional masculine model of employment' (one that ignores workers' home-life responsibilities and assumes that a woman will follow her partner's career [Brannen and Moss 1991]) disadvantages women and egalitarian couples. At some point three respondents had followed their partner's career because they felt that they could find a job more easily than their partners could. However, if one partner was settled in one location and unwilling or unable to move home, difficult decisions had to be made. Two respondents placed their relationships above a career move that would have required relocation. These respondents were both in valued relationships and had already established their careers. Unless both partners were highly committed in a relationship, career opportunities could bring a partnership to an untimely end. When faced with the decision whether to move for a career opportunity, or stay with a partner, six respondents chose to move. These women were usually in the early stages of career development. A further five respondents said that they would not relocate for a partner or expect their partner to relocate for them. This was the view expressed by Adrianne, who was a scientist:

> [*How central to you is work?*] It's a large part. I have put in a fair amount of effort to get to this point in my life. I wouldn't consider giving up my job and moving to another part of the country for somebody or anything like that, but equally I wouldn't expect anyone to do the same for me . . . I think the secret is to get involved with somebody who is in the right place in the first place—having had a long-distance relationship in the past, I don't think they are good for the sanity, but you can't always control who you fall in love with. (25)

Clearly, inequalities between women in terms of occupational status and/or circumstance can cause problems. Two women spoke of tensions arising when their partner was in a less rewarding job. As one woman commented, 'It is hard for a partner to understand why you work late every day, when they are in a poorly paid, nine-to-five job.' These strains brought a heavy toll and, consequently, these relationships tended to be short-lived. However, it must be remembered that, for a number of reasons, respondents were usually in relationships with women in broadly similar occupational circumstances.

Conclusion

There are two important interrelated factors shaping respondents' approaches to the balancing of employment and home commitments. First, lesbian relationships do not have the institutional backing of marriage to encourage longevity. Relationships are rarely entered on the assumption that they will last forever. This is not to say that lesbians do not take their relationships seriously, or that partners are dropped unceremoniously. The second important influence is economic. Respondents did not expect to enter a lifelong relationship with a woman who would be the main breadwinner. Nor did they desire this situation. They were aware of the problems associated with economic dependency. Consequently, respondents recognized that their lifestyle required that they be economically self-sufficient. . . . [T]his underpinned a perspective on employment that was lifelong. In many ways, employment rather than any particular relationship provided a source of continuity in their lives. This contributed to the understanding that neither partner had the right to place constraints on her partner's employment participation. Partners did, however, have to contend with differences relating to, for example, income, employment status, ethnicity, and education. Because of the absence of 'gender scripts', the intentional or unintentional operation of power in relationships was more clearly visible. Where possible they attempted to develop strategies aimed at neutralizing the effects of power imbalances, because they claimed to be uneasy about being dominated or dominant. Sometimes imbalances created a gulf that was too great to breach, which contributed to the breakup of a relationship.

The more balanced approach to domestic and employment commitments developed by the couples in my sample was, however, very much assisted by the similarities they experienced as women. Their relative freedom, in relationships, from operational constraints based on reciprocal gender identities ensured that tasks and achievements were not judged in the context of appropriate gender behaviour. Although 'butch/femme' relationships appear to be fairly *uncommon*, their existence does, in part, complicate this argument. Women in these kinds of relationships did emulate more polarized heterosexual domestic arrangements. However, as was said earlier, the more polarized division of domestic labour experienced did not extend to their approaches to employment. It is also worth mentioning that often the more 'masculine' partner earned less than her partner.

From respondents' accounts of their lesbian relationships it would appear that one partner's gender identity is not usually threatened by the employment successes of her lover. Nor is it contingent on monopolizing any one domain, insofar as neither partner usually feels the need to take responsibility for domestic tasks or 'breadwinning'. The achievement of more balanced task allocation at home, together with the emotional and practical support, characteristic of lesbian relationships, appears to be an important aspect of a lesbian's ability to engage in demanding employment. She does not have to sacrifice or forgo relationships for the sake of her career, as may be the case for other women. Nor does she have to subordinate her working life to a relationship, as is the case for many married or cohabiting single women.

The flexibility offered in women's relationships with each other, together with the similarities they shared, facilitated the operationalization of egalitarian ideals. This raises questions as to how far these more symmetric arrangements can be achieved by women and men who seek egalitarian relationships within the context of institutional heterosexuality. On the one hand, their efforts to bring about change may be limited by external social, economic, legal, and political structures and processes which serve to reproduce differences in the social, symbolic, and material conditions of individual women and men. On the other hand, gender inequalities are deeply embedded in the heterosexual gendered identities that these structures and processes constitute. This leads us to two thorny questions. First, if heterosexual desire is based on the eroticization of difference, what is so attractive about difference that is not related to the gendered power structures that feminists seek to undermine? Second, once processes supporting these gendered differences are undermined, how probable would a heterosexual outcome be? Unless we challenge and take seriously the role of institutionalized heterosexuality in shaping differences between women and men in most areas of social life, the feminist project will fail to move beyond the glass ceiling.

Notes

1. Relationships were described as 'exactly equal' by 48 per cent of heterosexual women, 38 per cent [of] gay men, and 40 per cent of heterosexual men.
2. See Blackburn (1988) and Chapters 1 and 3 of . . . [Dunne 1997] for a discussion of the empowering aspects of the questioning which novel situations in people's lives might prompt.
3. For general discussions of power, see Lukes (1974) and his edited volume (1986) and Merquior (1985, Ch. 8) on Foucault's approach to power. For a feminist consideration of power, see, for example, Griffin and Arnold (1991), Smart (1989), Fraser (1989) on Foucault, and the edited volume by Davis et al. (1991) on Lukes, Giddens, and Bourdieu.
4. As Smart (1989: 2) points out, feminists have often placed greater stress on the negative aspects of power, such as men holding all the power, women lacking power and being unable to make choices. This approach tends to obscure women's agency and the degrees to which power may be distributed unequally within the category 'woman'.
5. Women are more likely than men to take a more egalitarian stance on gender roles. The British Social Attitudes Survey noted that there was a statistically significant difference in male and female perspectives on this issue (Scott et al. 1993). Furthermore, constraints exist on heterosexual partners' ability to put egalitarianism into action. There appears to be a huge gulf between the advocation of egalitarian views and the operationalization of shared household task allocation (Witherspoon 1988: 185). I believe that an important reason for lesbian relationships offering greater possibilities for egalitarian outcomes is that it is in both partners' interests.
6. See note 11 below.
7. For an overview of the feminist debates on 'sameness' and 'difference', see, for example, Gross (1992), MacKinnon (1990), Scott (1990), Barrett (1987), and Phillips (1987).
8. See, for example, Green (1992) and Weston's (1991) research for a discussion of ways that ex-lovers become important in lesbian 'kinship' networks.
9. Research suggests that there is a less strictly gendered approach to domestic labour in African-American households (Miller and Garrison 1982: 242).
10. Sixty-nine per cent of lesbian respondents spent less than 10 hours on housework a week, as compared with 58 per cent of full-time employed cohabiting women and 56 per cent of full-time employed wives. In contrast, approximately 80 per cent of both married and cohabiting men spent less than 10 hours a week on housework (Blumstein and Schwartz 1985: 139–46).
11. I have recently begun a three-year project looking at divisions of labour between lesbian partners, particularly those with dependent children. I am working with Henrietta Moore, Bob Blackburn, and Kim Perren. This research uses a wide range of methodologies, including time-diaries and in-depth interviews. The early findings suggest that lesbians are developing very creative and

balanced approaches to the sharing of parenting, household tasks, and employment responsibilities. This research is funded by the Economic and Social Research Council, Grant No. R00023 4649.

12. The studies of lesbian couples referred to at the beginning of this chapter suggest that 'butch/ femme' couples are a very rare occurrence. See also Faderman (1992) and Weston (1991) for a more detailed discussion of the recent history of lesbian culture in the USA.

References

Barrett, M. 1987. 'The Concept of "Difference"', *Feminist Review* 26 (Summer): 29–41.

Blackburn, R.M. 1988. 'Ideologies of Work', in *Social Stratification and Economic Change*, ed. D. Rose (London: Hutchinson).

Blumstein, P., and P. Schwartz. 1985. *American Couples: Money, Work, Sex* (New York: Pocket Books).

———. 1990. 'Intimate Relationships and the Creation of Sexuality', in *Homosexuality/ Heterosexuality: Concepts of Sexuality*, eds D. McWhirter, D.D. Sanders, and J.M. Reinisch (Oxford: Oxford University Press).

Brannen, J., and P. Moss. 1991. *Managing Mothers: Dual Earner Households after Maternity Leave* (London: Unwin Hyman).

Caldwell, M.A., and L.A. Peplau. 1984. 'The Balance of Power in Lesbian Relationships', *Sex Roles* 10: 587–600.

Connell, R.W. 1987. *Gender and Power* (Cambridge: Polity).

Davis, K., M. Leijenaar, and J. Oldersma, eds. 1991. *The Gender of Power* (London: Macmillan).

Doucet, A. 1991. 'Striking a Balance: Gender Divisions of Labour in Housework, Childcare and Employment', *Sociological Research Group Working Paper Series*, University of Cambridge.

Duncombe, J., and D. Marsden. 1993. 'Love and Intimacy: The Gender Division of Emotion and Emotion Work', *Sociology* 27, 2: 221–42.

Faderman, L. 1992. *Odd Girls and Twilight Lovers: A History of Lesbian Life in Twentieth-century America* (London: Penguin).

Fraser, N. 1989. *Unruly Practices: Power, Discourse and Gender in Contemporary Social Theory* (Cambridge: Polity).

Green, S.F. 1992. 'The Politics of Gender, Sexuality and Identity: An Ethnography of Lesbian Feminists in London', unpublished PhD diss., University of Cambridge.

Griffin, C., and S. Arnold. 1991. 'Experiencing Power: Dimensions of Gender, "Race" and Class', paper presented at BPS/WIPS Women and Psychology Conference, University of Birmingham.

Gross, E. 1992. 'What Is Feminist Theory?', in *Knowing Women: Feminism and Knowledge*, eds H. Crowley and S. Himmelweit (Cambridge: Polity).

Hochschild, A. 1983. *The Managed Heart: Commercialization of Human Feeling* (Berkeley: University of California Press).

———. 1989. *The Second Shift* (New York: Viking).

Johnson, S. 1990. *Staying Power: Long Term Lesbian Couples* (Tallahassee, FL: Naiad Press).

Lindsey, L. 1990. *Gender Roles: A Sociological Perspective* (Englewood Cliffs, NJ: Prentice Hall).

Lukes, S. 1974. *Power: A Radical View* (London: Macmillan).

———, ed. 1986. *Power* (Oxford: Basil Blackwell).

MacKinnon, C.A. 1990. 'Legal Perspectives on Sexual Difference', in *Theoretical Perspectives on Sexual Difference*, ed. D. Rhode (London: Yale University Press).

Macklin, E. 1983. 'Non Marital Heterosexual Cohabitation: An Overview', in *Contemporary Families and Alternative Lifestyles*, eds E. Macklin and R.H. Rubin (Beverly Hills, CA: Sage).

McRae, S. 1986. *Cross-class Families: A Study of Wives' Occupational Superiority* (Oxford: Clarendon).

Mansfield, P., and J. Collard. 1988. *The Beginning of the Rest of Your Life? A Portrait of Newly-wed Marriage* (London: Macmillan).

Merquior, J.G. 1985. *Foucault* (London: Fontana).

Miller, J., and H.H. Garrison. 1982. 'Sex Roles: The Division of Labour at Home and in the Workplace', *Annual Review of Sociology* 8: 237–62.

Pahl, J. 1989. *Money and Marriage* (Basingstoke: Macmillan).

Pahl, R. 1984. *Divisions of Labour* (Oxford: Basil Blackwell).

Pateman, C. 1988. *The Sexual Contract* (Cambridge: Polity).

Peplau, L.A., and S.D. Cochran. 1990. 'A Relationship Perspective on Homosexuality', in *Homosexuality/Heterosexuality: Concepts of Sexuality*, eds D. McWhirter, D.D. Sanders, and J.M. Reinisch (Oxford: Oxford University Press).

———, K. Rook, and C. Padesky. 1978. 'Loving Women: Attachment and Autonomy in Lesbian Relationships', *Journal of Social Issues* 34, 3: 7–28.

Phillips, A., ed. 1987. *Feminism and Equality* (Oxford: Basil Blackwell).

Rubin, G. 1975. 'The Traffic in Women: Notes on the "Political Economy" of Sex', in *Towards an Anthropology of Women*, ed. R.R. Reiter (London: Monthly Review Press).

Scott, J. 1990. 'Women and the Family', in *British Social Attitudes: The 7th Report*, eds R. Jowell, S. Witherspoon, and L. Brook (Aldershot: Gower).

———, M. Braun, and D. Alwin. 1993. 'The Family Way', in *International Social Attitudes: The 10th BSA Report*, eds R. Jowell, L. Brook, and L. Dowds (Aldershot: Dartmouth).

Seymour, J. 1992. '"Not a Manly Thing to Do?": Gender Accountability and the Division of Labour', in *Inequalities in Employment: Inequalities in Home-life*, eds G.A. Dunne, R.M. Blackburn, and J. Jarman, Conference Proceedings for the Cambridge Social Stratification Seminar, University of Cambridge.

Smart, C. 1989. 'Power and the Politics of Child Custody', in *Child Custody and the Politics of Gender*, eds C. Smart and S. Sevenhuijsen (London: Routledge).

Weston, K. 1991. *Families We Choose: Lesbians, Gays, Kinship* (New York: Columbia University Press).

Witherspoon, S. 1988. 'Interim Report: A Woman's Work', in *British Social Attitudes: The 5th Report*, eds R. Jowell, S. Witherspoon, and L. Brook (Aldershot: Gower).

Chapter 25

Until recently, it was fairly rare for researchers who studied the allocation of household work between women and men in couples to consider the work involved in paying bills, keeping financial records, budgeting, and doing banking. Money matters are more invisible than other household work, it seems. Yet, in every household someone has to deal with the bills and the taxes, and worry about managing the finances. Sandra Colavecchia calls this work 'moneywork'. Based on her exploratory study, involving interviews with 31 married couples who were willing to talk about money matters with her, Colavecchia discusses who might be doing this work, and the gender differences in people's relationship to money.

Moneywork: Caregiving and the Management of Family Finances

Sandra Colavecchia

> Interviewer: Would you say that you're organized when it comes to money or not organized?
>
> Mary: Yeah, I would say I'm organized. Um, probably you know, anal, by most people's standards, yeah, yeah, I tend to be [a] very organized person and this is something that I'm, yeah, extremely organized. Um, you know I guess everybody has their own system set up. I like to organize the finances but, you know, I look after and I tend to keep things very organized and, you know, I like to track different things, you know in different areas, year over year, just to kind of see, you know, how we're doing and things like that, so I tend to be hyper organized.

Mary and her husband are one of the couples that participated in an exploratory qualitative study investigating how married couples organize their family finances. It is clear from Mary's comment that she is very involved in the day-to-day running of her family's financial affairs. Of course, the idea that a wife is responsible for keeping a family's financial house in order stands in contrast to long-standing beliefs about men's and women's roles within families. Yet Mary is not unique; she is representative of the women in my study, who typically take an active role in managing the finances in their families. This study addresses how a small group of married couples organize their family finances. I use the term 'moneywork' to underscore how this labour involving physical, mental, and emotional labour is viewed as housework.

An international body of research has shown that there are different arrangements by which heterosexual couples handle their money (see Fleming 1997; Nyman 1999; Pahl 1989; Singh 1997; Zelizer 1989). Nevertheless, the labour involved in handling family finances has not been systematically examined. Studies of women's domestic labour have overlooked the work involved in handling family finances, although some researchers have examined women's consumption work, including the work of shopping and finding ways to cut costs (see Bradbury 1993; DeVault 1991; Luxton 1980). The present study extends previous research by examining a wide range of activities involved in managing family finances.

Consistent with feminist methodology, it aims to 'excavate' the experiences of women to uncover what has been 'ignored, censored, suppressed' (DeVault 1999: 30).

The chapter outlines two separate sets of findings. The first set of findings examines the kinds of tasks that are involved in handling family finances and how this labour is viewed by participants, and the second set of findings describes important gender differences in spending. I begin with a brief description of the study, sample, analysis, and objectives of the study.

The Study

In 2002 and 2003, I interviewed 31 married couples with young children living in the Greater Toronto Area about their family finances. I studied families with young children because child-bearing is associated with a loss of income for most women, and because the economic inequality many women face in marriage is connected to their caregiving roles (Fox 2001; Nyman 1999). As recommended by other researchers, husbands and wives were interviewed separately (Pahl 1989; Woolley and Marshall 1994). Individual interviews give women the opportunity to speak freely about their marriages (Rubin 1976); given women's tendency to engage in conflict avoidance when it comes to money matters, separate interviews are especially important for women (Komter 1989; Nyman 1999; Wilson 1987). Semi-structured, open-ended interview questions were used to explore how participants accomplished the practical work of meeting financial obligations and their attitudes toward family finances, including their worries, anxieties, and stress related to family finances. Participants volunteered in response to posters advertising the study that were posted throughout the Greater Toronto Area in various locations, including small businesses and street posts.

In this non-random sample, the majority of participants are in their early to mid-thirties with one or two children. Most couples are in first-time marriages. There are six couples in which one of the spouses has been married previously; only two of these are making child-support payments. I focus on married couples because previous research indicates that money management varies across family types and is especially different for cohabiting couples (Burgoyne and Morison 1997; Fishman 1983; Singh and Lindsay 1996; Treas 1993). I also ensured variation among the couples with respect to the women's earnings relative to their husbands': I interviewed women who have either no regular earnings or only very minimal earnings (n = 8), women who earn less than their husbands (n = 13), women who earn the same as their husbands (n = 4), and women who earn considerably more than their husbands (n = 6). Eighteen of the couples are defined as middle class, as both spouses have university or college degrees with gross annual family incomes between $80,000 and $130,000. Six additional middle-class couples are university educated with gross annual family incomes between $40,000 and $50,000. These couples' low incomes are related to the fact that they are single-earner couples; all of the men work full-time and the women are self-defined stay-at-home mothers. Seven couples are low-income working-class families who do not have college or university degrees and have gross annual family incomes between $25,000 and $40,000. A lack of familiarity with university research and a greater likelihood of financial problems are no doubt just a few of the possible reasons why working-class couples were less interested in participating in this study. Most of the participants are white; there are nine visible minorities in the study, including Asians and blacks.[1]

The objective of the study is to understand how couples approach their family finances as a way to understand gender and power relations in marriage (Burgoyne 1990; Komter 1989; Pahl 1989; Singh 1997). One facet of family finances is the labour involved in handling financial matters. In this chapter I outline what this labour, or moneywork, entails, how it connects to women's responsibility for domestic labour, and the emotional consequences of this labour. A second facet of family finances concerns spending and I consider important differences in how men and women view personal spending. I describe how a 'relational' view of money, one that arises with the transition to motherhood, informs how women think about and actually spend money.

Uncovering the Labour of Family Finances

A major finding of the study is that handling family finances involves considerable physical, mental, and emotional labour. Interestingly, this labour has not been systematically examined in studies of unpaid work. Moneywork encompasses a range of activities that have been broadly categorized as bill paying, budgeting, shopping, and consumption work. It also includes learning about family finances from books, newsletters, and Internet sites. These activities are physical tasks that take time, and there are also mental and emotional aspects of the work that cannot be overlooked. I begin with a description of moneywork and an analysis of the gender differences that exist in how husbands and wives do this labour.

Bill Paying

Bill paying includes both paying a specific bill or a number of bills and coordinating bill paying. This kind of coordination work includes overseeing all bills and knowing when various bills are due, keeping track of bank balances to ensure that bills can be paid, contacting banks and other organizations to resolve problems, updating or checking accounts to see if bills have cleared, and figuring out pay dates in relation to when bills are due. In very tight financial circumstances, coordination work entails determining which bills can be paid when, and in what amounts. In the following passage, Tara describes how she carefully monitors the timing of when bills are due and how her husband relies on her to keep track of these financial transactions:

> Interviewer: Do you feel knowledgeable about your family's finances or not?
>
> Tara: I would say I'm the most knowledgeable of the two of us. I know when everything comes out of the bank. I know when the bills need to be paid, what gets paid at what time, when. My husband has direct deposit, so I know when it gets deposited and all that, so he is always asking questions . . . he would always ask questions about 'Can we get this? I have to make this payment, when does all this other stuff come out?' So he's not sure when the different bills come out of the bank account, and when they're due. So if he has something at work that he needs to bring in, like fifty dollars, which to us right now fifty dollars is a big amount, he'll ask, and I'll be like 'OK well can it wait to the next paycheque because so and so and so and so and so and so need to be paid.'

Among these couples, the women are more likely than the men to be responsible for the coordination of bill paying.

Budgeting

Budgeting entails short-term or long-term planning of earnings and spending, and often involves attempts to economize by limiting family spending. On one end of the spectrum are couples who do not use recorded budgets but instead use 'mental' budgets, which means keeping track of family expenditures 'in their heads'. On the opposite end of the spectrum are individuals who use very detailed recorded budgets to systematically track finances, which I refer to as 'high-intensity' budgeting. In high-intensity budgeting, all family expenditures are tracked, there is great attention to detail, and spending is closely monitored. Women are more likely than men to use budgets on a regular basis and they are also more likely to use recorded budgets, either pen and paper or electronic spreadsheets. When men use budgets they tend to rely on either mental budgets or to work out rough recorded budgets that include only a portion of family expenditures, typically larger expenditures such as mortgage and utilities. Women are more likely to engage in high-intensity budgeting and use exhaustive budgets that include large fixed expenditures such as mortgage and utilities, but also non-fixed expenses such as food, clothing and gifts, small expenditures, and miscellaneous spending. Matt and Tracy, university graduates working in white-collar non-professional jobs, are representative of the couples in my study. In the following comment Matt describes how he relies on Tracy's detailed and exhaustive budget when he attempts to do his own family budget:

> She'll take every little bill of everything we spend and she'll put it in the budget. Everything that we spend is in an Excel file in the budget on our computer. Home expenses, gas expenses, food, toys, everything. It's amazing really . . . I did a budget the other day at work and I just had her e-mail it to me 'cause I want to know how much hydro costs. I don't know how much that stuff costs, but once in a while when I do my budget I need her information so I can do my budget. (Matt)

His wife, Tracy, contrasts their different approaches to budgeting in the following remark:

> We differ in the sense that I am, I guess, anal. You know, I want everything in writing. I want to be able to see everything and in detail too, you know, every single item, whereas Matt, he, with pen and paper, just scribbles it down: this, that and that, and then once he's done with it he'll just throw it away and 'OK that's done.' But I need to keep a record of everything.

High-intensity budgeting, where all family expenditures are recorded and tracked, is done almost exclusively by women. Approximately half of the women engage in high-intensity budgeting; most have done so regularly throughout their marriage. Only one man does high-intensity budgeting, but he does so with the assistance of his wife who does the time-consuming work of tracking food bills—which she describes as 'picky' (Alice).

Learning about Finances

Women, especially those who engage in high-intensity budgeting, are also more likely than men to read about family finances in mass-market books, newsletters, and on the Internet. Mary, who has a master's degree in the health and medicine field but chose to be a stay-at-home mother, manages the finances in her household even though her husband's post-secondary education and professional work is in the financial field. Mary engages in high-intensity budgeting she learned from reading books about family finances.

> Mary: Yeah, he's definitely, we've both become a lot more frugal and as I became more frugal he became more frugal.
>
> Interviewer: Did you set the lead for that?
>
> Mary: I did and part of it I guess is, you know, as I said, I tend to be the one that has

> read the books or this and that and then you know we would discuss I would say you know I read this really neat book you know. I think it was at that time *Your Money or Your Life* [by Joe Dominguez and Vicki Robin]. I mean to read a book like that. And we'd talk about it and it gets your mind thinking and you know as I say with the baby, once you kind of get down that path, and having a baby's been a big, a big thing, you know you want to make sure that, you know he wants to make sure I don't have to go back to work. I want to make sure I don't go back. That's more important to both of us than having stuff. You know it just kind of makes you frugal.

One of the 'hooks' in the popular literature on finances is the promise to teach people how to save money. Interestingly, some of the guides are geared to stay-at-home mothers and families thinking of becoming single-earner families. With an eye to building their market, this literature connects money-saving strategies with ideas about the benefits, especially to children, of having a stay-at-home mother. The message that is conveyed is that in order to survive on one income women should engage in moneywork.

Shopping and Consumption Work

Moneywork includes shopping and consumption work. As retailers know, most of the shopping for food, gifts, and children's clothing and toys is done by women and viewed as women's responsibility. When men shop for the family it is typically in the context of buying groceries with their wives, or occasionally shopping for specific child-related items or gifts. The theme of women being 'careful' shoppers emerged during the interviews. Examples of careful shopping include meal planning to reduce food bills and various 'bargain-hunting' strategies such as waiting for sales, buying out-of-season items, using coupons, buying in bulk, comparison shopping, going through flyers, getting price adjustments when items that have been purchased later go on sale, shopping at discount grocery stores and warehouse outlets, and consignment shopping. This kind of careful shopping takes time and planning, although it is often viewed as a leisure activity (Luxton 1980). The women in this study are perceived to be better at 'spotting deals'; three women used the expression 'stretch a dollar' to describe their approach to shopping. Participants describe women as frugal and not impulsive and men as not frugal, and even impulsive in their spending. Troy's attitude with respect to shopping—'I'm not a real shop-around-look-for-the-best-deal-kind-of-person'—is shared by most of the men I interviewed.

Women are also more likely to engage in other activities to save money, and I refer to these various activities as 'consumption work'. These activities include borrowing items, for instance collecting hand-me-down clothing and toys; making items rather than purchasing them, for instance making birthday cards, gifts, clothing, diaper wipes, and husbands' lunches; researching financial products to save on bank fees; using 'points' cards to get free items like groceries; and selling clothing to consignment stores. Lesley's comment is representative of many of the women I interviewed: 'I don't spend a lot of money on things right now. Actually I'm really good at creative ways of saving money and bringing money in.' Women like Lesley, who left paid employment or reduced their hours of paid work, also look for ways to earn money that will not interfere with their childcare responsibilities, such as participating in market or medical research, taking in exchange students, and home-based businesses.

Moneywork as Care Work

The moneywork these women do is clearly an extension of the housework and caregiving work they typically do for their families. That is, attempts to economize food shopping are embedded in the work of planning and preparing meals, a task normally assigned to women (DeVault 1991). Similarly, women's responsibility for gift shopping is linked to their work in planning social events and women's consumption work is often associated with their responsibility for caregiving. For example, Bev buys and sells consignment clothing for her entire family in order to reduce family expenditures, operating a 'zero-based budget' for family clothing in order to work fewer hours outside of her home and spend more time with her child. Like Bev, many other women talked about finding ways to save or earn money that would allow them to be home with their children.

In a majority of the couples I interviewed women do more moneywork as well as more housework than their husbands. Although men shared or even did more housework than their wives in several couples, the women did more moneywork in these couples. Moreover, women's earnings relative to their husbands' do not affect whether or not they do the family's moneywork.

One of the consequences of doing moneywork is the related worry, stress, and anxiety that can accompany it. The people I interviewed talked about how it was the women who overwhelmingly experience these negative emotions. Moreover, the existence of a relationship between moneywork and harmful emotional reactions is supported by the fact that the three men in the study who take the lead on finances are also described as worriers. Of the remaining men, very few experience these negative emotions. Four men express fears about not being able to provide for their families; however these worries are temporary and linked to specific experiences of unemployment or illness. Because the men are more removed from the problematic aspects of finances, their lack of direct knowledge and responsibility for moneywork provides freedom from the worrying and stress that accompanies moneywork. These worries are greatest among families facing difficult financial circumstances, and particularly for women on maternity leave and stay-at-home mothers. They are also more pronounced for women who engaged in high-intensity budgeting, although some participants believe that high-intensity budgeting can be used to reduce worries and anxieties because detailed budgets provided some women with reassurance that things are better than they imagine them to be.

Personal Spending

Women's responsibility for moneywork and caregiving impacts women's attitudes about spending, especially their personal spending. Men and women consistently describe women as frugal, guilt-ridden, and neither impulsive nor spontaneous when it comes to spending money. In contrast, the men are described as not frugal, not feeling guilty about spending money, and impulsive in their spending. For example, Janice describes her husband Terry in the following way: 'I've never seen him restrain himself from buying something that he wants.' In contrast, the women spend time and effort to find ways to save their families' money. Paul describes his wife Jessica's efforts to save money as follows: 'She's very meticulous about what she buys, when she buys it. . . . everything that she purchases is well thought out. We need to upgrade the baby seat for example in the car and she did comparison shopping.' Women describe themselves as thinking through purchases more carefully than their husbands. For instance, Jessica contrasts her own and her husband Paul's approach to shopping:

> Like if he needs or wants something he's not one of those people that sort of goes 'Well should I buy it?' If he wants it, he'll get it, whereas I'm more contemplative. Like I'll go to the store and I'll see something I want and then I won't buy it, but I might come back two or three times before buying it. Do you know what I mean? . . . Whereas sometimes, even if I need it, or I think I need it, I don't always buy it right away. Like sometimes I'll wait for a sale or I'll go back a few times.

Women's efforts to save money must be understood in relation to their moneywork and the responsibility they bear for their families. Because women are responsible for moneywork they tend to know how much discretionary money there is, and because they are generally responsible for caregiving they also know what they need to buy. Their frugality often comes from knowing the relationship between their income and necessary expenses. Their resulting worries can explain their frugality. As a result, many women, both working class and middle class, state that they feel guilty about personal spending, and their husbands confirm this. Even women who earned more than their husbands felt such guilt. Joy, for example, links her husband's lack of guilt to his lack of awareness of the family finances: 'I don't think so, I don't think he's guilty about money. Maybe partially because he's not on top of it as much as I am, because I'm so aware of everything that goes in and out, where he just sort of hands me receipts.'

Even though women with regular earnings are just as likely to feel guilty as women without regular earnings, women who left paid employment to raise children sometimes connect their guilt to their lack of personal income. Alexis, a university-educated stay-at-home mother, views the guilt she feels about spending money as connected to the fact that she is not financially contributing to the household:

> Alexis: [I] very much feel guilty even for when it's groceries, if I feel like I haven't done my best job or the price even shocks when it adds up or when taxes are added onto the amount of [the] grocery bill, yeah, very much guilt involved there.
>
> Interviewer: And why do you think you feel guilty?
>
> Alexis: Probably, although I know that I'm staying at home and I want to stay at home, there's probably some guilt that I'm not actually contributing to the financial picture and yet I'm spending it, quite good at spending it, not earning it. And I know Adrian [her husband] supports me in our decision to stay home, I know that, but there's probably deep down some guilt.

Women who are not in paid employment have the lowest level of personal spending and their constraint in spending stems from feelings of guilt about not contributing financially and not feeling comfortable about spending, or entitled to spend, their husbands' earnings (Luxton 1980). Several husbands who have low earnings describe feeling guilty about spending money and this suggests that the ethic of altruism and sharing in marriage is overridden by the assumption that the one who earns money is entitled to spend it.

The Transition to Motherhood: A Relational View of Money

For women, the transition to motherhood brings about a change in how they feel about spending and how they actually spend money. Women repeatedly talked about reducing their own personal spending after having children. Janice, for example, noted: 'I think I am reluctant to spend money on myself. I think more so since we've had our son . . . I would rather spend money on him than on me. I don't think I need anything.' Another mother, Bev, said: 'I have been very creative and I would say my views towards money really shifted when my son came because I always liked nice things and shopping and so I had to find a way to feed that passion, but to do it on a shoestring. So I got into things like consignment.' Sarah uses the term 'new mommy syndrome' to describe the reduction in her personal spending and her awareness of other new mothers behaving similarly. These mothers contrast their current selves with their old selves before marriage and motherhood, and talk about how they used to spend more freely on items such as clothing and shoes before having children. Some men talk about spending less on themselves since hav-ing children, but they do not express feelings of guilt around personal spending. These mothers assert that their spending on children takes priority over personal spending:

> I don't ever buy things when we're totally broke and that I have to think 'Oh my goodness.' I am guilty sometimes, I feel guilty, when I buy for myself and I don't know if that's just, that's only been since being a mother that I think 'Oh should I buy this or is there something I could've bought the kids or are they gonna need something?' So I don't know if it just right now goes along with that, but my thoughts are always to, you know, something, do the kids need something. Not my husband, it's just my kids. (Tonya)

> I never used to feel guilty until I got married and then once you're married and you're a family, you know that it's like if you buy something for yourself sometimes you think, 'Well, you know, this money could go towards diapers or something.' So, you know, before I was married I never used to feel guilty about spending money. (Jessica)

> In a way I do [have difficulty spending money on myself] because I don't, I have trouble buying clothes and doing things like getting my hair cut. I guess that's changed since I had a child. I don't do those things as much. I don't spend money on those things. (Melanie)

For the couples in this study, parenthood brings greater reductions in women's personal spending than men's personal spending.

In these men's and women's comments about money, an important gender difference emerged: women talk about money in relational terms. For these women, the dollar spent on one item is a dollar that could be spent meeting family needs. One facet of this relational perspective is women's tendency to place the needs of family members ahead of their own needs. Dana is a university-educated professional who earns an income that is double what her husband earns. She connects her frugality to prioritizing the needs of other members of the family:

> Well some people would describe me as frugal. I can be frugal, for example, if I'm grocery shopping. If I see something that is on sale for a substantial reduction I'll buy extras so that if it's a non-perishable item I can save money on it. If it's something I would regularly buy, say a can of tuna, if it's on sale for fifty cents off, I'll buy a whole bunch to be, I guess, more frugal with the dollars that we have. 'Cause even though we have a good income I want to make sure we use it wisely because it's not just me that's, it's not just myself I have to think about. I have to think about the rest of the family.

This relational view of money helps to explain women's frugality, feelings of guilt, interest in getting deals and saving money, and their lower level of personal spending. Women view money spent on themselves as money that could have been spent on children or husbands, and they feel guilty because they view money spent on themselves as less money for their children. Husbands' higher levels of personal spending further constrain women's personal spending because of their relational perspective on money.

Women are also influenced by cultural norms about motherhood. Liz, for example, talks about feeling guilty about personal spending and describes a societal message that leads her to put her family's needs ahead of her own needs. Although she is not exactly sure where the message comes from, she knows that her feelings are typical among mothers:

> Interviewer: So what kinds of things might make you feel guilty?
>
> Liz: Probably around clothes. I think I have a real struggle around clothes . . . So if it's, you know right now I need a spring jacket but I'd actually love to get like two spring jackets, right? And so if I, and I'm going away this weekend to visit a friend and she may talk me into getting two spring jackets. I know I'll go through a period of feeling guilty over having two spring jackets and spending the money on something where I could do with one, and in fact I've got some really ugly old functional, you know, things that I could probably, that aren't, don't quite fit, or whatever that I could make, my mind tells me you can make do with that, sort of thing. So I think, you know, probably clothes is a good example of feeling guilty when I buy something that I can't completely justify needing.
>
> Interviewer: And why do you think you feel guilty?
>
> Liz: And I think this is like completely typical mom stuff that there is a finite piece of pie and that the bigger share of my pie is a smaller share of pie for other people . . . I can listen to it and just know that's the message. I don't know, where exactly it comes from, other than I know when I talk to my friends it's a very, very typical feeling.

Liz contrasts her childless friends with her friends who are mothers, and associates self-denial with only those friends who are mothers. Liz is representative of most of the other women in the study for whom a relational perspective of money derives from their involvement in moneywork and their broader responsibilities for caregiving.

Although a few of the men made references to money in relational terms, they did not consistently talk about spending and saving money in this way. Men refer to the cost of individual items and the affordability of items, but they do not seem to share the same relational view of money as the women. Indeed, several women told stories of husbands overpaying for items and this was interpreted as reflecting a lack of concern about the finiteness and relatedness of household resources. For instance, Liz relates a situation of her husband overpaying for a bike helmet for their daughter, and she described how the extra money could have been used for other necessary items.

Women's relational view of money means that they have a long-term view of money; they think about their finances with an eye to the future. Women express concerns about the future and ensuring that their families have enough money for the future. Paul's description of his wife was representative of women's long-term view of finances: 'She's organized, she's thorough, she's well-prepared, planned out, she looks to the future. She has a plan. She has set goals.' Women are especially concerned about providing for their children's future and being able to save money for their children's education. Although many men are described as good savers, women are more likely to be described that way. When men talk about saving, they talk about things like saving for retirement.

Women's guilt and lower levels of personal spending need to be understood within the context of women's caregiving in the family. Women are likely to recognize that they are putting others' needs ahead of their own and express this during their interviews. Several men also recognize that their wives do this. For example, Terry says of his wife, Janice: 'She's very responsible. She always thinks about the family first.'

Conclusion

These results show that the labour of managing family finances, or moneywork, is frequently taken on by women as part of their overall responsibilities for domestic labour. Moneywork involves more than the tasks of bill paying, shopping, and budgeting. It also involves mental and emotional labour, which can produce anxiety and worry.

Economists and sociologists have previously noted wives' lower level of personal spending as compared to husbands (Cantillon and Nolan 2001; Pahl 1989; Woolley and Marshall 1994). This study describes participants' interpretations of women's constraint in personal spending and elucidates the processes underlying gender differences in personal spending. Women's attitudes toward spending and reductions in personal spending are connected to a relational perspective on money that emerges with the transition to motherhood. This relational perspective is closely tied to women's responsibility for moneywork.

In addressing the labour involved in dealing with family finances, the present study highlights a form of household labour that has been overlooked by researchers. Results of this study suggest that given the time and emotional costs it entails, women's moneywork needs to be included in studies of women's household labour. By not considering moneywork researchers have likely underestimated the time women spend on household labour and gendered inequalities in the division of household labour.

Note

1. The qualitative method that I employ is a grounded theory approach to the analysis of interview data (Glaser and Strauss 1969). I conducted, recorded, and transcribed all interviews. Immediately after each interview notes were taken on reactions to interviews, initial impressions, key issues that stood out, preliminary ideas about emerging themes, comparisons to other couples, and comparisons between husbands and wives. After each interview was transcribed I coded the data, beginning with broad codes and moving to more refined codes as this process progressed. For example, initially all instances of bill paying were coded as 'bill paying' but as the coding process continued I developed the analytic code of 'the coordination of bill paying'.

References

Bradbury, Bettina. 1993. *Working Families: Age, Gender, and Daily Survival in Industrializing Montreal* (Toronto: Oxford University Press).

Burgoyne, C.B. 1990. 'Money in Marriage: How Patterns of Allocation Both Reflect and Conceal Power', *The Sociological Review* 38: 634–65.

———, and Victoria Morison. 1997. 'Money in Remarriage: Keeping Things Simple and Separate', *The Sociological Review* 45: 363–95.

Cantillon, Sara, and Brian Nolan. 2001. 'Poverty within Households: Measuring Gender Differences Using Non-monetary Indicators', *Feminist Economics* 7: 5–23.

DeVault, M. 1991. *Feeding the Family* (Berkeley, CA: University of California Press).

———. 1999. *Liberating Method: Feminism and Social Research* (Philadelphia: Temple University Press).

Fishman, Barbara. 1983. 'The Economic Behavior of Stepfamilies', *Family Relations* 32: 359–66.

Fleming, R. 1997. *The Common Purse: Income Sharing in New Zealand* (Auckland: Auckland University Press).

Fox, B. 2001. 'The Formative Years: How Parenthood Creates Gender', *Canadian Review of Sociology and Anthropology* 38, 4: 373–90.

Glaser, B.G., and A.L. Strauss. 1967. *The Discovery of Grounded Theory: Strategies for Qualitative Research* (Chicago: Aldine Publishing Company).

Komter, Aafke. 1989. 'Hidden Power in Marriage', *Gender and Society* 3: 187–216.

Luxton, M. 1980. *More Than a Labour of Love* (Toronto: Women's Press).

Nyman, Charlott. 1999. 'Gender Equality in "the Most Equal Country in the World?" Money and Marriage in Sweden', *The Sociological Review* 47: 766–93.

Pahl, J. 1989. *Money and Marriage* (London: Macmillan).

Rubin, Lillian B. 1976. *Worlds of Pain: Life in the Working-class Family* (New York: Basic Books).

Singh, Supriya. 1997. *Marriage Money: The Social Shaping of Money in Marriage and Banking* (Sydney: Allen and Unwin).

———, and Jo Lindsay. 1996. 'Money in Heterosexual Relationships', *Australia and New Zealand Journal of Sociology* 32: 57–69.

Treas, Judith. 1993. 'Money in the Bank: Transaction Costs and the Economic Organisation of Marriage', *American Sociological Review* 58: 723–34.

Wilson, Gail. 1987. *Money in the Family: Financial Organisation and Women's Responsibility* (Aldershot, UK: Avebury).

Woolley, Frances, and Judith Marshall. 1994. 'Measuring Inequality within the Household', *Review of Income and Wealth* 40: 415–31.

Zelizer, Viviana. 1989. 'The Social Meaning of Money: "Special Monies"', *American Journal of Sociology* 95: 342–77.

Chapter 26

There are many reasons why the division of household work based on gender has been resistant to change. The low status of care work in a capitalist economy and the fact that this kind of work is seen as 'women's work' are important cultural causes. The differences in the bargaining power of men and women, which in large part reflect their different positions in the paid labour force, are important structural causes. The fact that upper-middle- and upper-class couples have been able to employ women from Third World countries to do the work that they have no time for is an important cause as well.

In this chapter, Sedef Arat-Koc reviews the history of government policy that has continually chosen to enable couples with money to meet their childcare needs by shifting much of the work to the shoulders of a woman whose poverty gives her no other work options. As well, Arat-Koc examines the situation of these workers, and the factors that make them vulnerable to exploitation. Finally, she explains what it means for these domestic workers to leave their own families behind.

The Politics of Family and Immigration in the Subordination of Domestic Workers in Canada

Sedef Arat-Koc

Despite the sustained labour-force involvement of a majority of women, neither the availability and the quality of socialized childcare arrangements nor the division of household work between men and women appear to have changed radically. The structure, demands, and pressures of the labour market in Canada allow for little flexibility in the accommodation of family needs and responsibilities. Under these circumstances, housework and childcare remain private problems to be shouldered mainly by women, who must either work double and triple days or find substitutes.

In this context, the employment of live-in domestic workers has been a solution to the burdens of housework and childcare among high- and middle-income groups. Yet the way domestic service is organized in capitalist society in general, and the specific conditions of the majority of live-in domestic workers (98 per cent of whom are women), make this type of work particularly oppressive.

In discussing the implications of the domestic service 'solution' to the housework and childcare problem, I will document and analyze the structural and historical conditions of live-in domestic workers in Canada. My primary focus is on foreign domestic workers with temporary work permits. The conditions of this group best demonstrate the complex articulation of gender issues with those of class, race, and citizenship.

The Crisis of the Domestic Sphere

There has been a very significant increase in women's participation in the labour force in Canada since the 1960s. By 2006, 46.9 per cent of the labour force comprised women (Statistics Canada 2007). Moreover, the percentage of couples in the breadwinner/homemaker category was reduced to about 10 per cent from around 65 per cent in 1961 (The Task Force on Child Care 1986: 7; see Chapter 12). What is more interesting, however, is that the change has been most dramatic among women with family responsibilities. In 2004, the employment rate of women with children under 16 rose to 72.5 per cent, from 39 per cent in 1976 (National Council of Welfare 1999: 12; Statistics Canada 2007).

The response of society and the state to these changes in women's employment has been negligible. First, women continue to do significantly more housework and childcare than men, although men are now doing more housework and childcare than they used to (Marshall 2006). Even in dual-earner couples in which both partners work full-time women do considerably more household work than men (Marshall 2006: 13). Moreover, women continue to hold the responsibility for the household work that needs to be done every day (see Chapter 27).

Second, the childcare situation in Canada has been in a state of crisis for some time. Rather than keeping up with the need for adequate, affordable, and quality spaces, childcare in Canada in the 1990s had become, as Susan Prentice put it, 'less, worse, and more expensive' (Prentice 1999). There has been no substantial change since then because neither federal nor provincial governments have committed to providing childcare to every child who needs it (Mahon 2007). A very large percentage of children receiving non-parental care are in unlicensed arrangements, the quality and dependability of which are unknown. In 1998, regulated childcare spaces were available for only 10 per cent of all Canadian children under 13 years of age. In some provinces, the percentage of children served by regulated childcare locations was even lower: 3.9 per cent in Saskatchewan and 5 per cent in Newfoundland and Labrador (Childcare Resource and Research Unit 2000: 122). Even among children whose parents work or study more than 20 hours a week, access to licensed care is quite limited. In 1996, among children in this category, only 16 per cent of infants, 19 per cent of children 18 to 36 months old, 45 per cent of those three to six years of age, and 9 per cent of those between six and 13 years of age were served by regulated childcare (Human Resources and Development Canada 1997: 12–13).

A third factor that contributes to a crisis of the domestic sphere has to do with the inflexibility of work arrangements. Canadian employers and the state have provided little accommodation for the family responsibilities of working people. Except for an extended parental leave system, Canada lacks official recognition of recent changes in the labour force. Without the rights to refuse shift work and overtime and to work reduced hours or flexible workweeks (rights that are almost commonplace in Europe), working parents in Canada find that even privatized solutions fail to meet their needs (The Task Force on Child Care 1986; see Chapters 11 and 12).

As a result of the squeeze on working couples from pressures in the public and private spheres, there are signs that employment of domestic servants, a rare practice since the 1920s, has become widespread again. Decades ago, several governmental and mass-media sources mentioned the employment of domestic workers as a solution to the need for childcare (Royal Commission on the Status of Women 1970; Hook 1978; Vanstone 1986). There was evidence then that the employers of live-in domestic workers were overwhelmingly dual-career couples with small children. For 71.4 per cent of employers in the 1980s, the major reason for hiring a domestic was to 'free both spouses for the labour market' (The Task Force on Immigration Practices and Procedures 1981: 35–45). While the majority of employers have been in upper-middle to upper-income categories, there is a possibility that the demand for live-in domestic servants among middle-income families will continue to rise. An important reason for this is that user fees—as opposed to municipal, provincial, or national government financing—constitute a high proportion of childcare costs and middle-class families cannot get subsidies for such services in Canada. In 1995, the average parent fee for a three-year-old child was $753 per month (Prentice 1999: 139). Between 1989 and 1995, monthly daycare fees for preschoolers had increased by 11 to 40 per cent in different Canadian provinces (National Council of Welfare 1999: 50). It has been suggested that especially for parents with two or more preschool children, the employment of a live-in nanny costs significantly less than sending children to a daycare centre or hiring live-out help (Vanstone 1986: 51; Walmsley 1989: 129).

While the demand for domestic workers rises, the conditions of domestic service in general and live-in service in particular are so undesirable that it is very difficult to find Canadians willing to do the job. As a result, the Canadian Department of Immigration has devised mechanisms to bring in domestic workers, usually from the Third World, on temporary status. Most (96 per cent) of these workers are in live-in service (The Task Force on Immigration Practices and Procedures 1981: 53).

Although foreign domestic workers have certainly provided some solution to the pressures their employers face in meeting the demands of work and family, this solution is very questionable when one considers the working and living conditions of the workers involved. This paper starts with a short history of domestic service. The discussion of the conditions of domestic workers is divided into four parts. The first part examines the labour process in domestic service and analyzes what the domestic worker shares with the housewife. The second part focuses on the ambiguous status of the domestic as a special type of worker who is neither a member of the family nor an employee in the public sphere, enjoying some advantages of socialized work. In the third part, the citizenship status of foreign domestic workers in Canada is analyzed as a major factor contributing to, as well as perpetuating, the oppressiveness of their conditions. Finally, the status of domestic workers as mothers is briefly described.

History of Domestic Service

The emergence of domestic service, service provided by non-family members in the domestic sphere, is relatively recent, corresponding to the public/private split that came about with industrialization. Although servants were very widely employed in feudal Europe, the nature of their work and their status differed significantly from those of later domestic servants.

In feudal Europe, the labour requirements of most households—including those of most peasants and artisans—necessitated, at least during certain phases of their family cycle, the employment of servants. Servants were the children of poorer families and/or the children of families in different phases of their family life cycle. Social historians like Flandrin (1979) and Mitterauer and Sieder (1982) have clearly demonstrated that in an era when 'family' was synonymous with household, servants were very much a part of the patriarchal family, owing the same obedience to, and expecting the same protection and guidance as would, any family member, especially a child. In households that combined productive and reproductive work, servants performed unspecialized work alongside other family members, little of which had to do with the creation and maintenance of a comfortable domestic environment (Fairchilds 1984: 23–4).

With industrialization, the types of work performed by the family were divided and assigned to separate and gendered spheres. As the middle-class home sought to become a 'haven' in the competitive and harsh environment of early industrial society, the very purposes and nature of servant-keeping were transformed to serve the new emphasis on domestic comfort. Changes in the structure of society and the family in this period affected domestic service in more ways than one. Parallel to servants' work becoming exclusively 'domestic' for the first time was the 'feminization' of the occupation. As the home was defined to be women's sphere and housework to be women's work, domestic servants as well as their employers became predominantly female.

Another change that characterized this period of transformation was the increased social distance between master and servant. Two factors contributed to this. One was the increased privatization of the family, which defined it as a nuclear unit of parents and children and excluded servants as 'strangers' (Fairchilds 1984: 13–17; Rollins 1985: 33–6). Second, unlike the situation in feudal peasant and artisan households, where masters were direct producers, some of the bourgeois mistresses of the new domestic servants began to separate themselves from manual work. While the majority of middle-class women who could only afford one servant had to work side by side with them to keep up with highly demanding housework, upper-class women, committed to an ideology of domesticity, nevertheless began to maintain a clear distinction between their own managerial and supervisory roles in the home and the physical drudgery that servants undertook (Dudden 1983).

The history of domestic work in both Canada and the United States has been closely connected to histories of racial and ethnic relations and immigration, as well as to industrialization and urbanization. During the colonial period in the United States, domestic service was performed mainly by convicts, indentured servants, and black slaves. In this period, the low status and indignities that servants suffered were common in both the south and the north (Rollins 1985: 49).

From the American Revolution until about mid-nineteenth century, the exploitative and degrading treatment of black slaves in the American South coincided with relatively egalitarian master/servant relationships in the northern United States and Canada. The term *help* was used for the native-born whites in the American North, who partially replaced the foreign or black servants of the colonial period (Rollins 1985). Generally employed by farmers and small shopkeepers, the 'help' co-operated with the employer in the hard work of the household economy. The relationship of 'help' to their employers was quite egalitarian in the sense that they shared the conditions and the tables of the families for whom they worked. Also distinguishing the 'help' from past and future groups of domestic workers was the fact that theirs was less an occupation and lifelong status than an activity that allowed casual, temporary, and/or part-time employment (Dudden 1983). These conditions contrasted sharply with relations in bourgeois households in the cities, where the social distance between employers and employees was growing.[1]

From around the middle of the nineteenth century to the 1920s, the kinds of changes in domestic service that occurred in Europe as a result of industrialization and urbanization also prevailed in North America. As the urban middle-class family became more privatized, its emphasis on domestic comforts and luxury increased and therefore it became more dependent than ever on outsiders to actualize its standard of a private haven. While this substantially increased the demand for domestic workers, changes such as the decline in the general status of the domestic sphere, the 'bourgeoisification' of servant employers, and the distinction drawn between the family and non-family members precluded better working and living conditions for domestic workers.

Further contributing to a decline in the status of servants—or, in certain regions, the persistence of their low status—was the availability of groups of vulnerable workers. In the northeastern United States, immigrants like the Irish—many of them single women—were fleeing economic desperation in their own countries. Finding almost no alternatives to domestic work, they were particularly vulnerable. The term *servant*, which was rarely used in the democratic atmosphere of the post-revolution era in the American North, was reintroduced in this period (Steinberg 1981: 159; Rollins 1985: 51–2). In regions where there were large concentrations of people of colour, it was usually the women of the oppressed racial/ethnic groups who had to take domestic service positions.

> Despite differences in the composition of the populations and the mix of industries in the regions, there were important similarities in the situation of Mexicans in the southwest, African Americans in the south, and Japanese people in northern California and Hawaii. Each of these groups was placed in a separate legal category from whites, excluded from rights and protections accorded to full citizens. (Glenn 1992: 8)

Since the turn of the twentieth century, changes in the labour market as well as changes in the household have led to a decline in domestic service. First, alternative avenues of female employment opened up, as industrialization proceeded and some white-collar occupations were feminized. So, women rejected domestic service in favour of better working conditions elsewhere. Even when net wages from clerical, shop, or factory work were lower, women left domestic work to enjoy the relative independence of private life after work (Barber 1985). The demand for domestic workers also began to fall with improvements in household technology, falling birth rates, and the market production of goods previously produced in the household (Leslie 1974: 74). Since the beginning of the twentieth century, increased access to electricity, running water, and sewage systems; mechanization of heating, refrigeration, laundry; the development of food processing; and increased use of ready-made clothing meant for middle- and upper-class women that one person alone (in this case, the housewife) could do all the housework (Fox 1980; Luxton 1980). To the extent that domestic service survived, living-out became more widespread (Rollins 1985: 54).

In Canada, despite women's unwillingness to enter domestic service, employers were remarkably successful in maintaining a large supply of servants until World War II. Organized around church groups, YWCA, and other women's clubs and organizations, women seeking domestics were greatly helped by the Immigration Department (Leslie 1974; Roberts 1979). As domestic service in urban Canada became so undesirable that no native-born whites would do it, and as industrialization diverted women into other occupations, the Immigration Department became increasingly and more directly involved in ensuring a supply of domestics.

Although the demand for domestic workers decreased from the early part of the twentieth century until the late 1960s, it has always exceeded the supply. This has especially been the case for live-in jobs. As a result, the Department of Immigration developed new schemes in the post-war period to bring domestic workers to Canada, and to keep them doing domestic work.

The Material Conditions of Privatized Household Work

The geographic, economic, social, and ideological separation of the public work sphere from the home, which developed with socialized commodity production under capitalism, has led to a decline in the status of domestic labour—whether done by a housewife or a servant. One of the causes of this decline is the physical, economic, and ideological invisibility of domestic labour. Physically, what makes domestic labour 'invisible' is the service or maintenance nature of the work whose products are either intangible or consumed very quickly. The domestic labourer is at a disadvantage compared to the factory worker in this regard:

> The appropriate symbol for housework (and for housework alone) is not the interminable conveyor belt but a compulsive circle like a pet mouse in its cage spinning round on its exercise wheel unable to get off . . . (Williams, Twart, and Bachelli 1980: 114)

Also, domestic labour is performed in private, and perhaps is more isolated than ever before in human history. As the production of goods as well as services (such as education and health care) moved out of the home, as the husband and children left, and as the development of household technology made collaboration in certain tasks with other women less necessary, the household worker faced increased isolation, loneliness, and invisibility.

Economically, domestic labour is invisible because it is not part of capitalist production that utilizes wage labour to produce commodities (for the market) and profit. When performed by the housewife, domestic labour is unpaid; it produces use value and no profit. The work is more visible when carried out by a domestic servant because it is paid. As one domestic servant stated, however, it still can remain invisible, even in the eyes of the female employer:

> You know how housework is; you could tidy up the house and wash the dishes 20 times a day. At the end of each day, especially with three growing boy child, the house look like a hurricane pass through it, so when she is in a bad mood she wants to know what I do all day. (Noreen in Silvera 1983: 25)

Domestic labour involves physical and mental work, which goes into the reproduction of labour power and of the labour force. This is indispensable for the economy. Intertwined as it is with intimate, personal relations, however, domestic labour is considered a private matter, a 'labour of love'. As such, it is ideologically invisible as a form of real and hard work, a status that is hard to change even when it is paid.

Domestic labour generally does not appear on paycheques or in GNP figures; it is not considered 'real work', and is defined as 'non-productive'. Yet it involves very long working hours.[2] It is work that never ends. Especially for caregivers of young children who must be always on call, there is no clear boundary between work and leisure. For the housewife and the live-in domestic servant, the place of work is also the place of leisure. A domestic does not go to work, but wakes up to it. This makes her 'leisure' vulnerable to interventions and her work hours stretchable to 24 hours a day, seven days a week.

Contrary to its image as a place of comfort and safety, the home is a hazardous and stressful workplace for the domestic labourer. Besides working with dangerous chemicals and being involved in several activities that are accident prone, the domestic worker also experiences stress. Stress is typical for occupations that involve high demand and low control (Rosenberg 1986; 1987). In domestic work, the need to adjust the work to the different schedules of family members, and to juggle conflicting demands of housework and childcare, create stressful conditions. Being her own boss is largely a myth for the housewife. It is probably more so for the domestic worker whose schedule and standards of work are controlled by the employer.

Unlike wage labour which is—at least theoretically—changeable, the labour of the housewife is a lifelong, or at least marriage-long, commitment. Compared to the housewife, the domestic servant should fare better in this respect. This is only the case when we consider the free labourer, however. Domestic servants in Canada have very often been restricted in their ability to change employers, or even to decide whether or not to sell their labour power.

Although domestic labour under capitalism assumes several universal characteristics such as invisibility, isolation, and low status, the way these are experienced by individuals performing domestic labour may vary significantly by class, race, and citizenship. In the case of foreign domestic workers, the isolation and resulting loneliness imposed by the privatized nature of housework and childcare are perpetuated by racial, cultural, and linguistic barriers. Likewise, the invisibility of domestic labour and the low status attached to it are further reinforced by the powerlessness of domestic labourers when they are visible-minority women from the Third World on temporary work permits, who lack basic political rights.

Neither a Wife Nor a Worker: The Contradictions of the Domestic Worker's Status

While sharing with the housewife many of the material conditions of privatized housework and childcare, the domestic worker also has an ambiguous status: she is neither a wife nor a full-fledged worker with corresponding rights and privileges. Squeezed between the private and public spheres, she belongs to neither one nor the other, and probably experiences the worst aspects of both.

With the historical privatization of the family, the domestic worker has been excluded from membership in, or close bonding with, the employing family. Lost are the co-operation and companionship apparently characteristic of relations between 'help' and employers in rural America. The domestic worker today is like a stranger, 'being *in* the family, but not *of* it' (Leslie 1974: 87). She is involved in the work of a *house*, but not the pleasures and intimacies of a *home*. Positive aspects that are rightly or wrongly attributed to the private sphere—love, intimacy, nurturance, companionship—are not even part of her realistic expectations.

> I feel as if this is my home. It is my home, this is where I live. It's not like I come to work for them and then evening time I leave and go home. When you are living with them, they make you feel as if you really don't belong, and where the devil do you really belong? It's a funny thing to happen to us, because it make us feel like we don't know if we coming or going. This live-in thing really puts us in a funny situation. (Gail in Silvera 1983: 113)

Potentially, lack of intimacy with the employing family is liberating. Since class differences turn close employer–employee relationships into paternalistic ones, many domestic workers actually prefer maintaining a business-like professionalism. Professionalism in relations, however, is not possible for the domestic worker, since it requires relative power in social, political, and legal terms. Historically, the social construction of domestic work in Canada has deprived domestic workers from these forms of power.

In losing the close relationship to the family and becoming an employee, the domestic worker has not been compensated by the advantages other employees enjoy. The isolation of domestic service makes the organization of workers, as well as the standardization and regulation of working conditions, very difficult. This difficulty is greater for live-in workers for whom there is no separation between home and work. The result is generally a vulnerable and often exploited worker whose conditions are at the mercy of the employer:

> Wages are too often regulated by the employer's bank account, hours of service by his personal caprice, and moral questions by his personal convenience. (Salmon, cited in Leslie 1974: 112)

Labour standards legislation—which is under provincial jurisdiction in Canada and therefore not uniform—either does not apply or only partially applies to domestic workers. As of the mid-1980s, domestic employees in private homes were totally excluded from labour standards legislation in Alberta, New Brunswick, Nova Scotia, the Northwest Territories, and the Yukon. In other provinces they were only partially covered—in many, only with provisions providing lower than the general minimum wage, longer than the 40-hour workweek and rarely any overtime pay (The Task Force on Immigration Practices and Procedures 1981: 74–8; Estable 1986: 51–3).

In Ontario, which has about two-thirds of all domestic workers in Canada, the Employment Standards Act was extended finally to domestics in 1984. It set daily and weekly rates of pay based on a standard workweek of 44 hours. This change, however, was almost meaningless for live-in domestic workers because they were not covered by the hours of work and overtime pay provisions of the Act. Since it is not uncommon for live-in domestic workers to work or be on call 60 to 80 or more hours per week, the actual hourly wage can in many cases fall substantially below the minimum wage. Working very long hours and having little or no time off are actually some of the most common complaints of live-in domestic workers:

> I want something where I can go home to my house at night, close my door and pray to my God in peace. I want to know that when I go to bed at night, I don't have to listen out for people shouting at me to come and look after their food or come and change diapers. (Noreen in Silvera 1983: 26)

It took two years of negotiations with the Ontario government, and a Charter of Rights case against it (filed by the Toronto Organization for Domestic Workers' Rights, INTERCEDE) before Ontario acquired labour regulations (in October 1987) that gave live-in domestic workers the right to claim overtime pay after a 44-hour workweek.[3] Whether or not this provision is enforced depends on how much *de facto* bargaining power domestics have in relation to their employers. So far, even when protective legislation exists, governments have generally failed to enforce it. In practice, especially when they are dealing with vulnerable workers who have no choice but to remain in their jobs, employers are free to set work hours, duties, and pay rates.

In Ontario, provincial governments have not only failed to enforce existing legislation but also have prevented domestic workers from defending their rights in an organized, collective way. The Ontario Labour Relations Act denies the domestics employed in private homes the right to unionize. The same Act also denies domestics access to an impartial tribunal for unfair practices (Estable 1986: 51).[4] In the early 1990s, the NDP government in Ontario symbolically recognized the right of domestic workers, along with other groups of previously non-unionized workers, to unionize—but did not provide solutions for the practical difficulties of organizing from the private sphere. After the Conservative Party came to power in 1995, however, even this symbolic right was taken away (Fudge 1997).

In some cases, existing regulations may even sanction abuse. One serious problem domestic workers face is the lack of clear job definitions. The Canadian Classification and Dictionary of Occupations (which the Immigration Department uses in connection with employment authorizations) may add to the problem. In this system *babysitter* is defined as someone who, besides doing other work, 'keeps children's quarters clean and tidy' and 'cleans other parts of home'. The definition of *maid/domestic*, on the other hand, includes, 'may look after children' (The Task Force on Immigration Practices and Procedures 1981: 76). The specific combination of the class status of the domestic worker and the fact that domestic service takes place in the private sphere creates the potential for a very peculiar relation of domination between the employer and the domestic worker, especially if there is a live-in arrangement—which is compulsory for foreign domestic workers on temporary work permits.

There are social–psychological dimensions to the subordination of a domestic worker that make it different from the subordination of housewives (who also do domestic work) and workers (who also stand in an unequal class relation to their employers). While a factory worker experiences subordination and control during work, when she leaves her job at the end of the day she is a free person in relation to her employer. The live-in domestic worker, on the other hand, cannot leave her workplace and her employer's supervision. Sharing private space with the employers, and yet not being part of their family, the domestic finds it difficult to create her own private space and private life:

> Some domestics have to share a room with the children in the household or have their room used as a family room, TV room, sewing room, etc. One woman had to keep her door open at all times in case the children started to cry; others say their employers do not respect their privacy and walk in without knocking. In one case the piano was moved into the domestic's room for the children to practice on! (Epstein 1983: 26)

Living in the employer's home, it is also difficult to invite friends over. Other specific complaints about lack of privacy refer in certain cases to the domestic's mail and phones being watched, personal belongings searched, and inquiries into her activities after days off (Silvera 1981; 1983). Because live-in domestic service creates the possibilities of total scrutiny over both the work and the lives of domestic workers, it probably is not an exaggeration to call it a 'total institution' (Cock 1980: 58–60; Fairchilds 1984: 102–4).

Clearly, during its historical development, domestic service lost only some of the elements of the child-like status it had in earlier patriarchal households. Gone are the protection, security, and bonding to the family that were typical of service in feudal society; remaining are the supervision and the personal nature of the authority relationship that strip the domestic worker of full adult status. Linguistic practices are often reflective of this. For example, it is very common for both employers and domestics themselves to refer to domestics as 'girls', regardless of their age. It is also common for domestic workers to be called by their first names while they are expected to address their employers as Mr or Mrs (Hook 1978: 63; Rollins 1985: 158).

Besides heavy physical work, domestic service involves a personal relationship with the employer. Unlike factory work, which requires completion of clearly defined tasks in clearly defined ways, domestic service is very unstructured. Especially in live-in arrangements, a domestic is not just hired for specific tasks, 'but for general availability; above all, a servant ha[s] to take orders as well' (Leslie 1974: 83). Consequently, the deference, obedience, and submissiveness that the domestic is supposed to display can sometimes be as important or a more important part of her job than the actual physical work.[5] The domestic worker, therefore, is hired not for her labour alone but also for her personality traits.

Also unique to the employer–employee relationship in domestic service is that both the domestic and the mistress are designated, on the basis of gender, as responsible for domestic work. In different studies, all the female employers interviewed have indicated that they needed the domestic worker to help them because their husbands would not (Kaplan 1985; Rollins 1985). Employment of a domestic worker has enabled these women to avoid a confrontation with their husbands about sharing domestic work. In this sense, the presence of the domestic worker 'emphasizes the fact that women—all women—are responsible for cleaning the house, at the same time that it releases the housewife to become a lady of leisure or a career woman' (Kaplan 1985: 17). Given the gendered division of labour in the household, the labour of the housewife and the domestic worker are interchangeable: the domestic worker is employed to replace an absent full-time housewife; but when the domestic worker can't work, the housewife must. Given social degradation of domestic work and the class inequality between the domestic worker and the mistress, however, their shared subordination does not often lead to solidarity:

> the domestic represents the employer in the most devalued area of the employer's activities. . . . Any identification the employer has with the domestic is a negative identification. (Rollins 1985: 185)

Rather than solidarity, shared subordination can lead to 'housewife power strategies' through which 'many housewives seek to maintain class and race privileges vis-à-vis their domestics' (Kaplan 1985). Often, what characterizes servant–mistress relationships is deference from the worker and maternalism from the employer.

Good Enough to Work, Not Good Enough to Stay: Implications of Citizenship Status for Foreign Domestic Workers

From the nineteenth century on, the Canadian state has been very active in recruiting and controlling a domestic labour force (Leslie 1974; Barber 1986; Lindstrom-Best 1986). The amount of planning and energy that has gone into these activities tells us a great deal about the importance of domestic service for the Canadian economy and society. The low status and unfavourable conditions of the workers involved, however, stand in stark contrast to the attention their recruitment and control have received. In fact, the conditions have been so undesirable that not only has it been difficult to find Canadians interested in the job, but the only way of keeping immigrant domestics in domestic work has sometimes been through indenturing them.

Active state involvement in recruitment and control of domestic workers started in the late nineteenth century when industrialization diverted women into other occupations and it became difficult to find enough Canadian-born women interested in domestic service. This involvement ranged from making the immigration of domestics easier by sending immigration employees to England and Scotland to select domestics, to encouraging and even enforcing the so-called 'assisted passage' agreements that bonded servants to their employers for a certain period of time (Leslie 1974: 95–105). Bonding became such a necessary part of controlling the domestic labour force that the Department of Immigration sometimes evaded legislation in order to fulfill its policing function. For example, around the turn of the century, most provinces enacted master and servant legislation aimed to protect servants from an exploitative contract that they might have signed in order to immigrate. According to this legislation, contracts signed outside the province were not legally binding. The Immigration Department, however, in order to enforce bonded status, avoided this legislation by having immigrant domestics re-sign their contracts upon arrival in Canada (Leslie 1974: 122, 79ff).

Immigration of British and Scottish domestic workers in the late nineteenth and early twentieth centuries shared with later domestic immigration the practice of bonding. What made immigration practices in this period different from later periods, however, was that recruitment of domestics from abroad was closely linked to Canada's nation-building efforts. Until the 1920s, the middle-class women and social reformers involved in female immigration work voiced racist, nationalist, and moralistic concerns that went beyond a simple interest in meeting demands for the domestic labour force. Through their efforts in selecting, protecting, and supervising domestics, the organizations involved in female immigration wanted to make sure that the recruits would become more than servants—that these women of the 'right' national and racial stock and character would, in the long run, constitute the 'pure and virtuous mothers of the ideal Canadian home and the foundation of the moral Canadian nation' (Roberts 1979: 188–9). While these expectations were certainly restrictive for domestic workers, they also conveyed the message that these women 'belonged' in Canadian society, a message that would be missing in later immigration practices.

The West Indian Domestic Scheme

Although the demand for domestic servants has decreased since the early part of the twentieth century, it has still exceeded the supply. This has especially been the case for live-in jobs. As a result, the Department of Immigration has developed new schemes in the post-war period to bring domestic workers to Canada and to keep them doing domestic work. In 1955, for example, the Domestic Worker Program was started to import domestic workers from the Caribbean region (primarily from Jamaica). Under this scheme single women of good health, between 18 and 40 years of age, with no dependants and of at least Grade 8 education, were allowed into Canada as landed immigrants on the condition that they would spend at least one year as domestic servants before being free to choose other types of work (Arnopoulos 1979: 26). Through this program, between 1955 and 1960 an average of 300, and between 1960 and 1965 around 1,000, domestic workers were admitted per year (Bolaria and Li 1985: 178).

Even though the West Indian Domestic Scheme brought in domestics as landed immigrants, it involved special 'administrative controls' which were missing in previous immigration schemes involving white European domestics. Any domestic who broke her contract or was found 'undesirable' (e.g., upon becoming pregnant in her first year) would be deported to her country of origin at the expense of the Caribbean government. Also, unlike preferred domestics from western and northern Europe, West Indian domestics were not eligible to apply for interest-free travel loans from the Canadian government under the Assisted Passage Loan Scheme (Calliste 1989: 143).

The Introduction of Temporary Status

In the late 1960s, the demand for domestic workers started to increase in Canada. This was due to women's increasing participation in the labour force and the underdeveloped childcare system they faced. In this period, the Department of Immigration started to see the Domestic Worker Program as an inadequate solution to the labour shortage in domestic service because most women who came as domestics found their working conditions unacceptable and left service for other work once they fulfilled their one-year obligation. Rather than providing the mechanisms to improve the conditions of domestic work and make it attractive for people to stay in—by extending and effectively enforcing labour standards and human rights legislation to domestic workers, for example—the Canadian state opted for a solution that would force people to stay in domestic work.

In the 1960s and the early 1970s—in spite of the high and rising demand for domestic workers—immigration authorities arbitrarily lowered the rating for domestic work within the occupational demand category (Bakan and Stasiulis 1992). In 1973, the government started issuing temporary work permits that would only let these workers stay in the country for a specified period of time (usually a year), doing a specific type of work, for a specific employer. The temporary employment authorization system is a new version of indenture. From 1973 to 1981, foreign domestic workers could only come to Canada as 'guest workers'—instead of immigrants. As guest workers they had no rights to stay in Canada or claim social security benefits. Although foreign domestics could be allowed to change employers with special permission from immigration authorities, they could not leave domestic service without also having to leave Canada. Extension of the employment visa beyond the first year was possible and common, but the foreign worker inevitably had to leave Canada. Under this new scheme, increasing numbers of domestic workers were brought into Canada every year. The numbers of employment visas issued to domestics rose consistently from around 1,800 in 1973 to more than 16,000 in 1982 (Silvera 1983: 15; Bolaria and Li 1985: 178).

The official purpose of the employment visa system was to meet the urgent and temporary needs of Canadian employers to fill jobs that cannot be filled domestically without threatening the employment opportunities of Canadian residents (Wong 1984: 86). When we consider the case of domestic service, however, both the unwillingness of Canadians to take live-in work, as well as the century-long efforts of the Canadian state to import domestic workers from abroad, suggest that neither the need nor the solution has been temporary. Despite the persistence of a high-demand/low-supply situation, domestic workers have, since the 1970s, only been accepted to Canada with temporary status. Except for foreign agricultural workers—who do seasonal work—domestic workers have been the *only* occupational group to whom temporary work permits apply on a permanent basis.

When we look into Canada's immigration practices since the mid-1970s, we see an increasing tendency to resort to temporary employment visas as opposed to permanent immigration to meet labour demands not only in domestic service but also in several other job categories. Since 1975, the annual number of people entering Canada on temporary employment visas has consistently exceeded the number of landed immigrants destined for the labour force (Epstein 1983: 237; Wong 1984: 92). Migration to Canada, therefore, has changed in part from a movement of people to a movement of labour power. The benefits of this to Canada as a labour-importing country are enormous. As the literature on migrant workers in western Europe, South Africa, and California has demonstrated, recipient countries benefit not only by avoiding the costs of developing a young and healthy labour force but also by avoiding a commitment to supporting them during old age, sickness, and unemployment (Gorz 1970; Castles and Kosack 1980; Burawoy 1980). 'Behind the term "guest worker" [is] a belief that such workers [are] like replaceable parts. Like cogs in a machine, for every part that breaks down, there [is] a seemingly endless supply of replacements' (Rist 1979: 51).

There are also significant political advantages to employing workers without citizenship rights. Lacking electoral and political rights and freedoms, and dependent on their employers not only for wages but also for their continued stay in the country, workers on employment visas are expected to create a docile and acquiescent labour force. Historically, the presence of migrant workers has also frequently been associated with racist and xenophobic divisions in the working class. 'Canadians have the feeling that we are coming here to rob them, to take away their jobs, yet we are the ones who clean up their mess, pick up after them. We take the jobs they wouldn't take and yet they hate us so much' (Primrose in Silvera 1983: 100). One significant ideological implication of temporary work permits is that designation of a group of workers as temporary and foreign encourages a desensitized attitude toward their conditions. Hannah Arendt argues that with the development of nation-states and national sovereignty, basic human rights and freedoms were thoroughly implicated with the rights of citizenship (1966). In liberal democratic societies, where emphasis on formal equality has become a part of popular political discourse, separation of people into 'citizen' and 'non-citizen' categories, into 'insiders' (to whom rights apply) and 'outsiders', serves to legitimize inferior conditions and lesser rights for the latter group.[6]

The major effect of Canada's employment visa system on domestic workers has been the creation of a captive labour force, which has guaranteed that the turnover in domestic service would remain low no matter how bad the working and living conditions. Unable to leave domestic service without losing their rights to stay in Canada, foreign domestics have also found it difficult, in practice, to change employers. A foreign worker's status in Canada changes to that of visitor if she leaves or loses her job. While in practice workers are generally given a period of two weeks to find a new employer, the decision to issue a new employment visa is at the discretion of the individual immigration officer who judges whether the working conditions with the previous employer have in fact been intolerable (The Task Force on Immigration Practices and Procedures 1981: 26–7).[7] Besides the hassle given by individual immigration officers, there is a regulation that requires workers on employment visas to have a 'release letter' from the former employer before changing employers (Toughill 1986).[8]

Unlike other workers who enjoy the basic freedom to leave a particular job or employer, the only freedom that the foreign worker on an employment visa has is to return to her country of origin. In the case of many Third World women who come to Canada out of conditions of economic desperation, there is no choice but to stay in Canada. As Nancy Hook reported, compared to Canadian workers, foreign domestic workers on employment visas were more likely to live in the homes of their employer, to work more days per week, more overtime without pay, and receive a smaller hourly wage (Hook 1978: 107–8).[9]

Even though their status in Canada was by definition temporary, domestic workers on employment visas have been required to pay Canada Pension Plan, Unemployment Insurance premiums, and income tax (about one month's earnings a year) without being able to claim benefits.[10] The nature of the employment visa has made access to unemployment insurance benefits impossible because the worker either has to find a new employer or leave the country if she loses a job. Benefits from Canada Pension Plan have also been inaccessible because the 'guest worker' is expected to retire in the country of origin (The Task Force on Child Care 1986: 121). For services that they do not expect to receive, foreign domestics have paid a very high price. Revenue Canada has calculated the total of revenues from CPP and UIC premiums collected from foreign domestics between 1973–79 to be more than 11 million dollars (The Task Force on Immigration Practices and Procedures 1981: 70).[11]

The Foreign Domestic Movement (FDM) Program

In 1981, a federal task force was established to study the conditions of domestic workers on temporary work permits. Its report recommended that the Temporary Employment Authorization system be continued provided that opportunities for landing be broadened (The Task Force on Immigration Policies and Procedures 1981). The Foreign Domestic Movement (FDM) program which came into effect in November 1981 has enabled foreign domestics who have worked in Canada continuously for two years to apply for landed immigrant status without having to leave the country. While this was a progressive step, it failed to solve the problem of foreign domestic workers in Canada. First, the FDM continued to impose a two-year period of bonded service that the domestic had to fulfill before applying. In some ways, the practice of indenturing was strengthened by the entrenchment in the FDM of a mandatory live-in requirement for all participants in the program. Domestic workers who insisted on live-out arrangements would not only lose their rights to apply for landed immigrant status but would not even receive extensions on their employment authorization (Employment and Immigration Canada 1986: 17–18).[12]

Another problem with the FDM program has been that it gave no guarantee that landed immigrant status would be granted. Applicants needed to meet Immigration assessment criteria and demonstrate a 'potential for self-sufficiency'.[13] Reflecting societal notions about domestic labour in general, these women continued to get very low points for both the Specific Vocational Preparation category and, ironically, the Occupational Demand category (The Task Force on Immigration Practices and Procedures 1981: 18–21).[14] As a result, immigration officers required domestic applicants (again without any guarantees to grant them landing) to take upgrading courses (with high foreign student fees), to demonstrate adaptation and integration into Canadian society (through volunteer work in the community), and to prove financial management skills (through showing evidence of savings, etc.)—all special requirements applying to domestic workers only. For live-in foreign domestics, it has been difficult to afford both the time and the money to meet these requirements. Another problem has been that domestics with children (in the home country) and older domestics have faced special discrimination during assessment for immigrant status.[15]

> They say Immigration say any woman over 45 soon can't clean house and will be just a burden on the government, and woman with over two children will bring them into the country and take away the opportunities other Canadian children have. (Noreen in Silvera 1983: 29)

So-called 'rationalized' immigration policies, oriented toward the demands of the market, aim to import labour power rather than people. It is not, therefore, surprising to see dependants being treated as 'superfluous appendages' of the labour market (as they were called in South Africa).

The overall effect of the 1981 changes in the Temporary Employment Authorization Program has been to create the possibility for *individual* upward mobility of some domestic workers while providing no *structural* solution to the problems of domestic service or foreign domestic workers in general. Indeed, it is ironic that to accumulate enough points to get landed immigrant status, a domestic has had to move out of domestic service altogether. The implicit message that immigration policies and practices give is that domestic workers, as domestic workers, are 'good enough to work, but not good enough to stay' in this country. This message surely tells us a great deal about the status of domestic labour in general.

Furthermore, it is interesting to note the parallel between the modern attitude of the Canadian government and the historical treatment of domestic workers. Domestic servants did not receive legal equality and citizenship rights until the late nineteenth or early twentieth century. In France and England, for example, because they were considered to be too dependent on their masters to be recognized as civil persons, domestics (together with women) were the last groups to be enfranchised. Many of the basic workers' rights and freedoms we take for granted and often associate with capitalist society are, in fact, connected to citizenship rights. With the alleged attempt to meet the temporary labour requirements of the Canadian economy without threatening the jobs of Canadians, the employment visa system has created a *permanent* temporary workforce without citizenship rights.

By treating both the need and the presence of foreign workers as *temporary* the Canadian government has done nothing *permanent* either to improve significantly the conditions of workers or to find other solutions to problems of housework and childcare. As long as it has been able to maintain a captive labour force without citizenship rights to do live-in domestic service, the Canadian government has found little incentive for improving conditions for domestic work. Changes in immigration policy since the early 1990s also demonstrate this point.

The Live-in Caregiver Program (LCP)

In April 1992, the Ministry of Employment and Immigration introduced several changes to the previous FDM program and renamed it the 'Live-in Caregiver Program' (LCP). According to the new policy, women intending to do domestic work would be admitted to Canada on the basis of the education and training they have related to the care of children, seniors, and the disabled. Specifically, this would involve the successful completion of the equivalent of Canadian Grade 12 education plus proof of six months of full-time formal training in areas such as early childhood education, geriatric care, and pediatric nursing (CEIC 1992; *Domestics' Cross-cultural News* 1992). These new criteria were contested by domestic workers' advocacy organizations which argued that many potential applicants from Third World countries would not qualify under the new program. In many countries, basic schooling only goes to Grade 10 or Grade 11 and formal training in areas of child, elderly, and disabled care does not exist (DeMara 1992; *Domestics' Cross-cultural News* 1992). The government responded by revising the requirements to a high-school diploma and a minimum of work experience in caregiving, which would be counted as equivalent to six months of formal training.

The program introduced in 1992 lifted some of the extra requirements the earlier FDM placed on foreign domestics for landed status (i.e., doing skills upgrading, demonstrating successful adaptation by doing volunteer community work, and demonstrating financial management skills by having to show savings). To become a landed immigrant, a foreign domestic worker now had to demonstrate a minimum of two years employment as a full-time live-in domestic worker within 36 months after her arrival in Canada. Also, domestic workers no longer needed to obtain a 'release letter' from their employer in order to change employers. To receive a new employment authorization from immigration officers, domestic workers would instead have to get a 'record of employment' from their employers showing how long they were employed and a statement of their earnings (CEIC 1992).

Despite limited improvements on freedom of movement and the conditions for landed status, the LCP continues in the tradition of immigration policies regarding domestic workers by imposing the kind of status and conditions on workers that lead to abuse and an unfavourable working environment. Under the LCP, the temporary work permit system and the mandatory live-in requirement still prevail, while women have to prove higher qualifications to work as domestic workers. The new program 'enables Canadian employers to obtain higher qualified labour for less pay' (*Domestics' Cross-cultural News* 1992) while doing little to help domestic workers to improve their conditions.

Currently, the LCP is still under effect and the conditions and status of foreign domestic workers have hardly changed since the 1970s. There is also less hope for change in the short term. Compared to the 1970s, 1980s, and part of the 1990s, there is no longer a strong women's movement in Canada to take up the issue of domestic labour (in general and in its racialized forms) and struggle for change. Economic restructuring and neo-liberalism have also led to significant changes in employment norms, increasing precarious forms of work and reducing workers' protections and security. In addition, the category of temporary worker has become more widespread in Canadian immigration, especially since the early 2000s. In 2002, the federal government introduced a Foreign Worker Pilot Program which started to issue temporary visas to foreign workers in *any* occupation with a 'labour shortage'. In September 2007, the applications from employers under the program were expedited and the program further expanded, especially in Alberta where the economy has experienced a boom and in British Columbia where the upcoming Olympics are expected to create employment in several sectors. As of spring 2008, following an expansion of the program in Ontario, the federal government is planning significant changes to Canadian immigration policy. Justified as a way to reduce the backlog in the processing of immigrant applications, and introduced as part of the budget (therefore avoiding debate as major policy change), there are indications that the government may be moving to respond to many applications for permanent status from workers with temporary visas (Keung 2008a; 2008b).

As economic restructuring has pushed precarious work into the mainstream in the labour market, and changes in immigration policies continue to shift the status and conditions of migrant workers from anomaly to near normativity, the present situation presents more difficult challenges. But it also presents potentially positive possibilities for migrant domestic workers. On the one hand, in an environment where most workers experience a 'race to the bottom', changing the working and living conditions of domestic workers have become increasingly challenging, short of radical systemic changes. On the other hand, neo-liberalism and economic restructuring mean that conditions that have applied to migrant domestic workers are not only conditions for a highly racialized and gendered occupation that other workers can distance themselves from. Thus, we can also interpret current conditions as creating the possibility of potential solidarity among different sectors of labour.

Temporary Status and Transnational Families

According to research I have done in collaboration with Fely Villasin, one of the most negative implications of temporary immigration status and the living-in requirement for domestic workers is that women must come to Canada alone, having left their own families behind. All the immigration programs for domestic workers since the early 1970s are built on the premise that foreign domestic workers who arrive in Canada are—or should live as—single people. In reality, a significant percentage of domestic workers have children.

Canadian immigration regulations as well as individual employers assume that there is an incompatibility between this type of employment and parenting responsibilities of the worker. During interviews Fely Villasin and I conducted in 2000, a domestic worker explained how her employer did not allow her daughter, who was visiting her in Canada, to stay in her house; the employer warned her, 'don't forget you are working'. Sometimes the worker herself internalizes the notion of incompatibility between worker status and parenting that is imposed by the state and the employers. One of the respondents to our questionnaire replied to the question 'If you have children, did they come to Canada with you?' in the negative, explaining that she 'did not come to Canada as an immigrant but as a worker' (Arat-Koc with Villasin 2001: 21, 22).

Even though recent immigration programs for domestic workers allow them to apply for permanent resident status after two or three years of live-in service under temporary work permits, the time it takes for domestic workers to sponsor their families is, from the time of their arrival in Canada, on average, three to five years, and often longer. Moreover, for many domestic workers, Canada is not necessarily the first country they go to on a temporary work permit. When several years of work abroad are combined with an average of three to five years, and sometimes up to seven years of waiting in Canada, the experience and the impacts of separation are profound for domestic workers and for their families.

Several factors made the experience of family separation very painful for domestic workers. In addition to a profound sense of responsibility for the well-being of their children and feelings of guilt that they may be neglecting them by having to take employment abroad, domestic workers also suffer a sense of deprivation of intimacy and support. During the interviews, one domestic worker regretted being separated from her husband. She said that the deprivation of 'emotional and physical contact' caused her loneliness and depression. Another domestic worker summarized the effects of separation from her common-law spouse as a feeling of 'emptiness in the sense that [there is] no one who would comfort you when you have a problem or giving reassurance when you are down' (Arat-Koc with Villasin 2001: 29).

For most migrant domestic workers with children, the decision to leave their children was an extremely painful one. In addition to handling practical questions regarding whom to leave their children with and whether the children would be safe, well-cared for, happy, and healthy, domestic workers had to deal with heart-wrenching feelings during separation from their children. During her interview, one domestic worker described the time she bid her children goodbye and boarded the bus to Manila as follows: 'I could not walk up the bus, the driver had to carry me up. I was so weak and faint—leaving my kids and not knowing how long it would be before we could be together again' (Arat-Koc with Villasin 2001: 26).

Even though migrant workers were very aware of the significance of their remittances for their children's upkeep and future, they experienced a profound sense of guilt, anxiety over the well-being of the children, as well as a sense of sadness, loss, and loneliness. As one worker told us, 'My life will not be complete. A part of me will always be missing, wondering about how my child is doing' (Arat-Koc with Villasin 2001: 26). The mothers we interviewed constantly worried about their children. They tended to blame themselves when the children were maltreated, got into trouble, or did badly in school. Even when there were no apparent problems, there was anxiety about the unknown. One domestic worker said that her biggest regret was that she would 'not know what is going on inside them' and that she could not 'share their troubles and triumphs' (Arat-Koc with Villasin 2001: 27). Most mothers tried to maintain a good long-distance relationship with their children by spending large amounts on telephone bills.

Our surveys and our interviews with domestic workers as well as professionals dealing with immigrants' health revealed serious physical and mental health problems associated with separation from family. Complaints ranged from chronic stomach pain, muscle tension (specifically in the neck and shoulders), sleep problems, and frequent headaches, to severe anxiety and depression. Describing the effects of separation, one of the respondents to the questionnaire wrote about 'a gap, depression, frustration, and loneliness'. Another domestic worker dealt with similar feelings by 'always wanting to keep [herself] busy because [she] always felt sad if [she was] not doing something' (Arat-Koc with Villasin 2001: 27).

Mothers often assumed that the separation affected the children negatively, that they 'felt as orphans', deprived of the love of their parents. As one woman said, 'the effect of separation on my children was overwhelming. [They] felt insecure and unprotected while I was away. The trust on me as a parent was totally diminished by the time we got together in Canada' (Arat-Koc with Villasin 2001: 28). Some children were too young when the mothers left to know or remember them. Some older children were angry and resentful toward the mother, who, they thought, had betrayed them. Some children appreciated the economic necessity and the sacrifice but had deep feelings of longing and sadness. Other studies confirm this. Rhacel Salazar Parrenas (2003), who interviewed children of migrant domestic workers in the Philippines, reports on the profound sense of loss. When she asked Ellen, who was 10 when her mother left, how she felt about the children in her mother's care in New York, the girl responded:

> Very jealous. I am very, very jealous. There was even a time when she told the children she was caring for that they are very lucky that she was taking care of them while her children back in the Philippines do not even have a mom to take care of them. It's pathetic, but it's true. We were left alone by ourselves and we had to be responsible at a very young age without a mother. Can you imagine? (Parrenas 2003: 42)

Even as she experienced a sense of loss, Ellen was not unaware of her mother's dedication and commitment:

> I realize that my mother loves us very much. Even if she is far away, she would send us her love. She would make us feel like she really loved us. She would do this by always being there. She would just assure us that whenever we have problems to just call her and tell her . . . And so I know that it has been more difficult for her than other mothers. She has to do extra work because she is so far away from us. (in Parrenas 2003: 43)

Parrenas's research makes it clear that the children of transnational mothers who had positive surrogate parental figures and open, regular communication with their mothers were able to resolve the emotional challenges and focus on school. Even the well-adjusted, though, suffered the loss of family intimacy (Parrenas 2003). It was not unusual for some children to deal with feelings of loss and longing by emotionally withdrawing from the mother. Two of the respondents to our questionnaire who were still separated from their children said: 'I think they do not miss me any more or I don't exist. They don't care if I call or write to them.' 'They hardly know me . . . Even in my vacation in the Philippines, I could feel the gap between us' (Arat-Koc with Villasin 2001: 28, 29).

Problems did not end if/when families were reunited. When children met their mothers in Canada, they often met as strangers. Most mothers found it very hard to help their children get over feelings of abandonment. They also found it hard to undo the distance that had developed between themselves and their children. As one woman said, 'The children I take care of give me a hug as soon as I come to work, and hug me goodbye when I leave. They are much more affectionate than my own children who have joined me' (Arat-Koc with Villasin 2001: 33–4).

In addition to problems in establishing trust, love, and intimacy, mothers also found it difficult to establish authority over their children. As mothers tried to fulfill their maternal role, some children resented, resisted, and rejected this, questioning where she had been all these years and what right she had to control their lives (Arat-Koc with Villasin 2001: 34).

The difficulties in re-establishing parent–child ties sometimes lasted many years, sometimes never ended. In addition to the challenges of re-establishing authority, intimacy, and trust, mothers were confronted with the anger of children who were having difficulties adjusting to life in a new country. Feeling powerless about imposed emigration, the children tended to blame their difficulties on the person who seemed to be responsible for making this decision. One domestic worker related a moving story of how her kids were 'brainwashed' against her and how she has often 'fe[lt] alone against the world', despite all the efforts she put into providing for them and sponsoring them to move to Canada. It took five years before her children even 'began to understand' her. Still, she admitted, 'It is really hard for us to get reunited with them after a long time of separation' (Arat-Koc with Villasin 2001: 34).

As a result of the difficulties during separation, as well as the challenges faced after reunification, most migrant domestic workers in our research experienced forced family separation as a form of emotional abuse that emotionally scarred those involved for a long time, if not permanently.

Conditions of Domestic Work and the Role of the State

In Canada, the state has played a contradictory role in the organization of domestic work. It has underregulated working conditions while overregulating the workers. While the provincial labour standards laws, respecting 'the sanctity of the home', have either completely ignored or at best unequally treated the home as a workplace, the federal government, which has jurisdiction over immigration, has overregulated the workers (Luxton, Rosenberg, and Arat-Koc 1990: 15). In Canada, therefore, it has not simply been the generally low status of housework, or even the availability of a supply of foreign workers, that have created the conditions of domestic workers' vulnerability. As Castells (1975: 54) put it: 'immigrant workers do not exist because there are "arduous and badly paid" jobs to be done, but, rather, arduous and badly paid jobs exist because immigrant workers are present or can be sent for to do them'.

It is ironic that the consistently high and increasing demand for domestic work has corresponded with a deterioration of workers' conditions. This is due to the active role the state has played in structuring and controlling not only the volume but also the conditions of these workers. There is a striking contrast between the laissez-faire approach the liberal state has taken that favours private solutions to problems in the domestic sphere and its rigid intervention in the provision, organization, and control of 'help' for that sphere. Given the specific combination of state policies in areas of childcare provision, labour legislation, and immigration, domestic service is not simply a private but a politically constructed solution to the crisis of the domestic sphere.

The positions put forward by both the federal and provincial governments in childcare policy for the last three decades indicate the persistence of a clear preference for privatized solutions—with little concern about the quality and conditions for either children or caregivers. The absence of a universal childcare program or even a political commitment to increasing childcare spaces means that parents are left with no choice but to make private arrangements. While the pressures that many parents face in relation to childcare needs constitute a real and serious problem, the assumption in most legislative and policy debates and proposals has been that domestic workers should subsidize the inadequacy of the social childcare system through their underpaid and overworked conditions.

Current domestic service arrangements bring the interests of employers and employees into conflict. Given the pressures on budget and time that many middle-class working couples face, a domestic service relationship may turn into a zero-sum game in which the improvements in the pay and working conditions of domestic workers mean losses for the employers. As a relationship between female employers and workers, domestic service emphasizes most clearly the class, racial/ethnic, and citizenship differences among women which stand in the way of gender unity.

Feminism and Domestic Service

The domestic service question is a feminist question, not just because 98 per cent of domestic workers are women, or because it potentially may create divisions among women that feminism needs to solve to make 'sisterhood' a reality. It is also a feminist question because it is so closely implicated in the privatized nature of domestic labour in our society. Domestic service, as it is organized in Canada, is not just a question of human and workers' rights. It is a question of women's oppression and liberation. Women's liberation has been defined by some as the upward *mobility* of individual women *out of* some subordinate positions and occupations. According to this definition, 'women's liberation' can be compatible with a general devaluation of the subordinate positions and occupations many women hold.[16] If we choose, instead, to define women's liberation as a collective and transformative struggle—in addition to being one of individual liberation—that deals with class and racial inequalities and aims to restructure society to eliminate subordinate positions, live-in domestic service becomes a very backward 'solution' for the crisis of the domestic sphere.

Women's liberation is a multi-dimensional project which needs to involve challenging capitalism and the state as well as gender relations in the home. A domestic service 'solution' to the crisis of the domestic sphere means that neither the gender division of labour in the household nor the existing demands of the workplace, which refuse to address tensions between paid work and family responsibilities, are challenged. When adopted by wealthy and middle-class women, this 'solution' also leaves the state relieved of pressures and responsibility for providing collective solutions for people's needs. It leaves housework and childcare as women's work—still isolating, of low status and low value. Rather than solving the problem of gender inequality, it adds class and racial dimensions to it. Instead of housework and childcare being the responsibility of *all* women, it becomes the responsibility of *some* with subordinate class, racial, and citizenship status, who are employed and supervised by those they liberate from direct physical burdens.[17] Reinforcing divisions of mental and manual labour, this may perpetuate low status and pay for domestic service.

The domestic service 'solution' is also backward because it does not solve the problems posed by the separation of spheres. Given the availability of a cheap source of vulnerable workers, it discourages a struggle for socialized services and more flexible work arrangements.[18] Rather than easing the public/private split in society, therefore, this solution polarizes and deepens it with added class and racial dimensions. The crisis of the domestic sphere necessitates a search for creative solutions and an honest, open debate around each solution and its gender, class, and racial implications. In the absence of such a debate and a vision of concrete, constructive alternatives that would emerge from them, individualized ad hoc solutions may bring more harm than good to both individual women and to the struggle for the emancipation of all women.

Notes

This is a revised and updated version of a paper originally published in *Studies in Political Economy* 28 (Spring 1989) and M. Luxton, H. Rosenberg, and S. Arat-Koc, *Through the Kitchen Window*, 2nd edn (Toronto: Garamond, 1990). I am grateful to Pramila Aggarwal, Michal Bodemann, Bonnie Fox, Charlene

Gannage, Roberta Hamilton, Mustafa Koc, Meg Luxton, Barb Neis, Lynne Phillips, Ester Reiter, Harriet Rosenberg, Jane Ursel, and Fely Villasin for ideas and useful comments on different versions of the paper.

1. *The Canadian Settler's Handbook* advised immigrant domestics that they would enjoy 'social amenities' in rural Canada and that 'no lady should dream of going as a home-help in the cities, for there class distinctions (were) as rampant as in England' (cited in Lenkyj 1981: 10).
2. According to one study, in Sweden, 2,340 million hours are spent in housework annually, as compared to 1,290 million hours in industry (cited in Rowbotham 1973: 68).
3. Although these regulations may be a progressive step in recognizing the principle of overtime for domestic workers, they do not necessarily provide standard overtime protection since it is the employers who are given the option to negotiate with their employees to take the overtime in time off rather than in money for actual overtime worked. In this respect, regulations covering domestic workers still deviate from provisions of the provincial Employment Standards Act.
4. There is also the 'Subversive Activities' provision in the 1977 federal Immigration Act which, through its vague wording, provides an intimidating message to all non-citizen residents in Canada that engaging in union activities may become grounds for deportation (see Arnopoulos 1979: 41–5).
5. It is wrong, however, to confuse this appearance with real thoughts and feelings of the worker. Responding to Lockwood who referred to the domestic worker as the 'most socially acquiescent and conservative element' of the working class, Jacklyn Cock emphasizes the need to differentiate between deference and dependence. While the domestic recognizes her dependence on and powerlessness in relation to her employer, her deference is only 'a mask which is deliberately cultivated to conform to employer expectations, and shield the workers' real feelings' (Cock 1980: 104–6).
6. Here I have drawn on an argument made by Gerda Lerner in a different context. Commenting on the origins of slavery, Lerner has suggested that the process of marking a group of people as an out-group and 'designating th[is] group to be dominated as entirely different from the group exerting dominance', have been essential to the mental constructs involved in the institutionalization of slavery (see Lerner 1986: 76–7).
7. The criteria for tolerability used by immigration officers could sometimes be very flexible. Silvera reports the case of a domestic from the Caribbean who wanted to leave her employer for reasons of sexual assault. Because the assault was less than sexual intercourse, her complaint was not found legitimate and she was deported from Canada (see Silvera 1981: 58).
8. Although Employment and Immigration spokespersons have on a number of occasions announced that the practice of requiring release letters would be ended, a survey conducted among foreign domestic workers in Toronto suggests that it is very common (Arat-Koc and Villasin 1990: 12).
9. Research also shows that there is a very strong relationship between living-in (a requirement for foreign domestic workers) and working very long hours. According to a survey among 576 domestic workers in Toronto, only 35 per cent said they worked a standard workweek of 44 hours. Forty per cent worked for an average of 45 to 50 hours a week. Eighteen per cent worked 50 to 60 hours and 6 per cent worked more than 60 hours a week. Among the live-in domestics who did overtime work, only 34 per cent received the legal compensation. Twenty-two per cent said they received some, but less than the legal rates of compensation. An overwhelming 44 per cent of those doing overtime work stated that they received no compensation whatsoever! (Arat-Koc and Villasin 1990: 6).
10. In 1987 Canada had international agreements with only six countries (the United States, Jamaica, Italy, Greece, Portugal, and France) whose nationals could combine CPP contributions in Canada with pension contributions in their own countries (INTERCEDE 1987: 12).
11. Since 1986 the immigration department has been imposing fees for issuing, extending, and renewing employment authorizations. In addition to being underpaid and overtaxed in a

society that offers them no privileges and freedoms of citizenship, domestic workers are now being asked to 'take the burden off the Canadian taxpayer' and pay the costs of their own processing and policing.

12. The enforcement of the live-in requirement has been so strict that some domestics who lived-out have been threatened by deportation—even if their employer didn't have room and agreed with the arrangement (see 'Patriarch of the Month' 1992).
13. Many domestic workers who have had years of experience supporting themselves (and others) find it very offensive to have to prove such potential: 'I supported five children *before* I came here, and I've supported five children *since* I came here, and they want to know if I can manage on my own?' (Mary Dabreo, cited in Ramirez 1983/1984).
14. A point needs to be made about conceptions of the value of different occupations that immigration partly borrows from Canadian Classification and Dictionary of Occupations. CCDO has a rigid and static conception of skill as a 'thing' that is largely determined 'objectively' by the time spent in formal education. As Gaskell (1986) has argued, however, 'skill', far from being 'a fixed attribute of a job or a worker which will explain higher wages or unemployment', is a result of a political process determined by the relative power (through supply/demand advantages, organizational capabilities, etc.) of different groups of workers.
15. The 1978 case of 'seven Jamaican women' was fought on the basis that discrimination against women with children was discrimination on the basis of gender. Seven Jamaican women filed a complaint with the Canadian Human Rights Commission after being ordered deported for having failed to list their minor children in their applications to come to Canada. They won their case on the ruling that no married man had ever been deported for having to list his children (cited in Timoll 1989: 57).

    Although explicit and direct discrimination against women with dependent children has been eliminated, the practice still survives because those women who express their intention to stay in domestic service and also sponsor their dependants to Canada often fail to meet Immigration criteria on the grounds that they would not make enough income to make their families 'self-sufficient'.
16. This is Betty Friedan's position on housework. She approvingly cites others in *The Feminine Mystique* who think housework can be done by 'anyone with a strong enough back (and a small enough brain)' and find it 'peculiarly suited to the capacities of feeble-minded girls' (Friedan 1963: 206, 244).
17. With the emergence of surrogate motherhood, the same potential also applies to child-bearing. The employment of surrogate mothers of working-class backgrounds may indeed become the solution upper-class and career women opt for to avoid the time and inconvenience a pregnancy would cost.
18. During the 1920s, in the southern United States where there were more servants, the growth of commercial bakeries and laundries lagged behind such developments in the north and west (see Katzman 1978: 275).

References

Arat-Koc, S, and F. Villasin. 1990. 'Report and Recommendations on the Foreign Domestic Movement Program', prepared for INTERCEDE, Toronto Organization for Domestic Workers' Rights.

———, with F. Villasin. 2001. *Caregivers Break the Silence: A Participatory Action Research on the Abuse and Violence, Including the Impact of Family Separation, Experienced by Women in the Live-in Caregiver Program* (Toronto: INTERCEDE).

Arendt, H. 1966. *The Origins of Totalitarianism* (New York: Harcourt, Brace and World).

Arnopoulos, S.M. 1979. *Problems of Immigrant Women in the Canadian Labour Force* (Ottawa: Canadian Advisory Council on the Status of Women).

Bakan, A., and D. Stasiulis. 1992. 'Foreign Domestic Worker Policy in Canada and the Social Boundaries of Citizenship', unpublished paper.

Barber, M. 1985. 'The Women Ontario Welcomed:

Immigrant Domestics for Ontario Homes, 1870–1930', in *The Neglected Majority: Essays in Canadian Women's History*, eds A. Prentice and S.M. Trofimenkoff (Toronto: McClelland & Stewart).

———. 1986. 'Sunny Ontario for British Girls, 1900–30', in *Looking into My Sister's Eyes: An Exploration in Women's History*, ed. J. Burnet (Toronto: The Multicultural History Society of Ontario).

Bolaria, B.S., and P.S. Li. 1985. *Racial Oppression in Canada* (Toronto: Garamond Press).

Burawoy, M. 1980. 'Migrant Labour in South Africa and the United States', in *Capital and Labour*, ed. T. Nichols (Glasgow: Fontana).

Calliste, A. 1989. 'Canada's Immigration Policy and Domestics from the Caribbean: The Second Domestic Scheme', *Socialist Studies* 5.

Castells, M. 1975. 'Immigrant Workers and Class Struggles in Advanced Capitalism: The Western European Experience', *Politics and Society* 15, 1: 33–66.

Castles, S., and G. Kosack. 1980. 'The Function of Labour Immigration in Western European Capitalism', in *Capital and Labour*, ed. T. Nichols (Glasgow: Fontana).

CEIC. 1992. *Immigration Regulations, 1978*, as amended by SOR/92-214, P.C. 1992-685 (9 Apr.).

Childcare Resource and Research Unit. 2000. *Early Childhood Care and Education in Canada: Provinces and Territories 1998* (Toronto: Childcare Resource and Research Unit, University of Toronto).

Cock, J. 1980. *Maids and Madams: A Study in the Politics of Exploitation* (Johannesburg: Ravan Press).

DeMara, B. 1992. 'New Immigration Rules Racist Domestic Workers Rally Told', *Toronto Star*, 3 Feb.

Domestics' Cross-cultural News. 1992. Monthly newsletter of the Toronto Organization for Domestic Workers' Rights, June.

Dudden, F.E. 1983. *Serving Women: Household Service in Nineteenth-century America* (Middleton: Wesleyan University Press).

Employment and Immigration Canada. 1986. *Foreign Domestic Workers in Canada: Facts for Domestics and Employers*, pamphlet (Ottawa: Supply and Services, Cat. No. MP23-61/1986).

Epstein, R. 1983. 'Domestic Workers: The Experience in BC', in *Union Sisters: Women in the Labour Force*, eds L. Briskin and L. Yanz (Toronto: The Women's Press).

Estable, A. 1986. *Immigrant Women in Canada: Current Issues*, a Background Paper for the Canadian Advisory Council on the Status of Women, Mar. (Ottawa: Supply and Services).

Fairchilds, C. 1984. *Domestic Enemies: Servants and Their Masters in Old Regime France* (Baltimore: The Johns Hopkins University Press).

Flandrin, J.L. 1979. *Families in Former Times* (Cambridge: Cambridge University Press).

Fox, B. 1980. 'Women's Double Work Day: Twentieth Century Changes in the Reproduction of Daily Life', in *Hidden in the Household: Women's Domestic Labour under Capitalism*, ed. B. Fox (Toronto: The Women's Press).

Friedan, B. 1963. *The Feminine Mystique* (New York: Dell Publishing).

Fudge, J. 1997. 'Little Victories and Big Defeats: The Rise and Fall of Collective Bargaining Rights for Domestic Workers in Ontario', in *Not One of the Family: Foreign Domestic Workers in Canada*, eds A.B. Bakan and D. Stasiulis (Toronto: University of Toronto Press).

Gaskell, J. 1986. 'Conceptions of Skill and the Work of Women: Some Historical and Political Issues', in *The Politics of Diversity*, eds R. Hamilton and M. Barrett (Montreal: Book Centre).

Glenn, E.N. 1992. 'From Servitude to Service Work: Historical Continuities in the Racial Division of Paid Reproductive Work', *Signs* 18, 1.

Gorz, A. 1970. 'Immigrant Labour', *New Left Review* 61.

Hook, N.D. 1978. *Domestic Service Occupation Study: Final Report*, submitted to Canada Manpower and Immigration, Jan.

Human Resources and Development Canada. 1997. *Status of Daycare in Canada 1995 and 1996: A Review of the Major Findings of the National Daycare Study 1995 and 1996* (Ottawa: Author).

INTERCEDE. 1987. *Know Your Rights (A Guide for Domestic Workers in Ontario)* (Toronto: Oct.).

Kaplan, E.B. 1985. '"I Don't Do No Windows"' *Sojourner* 10, 10 (Aug.).

Katzman, D.M. 1978. *Seven Days a Week: Women and*

Domestic Service in Industrializing America (New York: Oxford University Press).

Keung, N. 2008a. 'Guest Labour Program Raises Troubling Questions', *Toronto Star*, 15 Mar.

———. 2008b. 'Tories to Shake up Immigration', *Toronto Star*, 14 Mar.

Lenkyj, H. 1981. 'A "Servant Problem" or a "Servant–Mistress Problem"? Domestic Services in Canada, 1890–1930', *Atlantis* 7, 1 (Fall).

Lerner, G. 1986. *The Creation of Patriarchy* (Oxford University Press).

Leslie, G. 1974. 'Domestic Service in Canada, 1880–1920', in *Women at Work, Ontario, 1850–1930* (Toronto: The Women's Press).

Lindstrom-Best, V. 1986. '"I Won't Be a Slave!"—Finnish Domestics in Canada, 1911–30', in *Looking into My Sister's Eyes: An Exploration in Women's History*, ed. J. Burnet (Toronto: The Multicultural History Society of Ontario).

Luxton, M. 1980. *More Than a Labour of Love* (Toronto: The Women's Press).

———, H. Rosenberg, and S. Arat-Koc. 1990. *Through the Kitchen Window: The Politics of Home and Family*, 2nd edn (Toronto: Garamond Press).

Mahon, Rianne. 2007. 'Challenging National Regimes from Below: Toronto Child-care Politics', *Politics and Gender* 3: 55–78.

Marshall, K. 2006. 'Converging Gender Roles', *Perspectives* (July), Cat. No. 75-001-XIE (Ottawa: Statistics Canada).

Mitterauer, M., and R. Sieder. 1982. *The European Family* (Chicago: University of Chicago Press).

National Council of Welfare. 1999. *Preschool Children: Promises to Keep: A Report by the National Council of Welfare* (Ottawa: Author).

Parrenas, R.S. 2003. 'The Care Crisis in the Philippines: Children and Transnational Families in the New Global Economy', in *Global Woman: Nannies, Maids and Sex Workers in the New Global Economy*, eds B. Ehrenreich and A.R. Hochschild (New York: Metropolitan Books).

'Patriarch of the Month'. 1992. *Herizons* 6, 3 (Fall).

Prentice, S. 1999. 'Less, Worse and More Expensive: Childcare in an Era of Deficit Reduction', *Journal of Canadian Studies* 34, 2 (Summer).

Ramirez, J. 1983/1984. 'Good Enough to Stay', *Currents* 1, 4.

Rist, R. 1979. 'Guestworkers and Post-World War II European Migrations', *Studies in Comparative International Development* 15, 2: 28–53.

Roberts, B. 1979. '"A Work of Empire": Canadian Reformers and British Female Immigration', in *A Not Unreasonable Claim: Women and Reform in Canada, 1880s–1920s*, ed. L. Kealey (Toronto: The Women's Press).

Rollins, J. 1985. *Between Women: Domestics and Their Employers* (Philadelphia: Temple University Press).

Rosenberg, H. 1986. 'The Home is the Workplace: Hazards, Stress and Pollutants in the Household', in *Through the Kitchen Window: The Politics of Home and Family* (Toronto: Garamond Press).

———. 1987. 'Motherwork, Stress, and Depression: The Costs of Privatized Social Reproduction', in *Feminism and Political Economy*, eds H.J. Maroney and M. Luxton (Toronto: Methuen).

Rowbotham, S. 1973. *Women's Consciousness, Man's World* (Harmondsworth, UK: Penguin).

Royal Commission on the Status of Women. 1970. *Report of the Royal Commission on the Status of Women* (Ottawa: Supply and Services).

Silvera, M. 1981. 'Immigrant Domestic Workers: Whose Dirty Laundry?', *Fireweed* 9.

———. 1983. *Silenced*, Talks with Working Class West Indian Women about Their Lives and Struggles as Domestic Workers in Canada (Toronto: Williams-Wallace Publishers).

Statistics Canada. 2007. <http://www40.statcan.ca/01/cst01/labor05.htm>.

Steinberg, S. 1981. *The Ethnic Myth: Race, Ethnicity, and Class in America* (Boston: Beacon Press).

The Task Force on Child Care. 1986. *Report of the Task Force on Child Care* (Ottawa: Supply and Services).

The Task Force on Immigration Practices and Procedures. 1981. *Domestic Workers on Employment Authorizations*, Report (Apr.).

Timoll, A.L. 1989. 'Foreign Domestic Servants in Canada', unpublished research essay, Department of Political Science, Carleton University, Ottawa.

Toughill, K. 1986. 'Domestic Workers Praise Rule Change', *Toronto Star*, 22 Sept.: C2.

Vanstone, E. 1986. 'The Heaven-sent Nanny', *Toronto Life* (Apr.).

Walmsley, A. 1989. 'Can a Working Mother Afford to Stay Home?', *Chatelaine* (Nov.).

Williams, J., H. Twart, and A. Bachelli. 1980. 'Women and the Family', in *The Politics of Housework*, ed. E. Malos (London: Allison & Busby).

Wong, L.T. 1984. 'Canada's Guestworkers: Some Comparisons of Temporary Workers in Europe and North America', *International Migration Review* 18, 1: 85–97.

Chapter 27

In this chapter, Meg Luxton examines the source of stress felt by many adults today: the incompatibility of the demands that our jobs and careers place on us and the needs of family members for our care. First, she situates dual-earner couples in a historical context that highlights the economic need most households have for two incomes. Then, relying on interviews with adults living in Toronto in 1999 and 2000, Luxton describes the kinds of dilemmas employed people face when close family need special attention and care. Finally, she reviews the different strategies that families and individuals might use to handle the joint demands of earning a livelihood and caring for family. In so doing, she pushes us to think about the relationships among families, the economy, and the state.

Family Coping Strategies: Balancing Paid Employment and Domestic Labour

Meg Luxton

Since the early twentieth century, the majority of families in Canada have made a living by combining paid employment and unpaid domestic labour.[1] To ensure an income, one or more family members sell their capacity to work, or their labour power, to an employer. On the job their labour power is consumed and they earn its monetary recompense, a wage or salary. In consumer markets and in their homes, people use those earnings and their unpaid labour to obtain and produce the goods and services that make up the means of subsistence for themselves and their families. Each day, the means of subsistence are prepared and consumed and family subsistence, including the capacity to work again, is produced. This labour of social reproduction ensures the survival of both individuals and the society as a whole (see Chapter 1). A man explained how this cycle of production and consumption played out in his daily life:[2]

> I like my job. It's interesting and it pays pretty good. I go to work every day, come home, and you know how it is, some of the money you make has to go to food and the mortgage and stuff you need for every day. So you have to keep working just to have enough money to live on. And you hope that maybe you can make a bit more than you need for every day. If you're lucky, maybe you do. (M A#27 1/00)

This particular form of family economy imposes conflicting demands on people whose livelihood depends on it. A young mother with two preschool children described her situation:

> I have to work and so does my husband. Without both incomes we wouldn't get by. But we have two little kids. So who is supposed to look after them? If I quit work, I could stay home with them, but we wouldn't be able to pay the bills. If we pay someone else to look after the kids, it takes almost all of my pay. Like it's almost impossible! I think maybe people won't be able to have families soon, unless something changes. (F A#26 1/00)

As her description implies, while such family livelihoods depend on both paid employment and domestic labour, the organization of the two different labour processes mean that the demands of one are at odds with the demands of the other. An office worker explained how she saw the issue:

> At my workplace they call it 'family friendly' policies and talk a lot about helping us employees 'balance work and family'. Mostly it just means you can come in a bit earlier and leave earlier, or it's okay to take unpaid time off occasionally if your kids are sick or that it's okay to have your kids call you at work. And though they call it 'family', they really mean women 'cause the guys never have to worry about that stuff. And it doesn't really help with the fact that if you're at work, you can't be at home looking after things. And if you stay home, you don't get paid. (F A#30 1/00)

As the comments of these two women indicate, the massive entry of women into the paid labour force has made it harder for individual families to manage their domestic responsibilities. As people struggled to find ways of improving the conditions of their lives, a range of social policies and practices have developed, some of which have made paid work and domestic labour a bit more compatible. These include universal services such as education and health care and a range of policies designed to ensure minimum income and employment standards, access to housing, childcare, and care of dependent adults (Ursel 1992). However, most social policies assume that individuals and their families are primarily responsible for personal caregiving and that women remain primarily responsible for managing the competing demands of the two labours necessary for family subsistence (Eichler 1988; 1997). A woman explained how this worked:

> My husband was injured at work. He was in hospital for weeks and we thought he was going to die. So I took time off work to stay with him. Then I had to go back to work. When he got out of hospital, he needed full-time care. Everyone—the doctors, the social workers, the nurses—they all assumed I would take care of him. When I said I couldn't, they acted like I was a monster! Surely if I was a good wife I would do anything for him. Like who was going to pay the bills? I said, he needs care, he should get it. That's what health care is for. Or, he was injured at work, the company should pay someone to care for him. It was a big struggle. I spent hours fighting to get him the care he needed. They really tried to make me do everything but I said I can't, I have to work. I felt terrible, but he understood. (F M#16 12/99)

Changing Patterns of Paid Employment

In the early twentieth century, the tensions between the two labours were mediated by the predominant family form, a heterosexual nuclear family, and its conventional divisions of labour based on gender and age. According to prevailing norms, adult men were 'breadwinners' whose primary responsibility was to earn an income for the family while adult women were 'housewives' whose primary responsibility was running the family home and caring for its members.[3] In practice, the higher the man's income and the more secure his employment, the less income other family members had to provide. Whether income-earning men were available or not, women were primarily responsible for domestic labour, and their participation in paid employment was always negotiated in relation to the needs of family members, especially when children were young or when there were family members who needed regular care related to illness, disability, or aging. Where necessary, many women augmented family incomes by intensifying domestic labour—making preserves, clothing, and other items for household use or engaging in a variety of home-based income-generating activities such as taking in laundry or sewing or renting rooms to boarders. Children were typically expected either to attend school as part of a strategy to strengthen their future employment chances or to get paid employment and contribute to the family economy by either contributing their earnings to the family household or reducing its expenses by moving away to set up their own household. Where necessary, older girls were expected to contribute to domestic labour, especially where there were a number of younger children or where their mother had income-generating work that made it difficult for her to handle all the domestic labour (Bradbury 1993).

This strategy, widely accepted as the norm, was idealized as the appropriate way to organize family life and naturalized in economic and social policies as diverse as wage rates and welfare regulations (Ursel 1992; Armstrong and Armstrong [1978] 1994). From the early twentieth century until the 1970s it was the dominant family form and division of labour (Armstrong and Armstrong [1978] 1994: 84–5). However, as Dionne Brand (1994) and Linda Carty (1994) have shown, African-Canadian women have a history of higher than average labour-force participation rates. Indigenous or Aboriginal women have had lower than average labour-force participation rates but have worked in mixed economies since colonization (Abele 1997). Immigration policies have permitted particular categories of women workers to enter Canada to fill certain types of labour needs (Stasiulis 1997; Preston and Giles 1997). Patterns of class, race, ethnicity, national origin, region, religion, and other cultural differences shaped the ways in which different populations both were located in the labour market and related to prevailing norms and the economic and social policies that presumed specific family forms and divisions of labour. A woman described her mother's experience as an immigrant:

> She came here in the fifties, as a domestic worker. She came because she had two daughters and in Jamaica she couldn't make enough to support us. The Canadian government wouldn't let her bring us so for years she sent money home and our grandmother raised us. (F A#13 11/99)

Another woman described how the prevailing norm of the income-earning husband and the homemaker wife created problems for her family in the 1960s:

> I remember how ashamed I used to feel because my father was unemployed—for years—and my mother went out to work. The worst was when teachers would tell me my mother should come to help at some school event, and I would have to explain that she couldn't. They would look at me and I always felt like scum of the earth. In those days, fathers worked and mothers stayed home and anyone who didn't conform was obviously of a lesser sort. (F A#15 1/00)

Never a satisfactory resolution, this strategy excluded those who did not live in heterosexual nuclear families and created pressures on people to marry. It depended on the man's ability to earn enough money to support a dependent wife and children, something few men actually achieved. It put pressure on men as the sole-income providers while isolating women in a demanding low status and unpaid job. It made women economically dependent on their husbands which left them vulnerable, especially if the relationship broke down (Luxton 1980). While it encouraged economic independence on the part of young-adult children, in low-income households it easily pitted parents and young-adult children against each other in struggles over family unity versus individual independence.[4] Parents might urge children to leave school to earn a living and contribute to the family household whereas children often preferred to stay in school or set up their own households. Parental demands often undercut girls' chances for staying in school by expecting them to help out at home.[5] This strategy also depended on families' capacities to make ends meet by expanding unpaid labour in the home to reduce expenses, something that became difficult as household expenses were increasingly monetary, such as mortgage payments and taxes—demanding income rather than useable goods (Parr 1999: 101–18).

Throughout the century, the participation rates of women in the formal labour force steadily increased, dramatically changing family economics and divisions of labour (see Table 27.1). Among cohabiting male–female couples in 1961, almost 70 per cent relied on the man as the single-income provider. By 1991 only 19 per cent did so, a number that has remained fairly constant since. In the majority of cohabiting male–female families (61 per cent), both adults had paid employment and, in 5 per cent, women were the sole-income providers (Oderkirk, Silver, and Prud'homme 1994). By 1997 women were the higher-income earners in 23 per cent of couples and the sole-income provider in about 20 per cent of couples (*Globe and Mail*, 21 Feb. 2000: A2). Most dramatically, the labour-force participation rates of married women with young preschool children increased from 49.4 per cent in 1981 to 69 per cent in 1991. By 2000, the vast majority of mothers with young children remained in the labour force.

There were many reasons for such changes. The growth of the service sector in the 1960s and

Table 27.1 Canadian Labour-force Participation Rates of All Men, All Women, and Married Women, 1901–1995

Year	All Men	All Women	Married Women	Women as a % of the Total Labour Force
1901	78.3	14.4	n.a.	13.3
1911	82.0	16.6	n.a.	13.3
1921	80.3	17.7	2.16	15.4
1931	78.4	19.4	3.45	16.9
1941	85.6*	22.9*	3.74	24.8
1951	84.4	24.4	9.56	22.0
1961	81.1	29.3	20.7	29.6
1971	77.3	39.4	33.0	34.4
1981	78.7	52.3	51.4	40.8
1991	75.1	58.5	61.7	45.4
1995	72.5	57.4	61.4	45.1

*Includes those in active service
Population 15 years of age and over

Sources: Leacy, F.H., ed., in *Historical Statistics of Canada*, 2nd edn, eds M.C. Urquhart and K.A.H. Buckley (Toronto: Macmillan, 1965), 107–23; Statistics Canada, *Historical Labour Force Statistics, 1995*, Cat. No. 71-201; *Labour Force Annual Averages*, Cat. No. 71-529; *Women in Canada*, Cat. No. 89503E, p. 78; 1961 Census, Cat. No. 94-536.

1970s created a particular demand for women workers (Marchak 1987). Birth rates have declined as women had fewer children, and as a result women spent less of their adult lives in active childcare. In 1961 the average number of children born per woman was 3.84 (Grindstaff 1995); by 1997 it was 1.6 (Statistics Canada 2000: 7). Changing gender ideologies, fuelled by the revitalization of the feminist movement, reflected women's interest in paid employment, as protection from the vulnerability of dependency on men, to augment their families' incomes, and because they liked the income, sociability, and status that paid employment secures. The potential consequences of women's economic dependency on men were revealed by a 1997 study which showed that men gained financially when their marriages ended; their incomes went up 10 per cent. In contrast, women and children did poorly; women lost about 23 per cent of their incomes. The only way women could regain their former financial status was by remarrying (*Toronto Star*, 10 Apr. 1997).

Men's earnings since the 1980s typically have been insufficient to support a family. The average earnings of men over 35 years of age have remained relatively unchanged while younger men's earnings have declined (Best 1995; Morissette 1997). The importance of women's earnings to total family income is reflected in the percentage of families whose income would fall below the Low Income Cut-off if women's earnings were not available.[6] In 1992, the average family had to work 77 weeks per year just to pay the bills. Since there are only 52 weeks in a year that meant either families had to go deeply into debt, or they had to rely on more than one income (*Toronto Star*, 7 Feb. 1998). In the same year, 4 per cent of dual-earner families had low incomes; if wives' earnings were deducted, this number would have increased to 16 per cent (Statistics Canada 1995b: 88). Between 1991 and 1996, average family incomes for all husband–wife families in Canada declined. Where the wife had no income, family income declined by 6.9 per cent, compared to families where the wife was employed whose incomes declined by 1.9 per cent (Statistics Canada 1998b: 3).

But, like men, most women seek paid employment for more than just financial benefits. A 1995 Statistics Canada survey found that 64 per cent of adult women said that having a paid job was important for their personal happiness and 55 per cent agreed that having a paid job was the best way for a woman to be an independent person (Ghalam 1997: 16). A mother who had stayed home for two years after her first child was born, refused to do so again. She explained why:

> When I stayed home, I hated it. I only did it because I really thought it was the best thing for the baby. I missed going to work, I was bored at home and I don't think it was so great for the baby to have me moping around. With what we're paying for childcare, it isn't financially worth our while me working, but a job is more than money. (F A#19)

By the early twenty-first century, women had become an integral part of the paid labour force and women's paid employment was an essential part of their household's livelihood. Employers depended on women's labour-force participation. In 2000, 54.8 per cent of women 24 years of age and over had paid employment and women were about 45 per cent of all paid workers (*Globe and Mail*, 21 Feb. 2000).

However, while women are increasingly in the paid labour force for most of their adult lives, their relationship to paid work continues to be quite different from men's. Jobs remain significantly sex segregated with women clustered in jobs that are typically low paid. Even when they do the same work, women often get paid less than men. In 1996 the top 10 jobs for men were (in descending order) truck drivers, retail sales, janitors, retail trade managers, farmers, sales reps and wholesale trade, motor vehicle mechanics, material handlers, carpenters, construction trade helpers. For women they were retail sales, secretaries, cashiers, registered nurses, accounting clerks, elementary teachers, food servers, general office clerks, babysitters, receptionists (*Toronto Star*, 18 Mar. 1998). Women's attachment to the labour force continues to be shaped by their responsibilities for domestic labour. Under pressure to manage things at home, they often take part-time or home-based employment. They are about 70 per cent of all part-time workers, 47 per cent of home-based employment (Ghalam 1993) and 29 per cent of all self-employed workers (Nadwodny 1996: 17). They are far more likely (62 per cent) than men (27 per cent) to have employment interruptions 'stopping working for pay for a period of six months or more' (Fast and Da Pont 1997: 3). The combination of job ghettos, reduced work time, work interruptions, and discriminatory pay rates means that women continue to earn less than men (Drolet 1999).

But just as domestic labour responsibilities shape women's attachment to paid employment, paid employment shapes men's and women's relationship to domestic labour. The assumption that men are income earners and do not have responsibility for domestic labour is central to the way most paid work is organized and fundamental to most male-dominated occupations (Luxton and Corman 2001). While employers need workers, they have no immediate interest in how their workers live, whether they support anyone else with their earnings, nor whether their workers have children or are responsible for caring for other people. Some employers have implemented 'family friendly' policies, and the labour and women's movements have won important policies such as paid maternity and parental leaves or unpaid personal leaves, but, for the most part, paid employment is organized on the principle that during working hours, workers are available for work and undistracted by other concerns. Typical male occupations usually assume that workers can do eight-hour shifts or longer, can be counted on to do overtime or travel, and don't expect time off for the birth of a child or to care for people who are sick or elderly. Many men assume that if they provide their family's main income, they have met their familial responsibilities and cannot be expected to take full responsibility for domestic labour as well.

As more women with young children and other pressing domestic responsibilities entered the paid labour force, they confronted directly the problems arising from the way paid employment fails to accommodate domestic labour. Caregiving to children, elderly, ill, or disabled people requires attention and energy, often unpredictably. The more dependent the person, the more likely their lives may depend on immediate care, regardless of the paid work responsibilities of the caregiver. A mother described how this played out in her life:

> I got a phone call at work. My supervisor came to tell me and he was pissed off. He said I was not ever to get calls at work again but he let me go. We're paid piece work so I don't know why he was so mad. He wasn't paying me when I stopped working. It was my daughter's teacher. She'd fallen and hurt her head and the ambulance was taking her to the hospital. I told the supervisor I had to go to the hospital. He said if I didn't go straight back to work I was fired! Well, I had no choice did I? (F M#14 12/99)

Changing Strategies for Managing Domestic Labour and Paid Employment

As the homemaker wife/income-earner husband strategy became increasingly less of an option, families developed a variety of other strategies to cope with the competing demands of domestic labour and paid employment. Where both partners have paid work, the responsibility for income generating is shared, providing the household with some protection from the insecurities of the labour market. A man explained:

> I got laid off with no warning. We showed up for work one night and the place was padlocked. They'd gone bankrupt and the owners had disappeared. Well, if it had happened two years earlier, we would have been in deep trouble, but as it was, my wife was working so we managed. (M A#19 12/99)

This arrangement not only reduces the onus on men to provide incomes for their families, it also reduces women's dependence on their husbands:

> I never thought about it before, but after I started working, I realized how much it meant to me not to have to ask him for every penny. I love having my own money. (F A#22 1/00)

However, with no one available to do domestic labour full-time, it is harder to get it done, caregivers for dependants have to be found and the relationships managed. There are additional expenses as well as complications arising from scheduling, coordinating, and planning. A woman with two school-aged children described her arrangements:

> I work 11–3 Mondays to Wednesdays and 3–9 on Thursdays and Fridays. My husband works rotating shifts so one week he's on days 7–3, then afternoons 3–11, then nights 11–7. So the way we do it is, if one of us is home, no problem. If it's a Thursday and my husband can't be there, the kids can go to a neighbour's after school and she will keep them till I get home. It's a bit late. They don't get to bed till 10 p.m. which means it's a struggle to get them up in time to go to school the next morning. If it's a Friday, either my girlfriend comes over to stay with them or I hire a babysitter—one of the kids from the local high school. Well, you can imagine how many phone calls it takes each week to make sure everything works! (F A#17 12/99)

Women's Strategies for Coping with the Double Day

Women who make the transition from being either childless employees or full-time mothers at home to being employed mothers often begin their new double day by trying to do both jobs so that neither detracts from the other. A woman with two preschool children described how she presented herself at work:

> When I came back to work after my maternity leave, I knew I had to act like I did before I had children, as if I had no kids. My workplace had been really good to me—no fuss about maternity leave either time. They gave me really nice showers for both babies. But I knew enough was enough. They expected me to leave anything to do with the kids at home and I couldn't let it come up at work. Occasionally my boss will ask how my children are, but he does it to be friendly. He doesn't really want to know. So I make sure, no matter what is happening, no one at work ever sees me dealing with family stuff. (F M#16 11/99)

Many women try to continue their domestic labour as if they had no other demands on their time and energy (Luxton 1990: 43). A woman recalled her efforts, when she first started her job, to maintain what she considered appropriate standards at home:

> I was running from morning till night, and late into the night at that. My house was spotless, my kids took home baking to

parents' night, I made their Halloween costumes myself, and I made sure we ate home-cooked meals every night. That lasted for about a year. Then I collapsed. I just couldn't keep it up and I stopped feeling like I should. (F M#18 1/00)

Few women can keep up such intensity for very long. While some maintain reduced involvement in paid employment, working part-time or trying to work from home, most end up relinquishing their exacting standards for domestic labour in order to reduce the amount of time they have to spend. The more hours women spend in paid employment, the more they cut back on household labour (Frederick 1995; Luxton and Corman 2001). They tolerate lower standards of cleanliness and tidiness, rely more on take-out foods, and as one woman put it:

just focus on what's important and let the rest go hang. What matters is spending time with the kids. If we do it in a messy house, so what? If I buy the snacks when it's my time to contribute to school lunches, so what? (F A#22 1/00)

It is much more difficult for most women to cut back on the amount of time and energy they put into caregiving. A mother described the difficult changes she had to make when her employer changed the time she had to start work:

My shift used to start at 10 a.m. That was very good. I got the children up and took them to the daycare. We had a lot of time. We could sing and tell stories and I didn't have to rush them. Mornings were a very good time. Now I have to be at work at 7 a.m. I let the children sleep until 5:30. Then I must wake them. It is very hard. They are so tired and do not want to get up and then I have to rush, rush, rush. My employer, he says if we are late three times we get fired so I am very mean to my children in the morning now. It makes me very sad. (F A#28 1/00)

The less time and energy mothers have available to them, the less they can attend to their children. One mother captured an important effect of time constraints and stress on her parenting:

Mostly for me it isn't the time *per se*. My kids know I am busy and they're fine with it. It's when I am so stretched and stressed that I lose my sense of delight in their lives. I get snappy. I'm short with them. My [15-year-old] son said the other day, 'Mom, when you're not here or you're upstairs working, and I don't see you, it's okay because I know you love me. But when you scream at me, I don't feel loved.' He's right. But sometimes I just lose it. I can't cope. (F M#18 11/99)

Women who are already stretched by employment and childcare responsibilities may find it impossible to care for others, imposing cruel choices on them. A single mother, struggling to manage on two part-time jobs, felt she had too little time for her three children, when her mother was suddenly taken ill:

I just cry all the time. I am too tired. I can't give my kids the attention they need. I am terrified I will lose my job and now this! My mama's in hospital and she needs me. Yesterday I didn't even get to visit her! But my youngest didn't come home from school so I went looking for him. I felt like God was making me choose between my mama and my son! (F M#25 3/00)

This strategy imposes serious strains on women. A national survey found that more than 28 per cent of women and slightly less than 16 per cent of men in relationships where both were employed full-time felt severely time crunched (Frederick 1993: 8). 'Nearly 50 per cent of full-time . . . mothers reported they would like to spend more time alone. The proportion for men never rises much above 25 per cent' (Frederick 1995: 58).

Sharing Domestic Labour with Men

As more and more women took on paid employment, there was a widespread assumption that their male partners would take on more domestic labour. Since the 1970s, popular media and academic studies alike have proliferated, claiming that men are beginning to increase their involvement in household labour, especially childcare (McMahon 1999). Public opinion polls in Canada show that since the 1970s there has been an increase from about 50 per cent to over 80 per cent of adults who agree that husbands should share domestic labour (Luxton 1990; Wilson 1991: 56). However, extensive studies of the impact of women's employment on domestic labour actually show that household labour remains sex segregated and that women do the bulk of it (Nakhaie 1995). As McMahon (1999: 13) documents, hundreds of studies from Australia, Europe, the United States, and Canada reveal that women's employment has a minimal impact on men's involvement in domestic labour, and men's domestic labour-participation rates remain consistent, regardless of race or social class differences across various countries: 'there are no significant cross-cultural and cross-class differences in men's performance of domestic labour'.[7]

A 1983 Canadian study of a national sample of 2,577 people investigated the extent to which men were taking on more traditionally female household tasks. In dual-earner couples, on average, women performed over 76 per cent of feminine-typed tasks, while men did less than 30 per cent (Brayfield 1992: 25). The 1992 General Social Survey found that even among young people 'young women did more unpaid work than young men and spent more time on the "traditionally female" chores such as cooking and housekeeping' (Frederick 1995: 14).[8] Only 10 per cent of men in dual-earner households claimed to have primary responsibility for domestic labour and an additional 10 per cent said they fully shared responsibilities (Marshall 1993). Since October 1990, fathers in Canada have been entitled to take a paid 10-week parental leave for a new baby. Of the 31,000 parents who have taken leave at the birth or adoption of a new baby, about 1,000 were fathers. Fathers as a percentage of all parents on leave have been about 3 per cent annually since 1991 (*Globe and Mail*, 29 Mar. 2000).

The 1996 census in Canada, which included questions on unpaid work for the first time, confirmed that there continued to be significant gender differences in the amount of time spent on unpaid work. Asked if they had spent time in the previous week doing housework or home maintenance, 25 per cent of women and 8 per cent of men said they spent 30 hours or more. Among those with full-time employment (30 hours or more), 51 per cent of wives reported spending 15 hours or more doing unpaid housework, compared with 23 per cent of husbands. Among men and women with full-time employment and children, 64 per cent of women and 39 per cent of men spent at least 15 hours a week on childcare. If at least one child was a preschooler, the numbers increased: 80 per cent of women and 49 per cent of men spent at least 15 hours a week on childcare. For those with no children under six, the proportion dropped to 51 per cent of women and 29 per cent of men (Statistics Canada 1998a: 17–18).

While survey research demonstrates general trends by comparing women and men, it does not investigate intra-household divisions of labour. Case studies based on interviews with both partners in a household, and especially longitudinal studies which trace domestic patterns over time reveal the interpersonal dynamics behind the time-use patterns. Typically, where households can afford to pay for services, they do so. Where household income is insufficient, men are drawn into domestic labour in limited ways, usually filling in while their wives are at their paid work (Luxton and Corman 2001). A majority of parents have organized their childcare by ensuring that parents work different shifts so that one of them can always be home. But while men may be providing care for their children, parenting is not gender-neutral, so the type of care fathers and mothers provide continues to be different. Women often talk about having to do additional work to compensate for men's approach to childcare. One couple's comments about their divisions of labour illustrate such gender differences at work. The man described his after-work routines:

> I get home before she does so I pick the kids up from the sitter and bring them home. I usually start dinner, then when she gets home we finish getting it ready together. We both put the kids to bed. (M A#16 11/99)

His wife elaborated:

> We both look after the kids. He picks them up and they usually get home about half an hour before I do. When I get in, it's crazy. The kids are hungry and squabbling so we rush to get dinner ready. Then we play a bit and do homework and read stories, then it's bath time and to bed. (F A#16 11/99)

She went on to explain the difficulties she had with their arrangement:

> He's great with the kids. He really is, but I wish he would be a bit more on top of things. Like, he never thinks to give them a snack when he comes home. He says it's too much bother and makes a mess and it will spoil their appetite for dinner. He'd rather just concentrate on getting dinner ready. But it means they are so cranky and strung out. I always have to break up fights and calm them down when I come in. And he never will get them doing their homework before dinner. He says they need time to play but it ends up I have to be the heavy saying 'homework now!' (F A#16 11/99)

He offered a different assessment:

> She's always fussing. She thinks I should make them do their homework after school but I don't like to pressure them. They need time to relax and I don't want to be always nagging them. Then she thinks I should give them snacks and play with them, but if I did that, dinner would be late. I don't like to eat late. (M A#16 11/99)

In effect, while he spent more time than she did, and both did the evening cooking and childcare together, he was ensuring that the basic work got done, while leaving the responsibility for emotional well-being and discipline to her.

There are a variety of explanations for why men have not taken on more responsibility for domestic labour. Prevailing cultural norms about and representations of domesticity, ranging from gender-specific toys such as dolls and play kitchens to ads for household products, typically assume that men are not involved in domestic labour. Men get little public validation or support for their involvement in domestic labour and may be subject to ridicule for doing 'women's work' (Luxton 1990: 50). A man described the reaction of his employer when he asked for reduced working hours to allow him to care for his elderly father:

> The request obviously threw him for a loop. He didn't want to say no outright but it made him uncomfortable, even though several women in the office have taken time off or reduced time to look after families and he had no problem with that. In fact, he is proud to say he is an enlightened employer. When I asked for the same thing, he hesitated, then he asked if my wife couldn't get time off her job. I said I wanted to look after my father. He was almost squirming but he finally agreed I could work four days and leave early two of those days. But he kept asking me if I really wanted to be doing it. It was like he couldn't believe I really wanted to do it. It was hard not to feel like a freak. (M M#23 1/00)

Even fewer men than women have paid jobs that in any way help workers accommodate family responsibilities, and in workplaces that are predominantly male, work practices typically have evolved to seriously preclude any such possibilities (Luxton and Corman 2001).

Existing sex-based differences in income reinforce sexual divisions in the home. In most households where both partners are employed, men are still typically the higher-income earners. If the woman's paid time is worth substantially less than her husband's, it makes sense financially for her to quit work in order to take care of a newborn or an elderly relative while her partner keeps his job. This apparently sensible coping strategy increases the pay gap between them, for in moving in and out of the labour force more frequently, her earning potential is diminished. The more continuous employment record of the man is rewarded with promotions, seniority, training opportunities, and so on. This strategy also reproduces gender differences because it reinforces women's involvement in caregiving while undermining men's possibilities of increasing theirs:

> Before the baby was born we agreed we both wanted to share childcare. But after she was born, I was home all the time so I just got better at caring for her and she knew me. He helps out a lot but it's not like what I do. (F A#24 1/00)

When men are the higher-income earners, both women and men can readily justify subordinating domestic demands to the requirements of his employment. Whether this means moving to accommodate his transfer and promotion, keeping the children quiet during the day while a shift worker sleeps or a professional works at home on the weekend, or accepting men's prolonged absence from the home as they work overtime to meet their job's expectations, most women accept the demands of men's paid employment as a legitimate reason for men's lack of domestic labour:

> He often stays late at work so how can I expect him to come home after such a long day and start housework. That's just too much. (F M#18 1/00)

The importance of economic earnings in shaping domestic divisions of labour is underscored by evidence that suggests that men's participation in domestic labour may increase in relation to the strength of their wives' labour-force attachment. The longer women are in paid employment and the greater the women's income is as a proportion of total household income, the more likely men are to do domestic labour (Luxton 1981; Marshall 1993).

But the power that accrues to most men who are income earners plays out in other ways as well. When so few men do domestic labour, those who do are often highly praised for even minimal contributions, a practice that can easily reinforce the notion that domestic labour is not expected of men. A woman conveyed her confusion about how to assess her husband's contributions:

Everyone tells me that he is so terrific around the house. They tell me I am so lucky to have a husband who does so much. All my friends are forever telling me they wish their husbands were half as helpful. So then, I feel so mean when I want to say he doesn't do nearly enough. Maybe I expect too much? And sometimes when we fight over it, he says, 'Well all your friends say I do more than my share. So what's your problem?' I don't know. (F M#19 1/00)

In the context of marriage and a commitment to making it work, many women hesitate to escalate their demands that men do more. They risk undermining their important and valued sense that their relationship is based on love and mutual caring if they challenge their partners to do more, and lose. If they force a serious confrontation about the distribution of domestic labour, they run the risk of provoking a major fight. In the interests of domestic harmony and of maintaining their sense of the value of their marriage, many women concede. Conversely, some women decide that struggles over the redistribution of household labour and responsibilities are not worth it. Growing numbers of young women and men are not marrying, more women are choosing to remain childless, and more women are having children without marrying (see Chapter 12; Oderkirk 1994: 5). Married women who are frustrated by their husbands' resistance may opt to leave the marriage. Charles Hobart (1996: 171) argues that one explanation for contemporary divorce rates is that:

paid employment has greatly reduced the time available to wives for domestic work, and having paycheques has empowered them, giving them increased influence and independence. Conflict has resulted, over (1) husbands' reluctance to share the domestic work fairly and (2) wives' refusal to be traditionally subservient.

The strategy of redistributing domestic labour between women and men is thus difficult to implement, both because the material conditions of social life work against it, and because, typically, men have the power in their own households to resist. It is not in their interests to take on more, unpaid, work, especially if their wives continue to do it if they refuse. Women's efforts to encourage men to do more are hampered by the private nature of family life. Their struggles are rarely understood as part of major changes in social divisions of labour; instead they are experienced as private conflicts between the individuals involved. Unlike struggles to change the occupational segregation of the paid labour force, where collective action by unions, legal challenges, and public campaigns have provided support for the workers involved, efforts to change household divisions of labour remain private, the interpersonal struggles of the couple involved.

Finally, systemic sexism means that not only do most men resist changing domestic divisions of labour, but there is little social recognition of the problem and widespread resistance to feminist efforts to make a political issue of the inequality. As McMahon (1999: vi) has argued, 'the central role men's material interests play in their motivation to defend the gendered status quo' has been 'systematically obscured or marginalized in both popular and academic discussion' because men have deeply vested interests in keeping the discussion of the existing inequalities in the gendered division of labour in the home 'blandly apolitical'.

Paying for Domestic Labour

One solution, for those who can afford it, is to hire replacement labour such as cleaners, babysitters, nannies, or nursing care, or to pay for services such as restaurant meals, nursery schools, or nursing homes. A wife's sole responsibility for housework and a husband's 'propensity for doing housework' both decline as each individual's income increases (Marshall 1993). The more money people have available to them, the more they are able, and inclined, to purchase services and labour instead of doing the work themselves (Brayfield 1992: 28). A lawyer described what she did when her mother was released from hospital needing full-time care:

> For the first few days, she came to my home and I hired round-the-clock nursing care. But it was very unsatisfactory. I couldn't rely on them. They kept phoning me to ask questions and I didn't really trust them around the house. So I contacted one of these services and got them to locate a good nursing home. It costs the earth, but I don't have to worry. (F M#15 11/99)

There are at least four problems with this solution. The first was identified by the same lawyer who was satisfied with the care her mother received but regretted her lack of personal involvement, a lack imposed by her need to work long hours in order to make enough money to pay for the care:

> I could afford it. That wasn't the problem. But I felt terrible. I want to be more involved, you know. If she could have stayed at home I could have seen her more often and been much more involved in her care every day. As it is, I go to visit early in the morning on the way to work and I pop in briefly at night. But it's not the same. (F M#15 11/99)

The second problem is that it makes no economic sense for families to pay more for services than the earnings of their lower earner. That means in effect that relatively low-earning women hire other women at even lower earnings or pay for services that are affordable only because the employees are paid low wages. Such dynamics perpetuate low-wage employment and trap immigrant women who come to Canada under government, foreign domestic worker plans in terrible working conditions (Giles and Arat-Koc 1994; Bakan and Stasiulus 1997). As Sedef Arat-Koc notes (1990: 97–8), they also pit women against each other:

> Current domestic service arrangements bring the interests of employers and employees into conflict. Given the pressures on their budget and time that some middle-class working couples do indeed face, a domestic service relationship may turn into a zero-sum game in which improvements in the pay and working conditions of domestic workers mean losses for the employers. As a relationship between female employers and workers, domestic service emphasizes, most clearly, the class, racial/ethnic, and citizenship differences among women at the expense of their gender unity.

A woman who had hired a foreign nanny described how such differences had a devastating effect on her children:

> At first we got along fine and the children loved her. She was always terrific with them. Gradually things got tense. If I was late getting home, she would be mad. Then she wanted more money and I just couldn't afford it. It was too uncomfortable and I was so relieved when she left but the children were devastated. They cried for months for their 'other mother'. (F M#13 12/99)

Strategies that involve purchasing services are attractive to many people because they are relatively straightforward and do not require people to engage in lengthy and complicated political negotiations to change legal and social policies. However, as they depend on maximizing individual family incomes, they encourage competition among people in a society. They generate tendencies for individuals to want higher pay and lower taxes even when reductions to government revenues mean cuts to the social services available to everyone. A unionized worker described the impact such views had on collective bargaining in her local:

> Up to now, we have always had a commitment to ensuring those at the lowest pay got the most. But recently, more and more members are saying they don't care about making pay rates more fair. They just want more money for themselves. It's very divisive. (F M#25 2/00)

A parent involved in his daughter's daycare centre made a similar point, showing how such practices increase inequalities:

> I'm on the board at our daycare centre. We are part of a large coalition of groups who have been fighting for a national childcare plan for Canada. We want the federal and provincial governments to fund great childcare centres everywhere. Economists have done the calculations. We could afford it. But so many people are calling for tax cuts. If governments have less money, they won't fund childcare. But the tax cuts won't give individual people enough money to buy childcare. They will just mean the rich get richer and the poor get less money and no services. (M A#25 2/00)

The most important problem with hiring or purchasing alternatives is that most households simply cannot afford to do so. The costs of childcare in a regulated centre, for example, were in 2000 about $9,000 a year for infants (*Toronto Star*, 11 Sept. 1999: A1, A30), a hefty chunk out of the average full-year full-time earnings for women of $31,506 per year (Drolet 1999: 25). The majority of households cannot sustain such expenditures over any length of time.

Changing Paid Employment—'Family Friendly' Workplaces

Another strategy for coping with the conflicting demands of paid employment and unpaid domestic labour has focused on changing the organization of paid work. As individuals, community activists, and union members, employees have struggled to make workplaces more accommodating of employees' personal lives (de Wolff 1994). They have fought for maternity, parental, and caregiving leaves (Heitlinger 1993; Mishra 1996). They have argued for flexible working hours that allow workers to coordinate their time more effectively with family demands. Employers have responded unevenly to such demands (Duxbury et al. 1992). Most are reluctant to implement such policies unless they see an obvious advantage to the success of their enterprise. Policy analyst Judith Maxwell (2000) argues that even though there is a tension between short-term goals of immediate growth in earnings and long-term goals of the viability of the enterprise and future productivity, business leaders have an interest in promoting more effective policies:

> Employers also have an immediate role to play in the way they support today's employees in their role as parents. Employers should ask these parents what working conditions they need to be the best that they can be at work, and still do their best for their children.

Workers who have access to such policies readily acknowledge that even limited programs help. However, they do not always work in ways that policy analysts expect. A study by Statistics Canada found that while such policies were originally intended to support women workers, typically men have benefited more from them (Frederick 1997). And the limits to such policies leave many people in crisis. A woman whose husband was hospitalized for three weeks said that her employer allowed her to have one week paid 'emergency' leave and two weeks unpaid leave. She was deeply grateful and made full use of both:

> It was so wonderful. I could just stay at the hospital and not have to even think about work. My company was really good to me. (F M#21 1/00)

However, her husband's illness lasted more than the time allowed her. She had to go back to work just when he was sent home, still too ill to care for himself. Like so many others in her situation, she found that existing policies are insufficient:

> I was in a state of panic for weeks. It was so difficult. I went to work, but how could I concentrate? I was frantic with worry about what was happening at home. (F M#21 1/00)

The more a workplace relies on women workers and the more skilled those workers are (and therefore harder to replace), the more likely the employer is to implement and permit workers to make use of such policies. Unionized workers have been more successful than non-unionized employees in winning such benefits. In a study of 11 workplaces that implemented policies intended to help employees mediate their paid employment and family responsibilities, Laura Johnson (1995: 63) concluded that: 'Employers and employees have provided ample opinion that they benefit from family friendly programs.'

Changing State Policies

Closely tied to efforts to reorganize working conditions in the paid labour force are struggles over government policies. Throughout much of the twentieth century, most government policies were based on the premise that women were wives and mothers with husbands to support them (Eichler 1988; 1997). A range of social policies provided some modest support for families in general, such as the family allowance, initiated in 1945 as a universal benefit to assist families with the costs of child rearing (Baker 1995: 128). Policies were developed for women, especially mothers, who did not have income-earning husbands to support them (Ursel 1992; Baker 1995). However, from the 1980s on, governments turned to neo-liberal economic policies aimed at reducing government provision of social services while fostering private for-profit businesses. The resulting government policies increasingly embodied a major ambivalence about the role of women in families and the labour market. In all areas of policy—from taxes, social assistance, legislated maternity and parental leaves to the absence of a national system of early childcare—governments reluctantly recognized that caregivers could not participate in the labour force without some government support. The policies that were developed, however, put pressure on individuals to provide as much care for themselves and others as possible (Armstrong 1996; Brodie 1996). As Chow, Freiler, and McQuaig (1999: 1) note: 'Not knowing whether to support women as mothers, workers, or both has led to a form of policy paralysis and an underdeveloped system of support to families with children.'

In the current context of limited assistance from certain policies and haphazard access to other services, families develop coping strategies that enable them to manage the competing demands of paid employment and domestic labour as best they can. A man described the decision-making process he and his wife went through after the birth of their first child. His comments indicate how vital even the limited support available was for them:

> My job wasn't very secure. I was afraid if I asked for time off I would get fired, so we weren't going to mess around there. My wife really liked her job. She could get maternity leave paid and even take some unpaid time too. So we did that. But then when it came time for her to go back, we weren't sure we could find childcare that wouldn't cost more than she was making. And we weren't sure what we thought about her being home with the baby—people say sitters or childcare are okay but how do you know? But she liked her job and didn't want to give it up. Once we found this daycare centre—it's great! Then we were set. (Values A#23)

What's at Stake? The Politics of Social Reproduction

A mother of two preschoolers tried to understand why unpaid domestic labour is such a problem:

> I really don't understand why it's so difficult to get men to do their fair share in their own homes or why employers and governments don't just see that it's in everyone's interests to ensure children get good care and parents can go to work secure in knowing their kids are having a wonderful time at daycare. It's almost like a conspiracy—it's just cheaper to get women to do everything for free. Do you think they just want women to carry the burden? (F M#17 12/99)

The United Nations (1991) estimates that women's unpaid work internationally is worth about $4 trillion annually. The General Social Survey indicates that in 1992 people in Canada performed at least 25 billion hours of unpaid work, 95 per cent of which was domestic labour—looking after children and caring for the home. Statistics Canada estimates that this labour is equivalent to about 13 million full-time jobs, is worth about $234 billion, equals about 40 per cent of Canada's gross domestic product and that women did two-thirds of it (Statistics Canada 1992; Chandler 1994; Statistics Canada 1995a).[9]

More importantly, this labour is the main source of caregiving for all children and for many dependent adults. As the labour that ensures households' livelihoods, it is critical for the personal well-being and daily survival of most people in Canada. If women were actually paid for all that work (especially at good wage rates), the wage bill would be enormous.[10] Conversely, if men had to take on even half of the work women do, they would add enormously to their workload; their leisure time would be seriously eroded. Employers and governments understand that provision of universal quality services by well-paid employees is expensive. They are typically resistant to reducing profits or spending public revenues unless there is widespread public support for doing so.

In countries where there has been a demand both for women's participation in the paid labour force and for increased birth rates, there have been well-developed policies to mediate the demands of both labours. Women have benefited by having long paid maternity leaves, as well as the right to have their former job back and retraining when they return to the job (Heitlinger 1979). In countries where there are public commitments to reduce wealth inequalities, and to ensure that all people have adequate care and decent standards of living, there are welfare state provisions available to all. Women and men have benefited from a range of policies and services that relieve the pressure on individuals and particularly women, such as lengthy parental leaves, free or low-cost, high-quality childcare centres, or home care for the ill and elderly (see Chapter 33).

Canada has never had a strong welfare state and since the late 1970s, the neo-liberal economic policies that federal, provincial, and territorial governments have implemented dramatically cut government provisions of social services and other measures that foster greater equality among people and between women and men (Brodie 1996). Jane Jensen and Sharon Stroick (1999: 3) describe what such changes have meant for parents and children:

> As Canada has done in the past, many countries pay family allowances or allow tax exemptions or credits for all children, whatever their parents' incomes may be. In Canada, recognition of this universal dimension of family life began to disappear in the 1970s, when targeting of social programs became popular. . . . [H]aving and raising a child was, in effect, treated as a 'private consumption decision' of adults, as if parents did not have legal or moral obligations to spend money on childcare.

A woman described the impact of such changes on her life as an employee:

> I used to work for a government agency as a home care provider. They privatized the agency, so I lost my job. Later I got another job in a private agency but it wasn't unionized and I make about half what I made before. And all they care about is making their money so we actually don't provide care to people any more. We go in and get out as fast as we can. I feel terrible about it. (F A#13 11/99)

Another woman described the impact on her unpaid domestic responsibilities when her husband was injured:

> So on top of my regular job I now have almost a second job, at home, looking after him. I have to get up with him at night, sometimes three or four times. I have to make sure he gets his medication at the right time. Sometimes if I get stuck in traffic on the way home I get so scared because he has to get his injections right on time and if I'm late, it's just so much a problem. (F M#16 12/99)

What these examples illustrate is the way most women, as the main people responsible for the work of social reproduction, maintain the standards of living for their household through their unpaid labour. When neo-liberal economic policies impose even more unpaid work on private family households, they rely on women's ability to increase their unpaid work, and in effect, force women to absorb the social costs.

While individual women and men engage in whatever strategies they can to get by, organized groups in the women's movement and the labour movement continue to struggle for policies that will redistribute more of the wealth in society to the majority of families, reduce the conflicts between paid employment and domestic labour, reduce the burdens on women and improve the quality of caregiving and the standards of living for the majority of the population. In 1995 at the United Nations Fourth International NGO Conference on Women at Beijing, China, Canadian delegates were among the 30,000 women from over 185 countries at the NGO Forum who identified prevailing neo-liberal policies as detrimental to most women around the world. Instead, they called for a new political orientation that took account of the needs of the majority of the world's people. In the years since then, Canadian feminist and labour groups have identified a range of policies that would help families secure their standards of living and improve the conditions of women's unpaid domestic labour.

In 2000, as part of an international campaign to eliminate women's poverty and violence against women, the main national labour organization, the Canadian Labour Congress (CLC), and the largest national women's organization, the National Action Committee on the Status of

Women (NAC) demanded (among other things) a right to social security, equality at work, childcare, and an end to violence against women:

> We demand full access to welfare and income security, fully-funded public health care and education, social housing, and adequate pensions. Working women demand improved labour standards, including a minimum wage above the poverty line—$10 an hour; the right to unionize; we want effective and enforceable pay and employment equity legislation; we need sexual, racial, sexual orientation, and personal harassment protection; and we demand the restoration of unemployment insurance to 1996 levels at a minimum. Women demand access to non-profit, state-funded childcare, paid maternity leave, parental leave, family leave, dependent care leave. (Canadian Women's March Committee 2000)

These demands illustrate what is at stake in the politics of social reproduction and show that negotiations between individuals in family households over how to balance paid employment and domestic labour are part of much larger struggles over standards of living, allocations of social resources and, ultimately, over the kind of society Canada will become.

Notes

1. This focus on the majority pattern tends to obscure the fact that capitalist class households acquire their income from investments and can hire workers to do all their domestic labour for them. Some households based on farming, fishing, arts and crafts, or other kinds of self-employment generate incomes by selling the products of their labour. Those who receive government transfer payments such as employment insurance, workers' compensation, or other forms of social assistance have to fight to ensure they receive enough to get by while those who have no secure sources of income typically live in precarious poverty.
2. The quotes cited in this paper come from interviews that are part of a study, 'Care Giving and Support among Family, Friends, Neighbours and Communities', a sub-project of a larger project funded by the Social Sciences and Humanities Research Council Grant # 410-94-1502, 'Rethinking Families: Canadian Social Policy and International Commitments to Conceptualize, Measure and Value Women's Family Work'. The interviews were conducted between September 1999 and January 2000. The identification in brackets indicates the sex (F or M), the situation they were interviewed about—either A for adult children living with their parents or M for people who had experienced an unexpected medical emergency, ID number of the speaker, and the date of the interview. The people interviewed lived in the Greater Toronto Area.
3. The term *breadwinner* with its assumption that bread is the main dietary staple illustrates the cultural specificity of this norm. Although it remains a popular term, I have used the culturally neutral term *income earner* instead.
4. Bettina Bradbury (1993: 119–27) documents for the late nineteenth century how parents and children negotiated and struggled over the competing dynamics of schooling, household needs for additional incomes, and children's commitment to contributing to their parental household or establishing their own. Similar struggles continued for working-class and low-income households throughout the twentieth century.
5. For poignant personal accounts of the impact on their lives of taking on family responsibilities when parents either needed help or were unavailable, see Campbell (1973), Crean (1995: 11), Joe (1996).
6. Statistics Canada identifies families or individuals as 'low income' if they spend on average at least

20 per cent more of their pre-tax income than the Canadian average on food, shelter, and clothing (Statistics Canada 1995b: 86).

7. As McMahon points out: 'Men's performance of domestic labour is one of the few sociological phenomena of which this can be said' (1999: 12).
8. The 1992 General Social Survey done by Statistics Canada (1992) was based on interviews with more than 9,000 people and was designed to find out about the amount and range of unpaid work done in Canada.
9. There are several different ways of calculating the economic value of unpaid work: replacement costs (what it costs to pay someone to do the work), opportunity costs (what the worker would earn if she or he were employed instead of doing domestic labour), or input/output costs (calculating the market equivalents to determine the price of household output) (Goldschmidt-Clermont 1993; INSTRAW 1995).
10. A 1992 study based on Statistics Canada data and using very low rates of pay as comparators calculated that the average annual cost of unpaid household work was between about $12,000 to $16,000 per year, per household. (Chandler 1994; Luxton 1997: 437).

References

Abele, F. 1997. 'Understanding What Happened Here: The Political Economy of Indigenous Peoples', in *Understanding Canada Building on the New Canadian Political Economy*, ed. W. Clement (Montreal and Kingston: McGill-Queen's University Press).

Arat-Koc, S. 1990. 'Importing Housewives: Non-citizen Domestic Workers and the Crisis of the Domestic Sphere in Canada', in *Through the Kitchen Window: The Politics of Home and Family*, 2nd edn, eds M. Luxton, H. Rosenberg, and S. Arat-Koc (Toronto: Garamond Press).

Armstrong, P. 1996. 'Unravelling The Safety Net: Transformations in Health Care and Their Impact on Women', in *Women and Canadian Public Policy*, ed. J. Brodie (Toronto: Harcourt Brace and Co.), 129–49.

———, and H. Armstrong. [1978] 1994. *The Double Ghetto: Canadian Women and Their Segregated Work*, 3rd edn (Toronto: McClelland & Stewart).

Bakan, A., and D. Stasiulis, eds. 1997. *Not One of the Family: Foreign Domestic Workers in Canada* (Toronto: University of Toronto Press).

Baker, M. 1995. *Canadian Family Policies: Cross-national Comparisons* (Toronto: University of Toronto Press).

Best, P. 1995. 'Women, Men and Work', *Canadian Social Trends* 36 (Spring): 30–3.

Bradbury, B. 1993. *Working Families: Age, Gender, and Daily Survival in Industrializing Montreal* (Toronto: McClelland & Stewart).

Brand, D. 1994. '"We Weren't Allowed to Go into Factory Work until Hitler Started the War": The 1920s to the 1940s', in *We're Rooted Here and They Can't Pull Us Up: Essays in African Canadian Women's History*, eds P. Bristow et al. (Toronto: University of Toronto Press).

Brayfield, A. 1992. 'Employment Resources and Housework in Canada', *Journal of Marriage and the Family* 54: 19–30.

Brodie, J. 1996. 'Canadian Women, Changing State Forms, and Public Policy', in *Women and Canadian Public Policy*, ed. J. Brodie (Toronto: Harcourt Brace and Co.), 1–28.

Campbell, M. 1973. *Halfbreed* (Halifax: Goodread Biographies).

Canadian Women's March Committee. 2000. *An Open Letter to Canadian Women*, 24 Jan. 2000.

Carty, L. 1994. 'African Canadian Women and the State: "Labour Only, Please"', in *We're Rooted Here and They Can't Pull Us Up: Essays in African Canadian Women's History*, eds P. Bristow et al. (Toronto: University of Toronto Press).

Chandler, W. 1994. 'The Value of Household Work in Canada', *1992 Canadian Economic Observer*, Statistics Canada, Cat. No. 11-010 (Apr.).

Chow, O., C. Freiler, and K. McQuaig. 1999. 'A National Agenda for All Families: Reframing the Debate about Tax Fairness', paper submitted to the Finance Sub-committee, Federal Government, 12 May.

Crean, S.G.H. 1995. *A Woman for Her Time* (Vancouver: New Star Books).

de Wolff, A. 1994. *Strategies for Working Families* (Toronto: Ontario Coalition for Better Child Care).

Drolet, M. 1999. 'The Persistent Gap: New Evidence on the Canadian Gender Wage Gap', Statistics Canada, Income Statistics Division (Ottawa: Industry).

Duxbury, L., C. Lee, C. Higgins, and S. Mills. 1992. *Balancing Work and Family: A Study of Canadian Private Sector Employees* (Ottawa: Carleton University).

Eichler, M. 1988. *Families in Canada Today: Recent Changes and Their Policy Consequences*, 2nd edn (Toronto: Gage Educational Publications).

———. 1997. *Family Shifts: Families, Policies, and Gender Equality* (Don Mills, ON: Oxford University Press).

Fast, J., and M. Da Pont. 1997. 'Changes in Women's Work Continuity', *Canadian Social Trends* 46 (Autumn): 2–7.

Frederick, J. 1993. 'Tempus Fugit . . . Are You Time Crunched?', *Canadian Social Trends* 31 (Winter): 6–9.

———. 1995. *As Time Goes By . . . Time Use of Canadians* (Ottawa: Industry).

———. 1997. Statistics Canada (Ottawa: Industry).

Ghalam, N. 1993. 'Women in the Workplace', *Canadian Social Trends* 28 (Spring).

———. 1997. 'Attitudes Toward Women, Work and Family', *Canadian Social Trends* 46 (Autumn) 13–17.

Giles, W., and S. Arat-Koc, eds. 1994. *Maid in the Market: Women's Paid Domestic Labour* (Halifax: Fernwood).

Goldschmidt-Clermont, L. 1993. 'Monetary Valuation of Unpaid Work', paper presented at the International Conference on the Measurement and Valuation of Unpaid Work, Statistics Canada, Apr.

Grindstaff, C.F. 1995. 'Canadian Fertility, 1951 to 1993', *Canadian Social Trends* 39 (Winter): 12–16.

Heitlinger, A. 1979. *Women and State Socialism: Sex Inequality in the Soviet Union* (Montreal: McGill-Queen's University Press).

———. 1993. *Women's Equality, Demography and Public Policy: A Comparative Perspective* (London: Macmillan Press).

Hobart, C. 1996. 'Intimacy and Family Life: Sexuality, Cohabitation, and Marriage', in *Families Changing Trends in Canada*, 3rd edn, ed. M. Baker (Toronto: McGraw-Hill Ryerson), 143–73.

INSTRAW (International Research and Training Institute for the Advancement of Women). 1995. Measurement and Valuation of Unpaid Contribution Accounting Through Time and Output, Santo Domingo, Dominican Republic.

Jensen, J., and S. Stroick. 1999. 'Finding the Best Policy Mix for Canada's Kids', *Perception* 23, 3 (Dec.): 3–5.

Joe, R. 1996. *Song of Rita Joe: Autobiography of a Mi'kmaq Poet* (Charlottetown, PEI: Ragweed Press).

Johnson, L. 1995. *Changing Families, Changing Workplaces Case Studies of Policies and Programs in Canadian Workplaces* for the Women's Bureau, Human Resources Development Canada (Ottawa: Supply and Services).

Luxton, M. 1980. *More Than a Labour of Love: Three Generations of Women's Work in the Home* (Toronto: The Women's Press).

———. 1981. 'Taking on the Double Day: Housewives as a Reserve Army of Labour', *Atlantis* 7, 1 (Fall): 12–22.

———. 1990. 'Two Hands for the Clock: Changing Patterns in the Gendered Division of Labour in the Home', in *Through the Kitchen Window: The Politics of Home and Family*, 2nd edn, eds M. Luxton, H. Rosenberg, and S. Arat-Koc (Toronto: Garamond Press).

———. 1997. 'The UN, Women, and Household Labour: Measuring and Valuing Unpaid Work', *Women's Studies International Forum* 20, 3: 431–9.

———, and J. Corman. 2001. *Getting By in Hard Times: Restructuring Class and Gender in Hamilton, Ontario 1980–1996* (Toronto: University of Toronto Press).

McMahon, A. 1999. *Taking Care of Men: Sexual Politics in the Public Mind* (Cambridge: Cambridge University Press).

Marchak, P. 1987. 'Rational Capitalism and Women as Labour', in *Feminism and Political Economy: Women's Work, Women's Struggles*, eds H.J. Maroney and M. Luxton (Toronto: Methuen).

Marshall, K. 1993. 'Dual Earners: Who's Responsible for Housework?', *Canadian Social Trends*, Cat. No. 11-008E (Spring/Winter): 11–14.

Maxwell, J. 2000. 'We Must Invest in Our Kids', *The Globe and Mail*, 24 Feb. 2000: A21.

Mishra, R. 1996. 'The Welfare of Nation', in *States Against Markets: The Limits of Globalization*, eds R. Boyer and D. Drache (London: Routledge), 316–33.

Morissette, R. 1997. 'Declining Earnings of Young Men', *Canadian Social Trends* 46 (Autumn): 8–12.

Nadwodny, R. 1996. 'Working at Home', *Canadian Social Trends* 40 (Spring): 16–20.

Nakhaie, M.R. 1995. 'Housework in Canada: The National Picture', *Journal of Comparative Family Studies* 26, 3 (Autumn): 409–25.

Oderkirk, J.C. 1994. 'Marriage in Canada: Changing Beliefs and Behaviours, 1600–1990', *Canadian Social Trends* (Summer): 2–7.

———, C. Silver, and M. Prud'homme. 1994. 'Traditional-earner Families', *Canadian Social Trends* 32 (Spring): 19–25.

Parr, J. 1999. *Domestic Goods: The Material, Moral, and the Economic in the Postwar Years* (Toronto: University of Toronto).

Preston, V., and W. Giles. 1997. 'Ethnicity, Gender and Labour Markets in Canada: A Case Study of Immigrant Women in Toronto', *The Canadian Journal of Urban Research* 6, 2 (Dec.): 135–59.

Stasiulis, D. 1997. 'The Political Economy of Race, Ethnicity, and Migration', in *Understanding Canada: Building on the New Canadian Political Economy*, ed. W. Clement (Montreal and Kingston: McGill-Queen's University Press).

Statistics Canada. 1992. Initial Data Release from the 1992 General Social Survey on Time Use (Ottawa: Author).

———. 1995a. 'Unpaid Work of Households', *The Daily* (20 Dec.).

———. 1995b. *Women in Canada: A Statistical Report* (Ottawa: Industry).

———. 1998a. *The Daily*, Cat. No. 11-001E (17 Mar.).

———. 1998b. *The Daily*, Cat. No. 11-001E (12 May).

———. 2000. *Canadian Social Trends*, Cat. No. 11-008, 56 (Spring).

United Nations. 1991. *The World's Women, 1970–1990: Trends and Statistics* (New York: United Nations Social Statistics and Indicator, Series K, No. 8).

Ursel, J. 1992. *Private Lives, Public Policy: One Hundred Years of State Intervention in the Family* (Toronto: The Women's Press).

Wilson, S. 1991. *Women, Families, and Work*, 3rd edn (Toronto: McGraw-Hill Ryerson).

PART FOUR

Families Negotiating Change, Changing Families

Chapter 28

Change is a constant feature of family life, if for no other reason than that family members age. But many Canadian families have experienced much more significant change than the aging of their members. The profound upheaval that immigration involves changes families in innumerable ways and, in the process, highlights both the impact of material and cultural context on families and people's agency in making (and remaking) their families.

In this chapter, Guida Man summarizes what she has learned of the changes that women from Hong Kong have experienced in their move to Canada. In explaining those changes, Man makes clear how profoundly family and gender relations are shaped by the organization of the communities in which people live. Her findings question the common assumption that gender relations become more equal in couples who move to Canada from cultures that are clearly patriarchal.

From Hong Kong to Canada: Immigration and the Changing Family Lives of Middle-class Women from Hong Kong

Guida Man

The Canadian government has historically adopted an approach characterized by pragmatism and economic self-interest in regard to immigration. Its immigration policies toward the Chinese have in the past been discriminatory in terms of race, gender, and class and continue to be partial to people from middle- and upper-class backgrounds. Hence, the entry of Chinese women and consequently the formation of Chinese families in Canada have been hampered by these restrictions.

The Canadian government's expansionist economic strategy toward immigration, and the way in which race, gender, and class operate as social relations, determine at any historical moment whether the Chinese are allowed into Canada and what category of Chinese are permitted. During the early periods of Chinese immigration, many racially discriminatory measures such as the head tax and the Chinese Exclusionary Act were imposed on the Chinese, but not on western European immigrants (see Abella and Troper 1982; Baureiss 1987; Hawkins 1988; Li 1988). And although some Chinese labourers were admitted into Canada to work on the railroad and the mines, the Canadian government prohibited Chinese women from entering Canada.[1] This measure effectively reduced the reproductive activities of the Chinese, and hence the formation of Chinese families.

While the head tax was imposed from 1885 to 1923, to prohibit Chinese labourers and their wives from entering Canada, affluent Chinese merchants and their wives were permitted entrance and an exemption from the head tax during the period 1911 to 1923 (Sedgewick 1973: 129; Wickberg 1982: 94, Man 1998: 120).[2] These wealthy merchants were useful in procuring trade for Canada, and therefore were accorded preferential treatment vis à vis their poor counterparts. Even during the exclusionary period between 1923 and 1947, when no Chinese was officially admitted, special privileges were granted to an elite class of Chinese who would otherwise have been prevented from entering Canada due to their race.[3] But the number of women who belonged to the elite class was minuscule, hence the population of

Chinese women in Canada remained very small.[4] Consequently, the number of Chinese families was low even as late as 1951.[5]

The pivotal shift occurred in 1967, when the Canadian government adopted a universal point system to select immigrants. The point system allowed the Chinese to be admitted under the same conditions as other groups (Hawkins 1988). The new initiative supposedly eliminated the racial and gender discriminatory elements of the Immigration Act, but the class discriminatory measures remained. The 1967 point system (and its subsequent revisions in 1978 and 1985) inevitably privileges people from middle- and upper-class backgrounds who have the opportunity to acquire the 'appropriate' educational, vocational, and language skills required by the Canadian government.

The 1967 revision of the Canadian immigration policy, coinciding with riots in Hong Kong triggered by skirmishes on the Chinese border, resulted in a large influx of Chinese immigrants from Hong Kong. Many of the Chinese who were admitted were middle-class professionals such as physicians and engineers. They were highly educated, cosmopolitan, with professional or technical skills, and proficient in either French or English. Many of the Chinese women who came into Canada at the time were sponsored by their husbands and relatives. But the selection policy also attracted some middle-class Chinese women professionals who had the educational and occupational skills to come in as independent applicants. By 1971, 83 per cent of the Chinese in Canada were recorded as belonging to a census family household (Statistics Canada 1971).

The universal point system of the 1967 immigration policy emphasized the educational and vocational skills of the new immigrants. Consequently, the 1986 census data gave a very positive picture of Chinese immigrant women's educational level (see Table 28.1) and their participation in the labour market (see Table 28.2), in comparison with their male counterparts and

Table 28.1 Level of Schooling for Foreign-born and Native-born Chinese Canadians and Other Canadians by Sex, 15 Years of Age and Over, 1986

	% Chinese Canadians				% Other Canadians	
	Foreign-born		Native-born			
Level of Schooling	Female	Male	Female	Male	Female	Male
Some High School or Less	50.4	38.8	26.7	30.8	45.5	43.1
Completed High School	11.6	10.0	15.0	10.0	14.3	11.3
Trade Certification or Diploma	0.6	0.9	0.5	0.8	2.1	4.2
Non-university without Diploma	5.3	6.0	7.4	6.2	7.0	6.6
Non-university with Trade or Diploma	9.2	9.4	17.2	9.5	14.5	14.6
Some University	10.1	12.7	13.9	22.1	8.7	9.0
University with Degree	12.8	22.2	19.3	20.6	7.9	11.2
TOTAL %	100	100	100	100	100	100
TOTAL SAMPLE	2,520	2,401	367	389	198,139	188,864

Source: Compiled from 1986 Public Use Microdata File on Individuals, a product of the 1986 Census of Canada. These data are based on a sample of 500,000 individuals, representing approximately 2 per cent of the population.

other Canadians. The data show that a higher percentage (12.8 per cent) of Chinese immigrant women ('foreign-born') have obtained a university degree than other immigrants, both female and male (7.9 per cent and 11.2 per cent respectively). However, fewer Chinese immigrant women than immigrant men and native-born women were able to enter the highly coveted managerial and professional occupations (14.4 per cent, as opposed to 25.4 per cent and 25.2 per cent respectively). At the same time, native-born Chinese Canadians are more likely to hold university degrees than other Canadians, both female and male (19.3 per cent and 20.6 per cent respectively), and also have higher participation rates in managerial and professional occupations (25.2 per cent and 26.7 per cent respectively).

In response to the transfer of government from British to Chinese sovereignty in Hong Kong in 1997, and the anticipated political, social, and economic uncertainty under Chinese rule, the 1980s saw a second wave of Chinese immigrants from Hong Kong to Canada. The Canadian media responded to the new immigrants by focusing on the wealthiest of the business immigrants. They are dubbed 'Gucci Chinese' (Cannon 1989) or 'yacht people' (*Calgary Herald*, 14 Feb. 1988: D3) by the media—in contrast with their poor Vietnamese cousins, the 'boat people'. Hence, a particular image of the immigrants has been created: that of affluent businessmen, driving Mercedes-Benzes and living in monster homes (*Halifax Chronicle Herald*, 25 Jan. 1988: 15; *Vancouver Sun*, 26 May 1989: B4; *Maclean's*, 7 Feb. 1994: 30). In fact, this image typifies only a small minority, and is far from the actual 'lived experiences' of most Chinese immigrants, particularly Chinese immigrant women.

Table 28.2 Occupations by Foreign-born and Native-born Chinese Canadians and Other Canadians by Sex, 1986

	% Chinese Canadians				% Other Canadians	
	Foreign-born		Native-born			
Occupations	Female	Male	Female	Male	Female	Male
Managerial, Administrative, and Related	4.5	9.0	7.4	12.1	4.5	10.1
Professional and Technical	9.9	16.4	17.8	14.6	12.4	10.3
Clerical and Related	17.3	6.0	31.3	12.6	20.1	5.5
Sales	4.7	6.4	8.2	10.3	5.8	7.1
Transport: Equipment Operating	0.0	1.7	0.3	2.8	0.4	4.8
Processing, Machining, and Construction	2.3	15.4	1.3	6.9	4.1	22.7
Service	13.7	21.4	10.1	12.3	10.2	8.2
Farming and Other Primary	0.6	0.4	0.5	1.8	1.7	6.8
Other	2.2	3.7	1.1	4.1	1.5	5.6
Not applicable	34.8	19.6	22.0	22.5	39.3	18.9
TOTAL %	100	100	100	100	100	100
TOTAL SAMPLE	2,520	2,401	367	389	198,139	188,864

Source: Compiled from 1986 Public Use Microdata File on Individuals, a product of the 1986 Census of Canada. These data are based on a sample of 500,000 individuals, representing approximately 2 per cent of the population.

Although the media image of the Hong Kong Chinese immigrants does not include women, since 1987 the number of Chinese immigrant women from Hong Kong has exceeded that of their male counterparts. For example, in 1992, 20,102 females versus 18,829 males immigrated to Canada from Hong Kong, and in 1993 the numbers of females and males were 18,800 and 17,685 respectively (EIC 1992, 1993). Despite their numbers and their contributions, Chinese women's experiences have remained invisible. This is congruent with the fact that the study of women was not legitimized as a topic of discourse, and that women's perspective has largely been ignored in academic research until fairly recently (Eichler 1985). Moreover, women's labour has almost always been incorporated into the family, or into their husbands' work (Luxton 1980). Consequently, their experience is seen to be either subsumed under that of men (Jacobson 1979) or tied to that of their male counterparts, and therefore they are perceived as not having a separate reality.

Theoretical Framework and Methodology

More recently, feminist theorists have ruptured the silence of women's experience. Hence since the 1980s, we have seen the emergence of studies on immigrant women in general (see, for example, Ng and Estable 1987; Boyd 1990; Ng 1998; Thobani 1998; Lee 1999), and on Chinese women in particular (see, for example, Nipp 1983; Adilman 1984; Yee 1987). Nipp's and Adilman's studies shed light on the historical accounts of Chinese immigrant women in Canada, while May Yee and the Chinese Canadian National Council's (1992) book project illuminated Chinese women's lives by making space for Chinese women to voice their stories from their own perspectives. These studies have found Chinese women to be actors who toiled and laboured alongside their male counterparts, and who were involved actively in political and community organizing.

Research on immigrants has typically derived its theoretical perspectives from work centred around the concepts of 'adaptation' and 'adjustment'. Such analyses assume that the onus is on the individual immigrant to adjust. The immigrant's failure to assimilate is seen to be her or his own fault. Studies based on these theoretical perspectives often focus only on microstructural processes (i.e., on the individual and the immediate family). Their analyses seldom go beyond the individual to investigate the interaction between her or him and the macrostructure, to look at how socially constructed opportunities and limitations rooted in institutional and organizational processes shape individual immigrants' lives. In my research, I have adopted a feminist methodology (Ng 1982; Hartsock 1983; Haraway 1985; Smith 1987; Hill-Collins 2000) which places women as 'subjects' of the study and takes into account both structural processes and individual negotiations. This methodology has enabled me to investigate how individual Chinese immigrant women as subjects account for their situations, and how their stories are as much their subjective experiences as they are shaped by objective structures in the form of organizational and institutional processes. Organizational and institutional processes are in fact interconnected. I have delineated them in order to obtain clarity in my exploration.

As mentioned previously, the Chinese come from diverse backgrounds and locations. I will focus on exploring the experiences of middle-class women in Chinese families that have recently immigrated from Hong Kong, and I will attempt to explain how their experiences in Canada have been transformed as a result of the difference in the social organization of the two societies. I have artificially categorized their experiences into topics: employment opportunities, housework and childcare, relationships with husbands and children, and social life. In actuality, people's everyday lives are not neatly delineated into categories. Human experiences and interactions with others occur in dialectical, rather than in linear relations. Events and feelings diverge and converge. Similarly, these categories overlap each other.

The Sample

The data for this study were generated through in-depth interviews with 30 recent middle-class Chinese immigrant women from Hong Kong. The women were all married, with at least one child. They had immigrated to Canada between 1986 and 1990. The majority of them (26 out of 30) came as dependants of their husbands. Five of them were living in Vancouver at the time of the interview, and the rest were living in Toronto. A snowball-sampling method was used to locate the interviewees. In other words, friends and colleagues were asked to refer women with the requisite characteristics. Women who were interviewed were then asked to suggest other women for inclusion in the study.

Each interview lasted between one and a half hours to three hours. An interview schedule was used as a guideline. All questions were open-ended. Interviewees were encouraged to talk freely about their experiences in Canada and in Hong Kong. Most of the interviews were conducted in Cantonese (a Chinese dialect spoken by most people in Hong Kong), interspersed with some English phrases—a mode of speaking favoured by most 'Chyuppies'.[6] Two interviewees preferred using the English language, and the interviews were conducted in English interspersed with Chinese phrases.

Institutional Processes

Institutional processes here refer to those processes and practices that are embedded in government, law, education, and professional systems. Such processes can engender and perpetuate social injustice in our society. In the previous section, I described how the institutionalized discriminatory process and practice of the Canadian immigration policies regulated the entrance of Chinese women into Canada. In this section, I will show how their opportunities for employment were restricted by institutionalized processes.

Employment Opportunities

Most of the women in this study came to Canada as dependants of their husbands who were the principal applicants under the 'Independent Class'[7] as 'business' or 'other independent' (professionals such as engineers, accountants, etc.) immigrants. These women therefore need not have high educational levels to score entry points. Due to their middle-class background, however, on the whole, their education is quite high. The majority have university degrees or post-secondary education. Their qualification is even higher than that of the average immigrant from Hong Kong. Despite the fact that these women were classified as 'dependants' by the immigration policy, and were therefore supposedly not destined for the labour market, many of these women had worked as professionals in Hong Kong. Although not all of these women actively sought employment when they first arrived, those who did were either underemployed or unemployed. Institutionalized practices in the form of the requirement of 'Canadian experience', and the lack of an accreditation system to calibrate their qualifications, have made it difficult for them to obtain employment commensurate with their qualifications. Consequently, some women found themselves economically dependent on their husbands for the first time in their lives. At the same time, immigrant men are subjugated to the same institutionalized discrimination.

The experiences of the husbands of these women were not unlike the experiences of other Chinese immigrants from Hong Kong. A study conducted in 1991 by the Alberta Career Development and Employment Policy and Research Division, the Hong Kong Institute of Personnel Management, and the Canadian Employment and Immigration Commission found that of 512 Hong Kong immigrants between the ages of 30 and 39 who entered Canada after 1980, 23 per cent reported no change in income, 46 per cent recorded a drop, and 31 per cent reported a rise in income. The majority (62 per cent) also experienced a drop in occupational status, 25 per cent experienced no change, and only 13 per cent had acquired a higher status (*Canada and Hong Kong Update* 1992: 7).

Another survey conducted in 1989, which focused specifically on Chinese immigrant women's needs in Richmond, BC (SUCCESS 1991), found that whereas 70 per cent of the women surveyed had worked prior to immigrating to Canada, fewer than 50 per cent were employed when surveyed. Of those who were employed, there was a significant degree of frustration and loss of self-esteem as a result of underemployment, low salaries, and limited opportunities for advancement. Nearly one-quarter of the respondents stated that their foreign education was not recognized in Canada. Over 46 per cent of these women had completed secondary education, and 41.2 per cent had post-secondary education which included college/university or professional training.

Chinese Canadians are concerned about the upsurge in racism. They feel that they are disadvantaged when it comes to getting jobs and being promoted—a 'glass ceiling' keeps them from advancing to management ranks. In a survey conducted for the Chinese Canadian National Council, 63 per cent of survey respondents from Chinese-Canadian organizations and 59 per cent from non-Chinese-Canadian social service organizations reported their belief that Chinese Canadians are being discriminated against (*Globe and Mail*, 26 Apr. 1991: A7).

These findings concur with my interview data. One of the women I interviewed, who has a postgraduate degree, and has worked as a translator and teacher in Hong Kong, got so exasperated with her job search that she gave up the idea of entering the labour force altogether. She lamented,

> It's a Catch-22. I cannot get a job because I don't have Canadian experience, and yet I don't see how I can possibly get Canadian experience without being hired in the first place!

Her frustration is echoed by other Chinese immigrant women.

A common strategy many immigrant women I interviewed adopted is what Warren (1986) terms a 'positive and pragmatic bridge' attitude toward their new positions. As one woman who worked as a Chief Executive Officer supervising over 300 employees when she was in Hong Kong rationalized:

> In terms of my employment here when I first arrived, I couldn't work as a manager as I didn't have Canadian experience; I couldn't work as a secretary because I was told I was overqualified. I was lucky to get a job with this company. They wanted to do business with Hong Kong. . . . That's why they hired me. They wanted someone to start the HK market. I was hired as an assistant. . . . They paid the B.Comm. graduates $1,200 a month. They paid me $1,500 a month. So they really respected me. . . . Either you don't work for someone, but if you work for them, you have to do your best, doesn't matter what the pay is. I kept telling myself that they were paying me to learn. I was in a new country. I didn't have a choice. I was paving my way for the future.

These women are cognizant of the futility of hoping for changes in processes that are institutionalized and embedded in the social system. Since they could not transform the macrostructure, they therefore resolved to change their own attitude toward their situations.

Organizational Processes

Organizational processes refer to the differences in the way societies are organized. Immigrants are often judged by their ability to 'adjust' to the host society. What is neglected, however, is an investigation into the differences between the social organization of the society from which the immigrant has come and the one to which she or he has immigrated. By uncovering how the individual woman's experience is shaped by the larger socio-economic structure, we can begin to understand the problems which seemingly dwell only on the micro level. The differences in the ways societies are organized determine the different ways people get their work done, conduct their lives, and relate to other people. In the following, I have attempted to demonstrate how Chinese immigrant women's everyday lives have been transformed because of the different organization of Hong Kong and Canadian societies.

Relationships with Husbands and Children

Being in a new country may change the relationships these women have with family members. The effects of their transformed relationships with husbands and family members vary depending on their labour-market participation and that of their husbands. Apart from the institutional processes that hamper immigrants' opportunities to enter the Canadian labour market, the differences between the social and organizational structures of Hong Kong and Canadian societies also contribute to new immigrants' unemployment and underemployment.

Under British colonial rule, Hong Kong adopted what economists consider a pure capitalist system. With an industrious workforce, this system created, on the one hand, a very low unemployment rate (around 3 per cent); on the other hand, it engendered a wide disparity between the rich and the poor, between professionals and low-level blue-collar workers. As well, unions have a relatively low profile, and workers enjoy few benefits. Although the Hong Kong economy has always been robust, the absence of a guaranteed minimum wage and the lack of an adequate social safety net (Cheng and Kwong 1992) make life extremely difficult for the poor and the unemployed. For the middle-class citizens, however, the situation is promising. The low unemployment rate, coupled with the brain drain due to emigration, allows professionals, whether men or women, to enjoy good salaries and excellent benefits.

In Canada, the situation is quite different. The relative strength of unions means that many workers, whether white- or blue collar, are protected. The wage gap between blue-collar workers and mid-level professionals is relatively narrow. Compared to Hong Kong, the average low-level worker in Canada fares better. Workers generally enjoy fairly good employee benefits, and comparable wages. But while there is a guaranteed minimum wage, the high cost of living has kept some people on welfare. And while the government strives to provide a social safety net for its citizens, the unemployment rate has remained high (hovering around 10 per cent). The continuing economic recession further exacerbates the situation. Competition for jobs is keen, and employers can be discriminatory about whom they hire. This does not provide an ideal situation for a new immigrant looking for work.

The changes these couples experience in their economic situation either improve or worsen their relationships. Some middle-class immigrant women professionals, who became unemployed or underemployed as a result of immigration, have found themselves economically dependent on their husbands for the first time in their lives. Such dependency has put some Chinese women in relatively powerless relationships with their husbands. Other women, however, have more positive experiences. They have found that their relationships with their husbands have improved because of their husbands' diminished career demands in Canada, which allows more time with their spouses. Their husbands have become underemployed or have reduced their business activities because of the lack of business connections and opportunities in a country with a less favourable economic environment. These women reported greater intimacy with their husbands. Spouses were drawn closer to each other by their common struggle to overcome obstacles in the new country, and to comfort each other when they were overwhelmed by feelings of isolation and alienation. As one woman whose husband used to be part owner of a manufacturing business in Hong Kong told me:

> My relationship with my husband has improved since we've emigrated. We are now much closer to each other. . . . In Hong Kong, my husband needed to entertain his clients, so he was out in the evenings a lot. He also used to travel back and forth to China quite often. So, even though we were living together, we led separate lives. Here, we only have a small business. He doesn't need to entertain any clients. Also he doesn't know that many business contacts, so he's home every evening. And because we are still struggling with the new business, I now help out in the store quite a bit, so we are together a lot. I'm really enjoying this togetherness. It's brought a new dimension to our marriage. We've discovered a renewed intimacy in our relationship. Now that we are together a lot, he really appreciates my help. He consults everything he does with me, something which he had never done when we were in Hong Kong. He used to consult with his mother, but not with me. They have a very close relationship, you see.

There were others, however, who found the isolation of being new immigrants and the stress of unemployment heightened their incompatibility and lack of communication, leading to marriage breakdown. One of the women I interviewed complained about her situation:

> My husband has been unemployed for over a year now. He had a very good position as an administrator with lots of benefits when he was in Hong Kong. The first year we were here, he found a job as a clerk. He was getting less than half of what he was making before. . . . But then the company went bankrupt, and he was unemployed. He's so depressed now that he is making me down too. He also kept blaming me for making him come here. We've had a lot of fights, and I'm not sure what will happen next. We talked about separating. I'm just living day-to-day at the moment.

Some of the husbands of the interviewed women who were either unable to complete the transfer of their businesses from Hong Kong to Toronto in time for their departure, or were afraid of relinquishing all their business contacts in Hong Kong, ended up spending half of the year in Hong Kong and away from their families in Toronto. These men are known among the Hong Kong immigrants as 'astronauts'.[8] This phenomenon also occurs among other immigrants who are reluctant to forgo their high-status, lucrative professional jobs in Hong Kong to face possible unemployment in Canada.[9] This long-distance arrangement has varying consequences for the wives. One astronaut's wife lamented the burden and the loneliness of maintaining the household on her own. She confided, 'I can't wait for the time when my husband can stop travelling back and forth. I'm tired of being here alone with the kids.' Her dissatisfaction is like that of women in the same situation in another study who expressed considerable worries stemming from their husbands' absence (SUCCESS 1991).

Another astronaut's wife in my study, in contrast, marvelled at her newfound independence, and attributed her heightened communication with her husband to his frequent absences. Interestingly, her positive reaction was similar to the findings of studies on dual-career commuting couples, which showed that some couples' relationships improved because of their time apart (Gerstel 1984; Man 1991; 1995). Here is what she told me:

> The first year when he [the husband] was still spending a lot of time in Hong Kong, he used to call me long distance all the time. We also wrote love letters to each other regularly. We were missing each other very much. We hadn't been that close together since we were married. And every time he came back to visit, it is like reliving our honeymoon again. It was really the sweetest year we have had for a long time.

One woman reported that she had been having problems with her two teenage children since they immigrated to Canada. What appear at first to be this family's adjustment problems due to immigration in fact have a concrete, material base. As this woman confided to me:

> Mothering is of course a lot easier in Hong Kong than here. There, the kids can be a lot more independent. My kids usually just hop on a cab right after school, and go to their respective tennis or music lessons. Afterwards, they just hop on a cab to go home. By the way, cabs are really cheap in Hong Kong. Also, Hong Kong is such a small place, you can go to any place within half an hour. I never had to worry about my children's transportation. The situation here is very different. It is too expensive for my kids to take cabs every day, and the public transportation in my area is not very good. I have to dovetail my work schedule with that of my children.

This woman now works late every night, so she can go straight after work to pick up her teenage son from his extracurricular activities. By the time she gets home, finishes making dinner, and cleans up, she is usually so exhausted that she just goes straight to bed. Her relationship with her children has become strained. Her son resents his loss of independence because he now has to wait for his mother to pick him up; and her daughter is annoyed that her mother cannot spend quality time with her. It is clear that what seem to be this woman's private, personal problems with her children in fact originate from external factors. The differences in social organization in Canada and the home country, such as the size of the city, the transportation system, and the high cost of living, have tremendous impact on the individual woman, affecting her everyday life, and the relationships of family members.

Housework and Childcare

In advanced capitalist societies such as Canada and Hong Kong, housework and childcare are privatized. Rather than acknowledging childcare as a public issue and allocating funds to establish childcare facilities, these governments have shifted the responsibility onto private households—that is, onto women (see Chapter 26). Despite the fact that economic demands have pushed many married women into the labour market, the unequal division of labour in the home has relegated women to primary responsibility for housework and childcare.

Feminist debates have located the family as the site of oppression for women, creating for housewives 'the problem with no name' (Friedan 1963); and housework as 'more than a labour of love' (Luxton 1980). Feminist research has also focused on the interconnectedness of housework and paid work (Connelly 1978; Armstrong and Armstrong 1984; Luxton and Reiter 1997; Man 1997; Hill-Collins 2000), and on how women must negotiate the conflicting demands of paid work and family responsibilities (Duffy, Mandell, and Pupo 1989).

Many upper-class women, and increasingly some middle-class women, try to 'resolve' the demands and pressures of juggling paid work, housework, and childcare by employing paid domestic help. Such a solution, however, inevitably creates a division among women along class lines, and threatens to undermine the collectivism within the feminist movement.

Although the gendered division of household labour is in some ways similar in Hong Kong and Canada, the differences in family structures and the social organization of these societies transform the situation of Chinese immigrant women, making their day-to-day living vastly different in Canada than in Hong Kong.

While the nuclear-family structure is prevalent in Hong Kong, many Chinese families (whether in Canada, Hong Kong, or elsewhere) retain vestiges of the extended-family form.[10] In such cases, three generations typically reside in the same residence. This extended-family arrangement is as much an adherence to the Confucian ideal (which stresses one's duty to care for the old) as a pragmatic arrangement in response to the high cost of housing and the shortage of state-subsidized homes for the aged. Very often, the arrangement is mutually beneficial for all parties. The grandparent (typically the grandmother) or the unmarried aunt is provided for; in return, they are able to help with housework and childcare. In cases where families adopt the nuclear-family structure, the small geographical area of the colony enables relatives to live in close proximity to each other, and thus promotes the development of close-knit support networks.

Regardless of whether the household in Hong Kong consists of a nuclear family or extended family (i.e., whether members of the extended family live together under one roof), the organization of the society enables members of the extended family to interact regularly and to lend support to each other if they so wish. The definition of family advocated by Fox and Luxton (see Chapter 1) urges ignoring household and focusing on personal support networks. It is evident that for Hong Kong Chinese families, who is in the household is less important than who interacts and helps each other to meet the needs of family members (see also Eichler 1988: 8–18). As one woman described her situation in Hong Kong:

> When we were in Hong Kong, my mother-in-law used to live with us. She did the cooking and the cleaning. She also picked up my oldest son after school so I didn't have to rush home right after work. My mother, on the other hand, lives close to my youngest son's school, so she used to pick him up after school and looked after him until I got to her place to pick him up after work. That's why my oldest son is very close to his maj-maj (paternal grandmother), and my youngest one is attached to his paw-paw (maternal grandmother)! You see, I had a lot of support in Hong Kong. Here, I have to do everything myself.

Beyond assistance in housework and childcare from members of the extended family, the class privilege of these middle-class Chinese women permitted some of them the luxury of hired help when they were in Hong Kong. This support system enabled them to pursue their career interests and allowed them free time for recreational or creative activities. Many of these women have taken this support system for granted.

Transplanted to Toronto, these women experience, first, a loss of support from the extended family (since many older parents are reluctant or unable to emigrate); and second, a decrease in their earning power due to the women's underemployment or unemployment, making it no longer economically feasible for them to have hired help. The extra burden of domestic labour is almost always assumed by the woman as her sole responsibility. Those women who tried to cope with a dual workload of housework and paid work often felt exhausted at the end of the day. Their predicaments are echoed by Chinese immigrant women in another study who described problems in childcare, household maintenance, and transportation (SUCCESS 1991). One woman described to me her typical day:

> I usually get up at seven, prepare breakfast for my kids and my husband, then take the TTC to go to work. It takes me at least one hour to get to work by public transit. We're a one-car family. I don't usually get to drive the car except when my husband is not around. Depending on where I work, I don't usually get home until six-thirty or seven, make dinner, clean up, and if I'm lucky, I get to watch a bit of television before going to bed. But usually, I need to do the ironing, washing, and mending, etc. I really don't have time to do much else. My husband and kids, though, they watch a lot of television.

A few women managed to recreate in Canada the support system they had in Hong Kong. Unlike other women, these women did not experience a drastic change in household duties, and were therefore able to maintain the balance of work and family responsibilities. Lily, whose parents had immigrated to Canada a few years prior, described how she maintained this mutually supportive network with her parents:[11]

> When I came here in 1987, I told my parents that I've brought money with me to buy a house. But I promised them that we'll live close by. . . . So we bought a house very close to theirs, so close that my younger daughter could go there after school. And we now eat dinner at my parents' place every night. . . . It's not only because of the fact that I don't know how to cook, but my mother felt that since my husband and I had to work, it would be better that we eat at their place. She told me that it's the same cooking for two people as cooking for six. At least this way, we get to see them every day. If we weren't eating there, I don't think we'd be driving there to see them every day. Also, because my younger daughter's school is very close to my parents' house, it's very convenient for my daughter as well. . . . So this is how my parents help us out. My mother cooks for us Monday to Friday, and on the weekends, I take them out for dinners. This way, my mother gets to have the weekends off. So, we take care of each other. . . . Also, it gives my mother something to look forward to every night when we go over there.

While in Hong Kong, many of these middle-class women did not actually engage in the physical labour of doing housework (cooking and cleaning), but rather the management of it. But since they clearly identified the management and control of the household as domestic labour, and as such an important task, they were proud to define themselves as capable housewives, in addition to being successful career women. For these women, power lies very much in the management and control of every aspect of family life. Nor is this image contradictory to their commitment to participation in the labour market in Hong Kong. These women were able to juggle the dual or triple workload of housework, paid work, and childcare because of the household support system they had when they were in

Hong Kong. There, many Chinese husbands took for granted that their wives would share the breadwinner role, as well as managing the household. Domestic harmony was maintained even though wives went out to work, because the husbands' daily sustenance was provided. Dinner still appeared on the table on time (although not prepared by the wife); shirts and pants were washed and ironed, ready to be worn the next morning (compliments of the mother or the hired help); and household maintenance chores were taken care of (by the hired workman). All this, however, did require skilful management by the wives. Husbands were relieved of virtually all of these tasks when they were in Hong Kong.

When asked whether her husband shared the housework in Canada or not, one of my interviewees laughed,

> No way! He had never lifted a finger all his life. Before we got married, he used to live at home, and his mother did everything for him. I would never dream of asking him to help me with housework. Besides, Chinese women don't do that. To ask your husband to help you with housework is to admit that you are incapable of being a good wife! It is a loss of face on the woman's part!

Since many of the husbands had never done housework before, they did not offer to help their wives after they immigrated to Canada. Nor do these women seek their help. As one woman explained:

> I feel that if I can manage it myself, I wouldn't ask. Furthermore, if my husband really wants to do it, he can offer to help. But he hasn't! As for my children, I would rather they spend their time studying or having fun. I don't really want them to waste their time on housework.

Some women, however, did get help from other family members, particularly with cleaning and grocery shopping:

> There's a lot of work. Fortunately, my husband and sons do help me with vacuuming. They also do the yardwork and cut the grass. Grocery shopping is very convenient here. There are also many Chinese supermarkets close to where we live. My husband loves to go grocery shopping. Usually, we just pick up some grocery on our way home from work. We shop several times a week because it's so convenient.

For some women, galvanizing the help of family members, with lots of planning and organization, were the keys to 'getting things done' in Canada:

> First of all, domestically, I have a lot of help. But I also have to be organized. My daughters are now older, so it's not like they would dirty up the walls, etc. Also being daughters they are much tidier than boys. I plan my schedule carefully. We only do laundry once a week. Every Friday night, we do the laundry. We also take turns ironing, me and my daughters usually. Sometimes my husband would offer to help. . . . Actually, there aren't too many things we buy that need ironing. I do everything the easy way; e.g., in terms of flowers, I buy pots of cactus. I change them only once every one or two months. . . . Also, there's not much dust here, so we only dust once a month. Once in a blue moon, we'll do a spring cleaning. Vacuum cleaning is my husband's responsibility. So is changing light bulbs, fixing the water faucet, gardening. He really enjoys gardening. We call him 'the gardener'.

Although cheaper housing costs allowed families to have bigger residences in Canada, these increase the amount of housework for women. Here is a comment from an interviewee:

> There seems to be more housework here. One reason could be that our house here is more than twice as big as our apartment in Hong Kong, so there's a lot more space to clean. As well, in Hong Kong, people usually have parquet floors, or tiled floors. Here, we have carpeting, which needs vacuuming more often.

In regard to doing other, more 'male-oriented' types of housework, Mabel revealed her and her husband's ignorance about this kind of work:

> Oh, he [husband] had never even used a hammer . . . and I'm definitely not handy myself either. I don't know how to fix a lock, or even to put up a nail. Most Canadians know how to do these things, but I never had to do it, so I didn't know how to do it at all. In the winter, I didn't know that I had to put caulking on my window. All these are little things, but they all add up. . . . In Hong Kong, services are so easily available people never think of doing anything themselves. You call up a handyman even just to put up a picture, or screw on a light bulb. It sounds ridiculous, but that's the reality there.

Both Mabel and her husband are highly educated professionals. They are capable and motivated people. However, they felt totally inadequate when they first came to Canada because they were not able to do small household maintenance chores like 'other Canadians'. This is due to the fact that the way in which the labour market is organized in Hong Kong is quite different from Canada. Until 1980, because of a constant flow of legal and illegal immigrants from China (Wong 1992), there had been a stable supply of cheap labour in Hong Kong, and services were relatively inexpensive. This in turn alleviates maintenance chores in middle-class households where both spouses participate full-time in the paid labour force. In Canada, because of the high cost of services, people are compelled to learn to do many household maintenance chores out of necessity.

In cases where the children are young, or when they participate in extracurricular activities which require the wife to chauffeur them back and forth, the women carry a triple burden of paid work, housework, and childcare. The way in which a society organizes its childcare facilities can have a tremendous impact on women who work full-time for pay. Kathy, a social worker, voiced her criticism of the inadequacy of daycare in Canada:

> I have a five year old and a two year old. I'm finding that daycare is a serious problem. Daycare is not flexible enough to accommodate working parents. Their hours of operation doesn't fill our gaps. We have to choose between quality or service. Sure, there are a few daycare centres now which run from 7 a.m. to 6 p.m. They are all privately run. They offer the service, but not necessarily the quality. So sometimes you don't want to put your child at risk. I have to choose very carefully. I have now found a very good quality daycare, and I can trust them very much . . . they have a lot of educational activities, lots of good materials which enable my children to learn a lot. On the other hand, they don't provide the service—i.e., their hours of operation are limited. So I have to juggle with my time to put my kids there. I am always dashing about like a mad woman. . . . I have no social life at all.

Most of the women I interviewed choose to live in areas within close proximity of friends and relatives, and which have easy access to Chinese grocery stores. However, the actual location of the houses is almost always determined by their children's schools and husbands' workplaces. Their own work location was not a determining factor in their initial decision. This can be attributed to the fact that children are considered the wives' responsibility. In order not to cause the women any more time loss in chauffeuring the children to and from school, it makes perfect good sense that homes be located close to schools.

Social Life

The immigrant women I interviewed have frequent interactions with other Hong Kong immigrants. Socializing with people who have common backgrounds and experiences creates for them a sense of continuity and is a stabilizing force in their new country (Warren 1986). Agnes, a secretary turned housewife, commented,

> I feel we have more in common with each other. We often get together and reminisce about our lives in Hong Kong. We also laugh about our ignorance of Canadian culture, and the little faux pas that we get ourselves into. Other times, we exchange information about schools, dentists, and other practical knowledge. Or we marvel at the high price we now pay for little things such as cooking wares and stockings. I have a feeling of solidarity when I talk to these people. They understand where I'm coming from.

Some women, however, also have friends from different ethnic groups. Usually, these friends are neighbours or parents of their children's friends, and occasionally friends they have met at work. This is in contrast to their lives in Hong Kong, where most working women customarily socialize with their colleagues. As well, social life there is more spontaneous. As one woman puts it succinctly, 'We usually just get together after work for movies and dinners; it's never planned.'

Although it is common and economically feasible for most people to organize frequent dinner parties at restaurants in Hong Kong, the astronomical cost of dinner parties at restaurants in Canada forces many to have small dinner parties at home, and only occasionally. This kind of change is seen by some as having positive effects. One woman expressed it this way:

> Life is comparatively quieter here. On the other hand, I now feel closer to my few friends. Our conversation is more personal and more meaningful, whereas before, I was always with a big crowd, and the conversation was usually superficial.

Nevertheless, women who have to juggle paid work, housework, and childcare typically are too exhausted at the end of the day to have much social life (Bernardo, Shehan, and Leslie 1987; Duffy, Mandell, and Pupo 1989). A mother of two who has a demanding career explained:

> I don't have any time for social life at all. Even if someone invites me for dinner on the weekend, I find it tiring to go. I don't know how everybody else does it here. There's no time for social life here at all. I have a lot of friends here, but I never have time to see them.

In Hong Kong, her situation was quite different:

> I was a member of a pottery club, calligraphy club, and an alumni choir. Here, I don't have any extracurricular activities. I simply don't have the time or energy. It seems foolhardy to drive an hour to go to a class when I don't even have enough time to manage my household chores. On the other hand, I really need this kind of outlet. But I don't have the kind of time and energy.

It is clear that the differences in social organization between Hong Kong and Canada, in terms of the household support system and the size and spread of the city, transform this woman's everyday experience.

Conclusion

Many migration studies have previously assumed that migration involves moving from a less developed to a more developed country, and from a rural to an urban area. It is further assumed that the entry of female migrants into the host labour market will lead to a rejection of their traditional roles and subjugated positions. These studies argue that the economic independence migrant women acquire through their engagement in waged work will assure them a higher status and a more equitable position in the family. Hence, migration has the positive effect of engendering equality of the sexes, as well as generating beneficial changes in domestic relations (Schwartz-Seller 1981; Morokvasic 1981).

I found that these migration theories are not applicable to middle-class Chinese immigrant women. Many of these highly educated, urbanized women do not necessarily enjoy a 'liberating' or 'less oppressive' experience when they settle in Canada. Because of the differences in the social organization of Hong Kong and Canada, these women's daily experiences have been transformed. While in Hong Kong, many of these middle-class women had help with their housework and childcare from either members of the extended family such as mothers or mothers-in-law, or hired help. This kind of support system enabled the women to pursue their career interests, and allowed them free time for social life and recreational activities.

Transplanted to Canada, these middle-class women lost the support system they had in Hong Kong. The lack of a support system exacerbated the workload of these middle-class women, making their struggle to negotiate the conflicting demands of family and career even more difficult. Furthermore, the physical spread of Canadian cities, and the lack of transportation systems in suburbia—where most of the Hong Kong immigrants reside—heighten children's dependency on their mothers, intensifying women's workloads. Consequently, some of them experience an intensification of traditional roles, unequal distribution of household labour, and gender and sexual oppression in the home. This, compounded with institutionalized discrimination which renders their previous work experience obsolete and the absence of an adequate accreditation system, has subjected some of them to unemployment and underemployment. These states, in turn, force them to become economically dependent on their husbands, who are themselves subject to the same discrimination.

Although some of the women I interviewed experienced improved family relations with their husbands after immigration, there were others who suffered communication problems, and marriage breakdowns. For some women, their power and status inside and outside the home deteriorated after they immigrated to Canada. Moreover, those who had professional careers in their home country experienced a loss of economic power through unemployment or underemployment (although some of their husbands also experienced such losses). They also experienced diminished buying power, and a general lack of opportunity.

Notes

1. Adilman (1984) made reference to the discussions of the immigration of Chinese women found in the Debates of the House of Commons (1923, v. 3, pp. 2310, 2311, 2314, 2318, 2384, and 2385); and in the Debates of the Senate (1923, pp. 1121–4). It is evident from these debates that the central concern in regard to the immigration of Chinese women into Canada was the proliferation of the Chinese population in Canada. In prohibiting Chinese women from coming into Canada, the government intended to effectively prevent the Chinese from settling permanently in Canada.
2. According to Sedgewick (1973), Immigration Policy at the time 'allowed merchants and their families exemption from the head tax and freedom to move in and out of the country' (136). However, the qualifications for 'merchant' status were not clearly defined. Hence, some labourers were able to immigrate in the guise of merchants.
3. According to Wickberg (1982: 141), the Chinese Immigration Act of 1923 contained the following provisions: abolition of the head tax; students below university age were no longer admitted; and only four groups of immigrants could enter Canada. All were categorized as temporary settlers. They were:
   (i) university students;
   (ii) merchants—(term was changed so as to exclude operators of laundries and restaurants, retail produce dealers, and the like). Merchant status was defined as 'one who devotes his undivided attention to mercantile pursuits, dealing exclusively in Chinese manufactures or produce or in exporting to China goods of Canadian produce or manufacture, who has been in such business for at least three years, and who has not less than $2,500 invested in it. It does not include any merchant's clerk, tailor, mechanic, huckster, peddler, drier or curer of fish, or anyone having any connection with a restaurant, laundry or rooming-house.';
   (iii) diplomatic personnel;
   (iv) native-borns returning from several years of education in China.
4. For example, in 1911, the ratio of Chinese men to Chinese women in Canada was approximately 28:1; in 1921, it was 15:1; and in 1931, it was still 12:1. Even as late as 1951, the ratio was 3.7:1 (see Li 1988: 61, Table 4.2).
5. As late as 1941, there were 20,141 'separated' families in the Chinese community, whereby the husbands resided in Canada, while the wives remained in their home country. In the same year, there were only 1,177 'intact' Chinese families in Canada in which both the husbands and wives resided in Canada. By 1951, the situation only improved slightly, and the discrepancy still remained very high: 12,882 'separated' families versus 2,842 'intact' families (see Li 1988: 67, Table 4.4).
6. Chinese yuppies.
7. 'Independent Class' immigrants are immigrants that are selected on criteria which are tied to the economic needs of Canada. They include skilled workers, also known as 'other independents', and 'business immigrants', which include entrepreneurs, investors, and the self-employed (see Margaret Young, *Canada's Immigration Program*, Library of Parliament, Research Branch, July 1992).
8. Some immigrants took advantage of an immigration clause (Immigration Pt. III, Ch. I-2, p. 17, 24 [2]) which allowed a permanent resident to be outside of Canada for 183 days in any one 12-month period without losing their permanent residency status, by continuing to conduct business between Hong Kong and Toronto. In fact, one husband I interviewed started his first year of immigration by conducting his business this way; and another husband was still commuting between Hong Kong and Toronto at the time of the interview.
9. For an in-depth study of the astronaut phenomenon, see Guida Man, 'The Astronaut Phenomenon: Examining Consequences of the Diaspora of the Hong Kong Chinese', in *Managing Change in Southeast Asia: Local Identities, Global Connections, Proceedings of the 21st Annual Conference of the Canadian Council for Southeast*

Asian Studies (University of Alberta, 1995).

10. This, however, is not to be collapsed with the popularized stereotypical image of Chinese families being largely patriarchal extended families with several generations living under the same roof. Ho et al. (1991) has reported empirical evidence which shows that the average size of the Chinese households has always been small, even prior to industrialization. The average size ranged from less than six from AD 755 to approximately five for the first half of the twentieth century. This is as much because of economic reasons as to the social customs of the time. The majority of the Chinese were poor peasants who subsisted on meagre means, and could not afford to support more than their immediate family members. Poverty and hunger governed the lives of these peasants. The idealistic Confucius conception of extended families were the entitlement of the few aristocratic gentry who numbered fewer than 10 per cent of the Chinese population.
11. The names mentioned here are pseudonyms, since the interviewees were assured anonymity. Most Chinese (especially the baby boomers and post-baby-boomer generation) who were brought up in the British educational system in colonized Hong Kong find themselves adopting English names over and above their Chinese names. Many Chinese in Hong Kong use their English names at school, at work, and for everyday use, but kept their Chinese names for official documents. In Canada, most Chinese maintain the same practice.

References

Abella, I., and H. Troper. 1982. *None Is Too Many: Canada and the Jews of Europe* (Toronto: Lester & Orpen Dennys).

Adilman, T. 1984. 'Chinese Women and Work in British Columbia', BA thesis, University of Victoria, Apr.

Armstrong, P., and H. Armstrong. 1984. *The Double Ghetto: Canadian Women and Their Segregated Work* (Toronto: McClelland & Stewart).

Baureiss, G. 1987. 'Chinese Immigration, Chinese Stereotypes, and Chinese Labour', *Canadian Ethnic Studies* 19, 3: 15–34.

Bernardo, D.H., C.L. Shehan, and G.R. Leslie. 1987. 'A Resident of Tradition: Jobs, Careers and Spouses' Time in Housework', *Journal of Marriage and the Family* 49: 381–90.

Boyd, M. 1990. 'Immigrant Women: Language, Socioeconomic Inequalities and Policy Issues', in *Ethnic Demography: Canadian Immigrant Racial and Cultural Variations*, eds S. Halli, F. Trovata, and L. Driedger (Ottawa: Carleton University Press).

Canada and Hong Kong Update. 1992. No. 7 (Summer).

Cannon, M. 1989. *China Tide* (Toronto: Harper & Collins).

Cheng, J.Y.S., and P.C.K. Kwong, eds. 1992. *The Other Hong Kong Report* (Hong Kong: The Chinese University Press).

Chinese Canadian National Council (CCNC), The Women's Book Committee. 1992. *Jin Guo: Voices of Chinese Canadian Women* (Toronto: The Women's Press).

Connelly, P. 1978. *Last Hired, First Fired: Women and the Canadian Work Force* (Toronto: The Women's Press).

Duffy, A., N. Mandell, and N. Pupo. 1989. *Few Choices: Women, Work and Family* (Toronto: Garamond Press).

Eichler, M. 1985. *On the Treatment of the Sexes in Research* (Ottawa: Social Sciences and Humanities Research Council of Canada).

———. 1988. *Families in Canada Today: Recent Changes and Their Policy Consequences* (Toronto: Gage).

Employment and Immigration Commissions (EIC). 1992, 1993. Immigration Statistics. Quarterly Statistics.

Friedan, B. 1963. *The Feminine Mystique* (New York: Dell Books).

Gerstel, N. 1984. 'Commuter Marriage', PhD diss., Columbia University.

Haraway, D. 1985. 'A Manifesto for Cyborgs: Science, Technology, and Socialist Feminism in the 1980s', *Socialist Review* 80.

Hartsock, N. 1983. 'The Feminist Standpoint:

Developing the Ground for a Specifically Feminist Historical Materialism', in *Discovering Reality*, eds S. Harding and M.B. Hintikka (Boston: D. Reidel), 293–310.

Hawkins, F. 1988. *Canada and Immigration: Public Policy and Public Concern*, 2nd edn (Kingston and Montreal: McGill-Queen's University Press).

Hill-Collins, P. 2000. *Black Feminist Thought* (New York: Routledge).

Ho, Lok-sang, et al. 1991. *International Labour Migration: The Case of Hong Kong* (Hong Kong: Hong Kong Institute of Asia-Pacific Studies, The Chinese University of Hong Kong).

Jacobson, H. 1979. 'Immigrant Women and the Community: A Perspective for Research', *Resources for Feminist Research* 8, 3 (Nov.): 17–21.

Lee, J. 1999. 'Immigrant Women Workers in the Immigrant Settlement Sector', *Canadian Women Studies* 19, 3.

Li, P.S. 1988. *The Chinese in Canada* (Toronto: Oxford University Press).

Luxton, M. 1980. *More Than a Labour of Love: Three Generations of Women's Work in the Home* (Toronto: Women's Educational Press).

———, and E. Reiter. 1997. 'Double, Double, Toil and Trouble. . . , Women's Experience of Work and Family in Canada 1980–1995', in *Women and the Canadian Welfare State: Challenges and Change*, eds P.M. Evans and G.K. Werkele (Toronto: University of Toronto Press).

Man, G. 1991. 'Commuter Families in Canada: A Research Report', report presented to the Demographic Review Secretariat, Health and Welfare Canada, Sept.

———. 1995. 'The Astronaut Phenomenon: Examining Consequences of the Diaspora of the Hong Kong Chinese', in *Managing Change in Southeast Asia: Local Identities, Global Connections* (Edmonton: University of Alberta), 269–81.

———. 1997. 'Women's Work Is Never Done: Social Organization of Work and the Experience of Women in Middle-class Hong Kong Chinese Immigrant Families in Canada', in *Advances in Gender Research,* Vol. II (Greenwich: JAI Press), 183–226.

———. 1998. 'Effects of Canadian Immigration Policies on Chinese Immigrant Women (1858–1986)', in *Asia-Pacific and Canada: Images and Perspectives* (Tokyo: The Japanese Association for Canadian Studies), 118–33.

Morokvasic, M. 1981. 'The Invisible Ones: A Double Role of Women in the Current European Migrations', in *Strangers in the World*, eds L. Eitinger and D. Schwarz (Bern, Stuggart, Vienna: Hans Huber).

Ng, R. 1982. 'Immigrant Housewives in Canada', *Atlantis* 8: 111–17.

———. 1998. 'Work Restructuring and Recognizing Third World Women: An Example from the Garment Industry in Toronto', *Canadian Women Studies* 18, 1: 21–5.

———, and A. Estable. 1987. 'Immigrant Women in the Labour Force: An Overview of Present Knowledge and Research Gaps', *RFR/DRF* 16, 1 (Mar.).

Nipp, D. 1983. 'Canada Bound: An Exploratory Study of Pioneer Chinese Women in Western Canada', MA thesis, University of Toronto.

Schwartz-Seller, M. 1981. *Immigrant Women* (Philadelphia: Temple University Press).

Sedgewick, C.P. 1973. 'The Context of Economic Change Continuity in an Urban Overseas Chinese Community', PhD diss., University of Victoria.

Smith, D. 1987. *The Everyday World as Problematic: A Feminist Sociology* (Toronto: University of Toronto Press).

Statistics Canada. 1971. Census of Canada.

———. 1986. Census of Canada, Public Use Sample Tape, Individual File.

SUCCESS, Women's Committee Research Group. 1991. Chinese Immigrant Women's Needs Survey in Richmond (Vancouver: SUCCESS).

Thobani, S. 1998. 'Nationalizing Citizens, Bordering Immigrant Women: Globalization and the Racialization of Women's Citizenship in Late 20th Century Canada', PhD diss., Simon Fraser University.

Warren, C.E. 1986. *Vignettes of Life* (Calgary: Detselig Enterprises).

Wickberg, E., ed. 1982. *From China to Canada: A History of the Chinese Communities in Canada* (Toronto: McClelland & Stewart).

Wong, S.L. 1992. 'Emigration and Stability in Hong Kong', *Asian Survey* 32, 10 (Oct.).

Yee, M. 1987. 'Out of the Silence: Voices of Chinese Canadian Women', *RFR/DRF* 16, 1 (Mar.).

Young, M. 1992. 'Canada's Immigration Program', background paper, Library of Parliament, Research Branch, July (Ottawa: Supply and Services).

Chapter 29

This chapter discusses general findings from a study of immigrant families living in and around Vancouver. Gillian Creese, Isabel Dyck, and Arlene McLaren draw on the results of focus groups and interviews to provide an overview of the changing experiences of the immigrants they talked to, and the multiple effects of immigration on them and their families. In so doing, they make clear that the impact of immigration is different for women and men; youth, adults, and children; and different racial groups. But for all, immigration unsettles and changes family relations.

Creese, Dyck, and McLaren also explore the variety of ways immigrants adapt to their new environment. Focusing on how immigrants rely on and create networks of support, they also indicate the ways family boundaries are extended and blurred, locally and transnationally, as people negotiate and renegotiate ways to solve the problems they encounter in establishing themselves and attempting to meet their objectives in immigrating—objectives that typically involve education and employment most importantly. Through this discussion, we see something about the ways immigration changes gender relations as well as parent–child relations.

Gender, Generation, and the 'Immigrant Family': Negotiating Migration Processes

Gillian Creese, Isabel Dyck, and Arlene Tigar McLaren

Academic research tends to view the immigrant family in two quite different ways. The dominant view for many years has been that 'the immigrant family' is a naturally bounded, unified whole. For example, it has been assumed that one can analyze 'the Greek-Canadian family', 'the Polish-Canadian family', and 'the Chinese-Canadian family' as if they were uniform entities (Ishwaran 1980). According to this idea, the immigrant family undertakes a linear journey to integration, moving from the home culture to the new culture. Such a model of immigration assumes the existence of two original, distinct cultures and a unidirectional process of adaptation; it also assumes that the primary dynamic exists between host and immigrant culture, ignoring dynamics within immigrant cultures as well as across them.

The notion that the two cultural poles of home and new culture are fixed or monolithic is difficult to sustain (Kibria 1997; Pizanias 1996). How can we say, for example, what is *the* Canadian family, when it can best be typified as diverse and in flux (Eichler 1997)? Or what is *the* 'Asian' family, differing as it does according to country, region, social class, ethnicity, religion, and so forth? Such monolithic visions are fictional families, bearing an uneasy relationship to people's daily experiences. Further complicating any definition of 'the immigrant culture' is the time of immigration, as well as processes of restructuring and globalization, and the emergence of diaspora cultures that stretch across national boundaries (Kibria 1997). Finally, such a model of immigrant family integration privileges cultural values and treats them as separate from everyday practices and social relations in families (including their power dynamics), discourses (including racist ideas), and structural constraints that provide barriers to integration.

A second way to understand immigrant families is to see families as fluid and constantly being negotiated and reconstituted both spatially and temporally (e.g., Lawson 1998). This view considers ways in which immigrant families are unfixed categories that are not discretely located in space. Families may adopt spatially extensive survival strategies incorporating multiple members in diverse places who remain part of a single income-pooling unit, or who continue to exercise influence over dynamics in the same household. As such, families may be situated in the home country, the new country, and elsewhere—the family is redefined as transnational (Hyndman and Walton-Roberts 1998). Moreover, boundaries between such transnational families can blur with local, national, and international networks that include kin, friends, and contacts. According to this second perspective, immigrant families (like other families) are heterogeneous, multiply positioned, and stratified—they differ in their composition, their social positions according to social class, ethnicity, race,[1] and locality, and in the experiences of various family members, especially in relation to gender and generation (e.g., Das Gupta 1995). Thus we cannot speak about *the* immigrant family because this denotes a far too static picture of what is a shifting set of complex social relations, with unpredictable outcomes.

Our research suggests that the second view of immigrant families as fluid and heterogeneous is the more fruitful way to understand migration processes, and families. Such processes may have more than a single country of origin and take place through a web of daily practices—within and between households—connected to immigration policy, neighbourhood, social networks, housing, the labour market, consumption, leisure, health, schooling, and so forth. Some immigrants celebrate this fluidity. In one of our focus groups, a woman from Poland, recently divorced (since coming to Canada) and a mother of a 13-year-old daughter, observed: 'The family here looks different.' She likes how the family looks in Canada: 'for me it's absolutely right that immigration changes the picture of the family'. In contrast, others voiced deep concern over the reconstitution of family dynamics. For example, a grandfather from India spoke about his disappointment over 'the breaking of the family' in Canada. These different views reflect the variety of family, gender, and generational anxieties and struggles that emerged as themes in our research and provide preliminary insights into different ways that people negotiate immigration and settlement.

Our study is based on 16 focus groups that we held in five districts in the Greater Vancouver region,[2] and multiple interviews with families in two of these neighbourhoods. We selected the five districts on the basis of their different residential type and unique history and profile of immigrant settlement: East Vancouver, Westside Vancouver (including Kerrisdale, Oakridge, and Shaughnessy), Richmond, North Surrey-Delta, and Tri-cities (Coquitlam, Port Coquitlam, and Port Moody). East Vancouver is an inner-city residential area that has long been a reception area for diverse groups of immigrants; Vancouver's affluent Westside, until recently largely British in ethnic origin, now has a large Chinese-origin population; Surrey is an outer suburb with a diverse immigrant mix, including a significant South Asian population; and Tri-cities is an outer suburb that has only recently begun to attract new immigrants among its residents. The focus groups varied in their composition. In all districts, we conducted focus groups with recently arrived immigrants. In most districts we also carried out focus groups with service providers, second-generation young adults, and women-only groups. And in one district, we organized a focus group with members of the 'host' community. The focus groups served as a preliminary stage of research to help familiarize ourselves with immigrant issues and as preparation for an in-depth longitudinal study of immigrant families in some districts. Over a five-year period, from 1997 through 2002, we interviewed 25 families (in most cases three or four times) in two neighbourhoods, East Vancouver and the Tri-cities. This paper draws largely from the focus groups with illustrations extracted from the family interviews. A more detailed analysis of the longitudinal family interviews is discussed elsewhere (Creese, Dyck, and McLaren 2006). These overlapping case studies, we believe, shed light on the complex connections between the everyday practices of immigrant families and how these interact with locality and larger regions.

Although talking about family in the public setting of focus groups is difficult, we were often struck by the animation of the discussions. In the focus groups, participants also discussed employment issues and relations with native-born people, which we have reported on elsewhere.[3] Our longitudinal interviews with families provided a more intimate portrayal of the complex and shifting nature of family relations. In this paper, we have chosen to report on three broad themes to do with the daily practices of family life that arose in the focus groups: network making; the dynamics of gender, generation, and racialization; and the negotiation of educational and employment opportunities. These themes—which we briefly illustrate—highlight the struggles, contingencies, heterogeneity, and fluidity of the everyday practices of immigrant families in a variety of localities.

1. Network Making

Immigrants may use informal networks of friends, relatives, or associates to help them settle into a new location; these may be used on their own or in conjunction with institutional service provision. Most immigrants are faced with a vast array of information that has to be accessed and processed in the first months of settlement as they attempt to find housing, jobs, and schools, and to negotiate everyday needs. This is often complicated by lack of English language ability, or French for those first settling in Quebec. Some immigrants have friends, relatives, or other contacts through ethnic affiliation who may be able to help; others have fewer resources in place when they arrive.

As some research has shown, immigrant families interact in various ways with local, national, and international networks (e.g., Hyndman and Walton-Roberts 1998). What struck us in the focus groups is the vast differences among networks, which vary from being densely organized (containing many people), and operating transnationally, to being thin (with few people) and confined to the localized context. For some immigrants, they are non-existent. Furthermore, such networks may extend, blur, and otherwise problematize the boundaries and meanings of family. For example, an Indo-Canadian participant from Surrey described a migration process including marriage and extended-family reunification that involved buying land, building houses together, setting up jobs for one another, and working together. He said, 'And that is where we all stayed together just like a network, like support mechanisms and everything, housing, food, set up a job, and those kinds of things. We always move together.'

Reciprocal support within families and across generations was important to some. The reunification of families allowed grandparents to support adult children, including those pursuing studies in Canada, through participation in the running of a household or caring for young children (see also McLaren's [2006] study of South Asian elderly women who were sponsored by their families to come to Canada and who contributed to running the households, caring for children, and providing family income from farm labour and other sources). Others from the Punjab mentioned common village origin (rather than just blood and marital relatives) as an important dimension of chain migration and available support on arrival in Canada, which expands notions of family in the new country. In our longitudinal interviews, we observed extensive shifts in family over time as in the case of chain migration in which individuals sponsored family members to join them in Canada. Two South Asian sisters, who had recently entered Canada as independent immigrants, applied to sponsor siblings, spouses, parents, and in-laws. All together for a period of time, seven adult family members of the extended family shared the accommodation of a two-bedroom basement suite and pooled resources. One of the sisters later moved to a suite nearby with her husband and baby.

In contrast to densely organized chain migration, a woman from Poland living in the Tri-cities talked about networks contingent upon changing family structure, migration, and different locales. When she first arrived in Toronto with her husband, they relied heavily on extended family and the Polish community for help in gaining crucial information: 'They were like the sailboat by this ocean of new information.' Later, after divorce and a move with her child to British Columbia, she profoundly missed the benefits of the large Polish community in Toronto. She deliberately sought Polish contacts, partly activated by links to Toronto that she maintained regularly through telephone and e-mail contact, to help her find housing and health service providers. Thus, she extended a network that had begun with family connections. Since then she has developed non-ethnically based social networks through volunteer work and through her daughter's school friends and sports activities. Friends made through her volunteer work have been helpful in providing her with job information and developing her career plans.

Such fluidity and blurred boundaries of families and networks, as illustrated in these examples, suggest that network making is far more complex than is captured in the often-used simple distinction between nuclear- and extended-family networks. The meaning of family structure and networks, how they operate and the purposes they serve, may be transformed as they interact with different spatial and social patterns. For example, Hong Kong's small geographical area enables nuclear families to be in close proximity to relatives not living in their households, a situation amenable to developing a close-knit family network that is in effect an extended family. Such an extension of family beyond the household may not be possible (or work in the same way) in more spatially stretched locations such as large Canadian cities (Man 1996). In our family interviews, a household from Hong Kong consisted of elderly parents, a son and daughter and their spouses, and another son who eventually married. Over time, the young couples began to migrate from their suburban location to another location with a greater concentration of Chinese immigrants, and they planned to move their parents to join them. On the other hand, immigrant families who lack the support networks of the extended family that were available to them in their home country (Man 1996; Pizanias 1996), may attempt to replicate them by symbolically adopting friends as relatives (Dhruvarajan 1996). In other words, networks may include a variety of family structures and contacts; these may change over time, and may extend beyond a specific neighbourhood to cross a sprawling city, a nation, or international borders. How families construct support networks is a critical element of the everyday practices of immigrant settlement.

2. The Dynamics of Gender, Generation, and Racialization

The fluidity of immigrant family life is perhaps nowhere more apparent than in the dynamics of gender, generation, and racialization. Immigration unsettles family relations in multiple ways and may give rise to new forms of independence, dependence, and identity. Recent research has shown, for example, how immigration policy, procedures, and discourses produce women's 'dependence' within families and other sites of interaction, including employment, by frequently categorizing family men as independent applicants and women as their dependents (Agnew 1996; Boyd 1997; Ng 1988; Vanderbijl 1998; McLaren and Black 2005). As Satzewich (1993) argues, immigration policy reinforces the myth of women's dependency (i.e., by categorizing them as if they were unemployable when in fact immigrant women have a high rate of employment) and promotes their marginalization (i.e., the stereotypes of dependency make it difficult for immigrant women to find decent employment). Thobani (1998) and Ng (1990) further argue that immigrant women are racialized. The very term 'immigrant women' connotes women who are racialized as non-white. White immigrant women more easily slough off their immigrant status whereas women of colour, whether immigrant or Canadian-born, may continue to be treated as immigrants, who really 'belong somewhere else' and who are a drain on Canada's resources. Immigration can, therefore, be understood as an ongoing process that in many ways promotes the marginalization of women of colour and those for whom English is a second language.

While immigration procedures may frequently inscribe women as dependent upon their husbands, focus group narratives revealed processes that were more complex and contradictory. A prominent narrative in the focus groups emphasized the independence from family that immigrant women may acquire in Canada. Participants from a variety of backgrounds talked about the position of women in the family as more equal in Canada, with its laws that protect them better than in their places of origin. As a woman from Hong Kong argued: 'I am better protected here. The laws in Canada are protecting the women.' Another participant, the woman from Poland who had divorced since coming to Canada, commented on the greater freedom that women enjoy in Canada, while acknowledging that new expectations placed additional stress on family relations:

> The woman has more freedom here. . . . For example, in my country still is this tradition to treat woman as the family person . . . the women are growing faster than the men . . . they are going to ask for some bigger freedom, some bigger partnership between them.

Women's improved social status was often double-edged, however, causing some participants to worry about increased conflict between spouses, the prevalence of divorce in Canada, and limited social support in the absence of extended kin nearby. Participants in a focus group linked to Tri-cities, for example, suggested that domestic violence is widespread and particularly exacerbated by women's vulnerability in the sponsorship process. Immigration to Canada can mean less independence and freedom for women, especially for those who are mothers.

Our family interviews suggest that greater 'freedom' for women was often not borne out in everyday practices, which are constrained both by the 'privatized' nuclear-family form in Canada (where parents are solely responsible for their children), and the systematic marginalization of immigrants—including skilled professionals—in the local labour market. Both downward mobility and the intensification of domestic labour were experienced by all the families we interviewed, with the brunt of additional work and stress borne by mothers. Women commonly put their own career aspirations on hold to look after children and to prioritize their husbands' (usually unsuccessful) attempts to remake their careers. This was particularly difficult for women who were professionals prior to migration. A former teacher from Iran, for example, talked about the health problems she experienced, which were related to isolation, marginal employment, and loss of her professional identity.

Our family interviews included some in which men adjusted to increased domestic demands by contributing more to domestic work in Canada. For example a father from Uganda worked nights so that he could care for his children after school and cook dinner for the family while his wife attended classes in the evening. But most men left the bulk of domestic work to their wives, creating a source of marital friction and additional stress for many women.

Some women were surprised to find just how difficult it was to care for children in Canada and, at the same time, pursue other activities. As a young woman from Latin America argued in a focus group, in Canada jobs are more essential to have yet more difficult to find, and mothering and employment harder to combine than in her country of origin where extended female kin shared child-rearing responsibilities. Many of the women were primarily responsible for negotiating childcare and, as a result, suffered severe isolation and often a sense of danger. As a single mother living in the outer suburban area of Tricities poignantly remembered:

> It is such a difficult time when you are landed, the language skills mostly are very crude during this time and the family, the child mostly—everything is your responsibility—and you don't have the communication skills, you don't have the knowledge about the country. Everything is strange, everything is danger almost. You have to do everything by yourself. It is really stressful and almost killing as an immigrant.

Some mothers feared that if they ever left their child unattended in Canada (as they had done in their country of origin) they could be accused of neglect. Generally, caring for children could be so time-consuming that it prevented women from being involved in the community, even though such involvement may be necessary for mothering and settlement more generally. As a woman living in East Vancouver commented:

> If you come as an immigrant woman you get that blockage whereby your children become your focus, and you have some hours when children are in school, which you can use to explore what it is about the community, because how do you know who [to go to] unless you have connections in the community?

Helping to organize other women in her community is now a central part of her life.

As these illustrations suggest, how mothers interact with the community is a vital issue for understanding settlement following immigration. Very little research, however, examines immigrant mothers' networks. Several writers (e.g., Boyd 1989; Pedraza 1991) note that research on social networks and migration has tended to be indifferent to gender. In focusing on immigrant families and the significance of social networks in providing various resources, Zhou (1997), for example, treats this process as if it were undifferentiated by gender, and ignores the specific requirements of mothering. Some studies examine the significance of mothers' networking as family and gendered strategies of providing for their children's well-being (e.g., Bell and Ribbens 1994; Dyck 1992), but few look at how mothers who have immigrated construct personal networks and make use of them. Our research attempts to understand how mothering, which is located spatially both within the home and outside it, is central to sustaining and transforming social relations (Dyck 1992) and the ways that mothers extend their practices beyond the household in ways that vary over time and space. For example, a young woman who had just arrived from India at the time of our first family interview had few connections with the local South Asian community (which she considered too conservative compared to her cosmopolitan upbringing in India) until after her daughter was born four years later; she then began to attend local Punjabi events and joined a Punjabi mother's group with her daughter.

As Man (1996; see Chapter 28) suggests, women's independence and control over their lives may be limited by the organization of Canadian cities, including the proximity of services, relatives, and transportation. In our research, the neighbourhood interacted in various ways to form new relations of dependence and restricted movement. A young woman from Hong Kong living in the Tri-cities, for example, commented on her dependence on her sister and father to get to school and visit friends until she got her driver's license. At the same time, her mother, who did not speak English, was now dependent on her and her sister to get out. Both the young woman and her mother resented these new forms of dependence, feeling constrained in their activity. The same young woman expressed a strong sense of loss accompanying the geographical and social dislocation of immigration: 'I felt like I lost my whole life, my own space.'

As a great deal of research suggests, immigrant family experiences can differ considerably according to generation (e.g., Maykovich 1980). Many participants, for example, suggested that parents struggle during migration while younger children adjust quickly and the second generation integrates more easily than the first. Not all agreed, however, that children adjust easily. Some participants talked about the isolation that many immigrant children feel, especially those who arrived in their teens. A woman expressed anxiety about teenaged children who often face greater difficulties than adults: 'I see a lot of the newcomers, immigrants, where the children are just sitting at home and they don't know what to do' and suggested 'the newcomers' children are mostly outsiders from our society', especially those in families with limited financial resources to pay for community activities. Other women talked of the feeling that children weren't welcome in Canada. One woman, for example, concluded from her difficult search to find housing that 'many people didn't like children'. And several participants, particularly in our family interviews, complained about their own children's behaviour as they adopted 'Canadian ways' of interacting that did not demonstrate appropriate respect for elders and deference to parental authority.

Two focus groups with second-generation young adults who grew up in the Lower Mainland—Chinese Canadians in Kerrisdale and Indo-Canadians in Surrey—highlighted the complex interaction of changing immigration policy, different family migration strategies, and changing settlement geographies in generating distinct and shifting generational identities and intergenerational relations. Conversation in these focus groups turned to young adults' feelings of being a racialized minority while growing up, often one of only a few Chinese- or Indian-origin children in their schools and neighbourhoods. Some expressed a sense of fragmented identities: 'All my friends were white and I thought of myself as white except when I got home I was Chinese. You don't notice until you look in the mirror that you are different.' As this comment illustrates, fragmented identities can be confusing and painful. The family interviews provided examples of the variability of identity, with youth who largely identified with their Canadian peers (for example just 'Canadian' for the teenage sons of a family from Uganda), those who identified as hyphenated Canadians (for example 'Spanish-Canadian' for the teenage children of a family from Guatemala), and those who identified primarily by their country of origin (including a teenage daughter from Iran who wished to return 'home' to raise her own children).

Unlike the diversity of identities evident among youth in the family interviews, most of the young men and women in the second-generation focus groups expressed an appreciation of their ability to move between cultures, to form, as it were, situational identities. This greater ease of moving between cultures and identities may be linked to the density of the local communities—Chinese-Canadian and Punjabi-Canadian—from which the youth focus groups were drawn. One young woman commented on speaking English at Pacific Centre (a downtown mall) and Chinese in areas of Chinese business concentration. In both cases decisions about language were tied to notions of what was appropriate in a specific place, and possible sanctions for contravening conventions. Similarly a young Indo-Canadian woman from Surrey commented: 'we all had a school personality and a home personality'. Yet this separation of school and home was not constant, but, according to participants, depended on the community in which the family lived—how white, multicultural, or Indo-Canadian it was—and how liberal, as several emphasized, the father was.

Second-generation participants also identified issues of parenting that set them apart from their peers. One may take for granted that parents, especially perhaps immigrant parents, should stress the importance of education and the need for scholastic achievement. However, some participants who had gone to school in the Lower Mainland reflected critically upon their parents' emphasis on scholastic achievement and the necessity to excel and work hard at school as a factor that inhibited their 'integration' with their white peers. Young Chinese-Canadian men and women in Kerrisdale, for example, mentioned that these family attitudes and expectations about education, such as attendance at Chinese school, limited their opportunities to make friends with white children. One commented: 'It was always "get the highest mark that you can".' The importance of education for this Chinese-Canadian group was further reflected in comments on how the family would support the children through school and university, and how this family lifestyle acted as a source of division between themselves and white students who were not supported in the same way.

Some young adults had lived through changes in immigration patterns, which meant the increased density of some Chinese-Canadian communities. This change made many participants feel less 'alone', and in some cases helped bridge the cultural/generation gap that existed between some children and their parents. As a participant said: 'In terms of my relationship with my parents, I can communicate so much better now. I talk to my friends in Chinese a lot now, so I'm a lot more articulate with my Chinese now than before.' For some Indo-Canadian participants, in contrast, strong patterns of family chain migration and extended-family settlement strategies produced early residential concentration and strong community ties. This was sometimes double-edged—especially for the young women who experienced support but also strong social pressure from the broader Indo-Canadian community which monitored their behaviour, even when parents were willing to allow them to become more 'Western'. In this context the boundaries of family that were not fixed and intact in the first place, became even less fixed and more permeable as the influence of community members filtered through the boundaries to control the behaviour of family members.

Overall, participants in our research identified ways that immigrant families were shaped by dynamics of gender, generation, and racialization. As immigrants, women and men had different experiences and, therefore, spousal relations often shifted in unsettling ways. There was no consensus, however, about whether or not coming to Canada meant that women improved their social position. But this was a topic of considerable interest to many participants. Despite the rhetoric that North American society promises more freedom for women, many participants suggested that immigration may lead to new dependencies and greater isolation. Mothers, for example, may face new constraints (e.g., legal, linguistic, spatial) while they take on the onerous responsibilities of settling themselves and their families in their new country and community. The social position of both men and women deteriorated after migration in terms of economic opportunities, but women also bore the brunt of the intensification of domestic labour as family strategies often prioritized men's quest for economic improvement. Generation was also a dimension that made for different experiences. Some parents, for example, became more dependent on their more linguistically able children, and many lamented the more permissive and child-centred milieu in Canada. Finally, racialization was a theme that second-generation participants were particularly concerned about, especially because it changed over time. These concerns were expressed, for example, in comments about changes in identity, ambiguous feelings of belonging, tensions with white residents, and ways that the increased density of communities of origin (particularly Chinese and South Asian) redefined daily life in Vancouver.

3. Negotiating Educational and Employment Opportunities

As countless research attests, education and employment are primary sites in which immigrants must negotiate their 'integration' into local neighbourhoods. More than any other topic, people in the focus groups told us over and over again how worried they were about employment issues. They also talked passionately about education. The disjuncture between hopes and actual experiences of schooling and employment often meant a fragile sense of the future and of family settlement in Canada. Many participants worried about their own opportunities as well as those of their spouses and children. But they were also hopeful. As a participant from Surrey commented, 'If children can pursue their education fully, they will have no problems in Canada.'

Research has not fully recognized the extent to which education and employment become family projects in which women, particularly as mothers, play a central role involving strategies that occur over time and space and that shift as negotiation takes place. Mothering practices are often shaped by the issue of their children's schooling and, because of recent changes in the labour market, a sense of educational urgency presses mothers more fully into the pursuit of educational opportunities for their children (Reay 1998).

Many of the parents in our focus group talked about coming to Canada because of the educational opportunities they thought this country promised their children. Families often pin their hopes for the future on their children's education. As a Kerrisdale focus group participant commented, 'the most important thing is the children's future'. At the same time, some family interviews raised concerns about Canadian education. For example a woman from Poland argued that her daughter would not be able to keep up to her peers if she were to return to school in Poland, thereby constraining her choice of whether to stay or leave Canada.

The focus group participants talked in ways that suggested that obtaining educational and occupational opportunities were central family projects varying from family to family. How families were able to support their children's education, for example, was dynamically related to their resources. A young woman suggested that due to differences in age of arrival and parents' financial security, her older brother had far fewer advantages than she did:

> I think my brother had a hard time. He is a smart guy. He would have liked to go to university and stuff but because of my parents' immigration process, I think it was hard for them to put him through university.

> So he started driving a taxi because my dad had a taxi at the time. He didn't have the same opportunities that me and my sister did.

Some parents who had adequate economic resources and knowledge about the local school chose to settle in specific neighbourhoods. Some had resources that allowed them to provide their children with tutoring, either paid or provided by members of their family or social network. Furthermore, some parents, especially those from Kerrisdale (a wealthy area of Vancouver), were knowledgeable about local schooling issues and talked about the ways that schools should be changed to reflect their interests (see Mitchell 2001 for an account of Chinese immigrant parents' attempts to change school curricula and pedagogy in a suburb of Vancouver). Some felt, for example, that schools kept children too long in English-as-Second-Language classes, and did not have enough Chinese-origin teachers relative to the student body. Overall, the research participants had mixed opinions about the quality of Canadian schools, pointing to how Canadian education is less rigorous, but also less stressful and more creative, than in their countries of origin.

Family strategies intersected with education, both locally and internationally, illustrating again the spatial fluidity of families. Some parents with adult children wanting to study in Canada migrated to support their children, in one case to provide childcare for grandchildren. In other families, parents maintained economic and residential ties with their country of origin while their children attended school or university in Canada. In one instance, a young woman who was pursuing a master's degree at a university in Vancouver had come to the realization that this education might not lead to good employment opportunities in Canada. She was considering the possibility of returning to Hong Kong, where her brothers were still living: 'I want a job that I can make progress [in] instead of just working as a cashier or helper. Because I'm young, I don't have a family myself, I want to develop my own career.' The importance of having a job is summed up by her statement: 'If you don't have a job you cannot see the future.'

Several participants talked of the transnational mobility and choice they had in employment due to their family resources, and some accounts referred to the phenomenon of the 'astronaut family', where the husband in a family goes back to Asia to pursue business. Family costs were attached to this strategy. For example, a Taiwanese woman perceived that such spatial separation of the family was a threat to family cohesion and encouraged marital discord. This spatial stretching of the family household can lead women to experience family life as lone parents, taking on the local responsibilities of child raising (see also Waters 2002).

Others without the choice to return to their countries of origin talked of stresses, discouragement and little income for family members who were unable to find paid employment. As they faced restricted employment opportunities, many participants adopted a family strategy that looked to the next generation for greater success—expected because of their locally attained education and potential to speak English fluently. At the same time many parents' desire for their children's integration was double-edged, simultaneously wanting it and fearing the loss of cultural identity that might result from it. Those who explicitly wanted their children to 'mix with other races' as one Kerrisdale participant put it, were also poignantly mindful of the many barriers that made this difficult. These barriers included living in a neighbourhood peopled by a specific cultural group which could inhibit acquiring fluency in English, and taking ESL classes which might unintentionally reinforce such networks.

Conclusion

Depictions in most texts of the immigrant family are strangely silent on the permeable nature of families as they experience dislocation and resettlement. To stress 'the unit of intimate partners', as do some texts, fails to capture the divisions and tensions within immigrant families and the shifting boundaries of their everyday experiences. Our research points to the inadequacy of normative views of nuclear and extended families, with examples of households with fluid and fluctuating social boundaries and whose physical boundaries may span several single-family dwellings and indeed several national borders. The use of networks in finding jobs, housing, and information about schools and other services appears to be a common, but not universal, strategy. Such networks take many forms that extend or blur the boundaries and meanings of family and also disrupt notions of a linear immigration process. As part of the process of immigration, family households are constituted and reconstituted in diverse ways that may involve complex and changing forms of dependence and renegotiation of family life. This renegotiation may also involve conflict and anxiety along the fault lines of gender, generation, and ethnic/racialized communities.

Notes

1. We acknowledge the social construction of all categories of ethnicity or race, whether in the census, research, or everyday language. Some researchers choose to signify this by using scare quotes around social categories such as 'Indo-Canadian', 'Chinese', or 'White'. We have chosen not to do this for consistency and stylistic reasons. The terms used by participants are preserved in quotations.
2. This paper is based on research that was conducted by a team of researchers who are part of the Vancouver RIIM Centre of Excellence: Gillian Creese, Isabel Dyck, Dan Hiebert, Tom Hutton, David Ley, Arlene Tigar McLaren, Geraldine Pratt. As well, the following researchers assisted us in our research: Wendy Mendes-Crabb, John Rose, Hugh Tan, Ann Vanderbijl, Margaret Walton-Roberts, and Priscilla Wei. We would like to thank the following agencies and their members for their participation in and help with the focus groups: City of Port Moody Parks, Recreation and Cultural Services; Coquitlam Leisure and Parks Services; Coquitlam School District; Vancouver and Lower Mainland Multi-cultural Family Support Services Society; Coquitlam Women's Centre; Greater Coquitlam Volunteer Centre; ISS; LINC; MOSAIC; Multicultural Family Centre; Progressive Intercultural Services; Richmond Police Department; Richmond Planning Department; Richmond Public Library; Richmond School District; Storefront Orientation Services; SUCCESS, Richmond Office; Surrey Delta Immigrant Society; Surrey Planning Department; Vancouver Community College; Vancouver Planning Department. We especially thank the focus group participants.
3. See Dan Hiebert, 'Immigrant Experiences in Greater Vancouver: Focus Group Narratives' <http://www. riim.metropolis.globalx.net>.

References

Agnew, V. 1996. *Resisting Discrimination: Women from Asia, Africa, and the Caribbean and the Women's Movement in Canada* (Toronto: University of Toronto Press).

Bell, L., and J. Ribbens. 1994. 'Isolated Housewives and Complex Maternal Worlds: The Significance of Social Contacts between Women with Young Children in Industrial Societies', *The Sociological Review* 42: 227–62.

Boyd, M. 1989. 'Family and Personal Networks in International Migration: Recent Developments and New Agendas', *International Migration Review* 23.

———. 1997. 'Migration Policy, Female Dependency and Family Membership: Canada and Germany', in *Remaking the Welfare State*, eds P. Evans et al. (Toronto: University of Toronto Press).

Creese, G., I. Dyck, and A.T. McLaren, 2006. 'The "Flexible" Immigrant: Household Strategies and the Labour Market', Vancouver Centre of Excellence, RIIM, Working Paper Series No. 06-19.

Das Gupta, T. 1995. 'Families of Native Peoples, Immigrants, and People of Colour', in *Canadian Families: Diversity, Conflict and Change*, eds N. Mandell and A. Duffy (Toronto: Harcourt Brace & Company), 141–74.

Dhruvarajan, V. 1996. 'Hindu Indu-Canadian Families', in *Voices: Essays on Canadian Families*, ed. M. Lynn (Toronto: Nelson Canada), 301–28.

Dyck, I. 1992. 'Integrating Home and Wage Workplace: Women's Daily Lives in a Canadian Suburb', in *British Columbia Reconsidered: Essays on Women*, eds G. Creese and V. Strong-Boag (Vancouver: Press Gang), 172–97.

Eichler, M. 1997. *Family Shifts: Families, Policies and Gender Equality* (Toronto: Oxford University Press).

Hanson, S., and G. Pratt. 1995. *Women, Work and Space* (London: Routledge).

Hyndman, J., and M. Walton-Roberts. 1998. 'Migration and Nation: Burmese Refugees in Vancouver', *The Bulletin* 11: 1–5.

Ishwaran, K., ed. 1980. *Canadian Families: Ethnic Variations* (Toronto: McGraw-Hill Ryerson).

Kibria, N. 1997. 'The Concept of "Bicultural Families" and Its Implication for Research on Immigrant and Ethnic Families', in *Immigration and the Family*, eds A. Booth et al. (Mahwah, NJ: Lawrence Erlbaum Assocs), 205–10.

Lawson, V.A. 1998. 'Hierarchical Households and Gendered Migration in Latin America: Feminist Extensions to Migration Research', *Progress in Human Geography* 22: 39–53.

McLaren, A.T. 2006. 'Parental Sponsorship—Whose Problematic? A Consideration of South Asian Women's Immigration Experiences in Vancouver', Vancouver Centre of Excellence, Research on Immigration and Integration in the Metropolis (RIIM), Working Paper Series No. 06-08.

———, and T.L. Black. 2005. 'Family Class and Immigration in Canada: Implications for Sponsored Elderly Women', Vancouver Centre of Excellence, Research on Immigration and Integration in the Metropolis (RIIM), Working Paper Series No. 05-26.

Man, G. 1996. 'The Experience of Middle-class Women in Recent Hong Kong Chinese Immigrant Families in Canada', in *Voices: Essays on Canadian Families*, ed. M. Lynn (Toronto: Nelson Canada), 271–300.

Maykovich, M.K. 1980. 'Acculturation Versus Familism in Three Generations of Japanese-Canadians', in *Canadian Families: Ethnic Variations*, ed. K. Ishwaran (Toronto: McGraw-Hill Ryerson), 65–83.

Mitchell, K. 2001. 'Education for Democratic Citizenship: Transnationalism, Multiculturalism, and the Limits of Liberalism', *Harvard Educational Review* 71, 1: 51–78.

Ng, R. 1988. *The Politics of Community Services: Immigrant Women, Class and the State* (Toronto: Garamond Press).

———. 1990. 'Immigrant Women: The Construction of a Labour Market Category', *Canadian Journal of Women and the Law* 4, 1: 96–112.

Pedraza, S. 1991. 'Women and Migration: The Social Consequences of Gender', *Annual Review of Sociology* 17: 303–25.

Pizanias, C. 1996. 'Greek Families in Canada: Fragile Truths, Fragmented Stories', in *Voices: Essays on Canadian Families*, ed. M. Lynn (Toronto: Nelson Canada), 329–60.

Reay, D. 1998. 'Engendering Social Reproduction: Mothers in the Educational Marketplace', *British Journal of Sociology of Education* 19, 2: 195–209.

Satzewich, V. 1993. 'Migrant and Immigrant Families in Canada: State Coercion and Legal Control in the Formation of Ethnic Families', *Journal of Comparative Family Studies* 24: 315–38.

Thobani, S. 1998. 'Nationalizing Citizens, Bordering Immigrant Women: Globalization and the Racialization of Citizenship in Late 20th Century Canada', unpublished PhD diss., Simon Fraser University.

Vanderbijl, A.E. 1998. 'The "Immigrant Family"', paper presented at the Western Association of Sociology and Anthropology Meetings, Vancouver, BC, 15–16 May.

Waters, J.L. 2002. 'Flexible Families? "Astronaut" Households and the Experiences of Lone Mothers in Vancouver, British Columbia', *Social & Cultural Geography* 3: 117–35.

Zhou, M. 1997. 'Growing up American: The Challenge Confronting Immigrant Children and Children of Immigrants', *Annual Review of Sociology* 23: 63–95.

Chapter 30

The economic restructuring that has been ongoing for some time has meant the 'downsizing' of firms and their workplaces and thus the firing of workers; it has also meant increases in bad jobs (e.g., jobs with low wages/salaries and poor benefits) and non-standard employment (e.g., part-time jobs, temporary jobs, jobs with few protections). This major trend in the economy has occurred at a time when the 'welfare state' is also being restructured and significantly reduced: social services have been cut back, moving work (such as health care) into the home, and therefore increasing the work typically done by women. Both sets of changes unsettle families in fundamental ways. Given women's greater responsibility for the daily care of their children and family members generally, these changes often affect women more directly than men.

In this chapter, Belinda Leach provides a description of the nature of rural economies and family livelihood in Ontario in the 1990s, and examines how economic restructuring affects rural women with families. She discusses how the women in her study responded to unemployment—a response affected by the necessary work they do for their families. She also considers the impact of economic restructuring, and the options women face, on the gendered divisions in their families.

Transforming Rural Livelihoods: Gender, Work, and Restructuring in Three Ontario Communities

Belinda Leach

> In November 1993, following months of speculation about the future of the company she worked for, and in particular its manufacturing plant in the community where she lived, Karen White, along with her husband and co-workers, was told that the plant would close in May of the following year. Walking home from work that day she made a detour and dropped into K-Brand, the other major factory in the town, which had been there a few months making sports clothing, such as baseball hats, and there she picked up two application for employment forms. She described her husband's reaction when she handed him one of them: 'I'm not working at K-Brand' he said. And that was the end of the discussion. Karen quit her industrial job which would terminate anyway five months later, and took what she was offered at K-Brand at minimum wage. As she put it, 'I knew at least I'd still be able to get home at lunchtime for Jason and Alex.' Six months later she was laid off from K-Brand, was unemployed for a couple of months, then found a part-time job in a local nursing home. Her husband took the layoff in May, and was unemployed for eight months until he found an industrial job about 60 kilometres away from home.
>
> —Field notes

This chapter draws on a qualitative study of the work lives of men and women who have been laid off from manufacturing jobs in rural communities in Wellington County, Ontario.[1] The findings of this study operate as a point of departure for thinking about how restructuring processes operate, are apprehended, and articulated within a gendered local culture. In the communities we have studied, men and women were employed alongside each other in factory work. When their workplaces closed, men and women workers faced the problem of finding new work on different terms. In this chapter I argue that at the moment of redundancy, factors came into play that directly affected women's strategies and options for new employment. Women not only confronted the new economy but dealt with gendered work expectations shaped in the rural cultural context.

The chapter then explores the way in which women's involvement in a rural labour process is bound to rural ideology, which incorporates powerful ideas about paid and unpaid work, as well as to the experience of restructuring. The caring labour expected of women, in both paid and unpaid forms, becomes significant when they explore new job possibilities. As all forms of women's work are restructured, the relations of caring are restructured as well. In the following case study, the attention women had to pay to their caring responsibilities led them into less economically secure forms of work and increased their economic dependence upon men.

A crucial argument here is that restructuring processes do not simply have local effects but are themselves shaped by rural ideologies and practices in multiple and complex ways. For example, cultural and ideological forces that shape gender relations and gender identity in the rural context also underpin the ways in which the rural emerges as an arena of consumption and as a locus of new service-sector jobs as part of the overall dynamic of restructuring toward a service economy.

Restructuring in Rural Communities

Since the 1970s Canadian workers have faced massive numbers of plant shutdowns. The Economic Council of Canada (1990: 15) concluded that plant closures signal permanent structural changes in the economy and are not simply signs of temporary conditions that will change with an upturn in the business cycle. Although there is considerable debate over what this means in terms of the jobs available to people in a restructured economy, it is clear that the service sector shows [the] most vitality, accounting for almost 90 per cent of job growth in Canada since 1967 (Economic Council of Canada 1990: 4–5; Betcherman and Lowe 1997). As well, there is a proliferation of so-called 'non-standard' forms of work. Part-time work grew through the 1980s from about 4 per cent of total employment to 15 per cent; and other kinds of non-standard work (such as short-term jobs, self-employment, and home-based work) also increased substantially and continue to grow. Correspondingly, long-term unemployment rates continue to increase, even in times of economic 'recovery' (Gera 1991: 99).

The downsizing and loss of rural manufacturing facilities has been largely responsible for the loss in rural community employment, retail trade, declining property values, and increased strain on community service capacity. As Janet Fitchen (1991) has argued in her work on rural upstate New York, some rural communities are even more dependent upon manufacturing activity than major metropolitan areas such as New York City. Similarly, the labour force in some Canadian rural communities with a manufacturing base has been more concentrated in goods-producing industries than the urban labour force, at least since 1971 (Bollman 1992, Ch. 1). The long-term decline in manufacturing, coupled with the continuation of the farm crisis, poses particular problems for rural communities.

Like workers facing restructuring outside rural areas, people in Fitchen's study were faced with accepting lower-paying, non-standard contingent work, with a decline in the quality of work on the job and a disproportionate impact on older workers and those with less education. Unlike non-rural workers, however, these people often had to commute farther to new jobs. Fitchen argues that the loss of factories in rural communities has had an even more pervasive and deeper impact than has the decline in farms (Fitchen 1991: 70).

While both manufacturing and agricultural jobs are in decline in rural areas, the service sector shows growth. Yet 1991 census data for Canadian rural communities indicate that employment rates in producer-services are only a third to a half of that in other regions (Canada 1995: 20), and it is producer-services that tend to provide many of the high-wage, high-skill jobs in the service sector. An assessment of the prospects for service-sector employment in American rural areas found a predominance of lower-paid jobs in food stores, car dealerships, gas stations, utility services, estate agents and insurance offices, government services, building material supply companies, agricultural services, transportation, and private household services (Miller and Bluestone 1988). Overall, Miller and Bluestone (1988) have concluded that the growth in the service economy tends to bring lower-wage jobs to rural areas, while growth in higher-paid service employment tends to be concentrated in urban areas. As well, the historical dependence of rural areas on high levels of public expenditure in infrastructure (for example, on relatively small hospitals and schools) makes them particularly vulnerable to the downsizing of the state. Although this kind of restructuring is happening apace and with much controversy, social scientists are only just beginning to explore it.

Our research with workers facing the aftermath of plant closures in North Wellington County, Ontario, a mainly rural county about 120 kilometres northwest of Toronto, has indicated a relatively higher incidence of service-sector, part-time work at a lower wage, accompanied by deteriorating work conditions and a disturbing proportion of older workers facing long-term unemployment (Leach and Winson 1995). However, my focus in this chapter is on a more detailed examination of the gendered nature of the restructuring of rural labour processes. For while superficially it would appear that men and women leaving similar jobs face common conditions in the labour market, I argue that in fact the experience of restructuring for men and for women is quite different.

Sarah Whatmore argues that despite the growth of European research interest in rural women in the 1980s, new work is needed that takes account of the contours of emerging rural economies, with serious attention to the rural context as a whole, recognizing the complex interactions and dependency between rural primary and secondary production, reproduction, and consumption (Whatmore 1994: 39). She argues that 'These global realignments . . . build on and, in turn, reshape rural gender relations' (Whatmore 1994: 40). She goes on to point out that one of the major theoretical challenges facing research on gender is to recognize the 'highly differentiated nature of women's experiences of rural restructuring as these are associated with particular social and environmental contexts'. As she says: 'Women's access to, and control over, the rural labour process is likely to revolve around . . . the double burden of combining so-called "productive" work with domestic labour responsibilities . . .' (Whatmore 1994: 47). In other words, women's caring labour at home will directly influence their capacity for taking on paid work outside the home.

The rich empirical studies emerging from feminist scholarship during the past couple of decades have shown how women are frequently segregated in particular occupations, such as clerical and caring work, and in particular types of work, for example, part-time and home-based. The specificity of women's experiences of the labour process historically are attributable at least in part (Beechey 1987) to their past and continuing responsibility for domestic labour—in other words, the unpaid kinds of caring labour—resulting in a different structural relationship to capitalism from that of men. One of the interesting features of our study is that men and women worked alongside each other, earned similar (though not exactly the same) wages for similar kinds of work and belonged to the same unions. While I am not arguing that men's and women's experiences of the labour process were the same, a key point is that the availability of jobs for women, which were comparable to men's and close to home for both, allowed them to meet on the shop floor on more equal terms. I am arguing that the degree of divergence that women experienced compared to men in trying to find a job after layoff, and in the jobs they eventually found, was disproportionate to the degree of difference in their job situations before layoff.

It is also worth noting that the women in the study were not women working off the farm to diversify the farm household income, as are many of the rural women mentioned in the literature. These were workers whose experience of work had been primarily non-agricultural as a result of the combined processes of the historical proletarianization of rural populations, as well as the more recent crisis in Canadian farming. It has been many generations since a majority of rural people in Ontario were directly connected to a farm. This is significant because the family farm is able to absorb surplus labour, at least in the short term, for example, if a farm wife is laid off from an off-farm job. In contrast, long-time proletarianized rural residents have no such cushion to absorb the impact of economic change.

There is now increasing evidence that in much the same way that labour processes are gendered, economic restructuring, too, affects women workers in ways that are quite specific. For example, women are less likely than men to find full-time jobs in the new economy (Armstrong 1996). Moreover part-time, short-term, and home-based jobs that are created as part of corporate flexibility strategies often appear rather insidiously to fulfill women's needs for flexible work options as they perform domestic labour. In fact, as I have argued from my work with industrial homeworkers, these kinds of work represent a particular gendering of restructuring that may lead to new forms of gender inequality (Jenson 1996; Leach 1993; 1996). As well, state cutbacks to social programs—such as cuts in childcare services, assistance to the elderly, or early release from hospital . . . place increased pressure on the domestic workload, in other words, on women. This occurs when other effects of restructuring—major ones like the loss of a household bread-winner's wage, or more everyday kinds like stagnant or declining real wages—make additional income even more essential (Redclift and Whatmore 1990: 193). When Canadian rural post offices, which had provided decent employment for women as rural postmasters, were about to be privatized, one analyst wrote that 'job loss, decreased wages, capricious job security, and lost employee benefits will exacerbate the existing economic instability that most rural women live' (Popaleni 1989: 138). Work such as this suggests that while feminist scholarship has shown the considerable variation in women's experience of paid and unpaid work in terms of race, class, and family status, it is also necessary to focus on the particular experience of work, layoff, and re-employment embedded in the rural context.

Taking a rural focus is in itself, however, problematic. There has been considerable debate in the rural sociology literature about what in fact constitutes 'the rural'. While it is not fruitful to revisit this debate here, it is important to make a number of points concerning the notion of rurality. There are some key features that distinguish a rural environment from an urban one. These features are not in dispute and are germane to the argument here. These include fewer opportunities for employment and lower population densities that create problems of distance and affect many areas of life, especially access to jobs, transportation, and childcare (McKinley Wright 1995: 218). While it could be argued that the material findings here are not specific to rural populations, the above factors are important in exacerbating the problems that result from restructuring. However, the changes taking place contribute in a number of ways to an overall process of urbanization, where people everywhere are tied into serving the urban market economy, and though integrated into the market in different ways, women in both rural and urban settings experience increasing commonality in their lives.[2]

Beyond this the notion of rurality as an ideological construct is more complex. Yet while it may be troublesome as an analytical category, it remains a key signifier to people themselves. People who live in rural areas, even when they are close to a city, define themselves in relation to, and as distinct from, urban people, drawing upon conceptions of rurality developed historically in specific localities. Mark Shucksmith (1994) has argued that the idea of rural is actually a contested domain within rural communities themselves. In his research, the definition of rural (as demonstrated by appropriate rural practices) was hotly disputed by groups with very different interests living in and around the same community. He argues that ultimately those best represented by local municipal officials won the day, and policy decisions were made in favour of their interests. In our own work we have seen how local municipal councillors publicly reacted to a newspaper report on our version of events and their outcomes, refuting our findings and questioning our methods, and denying the conclusions, which, they felt, reflected negatively on their community and its capacity to deal with restructuring (Leach and Winson 1999). The local press too involved itself, questioning the right of the workers involved to contribute to the discourse, asking 'Are unidentified workers who have just been fired from their job, the ones best qualified to say what happened and its effects on the community?' (*Mount Forest Olds* Apr./May 1996: 3). Taken together these reactions politically marginalize working people and diminish the significance of what working-class people have to say. At the same time they reinforce the dominance of those interests represented in municipal structures and the press.

Plant Closings in Wellington County

In our study men and women worked for two major employers in three communities in North Wellington County. This is a rural region comprising 11 municipalities with a total population in 1991 of 25,835. The local economy of the region is rooted in agriculture, and one of the firms, Canada Packers, had operated in the villages of Harriston and Elora since late in the last century, processing locally produced milk into a variety of dairy products. Both these plants had unionized early. In 1990 Canada Packers was acquired by the British food-processing giant, Hillsdown Holdings PLC, which restructured the company, concentrating on high-profit areas such as value-added food products and joint-venture operations with American agribusiness. These actions appear to have been intended to take advantage of the continental market opened up by the Free Trade Agreement with the United States. During the two-year restructuring period, Hillsdown sold off entire divisions and closed down 20 plants, including Harriston and Elora, in January 1991 (Winson 1993).

The other firm closure we examined was Westinghouse, which opened a custom-built facility in the town of Mount Forest in 1981, building electrical products for government, public utilities, and industry. This appears to have followed a 'greenfield' strategy, aimed at moving some operations away from the unionized plant in the heavily industrialized and unionized city of Hamilton, but a few workers relocated from Hamilton and the workforce was soon certified. During the real estate boom of the late 1980s, Westinghouse senior management made a foray into speculative real estate and other high-risk investments. The collapse of the North American real estate markets in 1990 as the recession took hold forced the company to write off $2.7 billion in assets and begin a massive restructuring program to cover bad loans (Baker, Dobrzynski, and Schroder 1992). This meant selling off whole corporate divisions and laying off several thousands of employees. In 1993 it was announced that the Mount Forest facility would close, and layoffs were staggered over more than a year until July 1994.

For our study we interviewed laid off plant workers in 1994 and obtained information on 68 workers, which included 14 couples working in the same firm. In the autumn of 1996 we went back to 34 of these people to find out what changes had taken place in their work lives. The following data indicates some of the changes that took place for these men and women between being employed in a steady job at either Canada Packers or Westinghouse to their personal situation in September and October of 1996.

Table 30.1 gives a sense of the differences between men's and women's full-time wages. These are not very far apart; the widest gap, about $2 an hour, was between men and women at Westinghouse in Mount Forest due to the different job classifications into which men and women were hired. Other differences between men and women included seniority, which has some impact on wages. For example, of 34 workers with more than 10 years' seniority at Canada Packers in Harriston, only eight were women.

Since for most people the plants were close to home, the juggling of domestic labour and the industrial labour process was less of an issue than it is in many work situations. This is not to say that conflict over this and inequality of responsibility in these areas were absent. As in most places, women remained primarily responsible for domestic tasks, which was clear from our interviews with them. But the ability to walk to work and 'pop back home' at lunchtime, to

Table 30.1 Pre- and Post-layoff Wages by Plant (CAD$)

	CP Harriston		CP Elora		Westinghouse, Mount Forest	
	Men	Women	Men	Women	Men	Women
Pre-layoff (n = 68)	$11.77	$11.07	$12.00	$10.93	$14.90	$12.98
1994 (n = 68)	$11.03	$9.18	$8.75	$7.90	$16.50	$8.29
1996 (n = 34)	$12.39	$8.62	$14.00	$11.19	$12.90	$10.22

pick up a few groceries, drive a child to a dental appointment, or visit an aging relative in the community made balancing work and family considerably easier for women and also enabled men to play a useful part in these activities.

This situation changed almost overnight as men and women workers laid off from similar industrial jobs found their re-employment trajectories markedly different. Some men and a few women were able to find comparable industrial jobs, but only if they were willing to commute considerable distances from home to small and medium-sized urban centres 50 or 60 kilometres away. One couple who commuted together to Toronto missed the social activities they used to engage in after work. While many men travelled long distances to work, the women who commuted to industrial jobs were those without young children living at home. Most of the women were more likely to be working closer to home so they could be available for school-aged or preschool children. One woman in Mount Forest with five children at home had been unable to find work since her layoff and she attributed her continued unemployment to her unwillingness to travel very far. The work that could be found locally was in more precarious, competitive industries, in informal work, or in part-time employment in the service sector. These factors reduced both women's wages and their access to the benefits for which they had been eligible in their old jobs.

When we contacted people in 1996, we found that their hourly wages had changed perhaps less dramatically than we might have expected. However, the change in annual income between the year in which they were last employed by Canada Packers or Westinghouse and 1995 is quite dramatic for most workers, both men and women. Pre-layoff average annual income was $31,000 for six men at Westinghouse and $24,000 for seven at Canada Packers. By 1995, five of the Westinghouse men had experienced a decrease in wages, reducing their average annual income to $25,000. Three Canada Packers men had considerable loss of income in 1995 when their earnings averaged $14,600.

For the women the situation was even more bleak. All except two of the 25 women experienced a decrease in their average annual wages, down from $29,000 at Westinghouse to $18,000, and from $23,000 to $12,000 at Canada Packers. These figures represent a loss of 38 per cent and 48 per cent respectively.

The difference between changes in hourly rates and annual income is attributable to the number of workers now employed in part-time jobs. By 1996, up to five years after layoff for the Canada Packers workers, 78 per cent of the women were in part-time work, compared to 25 per cent of the men. This does not, of course, account financially for the loss in benefits.

From the difference in average hourly rate for part-time work compared to full-time work, it is clear that the average wage of men dropped significantly when they accepted part-time work. By 1996, the difference between average full-time and part-time wages for women had widened. This seems to be attributable to a polarization between those (few) women who were willing to seek full-time jobs at some distance from their communities of residence, and those compelled (through their domestic responsibilities) to accept part-time jobs locally, where part-time wages dropped between 1994 and 1996. Our findings raise questions concerning the popular argument that women prefer 'flexible' forms of work. Certainly, for some, part-time work gave them more time with their children, yet a closer look at the women who felt this way reveals two significant factors. First, the part-time work they tended to be involved in was what we might call 'very part-time', i.e., approximately 15 hours per week. Second, all of these women had husbands with well-paid, relatively secure full-time jobs. One woman who had worked in part-time jobs as a single parent for 10 years described how the second income of her new husband made life

Table 30.2 Full- and Part-time Employment by Gender, 1994 and 1996

	Men			
	1994 (14)		1996 (12)	
	Full-time	Part-time	Full-time	Part-time
Total numbers	12 (85%)	2 (15%)	9 (75%)	3 (25%)
Average hourly wage	$12.20	$8.85	$13.54	$10.85
	Women			
	1994 (26)		1996 (18)	
	Full-time	Part-time	Full-time	Part-time
Total numbers	12 (46%)	14 (54%)	4 (22%)	14 (78%)
Average hourly wage	$8.11	$8.82	$11.00	$7.05

manageable and comfortable. Another woman who had suffered serious health problems following her layoff eventually divorced her husband and now has part-time jobs in two different communities. She told us, 'Life was a lot simpler and more organized when I worked at Canada Packers. Everything seemed to be thrown into chaos when I lost that job.'

Part-time jobs were often the only work that older women could find. One 60-year-old woman was working at three different part-time jobs and would have liked to quit one of them (a job working as a nurse's aide in a nursing home) because she found it extremely stressful as workers fought for the limited hours available. However, her husband, who was laid off at the same time that she lost her job, had been working at a gas station since then. Although he had just found a better job, she still needed to keep her three jobs, and neither of them could entertain the possibility of retirement for several years.

Women with part-time jobs without benefits and whose husbands had decent full-time jobs were able to rely on the health benefits associated with their husbands' jobs. This was another factor involved in the decision that men should seek work further afield since they were more likely to find jobs with benefits in the larger labour markets of Guelph, Kitchener– Waterloo, and Toronto. Women working at jobs in new local factories frequently found no job security. Rather, they faced a cycle of layoff (sometimes only weeks after being hired), unemployment, a new job or possibly recall to the old one, then layoff again. This was due to the instability of new companies operating in the competitive sector. Since in many workplaces benefits only come into effect after a probationary period of three months, these families needed the advantages that came from working in more stable industries, but these were usually at a distance.

Full-time jobs for women were found in only one of the three communities, indicating that the nature of the local labour market shapes post-layoff opportunities in important ways. In Harriston a majority of women found part-time jobs, and half of these had more than one. In Mount Forest, however, three-quarters of the women found full-time jobs in 1994, most of them at K-Brand, where Karen sought work. Even in 1996, by which time part-time work predominated in the other communities, in Mount Forest there was a more even division between full- and part-time work. The trade-off for the valuable asset of working full-time close to home, however, was a dramatic loss of income. The pre-layoff hourly wage for women at Westinghouse was $12.98, while those who moved to K-Brand averaged $6.90. These findings are remarkably similar to Fitchen's for rural New York State. She notes:

> Even where a factory closing was followed by an opening by another manufacturing firm, laid off workers who found new factory jobs suffered a substantial cut in pay not only because they were starting over, shorn of the seniority and raises they'd earned over the years and with little bargaining power in the employer's market, but also because the entire pay scale in the new manufacturing firms may be significantly lower than in the old firms. (Fitchen 1991: 70)

Many of the women lamented the loss of income that came with layoff and less well-paid replacement jobs. They usually talked about this in terms of the family activities they could no longer contemplate, such as taking vacations and moving out of rental accommodation into their own home. They also missed being able to help adult children and their families financially when they needed it. One woman, who had recently found a job after years of unemployment, said how happy she was 'to have my own money again and my own bank account'.

A few people indicated to us that they had turned to informal self-employment, such as catering, dog breeding, and small-engine repairs, but this usually happened after several unsuccessful attempts to rejoin the labour force and seemed in these cases to be an option of last resort. Overall, though, there is a significant shift in women's jobs away from the manufacturing sector and toward work in service industries. This shift echoes the broader shift in the economy and signals a crucial dynamic of restructuring.

It seems that rather than simply concluding that restructuring leads to a worsening in women's position vis-à-vis men, the divergence between men's and most women's post-layoff experiences of work needs further investigation and explanation. I argue that these differences are bound up in men's and women's respective relationships to caring labour, which are themselves shaped by particular ideologies and beliefs concerning appropriate gender roles.

Women's Work and Rural Culture

Recent studies examining restructuring and rural women in Britain and the United States indicate that women's employment options are tightly bound up with the particular cultural forms taken by gender relations in household and community in rural areas. Thus, we need to look at the ways in which gender and power relations are configured in the rural household and communities under study. Rather than seeing restructuring as a one-way street whereby social processes are determined by economic ones, it is necessary to consider how existing and dynamic gender and power configurations affect the experience of restructuring. In other words, the processes of social and economic change shape each other. This is particularly important because it permits agency and the possibility of resisting certain kinds of constructions of restructuring.

In writing about restructuring in small Iowa towns, Nancy Naples argues that 'traditional notions of rural community life' are used to try to make sense of the changing economic and social context, and to make a case against some of the changes people face (Naples 1994: 114). Similarly, Jo Little, in examining women's employment in three English rural communities, argues that while household livelihood strategies vary according to the employment opportunities available for women, they also depend on their consistency with the ideologies and value systems of rural communities (Little 1993: 14). She shows that 'the impact of restructuring is not only reflected in gender divisions but is also determined by them' (Little 1993: 22).

Deborah Fink (1992) has argued that, for the rural United States, agrarian ideology continues to influence ideas and behaviour profoundly in rural areas. Thus, the model for female behaviour is the farm wife, whose primary work is in the home, supporting her husband and raising her children to continue the farming tradition. Based on her extensive survey of the literature on women in rural areas of both industrialized and less-developed countries, Carolyn Sachs has extended this ideology beyond the United States. She says 'gender relations in rural areas continue to be steeped in vestiges of patriarchal relations in farm households' (Sachs 1996: 140). Agrarian ideology stresses a traditional gender division of labour and a two-parent, heterosexual family as the natural household form and idealizes and romanticizes women's role.

In the British literature a number of writers have argued that a strictly hierarchical local power structure evolved between landowner and agricultural labourer in rural communities that deliberately excluded women. This then combined with a set of moral values that reasserted men's sexual control over women to reinforce women's position in the home and the belief that they are responsible for the organization and maintenance of the household (Davidoff, L'Esperance, and Newby 1976). Following up on this work, others have argued that the historical stability of rural communities is attributable to the conservative nature of village life, and that both are central to gender relations in rural areas (McDowell and Massey 1984).

There is little literature dealing with gender ideology in the rural Ontario context and what does exist documents farm families, not those holding non-farm jobs. However, since rural life has been organized historically around agriculture and agriculture-related manufacturing and services, it seems reasonable to expect the existence of a local variant of agrarian ideology based on ideas emanating from the agricultural history of the region. On the basis of the findings of these studies, we would then expect both men and women to hold fairly conservative views about gender roles. A study by and of Ontario farm women published in 1983 stated: 'Though she may work hand in hand with her husband all morning, she can still be sure that she will be the one to put lunch on the table when they get to the house' (Ireland 1983: 38). A slightly later study describes the response of farm men to their wives' increased off-farm work and political activities as 'bewilderment' (Daley 1985). In a rare study focusing on the political views of women in rural Ontario, Louise Carbert (1995) found that while farm wives' views have been modified to some extent by their exposure to feminism, they exhibit conservatism both politically and with regard to gender roles. Yet there is increasing documentation of women's engagement with strong and effective rural women's organizations, fighting for recognition of women's work, clarification of their legal status, and improved rural services (Mackenzie 1995; Shortall 1994).

In certain respects the factory work that the women in this study engaged in, like some of the rural women's organizations, shatters the stereotype of rural women as it redraws the distinction between public and private. It is clear from some of the preceding comments that women did benefit from the power that came from having money of their own. It is notable that in contrast to the men, women were keen to tell us how much they had loved their old factory jobs. Their agency is apparent in the way they set about finding new jobs and obtaining them fairly quickly. Ironically, women's willingness to take work of almost any kind (as long as it was close to home) made it easier for men to wait until they found better jobs. Like Karen in the opening vignette, while women got on with making a living locally, men could seek out jobs comparable to their old ones at a more leisurely pace and in more distant labour markets.

Although these women may have avoided living the stereotype while they held industrial jobs, old ideas remained strong in the culture in which they lived and came into play constraining their choices after layoff. The dynamic of restructuring that shifts jobs from manufacturing to service also plays upon gendered, class, and urban/rural inequities, which are then used (though in different ways) by the social actors involved—women, their husbands, employers, and policy-makers.

Some of the strongly held local cultural ideas are reflected in the continued popularity of rural village fairs, where the emphasis is on growing, cooking and preserving skills, animal husbandry, and technical skills associated with farm work (such as tractor pulls). These lend support to an enduring ideology that privileges and romanticizes rural life and customs, and a prevailing set of gender roles and relations.

The popularity of rural village fairs, farmers' markets, and 'country crafts' gives a clue to understanding the trajectory of women's work lives after rural restructuring. Rural ideology, tied to a set of images and assumptions about rural spaces, is also important in shaping the use of rural areas. Little and Austin (1996) show how ideas about the 'rural idyll' in England, which invoke a nostalgia for the past and an escape from the modern, have shaped uses of rural areas. These include the exodus of urban populations to the country in search [of] a 'simpler' rural life, which affects the kinds of employment opportunities women are likely to find there. This is one kind of changing use of rural areas, many of which demonstrate rural communities' shift from production to theatres of consumption, with an associated service sector (Marsden 1992). This shift will be more pronounced in those rural areas within striking distance of significant population centres, and those more remote ones that have particular environments and experiences to offer. In Wellington County, urban dwellers are enticed to move to the 'estate-sized' housing lots bordering villages, to retire to cottages in idyllic communities, or move to long-term care facilities complete with breathtaking views. Urbanites are encouraged to visit and enjoy rural tourist attractions from summer theatre to berry picking, craft studios to restaurants featuring country-style cooking.

If we look more closely at these emerging attractions, we can see that rural communities are increasingly dependent on the consumption of their rural amenities for their continued survival. In addition, these attractions influence the restructured rural labour market in important ways, resulting in the kinds of service-sector jobs that the displaced women industrial workers in our study take. Like Karen working at the seniors' home in my opening vignette, working-class women are servicing the middle-class's consumption of rurality while their husbands cling to the vestiges of work in industrial production. At the same time, the jobs that are being created reinforce a conservative division of labour, picking up on gender-linked tasks such as nursing, food service, and handicrafts.

Conclusion

From a wide-ranging series of case studies, Carolyn Sachs concludes that restructuring relies heavily on rural women's labour (Sachs 1996). For this particular case, and as is clear from Karen's example, it seems possible to go further and argue that rural women are actually at the leading edge of the restructuring shift of emphasis from production to consumption. The shift from manufacturing jobs to service provision of care re-emphasizes the caring kinds of work traditionally associated with women, the perception of caring as involving essentially female qualities, and the association of men with manufacturing work. There are also resonances here with the notion of de-professionalization in the caring professions. . . . The women here are picking up the emerging unskilled caring jobs that result from the restructuring of professional caring work.

This divergence in men's and women's work trajectories has negative implications for women. The overall changes in men's and women's incomes indicate that women are likely to face (again, for some) a situation in which they are economically dependent upon men, an idea that is supported by the woman who described her life as much easier since she remarried and now had some access to a male wage. This, of course, is dependent upon the individual man's job security, which is not always certain, but it raises serious concerns, for example, for women in abusive relationships. The imbalance between men and women has further economic consequences as women with insecure part-time jobs lose pension, employment insurance, and benefit rights (Baldwin and Twigg 1991: 121).

The caring responsibilities are a constant burden for women that influence their other decisions, notably their choices concerning livelihoods. Women's flexibility in paid and unpaid work—their willingness to take on whatever is available and to construct a means of making a livelihood and caring for others in a patchwork fashion—is a key factor here. This flexibility is chosen by women because of their caring responsibilities at the same time that new, 'flexible' forms of work are increasingly the only ones available. This simultaneously contributes to their economic vulnerability, to the devaluing of all forms of women's work, and paradoxically to the survival of the household and the family. While life seems to continue as usual, in fact new forms of inequality built upon old ideas are being produced and reproduced.

Yet the important point here, as Nanneke Redclift and Sarah Whatmore (1990: 191) stress, is that livelihood and reproductive strategies together contribute to the overall processes of social stratification, not simply to a series of impacts. A focus on just the outcomes of restructuring reinforces the idea that change is generated from outside, and makes it difficult to see the ways in which economic processes are embedded in social and cultural contexts, and how the two are mutually constituting. This kind of analysis enables us to see how women resist certain forms of restructuring, possibly using the family, as bell hooks (1984: 133–4) has suggested for black American women, by using local cultural ideas and practices to insist on the primacy of caring relationships within the family over the pursuit of a masculine job model. Attention to these issues begins to provide the basis for a more nuanced understanding of the transformation of rural livelihoods, and of gendered restructuring processes more generally.

Notes

1. This study was carried out with Tony Winson and was funded through the Tricouncil Agro-Ecosystem Health Project.
2. I am grateful to Marie Campbell for pointing this out.

References

Armstrong, P. 1996. 'The Feminization of the Labour Force: Harmonizing Down in a Global Economy', in *Rethinking Restructuring: Gender and Change in Canada*, ed. I. Bakker (Toronto: University of Toronto Press), 29–54.

Baker, S., J.D. Dobrzynski, and M. Schroder. 1992. 'Westinghouse: More Pain Ahead', *Business Week* (7 Dec.): 32–4.

Baldwin, S., and J. Twigg. 1991. 'Women and Community Care: Reflections on a Debate', in *Women's Issues in Social Policy*, eds M. Maclean and D. Groves (London: Routledge), 117–35.

Beechey, V. 1987. *Unequal Work* (London: Verso).

Betcherman, G., and G.S. Lowe. 1997. *The Future of Work in Canada: A Synthesis Report* (Ottawa: Canadian Policy Research Networks Inc.).

Bollman, Ray, ed. 1992. *Rural and Small Town Canada* (Toronto: Thompson Educational Publishing).

Canada. 1995. *Rural Canada: A Profile* (Ottawa: Supply and Services).

Carbert, L. 1995. *Agrarian Feminism* (Toronto: University of Toronto Press).

Daley, N. 1985. 'Male Response to Change in Farm-wives' Sex Role in Rural Ontario', Rural Sociological Society Association Paper.

Davidoff, L., J. L'Esperance, and H. Newby. 1976. 'Landscape with Figures: Home and Community in English Society', in *The Rights and Wrongs of Women*, eds A. Oakley and J. Mitchell (Harmondsworth: Penguin), 139–75.

Economic Council of Canada. 1990. *Good Jobs, Bad Jobs* (Ottawa: Economic Council of Canada).

Fink, D. 1992. *Agrarian Women: Wives and Mothers in Rural Nebraska 1880–1940* (Chapel Hill: University of North Carolina Press).

Fitchen, J. 1991. *Endangered Spaces, Enduring Places: Change, Identity and Survival in Rural America* (Boulder, CO: Westview).

Gera, S. 1991. *Canadian Unemployment—Lessons from the 80s and Challenges for the 90s: A Compendium* (Ottawa: Economic Council of Canada).

hooks, b. 1984. *Feminist Theory: From Margin to Centre* (Boston: South End Press).

Ireland, G. 1983. *The Farmer Takes a Wife* (Chesley, ON: Concerned Farm Women).

Jenson, J. 1996. 'Part-time Employment and Women: A Range of Strategies', in *Rethinking Restructuring: Gender and Change in Canada*, ed. I. Bakker (Toronto: University of Toronto Press), 92–108.

Leach, B. 1993. '"Flexible" Work, Precarious Future: Some Lessons from the Canadian Clothing Industry', *Canadian Review of Sociology and Anthropology* 30, 1: 64–82.

———. 1996. 'Behind Closed Doors: Homework Policy and Lost Possibilities for Change', in *Rethinking Restructuring: Gender and Change in Canada*, ed. I. Bakker (Toronto: University of Toronto Press), 203–16.

———, and A. Winson. 1995. 'Bringing "Globalization" Down to Earth: Restructuring and Labour in Rural Communities', *Canadian Review of Sociology and Anthropology* 32, 3: 341–64.

———. 1999. 'Rural Retreat: The Social Impact of Restructuring in Three Ontario Communities', in *Restructuring Societies*, eds D.B. Knight and A.E. Joseph (Ottawa: Carleton University Press), 83–104.

Little, J. 1994. 'Gender Relations and the Rural Labour Process', in *Gender and Rurality*, eds T. Marsden, P. Lowe, and S. Whatmore (London: David Fulton), 335–42.

———, and P. Austin. 1996. 'Women and the Rural Idyll', *Journal of Rural Studies* 12, 2: 101–11.

McDowell, L., and D. Massey. 1984. 'A Woman's Place?', in *Geography Matters!*, eds D. Massey and J. Allen (Cambridge, UK: Cambridge University Press), 128–47.

Mackenzie, F. 1995. 'Is Where I Stand Where I Sit? The Ontario Farm Women's Network Politics and Difference', *Journal of Rural Studies* 10, 2: 101–15.

McKinley Wright, M. 1995. '"I Never Did Any Fieldwork, but I Sure Milked an Awful Lot of Cows!" Using Rural Women's Experience to Reconceptualize Modes of Work', *Gender & Society* 9, 2: 216–35.

Marsden, T. 1992. 'Exploring a Rural Sociology for the Fordist Transition: Incorporating Social Relations into Economic Restructuring', *Sociologia Ruralis* 32, 2, 3: 209–30.

Miller, J., and H. Bluestone. 1988. 'Prospects for Service Sector Employment Growth in Non-metro America', *Review of Regional Studies* 18 (Winter): 28–41.

Naples, N. 1994. 'Contradictions in Agrarian Ideology: Restructuring Gender, Race, Ethnicity and Class', *Rural Sociology* 59, 1: 110–35.

Popaleni, K. 1989. 'Shouldering the Burden for Canada Post: Privatization's Impact on Rural Women', *Resources for Feminist Research* 17, 3: 136–8.

Redclift, N., and S. Whatmore. 1990. 'Household Consumption and Livelihood: Ideologies and Issues in Rural Research', in *Rural Restructuring: Global Processes and Their Responses*, eds T. Marsden, P. Lowe, and S. Whatmore (London: David Fulton), 82–197.

Sachs, C. 1996. *Gendered Fields: Rural Women, Agriculture and Environment* (Boulder, CO: Westview).

Shortall, S. 1994. 'Farm Women's Groups: Community, Feminist or Social Movements?', *Canadian Review of Sociology and Anthropology* 28, 1: 279–91.

Shucksmith, M. 1994. 'Conceptualizing Post-industrial Rurality', in *Towards Sustainable Rural Communities*, ed. J. Bryden (Guelph: School of Rural Planning and Development, University of Guelph), 125–32.

Whatmore, S. 1994. 'Theoretical Achievements and Challenges of European Rural Gender Studies', in *Rural Gender Studies in Europe*, eds L. van der Plas and M. Fonte (Assen, Netherlands: Van Gorcum), 39–49.

PART FIVE

Other Family Matters

Chapter 31

Tragically, families may feature violence. This needs explaining. That this violence is not so rare suggests that some core features of intimate relations between women and men may themselves be at the heart of the problem. This article contains a review of the main findings of a large study of the women who were killed in Ontario between 1974 and 1994. Rosemary Gartner and her colleagues review their findings, and draw on other researchers' findings, to conclude that gender is indeed central to men's violence against women.

Confronting Violence in Women's Lives

Rosemary Gartner, Myrna Dawson, and Maria Crawford

Woman Killing: Intimate Femicide in Ontario, 1974–94

In March 1988, a young mother of two was killed by her estranged husband in a northern Ontario town. The killer had been visiting his wife who was staying in a shelter for abused women. Convinced that she was not going to return to him, he shot her twice at close range. Later that year, in a small-town outside of Edmonton, a woman was shot dead in her home by her estranged husband who then shot and killed himself. Miraculously, the woman's three-year-old girl, whom she was holding in her arms when she was shot, was not wounded. These women were two of the 202 female victims of homicide in Canada in 1988. They shared with 68 other female victims a marital relationship with their killers. These two women also shared the experience of having been clients and friends of women who worked in shelters for abused women in Ontario.

In response to these and other killings of women they had worked with, eight women met in January 1989 to share their experiences and provide each other emotional support. Within a few months the group had named itself the Women We Honour Action Committee, setting itself the task of learning more about the phenomenon of women killed by their intimate partners. With the support of a grant from the Ontario Women's Directorate, they conducted a literature review on women killed by their intimate partners, or intimate femicide.

That literature review led to a number of conclusions about the then-existing state of knowledge about intimate femicide (Women We Honour and R. Gartner 1990). First, obtaining an accurate estimate of the number of such killings in Canada or in Ontario from statistics in official publications was not possible because official publications restricted their classifications to 'spouse killings', which excluded killings by estranged common-law partners and current or former boyfriends. Second, information on the nature of intimate femicide—its dynamics as well as its structural and cultural sources—was incomplete. In part this reflected researchers' reliance on small, highly select samples, on offenders' recollections of their crimes, and on traditional psychological and psychiatric concepts and classifications. Third, much of the research had been conducted in the United States which is atypical in both the quantity and quality of its homicides. That is, spousal homicides make up a much smaller proportion of total homicides in the United States compared to many other nations. Moreover, the ratio of female to male victims of spouse killings is more balanced in the United States than in other countries (about 1.3: 1, compared to about 3:1 in Canada, Australia, Denmark, the UK, and other countries) (Wilson and Daly 1992b; Regoeczi and Silverman 1997).

It was to address these limitations that the Women We Honour Action Committee approached the Ontario Women's Directorate for funding to conduct their study of intimate femicide in Ontario. The study had three goals: to document for Ontario the incidence of killings of women by intimate partners, including legal spouses, common-law partners, and boyfriends, both current and estranged; to describe the characteristics of the people involved in and the circumstances surrounding these killings; and to present the stories of a small number of women who had been killed by their intimate partners. That study, completed in 1992, compiled and analyzed data on all intimate femicides known to authorities in Ontario from 1974 to 1990 (Crawford, Gartner, and the Women We Honour Action Committee 1992). A second study, designed to update the data through 1994, was completed in April 1997 (Crawford et al. 1997).

In this article, we describe the major findings of these two studies of intimate femicide. Our purpose is twofold: first, to provide an overview and statistical picture of intimate femicide in Ontario for the 21 years from 1974 to 1994; and, second, to locate this statistical picture in what is now a substantially larger and more sophisticated literature on violence against women by intimate partners. That literature encompasses studies similar in many ways to ours—that is, studies of the incidence and characteristics of relatively large numbers of femicides—as well as work designed to provide a theoretical and conceptual framework for understanding intimate femicide. We draw on that literature below in discussing our findings.

Framing the Issue of Intimate Femicide

After completing our literature review in 1989, we concluded that intimate femicide is a phenomenon distinct in important ways both from the killing of men by their intimate partners and from non-lethal violence against women; and, hence, that it requires analysis in its own right. This view was in contrast to much of the existing literature which treated 'spousal violence' as a relatively undifferentiated phenomenon arising out of the intense emotions, stresses, and conflicts that often characterize marital relations (Goode 1969; Boudoris 1971; Chimbos 1978; Blinder 1985). These analyses tended to locate the sources of 'spousal violence' in patterns of learning early in life, in the disinhibitory effects of alcohol consumption, and in dysfunctional patterns of communication between marital partners. Much of this early work also tended to devote limited attention and analysis to gender differences in spousal violence.

In response to this neglect of gender, a number of analysts have made gender a central feature of their accounts of spousal violence. Sex-role theorists highlight gender differences in socialization which teach males to view toughness, power, and control as masculine attributes. Evolutionary theorists argue that violence is an adaptive strategy for males facing the loss of status and control over their partners. Resource theorists view violence as the ultimate resource available to men when other means of exerting control over their partners are exhausted. General systems theorists argue that for men the rewards of violence against their wives are greater than the costs, because of society's failure to adequately sanction such violence. The arguments of these more gender-sensitive analyses resonated with the experiences of members of the Women We Honour Action

Committee. Power, control, and domination were themes that they encountered daily in talking with abused women and that they detected in relationships ending in intimate femicide.

In recent work specifically focused on women killed by their intimate partners, these themes have been elaborated and, in the case of feminist analyses, placed in a historical and institutional context (Campbell 1992; Kelkar 1992; Marcus 1994; Maloney 1994). For example, Wilson and Daly (1992a) cite 'male sexual proprietariness' as the predominant motive in the killing of wives across cultures and historical epochs. 'Men exhibit a tendency to think of women as sexual and reproductive "property" that they can own and exchange. . . . Proprietary entitlements in people have been conceived and institutionalized as identical to proprietary entitlements in land, chattels, and other economic resources.' They go on to note, 'That men take a proprietary view of female sexuality and reproductive capacity is manifested in various cultural practices', including claustration practices, asymmetrical adultery laws, and bride-prices. From this perspective, an extreme, if apparently incongruous, manifestation of male proprietariness is intimate femicide. If unable to control or coerce his partner through other means, a man may exert the ultimate control over her by killing her.

Thus, male proprietariness, or male sexual jealousy, has been placed at the centre of many empirical and theoretical analyses of intimate femicide. For example, research on intimate femicide and spousal homicide in Canada, Australia, Great Britain, and the United States (Dobash and Dobash 1984; Wallace 1986; Daly and Wilson 1988; Polk 1994) has identified a common core in these killings of 'masculine control, where women become viewed as the possessions of men, and the violence reflects steps taken by males to assert their domination over "their" women' (Polk 1994). This empirical work challenges many of the popular notions about the characteristics of such crimes, for example, the belief that they are explosive, unplanned, and unpredictable acts of passion. At the same time, it contests the validity and coherence of the concept 'spousal homicide' with its connotations of sexual symmetry in violence by revealing distinct differences between intimate partner killings by men and those by women. As Dobash et al. (1992) note:

> Men often kill wives after lengthy periods of prolonged physical violence accompanied by other forms of abuse and coercion; the roles in such cases are seldom if ever reversed. Men perpetrate familicidal massacres, killing spouses and children together; women do not. Men commonly hunt down and kill wives who have left them; women hardly ever behave similarly. Men kill wives as part of planned murder–suicides; analogous acts by women are almost unheard of. Men kill in response to revelations of wifely infidelity; women almost never respond similarly.

In sum, there have been significant advances in both empirical and conceptual analyses of lethal violence against women by their partners since the literature review that served as the impetus for our research. Those advances have not, however, filled all of the gaps identified in our earlier review. In particular, empirical research in Canada has continued to rely largely on official statistics from police sources, which exclude from their classification of spousal homicides killings by men of their estranged common-law partners and girlfriends. Relying on these official statistics also restricts analyses to the information and coding schemes employed by police agencies and personnel. Because of our concerns about the potential for lost information and for the introduction of unknown biases, we relied on a wider range of information sources than typically used in previous research. In this way, our study is unusual in the comprehensiveness of its data. As we see below, it is not however unique in its findings about the nature of intimate femicide.

Data Sources

We began our data collection by searching death records kept by the Office of the Chief Coroner for Ontario. Coroners' records provide a centralized source of information on all deaths in Ontario, and a means of identifying and assessing records for deaths identified by the Coroner's Office as homicides. These files frequently contain copies of police reports as well as medical reports on the condition of the body, the way in which the woman was killed and the violence suffered—details often not available from other sources. However, coroners' records, like all official sources of information on homicide, are imperfect measures of the actual number of deaths due to homicide. For example, cases of homicide in which no body has been found will not typically appear in coroners' records. As a consequence, we expect our estimates of the incidence of intimate femicide to undercount the true incidence, an issue we discuss in more depth below.[1]

We were able to cross-check and supplement data from coroners' records by reviewing police homicide investigation files for many of our cases.[2] In the second study, we were also able to review data from Crown Attorney files on many of the cases in which charges were laid between 1991 and 1994. In both studies, we supplemented our data from official sources with information from newspaper and magazine articles on some of the killings and on trials of some of the alleged offenders.

We compiled this information so that it could be used in both quantitative and qualitative analyses. Our final data collection instrument was designed to provide codes for approximately 52 variables, as well as space to record a narrative of the case where further information was available.[3]

The Incidence of Intimate Femicide in Ontario, 1974–94

Between 1974 and 1994, 1,206 women aged 15 and older were killed in Ontario, according to official records.[4] In 1,120 (93 per cent) of these cases, the crimes were solved and the killers were identified. In 705 (63 per cent) of the solved cases, the killers were the current or former legal spouses, common-law partners, or boyfriends of their victims. Thus, in Ontario over this 21-year period, intimate partners were responsible for the majority of all woman killings and an average of 34 women were victims of intimate femicide each year. These data indicate that the focus in official publications and some academic research on 'spousal homicides' of women provides an incomplete picture of the more general phenomenon of intimate femicide: excluding killings of women by their estranged common-law partners and current and former boyfriends underestimates the total number of intimate femicides by about 25 per cent.

The actual number of intimate femicides in Ontario during these years is undoubtedly higher than this. Intimate partners were certainly responsible for some portion of the cases in which no offender was identified or in which we had too little information to determine the precise nature of the relationship between victim and offender.[5] Adjusting for excluded cases, we estimate that intimate femicides may have accounted for as many as 76 per cent of all femicides in Ontario between 1974 and 1994. However, since it is impossible to know the number and characteristics of excluded cases, the analyses that follow focus only on those 705 cases in which the offender was officially identified as the current or former intimate partner of the victim.

Trends in Intimate Femicide

Between 1974 and 1994, the rate of intimate femicide (i.e., the number of victims of intimate femicide per 100,000 women in the general population) ranged from a low of 0.55 in 1978 to a high of 1.26 in 1991, but appears to follow no particular trend over time (see Figure 31.1).[6] Dividing the 21-year period in half suggests otherwise, however: the average annual rate for the second half of the period (1.01 per 100,000) was slightly higher than the rate for the first half (0.92 per 100,000).

On its own, this difference is insignificant statistically and, it might appear, substantively. However, when compared to the statistically significant decreases in other types of lethal violence, the slightly higher rate of intimate femicide in the latter period takes on greater importance. The annual rate at which women were killed by strangers or unknown assailants declined significantly from an average of 0.27 during 1974–83 to 0.16 during 1984–94. Moreover, the annual rate at which men were killed by their spouses also declined significantly, from an average rate of 0.31 during 1974–83 to 0.18 during 1984–94. In other words, during a period when women's risks from strangers and men's risks from spouses decreased, women's risks from their intimate partners increased slightly. Put another way, after 1984—a period of substantial expansion in services for abused women—men's risks of being killed by intimate partners decreased significantly whereas women's risks did not.

Figure 31.1 Trends in Rates of Lethal Violence, Ontario, 1974–94

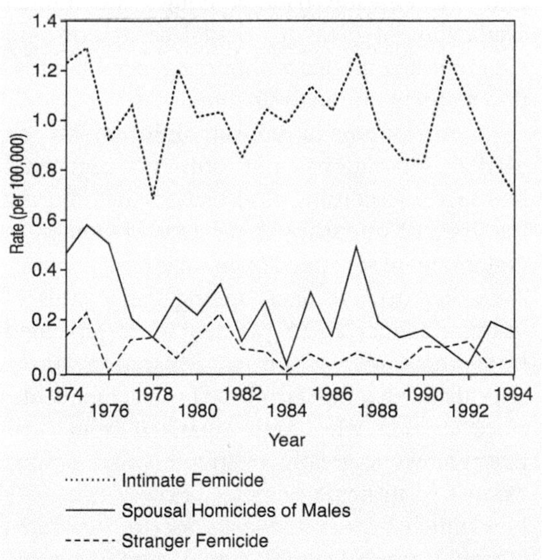

Without further analysis of these patterns—which is beyond the scope of this article—we can only speculate as to the reasons for this apparently counterintuitive finding. One possible explanation is that while the expansion of services for abused women may have resulted in the protection of abusive men from defensive violence by their intimate partners, these same services did not necessarily protect women from their male partners' violence. Research shows that women are most likely to kill their intimate partners after prolonged abuse and when they fear continued or more serious violence against themselves or their children (Browne 1987). Where services for abused women are available, women in abusive relationships have an alternative to killing their partners. As Browne and Williams (1989) note, 'By offering threatened women protection, escape and aid, [legal and extra-legal] resources can engender an awareness that there are alternatives to remaining at risk' and thus prevent 'killings that occur in desperation'. Their analysis of US data lends support to this interpretation: states with higher levels of services to abused women had lower rates of spouse killings of males, but not lower rates of spouse killings for females.

Characteristics of the Victims and Their Killers

In many respects, the women killed by their intimate partners and the men who killed them[7] are very similar to women and men in the general population of Ontario, as can be seen from the data in Table 31.1. For example, women killed by their intimate partners were, on average, about 37 years old; 51 per cent were employed; 80 per cent had children; and 76 per cent were born in Canada. These characteristics do not distinguish the victims from other women in Ontario.

In some other respect, however, victims of intimate femicide and their killers differed from women and men in the general population.[8] We can think of these differences as risk markers for intimate femicide because they tell us that some types of women and men face disproportionately high risks of intimate victimization or offending.[9] Each of the markers we discuss below has also been associated with increased risks of lethal violence against women in other research.

Table 31.1 Characteristics of Victims of Intimate Femicide and Their Killers, Ontario, 1974–94

Characteristics	Victims	Offenders
Total Number	705	705
Average Age	37	41
% born in Canada	76	70
% with children	80	77
Employment Status		
% employed	51	64
% unemployed	17	21
% homemakers	18	0
% students	5	2
% retired or on disability pension	9	13
Relationship of Victim to Offender		
% legal spouse, cohabiting	–	39
% legal spouse, separated	–	16
% common-law partner, cohabiting	–	18
% common-law partner, separated	–	7
% divorced spouse	–	<1
% current girlfriend	–	12
% estranged girlfriend	–	8
% Aboriginal	6	6

Relationship Status

Research based on data on spouse killings from Great Britain, Australia, the United States, and Canada shows that two indicators of the status of the relationship—estrangement and common-law status—are associated with a higher risk of spouse killings of women (Wallace 1986; Campbell 1992; Wilson and Daly 1993; Johnson 1996). We find similar patterns in our intimate femicide data, although the limited availability of data on marital separation and common-law unions within the general population restricts our analysis somewhat.

Census Canada collects information on marital separations, but only for registered marriages. According to census figures, during the years of our study, 3 per cent of women in Ontario were separated from their legal spouses. According to our data, among the victims of intimate femicide, 16 per cent were separated from their legal spouses. Separation, then, appears to be a risk factor for intimate femicide, since women who were separated from their partners were greatly overrepresented among victims of intimate femicide. However, exactly how much greater the risks are for separated women cannot be determined from our data. This is because our measure of separation and the census measure of separation are not precisely compatible: the census measure captures largely long-term and relatively well-established separations, whereas our measure is more sensitive and captures short-term as well as long-term separations. Thus our measure will yield a higher estimate of separated couples. Nevertheless, we expect that even correcting for this difference, we would find separation to be associated with higher risks of intimate femicide.

Data on the prevalence of common-law unions in the general population have been collected only since 1991, so we can estimate the risks to women living in common-law relationships only for the most recent years of our research. According to census data, 4 per cent of women were living in common-law unions in 1991 in Ontario. According to our data, during 1991–94, 21 per cent of the victims of intimate femicide were killed by common-law partners with whom they were living. Based on our calculations, the rate of intimate femicide for women in common-law unions was approximately six times greater than the average rate of intimate femicide in Ontario in the early 1990s.[10] Clearly, then, women in common-law unions were greatly overrepresented among victims of intimate femicide during the early 1990s, and perhaps in earlier years as well.

The higher risks associated with common-law status and estrangement have been interpreted in various ways. Compared to couples in registered marriages, common-law partners are more likely to be poor, young, unemployed, and childless—all factors associated with higher homicide rates. Compared to co-residing couples, estranged couples are more likely to have a history of domestic violence (Rodgers 1994; Johnson and Sacco 1995). This violence may be associated both with women's decisions to leave their relationships and with their greater risks of intimate femicide. In other words, 'the fact that separated couples constitute a subset of marriages with a history of discord could explain their higher homicide rates' (Wilson and Daly 1994).

Male sexual proprietariness could also play a role in the higher risks for common-law and estranged relationships. If, as some have speculated, 'husbands may be less secure in the proprietary claims over wives in common-law unions than in registered unions', they may be more likely to resort to serious violence to enforce those claims or to lethal violence when those claims are challenged (Wilson, Johnson, and Daly 1995: 343). Echoing a similar theme, several studies that have found elevated risks at separation have cited the male's inability to accept termination of the relationship and obsessional desires to maintain control over his sexual partner: 'He would destroy his intimate "possession" rather than let her fall into the hands of a competitor male' (Polk 1994: 29; see also Rasche 1989; Campbell 1992; Wilson and Daly 1993).

Ethnicity

Women in certain ethnic groups have risks of intimate femicide disproportionate to their representation in the population, according to several studies. For example, in the United States, African-American women face unusually high risks of intimate femicide. In Canada, such research is more difficult to do because of restrictions on the collection of crime statistics by race and ethnicity. However, Statistics Canada has collected data on Aboriginal victims of spousal homicides which indicate that Aboriginal women's rates of spousal homicide are between five and 10 times higher than the rates for non-Aboriginal women (Kennedy, Forde, and Silverman 1989; Silverman and Kennedy 1993).

We had initially hoped to explore ethnic and cultural differences in the risk of intimate femicide in our research. Our community advisory group, which was composed of women from various ethnic backgrounds active in community organizations, encouraged us to do so.[11] However, our research agreement with the

Ministry of the Solicitor General prevented us from compiling 'statistics based upon social, cultural, regional, linguistic, racial, or ethnic group' from the coroners' records. Nevertheless, we were able to document the number of Aboriginal victims of intimate femicide during these years by relying on other sources of data.[12]

We estimate that at least 6 per cent of the victims of intimate femicide in Ontario between 1974 and 1994 were Aboriginal women. Census data for these years indicate that just under 1 per cent of all women living in Ontario classified themselves as Aboriginal. Thus, Aboriginal women in Ontario appear to be overrepresented among the victims of intimate femicide. Conversely, Aboriginal men are overrepresented as offenders, since all but four of the Aboriginal victims were killed by Aboriginal men.

A number of factors might explain the disproportionate risks of intimate femicide faced by Aboriginal women. Aboriginal Canadians, similar to African Americans, are an economically impoverished and politically disenfranchised ethnic minority. Considerable research has shown that economic, social, and political disadvantages are associated with higher homicide rates generally, as well as higher rates of serious spousal violence. In addition, Aboriginal-Canadian heterosexual couples also have disproportionate rates of other risk markers for intimate partner violence, such as common-law marital status, low income, bouts of male unemployment, exposure to violence in childhood, alcohol abuse, overcrowded housing conditions, and social isolation—all of which have been cited as reasons for the higher rates of family violence in Aboriginal communities (Health and Welfare Canada 1990; Long 1995). Some analysts situate these risk factors within a structural approach that views them as consequences of internal colonialism: 'the conditions of colonialism [are] directly related to Aboriginal acts of political violence as well as rates of suicide, homicide, and family violence among the Aboriginal peoples' (Frank 1993; Bachmann 1993; Long 1995: 42).

Employment

Men's unemployment is commonly cited as a risk factor for wife assaults and is also associated with elevated risks of spousal homicide. Women's employment status, on the other hand, does not appear to be consistently associated with their risks of violence from their partners (Hotaling and Sugarman 1986; Brinkerhoff and Lupri 1988; Macmillan and Gartner 1996; Johnson 1996). The association between men's unemployment and violence against their female partners traditionally has been attributed to the stresses produced by unemployment and limited economic resources. But if this were the case, one would expect to find more evidence that women's unemployment is also associated with spousal violence, which is not the case. For those who see male violence against their partners as one resource for demonstrating power and control, the gender-specificity of the affects of unemployment is not surprising: men who lack more traditional resources (such as economic success) may 'forge a particular type of masculinity that centres on ultimate control of the domestic setting through the use of violence' (Messerschmidt 1993: 149).

Our data on intimate femicide are consistent with this interpretation. For women, employment status is not associated with differential risks of intimate femicide: 51 per cent of women in both the victim population and the general population were employed during the period of our study. For men, however, employment status is associated with differential risks. Among intimate femicide offenders, 64 per cent were employed, whereas among males in the general population, 73 per cent were employed. In Ontario, then, male unemployment appears to be associated with higher risks of intimate femicide offending.

Offenders' Violent Histories

Several studies have shown that men who kill their spouses frequently have histories of violent behaviour, both in and outside their marital relationships (Johnson 1996: 183–6). As Johnson notes, '[a]lthough some wife killings are the result of sudden, unforeseeable attacks by depressed or mentally unstable husbands and are unrelated to a history of violence in the family, most do not seem to fit this description' (183). Because of this, risk assessment tools designed to assess battered women's risk of lethal violence typically include measures of their partners' violence against their children and outside of the home, and threats of serious violence against their wives or others (Campbell 1995).

We also found evidence of unusual levels of violence in the backgrounds of the offenders in our sample. At least 31 per cent of them had an arrest record for a violent offence.[13] At least 53 per cent of them were known to have been violent in the past toward women they ultimately killed. This corresponds to data for Canada as a whole which indicates that in 52 per cent of spousal homicides of women between 1991 and 1993, police were aware of previous violent incidents between the spouses (Canadian Centre for Justice Statistics 1993). In addition, in at least 34 per cent of the cases of intimate femicide, the offenders were known to have previously threatened their victims with violence.[14] At least 10 per cent of the killings occurred while the offender was on probation or parole, or under a restraining order.

It is important to emphasize that these are *minimum* estimates of the number of offenders with violent and criminal histories. In over 200 of the 705 cases of intimate femicide we did not have enough information to determine if previous violence or police contact had occurred. Nevertheless, the information we were able to find clearly challenges the view that intimate femicides are typically momentary rages or heat-of-passion killings by otherwise non-violent men driven to act out of character by extreme circumstances.

A Summary of Risk Markers for Intimate Femicide

Women killed by their intimate male partners and the men who kill them are drawn from all classes, all age groups, all cultural and ethnic backgrounds. However, the victims of intimate femicide and their killers in our study did differ from other women and men in Ontario in some important respects: they were more likely than women and men in the general population to be separated from their partners, to be in common-law relationships, and to be Aboriginal. In addition, men who killed their intimate partners were also likely to be unemployed and to have histories of criminal violence. These risk markers for intimate femicide have been noted in other research on spousal homicides, and have been interpreted from within various theoretical frameworks. We suggest that they are perhaps most consistent with a framework which views intimate femicide as the manifestation of extreme (if ultimately self-defeating) controlling and proprietary attitudes and behaviours by men toward their female partners.

Characteristics of the Killings

An adequate understanding of the sources of intimate femicide will need to take account of the particular characteristics of these killings. Prior research has devoted much less attention to these characteristics than to the characteristics of the individuals involved in the killings.[15] As a consequence, we are limited in both the comparisons we can draw between our findings and the findings from other research and in the interpretations we can offer of these findings.

Intimate femicides are typically very private acts: three-quarters of the victims were killed in their own homes and, in almost half of these cases, in their own bedrooms. Less than 20 per cent occurred in public places, such as streets, parks, workplaces, or public buildings. The most typical method was shooting: one-third of the victims were killed with firearms. Virtually all the other methods required direct and often prolonged physical contact between offenders and their victims: about two-thirds of the offenders stabbed, bludgeoned, beat, strangled, or slashed the throats of their victims.

One of the distinguishing features of intimate femicide is the extent and nature of violence done to the victim. Unlike killings by women of their intimate partners, intimate femicides often involve multiple methods of far more violence than is necessary to kill the victim.[16] For example, in over half of the stabbings, offenders inflicted four or more stab wounds. Beatings and bludgeonings typically involved prolonged violence—leading some coroners to use the term 'over-kill' to describe them. In about 20 per cent of the cases, offenders used multiple methods against their victims, such as stabbing and strangling or beating and slashing. In about 10 per cent of the cases, we also found evidence that the victim's body had been mutilated or dismembered.

The violence in these killings is much more likely to be sexualized than when women kill their intimate partners.[17] Records on approximately half of the cases in our study provided sufficient information for us to determine whether sexual violence was present. In 27 per cent of these cases we found evidence that the victims had been raped, sodomized, or sexually mutilated; in another 22 per cent of the cases the victim's body was found partially or completely unclothed.

Consumption of alcohol by offenders and/or victims was no more common in intimate femicides than in other killings: 39 per cent of the offenders and 32 per cent of the victims had been drinking immediately prior to the killing. In only 3 per cent of the cases was there evidence of drug use by offenders or victims immediately prior to the killing.

Establishing the motives in these killings is fraught with difficulties, as suggested earlier. We made our own determination of the motive after reviewing all the information available to us. In about one-fourth of the cases we felt we had insufficient information to make a judgment about the offender's motive. In the remaining cases, one motive clearly predominated: the offender's rage or despair over the actual or impending estrangement from his partner. This motive characterized 45 per cent of the killings in which we identified a motive. In contrast, women who kill their intimate partners only rarely kill out of anger over an estrangement (Browne 1987; Daly and Wilson 1988).

Suspected or actual infidelity of the victim was the motive in another 15 per cent of the intimate femicides. In 10 per cent of the cases the killing appears to have been the final act of violence in a relationship characterized by serial abuse.[18] In only 5 per cent of the cases did stressful life circumstances—such as bankruptcy, job loss, or serious illness—appear to motivate the killer;[19] and in only 3 per cent of the cases was there evidence that the killer was mentally ill.

Another feature that distinguishes intimate femicide from intimate partner killings by women is the number of people who die as a result of these crimes. The 705 cases of intimate femicide resulted in the deaths of 977 persons. Most of these additional deaths were suicides by the offenders: 31 per cent of the offenders killed themselves after killing their female partners.[20] But offenders killed an additional 75 persons, most of whom were children of the victims. In addition, over 100 children witnessed their mothers' deaths; thus, while they may have escaped physical harm, they obviously suffered inestimable psychological harm.

Our documentation of these characteristics of intimate femicide cannot sufficiently convey the complexity and context surrounding these crimes. Nevertheless, it serves important purposes. Comparing characteristics of intimate partner killings by males and females shows the distinctiveness of these two types of killings—a distinctiveness that is obscured in studies that treat intimate partner killings by men and women as instances of a single phenomenon. Compared to killings of men by intimate female partners, intimate femicides are much more likely to involve extreme and sexualized violence, to be motivated by anger over separation, to be followed by the suicide of the offender, and to be accompanied by the killing of additional victims. These features highlight the gender-specificity of intimate partner killings and are consistent with a perspective on intimate femicide which views it as based in a larger system of gender[ed] inequality and stratification which perpetuates male control over women's sexuality, labour, and, at times, lives and deaths.

The Criminal Justice Response to Intimate Femicide

In our initial study of intimate femicide, we had not intended to collect and analyze data on the criminal justice responses to men who killed their intimate partners—in part because our primary interest was in the victims of intimate femicide and in part because we did not expect information on criminal justice responses to be consistently reported in coroners' and police records. However, contrary to our expectations, we were able to obtain information on charges laid, convictions, and sentencing in a substantial number of the cases. In 90 per cent of the 490 cases in which we were able to establish that offenders did not commit suicide, we found at least some information on criminal justice processing.

In 94 per cent of these cases, the offenders were charged with either first- or second-degree murder.[21] The proportion charged with first-degree murder increased over time, from 34 per cent of the cases in the first half of the period to 52 per cent in the second half. Of the 346 cases for which we found information on dispositions, 10 per cent were convicted of first-degree murder, 35 per cent of second-degree murder, and 38 per cent of manslaughter. Murder convictions increased over time: from 32 per cent of the dispositions in the first half of the period to 56 per cent in the second half. Acquittals accounted for a total of 13 per cent of the cases: 11 per cent were verdicts of not guilty by reason of insanity and 2 per cent were straight acquittals.

Sentencing information, available for 302 of the men convicted of killing their partners, also indicates that criminal justice responses to intimate femicide increased in severity over time. Prior to 1984, 7 per cent of convicted offenders received no jail time, 14 per cent were sent to secure mental institutions for indefinite periods, 25 per cent were sentenced to less than five years in prison, 38 per cent were sentenced to between five and 10 years, and 15 per cent received sentences of more than 10 years. After 1983, 4 per cent of convicted offenders received no jail time, 7 per cent were sent to secure mental institutions, 10 per cent received sentences of less than five years, 37 per cent received sentences of between five and 10 years, and 41 per cent were sentenced to prison for more than 10 years.

This evidence clearly shows that criminal justice responses to intimate femicide became increasingly punitive over the 21 years of our study. How much of this trend reflects increasing punitiveness toward all violent criminals and how much reflects growing public awareness and intolerance of violence against women is an issue requiring further research.[22]

The Gender-specific Nature of Intimate Femicide

We have alluded to the gender-specific nature of intimate femicide at various points in our analysis. Here, we develop our ideas about this gender-specificity by considering what is known about gender differences in homicide more generally. We base this discussion on a large body of criminological research on homicide, as well as on data on over 7,000 homicides collected by Rosemary Gartner and Bill McCarthy as part of a separate research project.

Among those who study homicide, it is well known that women and men are killed in different numbers, by different types of people, and in different circumstances. Women are less likely to be victims of homicide than men in virtually all societies. Canada and Ontario are no different: men outnumbered women as victims of homicide by a ratio of approximately 2:1 in Canada and in Ontario between 1974 and 1994.

This may appear to indicate that women have a sort of protective advantage over men—that, at least in this sphere of social life, women are not disadvantaged relative to men. However, if we consider gender differences in offending, a different picture emerges. Men accounted for 87 per cent of all homicide offenders in Ontario during these years; and males outnumbered females as offenders by a ratio of almost 7:1. When women were involved in homicides, then, they were almost three times more likely to be victims than offenders; when men were involved in homicides they were more likely to be offenders than victims. In other words, women are overrepresented among victims and underrepresented among offenders; for men the opposite is true.

Women were also much more likely than men to be killed by someone of the opposite sex, as these figures imply. Fully 98 per cent of all women killed in Ontario between 1974 and 1994 were killed by men. Only 17 per cent of adult male victims were killed by women. Thus, man killing appears to be primarily a reflection of relations *within* a gender, whereas woman killing appears to be primarily a matter of relations *between* the genders. Because women are the majority of victims in opposite-sex killings, such killings can be seen as one of the high costs to women of male dominance and desire for control in heterosexual relationships.

It is in intimate relationships between women and men that male dominance and control are most likely to erupt into physical violence. Women accounted for 75 per cent of all victims of spouse killings in Ontario during the last two decades.[23] So women outnumbered men among victims of spouse killings by a ratio of about 3:1. Moreover, spousal homicides accounted for over 50 per cent of all killings of women but less than 10 per cent of all killings of men.

If males, unlike females, are not killed primarily by their intimate partners, who are they killed by and under what circumstances? In Ontario, about 60 per cent of male victims are killed by acquaintances and strangers; another 20 per cent are killed by unknown assailants. Most male–male homicides are the result of arguments or disputes that escalate to killings. In many cases, both victim and offender have been drinking, and who becomes the victim and who the offender is a matter of happenstance.[24] One classic study of homicide (Wolfgang 1958) concluded that male–male homicides, as an instance of the more generally physically aggressive behaviour of males, converge with notions of masculine identity.

When males kill their intimate female partners, their methods of and motives for killing take on a character distinctive from male–male killings—a character that denotes the gender specificity of intimate femicide. As noted above, a substantial number of intimate femicides involved multiple methods, excessive force, and continued violence even after the women's deaths would have been apparent.[25] The violence in intimate femicides also frequently involves some form of sexual assault, a very rare occurrence in killings of men.

The motives in intimate femicide also point to its gender-specificity. The predominance of men's rage over separation as a motive in intimate femicides has no obvious counterpart in killings of men—even killings of men by their intimate female partners. We agree with others who see this motive as a reflection of the sexual proprietariness of males toward their intimate female partners.

In sum, our analysis of intimate femicide and our review of other research and data on gender differences in homicide suggest that women killing in general and intimate femicide in particular are uniquely gendered acts. By this we mean these killings reflect important dimensions of gender stratification, such as power differences in intimate relations and the construction of women as sexual objects generally, and as sexual property in particular contexts. Intimate femicide—indeed, probably most femicide—is not simply violence against a person who happens to be female. It is violence that occurs and takes particular forms because its target is a woman, a woman who has been intimately involved with her killer.

Conclusion

Our purpose in this article has been to document the incidence and provide a description of the phenomenon of intimate femicide. For some, our approach may be unsatisfying, because we have not proposed a systematic explanation of, nor outlined a detailed strategy for preventing, these killings. Obviously explaining and preventing intimate femicides are critical tasks, but both require comprehensive knowledge of the phenomenon. The statistical data we have gathered and analyzed are intended to contribute to this knowledge.

Nevertheless, we recognize that our overview of the extent and character of intimate femicide in Ontario between 1974 and 1994 has raised at least as many questions as it has answered. Why, for example, did women's risks of intimate femicide increase slightly when public concern over and resources available to abused women were also increasing; when other forms of lethal violence were decreasing; and when criminal justice responses to intimate femicide were becoming more punitive? Why did some women—such as those in common-law relationships and Aboriginal women—face disproportionately high risks of intimate femicide? Were there other types of women with elevated risks of intimate femicide—for example, immigrant women or women with disabilities—whom we couldn't identify because of the limitations of our data? Why are intimate partner killings by men and women so distinctively different? All of these questions deserve answers, but the answers will require research that goes beyond the data and analysis we have been able to present in this paper.

There are other types of questions raised by our research that are more immediately pressing, questions about how to prevent intimate femicides. Our research has shown that intimate femicides are not the isolated and unpredictable acts of passion they are often believed to be. Most of the killers in our study had acted violently toward their partners or other persons in the past and many had prior contact with the police as a consequence. Many of the victims had sought help from a variety of sources. In a substantial portion of these intimate femicides, then, there were clear signs of danger preceding the killing, signs that were available to people who might have been able to intervene to prevent the crime. We believe this information could be combined with what we know about the risk factors for intimate femicide—such as estrangement—to develop interventions that would save women's lives.

This is the question that has been at the core of our research and the recommendation that we tabled at the conclusion of both of our studies. We urged the establishment of a joint forces initiative that would include police, coroners, researchers, experts working in the field, as well as survivors of intimate violence, who would be charged with developing a system to respond more effectively to women when they are at greatest risk of intimate femicide. Such a response would need to be swift and focused on ensuring the victim's safety and deterring the offender from further violence or threats.

Of course, this kind of intervention must be coupled with efforts to address the underlying sources of intimate femicide. If, as we and others have argued, the sources lie at least in part in attitudes and behaviours that have been supported for centuries by patriarchal systems of power and privilege, those attitudes and behaviours, as well as the systems supporting them, must be confronted and contested. Some feminists argue that one means of doing this is through refining and reformulating law as a weapon against men's intimate violence against women. Isabel Marcus (1994), for example, argues for identifying domestic violence as terrorism and, as such, a violation of international human rights accords. Elizabeth Schneider (1994: 56) suggests redeploying the concept of privacy, not to keep the state out of intimate relationships as the concept has been used in the past but to emphasize individuals' autonomy and independence. She argues this affirmative aspect of privacy could frame a new feminist agenda against woman abuse.

As these and other analyses emphasize, preventing intimate femicides will require that the public as well as those working in fields relevant to the prevention of violence begin to see intimate femicide as a preventable crime. From our own and others' research on intimate violence, it should be apparent that these crimes are patterned and predictable. The danger lies in maintaining the view that violence is inevitable, unavoidable, and inherent in intimate relationships. Such fatalism must be challenged, so that women's safety in and outside their homes is seen as an achievable and pre-eminent goal.

Notes

Major funding for the studies described in this paper was provided by the Ontario Women's Directorate. The Ministry of Community and Social Services and the School of Graduate Studies at the University of Toronto each provided additional funding for one of the studies. The analyses and opinions in the paper are those of the authors and do not necessarily represent the views of any of these funders.

1. Coroners' records are limited in another obvious and unavoidable way: they are observations removed in time and space from the actual killing. As a consequence, the description in the records will be shaped by the interests and perspectives of the observer. A coroner's perspective is that of an investigator after the fact, and his/her primary interest is in determining the cause and means of death. Thus, the information recorded by coroners is intended to serve these purposes, not the interests of researchers.
2. Different procedures were used in the two studies to obtain access to municipal police and OPP records. These records are not centrally compiled and it was impossible to contact and obtain co-operation from all of the forces around Ontario which investigate and keep records on cases of homicide.
3. Obviously, the coded data provide only a partial and, in some respects, an incomplete portrayal of intimate femicide. The lives and deaths of the women represented in these statistics cannot be sufficiently understood from counts and categorizations. For this reason, we devoted a considerable portion of our first study to reconstructing the stories of some of the women who died through interviews with their family and friends.

4. Our research has looked only at killings of females aged 15 and older because the killing of children differs in distinctive ways from the killing of adults.
5. The number of intimate femicides is undercounted in official records for other reasons as well. For example, in some cases of intimate femicide, the woman's death may be incorrectly classified as due to suicide, accident, or natural causes. Among the intimate femicides in our study, at least eight were not initially classified as homicides and only reclassified after further investigation. Another example of this occurred while this article was being written: the body of a southern Ontario woman who died by hanging was exhumed and an investigation revealed she had not killed herself, as originally determined, but had been killed by her boyfriend.
6. Although there are no statistics on the rate of intimate femicide for Canada as a whole, there are statistics on the rate of spousal killings of women. Since the mid-1970s, trends in Ontario's rate have paralleled those for Canada as a whole; and the mean rate for Ontario (0.77) is very close to the mean rate for Canada (0.83).
7. Of the cases of intimate femicide between 1974 and 1994, we found only three in which the offender was a woman.
8. Identifying differences between victims or offenders and women and men in the general population requires establishing the proportion of victims (or offenders) with the particular characteristic and comparing this to the proportion of women (or men) in the general population of Ontario during the years 1974–94 with the same characteristics. If the former proportion is larger than the latter proportion, this indicates that women with that particular characteristic are overrepresented among victims of intimate femicide. Tests for statistically significant differences are not appropriate here because the data are based on populations, not samples. Because we used information from census reports to determine the characteristics of women in the general population of Ontario, we were limited in our search for risk markers of intimate femicide to characteristics which are measured in the census.
9. By highlighting these characteristics, we do not mean to obscure the fact that women from all types of backgrounds and in all types of relationships are victims of intimate femicide; nor do we mean to imply that certain characteristics of women make them likely targets for intimate violence. Rather, we would suggest that certain groups of women may be more vulnerable to intimate violence because they share characteristics that have isolated them, limited their access to resources for protection, or prevented them from obtaining a level of personal security that many Canadians take for granted.
10. The average annual rate of intimate femicide (per 100,000 women aged 15 and older) for the years 1991–94 was calculated by: (1) dividing the number of victims during those years (159) by the number of women aged 15 and older in the Ontario population in 1991 (4,130,450); (2) multiplying this figure by 100,000; and (3) dividing this figure by four (the number of years). This yields an average annual rate of 0.96 per 100,000 women aged 15 and older.

    The average annual rate of intimate femicides of women living in common law unions was calculated by: (1) dividing the number of victims living common-law during those years (45) by the number of women aged 15 and older in Ontario living in common-law unions in 1991 (182,155); (2) multiplying this figure by 100,000; and (3) dividing this figure by four. This yields an annual average rate of 6.18 per 100,000 women aged 15 and older living in common-law unions.
11. This group was formed at the beginning of our first study and met with the principal researchers regularly to review the research for cultural sensitivity and validity. At the completion of the first study, its members also reviewed and made contributions to the final report.
12. The final report for our first study (pp. 67–76) documents the problems with collecting information on race and cultural backgrounds of crime victims and offenders, as well as the procedures we followed to gather the data on Aboriginal victims.
13. Another 30 per cent had been arrested and charged with non-violent criminal offences.
14. In contrast, in only 6 per cent of the cases were

the victims known to have been violent toward their killers in the past; and in only 2 per cent of the cases were the victims known to have previously threatened their partners with violence.

15. What researchers can describe about homicide and femicide is largely determined by the types of information officials collect. This means that many details about the events leading up to the killing, the dynamics of the interaction immediately preceding the killing, or the states of mind of victim and offender are absent or at most only hinted at in official reports. Some characteristics of intimate femicide can be easily and reliably determined, such as where they occurred or whether weapons were involved. Other characteristics—such as the offender's motivation—are more susceptible to post hoc reconstructions that introduce the inevitable biases of observers and officials. When we collected and coded information, we reviewed all the information available to us and made our own best judgments about these characteristics. We recognize, however, that our judgments are necessarily based on limited information about extremely complex events. Our discussion of the characteristics of the killings therefore should be viewed with these limitations in mind.
16. We base this and other conclusions about the characteristics of intimate partner killings by women on data from an ongoing study by the first author of over 7,000 homicides in two Canadian cities and two US cities over the twentieth century.
17. Indeed, none of the data or research with which we are familiar indicates that women who kill their intimate partners exact sexual violence against their victims.
18. This does not mean that offenders who appeared to act for other motives had not engaged in systematic abuse of the women they killed. Rather, it indicates that in 10 per cent of the cases, the only motive we could identify was systematic, serial abuse that ultimately led to the woman's death.
19. Typically, offenders who kill under these circumstances are characterized as extremely depressed, and are more likely than other offenders to commit or attempt suicide after the killing. Nevertheless, some have argued that sexual proprietariness can still be seen in killings apparently motivated by stressful life circumstances (e.g., Daly and Wilson 1988). According to this view, when men kill their wives (and often their children as well) because they feel they can no longer provide for them, their acts suggest that they see their wives as possessions to dispose of as they see fit and/or that they cannot conceive of their wives having an existence separate from their own.
20. Other research has noted the high rates at which offenders suicide after intimate femicides, and has contrasted this to the rarity of suicides by women who kill their intimate partners (see, e.g., Carolyn R. Block and A. Christakos, 'Intimate Partner Homicide in Chicago over 29 Years', *Crime and Delinquency* 41 (1995): 496–526. Daly and Wilson (1988) have suggested that this pattern is grounded in males' feelings of possessiveness and ownership over their partners.
21. Murder is first-degree when the killing is planned and deliberate, when the victim is an officer of the law, or when a death is caused while committing or attempting to commit another offence, such as kidnapping. Any murder that does not fall within these categories is second-degree murder. According to the courts, the distinction between first- and second-degree murder is made solely for sentencing purposes. While anyone convicted of murder is sentenced to imprisonment for life, the parole ineligibility period varies between first- and second-degree murder.
22. Some analysts (e.g., Elizabeth Rapaport, 'The Death Penalty and the Domestic Discount', in *The Public Nature of Private Violence: The Discovery of Domestic Abuse*, eds M. Fineman and R. Mykitiuk [New York: Routledge, 1994], 224–51) have speculated that the killing of a woman by her intimate male partner is treated more leniently by the criminal justice system than other types of homicides, such as killings of men by female intimate partners. However, empirical evidence in this area is sparse and not conclusive.
23. We use the category 'spouse killings' here because we could find no statistics on the number of men killed by intimate partners, only statistics on men killed by spouses. To be comparable, we compare

these figures to the number of women killed by spouses—a subset of all intimate femicides.

24. Marvin Wolfgang has noted in *Studies in Homicide* (New York: Harper & Row, 1967) that where males are victims of homicide, victim precipitation of the violence is fairly common.

25. Wolfgang (1967) found a similar pattern in his study of homicides in Philadelphia.

References

Bachmann, R. 1993. *Death and Violence on the Reservation: Homicide, Family Violence, and Suicide in American Indian Populations* (New York: Auburn House).

Blinder, M. 1985. *Lovers, Killers, Husbands, and Wives* (New York: St Martin's Press).

Boudoris, J. 1971. 'Homicide and the Family', *Journal of Marriage and the Family* 32: 667–76.

Brinkerhoff, M., and E. Lupri. 1988. 'Interspousal Violence', *Canadian Journal of Sociology* 13: 407–34.

Browne, A. 1987. *When Battered Women Kill* (New York: The Free Press).

———, and K. Williams. 1989. 'Exploring the Effect of Resource Availability on the Likelihood of Female-perpetrated Homicides', *Law and Society Review* 23: 75–94.

Campbell, J. 1995. 'Prediction of Homicide of and by Battered Women', in Assessing Dangerousness: *Violence by Sexual Offenders, Batterers, and Child Abusers* (Thousand Oaks, CA: Sage), 96–113.

Campbell, J.C. 1992. 'If I Can't Have You No One Else Can': Power and Control in Homicide of Female Partners', in *Femicide: The Politics of Woman Killing*, eds J. Radford and D.E.H. Russell (New York: Twayne), 99–113.

Canadian Centre for Justice Statistics. 1993. *Homicide Survey*, unpublished statistics.

Chimbos, P.D. 1978. *Marital Violence: A Study of Interspousal Homicide* (San Francisco: R & E Associates).

Crawford, M., R. Gartner, and M. Dawson, in collaboration with the Women We Honour Committee. 1997. *Women Killing: Intimate Femicide in Ontario, 1991–1994* (Toronto: Women We Honour Action Committee).

———, and the Women We Honour Action Committee. 1992. *Woman Killing: Intimate Femicide in Ontario, 1974–1990* (Toronto: Women We Honour Action Committee).

Daly, M., and M. Wilson. 1988. *Homicide* (New York: Aldine de Gruyter).

Dobash, R.E., and R.P. Dobash. 1984. 'The Nature and Antecedents of Violent Events', *British Journal of Criminology* 24: 269–88.

Dobash, R.P., R.E. Dobash, M. Wilson, and M. Daly. 1992. 'The Myth of Sexual Symmetry in Marital Violence', *Social Problems* 39: 81.

Frank, S. 1993. *Family Violence in Aboriginal Communities: A First Nations Report* (British Columbia: Report to the Government of British Columbia).

Goode, W. 1969. 'Violence among Intimates', in *Crimes of Violence*, Vol. 13, eds D. Mulvihill and M. Tumin (Washington, DC: USGPO), 941–77.

Health and Welfare Canada. 1990. *Reaching for Solutions: Report of the Special Advisor to the Minister of National Health & Welfare on Child Sexual Abuse in Canada* (Ottawa: Supply and Services).

Hotaling, G., and D. Sugarman. 1986. 'An Analysis of Risk Markers in Husband to Wife Violence: The Current State of Knowledge', *Violence and Victims* 1: 101–24.

Johnson, H. 1996. *Dangerous Domains: Violence Against Women in Canada* (Toronto: Nelson Canada).

———, and V. Sacco. 1995. 'Researching Violence Against Women: Statistics Canada's National Survey', *Canadian Journal of Criminology* 3: 281–304.

Kelkar, G. 1992. 'Women and Structural Violence in India', in *Femicide: The Politics of Women Killing*, eds J. Radford and D.E.H. Russell (New York: Twayne), 117–23.

Kennedy, L.W., D.R. Forde, and R.A. Silverman. 1989. 'Understanding Homicide Trends: Issues in Disaggregating for National and Cross-national Comparisons', *Canadian Journal of Sociology* 14:

479–86.

Long, D.A. 1995. 'On Violence and Healing: Aboriginal Experiences, 1960–1993', in *Violence in Canada: Sociopolitical Perspectives*, ed. J.I. Ross (Don Mills, ON: Oxford University Press), 40–77.

Macmillan, R., and R. Gartner. 1996. 'Labour Force Participation and the Risk of Spousal Violence Against Women', paper presented at the 1996 Annual Meetings of the American Society of Criminology.

Maloney, M.A. 1994. 'Victimization or Oppression? Women's Lives, Violence, and Agency', in *The Public Nature of Private Violence: The Discovery of Domestic Abuse*, eds M.A. Fineman and R. Mykitiuk (New York: Routledge), 59–92.

Marcus, I. 1994. 'Reframing "Domestic Violence": Terrorism in the Home', in *The Public Nature of Private Violence: The Discovery of Domestic Abuse*, eds M.A. Fineman and R. Mykitiuk (New York: Routledge), 11–35.

Messerschmidt, J.W. 1993. *Masculinities and Crime: Critique and Conceptualization of Theory* (Lanham, MD: Rowman & Littlefield).

Polk, K. 1994. *When Men Kill: Scenarios of Masculine Violence* (Cambridge: Cambridge University Press).

Rasche, C. 1989. 'Stated and Attributed Motives for Lethal Violence in Intimate Relationships', paper presented at the 1989 Annual Meetings of the American Society of Criminology.

Regoeczi, W., and R. Silverman. 1997. 'Spousal Homicide in Canada: Exploring the Issue of Racial Variations in Risk', paper presented at the 1997 Annual Meetings of the American Society of Criminology.

Rodgers, K. 1994. *Wife Assault: The Findings of a National Survey* (Ottawa: Canadian Centre for Justice Statistics).

Schneider, E. 1994. 'The Violence of Privacy', in *The Public Nature of Private Violence: The Discovery of Domestic Abuse*, eds M. Fineman and R. Mykitiuk (New York: Routledge), 36–58.

Silverman, R., and L. Kennedy. 1993. *Deadly Deeds: Murder in Canada* (Toronto: Nelson Canada).

Wallace, A. 1986. *Homicide: The Social Reality* (New South Wales: NSW Bureau of Crime Statistics and Research).

Wilson, M., and M. Daly. 1992a. 'Til Death Do Us Part', in *Femicide: The Politics of Woman Killing*, eds J. Radford and D.E.H. Russell (New York: Twayne), 85.

———. 1992b. 'Who Kills Whom in Spouse Killings? On the Exceptional Sex Ratio of Spousal Homicides in the United States', *Criminology* 30: 189–215.

———. 1993. 'Spousal Homicide Risk and Estrangement', *Violence and Victims* 8: 3–16.

———. 1994. 'Spousal Homicide', *Juristat Service Bulletin* 14: 8.

———, H. Johnson, and M. Daly. 1995. 'Lethal and Nonlethal Violence against Wives', *Canadian Journal of Criminology* 37: 343.

Wolfgang, M. 1958. *Patterns in Criminal Homicide* (Philadelphia: University of Pennsylvania Press).

Women We Honour Action Committee, and R. Gartner. 1990. *Annotated Bibliography of Works Reviewed for Project on Intimate Femicide* (Toronto: Women We Honour Action Committee).

Chapter 32

Divorce has different consequences for women than for men, since women often suffer a significant drop in standard of living and economic security. It is the children we worry about most when divorce occurs, however. Frank Furstenberg and Andrew Cherlin are American researchers who have studied the effects of divorce on children, as well as many other issues in family life. This chapter from their book *Divided Families* presents an overview of the research findings on what most harms children, the extent of the damage, and how to prevent it.

Children's Adjustment to Divorce

Frank F. Furstenberg and Andrew J. Cherlin

As Helen watched, Sally, then three, walked over to where her six-year-old brother was playing and picked up one of his toy robots. Mickey grabbed the robot out of her hand, shouted 'No!' and pushed her away. The little girl fell backward and began to cry. Helen had just finished another frustrating phone call with Herb, who had told her he could no longer afford to pay as much child support as they had agreed. She was grateful to her parents for allowing her and the kids to live with them temporarily, but the crowded household was beginning to strain everyone's patience. She rushed over to her daughter, picked her up, and shouted at her son, 'Don't you hit her like that!' 'But it was mine', he said, whereupon he took another robot and threw it on the floor near his mother's feet. She grabbed his arm and dragged him to his room screaming at him all the way.

Then she sat down in the living room, with Sally in her lap, and reflected on how often scenes such as this were occurring. Ever since the separation eight months earlier, she had had a hard time controlling Mickey. He disobeyed her, was mean to his sister, and fought with friends at school. And when he talked back to her, she lost her temper. But that just made him behave worse, which in turn made her angrier, until he was sent to his room and she sat down, distraught.

Helen's problems with her son fit a pattern familiar to psychologists who study the effects of divorce on children, an escalating cycle of misbehaviour and harsh response between mothers and sons. But not all parents and children become caught up in these so-called coercive cycles after the breakup of a marriage. Studies show a wide range of responses to divorce. Some children do very well; others fare poorly. In this chapter we will examine these differences and inquire into why they occur.

We tend to think of divorce as an event that starts when a husband or wife moves out of their home. But it is often more useful to think of divorce as a process that unfolds slowly over time, beginning well before the separation actually occurs. In many cases it is preceded by a lengthy period of conflict between the spouses. It is reasonable to expect that this pre-disruption conflict, and the corresponding emotional upset on the part of the parents, may cause problems for children.

For example, when things began to heat up between Mickey and his mother, Helen naturally assumed that the problems between them were largely the result of the divorce. Perhaps she was right. But her guilty feelings made Helen conveniently forget that Mickey had had behavioural problems for several years—ever since the quarrelling between his parents became severe.

Almost two years before the separation, Mickey's preschool teacher had asked Helen if things were going all right at home. Mickey had displayed unusual fits of temper with his classmates and seemed distracted during play periods. If you had asked Mickey's teacher, she would have predicted that Mickey, although bright enough, was going to have adjustment problems in kindergarten. And so he did. True, Mickey's problems did get worse the year that his parents separated, but it is not obvious that his difficulties in school would have been avoided even if his parents had managed to remain together.

In fact, there is evidence that some children show signs of disturbance months, and sometimes even years, before their parents separate. In 1968 a team of psychologists began to study three year olds at two nursery schools in Berkeley, California. The psychologists followed these children and their families, conducting detailed personality assessments at ages four, five, seven, 11, and 14. When the study started, 88 children were living with two married parents. Twenty-nine of these children experienced the breakup of their parents' marriages by the time they were 14. Curious as to what the children were like before the breakup, the psychologists paged backward through their files until they found the descriptions of the children 11 years earlier, when they were age three.

The results were quite dramatic for boys. Years before the breakup, three-year-old boys whose families eventually would disrupt were more likely to have been described as having behavioural problems than were three-year-old boys whose families would remain intact. According to the researchers, Jeanne H. Block, Jack Block, and Per F. Gjerde, three-year-old boys who would eventually experience family disruption already were rated as more 'inconsiderate of other children, disorderly in dress and behaviour', and 'impulsive' and more likely to 'take advantage of other children'. Moreover, their fathers were more likely to characterize themselves as often angry with their sons, and both fathers and mothers reported more conflict with their sons. Much smaller differences were found among daughters.

Had the Berkeley researchers started their study when the children were age 14, they surely would have found some differences between the adolescents from the 29 disrupted families and the adolescents from the 59 intact families. And they probably would have attributed these differences to the aftermath of the disruption, as most other researchers do. But because they could look back 11 years, they saw that some portion of the presumed effects of divorce on children were present well before the families split up.

Why is this so? It is, of course, possible that some children have behavioural problems that put stress on their parents' marriages. In these instances divorce, rather than causing children's problems, may be the result of them. But it is doubtful that inherently difficult children cause most divorces. The Berkeley researchers suggest, rather, that conflict between parents is a fundamental factor that harms children's development and produces behavioural problems. In many families, this conflict—and the harm it engenders—may precede the separation by many years.

There are many other characteristics of divorce-prone families that might affect children. For example, people who divorce are more likely to have married as teenagers and to have begun their marriages after the wife was pregnant. They also are less religious. It is possible that these families may provide a less stable and secure environment and therefore cause children more problems even while the family is intact. But no researcher would suggest that all of the effects of divorce are determined before the actual separation. Much of the impact depends on how the process unfolds after the separation and how the children cope with it. Nearly all children are extremely upset when they learn of the breakup. For most, it is an unwelcome shock. Judith Wallerstein and Joan Kelly found that young children seemed surprised even in families where the parents were openly quarrelling and hostile. Although young children certainly recognize open conflict—and indeed may be drawn into it—they usually can't grasp the long-term significance and don't envisage the separation. Moreover, parents typically don't inform their children of the impending separation until shortly before it occurs.

When children do learn of the breakup, their reactions vary according to their ages. Preschool-aged children, whose ability to understand the situation is limited, are usually frightened and bewildered to find that their father or mother has moved out of the house. Preschoolers see the world in a very self-centred way, and so they often assume that the separation must be their fault—that they must have done something terribly wrong to make their parent leave. Three-year-old Sally promised never to leave her room a mess again if only Daddy would come home. Older children comprehend the situation better and can understand that they are not at fault. But they still can be quite anxious about what the breakup will mean for their own lives. And adolescents, characteristically, are more often intensely angry at one or both of their parents for breaking up their families.

Short-term Adjustment

The psychologists P. Lindsay Chase-Lansdale and E. Mavis Hetherington have labelled the first two years following a separation as a 'crisis period' for adults and children. The crisis begins for children with shock, anxiety, and anger upon learning of the breakup. (But as was noted, the harmful effects on children of marital conflict may begin well before the breakup.) For adults, too, the immediate aftermath is a dismaying and difficult time. It is especially trying for mothers who retain custody of the children, as about nine in 10 do.

Helen, for example, faced the task of raising her two children alone. Even when she was married, Helen had taken most of the responsibility for raising the children. But Herb had helped out some and had backed her up when the children were difficult. Now responsibility fell solely on her. What's more, she was working full-time in order to compensate for the loss of Herb's income. And all this was occurring at a time when she felt alternately angry at Herb, depressed about the end of her marriage, and anxious about her future. Harried and overburdened, she was sometimes overwhelmed by the task of keeping her family going from day-to-day. Dinner was frequently served late, and Sally and Mickey often stayed up past their bedtime as Helen tried to complete the household chores.

Children have two special needs during the crisis period. First, they need additional emotional support as they struggle to adapt to the breakup. Second, they need the structure provided by a reasonably predictable daily routine. Unfortunately, many single parents cannot meet both of these needs all the time. Depressed, anxious parents often lack the reserve to comfort emotionally needy children. Overburdened parents let daily schedules slip. As a result, their children lose some of the support they need.

A number of psychological studies suggest that the consequences of the crisis period are worse for boys than for girls; but it may be that boys and girls merely react to stress differently. Developmental psychologists distinguish two general types of behaviour problems among children. The first—externalizing disorders—refers to heightened levels of problem behaviour directed outward, such as aggression, disobedience, and lying. The second—internalizing disorders—refers to heightened levels of problem behaviours directed inward, such as depression, anxiety, or withdrawal. Boys in high-conflict families, whether disrupted or intact, tend to show more aggressive and antisocial behaviour. Hetherington studied a small group of middle-class families, disrupted and intact, for several years. She found coercive cycles between mothers and sons, like the ones between Helen and Mickey, to be prevalent. Distressed mothers responded irritably to the bad behaviour of their sons, thus aggravating the very behaviour they wished to quell. Even as long as six years after the separation, Hetherington observed this pattern among mothers who hadn't remarried and their sons.

The findings for girls are less consistent, but generally girls appear better behaved than boys in the immediate aftermath of a disruption. There are even reports of over-controlled, self-consciously 'good' behaviour. But we should be cautious in concluding that girls are less affected. It may be that they internalize their distress in the form of depression or lowered self-esteem. And some observers suggest that the distress may produce problems that only appear years after the breakup.

It is also possible that boys do worse because they typically live with their opposite-sex parent, their mother. A number of studies report intriguing evidence that children may fare better if they reside with a same-sex parent after a marital disruption. Families in which single fathers become the custodial parent, however, are a small and select group who may be quite different from typical families. Until recently, sole custody was awarded to fathers mainly in cases in which the mother had abandoned the children or was an alcoholic, drug abuser, or otherwise clearly incompetent. Until there is more evidence from studies of broad groups of children, we think it would be premature to generalize about same-sex custody.

To sum up, researchers agree that almost all children are moderately or severely distressed when their parents separate and that most continue to experience confusion, sadness, or anger for a period of months and even years. Nevertheless, the most careful studies show a great deal of variation in the short-term reactions of children—including children in the same family. Most of this variation remains unexplained, although differences in age and gender account for some of it. Part of the explanation, no doubt, has to do with differences in children's temperaments. Some probably are more robust and better able to withstand deprivation and instability. They may be less affected by growing up in a one-parent family, and they may also cope better with a divorce. In addition, clinicians have speculated that some children draw strength from adults or even peers outside of the household, such as grandparents, aunts, or close friends. But we are far from certain just how important each of the sources of resiliency is to the child's ability to cope with divorce.

Long-term Adjustment

Even less is known about the long-term consequences of divorce than about the short-term consequences. Within two or three years, most single parents and their children recover substantially from the trauma of the crisis period. Parents are able to stabilize their lives as the wounds from the breakup heal. With the exception of some difficulties between single mothers and their sons, parent–child relationships generally improve. And the majority of children, it seems, return to normal development.

But over the long run there is still great variation in how the process of divorce plays out. Without doubt, some children suffer long-term harm. It is easy, however, to exaggerate the extent of these harmful effects. In their widely read book that reports on a clinical study of 60 recently divorced middle-class couples from the San Francisco suburbs and their 131 children, aged two to 18, Judith Wallerstein and Sandra Blakeslee paint a picture of a permanently scarred generation. 'Almost half of the children', they write, 'entered adulthood as worried, under-achieving, self-deprecating, and sometimes angry young men and women.' Are these difficulties as widespread among children of divorce as the authors suggest? Despite their claim that the families were 'representative of the way normal people from a white, middle-class background cope with divorce', it is highly likely that the study exaggerates the prevalence of long-term problems. Its families had volunteered to come to a clinic for counselling, and many of the parents had extensive psychiatric histories. Moreover, there is no comparison group of intact families: instead, all of the problems that emerged after the breakup are blamed on the divorce.

We do not doubt that many young adults retain painful memories of their parents' divorces. But it doesn't necessarily follow that these feelings will impair their functioning as adults. Had their parents not divorced, they might have retained equally painful memories of a conflict-ridden marriage. Imagine that the more troubled families in the Wallerstein study had remained intact and had been observed 10 years later. Would their children have fared any better? Certainly they would have been better off economically; but given the strains that would have been evident in the marriages, we doubt that most would have been better off psychologically.

Studies based on nationally representative samples that do include children from intact marriages suggest that the long-term harmful effects of divorce are worthy of concern but occur only to a minority. Evidence for this conclusion comes from the National Survey of Children (NSC), which interviewed parents and children in 1976 and again in 1981. For families in which a marital disruption had occurred, the average time elapsed since the disruption was eight years in 1981. James L. Peterson and Nicholas Zill examined parents' 1981 responses to the question, 'Since January 1977 . . . has [the child] had any behaviour or discipline problems at school resulting in your receiving a note or being asked to come in and talk to the teacher or principal?' Peterson and Zill found that, other things being equal, 34 per cent of parents who had separated or divorced answered yes, compared with 20 per cent of parents of intact marriages.

Is this a big difference or a small difference? The figures can be interpreted in two ways. First, the percentage of children from maritally disrupted families who had behaviour or discipline problems at school is more than half again as large as the percentage from intact families. That's a substantial difference, suggesting that children from disrupted families have a noticeably higher rate of misbehaving seriously in school. (Although some of these children might have misbehaved even if their parents had not separated.) Second, however, the figures also demonstrate that 66 per cent of all children from maritally disrupted homes did not misbehave seriously at school. So one also can conclude that most children of divorce don't have behaviour problems at school. Both conclusions are equally valid; the glass is either half-full or half-empty, depending on one's point of view. We think that in order to understand the broad picture of the long-term effects of divorce on children, it's necessary to keep both points of view in mind.

The same half-full and half-empty perspective can be applied to studies of the family histories of adults. Based on information from several national surveys of adults, Sara McLanahan and her colleagues found that persons who reported living as a child in a single-parent family were more likely subsequently to drop out of high school, marry during their teenage years, have a child before marrying, and experience the disruption of their own marriages. For example, the studies imply that, for whites, the probability of dropping out of high school could be as high as 22 per cent for those who lived with single parents, compared with about 11 per cent for those who lived with both parents, other things being equal. Again, the glass is half-empty: those who lived with a single parent are up to twice as likely to drop out of high school. And it is half-full: the overwhelming majority of those who lived with a single parent graduated from high school.

In addition, the NSC data demonstrate that children in intact families in which the parents fought continually were doing no better, and often worse, than the children of divorce. In 1976 and again in 1981, parents in intact marriages were asked whether they and their spouses ever had arguments about any of nine topics: chores and responsibilities, the children, money, sex, religion, leisure time, drinking, other women or men, and in-laws. Peterson and Zill classified an intact marriage as having 'high conflict' if arguments were reported on five or more topics or if the parent said that the marriage, taking things all together, was 'not too happy'. They found that in 1981, children whose parents had divorced or separated were doing no worse than children whose parents were in intact, high-conflict homes. And children whose parents' marriages were intact but highly conflicted in both 1976 and 1981 were doing the worst of all: these children were more depressed, impulsive, and hyperactive, and misbehaved more often.

To be sure, even if only a minority of children experience long-term negative effects, that is nothing to cheer about. But the more fundamental point—one that all experts agree upon—is that children's responses to the breakup of their parents' marriages vary greatly. There is no ineluctable path down which children of divorce progress. What becomes important, then, is to identify the circumstances under which children seem to do well.

What Makes a Difference?

A critical factor in both short-term and long-term adjustment is how effectively the custodial parent, who usually is the mother, functions as a parent. We have noted how difficult it can be for a recently separated mother to function well. The first year or two after the separation is a difficult time for many mothers, who may feel angry, depressed, irritable, or sad. Their own distress may make it more difficult to cope with their children's distress, leading in some cases to a disorganized household, lax supervision, inconsistent discipline, and the coercive cycles between mothers and preschool-aged sons that have been identified by Hetherington and others. Mothers who can cope better with the disruption can be more effective parents. They can keep their work and home lives going from day-to-day and can better provide love, nurturing, consistent discipline, and a predictable routine.

Quite often their distress is rooted in, or at least intensified by, financial problems. Loss of the father's income can cause a disruptive, downward spiral in which children must adjust to a declining standard of living, a mother who is less psychologically available and is home less often, an apartment in an unfamiliar neighbourhood, a different school, and new friends. This sequence of events occurs at a time when children are greatly upset about the separation and need love, support, and a familiar daily routine.

A second key factor in children's well-being is a low level of conflict between their mother and father. This principle applies, in fact, to intact as well as disrupted families. Recall the finding from the NSC that children who live with two parents who persistently quarrel over important areas of family life show higher levels of distress and behaviour problems than do children from disrupted marriages. Some observers take this finding to imply that children are better off if their parents divorce than if they remain in an unhappy marriage. We think this is true in some cases but not in others. It is probably true that most children who live in a household filled with continual conflict between angry, embittered spouses would be better off if their parents split up—assuming that the level of conflict is lowered by the separation. And there is no doubt that the rise in divorce has liberated some children (and their custodial parents) from families marked by physical abuse, alcoholism, drugs, and violence. But we doubt that such clearly pathological descriptions apply to most families that disrupt. Rather, we think there are many more cases in which there is little open conflict, but one or both partners finds the marriage personally unsatisfying. The unhappy partner may feel unfulfilled, distant from his or her spouse, bored, or constrained. Under these circumstances, the family may limp along from day-to-day without much holding it together or pulling it apart. A generation ago, when marriage was thought of as a moral and social obligation, most husbands and wives in families such as this stayed together. Today, when marriage is thought of increasingly as a means of achieving personal fulfillment, many more will divorce. Under these circumstances, divorce may well make one or both spouses happier; but we strongly doubt that it improves the psychological well-being of the children.

A possible third key factor in children's successful adjustment is the maintenance of a continuing relationship with the non-custodial parent, who is usually the father. But direct evidence that lack of contact with the father inhibits the adjustment of children to divorce is less than satisfactory. A number of experts have stressed the importance of a continuing relationship, yet research findings are inconsistent. The main evidence comes from both the Hetherington and Wallerstein studies, each of which found that children were better adjusted when they saw their fathers regularly. More recently, however, other observational studies have not found this relationship.

And in the NSC, the amount of contact that children had with their fathers seemed to make little difference for their well-being. Teenagers who saw their fathers regularly were just as likely as were those with infrequent contact to have problems in school or engage in delinquent acts and precocious sexual behaviour. Furthermore, the children's behavioural adjustment was also unrelated to the level of intimacy and identification with the non-residential father. No differences were observed even among the children who had both regular contact and close relations with their father outside the home. Moreover, when the children in the NSC were re-interviewed in 1987 at ages 18 to 23, those who had retained stable, close ties to their fathers were neither more nor less successful than those who had had low or inconsistent levels of contact and intimacy with their fathers.

Another common argument is that fathers who maintain regular contact with their children also may keep paying child support to their children's mothers. Studies do show that fathers who visit more regularly pay more in child support. But it's not clear that they pay more because they visit more. Rather, it may be that fathers who have a greater commitment to their children both visit and pay more. If so, then the problem is to increase the level of commitment most fathers feel, not simply to increase the amount of visiting.

These puzzling findings make us cautious about drawing any firm conclusions about the psychological benefits of contact with non-custodial parents for children's adjustment in later life. Yet despite the mixed evidence, the idea that continuing contact with fathers makes a difference to a child's psychological well-being is so plausible and so seemingly grounded in theories of child development that one is reluctant to discount it. It may be that evidence is difficult to obtain because so few fathers living outside the home are intimately involved in child rearing. It is also likely that, even when fathers remain involved, most formerly married parents have difficulty establishing a collaborative style of child rearing. We remain convinced that when parents are able to co-operate in child rearing after a divorce and when fathers are able to maintain an active and supportive role, children will be better off in the long run. But we are certain that such families are rare at present and unlikely to become common in the near future.

Does Custody Make a Difference for Children?

The belief that the father's involvement is beneficial to children was an important reason why many states recently adopted joint-custody statutes. Supporters argued that children adjust better when they maintain a continuing relationship with both parents. They also argued that fathers would be more likely to meet child-support obligations if they retained responsibility for the children's upbringing. Were they correct? Joint custody is so recent that no definitive evidence exists. But the information to date is disappointing.

Joint legal custody seems to be hardly distinguishable in practice from maternal sole custody. A recent study of court records in Wisconsin showed no difference in child-support payments in joint-legal-custody versus mother-sole-custody families, once income and other factors were taken into account. The Stanford study found little difference, three and one-half years after separation, between joint-legal-custody (but not joint-physical-custody) families and mother-sole-custody families. Once income and education were taken into account, fathers who had joint legal custody were no more likely to comply with court-ordered child-support awards than were fathers whose former wives had sole legal and physical custody. They did not visit their children more often; they did not co-operate and communicate more with their former wives; and they didn't even participate more in decisions about the children's lives. The investigators concluded that joint legal custody 'appears to mean very little in practice'.

The handful of other small-scale studies of joint legal custody show modest effects, at most. It appears that joint legal custody does not substantially increase the father's decision-making authority, his involvement in child rearing, or the amount of child support he pays. Why is it so hard to increase fathers' involvement after divorce? For one thing . . . many men don't seem to know how to relate to their children except through their wives. Typically, when married, they were present but passive—not much involved in child rearing. When they separate, they carry this pattern of limited involvement with them; and it is reinforced by the modest contact most have with their children. Uncomfortable and unskilled at being an active parent, marginalized by infrequent contact, focused on building a new family life, many fathers fade from their children's lives.

Less is known about joint physical custody. But a few recent studies suggest that it isn't necessarily better for children's adjustment than the alternatives. Among all families in the Stanford study in which children still were seeing both parents about two years after the separation, parents in dual-residence families talked and coordinated rules more; but they quarrelled about the children just as much as did parents in single-residence families. Several colleagues of Wallerstein followed 58 mother-physical-custody families and 35 joint-physical-custody families for two years after the families had been referred to counselling centres in the San Francisco area. Many of the parents were disputing custody and visitation arrangements. Children from the joint-physical-custody families were no better adjusted than children from the mother-physical-custody families: their levels of behavioural problems, their self-esteem, their ease at making friends were very similar. What did make a difference for the children was the depression and anxiety levels of their parents and the amount of continuing verbal and physical aggression between them, regardless of the custody arrangement. The authors suggest that children whose parents are having serious disputes may have more behaviour problems, lower self-esteem, and less acceptance by friends if they shuttle between homes. They are exposed to more conflict, and their movement back and forth may even generate it.

The admittedly limited evidence so far suggests to us that custody arrangements may matter less for the well-being of children than had been thought. It is, of course, possible that when more evidence is available, joint custody will be shown to have important benefits from some families. As with father involvement, the rationale for joint custody is so plausible and attractive that one is tempted to disregard the disappointing evidence and support it anyway. But based on what is known now, we think custody and visitation matters less for children than the two factors we noted earlier: how much conflict there is between the parents and how effectively the parent (or parents) the child lives with functions. It is likely that a child who alternates between the homes of a distraught mother and an angry father will be more troubled than a child who lives with a mother who is coping well and who once a fortnight sees a father who has disengaged from his family. Even the frequency of visits with a father seems to matter less than the climate in which they take place.

For now, we would draw two conclusions. First, joint physical custody should be encouraged only in cases where both parents voluntarily agree to it. Among families in which both parents shared the child rearing while they were married, a voluntary agreement to maintain joint physical custody probably will work and benefit the children. Even among families in which one parent did most of the child rearing prior to the divorce, a voluntary agreement won't do any harm—although we think the agreement likely will break down to sole physical custody over time. But only very rarely should joint physical custody be imposed if one or both parents do not want it. There may be a few cases in which the father and mother truly shared the child rearing before the divorce but one of them won't agree to share physical custody afterward. These difficult cases call for mediation or counselling, and they may require special consideration. But among the vastly larger number of families in which little sharing occurred beforehand and one or both parents doesn't want to share physical custody afterward, imposing joint physical custody would invite continuing conflict without any clear benefits. Even joint legal custody may matter more as a symbol of fathers' ties to their children than in any concrete sense. But symbols can be important, and joint legal custody seems, at worst, to do no harm. A legal preference for it may send a message to fathers that society respects their rights and responsibilities for their children.

Our second conclusion is that in weighing alternative public policies concerning divorce, the thin empirical evidence of the benefits of joint custody and frequent visits with fathers must be acknowledged. All of the findings in this chapter have implications for the way in which we as a society confront the effects of divorce on children. A question to examine later is: Which public policies should have priority? What outcomes are the most important for society to encourage and support? In some cases, such as the economic slide of mothers and children, the problem is clear, and alternative remedies readily come to mind. In other cases, the problems are complex and the remedies unclear . . .

. . . [H]owever, we must note that a divorce does not necessarily mark the end of change in the family lives of children. A majority will see a new partner move into their home. A remarriage, or even a cohabiting relationship, brings with it the potential both to improve children's lives and to complicate further their adjustment.

Chapter 33

The social policies that are clearly needed to support families seem to have only a faint hope of becoming reality here. When social policies in Canada are compared to those that are common in Europe, however, it is clear that our stingy support of families is unusual. This chapter provides a comparison of Canadian and European policies. Written years ago, the details are dated, but the comparison is sufficient to make clear the differences in policy directions between Canada and many other countries.

Lessons from Europe: Policy Options to Enhance the Economic Security of Canadian Families

Shelley A. Phipps

As Canadians, we are used to thinking of ourselves as having social policies that are kinder and gentler than those of our neighbours in the United States. While this is partly true, it is essential for Canadians to realize that to European social policy experts, the similarities between Canada and the United States far outweigh the differences (Ringen 1987; Esping-Andersen 1990). European countries have policies that are very different from Canada's. More importantly, despite many similar macroeconomic and social trends, European policies have helped prevent the high levels of insecurity currently faced by many Canadian families. Hence, it makes sense to see what we might learn from the Europeans.

To explore new options for increasing the economic security of Canadian families with children, particularly young children, this chapter focuses on France, Germany, Finland, and Sweden. In all cases, these European countries offer more generous programs to assist families than we do, but the structure of available programs differs across the countries, providing a range of alternatives for Canadians to consider.

Policies in Sweden and Finland, two countries with social democratic histories, are most similar to one another. Programs in Germany and France look rather different. For example, German policy has been shaped by a strong belief that children are better off when cared for at home by their mothers until at least the age of three years. Swedish policy, on the other hand, has encouraged the labour-force participation of mothers in an attempt to achieve equality between men and women, both in the home and in the marketplace.

In general terms, however, the European countries have more in common with each other than with Canada, since the goals that have guided the development of social policy in the European countries have been quite different from our own. For example, pro-natalism was one important reason for the creation of the generous child allowances still available in each of the European countries studied. Increasing the birth rate has not been such an important goal in Canada except in Quebec, where family policy has also responded to this concern with, for example, sizable birth allowances ($8,000) for third and subsequent children. All of the European countries studied regard children as a major societal resource and hence a public as well as a private responsibility (Kamerman 1980), while Canadian policy generally reflects the attitude that, except as a last resort, children are the private responsibility of their parents. Canadian policy-makers worry about interfering with market outcomes; this has not been as important a consideration in the European countries.

Does it make any sense for Canadians to think about adopting policies developed elsewhere to meet possibly different goals? Yes. Regardless of why a policy idea appeared in the first place (e.g., to increase birth rates), if it seems likely to solve a problem we currently face (e.g., child poverty), we should consider using it, realizing, of course, that modifications may be required to use European ideas in the context of Canadian goals and institutions.

Socio-economic Change in Canada and Europe

The availability of more extensive programs for families is an important explanation for the fact that, despite quite similar underlying socio-economic trends, European families have avoided some of the problems Canadian families now face (Kamerman and Kahn 1988; Smeeding 1991; Jäntti and Danziger 1992; Wong et al. 1992). For example, rates of divorce or separation are high and single-parent families are increasingly common in all the countries, but extreme poverty among single-parent families is a Canadian and not a European phenomenon. Average family sizes have fallen and rates of labour-force participation for mothers have increased in all countries, but the Europeans offer more policies to help ease the strain of meeting both home and workplace responsibilities. Unemployment rates are high and the job market for young people has deteriorated in all the countries, but poverty among families with children is far worse in Canada. These important socio-economic patterns are outlined in more detail below.

First, Canada, Germany, and Sweden have almost identical and rather high divorce rates (Table 33.1); 44 per cent of marriages ended in divorce over the 1987 to 1990 period. Divorce rates are somewhat lower in Finland (38 per cent) and France (31 per cent). High rates of divorce can increase the economic vulnerability of women (if they had reasonable access to their husbands' incomes during marriage), since in all the countries studied, women have lower incomes than men. Canadian evidence indicates that men's standards of living typically rise by 30 per cent after separation (for the median non-custodial father who has not remarried). On the other hand, women's standards of living typically fall to 52 per cent of the pre-divorce level (for custodial mothers who have not remarried) (Finnie et al. 1994). Of course, these figures assume that husbands and wives had equal standards of living while married, which is not always the case.

In all the countries, divorce and separation are the main routes to single parenthood (Lefaucheur and Martin 1993; Kahn and Kamerman 1994). In both Canada and Sweden, 18 per cent of all families with children are single-parent families; in Finland, 15 per cent of all families with children are single-parent families; in France (where divorce rates are lower) and Germany, only 9 per cent and 7 per cent of families with children are single-parent families (Table 33.1). Because Germany still puts a heavy emphasis on preserving the traditional family, divorces are less likely for couples with children, and births outside marriage are much less common than in other countries (Kahn and Kamerman 1994). In all cases, however, there has been significant growth in the number of single-parent families in recent years.

All countries studied have experienced a significant decline in fertility rates between 1960 and 1991. However, the drop in fertility over this period is most extreme in Canada, where 1960 marked the end of the post-war baby boom. The ratio of the 1991 fertility rate to the 1960 fertility rate is about 50 per cent in Canada; about 65 per cent in Finland, France, and Germany; and about

Table 33.1 Demographic Indicators: Canada vs. Selected European Countries

	Canada	Finland	France	Germany	Sweden
Divorces (as % of marriages contracted 1987–90)[a]	43	38	31	44	44
Single-parent families (as % of all families with children)[b]	18	15	9	7	18
Ratio (%) of 1991 fertility rate to 1960 fertility rate[a]	47	66	65	62	89
Crude live-birth rates[c]	15.2	13.1	13.3	10.4	14.4

Sources: [a]United Nations Development Program, *Human Development Report* (Oxford: University Press, 1993); [b]Luxembourg Income Study; [c]United Nations, *Demographic Yearbook (1992)* (New York: United Nations, 1994).

90 per cent in Sweden. As of 1991, fertility rates were very similar in Canada and Sweden, slightly lower in Finland and France and significantly lower in Germany.

Smaller families have gone hand in hand with a second socio-economic pattern: increases in female labour-force participation rates in all countries (Table 33.2). Canada has experienced the sharpest increase of all countries studied. The ratio of 1990 female labour-force participation to 1960 labour-force participation is 2.4 in Canada, 1.9 in Sweden, 1.6 in France, and 1.3 in Finland and Germany. Labour-force participation is currently higher for Canadian women (69 per cent) than for women in France and Germany (58 per cent and 56 per cent, respectively). However, despite the rapid changes observed in Canada, current levels of female labour-force participation remain slightly lower than in Finland (73 per cent) and significantly lower than in Sweden (84 per cent). Swedish and Finnish women have a strong history of labour-force participation from which we can learn. It is also worth noting that nearly 40 per cent of Swedish women who are in the labour force work part-time, whereas in Canada 24 per cent work part-time (Nordic Council 1994: 3). In part, this difference is a result of policies that help women in Sweden combine paid work and child rearing (discussed later in this chapter).

Canada and the European countries can also be compared in terms of the percentage of mothers (married and single) with positive earnings.[1] In Sweden, 92 per cent of married mothers have paid employment; in Finland, 86 per cent; in Canada, 75 per cent; and in France and Germany, only 52 per cent and 41 per cent, respectively. In Germany, it is regarded as extremely important that a mother remain at home, particularly if she has children less than three years old. Percentages for single mothers with positive earnings are similar: 93 per cent in Sweden, 87 per cent in Finland, 75 per cent in France, 58 per cent in Canada, and 50 per cent in Germany. From the Canadian perspective, where much attention has recently focused on encouraging the labour-force participation of single mothers, it is interesting to note that single mothers are more likely than married mothers to have paid employment in all of the European countries, but less likely to have paid employment in Canada.

Table 33.2 Female Labour-force Participation: Canada vs. Selected European Countries

	Canada	Finland	France	Germany	Sweden
Female labour-force participation rate (%) 1990[a]	69.0	72.9	57.7	55.9	83.5
Ratio of 1990 female labour-force participation rate to 1960[a]	2.4	1.3	1.6	1.3	1.9
Married mothers with positive earnings (%)[b]	75	86	52	41	92
Single mothers with positive earnings (%)[b]	58	87	75	50	93
Female wages as a % of male wages (1990–91)[a]	63	77	88	74	89

Sources: [a]United Nations Development Program, *Human Development Report* (Oxford: University Press, 1993); [b]Luxembourg Income Study.

These trends in labour-force participation mean that, except in Germany, a majority of families do not have a 'stay-at-home mom' to take care of home and childcare responsibilities. Yet these responsibilities continue when mothers enter the labour force. For families without sufficient income to pay for help, the strain involved in balancing work and family is potentially significant. (Even when families have resources to pay for domestic help, there is still significant effort involved in coordination and in dealing with crises such as sickness.) Further, international evidence (Mikkola 1991; Wallace and Myles 1994) indicates that women still bear the greater share of family responsibilities even if they are full-time participants in the labour market. Thus, the strain of the double workday is felt by many women.

In addition, women earn less relative to men in Canada than in the European countries (Table 33.2). Female wages are 63 per cent of male wages in Canada, 89 per cent in Sweden, 88 per cent in France, 77 per cent in Finland, and 74 per cent in Germany. Thus, the potential vulnerability of families who rely on women's earnings is greatest in Canada. This includes families in which the husband's earnings are insufficient as well as families in which there is no man present.

A third socio-economic pattern and a serious problem in all countries is unemployment (see Table 33.3). In 1994, unemployment in Canada (10.8 per cent) was roughly similar to unemployment in France (12.3 per cent) and Germany (10 per cent), lower than unemployment in Finland (18.5 per cent) and higher than unemployment in Sweden (7.6 per cent).

Youth unemployment rates are much higher than overall unemployment rates in all countries but Germany (where much-admired apprenticeship training programs for young people apparently ease school-to-work transitions). For anyone concerned with the economic security of

Table 33.3 Macroeconomic Indicators: Canada vs. Selected European Countries

	Canada	Finland	France	Germany	Sweden
Unemployment rate (%)					
Total (1983–91)[a]	9.5	5.0	9.7	7.3	2.1
Total (1994)[a]	10.8	18.5	12.3	10.0	7.6
Youth (15–24) unemployment rate/total unemployment rate (1992)[b]	1.6	1.8	1.9	1.2	2.4
Earnings per employee, annual growth rate (1980–89)[b]	0.1	2.7	2.0	1.8	0.9
GNP per capita, % annual growth rate (1980–91)[b]	2.0	2.5	1.8	2.2	1.7
Average annual rate of inflation (%) (1980–91)[b]	4.3	6.6	5.7	2.8	7.4
Overall budget deficit/surplus (1991)[b]	–2.7	0.1	–1.4	–2.5	0.7

Sources: [a]OECD, *Employment Outlook* (OECD, 1994); [b]United Nations Development Program, *Human Development Report* (Oxford: University Press, 1994).

families, the labour-market difficulties faced by young people must be recognized. Unemployment today increases the likelihood of economic difficulties tomorrow, as skills deteriorate and experience is not acquired. Furthermore, economic difficulties for young adults must eventually translate into increases in child poverty as families are formed by people in their twenties and early thirties. In 1992, 60 per cent of Canadian children living with at least one parent aged less than 24 were poor (Sharif and Phipps 1994).

Since 1975, at least 30 per cent of new jobs created in most Canadian provinces have been part-time. A growing number of jobs are short-term (lasting less than six months), and an increasing number of individuals are self-employed without any employees of their own. Finally, temporary-help work tripled in the 1980s. These 'non-standard' forms of employment, which are especially likely to be experienced by youth and women, constitute nearly 30 per cent of total employment in Canada (Economic Council of Canada 1990). Similar trends are observable in the European countries studied here (OECD 1991, 1994).

Poverty or income inequality is a fourth socio-economic pattern (Table 33.4). Here, Canada's performance is consistently the worst. In terms of income inequality, the richest 20 per cent of Canadian households (1986 to 1989) have 7.1 times the income of the poorest 20 per cent of households. In Sweden, on the other hand, the richest households have 4.6 times the income of the poorest, and in Germany the richest have 5.7 times the income of the poorest.

Table 33.4 Poverty and Inequality Indicators: Canada vs. Selected European Countries

	Canada	Finland	France	Germany	Sweden
Ratio of income of richest 20% of households to poorest 20% (1986–89)[a]	7.1	6.0	6.5	5.7	4.6
Incidence of poverty among all families with children (%)[b]	18	5	12	9	5
Incidence of poverty among single-parent families (%)[b]	45	11	20	32	9

Sources: [a]United Nations Development Program, *Human Development Report* (Oxford: University Press, 1994); [b]Luxembourg Income Study.

A more stable distribution of income reduces economic insecurity.

The incidence of poverty among families with children is also significantly higher in Canada than in any of the European countries studied. Eighteen per cent of all Canadian families with children are poor, whereas in Finland and Sweden, only 5 per cent of all families with children are poor. Germany and France had intermediate records with 9 per cent and 12 per cent of families with children considered poor, respectively.

Single-parent families in Canada are particularly at risk of being poor. Forty-five per cent of Canadian single-parent families are poor, while only 9 per cent of Swedish single-parent families and 11 per cent of Finnish single-parent families are poor.[2] There are just as many single-parent families in Finland and Sweden as in Canada, so it is not small numbers that are enabling these countries to keep single parents out of poverty. France and Germany have intermediate records with 20 per cent and 32 per cent of single-parent families poor.

Of course, the poverty that is evident among single-parent families may have been hidden in households before separation if resources were not shared equally among all family members (Phipps and Burton 1995; Pulkingham 1995). Since women and children receive much smaller incomes, they may be poor within some families if men do not share. For example, traditional measures of poverty, which implicitly assume that wives have equal access to their husbands' incomes, indicate that 9 per cent of husbands and wives were poor in Canada in 1992. If, on the other hand, we assume that women have only very limited access to their husbands' incomes, poverty among wives increases to 25 per cent while poverty among husbands drops to 4 per cent (Phipps and Burton 1995).

To summarize, many of the same socio-economic trends are apparent in Canada and the four European countries studied. In Canada, high rates of unemployment and deteriorating labour-market conditions, especially for young adults, have left a large number of families in poverty or near-poverty. Many more families face the risk of deprivation and even families fortunate enough to have secure employment face significant strain in their attempts to juggle home and workplace responsibilities. In Europe, the same trends have not always resulted in the same problems.

Cash Transfers for Children in Canada and Europe

In the European countries, there has been 'a long history of acknowledging that children are a major societal resource and that the whole society should share in the costs of rearing them' (Kamerman 1980: 24). Universal cash transfers providing social support for all children are thus regarded as the core of family policy in these countries. In contrast, the Canadian attitude has increasingly been that children are the private responsibility of their parents, requiring state support only in the case of serious deprivation; therefore, Canada aims child benefits toward lower-income families.

Program Comparisons

France

Family allowances first appeared in France at the end of the nineteenth century as wage supplements paid by employers to employees with children as a means of avoiding more general wage increases. During the 1930s, the idea that these benefits could be used for pro-natalist purposes appeared, and all employers were required to contribute to a fund which then distributed benefits to all employees with children. The present system of family allowance payments, which emerged just after the Second World War, is regarded as one of the most extensive and generous systems in the world (Kahn and Kamerman 1994).

The pro-natalist spirit of the French system is still in evidence, with benefits that are relatively much more generous for larger families. Family allowances in France consist of a large number of different cash transfers. However, a basic universal benefit for all families with two or more children less than 16 years of age is by far the most important, accounting for about half of total expenditures. All political parties now agree on the merits of extending this basic benefit to families with just one child, although this has not yet been done in an era of fiscal restraint.

Over the past 20 years a concern with aiming benefits toward the most needy families has emerged. A number of means-tested or categorical (or both) child allowances have been established. For example, there are special benefits for children in single-parent families, for handicapped children, and for very young children (Kahn and Kamerman 1994). All child allowances are funded through a 7 per cent payroll tax levied on employers or on the self-employed (USDHHS 1992); family allowance transfers are not taxable income (OECD 1993). There is also tax relief for families with children.

Germany

The goal of preserving the traditional family has been the dominant influence on family policy in Germany. German family allowances were established in 1955 as a form of wage supplement and were originally payable only to fathers with three or more children. For obvious reasons, pronatalism could not be an explicit policy goal so soon after the Second World War, but the benefits had an implicit pro-natalist design. Over time, coverage was extended and the value of the transfers increased (Kahn and Kamerman 1994). Currently, all families with children under 16 (or under 21 if unemployed, or 27 if full-time students or invalids) receive family allowance payments financed from general revenue. Payments per child increase for additional children. For example, families receive twice as much for the second as for the first child, 4.4 times as much for the third as for the first and 4.8 times as much for the fourth and each subsequent child (USDHHS 1992). High-income families receive the same benefit as lower-income families for the first child, but only 1.4 times as much for the second child and 2.8 times for the third and each subsequent child (Gauthier 1993). As in France, family allowances are not subject to income taxation (OECD 1993).

Fathers, when present, are still the recipients of family allowance payments in Germany, in keeping with a policy perspective favouring the traditional family. However, it is also clear that family allowances are intended to help with the costs of child rearing. German family allowances (and tax concessions for children) were recently (1991) increased following a federal court ruling that all parents have the right to benefits that ensure a basic standard of living for their children (Kahn and Kamerman 1994).

Finland

Family allowances in Finland emerged in 1943 from a pro-natalist agenda. More recently, however, Finnish policy has been characterized as devoted to universalistic principles (Kahn and Kamerman 1994). Family allowances are viewed as a means of providing social support for all families with children. Benefits, financed through general revenue, are universally available to all families with children less than 16 years old. The real value of family allowances in Finland in 1990 was about three times what it was in 1951 and about 30 per cent above the 1982–87 value (Mikkola 1991).[3] Per-child payments increase as the number of children in the family increases (USDHHS 1992). In 1993, a young-child supplement to the family allowance as well as tax concessions for children were eliminated as a result of budgetary pressures. To help compensate for these measures, the level of basic family allowances was increased (Kahn and Kamerman 1994). Family allowances are not subject to income tax (OECD 1993).

Sweden

As in the other European countries, early family allowances in Sweden were intended to increase birth rates. However, as in Finland, concern has shifted over time to broader goals of economic security and equality (OECD 1994). Swedish family allowances, financed through general revenue, are now universally available to families with children under 16 (or less than 20 if full-time students). Higher per-child benefits are received for third and subsequent children: for the third child, the benefit is worth 150 per cent of that for the first; for the fourth child, 200 per cent; for the fifth and subsequent children, 250 per cent. The increments for additional children were increased to current levels in 1989 (Sundstrom 1991). Child allowances are paid monthly and are not subject to income taxation (OECD 1993).

Canada

In Canada, we have recently abandoned universal transfers for all families with children—which were similar in design to many of the European benefits but much lower in value—in favour of child benefits available only for children in lower-income families. We have thus moved away from the European approach of acknowledging social responsibility for all children and toward the US approach of regarding children as the private responsibility of their parents, except when parents are unable to supply basic needs. Canadians have been persuaded that it is somehow wasteful to pay family allowances to higher-income families, although there has not been the same general concern, for example, over the larger benefit well-to-do families receive from the childcare expense deduction.

Currently, the Canadian child benefit system consists of a basic child tax benefit and an earned income supplement. While the basic benefit is $1,020 per child per year, it is 'taxed back' so that only low-income families actually receive the full amount; middle-income families receive smaller and smaller benefits as their incomes increase; higher-income families receive nothing. The earned income supplement is a wage subsidy with a maximum value of $500 paid to parents with low but positive earnings. The earned income supplement also becomes smaller

Table 33.5 Cash Transfers for Children: Canada vs. Selected European Countries

	Canada 1991	Canada 1993	Finland 1991	France 1984	Germany 1984	Sweden 1987
Level of benefits						
Average child benefits received by families with children/median country gross income (%)	3.0[a]	3.5[a]	8.1[b]	13.3[b]	4.2[b]	7.7[b]

Sources: [a]Canada 1992 and Luxembourg Income Study; [b]Luxembourg Income Study.

and smaller as incomes increase, and disappears entirely for families with net incomes over $25,921. There is no general tax relief for dependent children.

The current Canadian child benefit system thus differs significantly from those of the European countries. Most importantly, the Canadian system is not universal; only about 62 per cent of families with children receive cash transfer (assuming that the post-1993 system of child tax benefits and earned income supplements delivers benefits to about the same proportion of families as the pre-1993 refundable child tax credit). Also, because benefits are delivered through the tax system, a family's benefit entitlements is always established with a lag—a fall in income will eventually mean an increase in benefits, but not until several months after the next income tax form is filed.

Finally, the level of benefits provided in Canada is much lower than that offered in any other countries studied (see Table 33.5). Before 1993, Canadian family allowances and refundable child tax credits provided transfers to families with children which, on average, constituted 3 per cent of median gross family income.[4] Since 1993, the average value of child tax benefits and earned income supplements is estimated to constitute 3.5 per cent of median family income. In Germany, the average value of family allowances constitute 4.2 per cent of median gross income; in Sweden, 7.7 per cent; in Finland, 8.1 per cent; and in France, 13.3 per cent. Moreover, the countries chosen for analysis in this chapter are not the ones with the most generous child benefit systems. Norway, Australia, Belgium, and Luxembourg provide even more generous child allowances than France (Gauthier 1993).

Advantages of the European Approach to Child Benefits

The European child benefit systems offer at least three advantages relative to that of Canada.

First, universal family allowance systems require no calculations to establish eligibility. Cheques can simply be mailed each month to all families with children. Administratively, it is an extremely simple program design.

Second, each of the European family allowance programs is a more effective poverty alleviation tool than the Canadian system. Canadians are not used to thinking of universal family allowance payments as a potential poverty alleviation tool—perhaps because our benefit levels have always been so low. Yet it has been shown that the higher the average level of child benefits, the more successful a country is likely to be at preventing poverty among families with children (Phipps 1995). Of course, simple arithmetic says that a fixed pot of money spent entirely on the poor could go further toward alleviating child poverty than the same funds distributed equally to all families. However, the key question is, would the same total funds always be available if child benefits were received only by the poor, particularly if the poor seemed to be receiving quite generous transfers? It is quite possible, particularly during difficult economic times, that benefits would be cut as a result of concerns about deficits or about transfers interfering with work incentives. In other countries, generous child allowance payments have proven extremely popular and their real value has increased over time, while the real value of Canadian benefits has been allowed to fall. When the Thatcher government attempted to replace universal family allowances with a child benefit aimed toward low-income families, public pressure led to the abandonment of this plan, leaving universal benefits in place (Gauthier 1993). Such popularity ensures that low-income households continue to receive generous benefits.

Third, the universal nature of the European benefits provides better security for families with children in an era when parental income is increasingly insecure. Generous child benefit cheques received monthly by all families with children in the European countries provide an excellent means of helping families cope with sudden reductions in income through, for example, the loss of a job. On the other hand, lack of responsiveness to year-to-year changes in family incomes is a characteristic of the new Canadian system (Kesselman 1993). In Canada, eligibility for any child benefit is assessed based on the previous year's income tax returns. Adjustments necessary as a result of changes in income are made 1 July. If an individual loses his or her job on 1 January of 1995 and is without employment throughout the year, evidence of the drop in income will not be available until April of 1996. Child benefits will not be adjusted until July of 1996. Thus, the family will wait from 1 January 1995, until 1 July 1996, for the receipt of any benefits. And, as noted above, economic insecurity is a fact of life for many Canadian families with children, particularly when parents are young.[5]

As well, longitudinal data for the United States indicates that many more families fall into poverty within a year than are measured to be poor based on annual income (Ruggles and Roberton 1989). Relatively few of these families have sufficient income to carry them through even a relatively short spell of reduced income. Yet most bills (rent, groceries) must be paid at least monthly, causing considerable hardship to families with even temporarily low income. A child allowance received monthly—particularly if it is relatively generous—can thus be an extremely effective and administratively simple way of increasing the economic security of Canadian families with children.

Maternity or Parental Benefits in Canada and Europe

In Canada, maternity and parental benefits are conceived as labour-market programs—benefits to provide parents who have significant past labour-force attachment with time at home with their new children before they return to paid employment. Administration of maternity or parental benefits through the unemployment insurance program is unique and clearly illustrates the labour-market orientation of the Canadian system. In contrast, while all of the European countries offer benefits that are linked with past earnings, they also offer at least some benefits to new parents without recent histories of paid employment. Thus, European maternity or parental benefits offer some assistance to all new parents; Canadian maternity or parental benefits assist only some paid employees who are new parents, and then only if they will be returning to their jobs. In general, the European programs offer benefits to more people, at a higher level of compensation and for a longer period than we do in Canada.

Program Comparisons

France

In France, pro-natalism is again very evident in the design of maternity and parental benefits that are considerably more generous for third and subsequent children. Maternity benefits have been available in France since 1946. To qualify for cash benefits, a woman must have had at least 1,200 hours of paid employment in the year before the child's birth and she must prove that her insurance coverage by the social security system has been in place for 10 months by the date of delivery (David and Starzec 1991).[6] The duration of benefits varies with the number of children the mother already has. For the first two children, she is entitled to 16 weeks of paid leave (six prenatal and 10 postnatal) at a basic rate of 84 per cent of daily earnings, with both a ceiling and floor (USDHHS 1992). For third and subsequent children, the mother is allowed 26 weeks of paid leave (eight weeks prenatal and 18 postnatal) at the same rate (David and Starzec 1991). (Employers often top up benefits to 100 per cent of previous earnings.) Additionally, all women are entitled to an income-tested child allowance from the fourth month of pregnancy, and nursing mothers are provided with a monthly allowance or milk coupons for four months (USDHHS 1992).

A child-rearing leave entitles parents with a minimum of one year of paid employment before the birth or adoption of the child to an additional two-year leave following the maternity leave. The child-rearing leave may be taken by either the mother or the father. During this period, the parent's job is protected, and he or she is entitled to social benefits from the job.

Since 1985, parents of a third or subsequent child have been eligible to receive a child-rearing allowance while on child-rearing leave. Eligibility is contingent only on previous work history (the parent claiming it must have had paid employment for at least two of the 10 years preceding the birth or adoption of the child); there is no income test. Benefits are paid until the child's third birthday (David and Starzec 1991). For one year preceding the child's third birthday, the parent receiving the allowance can return to work part-time, retaining half the cash benefit. Only one parent may claim the benefit. The allowance was about $547 per month (in 1990 terms) in 1989, over half the guaranteed minimum wage (David and Starzec 1991).

Germany

In Germany, two major programs exist for new parents. The first is a program for labour-force participants; the second offers payments to any new parents who remain at home to care for their young children. Since the payments for stay-at-home parents would not be enough to support a single parent with no other sources of income, and since the recipients are not supposed to engage in paid labour, the payments are clearly intended to reinforce the traditional family.

In Germany, all women with 12 weeks of insurance, or continuous employment from the tenth to the fourth month preceding confinement (this includes unemployment beneficiaries and the insured self-employed), are eligible for 14 weeks of paid maternity leave (six weeks before and eight weeks after the birth). Paid employees receive 100 per cent of their net covered earnings (based on an average for the past three months). The standard benefit is a flat rate, but employers must top up the flat-rate benefit for higher-income employees. Maternity benefits are not taxable.

In keeping with the desire to support traditional husband-and-wife families with stay-at-home mothers, a new government-financed child-rearing benefit was introduced in 1986. This benefit is available at a flat rate of about $405 per month (1990) for six months and on a means-tested basis for an additional 18 months. (This was increased from 12 months in 1993.)

Over 97 per cent of eligible families take the child-rearing benefit for the full period. Sometimes called 'an honorarium for motherhood', the benefit is intended to enable families to care for infants and toddlers at home. Legally, the benefit can be taken by either the father or the mother, but in practice it is almost always taken by the mother unless the father is unemployed. Families are eligible for benefits regardless of past employment status, so about half of all claimants are stay-at-home mothers without recent labour-force attachment (Kahn and Kamerman 1994). A beneficiary may not have more than 29 hours paid employment per week while receiving child-rearing benefits.

German parents (either mothers or fathers) are also entitled to an annual allotment of five days per child (compensated with 100 per cent of salary) for the care of sick children. Also, breast-feeding mothers are entitled to work two hours less per day with full salary (CACSW 1986).

Finland

The Finnish maternity and parental benefit system provides the most choices for new parents. Every new mother, regardless of previous employment status, is eligible to receive maternity allowance, provided she has resided in Finland for the six months preceding confinement (Mikkola 1991). The duration of cash maternity allowances is 105 days, which may be taken any time from five weeks before the baby's birth to 9.5 months after the birth; a further 170 days of parent's allowance, compensated at the same rate, may be taken by either mother or father, although the mother must decline to take the benefit for the father to be eligible.[7] The total duration of maternity and parental benefits is thus about 46 weeks.

For women with paid employment in the period preceding the birth, the benefit paid is 80 per cent of previous wages, not subject to a ceiling, while women who have no previous work history can collect the minimum allowance of about $277 per month (1990) (Mikkola 1991). While there is no ceiling, the earnings replacement rate is gradually reduced to 30 per cent for individuals with annual taxable income over approximately $22,849 (1990) in 1991 (USDHHS 1992). Cash benefits are taxable.

Finland also offers child-rearing allowances together with job-protected parental leaves from the end of the maternity or parental benefits until the child is three years old. These may be taken by either parent. Basic compensation during this period is equal to the minimum benefits for parental leave, about $277 (1990) per month. The allowance increases if there are at least two other children under the age of seven at home. Parents may also choose to use child-rearing funds to pay for childcare in or out of their own homes. About 80 per cent of eligible families take the child-rearing leave for, on average, an additional 14 months beyond the first 46 weeks of maternity or parental benefits (Kahn and Kamerman 1994).

Finally, Finnish parents are entitled to 60 days of paid leave per year to care for a sick child at home (USDHHS 1992).

Sweden

In Sweden, parental benefits are designed to encourage the continued labour-force participation of new parents. Mothers or fathers are entitled to 12 months of benefits compensated at 90 per cent of previous earnings, to a ceiling of about $78 (1990) per day in 1991, plus an additional three months with a small, flat-rate benefit. These benefits are universally available, regardless of previous labour-market participation, as long as the parent is covered by the national health insurance. Multiple births qualify the parent for an incremental six months of benefits for each additional child (Sundstrom 1991). Finally, and quite separately, parents are entitled to unpaid childcare leave until the child is 18 months. Since the paid leave may be taken at any time before the child reaches eight years, it is possible to arrange many different combinations of paid and unpaid leave, offering new parents a great deal of flexibility in their approaches to work and family life.

Parents are also entitled to paid temporary leave for the care of sick children (up to 10 years of age) of up to 60 days per child per year, compensated at 90 per cent of foregone earnings. Until the child is eight years, employers must grant parents the right to a six-hour workday with pro-rated pay (Gauthier 1993; Kahn and Kamerman 1994).

Canada

In Canada, maternity and parental benefits are available to some workers through the employment insurance system, although it is more difficult to qualify for maternity or parental benefits than for regular employment insurance (EI), and the maximum benefit period is shorter. To qualify for maternity or parental benefits, individuals must have 20 weeks of insurable earnings (with at least 15 hours per week or at least $121 of earnings per week in 1989). Successful claimants are then eligible for 15 weeks of maternity benefits compensated at 55 per cent to 60 per cent of previous earnings to a ceiling of $429 per week (1994). Parental benefits, which may be taken by either mothers or fathers, are available for a further 10 weeks on the same terms. Maternity and parental benefits are taxable income. Canada does not offer child-rearing benefits, a general program of paid leave for the care of sick children, or any special provisions for nursing mothers.

Advantages of the European Approach to Maternity and Parental Benefits

Reduced strain for two-earner and single-parent families

A first major advantage of all the European maternity and parental benefit systems is that they are better designed to reduce the strain that a growing number of Canadian families (both two-earner and single-parent) face—the strain of combining work outside the home with parenting responsibilities.

France and Germany offer basic paid maternity leaves that are comparable with the Canadian system, but also offer extended child-rearing leaves that allow new parents (either mother or father) the option of a longer period of time at home with new children without giving up jobs previously held. In Germany, this leave is paid. In France, the leave is paid only for third and subsequent children. French child-rearing leaves are contingent on past labour-force attachment. In Germany, on the other hand, child-rearing benefits are available to all families, regardless of past labour-force status. However, parents in receipt of child-rearing benefits can work no more than 19 hours per week and can only work at the job previously held. Thus, during the period of potential leave, a German parent is effectively forced to choose between paid employment and parenting; traditional gender roles are hence reinforced.

The Finnish system provides parents with more flexibility. The basic Finnish maternity or parental benefits are available, regardless of past labour-force status, for about double the potential duration of benefits in Canada; in addition, paid child-rearing leave is available until the child is three. Parents who choose to return to paid employment before the child is three have the option of working only six-hour days, retaining 25 per cent of the child-rearing allowance as partial compensation for the associated income loss; alternatively, the child-rearing allowance can be used to help pay for childcare for parents returning full-time to paid employment. Parents can thus choose the combination that best meets their needs.

In Sweden, new parents are encouraged to participate in the paid labour force; child-rearing leaves are not available. However, basic parental benefits are extremely flexible. A new parent can take an initial full-time leave, followed by part-time paid leave and part-time paid employment, in almost any combination. The intent is to support new parents in combining parenting and paid employment.

Finland, Sweden, and Germany also provide paid leave for the care of sick children, a reality that causes many Canadian parents logistical nightmares. Germany also recognizes the right of a new mother to paid time off for nursing.

The key point of all such policies is the recognition both that a growing majority of families now combine parenting and paid employment, and that without help from facilitative policies, enormous strains are created. Typically, these strains are disproportionately borne by mothers, since in all countries studied, traditional gender roles prevail despite the growth in female labour-force participation. In Germany, only 1.3 per cent of child-rearing leaves are taken by men, most of whom would otherwise be unemployed (Schiersmann 1991). In Finland, fathers took only 2 per cent of all parental-leave days (Mikkola 1991).

Longer paid leaves provide new parents with the option of spending more time with infants during their first years of life. Not only does this make life easier for sleep-deprived new parents but it may have important consequences for parent–child interactions. As one example, mothers breast-feed longer in the European countries than in Canada—an average of 8.5 months in Sweden (Waldenstrom and Nilsson 1994) compared to 4.3 months in Canada (Greene-Finestone et al. 1989).

Higher rates of compensation, especially for basic maternity or parental leaves, help European families cope with the financial strain of adding a new member to the family. Also, more families are covered. In Canada, relatively stringent eligibility conditions must be satisfied, resulting in the exclusion of, for example, the self-employed, workers with low weekly hours or earnings and workers with fewer than 20 weeks of work in the previous year. Given poor conditions in the labour market, particularly for young adults in their family formation years, significant numbers of new parents are excluded from benefits.

Increased equality between men and women in the paid labour market and increased economic security for women

The idea of parental rather than maternity leave is that by offering fathers the opportunity to stay home to care for their children, traditional gender roles will begin to erode, allowing both mothers and fathers to combine childcare and paid employment. However, as noted above, the reality everywhere still seems to be that mothers take the leaves. Thus, the real gender-equity advantage of the extensive child-related leaves, particularly in the Scandinavian states, seems to be that these policies make it easier for women to combine home and workplace responsibilities. More continuous labour-force participation contributes to increased job-related skills and experience with the likely outcome of higher wages. This may be one important reason why gender-earnings ratios are more favourable for women in the European countries than in Canada (see Table 33.2).

Better labour-market outcomes for women also have the distinct advantage that women are better able to support themselves financially in the increasingly likely event of divorce or separation. This helps to reduce the economic vulnerability of women both following a separation and within a marriage. A growing body of evidence indicates that women's power within marriage increases as their earned-income contributions increase (Phipps and Burton 1992). It is also true that women may be less likely to remain in a bad relationship if there is no economic need.

Furthermore, these facilitative policies offer an enormous advantage to single mothers, who must cope alone with both home and workplace responsibilities. The results in Europe seem very positive—rates of labour-force participation for European single mothers are high, especially in the Scandinavian countries where policies are most facilitative (see Table 33.2).

Advance Maintenance Payments

In each of the European countries studied, the state guarantees maintenance for the child by providing a cash transfer in cases where an absent parent does not pay child support, pays only infrequently, or does not pay enough. Like the European countries, Canada has a growing population of single-parent families. Unlike the European countries, single-parent families in Canada are extremely insecure. A study of the significant differences in outcomes for single parents in Europe versus Canada suggests one extremely important new policy option—advance maintenance payments.

While shockingly little information about the receipt of child support is available for Canada, a Department of Justice study indicated that 68 per cent of divorces involving children received court orders for child support. Of these, only two-thirds of non-custodial parents made payments regularly during the first year, and compliance is known to fall as time passes (Finnie et al. 1994). In Canada, some attention has recently been given to the design of enforcement mechanisms to ensure that non-custodial parents (typically fathers) pay. All provinces and territories now have automated, government-run enforcement programs, and the federal government contributes by garnisheeing funds such as income tax refunds and unemployment insurance when support payments are not being made. Guidelines for child support wards have also recently been recommended (Department of Justice 1995).

Despite these efforts, it is still true that if a non-custodial parent chooses not to contribute to the maintenance of his (or her) children or is unable to pay, the child suffers the consequences. Current child support policy thus treats children as the private responsibility of the parents. On the other hand, we offer disabled contributors' child benefits and orphans' benefits to the unmarried children of Canada Pension Plan contributors who become disabled or die. The availability of month benefits of $154 (1992) per child provides some insurance for children against the risk of income loss resulting from the death or incapacitation of a parent (Hess 1992). In effect, society shares in costs which would otherwise be borne exclusively by the child. The idea of advance maintenance payments is similar, providing children with some insurance against loss of income following the divorce, separation, or non-marriage of their parents. Such programs have been available in European countries for many years.

Program Comparisons

France

Family support allowances have been available in France since 1970 for children with a parent who is not meeting child-support obligations. The amount paid is about $87 (1990) per child.

Germany

In Germany, a limited system of tax-free advance maintenance payments has been available since 1980. These benefits are available only to single parents who do not receive support payments required by court order. Moreover, they are provided for a maximum of only three years or until the child reaches age six. The maximum payment is $158 (1989) per month. Thus payments are at a much lower level than those available, for example, in Sweden, and receipt of the child-support benefit results in a 50 per cent reduction in family allowance payments (Schiersmann 1991).

Sweden

The Swedish advance maintenance system is the oldest and most developed. Established in 1964, the basis for this system is the belief that children should not be penalized for an absent parent's inability or unwillingness to pay support (Kamerman and Kahn 1983). In 1990, advance maintenance payments were cash benefits equal to about $284 (1990) per month per child less than 18, tax free (Sundstrom 1991). The intent is that the cost of the advance should be recovered from the absent parent. In 1983, it was estimated that about 38 per cent of expenditures were recovered in this way (Kamerman and Kahn 1983). The effect of this comprehensive system of advance maintenance payments on the incomes of single mothers is striking—100 per cent of Swedish single mothers received child support (either directly from the non-custodial parent or from the state) (Phipps 1993). Maintenance payments are as important a source of income for Swedish single parents not in the labour force as social assistance (Kamerman 1984).

Finland

A similar program is available in Finland, where the monthly allowance in 1990 was $103 per month. Single parents who receive less than this amount in child support from absent parents (perhaps because of the non-custodial parent's inability to pay) receive a partial benefit from the state to bring them up to the state-guaranteed monthly level (Mikkola 1991). These child support payments are not income-tested and are not taxable.

Canada

The fact that we do not provide any publicly supported advance maintenance payments is another example of how Canadian policy tends to regard children as private rather than public responsibility. If the non-custodial parent is unable or unwilling to pay, the child suffers the consequences. With an advance maintenance system in place, the rest of society would share this burden.

How would advance maintenance payments work? One scenario is as follows:

- Child support payments would be set according to recommended guidelines and collected from the non-resident parent's income, just as income taxes are withheld or EI premiums are collected.
- The government would guarantee minimum child support payments for all children, regardless of the income of the custodial parent, financed through general revenue.[8]

The government would pay nothing in cases where support payments above the legislated minimum are received. But, just as any child is eligible for orphan benefits, any child not receiving sufficient child support would be eligible for the advance maintenance benefits, whether his or her mother is rich or poor (i.e., advance maintenance payments are not intended to be another form of social assistance). In practice, children with higher-income custodial mothers are more likely to be receiving child support because higher-income women are more likely to have been married to higher-income men who can subsequently afford to pay (Garfinkel 1994).

Summary Discussion

The discussion of socio-economic indicators for Canada at the start of this chapter indicated several sources of economic insecurity or strain for Canadian families: (1) an increasing number of two-earner and single-parent families who do not have a stay-at-home mother to cope with the inevitable day-to-day responsibilities of child- and home care (e.g., a sick child); (2) high rates of unemployment and growing 'non-standard' employment, particularly for younger Canadians, so that fewer families can rely on a continuous inflow of earnings; and (3) extremely high levels of economic vulnerability for a growing population of single-mother families.

Many of the same social trends are evident in Europe, but the associated negative outcomes are not always present (e.g., single-parent families are not particularly poor in the European countries). One very important reason for differences in outcomes between Canada and Europe is that the European countries offer more extensive and generous policies for families. Thus, when we look for solutions to our problems, Canadians can learn much from the Europeans.

Of course, there are differences that might make simply importing policies from one country to another difficult. For example, Canada is more heterogeneous in terms of geography, language, and ethnicity than the European countries studied. As well, the constitutional division of responsibilities between the federal and provincial governments seems to have made it more difficult to implement new social policies in Canada than in the other countries here.[9]

Obviously, the space constraints of a single chapter limit discussion to only a few policy areas. This chapter focuses on three European policies that are significantly different from those currently available in Canada, that would help to reduce economic insecurity for Canadian families and that seem most likely to have some hope of acceptance or adoption in Canada because they are reasonably consistent with some currently popular ideas about social policy in Canada. These popular ideas include (1) the belief that something should be done about high levels of child poverty; (2) the view that both fathers and mothers should try to enter the labour force to support themselves and their children; and (3) the concern that debts and deficits are out of control, and, hence, that we should not spend much more on almost anything. This chapter does not argue for or against these ideas, but merely suggests that they are not commonly held in Canada today. In the final analysis, we must be careful not to take currently popular ideas too seriously. One of the most important lessons to learn from international comparisons of policy is that our ideas are not the only ones possible—there really are different ways of thinking about social policy.

For each of the sources of vulnerability noted above, this review of European policies suggests at least one idea that could help and that we should seriously consider for adoption in Canada.

First, we should recognize the difficulties faced by a majority of Canadian families in balancing home and workplace responsibilities by offering more flexible maternity and parental leaves and benefits. This could remove an enormous burden of stress from Canadian families. For example, allowing parental leaves to be taken half-time (for twice as long) while parents returned to work half-time would not cost more but would increase the flexibility for families. Similarly, allowing parents even a small number of paid days off for the care of children each year would make life much easier for both two-earner and single-parent families without being extremely costly. Such changes are in the Swedish tradition of expecting labour-force participation of everyone. This seems more suited to current Canadian thinking than, say, a move to initiate a German-style child-rearing benefit to help support stay-at-home mothers. Child-rearing benefits would not be in keeping with the current Canadian emphasis on labour-force participation for all. Not only would more flexible maternity and parental leaves and sick days for children help families but they could also be expected to yield productivity gains that would help offset the costs as stress is removed from current employees and new workers are able to enter the labour market.[10]

In Sweden, Finland, and Germany, almost all new parents are eligible for some maternity, parental, or child-rearing benefits. Coverage in Canada is much narrower and shrinks as unemployment increases or non-standard employment grows. Since it is currently more difficult to qualify for maternity and parental benefits than to qualify for regular EI benefits, we should, as a first step, consider reducing entrance requirements to match those for regular EI benefits. This would extend coverage to many more new parents. As a second step, we should think about extending coverage to workers with low wages or low hours, perhaps with a flat-rate floor on benefits. This would provide maternity or parental benefits to the growing numbers of Canadians, particularly young people and women, who are in the labour force but who are unable to find 'good jobs'. While these changes in coverage would improve the economic security of many Canadian families, they would not involve major changes in the basic structure of existing programs. And, because EI is administered at the federal level, changes would be relatively easy to implement.

The maternity, parental, and child-rearing benefits available in the four European countries studied offer higher rates of compensation for a longer period of time than those available in Canada. Thus it would be desirable to increase expenditures on programs that are so potentially beneficial to both Canadian families and Canadian employers. Unfortunately, this might be a harder policy change to sell in the current Canadian policy environment. But if we do not expand benefits, we should at least be careful that we do not move even further away from international standards, if EI is downsized and maternity benefits, as part of the EI system, are reduced at the same time.

Second, the generous family allowances available in each of the European countries studied are central to their lower rates of child poverty. Thus, we should reinstate family allowances paid monthly to all families with children. Furthermore, the value of these allowances should be at least equal to the benefits currently received by low-income families. This would provide a reliable source of funds to help families with basic needs during periods of income shortfall and would be an important way of helping Canadian families face an increasingly insecure labour market. This is particularly true for young Canadian parents, many of whom are increasingly unlikely to be covered by EI.

Universal cash transfers for children are administratively simple, since no calculations of entitlement must be made. Universal cash transfers are also unlikely to discourage labour-force participation because no benefits are lost as earnings increase. Evidence from the European countries indicates that generous universal cash transfers for children are very effective in reducing child poverty. Thus, a return to universal family allowances would suit the Canadian social policy environment in many ways and, obviously, would be relatively easy to implement. The increased expenditures required to improve the generosity of family allowances might be opposed as too expensive, although obviously we can spend more on families and still be fiscally responsible if we are prepared to increase taxes or to make yet more cuts elsewhere.

Third, we should design a system of advance maintenance payments for single-parent families not receiving child support payments (or receiving only infrequent or inadequate payments). This system would help reduce the economic insecurity of single-mother families. With advance maintenance payments in place, we all share in the cost of non-payment by a defaulting non-custodial parent rather than forcing the child alone to pay.

It is important to note that many other family benefits are available in each of the European countries studied. For example, Finland, France, Sweden, and to a lesser extent Germany, offer much more comprehensive public childcare than we do in Canada. Housing allowances are also available in all four countries. While income-tested, these benefits are nonetheless received by 80 per cent of single-parent families and 30 per cent of two-parent families in Sweden (see Sundstrom 1991). There are also ideas from Europe that could help reduce the insecurity associated with high rates of unemployment in Canada. For example, all four European countries offer a second tier of unemployment insurance benefits to unemployed individuals without past labour-force attachment. These benefits are offered for an unlimited duration although at a lower level of compensation than the very generous basic UI benefits. (Second-tier UI benefits differ from social assistance in that individuals must be searching for work in order to qualify.) Such a program could be of particular benefit for Canadian youth.

Before concluding that any of these European policies should be considered for adoption in Canada, it is important to address the argument raised by critics of the European welfare states who claim that more generous programs necessarily mean a less efficient economy. Canada has the least generous welfare state of the countries studied here, so, by this argument, we should have the best economic performance. However, there is little evidence that this is true (see Table 33.3).[11] The average Canadian rate of unemployment for the period 1983 to 1991 was 9.5 per cent, while the equivalent for Finland was 5 per cent and for Sweden, 2.1 per cent. Canada has had the lowest growth in real earnings, although growth in GNP per capita is comparable with the other countries. Our inflation record is better than the group average, but our deficit position is worse. Similarly, Sweden and Finland offer the most generous social programs, and thus by the reasoning above should have the worst economic records. Again, this is not the case (Table 33.3). Historically, unemployment rates have been lower and inflation rates higher than in Canada. Growth of GNP per capita has been better in Finland and worse in Sweden compared to Canada. Earnings growth in both Finland and Sweden has been better than in Canada. Thus, it is not obvious from the historical data that less generous social programs—such as are available in Canada—mean better economic performance or that more generous social programs—such as are available in Sweden and Finland—lead to inferior economic records.

Critics of European welfare states have been delighted to hear of economic hardship in these countries in the last few years and have gleefully announced the 'death of the social democratic dream' (Klebnikov 1993). It is certainly true that economic conditions are currently extremely unfavourable in Finland and Sweden (see Table 33.3), but there is little evidence that welfare states are to blame. In Sweden, for example, an OECD report documents major expansion of the welfare state during the 1960s and 1970s followed by excellent economic performance with much lower rates of expenditure increases in the 1980s, which in turn was followed by poorer economic performance.[12] Other factors appear to have been more important than social programs in causing economic decline. For example, economic conditions in Finland took a dramatic turn for the worse following the breakup of the Soviet Union, which resulted in the sudden loss of 20 per cent of Finland's export market. Economic conditions deteriorated dramatically in Sweden after a major policy shift to deregulate financial markets. Unemployment rates for Germany increased significantly after reunification. (German data include East Germany from 1991 onward.)

Of particular interest is the fact that European family policies have remained basically untouched, despite very difficult times. In Finland, generous family allowances are a given, for all political parties (Kahn and Kamerman 1994). Similarly, in France, 'the likelihood that family policy will be spared cuts related to budgetary austerity is all the greater because of a broad political consensus on the principle of family protection' (David and Starzec 1991: 90).

The evidence so far is that no substantive cuts are being made to social welfare programs in the European countries studied here.[13] Apparently, people in these countries believe they can still afford generous social programs even though they are not as rich as we are in terms of per-capita income; indeed, most of these programs were introduced at a time when per-capita incomes were even lower than they are today. Can we afford more generous programs? The evidence says we can if we really want to. Perhaps, then, the most important thing to take from the Europeans is a vision of 'a society in which everyone is precious' (Kahn and Kamerman 1994) and social programs are a priority.

Conclusion

What can we learn from the Europeans about improving the economic security of Canadian families with children? Plenty. Although there are important differences across France, Germany, Finland, and Sweden, family policies in each of these countries reflect a tradition of acknowledging social responsibility for children; Canadian policies, like those in the United States, often reflect the attitude that children are the private responsibility of their parents. Policies offered in Europe are more extensive and generous, and outcomes for families in all cases look much better than outcomes in Canada. Finally, more generous welfare states have not led to economic disaster—our economic record is no better in Canada despite our rather cautious programs for families.

Notes

1. The term 'married' refers to both legal and common-law relationships.
2. Poverty estimates were obtained using microdata from the Luxembourg Income Study. For each country the most recent data available were used, but survey years differ across the countries. Data for Canada and Finland are from 1991; data for Sweden are from 1987; data for France and Germany are from 1984. To ensure consistency in poverty measurement across the countries, this chapter adopts the approach of defining a family as poor when gross income is less than 50 per cent of median gross income for the country. (All incomes are adjusted for differences in family needs using the equivalent scale recommended by the OECD, 1982.)
3. Finland also offers tax deductions for children worth about as much as the family allowances.
4. Since family allowances were subject to a clawback for high-income families and were counted as taxable income for the purposes of income tax, this overstates the level of benefits available in Canada at the time.
5. Of course, the current Canadian system could be made more responsive by income testing more often and reconciling benefits at tax time, but this would substantially increase administration costs.
6. Wives and daughters of insured persons can also be insured.
7. Multiple births qualify the parents for an additional 60 days of benefits (USDHHS 1992). Thus, total duration of benefits is 246 days for adoptions, 275 days for single births, and 335 days for multiple births.
8. Garfinkel recommends that advance maintenance be available only for children with court orders for child support (Garfinkel 1994). Eichler argues that all children be eligible (Eichler 1993).
9. While there are federal-state government disputes in Germany, they do not appear to be of the same magnitude as those in Canada, perhaps because Germany is geographically smaller and less economically and culturally diverse (Michelmann 1986).
10. A comprehensive childcare system would be an extremely important tool to facilitate labour-force participation by parents. I do not discuss this option here.
11. To avoid comparing performances in any given year when countries may be at different stages of

the business cycle, averages over a number of years for each indicator are reported in Table 33.3.

12. See OECD Economic Surveys (1994). Of course, it is true that deficits will increase when unemployment goes up in a country with generous transfer programs.

13. The only major change to transfer programs noted in the 1994 OECD report on Sweden was a reduction in the earnings replacement rate for social insurance programs to 80 per cent with the introduction of a one-day penalty without pay.

References

Canada. Canadian Advisory Council on the Status of Women (CACSW). 1986. *Report of the Task Force on Childcare* (Ottawa: Author).

———. Department of Justice. 1995. *Federal/Provincial/Territorial Family Law Committee's Report on Child Support* (Ottawa: Public Works and Government Services).

David, M.-G., and C. Starzec. 1991. 'France: A Diversity of Policy Options', in *Child Care, Parental Leave, and the Under 3s: Policy Innovation in Europe*, eds S.B. Kamerman and A.J. Kahn (Westport, CT: Auburn House).

Economic Council of Canada. 1990. *Good Jobs, Bad Jobs: Employment in the Service Economy* (Ottawa: Author).

Eichler, M. 1993. 'Lone Parent Families: An Instable Category in Search of Stable Policies', in *Single Parent Families: Perspectives on Research and Policy*, eds J. Hudson and B. Galaway (Toronto: Thomson Educational Publishing).

Esping-Andersen, G. 1990. *The Three Worlds of Welfare Capitalism* (Princeton, NJ: Princeton University Press).

Finnie, R., et al. 1994. *Child Support: The Guideline Options* (Montreal: Institute for Research on Public Policy).

Garfinkel, I. 1994. 'The Child-support Revolution', *American Economic Association Papers and Proceedings* 84, 2 (May): 81–5.

Gauthier, A.H. 1993. *Family Policies in the OECD Countries* (Oxford: University of Oxford, Department of Applied Social Studies and Social Research).

Greene-Finestone, L., et al. 1989. 'Infant Feeding Practices and Socio-demographic Factors in Ottawa–Carleton', *Canadian Journal of Public Health* 80, 3 (May/June): 173–6.

Hess, M. 1992. *The Canadian Fact Book on Income Security Programs* (Ottawa: Canadian Council on Social Development).

Jäntti, M., and S. Danziger. 1992. 'Does the Welfare State Work? Evidence on Antipoverty Effects from the Luxembourg Income Study', The Luxembourg Income Study, Working Paper 74.

Kahn, A.J., and S.B. Kamerman. 1994. *Social Policy and the Under 3s: Six Country Case Studies. A Resource for Policy Makers, Advocates and Scholars*, Cross-national Studies Research Program (New York: Columbia University School of Social Work).

Kamerman, S.B. 1980. 'Childcare and Family Benefits: Policies of Six Industrialized Countries', *Monthly Labour Review* 103, 11: 23–8.

———. 1984. 'Women, Children, and Poverty: Public Policies and Female-headed Families in Industrialized Countries', *Signs* 10, 2: 249–71.

———, and A.J. Kahn. 1983. 'Child Support: Some International Developments', in *The Parental Child-support Obligation*, ed. J. Cassety (Toronto: Lexington Books, D.C. Heath).

———. 1988. 'Social Policy and Children in the United States and Europe', in *The Vulnerable*, eds J.L. Palmer, T. Smeeding, and B.B. Zorrey (Washington: Urban Institute Press).

Kesselman, J.R. 1993. 'The Child Tax Benefit: Simple, Fair, Responsive?', *Canadian Public Policy* 19, 2: 109–32.

Klebnikov, P. 1993. 'The Swedish Disease', *Forbes* 151, 11: 78, 80.

Lefaucheur, N., and C. Martin. 1993. 'Lone Parent Families in France: Situation and Research', in

Single Parent Families: Perspectives on Research and Policy, eds J. Hudson and B. Galaway (Toronto: Thomson Educational Publishing).

Michelmann, H. 1986. 'Comparing Policy-making in Two Federations', in *Challenges to Federalism: Policy-making in Canada and the Federal Republic of Germany*, eds W. Chandler and C. Zollner (Kingston, ON: Institute of Intergovernmental Relations, Queen's University).

Mikkola, M. 1991. 'Finland: Supporting Parental Choice', in *Child Care, Parental Leave, and the Under 3s: Policy Innovation in Europe*, eds S.B. Kamerman and A.J. Kahn (Westport, CT: Auburn House).

Nordic Council. 1994. *Women and Men in the Nordic Countries: Facts and Figures 1994* (Copenhagen: Nordic Council of Ministers).

Organisation for Economic Co-operation and Development (OECD). 1991, 1994. *Employment Outlook* (Paris: Author).

———. 1993. *Taxation in OECD Countries* (Paris: Author).

———. 1994. *OECD Economic Surveys: Sweden* (Paris: Author).

Phipps, S.A. 1993. 'International Perspectives on Income Support for Families with Children', paper (Halifax: Department of Economics, Dalhousie University).

———. 1995. 'Taking Care of Our Children: Tax and Transfer Options for Canada', in *Family Matters: New Policies for Divorce, Lone Mothers, and Child Poverty*, eds J. Richards and W.G. Watson (Toronto: C.D. Howe Institute).

———, and P. Burton. 1992. 'What's Mine Is Yours? The Influence of Male and Female Incomes on Patterns of Household Expenditure', Discussion Paper 92-12 (Halifax: Department of Economics, Dalhousie University).

———. 1995. 'Sharing within Families: Implications for the Measurement of Poverty among Individuals in Canada', *Canadian Journal of Economics* 28, 1 (Feb.): 177–204.

Pulkingham, J. 1995. 'Investigating the Financial Circumstances of Separated and Divorced Parents: Implications for Family Law Reform', *Canadian Public Policy* 21, 1: 1–19.

Ringen, S. 1987. *The Possibility of Politics: A Study in the Political Economy of the Welfare State* (Oxford: Clarendon Press).

Ruggles, P., and W. Roberton. 1989. 'Longitudinal Measures of Poverty: Accounting for Income and Assets over Time', *Review of Income and Wealth* 35, 3: 225–82.

Schiersmann, C. 1991. 'Germany: Recognizing the Value of Child Rearing', in *Child Care, Parental Leave, and the Under 3s: Policy Innovation in Europe*, eds S.B. Kamerman and A.J. Kahn (Westport, CT: Auburn House).

Sharif, N., and S. Phipps. 1994. 'The Challenge of Child Poverty: Which Policies Might Help?', *Canadian Business Economics* 2, 3: 17–30.

Smeeding, T.M. 1991. 'US Poverty and Income Security Policy in a Cross National Perspective', The Luxembourg Income Study, Working Paper 70.

Sundstrom, M. 1991. 'Sweden: Supporting Work, Family and Gender Equality', in *Child Care, Parental Leave, and the Under 3s: Policy Innovation in Europe*, eds S.B. Kamerman and A.J. Kahn (Westport, CT: Auburn House).

United States Department of Health and Human Services (USDHHS). 1992. *Social Security Programs throughout the World—1991*, Social Security Administration Publication No. 61-006 (Washington: Author).

Waldenstrom, U., and C. Nilsson. 1994. 'No Effect of Birth Centre Care on Either Duration or Experience of Breastfeeding, but More Complications: Findings from a Randomised Controlled Trial', *Midwifery* 10, 1 (Mar.): 8–17.

Wallace, C., and J. Myles. 1994. *Relations of Ruling: Class and Gender in Postindustrial Societies* (Montreal: McGill-Queen's University Press).

Wong, Y.-L.I., et al. 1992. 'Single-mother Families in Eight Countries: Economic Status and Social Policy', The Luxembourg Income Study, Working Paper 76.

Index

Aboriginal peoples: in Malinowski's theory of family, 29–31; Montagnais-Naskapi family relations, 44–54; participation in labour force of, 455; and risk of intimate femicide, 530–2, 533, 537

abortion, 36, 129–30, 184, 219, 223; and pro-natalist policies, 14

Act to Secure to Married Women Certain Property Rights (1859), 87–8

adolescents/teenagers: and adoption, 23; and divorce, 544–5, 547, 549; and gender roles, 144; of immigrants, 485, 502; in modern England and France, 71; in nineteenth century, 127–8, 184; parenting in co-ops, 333–6; in post-war Canada, 138, 189; and sexuality, 11, 141, 149, 216; study of (girls), 220, 223–7, 232. *See also* boys; girls

adoption, 7, 23–4, 265, 311, 313, 461, 562; and 'putting out' children, 122, 125; by same-sex couples, 346, 359–60

adult care, 12–13, 15, 79, 91, 199, 202, 442, 458, 462–3, 468, 512; of women in nineteenth century, 93–4. *See also* elderly

African Americans: and breadwinner role, 189; as domestic workers, 432; and family unit, 8; and intimate femicide, 531–2; and single mothers, 293; social reproduction in, 15; support relations among, 200

African Canadians: participation in labour force of, 455; and single mothers, 293; support relations among, 301

agricultural/rural societies: and economic restructuring, 510–13, 518–20; family economies in, 57–8; family unit in, 14, 26–7; motherhood in, 121–4; and patriarchal relations of production, 85–6; women's economic contribution to, 74–5, 78

baby boom, 183, 186, 553; 'gayby' boom, 344

Barbie doll, 239

biology: and adoption, 23–4; and assumptions of family, 7–8, 34–5, 43; and assumptions of motherhood, 121, 277, 300, 312, 315, 346, 353–6, 361–2; beliefs about, 4; and fatherhood, 358–61; and kinship, 21–2, 27–8, 29; and sexuality, 11, 237

birth allowance. *See* child/family allowance

birth control, 63, 64–5, 149, 150, 184, 214, 225, 281–2, 311; and women's sexuality, 219

birth rates, 192–3; Canada and Europe compared, 553–4; in capitalist economy, 14, 125, 128–30; decline in, 183, 186, 188, 203; in modern England and France, 64–5; and pro-natalist government policies, 14, 552–4, 558–61, 562; in the 1950s, 136

boys: in agricultural societies, 122–4; and divorce, 544–6; and gender divisions, 98, 144, 148, 241, 488; in lesbian families, 347; in modern England and France, 61, 67, 71; place in family, 32; and sexuality, 11, 164. *See also* adolescents/teenagers

breast-feeding, 23, 126, 293, 297, 313, 318, 319, 370, 563, 565

capitalism: agricultural, 58, 85; birth rates and, 14, 125, 128–30; childcare in, 201; and domesticity, 112; and domestic workers, 430–2; and history of sexuality, 210; in Hong Kong, 483; kin relations in, 99–106, 106–9; and patriarchy, 98; role of mother in, 120, 124–7, 133; role of women in, 34; and theories about family, 33; and working-class families, 97

childcare: in Chinese immigrant households, 489; as collective, 176; government support of, 15–16, 466, 552 (*see also* government support of families); and housing, 326–7, 340; and ideologies of motherhood, 277, 372; trends in, 200–3. *See also* domestic workers; parenting

child/family allowance, 14, 149, 187, 467, 469, 552, 558–64, 566–7, 569–71. *See also* government support of families

children: birth rates, 14, 64–5, 192–3; decision to have, 265–6; disciplining of, 48, 51–2; and divorce, 196–7, 543–51; in family unit, 8, 12, 13, 197–9; and farm property rights, 89–94; feeding of, 62; government support for, 558–61, 566–7, 569–71; ideologies about nature of, 125, 128; and industrialization, 100–3, 104–6; life expectancy, 65–6; living in poverty, 553, 556–7; privatization of responsibility for, 201, 428; rates of illegitimacy, 63; as semi-dependent, 202; time spent caring for, 182–3; of widows/widowers, 68, 100; as women's responsibility, 80–2; working as servants, 58. *See also* government support of families; motherhood; orphans

Chinese Exclusionary Act, 477

Christianity, 49–53; and domesticity, 112, 113–14; and raising children, 122, 123–4; and role of mother, 126; in the 1950s, 139; sexual doctrine (Catholic), 219, 221, 222, 227–8, 231–3

class: and capitalism, 97–8, 124–5; and childcare, 199–200, 293; and consumption of rurality, 519; and domesticity, 111; and domestic workers, 429–30, 447; and gender, 186, 486; and immigration, 477–8, 491; and labour disputes, 176–7; and marriage, 71, 72–3; and money management, 418; and motherhood, 120, 185; and postpartum depression, 313; in the 1950s, 142–7; and single women, 69; and wage labour, 156; and women in family farms, 86

climate change, 10

Cold War, 137, 139–41, 143, 151

common-law families, 4, 180, 189, 194, 197–8, 202, 444; and children, 198–9, 294, 296; and immigration, 6; as nuclear, 197; perceptions of, 243; rates of,

190–2; and risk of intimate femicide, 525, 526–7, 528, 530–1, 532, 533, 537
Communism, 141
community: activity, 163; in co-operative housing, 331–40; support from, 200, 201
conception, 21–2
consumption and consumerism: as family activity, 148; of rural amenities, 519; in weddings, 251–2, 254, 255; as woman's responsibility, 421

daycare: class and, 200; cost of, 430, 466, 468; and division of labour, 15–16; government support for, 187, 194, 201, 203, 319, 467–8; housing and, 330; quality of, 489; workers, 317, 318
death rates, 65–6; infant mortality, 123, 128; and single women, 68
Depression, the, 138–9
deviance, 151, 171; during Cold War period, 140–2, 145–7; and gender roles in marriage, 148; and ideas of sexuality, 210–11, 389
diversity trends, 197–203
divorce and separation: Canada and Europe compared, 553–4; and children, 545–50, 566–7; and climate change, 10; and custody, 4, 550–1; increase in rates of, 149, 189, 242; and loss of domesticity, 274; in Montagnais society, 49; post-war, 142; and poverty, 11, 196–9, 202, 325; process leading to, 543–5; as risk of intimate femicide, 530–1, 537; and social change, 9; trends in, 194–7, 200–1
domestic economy. *See* family economies
domesticity, 111–16, 128; and Cold War, 139–40; in heterosexual relationship, 260–6, 273–4; and job opportunities, 266–71; and motherhood, 269–72, 279
domestic labour. *See* housework
domestic workers: and childcare, 200; demand for, 428–30, 432, 438–9, 443, 446; history of, 430–2, 437–8; and immigration status, 437–43, 446; separated from family, 443–6; status in household of, 434–7; wages of, 465. *See also* servants
dowry, 62–3, 68, 70, 73, 93
dual-earner families: earnings of, 457; gendered division of labour in, 201, 367–8, 373–6, 429, 461; lesbian, 391, 393; in long-distance relationships, 485; and need for childcare, 366; parenting ideology of, 369–73, 380–4; parenting in, 201–2, 376–8; trend of, 568

economic restructuring: and domestic workers, 443; individual experience of, 509; in rural context, 510, 513–17, 520; and trends in family, 189, 203
education: of Chinese-Canadian population by gender, 478–80; by colonizers, 48; and immigration, 478–9, 504–5; increase in formal, 185; and industrialization, 119–20; and literature on motherhood, 130–3; mothers as responsible for, 125–7, 129, 130; religious, 120, 123; requirements for domestic workers, 441; sex, 149, 184; and sexuality, 211, 229–30; and timing of motherhood, 277–8, 279; and timing of motherhood (study), 280–2, 287–8; of women, 111–12, 127, 131
elderly, 202, 498, 499, 502. *See also* adult care
employment insurance. *See* unemployment/employment insurance
Employment Standards Act (Ontario), 435
empty nest, 182–3
endogamy, 70–1
Equal Rights Amendment (US), 36
ethnicity: and risk of intimate femicide, 531–2; and sexuality, 220, 221, 223–7, 232–3. *See also* race
evolutionary theories, 33–4
extended families. *See under* kinship relations

familistic ideology, 8–9, 10, 12, 136
family: and conception, 21–2; definitions of, 6–8, 13, 15, 180; ideology of, 10, 29, 37–8; as labour unit and consumption unit, 62; as legal term, 5–6; mother–child unit in, 30–2; as social construct, 35–6; study of, 8; use of term, 3–4. *See also* family wage; households; kinship relations; privatization of family life
family allowance. *See* child/family allowance
family economies: and affordable housing, 327–31; and birth rate, 184; choice of domesticity, 263, 268, 273–4; combining paid and domestic work, 453–4; and divorce, 196–7; and extended families, 99–106, 198–9; and full-time homemakers, 198; households as centre of, 57; and industrial capitalism, 97; and inheritance, 62–3; in lesbian households, 391–9; and marriage, 62; and migration, 61–2; money management in, 417–26; and paid domestic labour, 428; and property, 63–4; role of married women in, 73–7, 79–80; role of single women in, 66–73, 87; role of widows in, 77–8; and single parents, 198, 201–2, 553, 557, 566–7, 568; single women in, 66–70; and women in workforce, 455–8. *See also* dual-earner families
family violence. *See* violence against women
family wage, 58, 60, 98, 185, 187, 189, 193–4, 197, 202
fathers: and adoption, 23–4; age of, 181–3; in definition of family, 31; and divorce, 4, 196–7, 548–9, 550–1; and gender-appropriate behaviour, 367, 380–3; in Germany, 559; in lesbian families, 361; and literature on motherhood, 130, 131–2; and paternity, 25–6; and sexuality of daughters, 227–8; of 1950s idealized families, 144, 145; as sperm donors, 347–8; trends

affecting, 194. *See also* men; parenting
femicide, intimate: characteristics of killings (Ontario study), 533–5; characteristics of victims and killers (Ontario study), 530–3; compared to US, 525–6; criminal justice response to (Ontario study), 535; in Ontario, 525–6; rates of (Ontario study), 528–9; study of, 537–8; theories about, 526–8. *See also* violence against women
feminism: changing gender ideologies, 457, 464; and childbirth, 314; defining family, 13; and domestic manufacture, 127; and domestic workers, 447; in family dynamic, 226, 228, 230; and gendered division of labour, 344, 388, 511–12, 518; and heterosexuality, 212–13, 216, 236, 237; and household work, 15, 485–6; and immigration, 480; and lesbian relationships, 386, 402–4, 414; models for family, 345, 350; and 'mummy', 358; on the nuclear family, 325; and parenting, 304; and postpartum depression, 310, 312, 318–19; and post-war period, 137; and social policy, 469; and theories of family, 4, 8–9, 31, 33; and violence against women, 242–3, 527, 538; and weddings, 256
food: bread riots, 62; in disciplining children, 52; and gender division of labour, 76; marketing of, 77; of the Montagnais, 44–5, 47–8; women providing and preparing, 79–80
foraging societies, 13, 14, 44, 48–9, 54
functionalism, 8, 29, 31, 33–6, 38, 217

gay, lesbian, bi, and trans people: assumptions about family, 8–9; assumptions about marriage, 5; and heterosexuality, 217; in ideology of 1950s, 145–7, 151; in immigration laws, 141–2; in Kinsey reports, 150; in liberation of urban life, 229; right to marry of, 211. *See also* lesbian families; same-sex partners
gender: and assumptions about family, 8–9; causes of differences in, 241; and difference in sexuality, 215–16; and divorce, 195–6, 545–6; and education in Chinese immigrants, 478–80; in ideology of family, 11–12, 517; and immigration, 499–504; relations and work, 160–1, 161–3; relations in foraging societies, 45; relations in marriage, 163–5; relations in Montagnais society, 47–8; role in violence against women, 525, 526, 535–7; and rural ideologies, 518–19; sexuality and equality, 216–17; and sexuality in marriage, 165–9; and structural identity, 344; in theories of morality, 33, 34–5; and wage comparisons, 514–17; and wedding planning, 250–2, 256. *See also* men; women
gendered division of labour, 8, 15–16, 203; assumptions of, 345; Canada and Europe compared, 555; changing patterns of, 343, 461–4, 468; in Chinese immigrant households, 486–90; and class, 486; as 'doing gender', 367–8; of domestic and paid, 158; and domestic workers, 429; and egalitarianism, 386; and emotional labour, 399–400, 462, 517; and government support, 562–6; in heterosexual couples, 192; of household, 200–1, 400–1; and household money management, 419–26; and identity, 428; in modern England and France, 79; and privatization of social reproduction, 325–6; in wedding planning, 251–2; women in workplace, 147–8. *See also* homemakers, full-time; parenting
generational relations, 502–4. *See also* adolescents/teenagers
girls: in agricultural societies, 123; and divorce, 545–6; education, 101, 456; and gender divisions, 241, 315, 455; in modern England and France, 61, 63, 67–72; in reference to domestic workers, 436; relationship with mother, 32; and sexuality, 11, 219; and weddings, 239, 252. *See also* adolescents/teenagers
government support of families, 187, 326–7, 429, 446, 466, 467–8, 468–70; in Canada and Europe, 558–61; Canada and Europe compared, 552, 562–7, 568–71; and dependence of women, 11; and issues of social policy, 568–71. *See also* child/family allowance
guilds, 58, 59–60, 72, 76–7

Harris, Mike, 5
healthcare, 66, 462–3, 467
heterosexuality, 212–17; as eroticized difference, 414; and fathers in lesbian families, 361; and gender inequality, 344–5; in ideology of family, 11, 385; as naturalized (heteronormativity), 236–8, 347, 351; and weddings, 237–8, 239–40. *See also* gendered division of labour
homemakers, full-time, 5, 8, 198; for childcare, 10, 12, 127, 131, 201, 290–1, 293; choosing to be, 259, 266, 269–71 (*see also* domesticity); decline of, 119–20, 188, 198; and divorce, 196; and economic dependence, 136, 189; and 'family values', 119; in Germany, 554, 562, 564, 568
homosexuality. *See* gay, lesbian, bi, and trans people
households: changing divisions of labour in, 459–68; and childbirth, 80–2; in definitions of family, 26–7; versus individuals, 56; as mode of production, 57, 60–1 (*see also* family economy); pre-industrial, 57; and social reproduction, 15–16; support among, 200; as unit of social reproduction, 14–15. *See also* family economies; homemakers, full-time; housework
housework: in Chinese immigrant households, 486–90; and divisions of labour, 373–6, 400–1, 455–8, 555; and emotional labour, 399–400, 462, 517; in lesbian households, 344, 349–50, 366, 386–91, 401–8; and the marketplace, 15; money management, 417–26; of single women (pre-industrial), 67–70; trends in, 200–1. *See also* gendered division of labour;

homemakers, full-time; parenting
housing: co-operative, 326–7, 340; co-operative and community, 331–8; co-operative as affordable, 327–31; co-operative as family, 338–9; and family, 26–7; government support for, 569–70; and home ownership, 396–9; and ideology of family, 12; as separate from work sites, 14, 158

identity: and gender, 111, 367, 428; and history of sexuality, 210; and immigration, 502–4; and sexual purity, 221, 226–7
ideologies: in analysis of 1950s, 137–8; common-sense, 4–5, 8; of family, 8–9, 10–12, 37–8, 136, 385, 517; of heterosexuality, 212–14, 216; of motherhood, 118, 119–21, 124, 126, 132, 133, 277, 372; of nature of children, 125, 128; of the nuclear family, 142–7, 151, 187; of rurality, 510, 512–13, 518–19; of shared parenting, 372–3, 383–4. *See also* capitalism; feminism; neo-liberalism
immigration: of Chinese to Canada, 477–80, 499; and domestic workers, 430, 431–2, 435, 437–46; dynamics of family and, 496–8, 506; employment opportunities, 481–3; and family definitions, 6, 148, 496–8; and family relations, 483–90; and income, 481–2; and language, 498, 500, 502–3, 505; laws regulating homosexuality, 141–2; and social life, 490–1; studies of women and, 480–1; and support networks, 498–9; and women's dependence, 484–5. *See also* migration
incest, 22–3, 25, 33–4
individualism, 9–10, 104–5, 148, 181, 219
inheritance systems, 61, 62–3
institutional processes, 481–3
isolation, 9–10, 162–3, 325, 331–3

Kinsey reports on sexuality, 149–51
kinship relations: assumptions about, 6, 506; and biology, 34; and childcare, 314–15; in the colonial family, 122; and conception, 21–2; and extended families, 46, 118, 199–200; and households, 26–7; for immigrant Chinese women, 486–90, 499; and immigration, 498–9, 503; and incest, 22–3; during industrialization, 99–106; lack of, 301, 500–1; and marriage, 24–6; in pre-industrial households, 57–8; reproduced by lesbian families, 344, 346–8, 348–51, 351–5, 355–60, 360–2; reproduced in co-operative housing, 325, 331, 335–9, 340; support among, 200, 202, 491; and weddings, 245–6, 256

legislation and domestic workers, 435, 440, 446. *See also* immigration
lesbian families: as different from heterosexual couples, 386–91; division of labour by, 344, 349–50, 366, 399–408, 405, 406–8; and egalitarianism, 386, 413–14; fathers in, 361; financial arrangements by, 391–9; marriage by, 7; parenting by, 344, 346–8, 360–2; wage labour and, 408–13. *See also* gay, lesbian, bi, and trans people; same-sex partners
life-course events, 181–3
life expectancy, 65–6
love and family relations, 32

Malinowski, Bronislaw, 29–33
marriage: and age, 62, 63, 73, 145, 181–3, 190–1; assumptions of, 24–6, 214; changes to, 147–8; courtship, 72–3; definitions of, 24–6; and definitions of family, 4; and domesticity, 114–15; and economic restructuring, 189; finding partners for, 70–1; gay and lesbian, 211; and ideology of 1950s, 145–7, 151, 187; and money management, 418; and property, 63–4, 87–92; rates of, 136, 180, 189–91, 242; relations and work, 160–1, 161–3; sex in, 147, 167–9; and sexuality, 219; trade regulations of, 63; traditional, 260–6; traditional (Germany), 553, 559, 562, 564; trends in, 186–7, 189–94; vows of, 156, 243, 253; of widows, 78; and women's low wages, 156–7. *See also* domesticity; gendered division of labour; weddings
Married Women's Act (1872), 88
masculinity: and family violence, 526–7, 532, 536; and gendered division of labour, 367; in lesbian relationships, 405; and occupations, 279; and paid work, 303, 356–7, 412–13, 520; in pre-industrial family, 122, 123; and sexuality, 215, 217, 385; shift in, 343, 347, 361, 365; in 1950s ideal, 143; and women in workforce, 147–8. *See also* men
matriarchy, 34
men: as breadwinners, 111, 170, 203, 303–4; division of domestic and paid labour, 158; and family wage, 58, 60, 98, 185, 189, 193–4, 197, 202; housework by, 200–1, 203; response to women in workplace, 147–8; sexuality and work, 166–9. *See also* fathers; masculinity; parenting
migration: after World War I, 138; and industrial capitalism, 98; and inheritance systems, 61; and kin relations in employment, 99, 106–9, 199–200. *See also* immigration
Moodie, Susanna, 91, 94
morality: and marriage, 4–5; in Montagnais society, 44, 48, 51, 52–3; in theories of family, 33–5, 38
motherhood: and adoption, 23–4; age of, 181–3, 193, 282; as alternative to wage work, 269–71, 271–2; choosing against, 286–7, 343–4; chosen by lesbians, 344–5, 360–2; in colonial America, 121–4; as compatible with other work, 119; and definition of family, 30–2; as 'doing gender', 367; and economics,

185; and feelings of isolation, 9–10; and female occupations, 278; ideologies of, 118, 119–21, 124, 126, 132, 133, 277, 295, 372; and immigration, 501–2; and industrialization, 124–7, 127–30; and literature on childcare, 130–3; and money management, 423–6; and paid work, 277; and postpartum depression, 310–19; postponing of, 284–6; in shared parenting, 378–80, 383–4; of 1950s idealized families, 144; timing of, 282–4; and women's dependence, 11–12, 299–301. *See also* children; parenting; women

mothers: assumption of love by, 32; and children in divorce, 548–9, 550–1; and education, 125–7, 129, 130; and gender-appropriate behaviour, 380–3; lone, 4–5, 11–12; reluctant, 264–5; and sexuality of daughters, 225–6; in workforce, 552, 553, 554–5, 564–6. *See also* parenting

nationalism and patriotism, 132–3

neo-liberalism: and deregulation of employment, 9; and domestic workers, 443; and 'family values', 5, 8, 119, 180, 293

nuclear family (heterosexual): and alternatives to childcare, 291, 325; assumptions of, 4–5, 8–9, 21, 180–1; and care of children, 197; changing divisions of labour in, 459–68; dynamics of wage labour in, 157–61, 455–8; gendered division of labour in, 365–6, 454–5; and immigration, 486, 499–500, 506; role of mother in, 121, 128–30, 133; in the 1950s, 142–7, 151, 186–7; and sociability in nineteenth century, 118; and wedding ceremonies, 243, 255–6

nurturance, 7–8, 31–2, 36–7, 39, 293, 379, 434

organizational processes, 483–91

orphans, 62, 65–6, 69–70

parental leave, 291, 561–4, 568–9. *See also* government support of families

parenting: choosing to have children, 295–6; and 'doing gender', 367–8; gender dynamics of, 295, 299–306, 325–6; by heterosexual couples, 292; in lesbian households, 344, 346–8, 360–2; literature on, 315–16; managing versus helping in, 373–6; and postpartum depression, 310–11; shared, 291, 369–72, 461–4; shared, expectations of, 293, 296–9, 306–7; shared, ideology of, 372–3, 383–4; shared, responses to, 380–3; socialization through, 376–8; study of first-time, 293–5; through community, 340. *See also* fathers; motherhood; mothers

patriarchy, 85–6, 94, 98; in weddings, 243, 252–3, 255; and women choosing domesticity, 262–3, 266

polygamy, 26–7, 49–50

popular culture: on being single, 12; masculinity in, 148; promotion of family by, 11; in the 1950s, 137, 140; and sexuality, 211; sexualization of, 149; and weddings, 249–50, 253–5, 257

postpartum depression, 310–14, 315–20

poverty: after World War II, 139; in children, Canada and Europe compared, 553, 556–7, 560–1; in children, high levels of, 198, 568, 569; and dependence of women, 428, 469–70; and divorce, 196–7; and family violence, 325; and housing, 328; and lone parent, 11, 202, 325; pre-industrial, 62–3, 78–9; and privatization, 5, 97, 112–13; in United States, 561; women coping with, 14–15

power relations: and domestic workers, 434; in European family, 48; and experience of restructuring, 517; on the family farm, 86, 94; in financial arrangements, 391–9; and gendered division of labour, 463–4 (*see also* gendered division of labour); and heterosexuality, 413–14; in lesbian couples, 388–91; in marriage, 9, 160–1, 163–7; in Montagnais society, 44–5, 47–8; and wage labour, 169–72, 177

privacy and ideology of family, 37. *See also* privatization of family life; public/private divide

privatization of family life, 12, 15–16, 325–6, 327, 331; and co-op living, 332, 338; and domestic workers, 429, 431, 434, 447; and immigrants, 500; and responsibility of children, 201, 203, 316, 320, 446; and social reproduction, 325

promiscuity, 29–30, 33, 71–3

property: in defining households, 61, 73; and family economies, 74; and male wage earner, 169; and marriage, 62–4; and rights, 87–94

Protestant Ethic, 184

public/private divide: and domestic workers, 447; and eroticism, 216–17; and family, 37. *See also* privatization of family life

race: in colonial Canada, 52; and domestic workers, 431, 438, 447; and immigration, 477–8, 499–504; and rates of women working, 455. *See also* ethnicity

restructuring. *See* economic restructuring

rituals: marriage, 22, 24–5, 71–2, 256; postpartum, 314–15. *See also* weddings

rural societies. *See* agricultural/rural societies

same-sex partners: childcare by, 291; and children, 198; increase in numbers of, 180; legal rights of, 6; as nuclear families, 197; in the 1950s, 187. *See also* lesbian families

servants: and marriage, 63–4, 71; in pre-industrial households, 57–8; single women as, 67, 69; in urban family economies, 59–60. *See also* domestic workers

sexuality: and Catholic doctrine, 222–3, 231–2; of daughters, 227–31; and ethnicity, 223–7, 233; and gender

difference, 215–16; and heteronormativity, 212–14, 238; and heterosexual intercourse, 214–15; history of ideas of, 210–11; influences on, 219; in intimate femicide, 534; Kinsey reports on, 149–51; and relations of power in marriage, 163–9; and secularization, 219–20, 221, 227–8; studies of, 220–1
slavery, 431
social reproduction: Canada and Europe compared, 558–61; family as unit of, 14–15; in households, 15–16; privatization of, 310–11, 325–6, 428; and unpaid domestic labour, 468–70. *See also* privatization of family life
spinsters, 69
standards of living: after divorce, 553; after World War II, 139. *See also* poverty
structural functionalism, 8

unemployment: Canada and Europe compared, 555–6; and intimate femicide, 532
unemployment/employment insurance, 187, 561, 569
unions, 176–7, 187, 483
urban society: and experience of sexuality, 227–31; family economies in, 58–60; single women in, 68–9, 330–1; women's economic contributions to, 75–7, 78–9

Vancouver Post Partum Counselling Service (PPCS), 312–15, 319
violence against women: and gender divisions of labour, 9; and industrial capitalism, 97; in pre-industrial households, 80; role of gender in, 525, 526, 535–7; and violent behaviour, 533; wage labour and, 171–2. *See also* femicide, intimate

weddings, 242; and division of labour, 250–2, 256; and heterosexuality, 239–40; meaning in details of, 247–52; study of, 243–4; symbolism of, 244–6, 252–5. *See also* rituals
widows/widowers, 66, 68, 77–9; property rights of, 89–92, 94; rates of, 190
women: and divorce, 553; as domestic workers, 432; and economic restructuring, 520; and egalitarianism, 386; employing domestic workers, 465; experience of restructuring, 510, 512; and family pattern trends, 203; and farm ownership, 86–94; in foraging societies, 13, 14; and heterosexuality, 212–14, 216–17; in history of family, 13–14; and identity in family economy, 111; and immigration, 481–3, 490–1, 500–2; and literature on childcare, 130–3; marriage and low wages, 156–7; and money management, 420–6; in Montagnais society, 47–8; and sexual double standard, 219–20; single in pre-industrial household, 66–70; as topic of discourse, 480; transition to adulthood, 223–7; as unpaid domestic labourers, 172–7, 468–9; wages compared to men, 555; as wet nurses, 75, 126; in workforce, 143, 147–8, 188–9, 200–1, 428–9, 454, 455–6, 459–68; in workforce, Canada and Europe compared, 554–5. *See also* domesticity; gender; homemakers, full-time; motherhood
work (paid): of Chinese-Canadian population by gender, 479–80; of children on the farm, 123; deregulation of, 3, 9; and domesticity, 116; employment rates, 139; employment rates, Canada and Europe, 555–6; and family violence, 171–2; flexibility of, 429, 462–3; gender and wage comparisons, 514–17; in household dynamic, 157–61, 169–72, 181; and ideologies of motherhood, 119–21; immigration and opportunities for, 504–5; impact of shift, 159, 163; importance of wage in, 157–8; institutional processes and, 481–3; and lesbian couples, 408–13; major trends in changes to, 184–8, 200–1; of married women (pre-industrial), 73–7, 79–80; and motherhood, 277, 278, 280, 282–6; and parental leave, 291, 562–6; participation in, 568; participation in (rates of), 456; part-time, 515–17; in pre-industrial household, 61, 70–2, 73; production and motherhood, 127–30; in relationship to housework, 172–7, 432–4, 453–4; and sexuality in marriage, 166–9; of single women (nineteenth century), 87; of single women (pre-industrial), 67–70; as tied to family, 60–1; urban (pre-industrial), 60–1, 76–7; of widows (pre-industrial), 77–8; women choosing domesticity over, 260–6, 266–71, 274. *See also* domestic workers; family economies; gendered division of labour; housework
World War I, 138–9
World War II: and birth rates, 183; and divorce rates, 142; and poverty, 139; and women's wage labour, 189

TCS Themes in
Canadian Sociology

This series of concise texts, the work of Canadian scholars, reflects recent research and trends in sociology. Lorne Tepperman and the late James Curtis were founding editors of the series, which is now edited by Tepperman and Susan A. McDaniel.

Children in Canada Today

PATRIZIA ALBANESE

This engaging text explores the process through which children become members of our society—how, where, when, and with whom children grow up to be socially 'functioning' adults. The roles played by various 'agents of socialization' and the places and situations in which socialization takes place are also discussed. Ideal for sociology courses dealing with children, family, socialization, the life cycle, social policy, and social problems, *Children in Canada Today* provides an accessible, insightful look at childhood in this country.

CONTENTS: 1. Histories of Childhood. 2. Social Theories of Childhood. 3. Doing Research on and with Children. 4. Parent(s) and Child(ren)—Socialization in the Home. 5. Schooling and Peer Groups. 6. Children, the Mass Media, and Consumerism. 7. Early Childhood Education and Care in Canada. 8. Immigrant, Refugee, and Aboriginal Children in Canada. 9. Child Poverty in Canada. 10. Divorce, Custody, and Child Support in Canada. 11. Child Abuse and Child Protection in Canada. 12. The Disappearance of Childhood? Glossary.

Paper, 2009, 248 pp., ISBN 9780195428896

Deconstructing Men and Masculinities

MICHAEL ATKINSON

This comprehensive introduction to masculine identity politics in Canada offers a range of viewpoints, narratives, and evidence about the contested nature of masculinity. Drawing primarily on author Michael Atkinson's ethnographic research of Canadian men over the past decade, the text explores the idea of masculinity in crisis and the attempt by many men to move beyond this perceived crossroads. Atkinson reviews the historical links between masculinity and social power, the cultural associations between masculinity and violence, the role of masculinity in sports cultures, the problems of masculinity for young men, the mass mediation of masculinity and misandry, and the rise of alternative and 'feminine' masculinities. Never before have men's social roles, statuses, and identities been so open to cultural critique and redefinition; *Deconstructing Men and Masculinities* provides an engaging sociological narrative to guide readers through this ground-breaking area of study.

CONTENTS: Introduction: Masculinity in Crisis? 1. Men, Power, and Pastiche Hegemony. 2. Violence, Residue, and Pastiche Hegemony. 3. The Lost (and Found) Boys. 4. Male Femininities, Metrosexualities, and Liquid Ubersexualities. 5. Sporting Masculinities. 6. Mass-Mediating Risk Masculinities. 7: The Unbearable Whiteness of Being. Epilogue.

Paper, 2011, 248 pp., ISBN 9780195430769

TCS **Themes in Canadian Sociology**

This series of concise texts, the work of Canadian scholars, reflects recent research and trends in sociology. Lorne Tepperman and the late James Curtis were founding editors of the series, which is now edited by Tepperman and Susan A. McDaniel.

Choices and Constraints in Family Life, Second Edition

MAUREEN BAKER

Designed specifically for sociology of the family courses, this text examines the choices and constraints placed on individuals, relationships, and marriages in light of both family circumstances and societal expectations. Using an interdisciplinary approach that draws on the latest research in sociology, psychology, anthropology, and social history, the author explores emerging patterns in family life, including rising rates of cohabitation among both heterosexual and same-sex couples; trends in birth rates; and higher rates of separation, re-partnering, and stepfamilies. With the most up-to-date statistical data, new information on aging and on women in the workforce, and extensive coverage of historical and theoretical perspectives, this new edition is a concise yet comprehensive examination of family life in Western society.

CONTENTS: 1. Conceptualizing Families. 2. Forming Relationships. 3. Cohabitation and Marriage. 4. Child-bearing, Child-rearing, and Childhood. 5. Household Work and Money. 6. Separation, Divorce, and Re-partnering. 7. Midlife, Aging, and Retirement. 8. Constraints on Personal Choices. Glossary.

Paper, 2010, 264 pp., ISBN 9780195431599

Understanding Health, Health Care, and Health Policy in Canada: Sociological Perspectives

NEENA L. CHAPPELL • MARGARET J. PENNING

This brief introduction to the sociology of health and health care emphasizes health (promotion, maintenance, and prevention) as well as illness (treatment, cure, and care), offering a broad and balanced treatment of the sociological debates within the field. The first half of the text introduces three important themes in the study of the sociology of health: (1) the importance of approaching health issues from a lifespan perspective; (2) the need to attend to both the public and the private, the micro and the macro, and the individual and the structural; and (3) issues of inequality as they intersect with health, health care, and health policy. The second half of the text focuses on self care, formal care, and informal care, along with Canada's health care policy. Discussion on topical issues such as obesity, smoking, homelessness, AIDS, stress, and mental illness is incorporated throughout the book.

CONTENTS: 1. Health and Health Care: Sociological History and Perspectives. 2. Health and Illness. 3. Self- and Informal Care. 4. Formal Care. 5. Health-Care Policy. 6. Conclusions: The Sociology of Health and Health Care in the Future. Glossary.

Paper, 2009, 296 pp., ISBN 9780195424768

TCS **Themes in Canadian Sociology**

This series of concise texts, the work of Canadian scholars, reflects recent research and trends in sociology. Lorne Tepperman and the late James Curtis were founding editors of the series, which is now edited by Tepperman and Susan A. McDaniel.

The Schooled Society: An Introduction to the Sociology of Education, Second Edition

SCOTT DAVIES • NEIL GUPPY

The Schooled Society examines how education has come to occupy a central place in society and how its function and form continue to evolve. Structured around the three core roles of modern schooling—selection, social organization, and socialization—the text integrates classical and contemporary theoretical approaches to discuss schooling within a sociological framework. This new edition has been revised and updated to include the latest data, research, and statistics, and includes new and expanded coverage on critical pedagogy, contemporary theory, lifelong learning/early learning, technology in the classroom, curriculum changes and policy controversies, legitimacy and integrity in Canadian universities, and teacher education and preparation. A completely revised and expanded chapter on inequality (Chapter 6) exposes students to this important topic in the sociology of education.

CONTENTS: I. Introduction. 1. Thinking Sociologically about the Schooled Society. 2. Classical Sociological Approaches to Education. 3. Contemporary Sociological Approaches to Schooling. II. Selection: Inequality and Opportunity. 4. Education Revolutionized: The Growth of Modern Schooling. 5. The Structural Transformation of Schooling: Accommodation, Competition and Stratification. 6. Unequal Student Attainments: Class, Gender, and Race. III. Social Organization and Legitimation. 7. The Changing Organization of Schooling. 8. Curriculum: The Content of Schooling. 9. The Sociology of Teaching. IV. Socialization. 10. Socialization: The Changing Influence of Schools on Students. 11. The Limits of School Socialization: Competing Influences on Students. V. Conclusion. 12. Future Directions for Canadian Education. Glossary.

Paper, 2010, 344 pp., ISBN 9780195431742

First Nations in the Twenty-First Century

JAMES S. FRIDERES

Focussing exclusively on First Nations peoples, this innovative new text addresses crucial issues such as the legacy of residential schools; intergenerational trauma; Aboriginal languages and culture; health and well-being on reserves; self-government and federal responsibility; the political economy of First Nations; and the federal Indian Affairs bureaucracy. Through an in-depth treatment of historical and contemporary topics, including recent court decisions and government legislations, students will learn about the experiences of First Nations peoples and their complex, evolving relationship with the rest of Canada.

CONTENTS: 1. Knowing Your History. 2. Who Are You? 3. Indigenous Ways of Knowing. 4. Aboriginal Residential Schools: Compensation, Apologies, and Truth and Reconciliation. 5. Intergenerational Trauma. 6. 'Hear' Today, Gone Tomorrow: Aboriginal Languages. 7. Well-Being and Health. 8. The Duty of Government and Fiduciary Responsibility. 9. Self-Government, Aboriginal Rights, and the Inherent Right of First Nations Peoples. 10. The Political Economy of First Nations. 11. The Bureaucracy: Indian and Northern Affairs Canada. 12. Surviving in the Contemporary World: The Future of First Nations Peoples in Canada. Conclusion. Glossary.

Paper, 2011, 272 pp., ISBN 9780195441437

TCs **Themes in Canadian Sociology**

This series of concise texts, the work of Canadian scholars, reflects recent research and trends in sociology. Lorne Tepperman and the late James Curtis were founding editors of the series, which is now edited by Tepperman and Susan A. McDaniel.

Mediated Society: A Critical Sociology of Media

JOHN D. JACKSON • GREG M. NIELSEN • YON HSU

Taking a sociological approach to the study of mass media, *Mediated Society* explores how the media affects individuals and society. Within this unique framework, the authors analyze media and mass communication as a social rather than as a technological construct while addressing issues such as democracy, citizenship, class, gender, and cultural diversity. Drawing attention to the way in which media frames everyday experiences and events, the text examines media and communication in urban, national, and global settings, as well as the power and structure of dominant mass media. With a wide range of Canadian and international examples, along with two real-life case studies and a wealth of pedagogical features throughout, this innovative, engaging text encourages students to consider how social identities, norms, and values are mediated by various forms of mass communication.

CONTENTS. I. Sociology, Media, and Citizenship. 1. Sources for a Critical Sociology of Mediated Society. 2. The Public Sphere. 3. Citizenship and Audiences. 4. Consumption and Advertising. 5. New Media, New World? II. Media Events and the Sociological Imagination. 6. Global Media Events. 7. National Media Events. 8. Urban Media Events: Toronto and Montreal Case Studies. III. Social Problems through Journalism and Media. 9. Reporting on Social Problems. 10. Journalism and Seriocomedy: Framing Poverty in Montreal Media. 11. Framing Immigration as a Social Problem in *The New York Times*. Glossary.

Paper, 2011, 296 pp., ISBN 9780195431407

Violence Against Women in Canada: Research and Policy Perspectives

HOLLY JOHNSON • MYRNA DAWSON

Examining a wide range of theoretical perspectives, empirical research, and policy responses, *Violence Against Women in Canada* emphasizes connections among different forms of violence—connections that have too often been ignored or downplayed. Taking a gendered sociological approach, the text reveals how violence against women stems from unequal access to power and resources. While gender is the central focus, the authors also show how intersections of race, ethnicity, class, and sexuality serve to deepen inequalities for particular groups. Comprehensive and concise, this text explores the evolution of methods to measure violence, the impact of these methods on the social framing of violence issues, the impact on victims, and current policy responses and their effectiveness.

CONTENTS: 1. Introduction. 2. Theoretical Debates. 3. Methods of Measuring Violence Against Women. 4. Intimate Partner Violence. 5. Sexual Assault. 6. Femicide. 7. Policy Outcomes and Impacts. Glossary.

Paper, 2011, 240 pp., ISBN 9780195429817

TCs

Themes in
Canadian Sociology

This series of concise texts, the work of Canadian scholars, reflects recent research and trends in sociology. Lorne Tepperman and the late James Curtis were founding editors of the series, which is now edited by Tepperman and Susan A. McDaniel.

Crime in Canadian Context: Debates and Controversies, Second Edition

WILLIAM O'GRADY

This concise, accessible introduction to criminology explores how crime is defined, measured, and controlled within a Canadian context. In-depth and well-balanced, the text covers the fundamentals of the discipline before exploring non-sociological explanations of crime, criminological theory, social inequality and crime, organizational crime, and intersections between the law and the criminal justice system. Drawing on the latest Canadian statistics and research, the text examines a range of contemporary topics from hate crime to homeless youth in an engaging and succinct style. Thoroughly updated with expanded discussions on policy, youth justice, and criminal law, along with boxed coverage of global and media issues, this second edition is essential reading for students studying criminology in Canada.

CONTENTS: 1. Crime, Fear, and Risk. 2. Measuring Crime. 3. Non-Sociological Explanations of Crime. 4. Classical Sociological Explanations of Crime. 5. Recent Sociological Approaches to Crime. 6. Crime and Social Exclusion. 7. Crime in the Context of Organizations and Institutions. 8. Responding to Crime. 9. Summary and Conclusions.

Paper, 2011, 296 pp., ISBN 9780195433784

Law and Society Redefined

GEORGE PAVLICH

Written by one of Canada's most prominent socio-legal scholars, *Law and Society Redefined* is a comprehensive introduction to law and society. Drawing on the foundational contributions of such prominent social theorists as Émile Durkheim, Max Weber, and Michel Foucault, author George Pavlich uses social theory to explore the relationship between law and society. With extensive coverage of many of the most important topics in socio-legal studies, including morality, race, gender, and violence, the text questions the traditional definition of the 'sociology of law' to determine how the field has developed, while also examining the ideas and critiques that might redefine it in the future.

CONTENTS: Introduction. I. Law *Sui Generis*. 1. Classical Natural Law. 2. Natural Law Theory: Morality and Law. 3. Positing Law. 4. Realizing Sociological Jurisprudence. II. Society *Sui Generis*. 5. Durkheim Socializes the Law. 6. Law, Ideology, and Revolutionary Social Change. 7. Max Weber, Modern Disenchantment, and the Rationalization of Law. 8. Critical Confrontations: Law, Race, Gender, and Class. III. Promising Justice: The *Becoming* of Law and Society. 9. Michel Foucault: The Power of Law and Society. 10. Contested Sovereignties, Violence, and Law. 11. Just Events: Law and Society. Conclusion: After Law and Society?

Paper, 2011, 248 pp., ISBN 9780195429800

TCs **Themes in Canadian Sociology**

This series of concise texts, the work of Canadian scholars, reflects recent research and trends in sociology. Lorne Tepperman and the late James Curtis were founding editors of the series, which is now edited by Tepperman and Susan A. McDaniel.

'Race' and Ethnicity in Canada: A Critical Introduction, Second Edition

VIC SATZEWICH • NIKOLAOS LIODAKIS

'Race' and Ethnicity in Canada: A Critical Introduction provides students with a comprehensive look at the major approaches and explanations to the key concepts in this field of study. Through their exploration of the central issues that affect Canadians today—immigration, multiculturalism, assimilation, racism, and Aboriginal and non-Aboriginal relations—the authors argue that race is not a biologically real category, but rather, a socially constructed label used to describe and explain certain kinds of human difference. The text questions whether there are patterns of race and ethnic relations that are truly unique to Canada and puts Canada into a wider global context. Fully updated and revised, *'Race' and Ethnicity in Canada*, second edition, includes new discussions of the economy, education, and policing and their impact on race and ethnic relations, as well as new coverage of French–English relations, racism, globalization, and ethnic and religious fundamentalism.

CONTENTS: 1. Theories of Ethnicity and 'Race'. 2. The Dynamics of Nation-Building: French/English Relations, Aboriginal/Non-Aboriginal Relations, and Immigration in Historical Perspective. 3. Immigration and the Canadian Mosaic. 4. Understanding Social Inequality: The Intersections of Ethnicity, Gender, and Class. 5. Identity and Multiculturalism. 6. Racism. 7. Aboriginal and Non-Aboriginal Relations. 8. Transnationals or Diasporas? Ethnicity and Identity in a Globalized Context.

Paper, 2010, 344 pp., ISBN 9780195432299

Gender Relations in Canada: Intersectionality and Beyond

JANET SILTANEN • ANDREA DOUCET

Today it is widely recognized that the experience of inequality depends on the intersections of gender, race, and class in each individual life. This text traces the way the implications of gender play out for women and men throughout the life course, from the formation of gender identity in childhood through the identity struggles of adolescence to adulthood, where gender continues to play a major role in the structure of work and family life alike. At the same time the authors underline the importance of moving beyond intersectionality as a framework for research in this area.

CONTENTS: 1. Sociology and the Analysis of Gender Relations. 2. The Multiple Genders of Childhood. 3. Gender Intensification: Adolescence and the Transition to Adulthood. 4. Diverse Paths: Gender, Work, and Family. 5. Making Change: Gender, Careers, and Citizenship (by Mary Ellen Donnan). 6. Analyzing the Complexity of Gender: Intersectionality and Beyond. Glossary.

Paper, 2008, 204 pp., ISBN 9780195423204

About Oxford University Press Canada

The Canadian branch of Oxford University Press was established in 1904. It was the first overseas branch to be set up after an office was established in New York in 1896. Although the branch did not open until 1904, the first book published for the Canadian market actually appeared eight years earlier—a hymnal for the Presbyterian Church of Canada.

OUP Canada's first home, at 25 Richmond Street West in Toronto.

Before the twentieth century, the main suppliers of books to the trade in Canada were the Copp Clark Company, the W.J. Gage Company, and the Methodist Bookroom (in 1919 renamed The Ryerson Press after its founder, Egerton Ryerson). These three firms acted as 'jobbers' for other lines that were later to be represented either directly by branches of their parent houses or by exclusive Canadian agents. Prior to 1904, Oxford books had been sold in Canada by S.G. Wilkinson, who, based in London, England, travelled across Canada as far west as Winnipeg. Wilkinson did a large trade with S.B. (Sam) Gundy, the wholesale and trade manager of the Methodist Bookroom. When Oxford University Press opened its own branch in Canada, Gundy, already familiar with Oxford books, was invited to become its first manager. The premises were at 25 Richmond Street West and, lacking an elevator of any kind, were hardly ideal for a publishing house.

An etching of Amen House on University Avenue, created by Stanley Turner.

The original reception area and library at 70 Wynford Drive. The library was later removed to make room for offices.

In 1929, the branch moved to Amen House, located at 480 University Avenue, and in 1936, after Gundy's death, the branch became closely allied with Clarke, Irwin and Company under W.C. Clarke. This association continued until 1949 when Clarke, Irwin moved to a separate location on St Clair Avenue West. In 1963, the Press moved to a new building at 70 Wynford Drive in Don Mills, which served it well for the next 46 years. By 2009, however, the branch had outgrown the 70 Wynford site. An extensive search process culminated in the move that November to a split-site configuration. The offices relocated to new premises at the Shops at Don Mills, an innovative retail/office/residential development, while the warehouse moved to a site in Brampton that not only offered more affordable rent and carrying charges but also provided a modern high-bay space much closer to major customers and Pearson International Airport.

Today OUP Canada is a major publisher of higher education, school, and English-as-a-second-language textbooks, as well as a significant trade and reference publisher. The Higher Education Division publishes both introductory and upper-level texts in such disciplines as sociology, anthropology, social work, English literature and composition, geography, history, political science, religious studies, and engineering. The division publishes more than 60 new Canadian texts and 150 student and instructor supplements each year, and derives about 60 per cent of its total sales from books and other learning materials written, edited, and published in Canada.

Some of the many books recently published by Oxford University Press Canada.